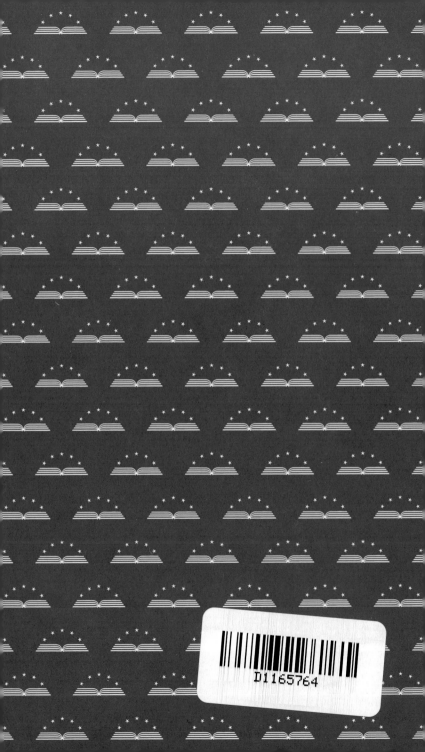

ARTHUR MILLER

ARTHUR MILLER

COLLECTED PLAYS 1964–1982

THE LIBRARY OF AMERICA

TONY KUSHNER
IS THE EDITOR OF THIS VOLUME

Contents

AFTER THE FALL

THE CHARACTERS

QUENTIN
FELICE
DAN
MOTHER
ELSIE
LOUISE
CARRIE
CHAIRMAN
HOLGA
FATHER
MAGGIE
LOU
MICKEY
LUCAS
HARLEY BARNES

Nurses, porter, secretary, hospital attendant,
a group of boys, and passers-by

ACT ONE

The action takes place in the mind, thought, and memory of Quentin.

Except for one chair there is no furniture in the conventional sense; there are no walls or substantial boundaries.

The setting consists of three levels rising to the highest at the back, crossing in a curve from one side of the stage to the other. A stairway, center, connects them. Rising above all, and dominating the stage, is the blasted stone tower of a German concentration camp. Its wide lookout windows are like eyes which at the moment seem blind and dark; bent reinforcing rods stick out of it like broken tentacles.

On the two lower levels are sculpted areas; indeed, the whole effect is neolithic, a lavalike, supple geography in which, like pits and hollows found in lava, the scenes take place. The mind has no color but its memories are brilliant against the grayness of its landscape. When people sit they do so on any of the abutments, ledges, or crevices. A scene may start in a confined area, but spread or burst out onto the entire stage, overrunning any other area.

People appear and disappear instantaneously, as in the mind; but it is not necessary that they walk off the stage. The dialogue will make clear who is "alive" at any moment and who is in abeyance.

The effect, therefore, will be the surging, flitting, instantaneousness of a mind questing over its own surfaces and into its depths.

The stage is dark. Now there is a sense that some figure has moved in the farthest distance; a footstep is heard, then others. As light dimly rises the persons in the play move in a random way up from beneath the high back platform. Whispering emanates from them. Some sit at once, others come farther downstage, seem to recognize one another; still others move alone and in total separateness; in short, there is a totally random congeries of movements in a slow but not dreamlike rhythm. One of them, Quentin, a man in his forties, moves out of this mass and down the depth of the stage to the chair. This chair faces front, toward the audience. A sharp light now isolates it. All movement ceases. Quentin reaches forward over the chairback to shake the hand of the Listener, who, if he could be seen, would be sitting just beyond the edge of the stage itself.

QUENTIN: Hello! God, it's good to see you again! I'm very well. I hope it wasn't too inconvenient on such short notice. Fine, I just wanted to say hello, really. Thanks. *He sits on invitation.* How've you been? You look sunburned. . . . Oh! I've never been to South America, you enjoy it? That's nice. . . . Do I? I guess I am, I'm quite healthy—I do a lot of walking now. *Slight pause.* I started to call you a couple of times this year. Last year too. . . . Well, I lost the impulse; I wasn't sure what I wanted to say, and at my age it's discouraging to still have to go wandering around in one's mind. Actually, I called you on the spur of the moment this morning; I have a bit of a decision to make. You know—you mull around about something for months and all of a sudden there it is and you're at a loss for what to do. Were you able to give me two hours? It might not take that long, but I think it involves a great deal and I'd rather not rush. Fine.

He sets himself to begin, looks off.

Ah . . .

Interrupted, he turns back to Listener, surprised.

I've quit the firm, didn't I write you about that? Really! I was sure I'd written. . . . Oh, about fourteen months ago; a few weeks after Maggie died. . . . No, no. I've withdrawn completely. I still hold my interest, such as it is, but I'm out of it. . . . Well, it just got to where I couldn't concentrate on a case any more; not the way I used to. It's hard to describe; it all lost its necessity; I was going on because I'd started out to become a successful attorney, and I'd become one—I felt I was merely in the service of my own success. There has to be some semblance of a point, and I couldn't find it any more. Although I do wonder sometimes if I am simply trying to destroy myself. . . . Well, I have walked away from what passes for an important career. . . . Not very much, I'm afraid; I still live in the hotel, see a few people, read a good deal—*Smiles*—stare out the window. I don't know why I'm smiling; maybe I feel that's all over now, and I'll harness myself to something again. Although I've had that feeling before and done nothing about it, I—

Again, interrupted, he looks surprised.

God, I wrote you about *that*, didn't I? Maybe I dream these letters. . . . Mother died. Oh, it's four, five months ago, now. Yes, quite suddenly; I was in Germany at the time and . . . it's one of the things I wanted to talk to you about. I . . . met a woman there. *He grins.* I never thought it could happen again, but we became quite close. In fact, she's arriving tonight for some conference at Columbia. She's an archaeologist. . . . I'm not sure, you see, if I want to lose her, and yet it's outrageous to think of committing myself again. . . . Well, yes, but look at my life. A life, after all, is evidence, and I have two divorces in my safe-deposit box.

He stands, moves, thinks.

I tell you frankly I'm a little afraid. . . . Of who and what I'd be bringing to her. And I thought if I could say aloud what I see when I'm alone . . . Well, for example, this:

He sits again, leans forward.

You know . . . more and more I see that for many years I looked at life like a case at law. It was a series of proofs. When you're young you prove how brave you are, or smart; then, what a good lover; then, a good father; finally, how wise, or powerful or what-the-hell-ever. But underlying it all, I see now, there was a presumption. That one moved not in a dry circle but on an upward path toward some elevation, where . . . God knows what . . . I would be justified, or even condemned. A verdict, anyway. I think now that my disaster really began when I looked up one day . . . and the bench was empty. No judge in sight. And all that remained was the endless argument with oneself, this pointless litigation of existence before an empty bench. . . . Which, of course, is another way of saying—despair, and no great news. Some of the best, most energetic lawyers I know believe in nothing, and even find a joy in proving again and again that men are worthless, including their own clients. Despair can be a way of life, providing you believe in it. And I say to myself, pick it up, take it to heart, and move on again. Instead, I seem to be hung up, waiting for some . . . believable sign. And the days and the months . . . and now the years . . . are draining away. *Slight pause.* A couple of weeks ago I became aware of a strange fact. With all this darkness, the truth is that every morning when I awake, I'm full of hope! With everything I know . . . I open up my eyes . . . I'm like a boy! For an instant there's some . . . unformed promise in the air. I jump out of bed, I shave, I can't wait to finish breakfast—and then . . . it seeps in my room, the world, my life, and its pointlessness. And I thought . . . if I could corner that hope, find what it consists of, and either kill it for a lie, or really make it mine . . .

Felice enters in sweater and skirt, sits on the floor.

FELICE: I just saw you walking by, that's all, and I thought, why don't I talk to you? You do remember me, don't you?

QUENTIN, *with a glance at Felice:* For instance, I ran into a girl on the street last month; I'd settled her divorce a few years ago and she recognized me. And I hadn't had a woman in so long and she obviously wanted to . . .

FELICE: No! I just wanted to be near you. I love your face. You have a kind face. . . . You remember in your office, when my husband was refusing to sign the papers?

QUENTIN, *to Listener:* It's this: somehow, whatever I look at, I seem to see its death.

He turns to her.

FELICE: Well, see, he was always so childish alone with me; like a little stubborn boy. And when you talked to him—I could see it, he felt like a man. Like he had dignity. And me too. I felt like a grown-up woman. And I swear . . . when we walked out of your office, I . . . I almost loved him! And he asked me something when we got down in the street. Should I tell you? Or do you know already?

QUENTIN, *in frustration:* I'm afraid it's pointless, I don't know why I—

Breaks off, still to Listener.

Well, just that he asked her to go to bed with him, one last time . . .

FELICE: How did you know that!

QUENTIN—*he is caught by her suddenly; his tone is answering her:* Because it's very hard to see the death of love, and simply walk away. *He is now turning to face her.*

FELICE: You think I should have?

QUENTIN: Well, what harm would it have done?

FELICE: That's what *I* wondered! Except, it would be funny, wouldn't it? The same day we got a divorce? See, I wanted it to mean something, the divorce!

QUENTIN: Honey . . . you never stop loving whoever you loved. Hatred doesn't wipe it out.

Louise appears, brushing her hair. Maggie sits up from the upper platform, her breathing beginning to be heard. And Quentin becomes active and agitated, and speaks to the Listener.

Why do I make such stupid statements? I don't believe that! These goddamned women have injured me; have I learned nothing?

Holga appears beneath the tower, her arms full of flowers.

HOLGA: Would you like to see Salzburg? I think they play *The Magic Flute* tonight.

Quentin is facing up to her. A pause. He turns back to Listener.

QUENTIN: It's that . . . I don't know what I'd be bringing to that girl.

Holga is gone, and Maggie and Louise.

I don't know what I believe about my own life! What? *He turns to Felice.* Well, death in the sense that she was trying so damned hard to be hopeful, and I . . .

FELICE: I don't deny he loved me, but . . . everything came down to how much mileage you got on a Volkswagen! I just wished we could get lost in some goddamn wilderness or something, and scream and bite each other and . . . and start going *toward* something!

QUENTIN: Well, you're in the wilderness now, aren't you? You live alone, leave the bed unmade, get a hamburger at three in the morning, sleep with who you like. You feel you're going toward something?

FELICE: I think so. I feel I'm good now, as a dancer . . . or almost. I almost feel free, when I dance. Not quite, but . . . sometimes I only have to think high and I go high; I have a long thought and I fly across the floor; sometimes, sometimes I'm almost exactly what I imagine, and when that happens . . .

She has danced out of sight.

QUENTIN: Death in this sense: I'm sure her hope is real to her, but I sit there and see the day her legs will lose their spring, and her body will no longer follow those high leaping thoughts. . . . Yes, but there's always time to die, why reach for it? In fact, she came back again the other night, almost flew into my room! And it struck me with great force—how little I really believe in life.

Felice appears, standing, with a coat on; she is straight, nearly ecstatic.

FELICE: I had my nose fixed! Are you very busy? The doctor took the bandage off but I put it back on. I wanted you to be the first. Do you mind?

QUENTIN: No. But why me?

FELICE: Because . . . remember that night when I came up here? I was trying to make up my mind . . . I mean there's something sort of insincere about changing your nose. I mean there could be. If that's all that makes or breaks you, the shape of a piece of cartilage? I mean if you're going to go through life building everything on *that* . . . You don't absolutely have to answer, but . . . I think you wanted to make love to me that night. Didn't you?

QUENTIN: I did, yes.

FELICE: I knew it! And it just clicked something for me. Because you really listened to me and didn't just try to roll me over. I felt it didn't matter what kind of nose I had, so I—I might as well have a short one! Can I show it to you?

QUENTIN: I'd like very much to see it.

FELICE: Close your eyes.

He does. She lifts the invisible bandage.

Okay.

He looks. She raises her arm in blessing.

I'll always bless you. Always!

He turns away, slowly returns to the chair as she walks into darkness.

QUENTIN, *to the Listener:* Maybe it's this; she meant nothing to me, it was a glancing blow, and yet it's not impossible that I stand in her mind like some corner she turned in her life. I feel like a mirror in which she somehow saw herself as . . . glorious. The truth is, I even liked her first nose better!

Two pallbearers in the distance carry an invisible coffin.

It's like my mother's funeral; I still hear her voice in the street sometimes, loud and real, calling my name. She's under the ground but she's not impressively dead to me. That whole cemetery . . . I saw it like a field of buried mirrors in which people saw themselves. I don't seem to know how to grieve. Or is it just some hardness in it bothers me?

Holga appears above, flowers in her arms.

God, maybe I ought to live alone; or maybe I don't believe that grief is grief unless it kills you.

Holga is gone. Dan appears. A nurse is whispering in his ear.

Like when I flew back and met my brother in the hospital.

The nurse hurries out, and Dan speaks to the empty air.

DAN: I'm so glad you got here, kid; I wouldn't have wired you but I don't know what to do. You have a good flight?

Now Father appears in a "bed." The same nurse is puffing up his pillow.

FATHER: Is that my sons in the hall? Where's my wife?
QUENTIN, *to Dan:* But what's the alternative? She's dead, he has to know.
FATHER: Why don't they come in? Where's my daughter?

DAN: But he was only operated on this morning. How can we walk in and say, "Your wife is dead"? It's like sawing off his arm. Suppose we tell him she's on her way, then give him a sedative?

QUENTIN: But Dan, I think it belongs to him, doesn't it? After fifty years you . . . owe one another a death?

DAN, *in agony:* Kid, the woman was his right hand. Without her he was never very much, you know. He'll fall apart.

QUENTIN: I can't agree; I think he can take it, he's got a lot of stuff.

Without halt, to the Listener:

Which is hilarious! . . . Well, because! He was always the one who idolized the old man, and I saw through him from the beginning; suddenly we're changing places, like children in a game! I don't know what I am to anybody!

DAN, *as though he had come to a decision:* All right; let's go in, then.

QUENTIN: You want me to tell him?

DAN, *unwillingly, afraid but challenged:* I'll do it.

QUENTIN: I could do it, Dan.

DAN, *relieved:* All right; if you don't mind.

They turn together toward Father in the "bed." He does not see them yet. They move with the weight of their news.

QUENTIN: It belongs to him, Dan, as much as his wedding.

He turns to the Listener as he walks.

Or is it simply that . . .

They have come to a halt near Father's "bed."

. . . I am crueler than he?

The nurse glances up at them and goes upstage, but waits there, apparently squinting into an upheld hypodermic needle. Now Father sees them and raises up his arm.

FATHER: For cryin' out loud! Look who's here! I thought you were in Europe!

QUENTIN: Just got back. How are you?

DAN: You look wonderful, Dad.

FATHER: What do you mean, "look"? I *am* wonderful! I tell you, I'm ready to go through it again!

They laugh proudly with him.

I mean it—the way that doctor worries, I finally told him, "Look, if it makes you feel so bad you lay down and I'll operate!" Very fine man. I thought you'd be away couple months more.

QUENTIN, *hesitantly:* I decided to come back and—

DAN, *breaking in, his voice turning strange:* Sylvia'll be right in. She's downstairs buying you something.

FATHER: Oh, that's nice! I tell you something, fellas—that kid is more and more like Mother. Been here every day . . . Where is Mother? I been calling the house.

The slightest empty, empty pause.

DAN: One second, Dad, I just want to—

Crazily, without evident point, he starts calling, and moving upstage toward the nurse. Quentin is staring at his father.

Nurse! Ah . . . could you call down to the gift shop and see if my sister . . .

FATHER: Dan! Tell her to get some ice. When Mother comes you'll all have a drink! I got a bottle of rye in the closet.

To Quentin, as Dan comes in closer:

I tell you, kid, I'm going to be young. I've been thinking all day since I woke up—Mother's right; just because I got old I don't have to act old. I mean we could go to Florida, we could—

QUENTIN: Dad.

FATHER: What? Is that a new suit?

QUENTIN: No, I've had it.

FATHER, *remembering—to Dan, of the nurse:* Oh, tell her glasses, we'll need more glasses.

Dan feels forced to turn and start out.

QUENTIN: Listen, Dad.

Dan halts, and turns back.

FATHER, *totally unaware:* Yeah?

QUENTIN—*he takes Father's hand:* Mother died.

Father's hand grips his abdomen as though he were stabbed; his right arm rises like a policeman ordering a stop. A gasp flies out of him.

She had a heart attack last night on her way home.

FATHER: Oh, no, no, no, no.

QUENTIN, *grasping his hand again:* We didn't want to tell you but—

FATHER: Ahhh! Ahhh, no, no, no.

DAN: There's nothing anybody could have done, Dad.

FATHER—*he claps his hands together:* Oh! Oh! Oh!

QUENTIN, *grasping his hand again:* Now look, Dad, you're going to be all right, you'll—

FATHER—*it is all turning into a deep gasping for breath; he struggles on his "bed," half trying to get off, his head constantly turning as though he were looking for his wife:* Oh boy. Oh boy! No, no.

DAN: Now look, Dad, you're a hell of a fella. Dad, listen—

FATHER: Goddamn it! I couldn't take care of myself, I knew she was working too hard!

QUENTIN: Dad, it's not your fault, that can happen to anyone.

FATHER: But she was sitting right here. She was . . . she was right here!

Now he weeps uncontrollably into his hands. Quentin puts an awkward arm around him.

QUENTIN: Pa . . . Pa . . .

Now Quentin grips him with both arms. Dan moves in close as though to share him. He lays a hand on Father's shoulder.

FATHER: Oh, boys—she was my right hand!

He raises his fist and seems about to lose his control again.

DAN: We'll take care of you, Dad. I don't want you to worry about—

FATHER: No-no. It's . . . I'll be all right. I'll . . . God! . . . Now I'm better! Now, *now* I'm better!

They are silent; he keeps shaking his head.

So where is she?

QUENTIN: In the funeral parlor.

FATHER, *shaking his head—an explosive blow of air:* Paaaaaah!

QUENTIN: We didn't want to tell you but we figured you'd rather know.

FATHER: Ya. *Pats Quentin's hand.* Thanks. Thanks. I'll . . . *He looks up at Quentin.* I'll just have to be stronger.

QUENTIN: That's right, Dad.

FATHER, *to no one:* This . . . will make me stronger. *But the weeping threatens; he clenches his jaws, shakes his head, and indicates a point.* She was right here!

Lights go out on him and Dan. Quentin comes slowly to the Listener.

QUENTIN: Yes, I'm proud I didn't kid him, it bothers me. I don't know, maybe that he took it so for granted I was also devastated. . . . This? I hadn't thought of this as grief. I hope it is.

The tower gradually begins to light.

Still, a couple months later he bothered to register and vote. . . . Well, I mean . . . it didn't kill him either, with all his tears. I don't know what the hell I'm driving at! I—*He is caught by the bright tower.* I don't get the connection at the moment but . . . I visited a concentration camp in Germany. . . .

He has started toward the tower when Felice appears, raising her arm in blessing.

FELICE: Close your eyes, okay?

QUENTIN, *turned by her force:* I don't understand why that girl sticks in my mind. . . . Yes!

He moves toward her now.

She did; she offered me some . . . love, I guess. And if I don't return it . . . or if it doesn't change me somehow, it . . . it's like owing for a gift you didn't ask for.

FELICE: I'll always bless you!

Her arm raised, she walks into darkness.

QUENTIN: When she left, I did a stupid thing. I don't understand it. There are two light fixtures on the wall of my hotel room. *Against his own disgust.* I noticed for the first time that they're . . . a curious distance apart. And I suddenly saw that if you stood between them—*He spreads out his arms*—you could reach out and rest your . . .

Just before he completely spreads his arms Maggie sits up; her breathing sounds. He drops his arms, aborting the image. Maggie goes dark.

Maybe I can get to it later. I can't now. . . .

Now Holga appears and is bending to read the legend fixed to the wall of a torture chamber.

Yes, with this woman . . . Holga. She took me there.

HOLGA, *turning to "him":* It's a general description. No, I don't mind, I'll translate it.

She returns to the legend; he slowly approaches behind her.

"In this camp a minimum of two hundred thousand Dutch, Belgian, Russian, Polish, French, and Danish prisoners of war were killed. Also, four thousand two hundred and seven refugees from the Spanish Republican Army. The door to the left leads into the chamber where their teeth were extracted for gold; the drain in the floor carried off the blood. At times instead of shooting, they were individually strangled to death. The barracks on the right were the bordello where women prisoners were forced to—"

QUENTIN, *touching her shoulder:* I think you've had enough, Holga.

HOLGA: No, if you want to see the rest . . . *She bursts into tears, but in silence, and quickly turns away.* Come, I don't mind.

QUENTIN, *taking her arm:* Let's walk, dear. Country looks lovely out there.

They walk. The light changes to day.

Here, this grass looks dry; let's sit down.

They sit. Pause.

I always thought the Danube was blue.

HOLGA: Only the waltz. Although it does change near Vienna. Out of some lingering respect for Strauss, I suppose.

QUENTIN: I don't know why this hit me so; I suddenly got a cracking headache in there.

HOLGA: I'm sorry. It's just that you seemed so interested in the Nazi period, and we were passing so close . . .

QUENTIN: No, I'm glad I saw it.

HOLGA, *starting to rise; she senses an estrangement:* I have some aspirin in the car.

QUENTIN, *lightly touching her:* We'll go soon. I just want to . . . sit for a minute.

HOLGA, *to raise his spirits:* You still want to see Salzburg?

QUENTIN: Oh, sure.

HOLGA: I'd love to show you Mozart's house. And the cafés are excellent there.

QUENTIN, *turning to her now:* Was there somebody you knew died here?

HOLGA: Oh, no. I feel people ought to see it, that's all. No one comes here any more. I've brought foreign colleagues once or twice.

QUENTIN: But why do you come back? It seems to tear you apart.

HOLGA: I suppose . . . one doesn't want to lose the past, even if it's dreadful. You're the first person I've met in a very long time who wants to talk about it.

QUENTIN: Yes, but I'm an American.

HOLGA: Oh, Americans too. In fact, when I first visited America after the war I was three days under questioning before they let me in. It was impossible to explain to them. How could one be in forced labor for two years if one were not a Communist? And of course, not being Jewish either, it was very suspicious. I was ready to turn back, I was so frightened. In fact, it was only when I told them I had blood relatives in several Nazi ministries that they were reassured. You see? Here it's not talked about, and outside it's not understood. It's as though fifteen years of one's life had simply vanished in some insane confusion. So I was very glad you were so interested.

QUENTIN, *glancing up at the tower:* I guess I thought I'd be indignant, or angry. But it's like swallowing a lump of earth. It's strange.

He starts to cover his eyes and she presses him to lie down, and speaks cheerfully . . .

HOLGA: Come, lie down here for a while and perhaps—

QUENTIN: No, I'm—*He has fended off her hand.* I'm sorry, dear, I didn't mean to push you away.

HOLGA, *rebuffed and embarrassed:* I see wildflowers on that hill; I'll pick some for the car!

She gets up quickly.

QUENTIN: Holga?

She continues off. He jumps up and hurries to her, turning her.

Holga.

He does not know what to say.

HOLGA, *holding back tears:* Perhaps we've been together too much. I could rent another car at Linz; perhaps we could meet in Vienna sometime.

QUENTIN: I don't want to lose you, Holga.

HOLGA: I understand that you're leaving soon. I never expected any . . .

QUENTIN: But you do expect something, everybody does. You're not a woman to go to bed just for the ride.

HOLGA: No, I'm not. But I have settled since several years to live for my work. I am not helpless alone. It's simply that from the moment you spoke to me I felt somehow familiar, and it was never so before. . . . It isn't a question of getting married; I am not ashamed this way. But I must have *something*.

QUENTIN: I don't give you anything? Tell me; because I've been told that before, but never so calmly.

HOLGA: You give me very much. . . . It's difficult for me to speak like this—I am not a woman who must be reassured every minute, those women are stupid to me.

QUENTIN: We're good friends, Holga; say it to me.

HOLGA: You have nothing; but perhaps that's all you want. I can understand that after what you've lived.

QUENTIN: That's not it, Holga; there's nothing as dull as adventure. I've had all I can use.

HOLGA: But perhaps that's all there is for you.

QUENTIN—*he turns her face to him:* Holga. Are you weeping . . . for *me?*

HOLGA: Yes.

QUENTIN, *struck:* Don't go away; not yet. Will you?

HOLGA: I hear your wings opening, Quentin.

QUENTIN: I don't want to abuse your feeling for me, you understand? The truth is—and I couldn't say this if I didn't trust you—I swear I don't know if I have lived in good faith. And the doubt ties my tongue when I think of promising anything again.

HOLGA: But how can one ever be sure of one's good faith?

QUENTIN, *surprised:* God, it's wonderful to hear you say that. All my women have been so goddamned sure!

HOLGA: But how can one ever be?

QUENTIN—*he kisses her gratefully:* Why do you keep coming back to this place?

Pause. Holga is disturbed, uncertain.

HOLGA: I . . . don't know. Perhaps . . . because I didn't die here.

QUENTIN—*turns quickly to Listener:* What?

HOLGA: Although that would make no sense! I don't really know!

QUENTIN—*goes to the chair:* That people . . . what? "Wish to die for the dead"? No, no, I can understand it; survival can be hard to bear. But I . . . I don't think I feel that way . . .

Maggie again appears in bed on the upper level; she begins to heave for breath. Her face is still indistinguishable. Instantly Quentin turns away as from an opposite side of the stage a piano is heard and a woman, Mother, is in midsong with a romantic ballad from a musical of the twenties.

Although I do think of my mother now, and she's dead. Yes!

He turns to Holga.

Maybe the dead do bother her.

HOLGA: It was the middle of the war. I had just come out of a class and there were leaflets on the sidewalk. A photograph of a concentration camp. And emaciated people. It was dropped there by British Intelligence; one tended to believe the British. I had had no idea. Truly. Any more, perhaps, than Americans know how a Negro lives. I was seventeen; I lived in my studies; I planned how to cut my hair differently. It is much more complicated than it seems later. There were many officers in my family. It was our country. It isn't easy to turn against your country; not in a war. There are always reasons —do Americans turn against America because of Hiroshima? No, there are reasons always.

Pause.

And I took the leaflet to my godfather—he was still commanding our Intelligence. And I asked if it were true. "Of course," he said, "why does it excite you"? And I said, "You are a swine. You are all swine." I threw my briefcase at him. And he opened it and put some papers in and asked me to deliver it to a certain address. And I became a courier for the officers who were planning to assassinate Hitler. . . . They were all hanged.

QUENTIN: Why not you?

HOLGA: They didn't betray me.

QUENTIN: Then why do you say good faith is never sure?

HOLGA, *after a pause:* It was my country . . . longer perhaps than it should have been. But I didn't know. And now I don't know how I could not have known. I can't imagine not knowing, now.

QUENTIN: Holga . . . I bless your uncertainty. Maybe that's why you're so wonderful to be with. You don't seem to be looking for some goddamned . . . moral *victory*. Forgive me, I didn't mean to be distant with you. I—*Looks up at the tower*—think this place frightens me! And how is that possible? All empty!

HOLGA: I'll get the flowers. And maybe we can buy some cheese and apples and eat while we drive!

She starts away.

QUENTIN: And you forgive me?

HOLGA—*turns, and with great love:* Yes! I'll be right back! And we'll go right away!

She hurries away.

Quentin stands in stillness a moment; the presence of the tower bores in on him; its color changes; he now looks up at it and addresses the Listener.

QUENTIN: But it's empty now! In fact, the view from here is rather pastoral; and the stone walls are warm in the sun, and quiet. I think . . . I may have imagined it more monstrous. Or bizarre. I helped a mason years ago before I went to college—I see the problem building such high walls in sandy soil . . . how dare one think of that? I think of the footings —they must go ten feet down. At least ten! I know footings! But I never thought the stones would look so ordinary.

Now he turns out.

Why do I *know* something here? Even hollow now and empty, it has a face; and asks a sort of question: "What do you believe . . . as true as this?" Yes! Believers built this, maybe that's the fright—and I, without belief, stand here disarmed. I can see the convoys grinding up this hill; and I inside; no one knows my name and yet they'll smash my head on a concrete floor! And no appeal.

He turns quickly to the Listener.

Yes! It's that I no longer see some last appeal, and here there was none either! Socialism once, then love; some final hope is gone that always saved before the end!

Mother appears; at the same time her coffin appears above.

MOTHER: Not too much cake, darling, there'll be a lot of food at this wedding. *Calling upstage.* Fanny? Cut him a small piece . . . well, not *that* small!

QUENTIN: Mother! That's strange. And murder. Or is it her comfort brings her to me in this place?

MOTHER: Fanny? Not too hot ironing my husband's dress shirt! *Turns suddenly to an invisible boy.* You are going to wear garters tonight, Quentin, and don't argue with me. . . . Because it's my brother's wedding and your stockings are not to hang over your shoes!

QUENTIN—*he has started to laugh but it turns into:* Why can't I mourn her? And Holga wept in there . . . why can't I weep? Why do I feel an understanding with this slaughter-house?

Now Felice appears, raising her arm.

I don't understand what I'm supposed to be to anyone!

Felice is gone. Mother laughs. He turns to her, addressing the Listener.

I don't know, some wedding in the family. I don't get it.

MOTHER—*her laughter turning bitter:* God! Why must every wedding in this family be a catastrophe! . . . Because the girl is pregnant, darling, and she's got no money, she's stupid, and I tell you this one is going to end up with a mustache! Five beautiful men like that and one after the other . . . I don't know where they *find* such women!

QUENTIN, *watching her, seated:* But what the hell has this to do with a concentration camp?

MOTHER: And wants a tight gown! As though she's fooling somebody! That's why, darling, when you grow up, I hope you learn how to disappoint people. Especially women. Never forget it, dear, you're a man, and a man has all the choices. Will you stop playing with matches? *Slaps an invisible boy's hand.* You'll pee in bed! Why don't you practice your penmanship instead? You write like a monkey, darling.

QUENTIN, *shaking his head, glancing up at the tower:* I don't get it.

Father suddenly appears, holding an invisible phone to his ear. Quentin instantly stands.

MOTHER: And where is your father? If he went to sleep in a Turkish bath again, I'll . . .

Quentin is moving toward Father as though wanting to hear

what he is saying in phone; he is making a shushing gesture to Mother.

What are you talking about, I didn't end up calling all the Turkish baths the night my brother Herbert got married? Forgot all about it . . . and nothing bothers him!

She laughs warmly. Quentin has arrived at Father, peers at his profile.

FATHER: Herman? Cable Hamburg.
MOTHER: Like the night of the Dempsey-Tunney fight.
QUENTIN: Ssh!

He turns back, eager to hear what Father is saying.

MOTHER: . . . The men's-room door gets stuck so by the time he gets out there's a new champion. Cost him a hundred dollars to go to the men's room!
FATHER: No, sixty thousand tons; sixty; Vera Cruz, the *Bismarck*'s due.
MOTHER: But you mustn't laugh at him, he's a wonderful man, it's just that sometimes he can drive you out of your mind.
FATHER: Then cable Southampton, turn him back to Finland Monday. A.T.O.
MOTHER: My wedding? Oh, no dear, my wedding . . . there was happiness.

Quentin turns to her.

Well, look at your father; to this day he walks into a room you want to bow! Not like my sisters, one after the other running into the house, "Mama, I'm in love!" And with what? With who? I wasn't allowed to *see* your father till his father and Grandpa had agreed! . . . *Because*, I decided for once somebody was not going to break my mother's heart. . . . What are you talking about, of course I loved him! *Warmly.* He'd take me to a restaurant—one look at him and the waiters started moving tables around; if he saw a thick water glass he'd walk out; there could be a line around the block to a Broadway show, he'd go right up to the box office and they'd find two tickets. *Because*, dear—people know that this is a *man*. Even Doctor Strauss, at my wedding he came over to me says, "Rose, I can see it looking at him, you've got a wonderful man," and he was always in love with me, Strauss. . . . Oh, sure, but he was only a medical student then, didn't have a penny, my father wouldn't let him in the house. Who knew he'd end up so big in gallstones? That poor boy—used to bring me novels to read, poetry, philosophy, God knows what! One time we even sneaked off to hear Rachmaninoff together. . . .

She laughs sadly; with wonder more than bitterness:

That's why, you see, two weeks after we were married; sit down to dinner and Papa hands me a menu, and asks me to read it to him. . . . Couldn't *read*! I got so frightened I nearly ran away! . . . "Why"? Because your grandmother is such a fine, unselfish woman; two months in school and they put him into the shop! That's what some women are, my dear . . . and now he goes and buys her a new Packard every year and two more for his brothers! Damned fool, I could kill him! And what are we paying a chauffeur for, I can't find him half the time anyway! . . . Because if they're going to have chauffeurs I'm going to have a chauffeur—it's all our money anyway!

With a strange and deep fear:

Please, darling, I want you to *draw* the letters, that scribbling is ugly, dear; and your posture, your speech, it can all be beautiful! Ask Miss Fisher, for years they kept my handwriting pinned up on the bulletin board; they made up a special new prize to give me on graduating day. God, I'll never forget it, valedictorian of the class with a scholarship to Hunter in my hand—*A blackness flows into her soul*—and I come home, and Grandpa says, "You're getting married!" It had never come into my mind! I was like . . . like with small wings, just getting ready to fly; I slept all year with the catalogue under my pillow. To learn, to learn everything! Oh, darling, the whole thing is such a mystery!

Father enters the area, talking to the young, invisible Quentin.

FATHER: Quentin, would you get me the office on the phone?

To Mother as he kisses her lightly on the cheek: Why would you call the Turkish bath?

MOTHER: I thought you forgot about the wedding.

FATHER: I wish I could but I'm paying for it.

MOTHER: He'll pay you back!

FATHER: I believe it, I just wouldn't want to hang by my hair that long.

He turns, goes to an invisible phone, stands.

Herman? Hold the wire. *To Mother:* Why don't you both go up and get dressed?

MOTHER, *moving up the stairs:* I don't want to be late, now.

FATHER: There's time; she won't give birth if we're a half-hour late.

MOTHER: Don't be so smart! He fell in love, what's so terrible about that?

FATHER: They all fall in love on my money. Only I can't fall in love unless I pay for it. I married into a love nest! *He turns to the invisible Quentin, warmly smiling.* Did they pass a law that kid can't get a haircut? *Reaching into his pocket, tossing a coin.* Here, at least get a shine. *To Mother:* I'll be right up, dear, go ahead, get dressed. *In "phone":* Herman? The accountant still there? Put him on.

QUENTIN, *suddenly, recalling:* Oh, yes!

MOTHER: I'll put in your studs. God, he's so beautiful in a tuxedo!

She goes a distance out of the area but halts on the stair, turns, eavesdrops.

FATHER: Billy? You finished? Well what's the story, where am I?

Quentin now turns up toward Mother on the stairs.

QUENTIN: . . . Yes!

FATHER: Don't you read the papers? What'll I do with Irving Trust, I can't give it away. What bank?

Mother descends a step, alarmed.

I been to every bank in New York, I can't get a bill paid, how the hell they going to lend me money? No-no, there's no money in London, there's no money in Hamburg, there ain't a cargo moving in the world, the ocean's empty, Billy. . . . Now tell me the truth, where am I?

Pause. Mother descends another step. Quentin is below, watching her. Now Mother descends into the area. Father stands almost stiffly, as though to take a storm.

MOTHER: What's that about? What are you "winding up"?

Father stands staring; he speaks unheard, but she seems to have heard an additional shocking fact, then another, and another.

What are you talking about? When did this start? . . . Well, how much are you taking out of it? . . . You lost your mind? You've got over four hundred thousand dollars' worth of stocks, you can sell the . . . You sold those wonderful stocks! When? . . . Eight months! I just bought a new grand piano, why didn't you say something? And a silver service for my brother, and you don't say anything? . . .

More subdued, walks a few steps in thought.

Well then, you'd better cash your insurance; you've got at least seventy-five thousand cash value. . . .

Halts, turning in shock.

When?

Father is gradually losing his stance, his grandeur; he pulls his tie loose.

All right, then—we'll get rid of my bonds. Do it tomorrow. . . . What do you mean? Well you get them back, I've got ninety-one thousand dollars in bonds you gave me. Those are my bonds. I've got bonds. . . .

Breaks off; open horror on her face and now a growing contempt.

You mean you saw everything going down and you throw good money after bad? Are you some kind of a moron?

FATHER: You don't walk away from a business; I came to this country with a tag around my neck like a package in the bottom of the boat!

MOTHER: I should have run the day I met you!

FATHER, *as though stabbed:* Rose!

He sits, closing his eyes, his neck bent.

MOTHER: I should have done what my sisters did, tell my parents to go to hell and thought of myself for once! I should have run for my life!

FATHER: Sssh, I hear the kids.

A sharp shaft of light opens a few yards away and he glances toward it.

MOTHER: I ought to get a divorce!

FATHER: Rose, the college men are jumping out of windows!

MOTHER: But your last dollar? *Bending over, into his face:* You are an idiot!

Her nearness forces him to stand; they look at each other, strangers.

QUENTIN—*he looks up at the tower:* Yes! For no reason—they don't even ask your name!

FATHER—*he looks toward the column of light:* Somebody crying? Quentin's in there. You better talk to him.

Quentin walks upstage, away from the light. She goes in some trepidation toward it. A foot or so from it she halts.

MOTHER: Darling? You better get dressed. Don't cry, dear, it'll be all right. He'll come back bigger than ever!

She is stopped short by something "Quentin" has said.

What *I* said? Why, what did I say? . . . Are you crazy? I'd never say a thing like that, I thought you were upstairs. Well I was a little angry, that's all, but I never said *that*. I think he's a wonderful man! *Laughs.* How could I say a thing like that? Quentin!

The light rapidly fades, and as though he is disappearing she extends her arms toward the fading light.

But I didn't say anything!

With a cry toward someone lost.

Darling, I didn't say anything!

Instantly Holga appears beneath the tower, with flowers in her arms. She looks about for him.

HOLGA: Quentin? Quentin?

He is still staring at Mother, from whom he turns toward Holga. Now Holga sees him and comes down to him.

Look! The car will be all sweet inside!

QUENTIN—*he absently sniffs the flowers, staring at her:* You love me, don't you?

HOLGA: Yes.

QUENTIN, *glancing up at the tower:* Do you ever feel when you come here some vague . . . complicity?

HOLGA: Quentin . . . no one they didn't kill can be innocent again.

QUENTIN—*slight pause:* Then how do you get so purposeful, Holga? You work so hard, you seem so full of joy and hope.

HOLGA: While I was getting the flowers just now I thought I ought to tell you something. In a bombing once I lost my memory, and wandered everywhere with crowds across the countryside looking for a safe place. Every day, one turned away from people dying on the roads. Until one night I tried to jump from the railing of a bridge. An old soldier pulled me back and slapped my face and made me follow him; he'd lost a leg at Stalingrad, was furious that I would kill myself; I walked behind his crutches over Germany looking for some sign of who I'd been. And suddenly there was a door with a tremendous lion's-head brass knocker; I ran; I knocked; my mother opened it. My life came back! And I turned to ask the soldier in; to thank him; to feed him; to give him everything I had! But he was gone. I've been told that I imagined him, but even now at times I turn a corner and expect to find him. If we could even . . . nod to one another! I know how terrible it is to owe what one can never pay. And for a long time after I had the same dream each night—that I had a child; and even in the dream I saw that the child was my life; and it was an idiot. And I wept, and a hundred times I ran away, but each time I came back it had the same dreadful face. Until I thought, if I could kiss it, whatever in it was my own, perhaps I could rest. And I bent to its broken face, and it was horrible . . . but I kissed it.

QUENTIN: Does it still come back?

HOLGA: At times. But it somehow has the virtue now . . . of being mine. I think one must finally take one's life in one's arms, Quentin.

She takes his hand.

Come, I think they play *The Magic Flute* tomorrow. You like *The Magic Flute*?

QUENTIN—*he kisses her:* One thing about you, you tell the goddamned funniest stories!

HOLGA—*hits him and mock-pouts:* You're making fun of me!

QUENTIN: Let's get out of this dump, and . . . where we going?

HOLGA, *laughing:* Salzburg!

QUENTIN: I'll race you to the car, last one there's a rotten egg. Or do you say a rancid wurst?

HOLGA, *laughing:* Okay, I'm racing!

She gets set.

QUENTIN: Go!

They start running, but while she goes off into darkness Quentin comes down to the chair.

QUENTIN: I miss her badly. And yet, I can't sign my letters to her "With love." I put "Sincerely" or "As ever," some such brilliant evasion. I've lost the sense of some absolute necessity, I think. Living alone does that; I walk down the street, I see the millions of apartment windows lighting up—I swear I don't understand how each man knows which door to go to. Can they all be in love? Is that what sorts them out? I don't think so; it's some kind of innocence, a deep belief that all their destinations are ordained. With me, whether I open a book or think of marrying again, it's so damned clear I've chosen what I do—it cuts the strings between my hands and heaven. It sounds foolish, but I feel . . . unblessed. And I look back at when there seemed to be a kind of plan, some duty in the sky. I had a dinner table, and a wife, a child, and the world so wonderfully threatened by injustices I was born to correct! How fine! Remember? When there were good people and bad people? And how easy it was to tell! The worst son of a bitch, if he loved Jews and Negroes and hated Hitler—he was a buddy. Like some kind of paradise compared to this. . . . Until I begin to look at it.

Elsie appears, a beach robe hanging from her shoulders, her arms out of the sleeves, her back to us; she is fixing her wet hair in an invisible mirror.

God, when I think of what I believed, I want to hide!

He stands, moves toward her.

. . . Yes, but I wasn't all that young! You would think a man of thirty-two would know that when a guest, changing out of a wet bathing suit in his bedroom . . .

Elsie, as he approaches, turns to him, and her robe slips off one shoulder.

and just stands there with her two bare faces hanging out . . .

ELSIE: Oh, are you through working? Why don't you swim now? The water's just right.

QUENTIN, *with a laugh of great pain, crying out:* I tell you I believed she didn't know she was naked! It's Eden! . . . Well, she was *married*! How could a woman who can tell when the Budapest String Quartet is playing off key, who refuses to wear silk stockings because the Japanese have invaded Manchuria, whose husband—my friend, a saintly professor of law—is editing my first appeal to the Supreme Court on the grass outside that window—I could see the top of his head past her tit, for God's sake! . . . Of course I understood, but it's what you allow yourself to admit! To admit what you see endangers principles!

Elsie leaves the "room" and crosses to where Louise sits. Quentin turns to them. They are talking in an intense whisper. He now approaches them from behind, halts, turns to the Listener.

You know? When two women are whispering, and they stop abruptly when you appear . . .

ELSIE and LOUISE, *turning to him after an abrupt stop to their talking:* Hi.

In the background Lou appears, reading a brief—a tender, kindly man, in shorts.

QUENTIN: . . . The subject must have been sex. And if one of them is your wife . . . she must have been talking about you.

ELSIE, *as though to get him to go:* Lou's behind the house, reading your brief. He says it's superb!

QUENTIN: I hope so. I've been kind of nervous about what he'd say.

ELSIE: I wish you'd tell him that, Quentin! Will you? Just how much his opinion means to you. It's important you tell him.

QUENTIN: I'll be glad to. *Awkwardly glancing from Louise back to her:* Nice here, isn't it?

ELSIE: It's enchanting. *Taking in Louise:* I envy you both so much!

QUENTIN: See you. Glad you could come.

ELSIE—*gets up, goes past Lou:* I want one more walk before the train, dear. Did you comb your hair today?

LOU, *closing the brief:* I think so. Quentin! This is superb! It's hardly like a brief at all; there's a majestic quality, like a classic opinion! *Chuckling, tugs Quentin's sleeve.* I almost feel honored to have known you!

Elsie is gone.

QUENTIN: I'm so glad, Lou—your opinion means . . .

LOU: Your whole career will change with this, Quentin. But do me a favor, will you?

QUENTIN: Oh, anything, Lou.

LOU: Would you offer it to Elsie to read? I know it seems an extraordinary request, but . . .

QUENTIN: No, I'd be delighted!

LOU, *secretively:* It's shaken her terribly, my being subpoenaed and all those damned headlines. Despite everything, it does affect one's whole relationship. So any gesture of respect becomes terrifically important. For example, I gave her the manuscript of my new text to read, and I've even called off publication for a while to incorporate her criticisms. It may be her psychoanalysis, but she's become remarkably acute.

QUENTIN: But I hope you don't delay any more, Lou; it'd be wonderful if you published something now. Just to show those bastards.

LOU: Yes . . .

Glancing toward the women, he takes Quentin's arm and strolls with him.

I've been thinking of calling you about that, Quentin. You see, it's a textbook for the schools, and Elsie feels that it will only start a new attack on me.

QUENTIN: But they've investigated you, what more damage could they do?

LOU: Who knows? Another attack might knock me off the faculty. It's only Mickey's vote that saved me the last time.

QUENTIN: Really! I didn't know that.

LOU: Oh, yes, he made a marvelous speech at the Dean's meeting when I refused to testify.

QUENTIN: Well, that's Mickey.

LOU: Yes, but Elsie feels . . . I'd just be drawing down the lightning again to publish now. She even feels it's some unconscious wish for self-destruction on my part. And yet, if I put the book away, it's like a kind of suicide to me. Everything I know is in that book. . . . What's your opinion?

QUENTIN: Lou, you have a right to publish; a radical past is not leprosy. We only turned Left because it seemed the truth was there. You mustn't be ashamed.

LOU, *in pain:* Goddamn it, yes! Except . . . I never told you this, Quentin. . . .

QUENTIN—*comes down to the Listener:* What am I going into this for? *Listens.* Yes—in a way it was—the day the world ended, it all fell down, and nobody was innocent again. And yet, we never were! What am I looking for?

LOU: When I returned from Russia and published my study of Soviet law—*Breaks off.* I left out many things I saw. I . . . lied. For a good cause, I thought, but all that lasts is the lie. It's so strange to me now—I have many failings, but I have never been a liar. And I lied for the Party. Over and over, year after year. And that's why, now . . . with this book of mine, I want to be true to myself. You see, it's no attack I fear, but being forced to defend my own incredible lies!

Elsie appears, approaching, hearing.

ELSIE: Lou, I'm quite surprised. I thought we'd settled this.
LOU: Yes, dear, I only wanted Quentin's feeling . . .
ELSIE: Your shirt's out, dear.

He quickly tucks it into his shorts. And to Quentin:

You certainly don't think he ought to publish.
QUENTIN: But the alternative seems—
ELSIE, *with a volcanic, suppressed alarm:* But, dear, that's the *situation*! Lou's not like you, Quentin; you and Mickey can function in the rough and tumble of private practice, but Lou's a purely academic person. He's *incapable* of going out and . . .
LOU, *with a difficult grin and chuckle:* Well, dear, I'm not all that delicate, I—
ELSIE—*a sudden flash of contempt; to Lou:* This is hardly the time for illusions!

With a smash of light Mother appears, and Father slumped in a chair beside her.

MOTHER: You *idiot*!

Quentin is shocked, turns quickly to Mother.

My *bonds*?

She and Father are gone. Instantly, as before, Holga appears under the tower, flowers in her hand, looking about for him.

HOLGA: Quentin?

He quickly turns his head toward her. She is gone.

QUENTIN, *alone:* How do you believe again?

Felice appears.

FELICE: I'll always bless you!

She turns and walks into the dark. The wall appears with the two light fixtures.

QUENTIN: The other night, when that girl left . . . I . . .

Turns to the wall. The fixtures light up. But he turns away, agonized.   .

I'll try to get to it . . .

ELSIE: Come, dear, you haven't even swum. Let's enjoy this weekend!

She walks off with Lou, kissing his cheek.

QUENTIN, *watching them go:* Then why does something seem to fall apart? Was it ever whole?

Louise now stands up from the beach chair. She turns, addresses an empty space.

LOUISE: Quentin?

QUENTIN—*he turns his eyes to the ground, then speaks to the Listener:* Wasn't that a terrifying thing, what Holga said?

LOUISE: I've decided to go into psychoanalysis.

QUENTIN, *still to Listener:* To take up your life, like an idiot child?

LOUISE: I want to talk about some things with you.

QUENTIN: But can anybody really do that?

He turns toward Louise now guiltily.

Kiss his life?

LOUISE, *as though he had not answered—speaking toward the empty space:* Quentin?

He is drawn to the spot she is concentrating her gaze on. Tension rises in him as he arrives in her line of sight and faces her.

You don't have to pick up Betty now, she enjoys playing there. *Steeling her shy self.* I've got to make a decision.

QUENTIN: About what?

LOUISE, *in fear:* About everything.

QUENTIN: What do you mean?

LOUISE—*at a loss for an instant:* Sit down, will you?

She sits, gathering her thoughts. He hesitates, as though pained at the memory, and also because at the time he lived this it was an agony. And as he approaches his chair he speaks to the Listener.

QUENTIN: It was like . . . a meeting. In seven years we had never had a meeting. Never, never what you'd call . . . a meeting.

LOUISE: We don't seem . . .

A long pause while she peers at a forming thought—

married.

QUENTIN: We?

LOUISE—*it is sincere, what she says, but she has had to learn the words, so there is the faintest air of a formula in her way of speaking:* You don't pay any attention to me.

QUENTIN, *puzzled:* When?

LOUISE: You never did. But I never realized it till . . . recently.

QUENTIN, *to help her:* You mean like Friday night? When I didn't open the car door for you?

LOUISE: Well, that's a small thing, but it's part of what I mean, yes.

QUENTIN: But I told you; you always opened the car door for yourself.

LOUISE: I've always done everything for myself, but that doesn't mean it's right. Everybody notices it, Quentin.

QUENTIN: What?

LOUISE: The way you behave toward me. I don't . . . *exist.* People are supposed to find out about each other. I am not all this uninteresting, Quentin. Many people, men *and* women, think I *am* interesting.

QUENTIN: Well, I—*Breaks off.* I—*Breaks off.* I . . . don't know what you mean.

LOUISE: I know you don't. You have no conception of what a woman is. You think I'm some sort of . . . I don't know what I am to you.

QUENTIN: But I do pay attention—just last night I read you my whole brief.

LOUISE: Quentin, you think reading a brief to a woman is talking to her?

QUENTIN: But that's what's on my mind.

LOUISE: But if that's all on your mind what do you need a wife for?

QUENTIN: Now what kind of a question is that?

LOUISE: Quentin, that's the question!

QUENTIN—*slight pause; with fear, astonishment:* What's the question?

LOUISE: What am I to you? Do you . . . do you ever *ask* me anything? Anything personal?

QUENTIN, *with rising alarm:* But Louise, what am I supposed to ask you? I *know* you!

LOUISE: No.

She stands with dangerous dignity.

You don't know me.

Pause. She proceeds now with caution.

I don't intend to be ashamed of myself any more, I used to think it was normal; or even that you don't see me because I'm not worth seeing. But I think now that you don't really see any woman. Except in some ways your mother. You do sense her feelings; you do know when she's unhappy or anxious, but not me. Or any other woman.

Elsie appears, about to drop her robe.

QUENTIN: That's not true, though. I . . .

LOUISE: Elsie's noticed it too.

QUENTIN, *guiltily snapping away from the vision of Elsie:* What?

LOUISE: She's amazed at you.

QUENTIN: Why, what'd she say?

LOUISE: You don't seem to . . . register the fact that a woman is *present.*

QUENTIN: Oh. *He is disarmed, confused, and silent.*

LOUISE: And you know how she admires you.

Quentin nods seriously. Suddenly he turns out to the Listener and bursts into an agonized, ironical laughter. He abruptly breaks it off, and returns to silence before Louise.
Louise speaks with uncertainty; it is her first attempt at confrontation.

Quentin?

He stands in silence.

Quentin?

He is silent.

Silence is not going to solve it any more. I can't live this way. Quentin?

QUENTIN—*pause; he gathers courage:* Maybe I don't speak because the one time I did tell you my feelings you didn't get over it for six months.

LOUISE, *angered:* It wasn't six months, it was a few weeks. I did overreact, but it's understandable. You come back from a trip and tell me you'd met a woman you wanted to sleep with?

QUENTIN: That's not the way I said it.

LOUISE: It's exactly the way. And we were married a year.

QUENTIN: It is not the way I said it, Louise. It was an idiotic thing to tell you but I still say I meant it as a compliment; that I did not touch her because I realized what you meant to me. And for damn near a year you looked at me as though I were some kind of a monster who could never be trusted again.

LOUISE: Well that's in *your* mind. I've completely forgotten it.

QUENTIN: Is it only in my mind if you can still distort it this way?

LOUISE: Quentin, I am not your mother or some third party to whom you can come running with reports of your conquests!

QUENTIN: You see? This is what I mean! What conquests? How can I talk if you are going to blow everything up into a—a—

LOUISE: Quentin, I didn't bring her up, you did.

QUENTIN: Because I know you have never forgiven it, and I can't talk if I have to watch every word I say.

LOUISE, *astonished:* You mean you have to watch every word you say?

QUENTIN: Well, not every word, but—but—

LOUISE, *looking at him with new eyes:* Well, I had no idea!

QUENTIN, *pleading:* Now, look, Louise . . . I didn't mean it exactly that way!

LOUISE, *horrified:* I had no idea you were . . . dishonest with me.

QUENTIN, *drowning in guilt:* Well what did I say? What are you looking at me like that for?

With her hands thrust into her hair she rushes away, a stifled cry in her throat. He calls after her.

Louise!

Immediately to the Listener:

And why do I believe she's right? . . . That's the point! . . . Yes, now, now! It's innocence, isn't it? The innocent are always better, aren't they? Then why can't I be innocent?

Elsie appears, about to drop her robe.

Why couldn't I simply say, "Louise, your best friend is treacherous; your newfound dignity suits her purpose"? . . . No, no, it isn't only that Elsie tempted me, it's worse. If I see a sin why is it in some part mine?

Elsie vanishes as the tower appears.

Even this slaughterhouse! Could I kill Jews? Throw ice water on prisoners of war and let them freeze to death? Why does something in this place touch my shoulder like an accomplice? . . . Huh? Please, yes, if you think you know.

Mother appears. He turns to her.

In what sense treacherous?

MOTHER: What poetry he brought me! He understood me, Strauss. And two weeks after the wedding, Papa hands me the menu. To *read*!

QUENTIN: Huh! Yes! And to a little boy . . . who knows how to read; a powerful reader, that little boy!

MOTHER: I want your handwriting beautiful, darling; I want you to be . . .

QUENTIN: . . . an accomplice!

MOTHER, *turning on Father, who sits dejectedly:* My *bonds*? And you don't even tell me anything? Are you a moron?

QUENTIN—*he watches her go dark, and speaks to the Listener. The tower remains alive:* Yes, yes, I understand, but . . . Why is the world so treacherous? Shall we lay it all to mothers? You understand? The sickness is much larger than my skull; aren't there mothers who keep dissatisfaction hidden to the grave, and do not split the faith of sons until they go in guilt for what they did not do? And I'll go further—here's the final bafflement for me—is it altogether good to be not guilty for what another does?

Mickey appears coming to Quentin, who turns to him.

MICKEY: The brief is fine, kid; I swear it almost began to move me. *To Louise, grinning:* You proud of him?

LOUISE—*she starts off:* Yes! Lou and Elsie are here.

MICKEY: Oh! I didn't know. You look wonderful, Louise, look all excited!

LOUISE: Thanks! It's nice to hear.

She shyly, soundlessly laughs, glancing at Quentin, and goes.

MICKEY—*pause; his smile transforms instantly to a shy grin:* You got trouble?

QUENTIN, *embarrassed:* I don't think so. She's going into psychoanalysis.

The tower dies out.

MICKEY: You got trouble, then. *Laughs.* But she'll be more interesting. Although for a while she'll probably be talking about her rights.

QUENTIN: Really? That's just what she was talking about!

MICKEY—*shakes his head, laughing joyfully:* I love women! I think maybe you got married too young; I did too. Although, *you* don't fool around, do you?

QUENTIN: I don't, no.

MICKEY: Then what the hell are you so guilty about?

QUENTIN: I am?

MICKEY: She loves you, Quent.

QUENTIN: I guess so, ya.

MICKEY: Maybe you ought to— See, when it first happened to me, I set aside five minutes a day just imagining my wife as a stranger. As though I hadn't made her yet. You got to generate some respect for her mystery. Start with five minutes; I can go as long as an hour, now.

QUENTIN: Makes it seem like a game though, doesn't it?

MICKEY: Well it is, isn't it, in a way? As soon as there's two people you can't be absolutely sincere, can you? I mean she's not your rib.

QUENTIN: I guess that's right, yes.

Pause.

MICKEY: Where's Lou?

QUENTIN, *pointing:* They're down swimming. You want to swim?

MICKEY: No.

He walks to a point, looks down as over a cliff.

That dear man; look at him, he never learned how to swim, always paddled like a dog. I used to love that man. I still do.

He sits on his heels, draws in the earth.

I'm sorry you didn't get into town two weeks ago when I called you.

QUENTIN: Why, is there some . . . ?

MICKEY: Well, I called you, Quent, I called you three times wanting to talk to you.

He gets up, stands, hands in pockets, glancing at the ground.

I've been subpoenaed.

QUENTIN, *shocked:* Oh, God! The Committee?

MICKEY: Yes. I wish you'd have come into town. . . . But it doesn't matter now.

QUENTIN: I had a feeling it was something like that. I guess I . . . didn't want to know any more. I'm sorry, Mick.

To Listener:

Yes, not to see, not to see!

A long pause. They find it hard to look directly at each other. Mickey picks up a stick, gouges at it with his thumbnail.

MICKEY: I've been going through hell, Quent. It's a strange thing—to have to examine what you stand for; not theoretically, but on a life-and-death basis. A lot of things don't stand up.

QUENTIN: I guess the main thing is not to be afraid.

MICKEY: Yes. *Pause.* I don't think I am, any more. I was, two weeks ago; I shook when the marshal came into the office and handed me that pink piece of paper. I really shook. It was dreadful. My knees shook.

A pause. Both sit staring ahead. Finally, Mickey turns and looks at Quentin, who now faces him. Mickey tries to smile.

You may not be my friend any more.

QUENTIN—*tries to laugh it away, a terror rising in him:* Why?

MICKEY: I'm going to tell the truth.

Pause.

QUENTIN: How do you mean?

MICKEY: I'm . . . going to name names.

QUENTIN, *incredulously:* Why?

MICKEY: Because . . . I want to. I don't want this conceal-ment any more. Fifteen years, wherever I go, whatever I talk about, the feeling is always there that I'm deceiving people. Like living in an occupied country, half in the dark.

QUENTIN: But you only belonged for a few months, didn't you?

MICKEY: Yes, but it was a commitment, Quent. I'm sorry we never got to talk about it; I've never really gone along with this Fifth Amendment silence, I think it's insincere; a man ought to take the rap for what he's been.

QUENTIN: But why couldn't you just tell about yourself?

MICKEY: I have. They're playing for keeps, kid; they want the names, and they mean to destroy anyone who—

QUENTIN: I think it's a mistake, Mick. All this is going to pass, and I think you'll regret it. And anyway, how can they de-stroy you?

MICKEY—*slight pause:* Quent, I'll be voted out of the firm if I don't testify.

QUENTIN: Oh, no! Max has always talked against this kind of thing!

MICKEY: I've had it out with Max.

QUENTIN: I can't believe it! What about DeVries?

MICKEY: DeVries was there, and Burton, and most of the others. I wish you'd have seen their faces when I told them. Men I've worked with for thirteen years. Played tennis; intimate friends, you know? And as soon as I said I had been —stones.

The tower lights.

QUENTIN, *to the Listener:* Everything is one thing! You see? I don't know what we are to one another! Or rather, rather what we ought to be!

MICKEY: Quent, I could feel their backs turning on me. It was horrible! As though—they would let me die.

Maggie appears in her bed, and her breathing is heard.

MAGGIE: Quentin?

Quentin barely glances at her and turns away, pacing up and down before the Listener. As Mickey resumes, Maggie and her deep-drawn breathing fade away.

MICKEY: I only know one thing, Quent, I want to live an open life, a straightforward, open life!

Lou enters in bathing trunks, instantly overjoyed at seeing Mickey.

LOU: Mick! I *thought* I heard your voice! *Grabs his hand.* How are you?

Holga appears beneath the tower with flowers, and in a moment disappears.

QUENTIN: How do you dare make promises again? I have lived through all the promises, you see?

MICKEY: Pretty good, Lou. I intended to call you tomorrow.

LOU: Really? I was going to call *you*; about a little problem I—*Uncertain: May* I?

MICKEY: Of course, Lou! You can always call me. I've got guests at home. *Grasps Lou's arm.* Give my best to Elsie.

LOU, *relieved:* I'll ring you tomorrow! And thank you, Mickey!

The gratitude seems to stab Mickey, who is already a few yards away, and he turns back, resolves *to turn back.*

MICKEY: What . . . was the problem, Lou?

LOU, *relieved, hurrying to him like a puppy:* Just the question of publishing my book now. Elsie's afraid it will wake up all the sleeping dogs again. . . .

MICKEY—*pause:* But don't you have to take that chance? I think a man's got to take the rap, Lou, for what he's done, for what he is. I think what you hide poisons you. After all, it's your work.

LOU: I feel exactly that way! *Grabs his arm.* Golly, Mick! Why don't we get together as we used to? I miss all that wonderful talk! Of course I know how busy you are now, but—

MICKEY: Lou.

Pause.

LOU: Yes, Mick. I'll meet you anywhere you say!

MICKEY: Elsie coming up?

LOU: You want to see her? I could call down to the beach.

He starts off; Mickey stops him.

MICKEY: Lou.

LOU, *sensing something odd:* Yes, Mick.

QUENTIN, *facing the sky:* Dear God.

MICKEY: I've been subpoenaed.

LOU: No!

Mickey nods, looks at the ground. Lou grips his arm.

Oh, I'm terribly sorry, Mick. I was afraid of that when they called me. But can I say something—it might ease your mind: once you're in front of them it all gets remarkably simple!

QUENTIN: Oh, dear God!

LOU: Really, it's not as terrible as it seems to you now; everything kind of falls away excepting one's . . . one's self. One's truth.

MICKEY—*slight pause:* I've already been in front of them, Lou. Two weeks ago.

LOU: Oh! Then what do they want with you again?

MICKEY—*pause. A fixed smile on his face:* I asked to be heard again.

LOU, *puzzled, open-eyed:* Why?

MICKEY—*he carefully forms his thought:* Because I want to tell the truth.

LOU, *with the first rising of incredulous fear:* In . . . what sense? What do you mean?

MICKEY: Lou, when I left the hearing room I didn't feel I had spoken. Something else had spoken, something automatic and inhuman. I asked myself, what am I protecting by refusing to answer? Lou, you must let me finish! You must. The Party? But I despise the Party, and have for many years. Just like you. Yet there is something, something that closes my throat when I think of telling names. What am I defending? It's a dream, now, a dream of solidarity, but hasn't that died a long time ago? The fact is, I have no solidarity with the people I could name—excepting for you. And not because we were Communists together, but because we were young together. Because we—when we talked it was like—monks probably talk, like some brotherhood opposed to all the world's injustice. It's you made my throat close, just the love whenever we saw one another. But what created that love, Lou? Wasn't it a respect for truth, a hatred of hypocrisy? Therefore, in the name of that love, I ought to be true to myself now. It would be easier, in a sense, to do what you did and stick with it; I would keep your friendship, but lose myself. Because the truth, Lou, my truth, is that I think the Party *is* a conspiracy. . . . Let me finish. I think we *were* swindled; they took our lust for the right and used it for Russian purposes. And I don't think we can go on turning our backs on the truth simply because reactionaries are saying it. What I propose—is that we try to separate our love for one another from this political morass. It was not the Party we loved, it was each other's truth. And I've said nothing just now that we haven't told each other for the past five years.

LOU: Then . . . what's your proposal?

MICKEY: That we go back together. Come with me. And answer the questions. I was going to tell you this tomorrow.

LOU: Name . . . the names?

MICKEY: Yes. I've talked to all the others in the unit. They've agreed, excepting for Ward and Harry. They cursed me out, but I expected that.

LOU, *dazed:* Let me understand—you are asking my permission to name me? *Pause.* You may not mention my name. *He begins physically shaking.* And if you do it, Mickey, you are selling me for your own prosperity. If you use my name I will be dismissed. You will ruin me. You will destroy my career.

MICKEY: Lou, I think I have a right to know exactly why you—

LOU: Because if everyone broke faith there would be no civilization! That is why that Committee is the face of the Philistine! And it astounds me that you can speak of truth and justice in relation to that gang of cheap publicity hounds! Not one syllable will they get from me! Not one word from my lips! No—your eleven-room apartment, your automobile, your money are not worth this.

He strides toward the edge of the area.

MICKEY, *stiffened:* That's a lie! You can't reduce it all to money, Lou! *That is false!*

LOU, *turning on him:* There is only one truth here. You are terrified! They have bought your soul!

He starts out again.

MICKEY, *angrily, but contained:* And yours? Lou! Is it all yours, your soul?

LOU, *beginning to show tears:* How dare you speak of my—?

MICKEY, *quaking with anger:* You've got to take it if you're going to dish it out, don't you? Have you really earned this high moral one—this . . .

Elsie appears in the farthest distance, slowly coming toward them as though from a beach, her robe open, her head raised up toward the breeze, toward longing, toward the sky.

perfect integrity? I happen to remember when you came back from your trip to Russia; and I remember who made you throw your first version into my fireplace!

LOU, *almost screaming—after a glance toward Elsie:* The idea!

MICKEY: I saw you burn a true book and write another that told lies! Because she demanded it, because she terrified you, because she has taken your soul!

LOU, *shaking his fist in the air:* I condemn you!

MICKEY: But from your conscience or from hers? Who is speaking to me, Lou?

LOU: You are a monster!

He bursts into tears, walks off toward Elsie; he meets her in the near distance, says a few words, and her face shows horror. At the front of stage Mickey turns and looks across the full width toward Quentin at the farthest edge of light, and, reading Quentin's feelings:

MICKEY: I guess you'll want to get somebody else to go over your brief with you.

Quentin, indecisive, but not contradicting him, now turns to him.

Good-bye, Quentin.
QUENTIN, *in a dead tone:* Good-bye, Mickey.

Mickey goes out as Elsie and Lou rush down, she in a near-hysteria. As they arrive, Louise appears, stands watching.

ELSIE: Did you hear? *Including Louise in her glance.* Did you hear? He's a *moral idiot*!

Quentin turns to her; something perhaps in his gaze or in the recesses of her mind makes her close her robe, which she holds tightly shut. And to Quentin . . .

Isn't that *incredible?*
QUENTIN, *quietly:* Yes.
ELSIE: After such friendship! Such love between them! And for so many years!

The camp tower comes alive, and Quentin moves out of this group, slowly toward it, looking up.

LOU, *stunned:* And only this spring, brought me an expensive briefcase for my birthday!
ELSIE: And named his son Louis after you! Who can understand this?

Above, Holga appears as before, carrying flowers. She is a distance away from Quentin, who turns to her.

QUENTIN: You love me, don't you?
HOLGA: Yes.

An instant's hesitation and he turns quickly to Listener, and cries out.

QUENTIN: Is it that I'm looking for some simple-minded constancy that never is and never was?

He turns to Elsie, who is lifting Lou to his feet and kisses him.

How tenderly she lifts him up—now that he is ruined.

Elsie walks off with Lou, her arm around him, and kissing his cheek. Quentin watches them go.

Still, that could be a true kiss. Or is there no treason but only man, unblamable as trees or cats or clouds? . . . Yes, I do, I see it; but if that is what we are, what will keep us safe?

Louise appears.

Or is the question foolish?

LOUISE: I had a dream. I want to tell you about it.

QUENTIN, *in pain:* Are we ever safe?

LOUISE: I was standing beside a high mountain. With my legs cut off.

He picks up a brief, looks into it.

Must you work tonight?

QUENTIN: It's Lou's case. I have a pile of stuff. *Slight pause.* Well, I can do it later. What is it?

LOUISE: Never mind.

QUENTIN—*he sits at once, as though remembering some resolution to act well:* I'm sorry, Louise. What'd you want to say?

LOUISE: I'm trying to understand why you got so angry with me at the party the other night.

QUENTIN: I wasn't *angry*; I simply felt that every time I began to talk you cut in to explain what I was about to say.

LOUISE: Well, I'd had a drink; I was a little high. I felt happy, I guess, that you weren't running for cover when everybody else was.

QUENTIN: Yes, but Max was there, and DeVries, and they don't feel they're running for cover. I only want to win Lou's case, not some moral victory over the firm. I felt you were putting me out on a limb.

LOUISE: Quentin, I saw you getting angry when I was talking about that new anti-virus vaccine.

He tries to remember, believing she is right.

What is it? Don't you want me to speak at all?

QUENTIN: That's ridiculous, Louise, why do you—

LOUISE: Because the moment I begin to assert myself it seems to threaten you. I don't think you *want* me to be happy.

QUENTIN—*there is a basic concession made by his tone of admitted bewilderment:* I tell you the truth, Louise—I don't think I feel very sure of myself any more. I feel sometimes that I don't see reality at all. I'm glad I took on Lou, but it only hit me lately that no respectable lawyer would touch him. It's like some unseen web of connection between people is simply not there. And I always relied on it, somehow; I never quite believed that people could be so easily disposed of. And it's larger than the political question. I think it's got me a little scared.

LOUISE, *with a wish for his sympathy, not accusing:* Well then, you must know how I felt when I found that letter in your suit.

QUENTIN—*he turns to her, aware:* I didn't do that to dispose of you, Louise.

She does not reply.

I thought we'd settled about that girl.

She still does not reply.

You mean you think I'm still . . .

LOUISE: I don't know what you're doing.

QUENTIN, *astounded:* What do you mean, you don't know?

LOUISE, *directly at him:* I said I don't know! I thought you told the truth about the other girl years ago, but after what happened again this spring—I don't know anything.

QUENTIN—*pause:* Tell me something; until this party the other night—in fact this whole year—I thought you seemed much happier. You were, weren't you?

LOUISE: Quentin, aren't you aware I've simply been staying out of your way this year?

QUENTIN, *amazed, frightened for his sense of reality:* Staying out of my way!

LOUISE: Well, can you remember one thing I've said about myself this year?

QUENTIN, *angrily, still amazed:* I swear to God, Louise, I thought we were building something till the other night!

LOUISE: But why?

QUENTIN: Well, I can't give you a bill of particulars, but it seems pretty obvious I've been trying like hell to show what I think of you. You've seen that, haven't you?

LOUISE: Quentin, you are full of resentment; you think I'm blind?

QUENTIN: What I resent is being forever on trial, Louise. Are you an innocent bystander here? I keep waiting for some contribution you might have made to what I did, and I resent not hearing it.

LOUISE: I said I did contribute; I demanded nothing for much too long.

QUENTIN: You mean the summer before last you didn't come to me and say that if I didn't change you would divorce me?

LOUISE: I never said I was *planning* a—

QUENTIN: You said if it came down to it you would divorce me—that's not a contribution?

LOUISE: Well, it certainly ought not send a man out to play doctor with the first girl he could lay his hands on!

QUENTIN: How much shame do you want me to feel? I hate what I did. But I think I've explained it—I felt like nothing; I shouldn't have, but I did, and I took the only means I knew to—

LOUISE: This is exactly what I mean, Quentin—you are still defending it. Right now.

He is stopped by this truth.

And I know it, Quentin.

QUENTIN: And you're . . . not at all to blame, heh?

LOUISE: But how?

QUENTIN: Well, for example . . . you never turn your back on me in bed?

LOUISE: I never turned my—

QUENTIN: You have turned your back on me in bed, Louise. I am not insane!

LOUISE: Well what do you expect? Silent, cold, you lay your hand on me?

QUENTIN, *fallen:* Well, I . . . I'm not very demonstrative, I guess.

Slight pause. He throws himself on her compassion.

Louise . . . I worry about you all day. And all night.

LOUISE—*it is something, but not enough:* Well, you've got a child; I'm sure that worries you.

QUENTIN, *deeply hurt:* Is that all?

LOUISE, *with intense reasonableness:* Look, Quentin, it all comes down to a very simple thing; you want a woman to provide an . . . atmosphere, in which there are never any issues, and you'll fly around in a constant bath of praise . . .

QUENTIN: Well I wouldn't mind a little praise, what's wrong with praise?

LOUISE: Quentin, I am not a praise machine! I am not a blur and I am not your mother! I am a separate person!

QUENTIN—*he stares at her, and what lies beyond her:* I see that now.

LOUISE: It's no crime! Not if you're adult and grown-up.

QUENTIN, *quietly:* I guess not. But it bewilders me. In fact, I got the same idea when I realized that Lou had gone from one of his former students to another and none would take him . . .

LOUISE: What's Lou got to do with it? I think it's admirable that you . . .

QUENTIN: Yes, but I am doing what you call an admirable thing because I can't bear to be a separate person! I think so. I really don't want to be known as a Red lawyer; and I really don't want the newspapers to eat me alive; and if it came down to it, Lou could defend himself. But when that decent, broken man, who never wanted anything but the good of the world, sits across my desk . . . I don't know how to say that my interests are no longer the same as his, and that if he doesn't change I consign him to hell because we are separate persons.

LOUISE: You are completely confused! Lou's case has nothing—

QUENTIN, *grasping for his thought:* I am telling you my confusion! I think Mickey also became a separate person.

LOUISE: You're incredible!

QUENTIN: I think of my mother, I think she also became—

LOUISE: Are you identifying *me* with—

QUENTIN: Louise, I am asking you to explain this to me because this is when I go blind! When you've finally become a separate person, what the hell is there?

LOUISE, *with a certain unsteady pride:* Maturity.

QUENTIN: I don't know what that means.

LOUISE: It means that you know another person exists, Quentin. I'm not in analysis for nothing!

QUENTIN, *questing:* It's probably the symptom of a typical case of some kind, but I swear, Louise—if you would just once, of your own will, as right as you are—if you would come to me and say that something, something important was your fault and that you were sorry . . . it would help.

In her pride she is silent, in her refusal to be brought down again.

Louise?

LOUISE: Good God! What an idiot!

She begins to weep helplessly for her life, and vanishes. Light rises on a park bench with the sound of traffic. A young Negro hurries past, neat, wearing sunglasses, on the lookout, halts to flick dust off his shined shoes, goes on. An old woman in shapeless dress carries a shopping bag and a parrot in a cage across, limping. Quentin strolls on and sits on the bench, briefcase on his lap.

QUENTIN: How few the days are that hold the mind in place; like a tapestry hanging on four or five hooks. Especially the day you stop becoming; the day you merely are. I suppose it's when the principles dissolve, and instead of the general gray of what ought to be you begin to see what is. Even the bench by the park seems alive, having held so many actual men. The word "Now" is like a bomb through the window, and it ticks.

The old woman recrosses with the parrot.

Now a woman takes a parrot for a walk. Everything suddenly has consequences; she probably worries what will happen to it when she's gone.

A plain girl in tweeds passes, reading a paperback.

And how brave a homely woman has to be! How disciplined of her, not to set fire to the museum of art.

The Negro passes, flicking dust off his shoe, comes to Quentin demanding a light for his cigarette. Quentin lights it.

And how does he keep so neat, and the bathroom on another floor? He must be furious when he shaves.

The Negro sees his girl upstage, walks off with her.

And whatever made me think that at the end of the day, I absolutely had to go home? You understand? That day when, suddenly, nothing whatsoever is ordained. Only . . . "Now," ticking away.

Maggie appears, looking about for someone.

Now there's a truth; symmetrical, lovely skin, undeniable.

MAGGIE: S'uze me, did you see a man with a big dog?

QUENTIN: No. But I saw a woman with a little bird.

MAGGIE: No, that's not him. Is this the bus stop?

QUENTIN: Ya, the sign says . . .

MAGGIE—*sits beside him:* I was standing over there and a man came with this big dog and just put the leash in my hand and walked away. So I started to go after him but the dog wouldn't move. And then this other man came and took the leash and went away. But I don't think it's really his dog. I think it's the first man's dog.

QUENTIN: But he obviously doesn't want it.

MAGGIE: But maybe he wanted for me to have it. I think the other man just saw it happening and figured he could get a free dog.

QUENTIN: Well, you want the dog?

MAGGIE: How could I keep a dog? I don't even think they allow dogs where I live. They might, but I never saw any dog. Although I'm not there much. What bus is this?

QUENTIN: Fifth Avenue. This is the downtown side. Where did you want to go?

MAGGIE—*thinks:* Well, I could go there.

QUENTIN: Where?

MAGGIE: Downtown.

QUENTIN: Lot of funny things go on, don't they?

MAGGIE: Well, he probably figured I would like a dog. Whereas

I would if I had a way to keep it, but I don't even have a refrigerator.

QUENTIN: Yes. *Pause.* I guess he thought you had a refrigerator; that must be it.

She shrugs. Pause. He looks at her as she watches for the bus. He has no more to say. Louise lights up.

LOUISE: You don't talk to any woman—not like a *woman*! You think reading your brief is *talking* to me?

She goes dark. In tension Quentin leans forward, arms resting on his knees. He looks at Maggie again. Anonymous men appear, lounge about, eying her.

QUENTIN, *with an effort:* What do you do?

MAGGIE, *as though he should know:* On the switchboard.

QUENTIN: Oh, telephone operator?

MAGGIE—*laughs:* Don't you remember me?

QUENTIN, *surprised:* Me?

MAGGIE: I always sort of nod to you every morning through the window.

QUENTIN—*an instant:* Oh. In the reception room!

MAGGIE: Sure!

QUENTIN: What's your name?

MAGGIE: Maggie.

QUENTIN: Of course! You get my numbers sometimes.

MAGGIE: Did you think I just came up and started talking to you?

QUENTIN: I had no idea.

MAGGIE—*laughs:* Well what must you have thought!

QUENTIN: I didn't know what to think.

MAGGIE: I guess it's that you never saw me altogether. I mean just my head through that little window.

QUENTIN: Yes. Well, it's nice to meet all of you, finally.

MAGGIE—*laughs:* You go back to work again tonight?

QUENTIN: No, I'm just resting for a few minutes.

MAGGIE, *with a sense of his loneliness:* Oh.

She looks idly about. He glances down her body.

QUENTIN: It's a pity you have to sit behind that little window.

She laughs, gratefully. Her eye catches something.

MAGGIE, *rising:* Is that my bus down there?

QUENTIN: I'm not really sure where you want to go.

A man appears, eyes her, glances up toward the bus, back to her, staring.

MAGGIE: I wanted to find one of those discount stores; I just bought a phonograph but I only have one record. I'll see you!

She is half-backing off toward the man.

MAN: There's one on Twenty-seventh and Sixth Avenue.

MAGGIE, *turning, surprised:* Oh, thanks!

QUENTIN, *standing; moving toward her as though not to lose her to the man:* There's a record store around the corner, you know.

MAGGIE: But is it discount?

QUENTIN: Well they all discount—

MAN, *slipping his hand under her arm:* What, ten per cent? Come on, honey, I'll get you easy fifty off.

MAGGIE, *moving off on his arm:* Really? But Perry Sullivan?

MAN: Look, I'll give it to you—I'll give you two records! Come on!

MAGGIE—*she halts, suddenly aware; disengages her arm, backs:* S'uze me, I . . . I . . . forgot something.

MAN, *lathering:* Look, I'll give you ten records. *Calls off.* Hold that door! *Grabs her.* Come on!

QUENTIN, *moving toward him:* Hey!

MAN, *letting her go—to Quentin:* Ah, get lost! *He rushes off.* Hold it, hold the door!

Quentin watches the "bus" go by, then turns to her. She is absorbed in arranging her hair—but with a strangely doughy expression, removed.

QUENTIN: I'm sorry, I thought you knew him.

MAGGIE: No. I never saw him.

QUENTIN: Well . . . what were you going with him for?

MAGGIE: Well he said he knew a store.

QUENTIN—*mystified, intrigued, looks at her, then nods inconclusively:* Oh.

MAGGIE: Where's the one you're talking about?

QUENTIN: I'll have to think a minute. Let's see . . .

MAGGIE: Could I sit with you? While you're thinking?

QUENTIN: Sure.

They return to the bench. He waits till she is seated; she is aware of the politeness, glances at him as he sits. Then she looks at him fully, for some reason amazed.

That happen to you very often?

MAGGIE: Pretty often.

It is impossible to tell if she likes it or not.

QUENTIN: It's because you talk to them.

MAGGIE: But they talk to me, so I have to answer.

QUENTIN: Not if they're rude.

MAGGIE: But if they talk to me . . .

QUENTIN: Just turn your back.

MAGGIE—*she thinks about that, and indecisively:* Oh, okay. *As though remotely aware of another world, his world:* . . . Thanks, though . . . for stopping it.

QUENTIN: Well, anybody would.

MAGGIE: No, they laugh. It's a joke to them. *She laughs in pain. Slight pause.* You . . . going to rest here very long?

QUENTIN: Just a few minutes. I'm on my way home. I never did this before.

MAGGIE: Oh! You look like you always did.

QUENTIN: Why?

MAGGIE: I don't know. You look like you could sit for hours, under these trees . . . just thinking.

QUENTIN: No. I usually go right home. *Grinning:* I've always gone right home.

MAGGIE—*she absorbs this:* Oh. *Coming awake:* See, I'm still paying for the phonograph, whereas they don't sell records on time, you know.

QUENTIN: They're afraid they'll wear out, I guess.

MAGGIE: Oh, that must be it! I always wondered. Cause you *can* get phonographs. How'd you know that?

QUENTIN: I don't. I'm just guessing.

MAGGIE: It sounds true, though. *Laughs.* I can never guess those things! I don't know why they do anything half the

time! *She laughs more deeply. He does.* I had about ten or
twenty records in Washington, but my friend got sick, and I
had to leave. Although maybe they're still there.

QUENTIN: Well, if you still have the apartment . . .

MAGGIE: I'm not sure I do. I got a letter from them couple
months ago, the Real Estate. *Pause. Thinks.* I better open it.
He lived right over there on Park Avenue.

QUENTIN: Oh. Is he better?

MAGGIE: He died. *Tears come into her eyes.*

QUENTIN, *entirely perplexed:* When was this?

MAGGIE: Friday. Remember they closed the office for the day?

QUENTIN: You mean—*Astounded*—Judge Cruse?

MAGGIE: Ya.

QUENTIN, *with lingering surprise:* Oh, I didn't know that
you . . . He was a great lawyer. And a great judge, too.

MAGGIE, *rubbing tears:* He was very nice to me.

QUENTIN: I was at the funeral; I didn't see you, though.

MAGGIE, *with difficulty against her tears:* His wife wouldn't let
me come. But I got into the hospital before he died. But as
soon as I opened the door of his room the family pushed me
out and . . . I could hear him calling, "Maggie! Maggie!"
Pause. They kept trying to offer me a thousand dollars. But
I told them, I don't want anything, I just wanted to say
good-bye to him!

She opens her purse, takes out an office envelope, opens it.

I have a little of the dirt. See? That's from his grave. His
chauffeur drove me out—Alexander.

QUENTIN—*looks at the dirt, at her face:* Did he leave you very
much?

MAGGIE: No, he didn't leave me anything.

She puts the envelope back, closes the purse, stares.

QUENTIN: Did you love him very much?

MAGGIE: No. But he was very nice. In fact, a couple of times I
really left him.

QUENTIN: Why didn't you altogether?

MAGGIE: He didn't want me to.

QUENTIN: Oh. *Pause.* So what are you going to do now?

MAGGIE: I'd love to get that record if I knew where they had a discount.

QUENTIN: No, I mean in general.

MAGGIE: Why, they going to fire me now?

QUENTIN: Oh, I wouldn't know about that.

MAGGIE: Although I'm not worried, whereas I can always go back to hair.

QUENTIN: To where?

MAGGIE: I used to demonstrate hair preparations. *Laughs, squirts her hair with an imaginary bottle.* You know, in department stores? I was traveling even, they sent me to Boston and New Orleans and all over. *Tilting her head under his chin:* It's because I have very thick hair, you see? I have my mother's hair. And it's not broken. You notice I have no broken hair? Most women's hair is broken. Here, feel it, feel how— *She has lifted his hand to her head, and suddenly lets go of it.* Oh, s'uze me!

QUENTIN: That's all right.

MAGGIE: I just thought you might want to feel it.

QUENTIN: Sure.

MAGGIE: Go ahead. I mean if you want to.

She leans her head to him again. He touches the top of her head.

QUENTIN: It is, ya! Very soft.

MAGGIE, *proudly:* I once went from page boy to bouffant in less than ten minutes!

QUENTIN: What made you quit?

MAGGIE—*the dough comes into her eyes again:* They start sending me to conventions and all. You're supposed to entertain, you see.

QUENTIN: Oh, yes.

MAGGIE: There were parts of it I didn't like any more.

A long moment. A student goes by, reading. He looks up from his book, shyly glances at her, goes on reading. She laughs.

Aren't they sweet when they look up from their books!

She turns to him with a laugh. He looks at her warmly, smiling.

S'uze me I put your hand on my head.

QUENTIN: Oh, that's all right. . . . I'm not *that* bad. *He laughs softly, embarrassed.*

MAGGIE: You're not bad.

QUENTIN: I don't mean bad, I mean . . . shy.

MAGGIE: It's not bad to be shy. *She gives him a long look, absorbed.* I mean . . . if that's the way you are.

QUENTIN: I guess I am, then.

Pause. They look at each other.

You're very beautiful, Maggie.

She smiles, straightens as though his words had entered her.

And I wish you knew how to take care of yourself.

MAGGIE: Oh . . . *Holding out a ripped seam in her dress:* I got this torn on the bus this morning. I'm going to sew it home.

QUENTIN: I don't mean that.

She meets his eyes again—she looks chastised.

Not that I'm criticizing you. I'm not at all. Not in the slightest. You understand?

She nods, absorbed in his face. He stands.

I've got to go now.

She stands, staring at him, giving herself. He sees this. His hand moves, but it becomes a handshake.

You could look up record stores in the phone book.

MAGGIE: I think I'll take a walk in the park.

QUENTIN: You shouldn't. It's getting dark.

MAGGIE: But it's beautiful at night. I slept there one night when it was hot in my room.

QUENTIN: God, you don't want to do that! I know this park. Most of the animals are not in the zoo.

MAGGIE: Okay. I'll get a record, then. *She backs a step.* S'uze me about my hair if I embarrassed you.

QUENTIN—*laughs:* You didn't.

MAGGIE—*backing to leave, she touches the top of her head:* It's just that it's not broken.

He nods. She halts some yards away, holds out her torn seam.

I'm going to sew this home.

He nods. She indicates the park, upstage.

I didn't *mean* to sleep there. I just fell asleep.

Two young guys appear, pass Quentin, slow as they pass her, and halt in the far periphery of the light, waiting for her.

QUENTIN: I understand.
MAGGIE: Well . . . see you! *Laughs.* If they don't fire me!
QUENTIN: 'Bye.

She passes the two men, who walk step for step behind her, whispering in her ear together. She doesn't turn or answer but shows no surprise.

QUENTIN—*in anguish he hurries after her:* Maggie! *He catches her arm and brings her clear of the men, takes a bill from his pocket.* Here, why don't you take a cab? It's on me. Go ahead, there's one right there. *Points and whistles.* Go on, grab it!
MAGGIE, *backing in the opposite direction from the waiting men:* Where . . . where will I tell him to go but?
QUENTIN: Just cruise in the forties—you've got enough there.
MAGGIE: Okay, 'bye! *Backing out:* You . . . you just going to rest more?
QUENTIN: I don't know.
MAGGIE, *wondrously:* Golly, that's nice!

She hurries off. He stands staring after her. Likewise, the men watch the "cab" going by, then walk off.

Lights rise on Louise reading in a chair. Quentin, clasping his briefcase behind his back, walks slowly into the area, stands a few yards from her, staring at her. She remains unaware of him, reading and smoking.

QUENTIN: Yes. She has legs, breasts, mouth, eyes. How wonderful—a woman of my own! What a miracle! In my own house!

He walks to her, bends and kisses her. She looks up at him surprised, perplexed.

Hi.

She keeps looking up at him, aware of some sealike opening in the world.

What's the matter?

She still doesn't speak.

Well, what's the matter?

LOUISE: Nothing.

She returns to her book. Mystified, disappointed, he stands watching, then opens his briefcase and begins taking out papers.

Close the door if you're going to type.

QUENTIN: I always do.

LOUISE: Not always.

QUENTIN: Almost always.

He almost laughs, he feels loose, but she won't be amused, and returns again to her book. He starts for the bedroom, halts.

How about eating out tomorrow night? Before the parents' meeting?

LOUISE: What parents' meeting?

QUENTIN: The school.

LOUISE: That was tonight.

QUENTIN, *shocked:* Really?

LOUISE: Of course. I just got back.

QUENTIN: Why didn't you remind me when I called today?

LOUISE: You knew it as well as I.

QUENTIN: But you know I often forget those things. I told you I wanted to talk to her teacher.

LOUISE, *a little more sharply:* People do what they want to do, Quentin.

QUENTIN: But Louise, I was talking to you at three o'clock this afternoon . . .

LOUISE—*an unwilling shout:* Because you said you had to work tonight!

She glares at him meaningfully; returns to her book. He stands, alarmed.

QUENTIN: I didn't work.

LOUISE, *keeping to her book: I* know you didn't work.

QUENTIN, *surprised:* How did you know?

LOUISE: Well for one thing, Max called here at seven-thirty.

QUENTIN: Max? What for?

LOUISE: Apparently the whole executive committee was in his office waiting to meet with you tonight.

His hand goes to his head; open alarm shows on his face.

He called three times, as a matter of fact.

QUENTIN: I forgot all about it! *He hurries to the phone, stops.* How is that possible? It completely—

LOUISE: Well they wouldn't be there any more now. *Pointedly:* It's ten-thirty.

QUENTIN: My God, I— How could I do that? What's his home number?

LOUISE: The book is in the bedroom.

QUENTIN: We were supposed to discuss my handling Lou's case. DeVries stayed in town tonight just to . . . settle everything. And I go and walk out as though . . . nothing . . . *Breaks off. Picks up phone.* What's Max's number, Murray Hill 3 . . . what is it?

LOUISE: The book is next to the bed.

QUENTIN: You remember it, Murray Hill 3, something.

LOUISE: It's in the book.

Pause. He looks at her. Puzzled.

QUENTIN: What are you doing?

LOUISE: I'm saying the book is in the bedroom.

QUENTIN—*slams the phone down, and, as much in fright as in anger:* But you remember his number!

LOUISE: I'm not the keeper of your phone numbers. You can remember them just as well as I.

QUENTIN: Oh, I see. *Nods ironically, starts out.*

LOUISE: Please don't use that phone, you'll wake her up.

QUENTIN—*turns:* I had no intention of calling in there.

LOUISE: I thought you might want to be private.

QUENTIN: There's nothing private about this. This concerns you as much as me. The food in your mouth and the clothes on your back.

LOUISE: Really! When did you start thinking of us?

QUENTIN: The meeting was called to decide whether I should

separate from the firm until Lou's case is over—or permanently, for all I know.

Quentin goes toward the phone. She stands staring in growing fright.

Murray Hill 3 . . .

He picks it up, dials one digit.

LOUISE, *much against her will:* That's the old number.

QUENTIN: Murray Hill 3-4598.

LOUISE: It's been changed. *A moment; and finally:* Cortland 7-7098.

QUENTIN—*she is not facing him; he senses what he thinks is victory:* Thanks.

Starts again to dial, puts down the phone. She sits; there is an admission of the faintest sort of failing in her.

I don't know what to say to him.

She is silent.

We arranged for everybody to come back after dinner. It'll sound idiotic that I forgot about it.

LOUISE: You were probably frightened.

QUENTIN: But I made notes all afternoon about what I would say tonight! It's incredible!

LOUISE, *with an over-meaning:* You probably don't realize how frightened you are.

QUENTIN: I guess I don't. He said a dreadful thing today—Max. He was trying to argue me into dropping Lou and I said, "The law is the law; we can't adopt some new behavior just because there's hysteria in the country." I thought it was a perfectly ordinary thing to say but he—he's never looked at me that way—like we were suddenly standing on two distant mountains; and he said, "I don't know of any hysteria. Not in this office."

LOUISE, *without rancor:* But why does all that surprise you?

QUENTIN—*slight pause:* I don't understand exactly what you're getting at.

LOUISE: Simply that there are some issues you have to face. You tend to make relatives out of people. Max is not your

father, or your brother, or anything but a very important
lawyer with his own interests. He's not going to endanger
his whole firm to defend a Communist. I don't know how
you got that illusion.

QUENTIN: You mean—

LOUISE: I mean you can't have everything; if you feel this
strongly about Lou you probably will have to resign.

QUENTIN—*pause:* You think I should?

LOUISE: That depends on how deeply you feel about Lou.

QUENTIN: I'm trying to determine that; I don't know for sure.
What do you think?

LOUISE, *in anguish:* It's not my decision, Quentin.

QUENTIN, *puzzled and surprised:* But aren't you involved?

LOUISE: Of course I'm involved.

QUENTIN, *genuinely foxed:* Is it that you're not sure of how you
feel?

LOUISE: I know how I feel but it is not my decision.

QUENTIN: I'm only curious how you—

LOUISE: You? Curious about me?

QUENTIN: Oh. We're not talking about what we're talking about,
are we?

LOUISE, *nodding in emphasis:* You have to decide what you feel
about a certain human being. For once in your life. And
then maybe you'll decide what you feel about other human
beings. Clearly and decisively.

QUENTIN: In other words . . . where was I tonight.

LOUISE: I don't care where you were tonight.

QUENTIN—*pause:* I sat by the park for a while. And this is what
I thought. I don't sleep with other women, but I think I
behave as though I do.

She is listening. He sees it, is enlivened by hope.

Maybe I invite your suspicion on myself in order to . . . to
come down off some bench, to stop judging others so perfectly. Because I do judge, and harshly, too—when the fact is
I'm bewildered. I even wonder if I left that letter for you to
read . . . about that girl . . . in order to . . . somehow
join the condemned; in some way to start being real. Can
you understand that?

LOUISE: But . . . *She is digging in her heels against being taken.* Why should you be condemned if you're not still doing anything?

QUENTIN, *uneasily again:* But don't you continue to feel ashamed for something you've done in the past? You can understand that, can't you?

LOUISE: I don't do things I'll be ashamed of.

QUENTIN, *now astonished, and moving toward anger:* Really and truly?

LOUISE—*starts to rise:* I'm going to bed.

QUENTIN: I have to say it, Louise; whenever our conversations verge on you, they end. You say you want to talk, but is it only about my sins?

LOUISE: Now you listen here! You've been "at the office" one night a week since last winter. It's not my forgiveness you want, it's the end of this marriage! But you haven't the courage to say so!

QUENTIN: All right, then. *Against his own trepidation, striving for a clear conscience:* I think I won't be ashamed either. I met a girl tonight. Just happened to come by, one of the phone operators in the office. I probably shouldn't tell you this either, but I will.

She sits, slowly.

Quite stupid, silly kid. Sleeps in the park, her dress is ripped; she said some ridiculous things, but one thing struck me, she wasn't defending anything, upholding anything, or accusing—she was just *there*, like a tree or a cat. And I felt strangely abstract beside her. And I saw that we are killing one another with abstractions. I'm defending Lou because I love him, yet the society transforms that love into a kind of treason, what they call an issue, and I end up suspect and hated. Why can't we speak below the "issues"—with our real uncertainty? I walked in just now—and I had a tremendous wish to come out—to you. And you to me. It sounds absurd that this city is full of people rushing to meet one another, Louise. This city is full of lovers. . . .

LOUISE: And what did she say?

QUENTIN: I guess I shouldn't have told you about it.

LOUISE: Why not?

QUENTIN: Louise, I don't know what's permissible to say any more.

LOUISE—*nods:* You don't know how much to hide.

QUENTIN—*he angers:* All right, let's not hide anything, it would have been easy to make love to her.

Louise reddens, stiffens.

And I didn't because I thought of you, and in a new way . . . like a stranger I had never gotten to know. And by some miracle you were waiting for me, in my own home. I came into this room, Louise, full of love . . .

LOUISE: What do you want, my congratulations? You expect me to sit here and enjoy your latest conquest? You take me for a Lesbian?

QUENTIN, *perplexed:* What's a Lesbian got to do with . . .

LOUISE: Ask your friend with the torn dress. You don't imagine a real woman goes to bed with any man who happens to come along? Or that a real man goes to bed with every woman who'll have him? Especially a slut, which she obviously is?

QUENTIN: How do you know she's a—

LOUISE—*laughs:* Oh, excuse me, I didn't mean to insult her! You're unbelievable! Supposing I came home and told you I'd met a man—a man on the street I wanted to go to bed with . . .

He hangs his head, defeated.

because he made the city seem full of lovers. What would you feel? Overjoyed for my discovery?

QUENTIN—*pause; struck:* I understand. I'm sorry. I guess it would anger me too. *Slight pause.* But if you came to me with such a thing, I think I would see that you were struggling. And I would ask myself—maybe I'd even be brave enough to ask you—how *I* had failed.

LOUISE: Well, you've given me notice; I get the message.

She starts out.

QUENTIN: Louise, don't you ever doubt yourself?

She slows, but does not turn.

Is it enough to prove a case, to even win it—*Shouts*—when we are dying?

LOUISE—*turns in full possession:* I'm not dying. I'm not the one who wanted to break this up. And that's all it's about. It's all it's been about the last three years. You don't want me!

She goes out.

QUENTIN: God! Can that be true?

Mickey enters as he was in his scene, dressed in summer slacks.

MICKEY: There's only one thing I can tell you for sure, kid—don't ever be guilty.

QUENTIN: Yes! *Seeking strength, he stretches upward.* Yes! *But his conviction wavers; he turns toward the vision.* But if you had felt more guilt, maybe you wouldn't have . . .

Elsie rushes into this light as before, her robe open to her tight bathing suit.

ELSIE: He's a moral idiot!

QUENTIN: Yes! That is right. And yet. . . .

He turns and faces her, and she slowly, under his gaze, draws her robe together in a way to conceal her own betrayal, and she and Mickey are gone. Quentin stands staring out.

What the hell is moral? What does that really mean? And what am I . . . to even ask that question? A man ought to know . . . a decent man knows that like he knows his own face!

Louise enters with a folded sheet and a pillow which she tosses into the chair.

LOUISE: I don't want to sleep with you.

QUENTIN: Louise, for God's sake!

LOUISE: You are disgusting!

QUENTIN: But in the morning Betty will see . . .

LOUISE: You should have thought of that.

The phone rings. He makes no move to answer.

Did you give her this number?

The phone rings again.

LOUISE: Did you give her this number? *With which she strides to the phone.* Hello! . . . Oh, yes. He's here. Hold on, please. *To him:* It's Max.

For a moment, he stands touching the sheets, then looks at her, picks up the sheets, and hands them to her.

QUENTIN: I can't sleep out here; I don't want her to see it.

But she adamantly lets the sheets fall to the floor. He goes to the phone with a look of hatred.

Max? I'm sorry, the whole thing just slipped my mind. I don't know how to explain it, Max, I just went blank, I guess, I— *Pause.* The radio? No, why? *What?* When? *Long pause.* Thanks . . . for letting me know. Yes, he was. Good night . . . ya, see you in the morning. *Pause. He stands staring.*

LOUISE: What is it?

QUENTIN: Lou. Was killed by a subway train tonight.

LOUISE—*gasps:* How?

QUENTIN: They don't know. They say "fell or jumped."

LOUISE: He couldn't have! The crowd must have pushed him!

QUENTIN: There is no crowd at eight o'clock. It was eight o'clock.

LOUISE: But *why?* Lou *knew* himself! He knew where he *stood!* It's impossible!

QUENTIN, *staring:* Maybe it's not enough—to know yourself. Or maybe it's too much. I think he did it.

LOUISE: But *why?* It's inconceivable!

QUENTIN: When I saw him last week he said a dreadful thing. I tried not to hear it.

LOUISE: What?

QUENTIN: That I turned out to be the only friend he had.

LOUISE, *genuinely:* Why is that dreadful?

QUENTIN, *evasively, almost slyly:* It just was. *He starts moving.* I don't know why.

He arrives at the edge of the stage, tears forming in his eyes.

I didn't dare know why! But I dare now. It was dreadful because I was not his friend either, and he knew it. I'd have stuck it to the end but I hated the danger in it for myself, and he saw through my faithfulness; and he was not telling me what a friend I was, he was praying I would be— "Please be my friend, Quentin," is what he was saying to me, "I am drowning, throw me a rope!" Because I wanted out, to be a good American again, kosher again—and he saw it, and proved it in the joy . . . the joy . . . the joy I felt now that my danger had spilled out on the subway track! So it is not bizarre to me. . . .

The tower blazes into life, and he walks with his eyes up.

Holga appears with flowers.

This is not some crazy aberration of human nature to me. I can easily see the perfectly normal contractors and their cigars; the carpenters, plumbers, sitting at their ease over lunch pails, I can see them laying the pipes to run the blood out of this mansion; good fathers, devoted sons, grateful that someone else will die, not they. And how can one understand that, if one is innocent; if somewhere in the soul there is no accomplice . . .

The tower fades, Holga too. Louise brightens in light where she was standing before.

. . . of that joy, that joy, that joy when a burden dies . . .

He moves back into the "room."

. . . and leaves you safe?

Maggie's breathing is heard.

MAGGIE: Quentin?

He turns in pain from it, comes to a halt on one side of the sheets and pillow lying on the floor. Louise is on the other side. He looks down at the pile.

QUENTIN: I've got to sleep; I'm very tired.

He bends to pick up the sheets. A split second later she starts to. And while he is still reaching down . . .

LOUISE, *with great difficulty:* I . . .

He stands with the sheets in hand, the pillow still on the floor; now he is attending her, sensing a confession.

I've always been proud you took Lou's case.

He barely nods, waiting.

It was . . .

She picks up the pillow.

courageous.

She stands there with the pillow, not fully looking at him.

QUENTIN: I'm glad you feel that way.

But he makes no move. The seconds are ticking by. Neither can let down his demand for apology, for grace. With difficulty:

And that you told me. Thanks.
LOUISE: You are honest—that way. I've often told you.
QUENTIN: Recently?
LOUISE—*bridles, hands him the pillow:* Good night.

He takes the pillow; she starts away, and he feels the unwilling-ness with which she leaves.

QUENTIN: Louise, if there's one thing I've been trying to do it's to be honest with you.
LOUISE: No. You've been trying to arrange things, that's all—to keep the home fires burning and see the world at the same time.
QUENTIN: So that all I am is deceptive, and cunning.
LOUISE: Not all, but mostly.
QUENTIN: And there is no struggle. There is no pain. There is no struggle to find a way back to you?
LOUISE: That isn't the struggle.
QUENTIN: Then what are you doing here?
LOUISE: I . . .
QUENTIN: What the hell are you compromising yourself for if you're so goddamned honest?

On the line he starts a frustrated clench-fisted move toward her and she backs away, terrified, and strangely alive. Her look takes note of the aborted violence and she is very straight and yet ready to flee.

LOUISE: I've been waiting for the struggle to begin.

He is dumbstruck—by her sincerity, her adamance. With a straight look at him, she turns and goes out.

QUENTIN, *alone, and to himself:* Good God, can there be more? Can there be worse?

Turning to the Listener:

See, that's what's incredible to me—three years more! What did I expect to save us? Suddenly, God knows why, she'd hold out her hand and I hold out mine, and laugh, laugh it all away, laugh it all back to `.` . . . her dear, honest face looking up to mine. . . .

Breaks off, staring.

Back to some hidden, everlasting smile that saves. That's maybe why I came; I think I still believe it. That underneath we're all profoundly friends! I can't believe this world; all this hatred isn't real to me!

Turns back to his "living room," and the sheets.

To bed down like a dog in my living room, how can that be necessary? Then go in to her, open your heart, confess the lechery, the mystery of women, say it all . . . the truth must save!

He has moved toward where she exited, now halts.

But I did that. So the truth, after all, may merely be murderous? The truth killed Lou; destroyed Mickey. Then what else is there? A workable lie? Maybe there is only one sin, to destroy your own credibility. Strength comes from a clear conscience or a dead one. Not to see one's own evil—there's power! And rightness too! So kill conscience. Kill it.

Glancing toward her exit.

Know all, admit nothing, shave closely, remember birthdays, open car doors, pursue Louise not with truth but with attention. Be uncertain on your own time, in bed be absolute. And thus, be a man . . . and join the world.

Reflectively he throws the sheet open on the couch, then stops.

And in the morning, a dagger in that dear little daughter's heart!

Flinging it toward Louise's exit.

Bitch!

Sits.

I'll say I have a cold. Didn't want to give it to Mommy.

With disgust.

Pah! Papapapapa.

Sniffs, tries to talk through his nose.

Got a cold in my dose, baby girl . . .

He groans. Pause. He stares; stalemate. A jet plane is heard. An airport porter appears, unloads two bags from a rolling cart as Holga, dressed for travel, appears opening her purse, tipping him, and now looking about for Quentin. A distant jet roars in take-off. Quentin glances at his watch, and, coming down to the chair:

Six o'clock, Idlewild.

Now he glances at Holga, who is still looking about him as in a crowd, and speaks to the Listener.

It's that the evidence is bad for promises. But how do you touch the world without a promise? And yet, I mustn't forget the way I wake; I open up my eyes each morning like a boy, even now, even now! That's as true as anything I know, but where's the evidence? Or is it simply that my heart still beats? . . . Certainly, go ahead.

He smiles and sits, following the departing Listener with his eyes; a light moves upstage, going away. He talks upstage.

You don't mind my staying? Good. I'd like to settle this. Although actually, I—*Laughs*—only came by to say hello.

He turns front. The Listener's light is gone. Alone now, he stares ahead, a different kind of relaxation on him. From the darkness high on the upper level, the sucking breathing is heard; light dimly shows Maggie, her back to us, sitting up in the "bed."

MAGGIE: Quentin?

QUENTIN, *in agony:* I'll get to it, honey.

He closes his eyes.

I'll get to it.

He stands, and as though wandering in a room he moves at random, puts a cigarette in his mouth, and strikes sparks from his lighter as darkness covers him.

CURTAIN

ACT TWO

The stage is dark. A spark is seen; a flame fires up. When the stage illuminates, Quentin is discovered lighting his cigarette—no time has passed. He continues to await the Listener's return, and walks a few steps in thought and as he does a jet plane is heard, and the garbled airport announcer's voice: ". . . from Frankfurt is now unloading at gate nine, passengers will please . . ." It becomes a watery garble and at the same moment Holga, beautifully dressed, walks onto the upper level with an airport porter, who leaves her bags and goes. She looks about as in a crowd—then, seeing "Quentin," stands on tiptoe and waves.

HOLGA: Quentin! Here! Here!

She opens her arms as he evidently approaches.

Hello!

She is gone as Louise rushes on from another point, a ribbon in her hair, a surgical mask hanging from her neck, a lab technician's smock open to show her sweater and long skirt of the thirties. A hospital attendant is mopping the floor behind her. She sees "Quentin."

LOUISE: Hello! I just got my final grades! I got an A on that paper you wrote! Ya—the one on Roosevelt. I'm a Master! *Laughs.* And guess what Halliday said. That my style has immeasurably improved! *Laughs; and now she walks with "him."* If it wasn't for the mop I'd think you were an intern in that uniform; you look well in white. *Her face falls; she halts.* Oh! Then when would you be leaving? . . . No, I'm glad, I always heard Columbia Law was the best. *Shyly:* Actually, I could try some labs in New York, it'd be cheaper if I lived at home. . . . Well, then, I'd look for something else; anyway there are more bacteriologists than bugs these days. *With dread and shyness:* Unless you wouldn't want me to be there. *She bursts into an adoring smile.* Okay! You want a malt later? I have some money, I just sold all my textbooks! Oop! *She stops abruptly, looking down at the floor.* I'm sorry! I forgot it was wet! See you!

With a happy wave of her hand she picks her way on tiptoe over a wet floor into darkness as a door is heard opening upstage and a light moves downstage, over the floor; Quentin turns toward the returning Listener and smiles.

QUENTIN: Oh, that's all right, I didn't mind waiting. How much time do I have?

He looks at his watch, coming down to the chair. Maggie appears, above, in a lace wedding dress; Lucas, a designer, is on his knees finishing the vast hem. Carrie, a maid, stands by, holding gloves. Maggie is nervous, on the edge of life, looking into a "mirror."

Quentin sits in the chair. He looks forward now, to speak.

I, ah . . .

Lucas gets up and quickly goes as . . .

MAGGIE, *in an ecstasy of fear and hope:* All right, Carrie, tell him to come in! *As though trying the angular words:* . . . My husband!

CARRIE, *walking a few steps to a point, halts:* You can see her now, Mister Quentin.

They are gone. He continues to the Listener.

QUENTIN: I think I can be clearer now, it shouldn't take long. I am bewildered by the death of love. And my responsibility for it.

Holga appears again, looking about for him at the airport.

This woman's on my side; I have no doubt of it. And I wouldn't want to outlive another accusation. Not hers. *He stands, agitated.* I suddenly wonder why I risk it again. Except . . . *Slight pause; he becomes still.* You ever felt you once saw yourself—absolutely true? I may have dreamed it, but I swear, I feel that somewhere along the line—with Maggie I think—for one split second I saw my life; what I had done, what had been done to me, and even what I ought to do. And that vision sometimes hangs behind my head, blind now, bleached out like the moon in the morning; and if I could only let in some necessary darkness it would shine again. I think it had to do with power.

Felice appears, about to remove the bandage.

Maybe that's why she sticks in my mind; she brings some darkness. Some dreadful element of power. *He walks around her, peering. . . .* Well, that's power, isn't it? To influence a girl to change her nose, her life? . . . It does, yes, it frightens me, and I wish to God . . .

FELICE, *raising her arm:* I'll always . . .

QUENTIN: . . . she'd stop blessing me! *He laughs uneasily, surprised at the force of his fear. . . .* Well, I suppose because there is a fraud involved; I have no such power.

Maggie suddenly appears in a "satin bed," talking into a phone.

MAGGIE, *with timid idolatry:* Hello? Is . . . How'd you know it's me? *Laughs.* You really remember me? Maggie? From that park that day? Well 'cause it's almost four years so I . . .

He comes away from her; she continues talking unheard. He halts near the chair. He glances toward a point where again Felice appears, raising her arm in blessing, and instantly disappears, and he speaks to the Listener.

QUENTIN: I do, yes, I see the similarity.

Laughter is heard as Holga appears at a "café table," an empty chair beside her.

HOLGA: I love the way you eat! You eat like a pasha, a grand duke!

QUENTIN—*looks toward her, and to Listener:* Yes, adored again! But . . . there is something different here.

As he moves toward Holga, he says to Listener:

Now keep me to my theme. I spoke of power.

He sits beside her. As he speaks now, Holga's aspect changes; she becomes moody, doesn't face him, seems hurt. And sitting beside her he tells the Listener:

We were in a café one afternoon in Salzburg, and quite
suddenly, I don't know why—it all seemed to be dying between us. And I saw it all happening again. You know that
moment, when you begin desperately to talk about architecture?

HOLGA: Fifteen-thirty-five. The archbishop designed it himself.

QUENTIN: Beautiful.

HOLGA, *distantly:* Yes.

QUENTIN—*as though drawing on his courage, he suddenly turns
to her:* Holga. I thought I noticed your pillow was wet this
morning.

HOLGA: It really isn't anything important.

QUENTIN: There are no unimportant tears. *Takes her hand,
smiles.* I know that much, anyway. Unless it doesn't concern
me. Is it about the concentration camp?

She wipes her eyes, unhappy with herself.

Even during the day, sometimes, you seem about to weep.

HOLGA: I feel sometimes . . . *Breaks off, then:* . . . that I'm
boring you.

Louise appears.

LOUISE: I am not all this uninteresting, Quentin!

Louise is gone.

HOLGA: I really think perhaps we've been together too much.

QUENTIN: Except, it's only been a few weeks.

HOLGA: But I may not be all that interesting.

*Quentin stares at her, trying to join this with his lost vision,
and in that mood he turns out to the Listener.*

QUENTIN: The question is power, but I've lost the connection.

Louise appears brushing her hair.

Yes!

He springs up and circles Louise.

I tell you, there were times when she looked into the mirror
and I saw she didn't like her face, and I wanted to step

between her and what she saw. I felt guilty even for her face!
But . . . that day . . .

He returns to the café table and slowly sits.

there was some new permission . . . not to take a certain
blame. There was suddenly no blame at all but that . . .
we're each entitled to . . . our own unhappiness.

HOLGA: I wish you'd believe me, Quentin; you have no duty
here.

QUENTIN: Holga, I would go. But the truth is, I'd be looking
for you tomorrow. I wouldn't know where the hell I thought
I had to be. But there's truth in what you feel. I see it very
clearly; the time does come when I feel I must go. Not toward anything, or away from you. But there is some freedom
in the going. . . .

Mother appears, and she is raising her arm.

MOTHER: Darling, there is never a depression for great people!
The first time I felt you move, I was standing on the beach
at Rockaway. . . .

*Quentin has gotten up from the chair, and, moving toward
her:*

QUENTIN: But power. Where is the—?

MOTHER: And I saw a star, and it got bright, and brighter, and
brighter! And suddenly it fell, like some great man had died,
and you were being pulled out of me to take his place, and
be a light, a light in the world!

QUENTIN, *to Listener:* Why is there some . . . air of treachery
in that?

FATHER, *suddenly appearing—to Mother:* What the hell are you
talking about? We're just getting a business started again. I
need him!

Quentin avidly turns from one to the other as they argue.

MOTHER: You've got Dan, you don't need him! He wants to
try to get a job, go to college, maybe—

FATHER: He's got a job!

MOTHER: He means with pay! I don't want his young years
going by. . . . He wants a life!

FATHER, *indicating Dan:* Why don't he "want a life"?
MOTHER: Because he's different!
FATHER: Because *he* knows what's *right*!

Indicating Mother and Quentin together:

You're two of a kind—what you "want"! Chrissake, when I was his age I was supporting six people!

He comes up to Quentin.

What are you, a stranger? *What are you?*

Quentin is peering into the revulsion of his Father's face. And he turns toward Holga in the café and back to Father.

QUENTIN: Yes, I felt a power in the going . . . and treason in it. . . . Because there's failure, and you turn your back on failure.

DAN: No, kid, don't feel that way. I just want to see him big again, but you go. I'll go back to school if things pick up.

QUENTIN, *peering at Dan:* Yes, good men stay . . . although they die there.

DAN, *indicating a book in his hand:* It's my Byron, I'll put it in your valise, and I've put in my new argyles, just don't wash them in hot water. And remember, kid, wherever you are . . .

Dan jumps onto a platform, calling. A passing train is heard.

. . . wherever you are this family's behind you! You buckle down, now. . . . I'll send you a list of books to read!

MAGGIE, *suddenly appearing on her bed; she is addressing an empty space at the foot:* But could I read them!

QUENTIN—*spins about in quick surprise:* Huh!

All the others are gone dark but he and Maggie.

MAGGIE: I mean what kind of books? 'Cause, see . . . I never really graduated high school. *She laughs nervously.* Although in Social Science he liked me so he let me keep the minutes. Except I didn't know what's a minute! *Laughs.* I like poetry, though.

QUENTIN—*breaks his stare at her, and quickly comes down to the*

Listener: It's that I can't find myself in this vanity, any more. It's all contemptible! *He covers his face.*

MAGGIE, *enthralled, on the bed:* I can't hardly believe you came! Can you stay five minutes? I'm a singer now, see? In fact— *With a laugh at herself*—I'm in the top three. And for a long time I been wanting to tell you that . . . none of it would have happened to me if I hadn't met you that day.

QUENTIN: . . . Yes, I see the power she offered me; but I saw beyond it once, and there was some . . . salvation in it. . . . All right. I'll . . .

He turns to her, walking into her line of sight.

. . . try.

MAGGIE: I'm sorry if I sounded frightened on the phone but I didn't think you'd be in the office after midnight. *Laughs at herself nervously.* See, I only pretended to call you. Can you stay like five minutes?

QUENTIN, *backing into the chair:* Sure. Don't rush.

MAGGIE: That's what I mean, you know I'm rushing! Would you like a drink? Or a steak? They have two freezers here. Whereas my agent went to Jamaica, so I'm just staying here this week till I go to London Friday. It's the Palladium, like a big vaudeville house, and it's kind of an honor, but I'm a little scared to go.

QUENTIN: Why? I've heard you; you're marvelous. Especially . . .

He can't remember a title.

MAGGIE: No, I'm just flapping my wings yet. I mean if you ever heard like Ella Fitzgerald or one of those . . . But did you read what that *News* fellow wrote? He keeps my records in the 'frigerator, case they melt!

QUENTIN—*laughs with her:*—"Little Girl Blue"—it's very moving the way you do that.

MAGGIE, *surprised and pleased:* Really? 'Cause see, it's not I say to myself "I'm going to sound sexy," I just try to come *through* . . . like, in love or . . . *Laughs.* I really can't believe you're here!

QUENTIN: Why? I'm glad you called. I've often thought about

you the last couple of years. All the great things happening to you gave me a secret satisfaction for some reason.

MAGGIE: Maybe 'cause you did it.

QUENTIN: Why do you say that?

MAGGIE: I don't know, just the way you looked at me . . . I didn't even have the nerve to go see an agent before that day.

QUENTIN: How did I look at you?

MAGGIE, *squinching up her shoulders, feeling for the mystery:* Like . . . out of your *self.* See, most people they . . . just look *at* you. I can't explain it! And the way you talked to me . . .

Louise appears.

LOUISE: You think reading your brief is talking to me?

And she is gone.

QUENTIN, *to Listener, of Louise:* Yes, I see that, but there was something more. And maybe power isn't quite the word . . .

MAGGIE: What did you mean . . . it gave you a secret satisfaction?

QUENTIN: Just that . . . like in the office, I'd hear people laughing that Maggie had the world at her feet. . . .

MAGGIE, *hurt, mystified:* They laughed!

QUENTIN: In a way.

MAGGIE, *in pain:* That's what I mean; I'm a joke to most people.

QUENTIN: No, it's that you say what you mean, Maggie. You don't seem to be upholding anything, or . . . You're not ashamed of what you are.

MAGGIE: W—what do you mean of what I am?

Louise appears; she is playing solitaire.

QUENTIN, *suddenly aware he has touched a nerve:* Well . . . that you love life, and . . . It's hard to define, I—

LOUISE: The word is tart. But what did it matter as long as she praised you?

QUENTIN, *to Listener, standing, and moving within Maggie's area:* But there's truth in it—I hadn't had a woman's praise, even a girl I'd laughed at with the others . . .

MAGGIE: But you didn't, did you?

He turns to her in agony; Louise vanishes.

Laugh at me?
QUENTIN: No.

He suddenly stands and cries out to Listener:

Fraud—from the first five minutes! . . . Because—I should have agreed she *was* a joke, a beautiful piece trying to take herself seriously! Why did I lie to her, play this cheap benefactor, this . . . What? *Listens, and now, unwillingly:* Yes, that's true too; she had; a strange, surprising honor.

He turns back to her.

MAGGIE: Oh, hey? I just bought back two records I made!
QUENTIN: Bought them back how?
MAGGIE: Well, they're no good, just stupid rock-and-rolly stuff, and I start to think—*Laughs shyly*—maybe you'd turn on your radio, and I didn't want you to hear them. Is that crazy?
QUENTIN: No, but it's pretty unusual to care that much.
MAGGIE: I didn't used to, either. Honest.
QUENTIN, *mystified:* But I hardly said anything to you that day.
MAGGIE: Well, like—*Afraid she is silly*—when you told me to fix where my dress was torn?
QUENTIN: What about it?
MAGGIE: You wanted me to be . . . proud of myself. Didn't you?
QUENTIN, *surprised:* I guess I did, yes. . . . I did.
MAGGIE, *feeling she has budged him:* Would you like a drink?
QUENTIN, *relaxing:* I wouldn't mind. *Glancing around:* What's all the flowers?
MAGGIE, *pouring:* Oh, that's that dopey prince or a king or whatever he is. He keeps sending me a contract . . . whereas I get a hundred thousand dollars if we ever divorce. I'd be like a queen or something, but I only met him in El Morocco *once*! And I'm supposed to be his girl! *She laughs, handing him his drink.* I don't know why they print those things!
QUENTIN: Well, I guess everybody wants to touch you now.
MAGGIE: Cheers!

They drink; she makes a face.

I hate the taste but I love the effect! Would you like to take off your shoes? I mean just to rest.

QUENTIN: I'm okay. I thought you sounded on the phone like something frightened you.

MAGGIE, *evasively:* No. I . . . You have to go home right away?

QUENTIN: You all alone here?

MAGGIE, *with a strong evasiveness:* I don't mind that, I've always been alone. Oh, hey!

As though afraid to lose his interest, she digs into a pile of papers beside the bed, coming up with a small framed photo.

I cut your picture out of the paper last month. When you were defending that Reverend Harley Barnes in Washington? See? I framed it.

QUENTIN, *pleased and embarrassed:* What'd you do that for?

MAGGIE: It's funny how I found it. I was on the train . . .

QUENTIN: Is something frightening you, Maggie?

MAGGIE: No, don't worry! I'm just nervous you're here. See, what I did, they kept interviewing me and asking where you were born and all, and I didn't know what to answer. Whereas my father, see, he left when I was like eighteen months, and I just thought . . . if I could see him. And maybe he would like me. Or even not. Just so he'd look. I can't explain it.

QUENTIN: Maybe so you'd know who you were.

MAGGIE: Yes! So I took the train, he's got a business upstate there, and I called him from the station. And I said, "Can I see you?" And he said, "Who is it?" And I said, "It's Maggie, your daughter." Whereas he said I wasn't from him, although my mother always said I was. And he said, "I don't know who you are, see my lawyer." And I told him, "I just want you to look at me and—" And he hung up. *She laughs, lightly.* So I had time and I walked around the town and I thought maybe if I could find where he eats. And I would go in, and he'd see me and maybe . . . pick me up! *Laughs.* 'Cause my mother said he always liked beautiful girls!

QUENTIN: And then you'd tell him?

MAGGIE: I don't know. Maybe. Maybe . . . afterwards. I don't know why I tell you that . . . Oh, yes! On the train back I found this picture in the paper. And you see the way you're looking straight in the camera? That's very hard to do, you know . . . to look absolutely straight in?

QUENTIN: You mean I was looking at you.

MAGGIE: Yes! And I said, "I know who I am. I'm Quentin's friend." *Afraid she's gone too fast:* You want another drink or . . . I mean you don't have to do anything. You don't even have to see me again.

QUENTIN: Why do you say that?

MAGGIE: 'Cause I think it worries you.

QUENTIN: It does, yes.

MAGGIE: But why? I mean, can't you just be somebody's friend?

QUENTIN—*slight pause, and with resolve:* Yes. I can. It's that you're so beautiful, Maggie. I don't mean only your body and your face.

MAGGIE, *with a sudden rush of feeling:* I would do anything for you, Quentin. You—*It bursts from her*—you're like a god! S'uze me I say that but I—

QUENTIN, *with half a laugh:* Maggie, anybody would have told you to mend your dress.

MAGGIE: No, they wouldn't.

QUENTIN: What then?

MAGGIE, *in great pain:* Laugh. Or just . . . try for a quick one. You know.

QUENTIN, *to Listener:* Yes! It's all so clear: the honor! The first honor . . . was that I hadn't tried to go to bed with her! God, the hypocrisy! . . . Because, I was only afraid, and she took it for a tribute to her . . . "value"! No wonder I can't find myself here!

He has gotten to his feet in agony.

MAGGIE: Oh, hey—I christened a submarine! But you know what I did?

QUENTIN: What?

MAGGIE: I was voted the favorite of the Groton Shipyard! You know, by the workers. So the Admiral handed me the champagne bottle and I said, how come there's no workers in the ceremony, you know? And they all laughed! So I yelled down, and I got about ten of them to come up on the platform! Whereas they're the ones built it, right?

QUENTIN: That's wonderful!

MAGGIE: And you know what the Admiral said? I better watch out or I'll be a Communist. Honestly! So I said, "I don't know what's so terrible. . . . I mean they're for the poor people." Aren't they? The Communists?

QUENTIN: It's a lot more complicated, honey.

MAGGIE: But I mean, like when I was little I used to get free shoes from the Salvation Army. Although they never fit. *Embarrassed, with waning conviction:* But if the workers *do* everything why shouldn't they have the honor? Isn't that what you believe?

QUENTIN: I did, yes. But the question is whether the workers don't end up just where they are, and some new politicians on the stand.

MAGGIE: Oh. *With open longing and self-loss:* I wish I knew something!

QUENTIN: Honey, you know how to see it all with your own eyes; that's more important than all the books.

MAGGIE: But I don't know if it's true, what I see. But you do. You see and you know if it's true.

QUENTIN: What do you think I know?

MAGGIE, *some guard falling, her need rising:* Well like . . . that I was frightened.

QUENTIN: You frightened *now?* . . . You are, aren't you?

Maggie stares at him in tension; a long moment passes.

What is it, dear? You frightened to be alone here?

An involuntary half-sob escapes her. He sees she is in some great fear.

Why don't you call somebody to stay with you?

MAGGIE: I don't know anybody . . . like that.

QUENTIN—*slight pause:* Can I do anything? Don't be afraid to ask me.

MAGGIE—*in a struggle she finally says:* Would you . . . open that closet door?

QUENTIN—*he looks off, then back to her:* Just open it?

MAGGIE: Yes.

He walks into the dark periphery; she sits up warily, watching. He returns. And she lies back.

QUENTIN: Do you . . . want to tell me something?

MAGGIE: I just never know what's right to say and I—

QUENTIN: Well, say it, and find out; what are people for? I'm not going to laugh. *Sits.* What is it?

MAGGIE, *with great difficulty:* When I start to go to sleep before. And suddenly I saw smoke coming out of that closet under the door. It started to fill the whole room! *She breaks off, near weeping.*

QUENTIN—*reaches and takes her hand:* Oh, kid, that's nothing to—

MAGGIE: But it kept coming and coming!

QUENTIN: But look—you've often dreamed such things, haven't you?

MAGGIE: But I was awake!

QUENTIN: Well, it was a waking dream. It just couldn't stay down till you went to sleep. These things can be explained if you trace them back.

MAGGIE: I know. I go to an analyst.

QUENTIN: Oh . . . then tell him about it, you'll figure it out.

MAGGIE: It's when I start to call you before.

She is now absorbed in her own connections.

See, my mother . . . she used to get dressed in the closet. She was very . . . like moral, you know? But sometimes she'd smoke in there. And she'd come out—you know?— with a whole cloud of smoke around her.

QUENTIN: Well . . . possibly you felt she didn't want you to call me.

MAGGIE, *astounded:* How'd you know that?

QUENTIN: Because you said she was so moral. And here you're calling a married man.

MAGGIE: Yes! See, she tried to kill me once with a pillow on my face, whereas . . . I would turn out bad because of her . . . like her sin. And I have her hair, and the same back.

She turns half from him, showing a naked back.

'Cause I have a good back, see? Every masseur says.

QUENTIN: Yes, it is. It's beautiful. But it's no sin to call me.

MAGGIE, *shaking her head like a child—with a relieved laugh at herself:* Doesn't make me bad. Right?

QUENTIN: You're a very moral girl, Maggie.

MAGGIE, *delicately and afraid:* W—what's moral?

QUENTIN: You tell the truth, even against yourself. You're not pretending to be . . .

Turns out to the Listener, with a dread joy.

. . . innocent! Yes, that suddenly there was someone who— would not club you to death with their innocence! It's all laughable!

Felice begins to brighten, her arms raised, just as Mother appears and she is raising her arm . . .

MOTHER: I saw a star. . . .

MAGGIE: I bless you, Quentin!

Mother and Felice vanish as he turns back to Maggie, who takes up his photo.

Lot of nights when I go to sleep, I take your picture, and I bless you. You mind?

She has pressed the picture against her cheek. He bends to her, kisses her; for an instant she is unprepared, then starts to raise her arms to hold him. But he stands and backs away.

QUENTIN: I hope you sleep.

MAGGIE: I will now! *Lies back.* Honestly! I feel . . . all clear!

QUENTIN, *with a wave of his hand, backing away:* Good luck in London.

MAGGIE: And . . . what's moral, again?

QUENTIN: To live the truth.

MAGGIE: That's you!

QUENTIN: Not yet, dear; but I intend to try.

He halts. Across the room they look at one another. He walks back to her; now he bends in and she embraces him this time, offering herself, raising her body toward him. He stands, breaking it off. And as though he knows he is taking a step . . .

Don't be afraid to call me if you need any help.

She is suddenly gone. Alone, he continues the thought.

Any time . . .

Dan appears in crew-necked sweater with his book.

. . . you need anything, you call, y'hear?
DAN: This family's behind you, Quentin.

Backing into darkness, with a wave of farewell.

Any time you need anything . . .

Quentin, surprised, has turned quickly to Dan, who disappears.

QUENTIN, *to the Listener, as he still stares at the empty space Dan has left:* You know? It isn't fraud, but some . . . disguise. I came to her like Dan . . . his goodness! No wonder I can't find myself!

Felice appears, about to remove the "bandage," and he grasps for the concept.

. . . And that girl the other night.

Felice turns and goes.

When she left. It's still not clear, but suddenly those two fixtures on my wall . . .

He walks toward a "wall," looking up.

I didn't do it, but I wanted to. Like . . .

He turns and spreads his arms in crucifixion.

. . . this!

In disgust he lowers his arms.

. . . I don't know! Because she . . . *gave* me something! She . . . let me change her! As though I—*Cries out*—felt something! *He almost laughs.* What the hell am I trying to do, love *everybody*?

The line ends in self-contempt and anger. And suddenly, extremely fast, a woman appears in World War I costume—a Gibson Girl hat and veil over her face, ankle-length cloak, and in her hand a toy sailboat. She is bent over as though offering the boat to a little boy, and her voice is like a whisper, distant, obscure.

MOTHER: Quentin? Look what we brought you from Atlantic City—from the boardwalk!

The boy evidently runs away; Mother instantly is anxious and angering and rushes to a point and halts, as though calling through a closed door.

Don't lock this door! But darling, we didn't trick you, we took Dan because he's older and I wanted a rest! . . . But Fanny told you we were coming back, didn't she? Why are you running that water? Quentin, stop that water! Ike, come quick! Break down the door! Break down the door!

She has rushed off into darkness, and Quentin has started after her as though to complete the memory. He halts, and speaks to the Listener.

QUENTIN: . . . They sent me for a walk with the maid. When I came back the house was empty for a week. God, why is betrayal the only truth that sticks! . . . Yes! *He almost laughs.* "Love everybody!" And I can't even mourn my own mother. It's monstrous.

The "park bench" lights. Maggie appears in a heavy white man's sweater, a red wig over a white angora skating cap, moccasins, and sunglasses.

MAGGIE, *to the empty bench:* Hi! It's me! *Lifting the glasses.* Maggie!

QUENTIN, *looking toward Maggie:* Or mourn her, either. Is it simply grief I want? . . . No, this isn't mourning! . . . Because there's too much hatred in it!

He has come away from the adoring Maggie to the chair, shaking his head.

. . . No, it's not that I think I killed her. It's—

An anonymous man passes Maggie, glances, and goes on out.

MAGGIE, *to the empty bench:* See? I told you nobody recognizes me! Like my wig?

QUENTIN: . . . that I can't find myself in it, it's like another man. Only the guilt comes. Yes, or the innocence!

MAGGIE, *sitting beside "him" on the bench:* When you go to

Washington tonight . . . you know what I could do? I
could get on a different car on the same train!

QUENTIN, *to Listener:* But is it enough to tell a man he is not
guilty? *Glances at her.* My name is on this man! Why can't I
say "I"? *Turning toward her:* I did this. I want what I did!
And I saw it once! I saw *Quentin* here! For one moment like
the moon sees, I saw us both unblamed!

MAGGIE: Golly, I fell asleep the minute you left the other night!
I didn't even hear you close the door! You like my wig? See?
And moccasins!

Slight pause. Now he smiles.

QUENTIN: All you need is roller skates.

MAGGIE, *clapping her hands with joy:* You're funny!

QUENTIN, *half to Listener:* I keep forgetting . . . *Wholly to
her:* . . . how beautiful you are. Your eyes make me shiver.

She is silent, adoring. He breaks it, sitting.

MAGGIE: Like to see my new apartment? There's no elevator
even, or a doorman. Nobody would know. If you want to
rest before you go to Washington.

He doesn't reply.

'Cause I just found out, I go to Paris after London. I'm on
for two weeks, which is supposed to be unusual. But I won't
be back for a while.

QUENTIN: How long will you be gone?

MAGGIE: About . . . six weeks, I think.

*They both arrive at the same awareness: the separation is pain.
Tears are in her eyes.*

Quentin?

QUENTIN: Honey . . . *Takes her hand.* Don't look for anything more from me.

MAGGIE: I'm not! See, all I thought, if I went to Washington—

QUENTIN, *with a laugh:* What about London?

MAGGIE: Oh, they'll wait. 'Cause I could register in the hotel
as Miss None.

QUENTIN: N-u-n?

MAGGIE: No—"n-o-n-e"—like nothing. I made it up once, 'cause

I can never remember a fake name, so I just have to think of nothing and that's me! *She laughs with joy.* I've done it.

QUENTIN: It *is* a marvelous thought. The whole government's hating me, and meanwhile back at the hotel . . .

MAGGIE: That's what I mean! Just when that committee is knocking on your head you could think of me like naked. . . .

QUENTIN: What a lovely thought.

MAGGIE: And it would make you happy.

QUENTIN, *smiling warmly at her:* And nervous. But it is a lovely thought.

MAGGIE: Because it should all be one thing, you know? Helping people, and sex. You might even argue better the next day!

QUENTIN, *with a new awareness, astonishment:* You know?— There's one word written on your forehead.

MAGGIE: What?

QUENTIN: "Now."

MAGGIE: But what else is there?

QUENTIN: A future. And I've been carrying it around all my life, like a vase that must never be dropped. So you cannot ever touch anybody, you see?

MAGGIE: But why can't you just hold it in one hand?

He laughs.

And touch with the other! I would never bother you, Quentin.

He looks at his watch, as though beginning to calculate if there might not be time.

Can't somebody just give you something? Like when you're thirsty. And you drink, and walk away, that's all.

QUENTIN: But what about you?

MAGGIE: Well . . . I would have what I gave. *Slight pause.*

QUENTIN: You're all love, aren't you?

MAGGIE: That's all I am! A person could die any minute, you know. *Suddenly:* Oh, hey! I've got a will! *She digs into her pocket and brings out a folded sheet of notepaper.* Could . . . I show it to you?

QUENTIN, *taking it:* What do you want with a will?

MAGGIE: Well I'm going to do a lot of flying now and I just got my payment yesterday. Should I tell you how much?

QUENTIN: How much?

MAGGIE: Two hundred thousand dollars.

QUENTIN: Huh! You remember we sat right here, and I gave you five dollars?

MAGGIE, *with great love:* Yes!

They stare at each other.

Really, Quentin, there's not even an elevator man.

QUENTIN: You want me to look at that? Honey, I've got to do one thing at a time. *He opens the will.*

MAGGIE: I understand!

He starts reading the will.

See, I'm supposed to be like a millionaire in about two years!

Laughs; he goes on reading.

Is it legal if it's not typewritten?

QUENTIN—*looks at her:* Who wrote this?

MAGGIE: My agency; mostly Andy. Whereas he had to leave for London this morning to set everything up. And it was in a big rush.

Not comprehending, he nods and reads on.

But he's got a copy and I've got a copy.

He glances at her, bewildered.

I mean, that's what he said; that we both have copies.

He turns the page, reads on.

You got a haircut. I love the back of your head, it's sweet.

His brows knit now as he reads.

I'll shut up.

Finished reading, he stares ahead.

Or does it have to be typed?

QUENTIN: Who's this other signature?

MAGGIE: That's Jerry Moon. He's a friend of Andy in the

building business, but he knows a lot about law so he signed it for a witness. I saw him sign it. In my bedroom. Isn't it good?

QUENTIN: It leaves everything to the agency.

MAGGIE: I know, but just for temporary, till I can think of somebody to put down.

QUENTIN: But what's all the rush?

MAGGIE: Well in case Andy's plane goes down. He's got five children, see, and his—

QUENTIN: But do you feel responsible for his family?

MAGGIE: Well, no. But he did help me, he loaned me money when I—

QUENTIN: A million dollars?

MAGGIE, *with a dawning awareness:* Well, not a million. *With fear:* You mean I shouldn't?

QUENTIN: Who's your lawyer?

Two boys with bats and gloves pass, see her, walk off backward, whispering.

MAGGIE: Well, nobody. Jerry has a lawyer and he checks. I mean what's good for Andy's good for me, right?

QUENTIN—*with a certain unwillingness, even a repugnance, about interfering, he sounds neutral:* Didn't anybody suggest you get your own lawyer?

MAGGIE, *with fading conviction:* But if you trust somebody, you trust them. . . . Don't you?

QUENTIN—*a decision seizes him; he takes her hand:* Come on, I'll walk you home.

MAGGIE, *standing:* Okay! 'Cause I mean if you trust somebody!

QUENTIN: I'm sorry, honey, I can't advise you. Maybe you get something out of this that I don't understand. Let's go.

MAGGIE: No, I'm not involved with Andy. I . . . don't really sleep around with everybody, Quentin.

QUENTIN: Come on.

MAGGIE, *suddenly brightening:* 'Cause . . . I was never a prostitute. I was with a lot of men, but I never got anything. Not even for a job. I mean I'm changing. My analyst says I used to think it was like charity—sex. Like I give to those in need? *Laughs shyly.* Whereas I'm not an institution! Will you come in for a minute, too?

QUENTIN, *taking her arm:* Sure.

A small gang of boys with baseball equipment obstructs them; one of the first pair points at her.

FIRST BOY: It's Maggie, I told you!

MAGGIE, *pulling at Quentin's arm, defensively:* No, I just look like her, I'm Sarah None!

SECOND BOY: I can hear her voice!

QUENTIN: Let's go!

He tries to draw her off, but the boys grab her, and strangely, she begins accepting pencils and pieces of paper to autograph.

Hey!

CROWD: How about an autograph, Maggie?

> Whyn't you come down to the club?
> When's your next spectacular?
> Hey, Mag, I got all your records!
> Sing something!

Handing over a paper for her to sign.

> For my brother, Mag!
> Take off your sweater, Mag, it's hot out!
> How about that dance like you did on TV?

A boy wiggles sensually.

Quentin has been thrust aside; he now reaches in, grabs her, and draws her away as she walks backward, still signing, laughing with them. The boys gone, she turns to him.

MAGGIE: I'm sorry!

QUENTIN: It's like they're eating you. You like that?

MAGGIE: No, but they're just people. Could you sit down till the train? All I got so far is this French Provincial. *Taking off her sweater:* You like it? I picked it out myself. And my bed, and my record player. But it could be a nice apartment, couldn't it?

In silence Quentin takes her hand; he draws her to him; he kisses her.

Enflamed:

I love you, Quentin. I would do anything for you. And I would never bother you, I swear.

QUENTIN: You're so beautiful it's hard to look at you.

MAGGIE: You didn't even see me! *Backing away.* Why don't you just stand there and I'll come out naked! Or isn't there a later train?

QUENTIN—*pause:* Sure. There's always a later train.

He starts unbuttoning his jacket.

MAGGIE: I'll put music!

QUENTIN—*now he laughs through his words:* Yeah, put music!

She rushes into the dark, and he strives for his moment. To the Listener as he opens his jacket:

Here, it was somewhere here! . . . I don't know, a . . . a fraud!

A driving jazz comes on and she comes back, still dressed.

MAGGIE: Here, let me take off your shoes!

She drops to his feet, starting to unlace. Stiffly, with a growing horror, he looks down at her. Now shapes move in the darkness. He moves his foot away involuntarily.

QUENTIN: Maggie?

MAGGIE, *looking up from the floor, leaving off unlacing:* Yes?

He looks around in the darkness, and suddenly his Father charges forward.

FATHER: What you *want*! Always what you *want*! Chrissake, *what are you*?

Now Louise appears, reading a book, but Dan is standing beside her, almost touching her with his hand.

DAN: This family's behind you, kid.

And Mother, isolated, almost moving sensuously—and Quentin is moved, as though by them, away from Maggie.

MOTHER: Oh, what poetry he brought me, Strauss, and novels and . . .

QUENTIN—*he roars out to all of them, his fists angrily in air against them:* But where is *Quentin?*

Going toward Mother in her longing.

Yes, yes! But I know that treason! And the terror of complicity in that desire.

Turns toward Dan, who has moved alongside Father. The music breaks off.

Yes, and to not be unworthy of those loyal, failing men! But where is Quentin? Instead of taking off my clothes, this—*He bends to Maggie, raises her to her feet*—posture!
MAGGIE: Okay. Maybe when I get back we—
QUENTIN: I have to say it to you, Maggie.

To Listener.

Here it is, right here the killing fraud begins. *Pause.* You . . . have to tear up that will.

To Listener.

Can't even go to bed without a principle! But how can you speak of love, she had been chewed and spat out by a long line of grinning men! Her name floating in the stench of locker rooms and parlor-car cigar smoke! She had the truth that day, I bought the lie that she had to be "saved"! From what—except my own contempt? . . . Heh?

He is evidently caught by the Listener's contradicting him, steps closer to the chair, avidly listening.

MAGGIE, *to the empty space where Quentin was:* But I showed the will to my analyst, and he said it was okay. 'Cause a person like me has to have *somebody.*
QUENTIN: Maggie . . . honest men don't draw wills like that.
MAGGIE: But it's just for temporary. . . .
QUENTIN: Darling, if I went to Andy, and this adviser, and the analyst too, perhaps, I think they'd offer me a piece to shut up. They've got you on a table, honey, and they're carving you.
MAGGIE: But . . . I can't spend all that money anyway! I can't even *think* over twenty-five dollars!

QUENTIN: It's not the money they take, it's the dignity they destroy. You're not a piece of meat; you seem to think you owe people whatever they demand!

MAGGIE: I know. *She lowers her head with a cry, trembling with hope and shame.*

QUENTIN, *tilting up her face:* But Maggie, you're somebody! You're not a kid any more running around looking for a place to sleep! It's not only your success or that you're rich— you're straight, you're serious, you're first-class, people *mean* something to you; you don't have to go begging shady people for advice like some . . . some tramp.

With a sob of love and desperation, she slides to the floor and grasps his thighs, kissing his trousers. He watches, then suddenly lifts her and, with immense pity and joy:

Maggie, stand up!

The music flies in now, and she smiles strangely through her tears, and with a kind of statement of her persisting nature begins unbuttoning her blouse, her body writhing to the beat within her clothing. And as soon as she starts her dance his head shakes . . . and to the Listener:

No, not love; to stop impersonating, that's all! To live— *Groping:*—to live in good faith if only with my guts! To . . .

Suddenly Dan and Father appear together; and to them:

Yes! To be "good" no more! Disguised no more! Afraid no more to show what Quentin, Quentin, Quentin . . . is!

Louise appears, talking.

LOUISE: You haven't even the decency to—

QUENTIN: That decency is murderous! Speak truth, not decency—I curse the whole high administration of fake innocence! I declare it, I am not innocent! Nor good!

A high tribunal dimly appears; a chairman bangs his gavel once; he is flanked by others looking down on Quentin from on high. Maggie is dropping her blouse.

CHAIRMAN: But rarely Reverend Barnes cannot object to

answering whether he attended the Communist-run Peace
Congress in Prague, Czechoslovakia. No—no, counsel will
not be allowed to confer with the witness, this is not a trial!
Any innocent man would be . . .

QUENTIN: And this question—innocent! How many Negroes
you allow to vote in your patriotic district? And which of
your social, political, or racial sentiments would Hitler have
disapproved? And not a trial? You fraud, your "investigators"
this moment are working this man's church to hound him
out of it!

HARLEY BARNES—*appears rising to his feet; he has a clerical collar:* I decline on the grounds of the First and Fifth Amend-
ments to the Constitution.

QUENTIN, *with intense sorrow:* But are we sure, Harley—I ask
it, I ask it—if the tables were turned, and they were in front
of you—would you permit *them* not to answer? Hateful men
that they are?

Harley looks at him indignantly, suspiciously.

I am not sure what we are upholding any more—are we
good by merely saying no to evil? Even in a righteous "no"
there's some disguise. Isn't it necessary . . . to say . . .

*Harley is gone, and the tribunal. Maggie is there, snapping her
fingers, letting down her hair.*

. . . to finally say yes . . . to *something*?

*A smile of pain and longing has come into his face, and Mag-
gie expands now, slipping out of her skirt, dancing in place. He
goes to her and grasps her body, moving with her serpentine
motion.*

A fact . . . a fact . . . a thing.

*Maggie embraces him and then lies down on the "bed" with the
imagined Quentin.*

MAGGIE: Sing inside me.

*Quentin moves to the chair facing the Listener; she continues
on the bed behind him as he sits.*

QUENTIN: Even condemned, unspeakable like all truth!

MAGGIE: Become happy.

QUENTIN, *still to Listener:* Contemptible like all truth.

MAGGIE: That's all I am.

QUENTIN: Covered like truth with slime; blind, ignorant.

MAGGIE: But nobody ever said to me, stand up!

QUENTIN: The blood's fact, the world's blind gut . . . yes!

MAGGIE: Now.

QUENTIN: To this, yes.

MAGGIE: Now . . . now.

Her recorded number ends and only the thumping needle in the empty groove is heard through the lengthening darkness. Then her voice, pillowed and soft.

Quentin?

Light finds her prone on a bed, alone on the stage, a sheet partly covering her naked body. Her chin rests languidly on her hands. She glances toward a point, off.

Quenny? That soap is odorless, so you don't have to worry.

Slight pause.

It's okay! Don't rush; I love to wait for you!

Her eye falls on his shoe on the floor. She picks it up, strokes it.

I love your shoes. You have good taste!

Slight pause.

S'uze me I didn't have anything for you to eat, but I didn't know! I'll get eggs, though, case maybe in the mornings. And steaks—case at night. I mean just in case. You could have it just the way you want, just any time.

Quentin stands looking front; she speaks to empty space from the bed.

Like me?

He glances back at her adoring face, as Holga appears above in the airport, looking about for him. Maggie remains on the bed, stroking his shoe.

QUENTIN, *glancing at Maggie:* It's all true, but it isn't the truth.

I know it because it all comes back too cheap; my bitterness is making me lie. I'm afraid. To make a promise. Because I don't know who'll be making it. I'm a stranger to my life.

MAGGIE—*she has lifted a tie off the floor:* Oh, your tie got all wrinkled! I'm sorry! But hey, I have a tie! *Jumping up with the sheet around her.* It's beautiful, a regular man's tie—*Catching herself:* I . . . just happen to have it!

She tries to laugh it off and goes into darkness. Holga is gone.

QUENTIN: I tell you, below this fog of tawdriness and vanity, there is a law in this disaster, and I saw it once as hard and clear as a statute. But I think I saw it . . . with some love. Or simply wonder, but not blame. It's . . . like my mother; so many of my thoughts of her degenerate into some crime; the truth is she was a light to me whenever it was dark. I loved that nut, and only love does make her real and mine. Or can one ever remember love? It's like trying to summon up the smell of roses in a cellar. You might see a rose, but never the perfume. And that's the truth of roses, isn't it—the perfume?

Maggie appears in light in a wedding dress; Carrie, the maid, is just placing a veiled hat on her head; Lucas, the designer, is on his knees hurriedly fixing the last hem. Maggie is turning herself wide-eyed in a mirror. Quentin begins to rise.

MAGGIE: Okay! Let him in, Carrie! Thanks, Lucas, but I don't want him to wait any more, the ceremony is for three! Hurry, please!

Lucas sews faster; Carrie goes to a point, calls down.

CARRIE: Mister Quentin? You can see her now.

QUENTIN: I want to see her with . . . that love again! Why is it so hard? Standing there, that wishing girl, that victory in lace. We had turned all mockery to purpose, and purpose moved around us like the natural shadows of the day!

MAGGIE, *looking ahead on the edge of life as Lucas bites off the last threads:* You won't hardly know me any more, Lucas! He saved me, I mean it! I've got a new will and I even changed my analyst, I've got a wonderful doctor now! And we're going to do all my contracts over, which I never got properly paid. And Ludwig Reiner's taking me! And he won't take even opera singers unless they're, you know, like artists! No matter how much you want to pay him. I didn't even dare but Quentin made me go—and now he took me, imagine! Ludwig Reiner!

She turns, seeing Quentin entering. An awe of the moment takes them both; Lucas goes. Carrie lightly touches Maggie's forehead and silently prays, and walks off.

QUENTIN: Oh, my darling. How perfect you are.

MAGGIE: Like me?

QUENTIN: Good God—to come home every night—to *you*!

He starts for her open-armed, laughing, but she touches his chest, excited and strangely fearful.

MAGGIE: You still don't have to do it, Quentin. I could just come to you whenever you want.

QUENTIN—*it hurts him but he tries to laugh again:* You just can't believe in something good really happening. But it's real, darling, you're my wife!

MAGGIE, *with a hush of fear on her voice:* I want to tell you something.

QUENTIN: I know enough. Come.

MAGGIE, *slipping her hand out of his:* I just want to tell you!

QUENTIN: Darling, you're always making new revelations, but that stuff doesn't matter any more.

MAGGIE, *pleased, and like a child wanting some final embrace:* But the reason I went into analysis! I never told you *that*!

QUENTIN, *smiling above his own foreboding:* All right, what?

MAGGIE: 'Cause you said we have to love what happened, didn't you? Even the bad things?

QUENTIN, *seriously now, to match her intensity:* Yes, I did.

MAGGIE: I . . . was with two men . . . the same day. *She has turned her eyes from him.* I mean the same day, see. But I didn't realize it till that night. And I got very scared. *She almost weeps now, and looks at him, subservient and oddly chastened.* I'll always love you, Quentin. But don't be afraid what people say, we could just tell them we changed our mind, and get in the car and maybe go to a motel. . . .

Anonymous men appear in the farthest distance and vanish as Quentin shakes his head.

QUENTIN: Look, darling. It wasn't you. . . . *Reaching for her hand again:* Come now.

MAGGIE: But maybe in a way it was. In a way! I don't know!

QUENTIN: Sweetheart, everyone does things that . . .

To Listener, with sudden realization:

Here, here is part of it! One part is that . . .

Back to her:

An event itself, dear, is not important; it's what you took from it. Whatever happened to you, this is what you made of it and I love this.

To Listener, rapidly:

. . . Yes! That we conspired to violate the past, and the past is holy and its horrors are holiest of all!

Turning back to Maggie:

And . . . something . . . more . . .

MAGGIE, *with hope now:* Maybe . . . it would even make me a better wife, right?

QUENTIN, *with hope against the pain:* That's the way to talk!

MAGGIE, *with gladness, seeing a fruit of the horror:* 'Cause I'm not curious! You be surprised, a lot of women, they smile and their husbands never know, but they're curious. But I *know*—I have a king, and *I know!*

A wedding march strikes up. It shatters her fragile vision; he takes her arm.

There's people who . . . going to laugh at you.

QUENTIN: Not any more, dear, they're going to see what I see. Come!

MAGGIE, *not moving with him:* What do you see? Tell me! *Bursting out of her:* 'Cause I think . . . you were ashamed once, weren't you?

QUENTIN: I see you suffering, Maggie; and once I saw it, all shame fell away.

MAGGIE: You . . . were ashamed!?

QUENTIN, *with difficulty:* Yes. But you're a victory, Maggie, for yourself and me. And somehow for everyone. *He kisses her hand.* Believe it, darling, you're like a flag to me, a kind of proof, somehow, that people can win.

MAGGIE: And you . . . you won't ever look at any other woman, right?

QUENTIN: Darling, a wife can be loved! You never saw it but . . .

MAGGIE, *with a new intensity of conflict:* Before, though—why did you kiss that Elsie?

QUENTIN: Just hello. She always throws her arms around people.

MAGGIE: But . . . why'd you let her rub her body against you?

QUENTIN—*laughs:* She wasn't rubbing her . . .

MAGGIE, *downing a much greater anxiety:* I saw it. And you stood there.

QUENTIN, *trying to laugh:* Maggie, it was a meaningless gesture.

MAGGIE: But you told me yourself that I have to look for the meaning of things, didn't you? You want me to be like I used to be? Like nothing means anything, it's all a fog? *Now pleadingly, and vaguely wronged:* I'm just trying to understand; you mustn't laugh. Why did you let her do that?

QUENTIN: She came up to me and threw her arms around me, what could I do?

MAGGIE—*a flash of contemptuous anger:* What do you mean? You just tell her to knock it off!

QUENTIN, *taken aback:* I . . . don't think you want to sound like this, honey.

MAGGIE, *frightened she has shown a forbidden side:* Sound like what?

QUENTIN, *trying to brush it away:* Darling, you're just frightened and it magnifies every threat. Come, they're waiting.

He puts her arm in his; they turn to go.

MAGGIE, *almost in tears:* Teach me, Quentin! I don't know how to be!

QUENTIN: Yes, darling. Now we start to be. Both of us.

They begin moving in processional manner toward a group of guests.

MAGGIE: It's that nobody's here . . . from me. I'm like a stranger here! If my mother or my father or anybody who loved me—

QUENTIN: Be calm, dear, everyone here adores you.

Now as Maggie speaks she continues in processional tread, but he remains behind, staring at her; and she goes on with "him," her arm still held as before, but in midair now.

MAGGIE: I'm sorry if I sounded that way, but you want me to say what I feel, don't you? See, till you, I never said anything, Quentin; you like gave me my feelings to say! You don't want me just smiling, like most women, do you?

During her speech Louise has appeared.

QUENTIN, *as against the vision of Louise:* No. *Say* what you feel; the truth is on our side; always say it!

Louise is gone.

MAGGIE, *faltering, but going on:* You're not holding me!

QUENTIN, *half the stage away now, and turning toward the empty air:* I am, darling, I'm with you!

MAGGIE, *as she walks into darkness:* I'm going to be a good wife, I'm going to be a good wife. . . . Quentin, I don't feel it!

QUENTIN, *both frustrated and with an appeal to her:* I'm holding you! See everybody smiling, adoring you? Look at the orchestra guys making a V for victory! Everyone loves you, darling! Why are you sad?

Suddenly, the Wedding March is gone as from the far depths of the stage, her shape undefined, she calls out with a laugh.

MAGGIE: Surprise! You like it? They rushed it while we were away!

QUENTIN—*a slight pause; they are half a stage apart:* Yes, it's beautiful!

The dialogue is now condensed, like time swiftly passing in the mind.

MAGGIE: See how large it makes the living room? And I want to take down that other wall too! Okay?

QUENTIN, *not facing her direction; to his memory of it:* But we just finished putting those walls in.

MAGGIE: Well it's only money; I want it big, like a castle for you! You want it beautiful, don't you?

QUENTIN: It's lovely, dear, but . . . maybe wait till next year with the other wall. We're behind in the taxes, darling.

MAGGIE: But we could die tomorrow! Used to say, I have one word written on my forehead—why can't it be beautiful now? I get all that money next year.

QUENTIN: But see, dear, you owe almost all of it. . . .

MAGGIE: Quentin, don't hold the future like a vase—touch now, touch me! I'm here, and it's now!

QUENTIN: Okay! Tear it down! Make it beautiful! Do it now! Maybe I *am* too cautious. Forgive me.

Her voice is suddenly heard in a vocal number. He breaks into a genuine smile of joy.

Maggie, sweetheart—that's magnificent!

Now she appears, in blouse, leotards, high heels, listening and pacing. Several executives in dark suits appear, listening carefully.

MAGGIE: No! Tell me the truth! That piano's off, you're not listening!

QUENTIN: But nobody'll ever notice that.

A pianist moves near her out of the executive group.

MAGGIE: I know the difference! Don't you want me to be good? I *told* Weinstein I wanted Johnny Block but they give me this fag and he holds back my beat! Nobody listens to me, I'm a joke!

QUENTIN: All right, dear, maybe if I talked to Weinstein—

MAGGIE: No, don't get mixed up in my crummy business, you've got an important case . . .

QUENTIN—*he moves to a point and demands:* Weinstein, get her Johnny Block!

The music turns over into another number and her voice, swift, sure.

There now! Listen now!

She listens in suspense; he almost struts with his power.

See? There's no reason to get upset, just tell me and I'll talk to these people any time you—

MAGGIE: Oh, thank you, darling! See? They respect you. Ask Ludwig, soon as you come in the studio my voice flies! Oh, I'm going to be a good wife, Quentin, I just get nervous sometimes that I'm—*She sits as the music goes out*—only bringing you my problems. But I want my stuff to be perfect, and all they care is if they can get rich on it.

The executives are gone.

QUENTIN: Exactly, dear—so how can you look to them for your self-respect? Come, why don't we go out for a walk? We never walk any more. *He sits on his heels beside her.*

MAGGIE: You love me?

QUENTIN: I adore you. I just wish you could find some joy in your life.

MAGGIE: Quentin, I'm a joke that brings in money.

QUENTIN: I think it's starting to change, though—you've got a great band now, and Johnny Block, and the best sound crew. . . .

MAGGIE: Only because I fought for it. You'd think somebody'd come to me and say, Look, Maggie, you made us all this money, now we want you to develop yourself, what can we do for you?

QUENTIN: Darling, they'd be selling frankfurters if there were more money in it, how can you look to them for love?

MAGGIE, *alone, alone:* But where will I look?

QUENTIN, *thrown down:* Maggie, how can you say that?

MAGGIE—*she stands; there is an underlying suspiciousness now:* When I walked into the party you didn't even put your arms around me. I felt like one of those *wives* or something!

QUENTIN: Well, Donaldson was in the middle of a sentence and I—

MAGGIE: So what? *I walked into the room!* I hire him, he doesn't hire me!

QUENTIN: But he is directing your TV show and I was being polite to him.

MAGGIE: You don't have to be ashamed of me, Quentin. I had a right to tell him to stop those faggy jokes at my rehearsal. Just because he's cultured? I'm the one the public pays for, not Donaldson! Ask Ludwig Reiner what my value is!

QUENTIN: I married you, Maggie, I don't need Ludwig's lecture on your value.

MAGGIE, *looking at him with strange eyes—with a strange laugh:* Why . . . why you so cold?

QUENTIN: I'm not cold, I'm trying to explain what happened.

MAGGIE: Well, take me in your arms, don't explain.

He takes her in his arms, kisses her, and she plaintively instructs:

Not like that. *Hold* me.

QUENTIN—*he tries to hold her tighter, then releases her:* Let's go for a walk, honey. Come on . . .

MAGGIE, *sinking:* What's the matter?

Louise appears, playing solitaire.

QUENTIN: Nothing.

MAGGIE: But Quentin . . . you should look at me more. I mean . . . like I *existed* or something. Like you used to look—out of your *self*.

Louise vanishes. Maggie moves away into darkness, deeply discouraged.

QUENTIN, *alone:* I adore you, Maggie; I'm sorry; it won't ever happen again. Never! You need more love than I thought. But I've got it, and I'll make you see it, and when you do you're going to astound the world!

A rose light floods a screen; Maggie emerges in a dressing gown, indicating an unseen window.

MAGGIE: Surprise! You like it? See the material?

QUENTIN: Oh, that's lovely! How'd you think of that?

MAGGIE: All you gotta do is close them and the sun makes the bed all rose.

QUENTIN, *striving for joy:* Yes, it's beautiful! You see? An argument doesn't mean disaster! Oh, Maggie, I never knew what love was! *Takes her in his arms.*

MAGGIE, *her spirit gradually falling:* 'Case during the day, like maybe you get the idea to come home and we make love again in daytime. *She ends sitting in a weakness; nostalgically:* Like last year, remember? In the winter afternoons? And once there was still snow on your hair. See, that's all I am, Quentin.

QUENTIN: I'll come home tomorrow afternoon.

MAGGIE: Well don't *plan* it.

He laughs, but she looks at him; her stare is piercing. His laugh dies.

QUENTIN: What is it? See, I don't want to hide things any more, darling. The truth saves, always remember that—tell me, what's bothering you?

MAGGIE, *shaking her head, seeing:* I'm not a good wife. I take up so much of your work.

QUENTIN: No, dear. I only said that because you—*Striving, against his true resentment*—you kind of implied that I didn't fight the network hard enough on that penalty, and I got it down to twenty thousand dollars. They had a right to a hundred when you didn't perform.

MAGGIE, *with rising indignation:* But can't I be sick? I was sick!

QUENTIN: I know, dear, but the doctor wouldn't sign the affidavit.

MAGGIE, *furious at him:* I had a pain in my side, for Christ's sake, I couldn't stand straight! You don't believe me, do you!

QUENTIN: Maggie, I'm only telling you the legal situation.

MAGGIE: Ask Ludwig what you should do! You should've gone in there roaring! 'Stead of a polite liberal and affidavits and—

QUENTIN, *hurt:* Don't say that, Maggie.

MAGGIE: Well, ask him! You don't know what a star's rights are! I make millions for those people!

QUENTIN: Maggie, I always thought I was a pretty good lawyer. . . .

MAGGIE: I'm not saying Ludwig is a lawyer.

QUENTIN: I know, dear, but he's always got these brave solutions but the two-three times I've tried to pin him down to specifics he gets full of oxygen.

MAGGIE: Now you're hurt! I can't *say* anything!

QUENTIN: Well, honey, I'm putting in forty per cent of my time on your problems.

MAGGIE: You are not putting—

QUENTIN, *horrified she doesn't know—an outburst:* Maggie, I keep a log; I know what I spend my time on!

She looks at him shaking her head; mortally wounded, tears in her eyes. She goes to a bottle and pours.

I'm sorry, darling, but when you talk like that I feel a little . . . like a fool. Don't start drinking; please.

She drinks.

Look, I don't object to the time I spend, I'm happy to do it, but—

MAGGIE: Should never gotten married. I knew it. Soon's they got married it all changes. Every man I ever knew they hate their wives.

QUENTIN: Honey, it always comes down to the same thing, don't you see? Now listen to me. *Turns her.* You're still proceeding on the basis that you're alone. That you can be disposed of. And the slightest contradiction of your wishes makes the earth tremble. But—

MAGGIE: You taught me to speak out, Quentin, and when I do you get mad.

QUENTIN: I'm not mad, I'm frustrated that you can't seem to pick up the joy we could have. My greatest happiness is when I know I've helped to make you smile, to make you—

MAGGIE: But the only reason I went to see Ludwig was so you'd be proud of me, so you could say, "See? I found her she was a little lost nut, and look, look what became of Maggie!" It's all for you, that's why I want it good!

QUENTIN: Then what are we arguing about? We want the same thing, you see?

Suddenly to Listener:

Power! Yes, the power, the power to . . . to . . . Wait a minute, I had it, and I lost it.

MAGGIE, *pouring another drink:* So maybe the best thing is if I get a lawyer . . . you know, just a stranger.

QUENTIN—*slight pause; hurt:* Okay.

MAGGIE: It's nothing against you; but see, like that girl in the orchestra, that cellist—I mean, Andy took too much but he'd have gone in there and got rid of her. I mean, you don't laugh when a singer goes off key.

QUENTIN: But she said she coughed.

MAGGIE, *furiously:* She didn't cough, she laughed! And you stand there going ho-ho-ho to her high-class jokes! Christ sake, just because she played in a symphony?

QUENTIN: Maggie, I stopped by to pick you up, I said hello to her and—

MAGGIE: I'm not finishing this tape if she's in the band tomorrow! I'm entitled to my conditions, Quentin! *Commanding:* And I don't have to plead with anybody! I want her out!

QUENTIN, *quietly:* All right. I'll call Weinstein in the morning.

MAGGIE: You won't. You're too polite.

QUENTIN: I've done it before, Maggie; three others in three different bands.

MAGGIE: Well, so what? You're my husband. You're supposed to do that. Aren't you?

QUENTIN: But I can't pretend to enjoy demanding people be fired.

MAGGIE: But if it was your daughter you'd get angry, wouldn't you? Instead of apologizing for her?

QUENTIN—*envisions it:* I guess I would, yes. I'm sorry. I'll do it in the morning.

MAGGIE, *with desperate warmth:* That's all I mean. If I want something you should ask yourself why, why does she want it, not why she shouldn't have it. That's why I don't smile, I feel I'm fighting all the time to make you *see.* You're like a little boy, you don't see the knives people hide.

QUENTIN: I see the knives, but . . . It's the same thing again. You still don't believe you're not alone.

MAGGIE: Then make me believe it!

QUENTIN: I'm trying, darling, but sometimes you say a thing that cuts me down like a . . . Maggie, I'm not cold to you.

MAGGIE: I didn't mean you're cold. It's just . . . I've seen such terrible things, Quentin. I never told you most of it. And when you're alone all you have is what you can see. Ask my doctor—I see more than most people, 'cause I had to protect myself.

QUENTIN: But sweetheart, that's all gone. You've got a husband now who loves you.

Pause. She seems to fear greatly.

MAGGIE: But it's not all gone. When your mother tells me I'm getting fat, I know where I am—and when you don't do anything about it.

QUENTIN: But what can I do?

MAGGIE: Slap her down, that's what you do!

QUENTIN: But she says anything comes into her head, dear.

MAGGIE: She insulted me! She's jealous of me!

QUENTIN: Maggie, she adores you.

MAGGIE: What are you trying to make me think, I'm crazy?

QUENTIN: Why does everything come down to—

MAGGIE: I'm not crazy!

QUENTIN, *carefully, on eggs:* The thought never entered my mind, darling. I'll . . . talk to her.

MAGGIE, *mimicking him as though he were weak:* "I'll talk to her." She hates me!

QUENTIN: I'll tell her to apologize.

MAGGIE: But at least get a little angry!

QUENTIN: All right, I'll do it.

She drinks.

MAGGIE: I'm not going to work tomorrow.

She lies down on the "bed" as though crushed.

QUENTIN: Okay.

MAGGIE, *half springing up:* You know it's not "okay"! You're scared to death they'll sue me, why don't you say it?

QUENTIN: I'm not scared to death; it's just that you're so wonderful in this show and it's a pity to—

MAGGIE, *sitting up furiously:* All you care about is money! Don't shit me!

The anonymous men appear in the distance.

QUENTIN, *quelling a fury—his voice very level:* Maggie, don't use that language with me, will you?

MAGGIE: Calling me vulgar, that I talk like a truck driver! Well, that's where I come from. I'm for Negroes and Puerto Ricans and truck drivers!

QUENTIN: Then why do you fire people so easily?

MAGGIE—*her eyes narrowing, she is seeing him anew:* Look. You don't want me. What the hell are you doing here?

QUENTIN, *with a quavering, mountainous restraint:* I live here. And you do too, but you don't know it yet. But you're going to. I . . .

Father appears.

FATHER: Where's he going, I need him! What are you?

And he is gone.

QUENTIN: I'm here, and I stick it. And one day you're going to catch on. Now go to sleep, I'll be back in ten minutes, I'd like to take a walk.

He starts out and she comes to attention.

MAGGIE: Where are going to walk?
QUENTIN: Just around the block.

She watches him carefully. He sees her suspicion.

There's nobody else, kid; I just want to walk.
MAGGIE, *with great suspicion:* 'Kay.

He goes a few yards, halts, turns to see her taking a pill bottle and unscrewing the top.

QUENTIN, *coming back:* You can't take pills on top of whiskey, dear.

He has reached for them; she pulls them away but he grabs them again and puts them in his pocket.

That's how it happened the last time. And it's not going to happen again. Never. I'll be right back.
MAGGIE—*she pours again:* Why you wear those pants?

He turns back to her, knowing what is coming.

I told you the seat is too tight.

QUENTIN: Well, they made them too tight, but I can take a walk in them.

MAGGIE: Fags wear pants like that; I told you.

She drinks again. It is so pathological he looks with amazed eyes.

They attract each other with their asses.

QUENTIN: You calling me a fag now?

MAGGIE—*she is very drunk:* Just I've known fags and some of them didn't even know themselves that they were. And I didn't know if you knew about that.

QUENTIN: That's a hell of a way to reassure yourself, Maggie.

MAGGIE, *staggering slightly:* I'm allowed to say what I see . . .

QUENTIN: You trying to get me to throw you out? Is that what it is? So it'll get real?

MAGGIE, *pointing at him, at his control:* Wha's that suppose to be, strong and silent? I mean what is it?

She stumbles and falls. He makes no move to pick her up.

QUENTIN, *standing over her, quite knowing she is beyond understanding:* And now I walk out, huh? And it's real again, huh?

He picks her up angrily.

Is that what you want?

MAGGIE, *breaking from him:* I mean what *is it*?

She pitches forward; he catches her and roughly puts her on the bed.

Wha's the angle? I mean what is it?

She gets on her feet again.

You gonna wait till I'm old? You know what another cab driver said to me today? "I'll give you fifty dollars."

An open sob, wild and contradictory, flies out of her.

You know what's fifty dollars to a cab driver?

Her pain moves into him, his anger is swamped with it.

Go ahead, you can go; I can even walk a straight line, see? Look, see?

She walks with arms out, one foot in front of the other.

So what is it, heh? I mean what is it? I mean you want dancing? You want dancing?

QUENTIN: Please don't do that.

Breathlessly she turns on the phonograph and goes into a hip-flinging, broken ankle step around him.

MAGGIE: I mean what do you want! What is it?

He hasn't been looking at her, but beyond her, and now she starts tumbling about and he catches her and lays her down on the bed.

I mean, you gonna wait till I'm old? Or what? I mean what is it?

She lies there gasping. He stares down at her, addressing the Listener.

QUENTIN: That there is a love; limitless; a love not even of persons but blind, blind to insult, blind to the spear in the flesh, like justice blind, like . . .

Felice appears. Quentin slowly raises up his arms; holds them there. But his face is drawn together in his quest. Maggie speaks from the bed, half-asleep.

MAGGIE: Hey? Why?

Felice vanishes. He lowers his arms, peering for his answer, as . . .

I mean what do you want? Whyn't you beat it? I mean what is it?

Father appears.

FATHER: What are . . .

Quentin shakes his head, an unformed word of negation in his mouth.

Dan appears.

DAN: This family is always behind you, boy; anything you need, just . . .

Mickey appears: Quentin moves toward him.

MICKEY: . . . That we both go back, Lou, you and I together; and name the names.

QUENTIN, *shaking the vision out of his head as false and crying out—as Dan and Father disappear:* No! I had it! In whose name you turn your back! I saw it clear! I saw the name!

Lou appears on high; the approaching sound of a subway train is heard and he seems to fall off a platform to the wracking squeal of brakes, crying.

LOU: Quentin!

He is gone, and Mickey is gone. Quentin's hands are a vise against his head. The tower lights as . . .

QUENTIN, *on new level of angry terror:* In whose name? In whose blood-covered name do you look into a face you loved, and say, Now, you have been found wanting, and now in your extremity you die! It had a name, it . . .

Behind his back, in the farthest extremity of the stage, hardly visible excepting as a bent-over shape, Mother appears in pre–World War I costume, calling in a strange whisper:

MOTHER: Quentin? Quentin?

She is moving rapidly through shadow. He hurries toward her, but in fear.

QUENTIN: Hah? Hah?

MOTHER: See what we brought you from Atlantic City! From the boardwalk!

A tremendous crash of surf spins him about, and Mother is gone and the light of the moon is rising on the pier.

QUENTIN: . . . By the ocean. That cottage. That last night.

Maggie in a rumpled wrapper, a bottle in her hand, her hair in snags over her face, staggers out to the edge of the "pier" and stands in the sound of the surf. Now she starts to topple over the edge of the "pier" and he rushes to her and holds her in his hands. She slowly turns around and sees it's he. Now the sound of jazz from within is heard, softly.

MAGGIE: You were loved, Quentin; no man was ever loved like you.

QUENTIN, *releasing her:* Carrie tell you I called? My plane couldn't take off all day. . . .

MAGGIE, *drunk, but aware:* I was going to kill myself just now. *She walks past him. He is silent. She turns.* Or don't you believe that either?

QUENTIN, *with an absolute calm, a distance, but without hostility:* I saved you twice, why shouldn't I believe it? *Going toward her:* This dampness is bad for your throat, you oughtn't be out here.

MAGGIE—*she defiantly sits, her legs dangling:* Where've *you* been?

QUENTIN: I've been in Chicago. I told you. The Hathaway estate.

MAGGIE—*a sneer:* Estates!

QUENTIN: Well, I have to make a living before I save the world.

He goes into the bedroom, removing his jacket.

MAGGIE, *from the pier:* Didn't you hear what I told you?

QUENTIN: I heard it. I'm not coming out there, Maggie, it's too wet.

She looks out a moment, wide-eyed at the neutrality of his tone; then gets up and unsteadily comes into the room. He is taking off his tie.

MAGGIE: What's *this* all about?

QUENTIN: Just going to sleep. I'm very tired. I don't feel too hot.

MAGGIE: Tired.

QUENTIN: Yep. I can get tired too.

MAGGIE: Poor man.

QUENTIN: Not any more, no.

He sits on the bed unlacing his shoes. Sensing, she sits on a chair, the pill bottle in her hand.

MAGGIE, *like a challenge to him:* I didn't go to rehearsal today.

QUENTIN: I didn't think you did.

MAGGIE: I called Weinstein; I'm not working on his label any more and I don't care if he's got ten contracts. And I called the network; I'm not doing that stupid show, and I don't owe it to them regardless of any promise you made me make. I'm an artist and I don't have to do stupid shows no matter what contract!

QUENTIN: Maggie, I'm not your lawyer any more; tell it to—

MAGGIE: I told him. And he's getting me out of both contracts. And no arguments either.

QUENTIN: Good. I'll sleep in the living room. I've got to rest.

He starts out.

MAGGIE, *holding up the bottle:* Here, count them if you want to, I only took a few.

QUENTIN: I'm not counting pills any more, Maggie, I've given up being the policeman. But if you want to, I wish you'd tell me how many you had before I came. 'Cause they should know that in case they have to pump you out tonight.

MAGGIE, *hurt and bewildered:* What is this?

QUENTIN: Just that I can't pull on the other end of that rope any more. And I see the signs, honey, so I'm telling you in advance. The last two times when we got you out of it you thanked me for saving your life, and for days everything was warm and sweet. I'm not your analyst, but if this is how you create a happy reunion, forget it—this time I call the ambulance, so if you do wake up it'll be in the hospital, and that means the newspapers. I'm just trying to remove one of the motives, if a happy reunion is one of them—because I'm not going to be the rescuer any more. It's only fair to tell you, I just haven't got it any more. They're your pills and your life; you keep the count.

He starts out.

MAGGIE: What. . . . what's all this? Well, don't run away like a kid. What is all this?

QUENTIN—*halts; a pause:* Well . . . one thing is that I've been fired. And that's what I've been doing in Chicago. Max is there and I went to convince him that I oughtn't be let out of the firm.

MAGGIE: You're not fired.

QUENTIN: In fact, it's the second time in six months. I can't make a decision any more without something sits up inside me and busts out laughing.

MAGGIE: That my fault, heh?

QUENTIN: Maggie, I only tell it to you so you'll understand that the question is no longer whether you'll survive, but also whether I will. Because I'm backed up to the edge of the cliff, and I haven't one inch left behind me. And that's the difference tonight, Maggie. So take care what you ask me, dear, because all I've got left is the truth. You know that feeling?

They hold each other's gaze. She unscrews the bottle and takes out a pill and swallows it.

Okay.

He sits on the bed, and puts his shoes on again.

MAGGIE: What are you doing?

QUENTIN: I'll sleep at the inn tonight. I think you're safer without me here. I think I've turned into some kind of ogre to you; and I haven't the strength to try to correct it any more.

He gets his tie.

MAGGIE—*her speech thicker, but she is doped rather than drunk:* Don't . . . do that.

He looks at her lost face.

Please. Please . . . sit down.

And as she did when they first met, but in a caricature of that invitingness, she indicates a chair.

Could you . . . just while I . . . go to sleep? Please?

QUENTIN, *gently moved:* Okay, if you lie down and go to sleep.

MAGGIE: I'll . . . lie down here. See?

She quickly goes to the bed, clutching her pills, and lies down.

See?

He sits facing her, a yard away. Silence.

'Member? How used talk to me till I fell asleep?

QUENTIN: I've sat beside you for days and weeks at a time, Maggie, but you never remember. I've taken you for long drives to soothe you; sailed you around the bay for hours and my office looking high and low for me, but all you remember is the bad.

MAGGIE: Could you stay . . . like five minutes?

QUENTIN—*pause; he tries not to weep:* Yes.

MAGGIE—*slight pause; suddenly she puts the pills on the floor:* See? I'm not taking any more.

He is silent.

I only had . . . about fifteen, I think. You . . . you can have the bottle if you want, even.

QUENTIN, *without rancor; explaining:* I don't want the bottle; I'm not the policeman any more.

MAGGIE: Please don't call the ambulance.

QUENTIN: Then don't take any more. I just can't go through it alone again, and I'm telling you.

MAGGIE—*slight pause:* You going back to your former wife, right?

QUENTIN: No, I've . . . *been* there.

MAGGIE: What then?

QUENTIN—*long pause:* Well, the first thing I've got to do is . . . get somebody to take care of you.

MAGGIE, *very carefully:* What do you mean, take care of me?

QUENTIN—*pause; under terrific stress he begins to touch his face, then puts his hand down:* I talked to your doctor this afternoon.

MAGGIE—*the terror growing:* About what? Thought you said your plane didn't take off.

QUENTIN: I was lying again, but there's no point to it any more. I just didn't want to have this conversation when you—

MAGGIE: I hear everything; what'd you talk to my doctor about? You going to put me somewhere? Is that it?

QUENTIN: No. But you should be supervised. And I shouldn't be with you any more. I shouldn't have been for at least a year, in fact.

MAGGIE: Well now you got what you wanted, didn't you.

QUENTIN: No, exactly the opposite. But he's trying to get a plane up here; if he can he'll spend the night with you; and you can decide with him what to do. But we shouldn't argue any more. It's between you and him.

MAGGIE, *with a knowing, determined smile:* You're not going to put *me* anywhere, mister.

QUENTIN: I've nothing to do with that, Maggie, it's you and him.

MAGGIE: Why, what'd you say to him?

QUENTIN: Maggie, you want to die and I don't know any more how to prevent it. Maybe it was just my being out in the real world for twenty-four hours again, but it struck me that I'm playing with your life out of some idiotic hope of some kind that you're suddenly going to come out of this endless spell. I think somebody ought to be with you who has no illusions of that kind, and simply watches constantly to prevent it.

MAGGIE: Maybe a little love would prevent it.

QUENTIN: But how would you know, Maggie? Not that I love you, but if I did, would you know any more? Do you know who I am? Aside from my name? I'm all the evil in the world, aren't I? All the betrayal, the broken hopes, the murderous revenge?

MAGGIE: And how'd that happen? Takes two to tango, kid.

With a sneer she opens the bottle. He stands at once.

QUENTIN: I'm not sitting here if you take anymore. Especially on top of whiskey; that's the way it happened the last time.

She spills out a few into her palm and he walks a step away.

Okay. Carrie's in her room; I've told her to look in here every few minutes, and if she sees the signs she's to call the ambulance. Good night.

MAGGIE: She won't call the ambulance, she loves me.

QUENTIN: That's why she'll call the ambulance. Which is what I would have done last year if I'd loved you instead of loving myself. I'd have done it two years ago, in fact, but I didn't know what I know now.

MAGGIE, *sneering:* What do you know now? You're spoiled. What do you know?

QUENTIN: A suicide kills two people, Maggie. That's what it's for. So I'm removing myself and perhaps it will lose its point.

She appears to consider for a moment; then carefully takes two pills and swallows them.

Right.

He walks, determined, upstage. And when he is a far distance:

MAGGIE, *on a new level; softly, and without any antagonism:* What's Lazarus?

He halts, without turning back. She looks about for him, not knowing he has left.

Quentin?

Not seeing him, she starts up off the bed; a certain alarm . . .

Quen?

He comes halfway back.

QUENTIN: Jesus raised him from the dead. In the Bible. Go to sleep now.

MAGGIE: Wha's 'at suppose to prove?

QUENTIN: The power of faith.

MAGGIE: What about those who have no faith?

QUENTIN: They only have the will.

MAGGIE: But how you get the will?

QUENTIN: You have faith.

MAGGIE: Some apples.

He smiles, turns again to go.

I want more cream puffs.

He turns back; doesn't answer.

And my birthday dress? If I'm good? Mama? I want my mother.

She sits up, looks about as in a dream, turns and sees him.

Why you standing there?

She gets out of bed, squinting, and comes up to him, peers into his face; her expression comes alive.

You . . . you want music?

QUENTIN: All right, you lie down, and I'll put a little music on.

MAGGIE: No, you; you, sit down. And take off your shoes. I mean just to rest. You don't have to do anything. *She goes to the machine, turns it on; jazz.* Was I sleeping?

QUENTIN: For a moment, I think.

MAGGIE: Was she. . . . was anybody else here?

QUENTIN: No. Just me.

MAGGIE: Is there smoke?

QUENTIN: Your mother's dead and gone, dear, she can't hurt you any more, don't be afraid.

MAGGIE, *in a helpless voice of a child:* Where you going to put me?

QUENTIN, *his chest threatening a cry:* Nowhere, dear—he'll decide with you. He might be here tonight.

MAGGIE: See? I'll lay down. *She hurries to the bed, lies down.* See?

QUENTIN: Good.

MAGGIE: 'Member how used to talk to me till I went to sleep?

QUENTIN: Yes, dear. *He sits beside the bed.*

MAGGIE—*she struggles for lucidity, for some little pose of quiet charm:* It nice in Chicago?

QUENTIN: Yes, very nice. *The caricature of the pleasantry nearly shakes off the world.* Was it nice here?

MAGGIE—*she takes a strange, deep breath:* Ya. Some birds came. And a mouse. You . . . you could have the pills if you want.

QUENTIN—*stands:* I'll have Carrie come in and take them. *He starts to move.*

MAGGIE, *clutching the bottle:* No. I won't give them to Carrie.

QUENTIN: Why do you want me to have them?

MAGGIE, *extending them:* Here.

QUENTIN—*pause:* Do you see it, Maggie? Right now? You're trying to make me the one who does it to you? I take them; and then we fight, and then I give them up, and you take

the death from me. You see what's happening? You've been
setting me up for a murder. Do you see it? *He moves backward.* But now I'm going away; so you're not my victim any
more. It's just you, and your hand.

MAGGIE, *slowly retracting her hand, looking at it:* But ask Ludwig—I only wanted to be wonderful so you be proud,
and you—

QUENTIN: And for yourself, dear, mostly for yourself. You were
ambitious; it's no crime. You would have been everything
you are without me.

MAGGIE, *about to weep:* You ran out of patience, right?

QUENTIN: That's right. Yes.

MAGGIE: So you lied. Right?

QUENTIN: Yes, I lied. Every day. We are all separate people.

MAGGIE: You wanted a happy whore. Right?

QUENTIN: Not a whore, but happy, yes. I didn't want too much
trouble.

MAGGIE: But Jesus must have loved her. Right?

QUENTIN: Who?

MAGGIE: Lazarus?

QUENTIN—*pause; he sees, he gropes toward his vision:* That's
right, yes! He . . . loved her enough to raise her from the
dead. But he's God, see . . .

Felice appears, raising her arm in blessing.

. . . and God's power is love without limit. But when a
man dares reach for that . . .

He has moved toward Felice, pursuing his truth.

he is only reaching for the power. Whoever goes to save another person with the lie of limitless love throws a shadow
on the face of God. And God is what happened, God is what
is; and whoever stands between another person and her
truth is not a lover, he is . . .

*He breaks off, lost, peering, and turns back to Maggie for his
clue, and as Felice vanishes . . .*

And then she said.

He goes back to Maggie, crying out to invoke her.

And then she said!

MAGGIE—*she is trying to wipe a film from before her thought:*
But . . . but . . . will my father find me if you put me
. . . No. I mean . . . what's moral?

QUENTIN, *in the tension of trying to recall:* To tell the truth.

MAGGIE: No-no . . . against yourself even.

QUENTIN: Yes.

MAGGIE—*she turns to him; her look is insane, and the truth is
purified of all restraint:* Well?

*A cry is gathering in her, as though only now did she know
there was no return.*

I hear you. Way inside. Quentin? My love? I hear you! Tell
me what happened!

Her tears tell her sanity. He weeps facing her.

QUENTIN, *on the verge of the abyss:* Maggie, we . . . used one
another.

MAGGIE, *weeping, calling:* Not me, not me!

QUENTIN: Yes, you. And I. "To live," we cried, and "Now," we
cried. And loved each other's innocence as though to love
enough what was not there would cover up what was. But
there is an angel, and night and day he brings back to us
exactly what we want to lose. And no chemical can kill him,
no blindness dark enough to make him lose his way; so you
must love him, he keeps truth in the world. You eat those
pills like power, but only what you've done will save you. If
you could only say, I have been cruel, this frightening room
would open! If you could say, I have been kicked around,
but I have been just as inexcusably vicious to others; I have
called my husband idiot in public, I have been utterly selfish
despite my generosity, I have been hurt by a long line of
men but I have cooperated with my persecutors. . . .

MAGGIE—*she has been writhing, furious at this exorcism:* Son of
a bitch!

QUENTIN: And I am full of hatred, I, Maggie, the sweet lover
of all life—I hate the world!

MAGGIE: Get out of here!

QUENTIN: Hate women, hate men, hate all who will not grovel
at my feet proclaiming my limitless love for ever and ever!

She spills a handful of pills into her palm. He speaks desperately, trying not to physically take the pills from her.

Throw them in the sea; throw death in the sea and drink your life instead; your rotten, betrayed, hateful mockery of a life. That power is death, Maggie! Do the hardest thing of all—see our own hatred, and live!

Dumbly, she raises her hand toward her open mouth. He cannot hold back his hand and grips her wrist.

MAGGIE: What are you, goddamn judge or something? Let go. You no judge.

He lets go.

You know when I wanted to die. When I read what you wrote, judgey. Two months after we were married, judgey.

QUENTIN, *stricken, afraid, but remorseless:* Let's keep it true. It's not some words on a piece of paper destroyed us. You told me you tried to die long before you met me.

MAGGIE: So you're not even there, huh. I didn't even meet you. *Tries to laugh.* You coward. Coward!

She staggers to her feet; he finds it hard to look directly at her. A clear line of accusation momentarily seems to steady her, and with the pills in her palm she stands straight.

I was married to a king, you son of a bitch! I was looking for a fountain pen to sign some autographs. And there's his desk . . .

She is speaking toward some invisible source of justice now, telling her injury.

. . . and there's his empty chair where he sits and thinks how to help people. And there's his handwriting. I wanted to touch his handwriting. And there's some words . . .

She almost literally reads in the air, and with the same original astonishment.

"The only one I will ever love is my daughter. If I could only find an honorable way to die."

Now she turns to him.

When you gonna face that, judgey? Remember how I fell
down fainted? On the new rug? 'Member? That's what killed
me, judgey. Right?

She staggers up to him and into his face.

'Zat right? When you gonna face that one, kiddo?

QUENTIN—*a pause; he is struggling with her accusation and his
guilt:* All right. You pour them back and I'll tell you the
truth about that.

MAGGIE: You won't tell truth.

QUENTIN: I will now. *He tries to tip her hand toward the bottle,
holding both her wrists.* You can hold the bottle, just pour
them back.

MAGGIE, *closing her hand on the pills:* But that's why, right?

QUENTIN, *with difficulty:* We'll see. Pour them back, first.

*She lets him pour them back, but she keeps the bottle. She sits
staring on the bed, holding it in two hands.*

MAGGIE—*she takes a deep breath:* Liar.

QUENTIN, *in quiet tension against his own self-condemnation:*
We'd had our first party in our own house. Some important
people, network heads, directors . . .

MAGGIE: And you were ashamed of me. Don't lie now! You're
still playing God! That's what killed me, Quentin!

QUENTIN: All right. I wasn't . . . ashamed. But . . . afraid.
Pause. I wasn't sure if any of them . . . had had you.

MAGGIE, *astounded:* But I didn't know any of those!

QUENTIN, *not looking at her:* I didn't know. But I swear to you,
I did get to where none of it meant anything to me, I
couldn't imagine what I'd ever been ashamed of. But it was
too late. I had written that, and I was like all the others
who'd betrayed you, and I could never be trusted again.

MAGGIE, *shaking her head; it is all corroborated:* You never gave
me a chance!

QUENTIN, *consumed, desperate for the slightest absolution:* I did,
Maggie, but it was too late. I laid down my life for you. But
it was all too late.

MAGGIE, *with a mixture of accusation but near-sympathy:* Why
did you write that? *She sobs, once.*

QUENTIN: Because when the guests had gone, and you suddenly

turned on me, calling me cold, remote, it was the first time I saw your eyes that way—betrayed, screaming that I'd made you feel you didn't exist.

MAGGIE: Don't mix me up with Louise!

QUENTIN: That's just it. That I could have brought two women so different to the same accusation—it closed a circle for me. And I wanted to face the worst thing I could imagine—that I could not love. And I wrote it down, like a letter . . . from myself.

She pours pills into her hand again.

I've told you the truth. That's rock bottom. What more do you want?

She starts to raise her hand to her mouth, and he steps in and holds her wrist.

What more do you *want*?

She looks at him, her eyes unreadable.

Maggie, we've got to have some humility toward ourselves; we were both born of many errors, a human being has to forgive himself! You want me to say I killed you? All right, I killed you. Now what? What do you want?

A strange calm overtakes her. She lies back on the bed. The hostility seems to have gone.

MAGGIE: Just . . . be human. And help me. And stop arguing.

He lets her hand go; it falls to the bed.

And love me. Sit on the bed.

He sits down.

Cover me.

He covers her.

And take down the sand dune. It's not too expensive. I wanted to hear the ocean when we made love in here but we could never hear the ocean.

QUENTIN: We're nearly broke, Maggie; and that dune keeps the roof from blowing off.

MAGGIE: Then you get a new roof. You'll have them take it away, right?

He doesn't answer.

I'm cold. Lie on me.

QUENTIN: I can't do that again, not when you're like this.

MAGGIE: Please. Just till I sleep!

QUENTIN, *breaking down:* Maggie, it's a mockery. Leave me *something.*

MAGGIE: Just out of humanness! I'm cold!

Downing self-disgust, he lies down on her but holds his head away. Pause.

If you don't argue with me any more, I'll get rid of that other lawyer. 'Kay? If you don't argue? Ludwig doesn't argue.

He is silent.

And don't keep saying we're broke? And the sand dune?

The fear of his own total disintegration is growing in his face.

'Cause I love the ocean sound; like a big mother—sssh, sssh, sssh.

He slips off and stands looking down at her. Her eyes are closed.

You gonna be good now? 'Cause all I am . . . is love. And sex.

She takes a very deep, jagged breath.

Quentin reaches in carefully and tries to slip the bottle out of her hand; she grips it.

Whyn't you lie on me?

QUENTIN, *as a fact, simply:* It disgusts me.

MAGGIE: But if Lazarus . . .

QUENTIN: I am not the Savior and I am not the help. . . . You are not going to kill me, Maggie, and that's all this is for!

MAGGIE: You liar!

QUENTIN: Not any more—I am not guilty for your life! I can't be. But I am responsible for it now. And I want those pills. I don't want to fight you, Maggie. Now put them in my hand.

She looks at him; then quickly tries to swallow her handful, but he knocks some of them out—although she swallows many. He grabs for the bottle but she holds and he pulls, yanks; she goes with the force and he drags her onto the floor, trying to pry her hands open as she flails at him and tears at his face, digs at his eyes. Her strength is wild and no longer her own, and, strangely, she is smiling, almost laughing. He grabs her wrist and squeezes it with both his fists.

Drop them, you bitch! You won't kill me!

She holds on, still smiling with a profound certainty, and suddenly, clearly, he lunges for her throat and lifts her with his grip.

You won't kill me! You won't kill me!

She drops the bottle as from the farthest distance Mother rushes to a point crying out—the toy sailboat in her hand—

MOTHER: Darling, open this door! I didn't trick you! I told Fanny to tell you we'd gone as soon you got up from your nap! I didn't trick you!

Quentin springs away from Maggie, who falls back to the floor; his hands are open and in air.

Quentin, why are you running water in there?

The sound of the sea comes up. Mother backs away in horror.

Stop that water! Quentin, I'll die if you do that! I saw a star when you were born, a light, a light in the world!

He stands transfixed as Mother backs into his hand, and he begins to squeeze her throat and she to sink to the floor gasping for breath. He releases her in horror.

QUENTIN: Murder?

Mother stumbles into darkness, her hands in prayer, whispering, "I will die, I will die." He turns to Maggie, who is now getting to her hands and knees, gasping. He rushes to help her, terrified by his realization, but she flails out at him, and on one elbow looks up at him in a caricature of laughter, her eyes victorious and wild with fear.

MAGGIE: Now we both know. You tried to kill me, mister. I been killed by a lot of people, some couldn't hardly spell, but it's the same, mister. You're on the end of a long, long line, Frank.

As though to ward off the accusation he desperately reaches again to help her up, and in absolute terror she skitters away across the floor.

Stay 'way! . . . No! No—no, Frank! Don't you do that!

Cautiously, as though facing a wild, ravening beast.

Don't you do that . . . or I call Quentin if you do that.

She glances off and calls quietly, but never leaving him out of her sight.

Quentin? Qu—?

She falls unconscious, crumpled on the floor, now with deep, strange breathing. He quickly goes to her, throws her over onto her stomach, starts artificial respiration, but just as he is about to start, he stands. He calls upstage.

QUENTIN: Carrie? Carrie!

Carrie appears, praying, with open hands almost shielding her eyes. And, as though it were a final farewell:

Quick! Call the ambulance.

Carrie bends to exorcise Maggie's demons.

Stop wasting time! Call the ambulance!

Carrie hurries out.

Felice appears; he hardly glances at her, comes down to the dock, halts. Felice remains behind him.

. . . No-no, we saved her. It was just in time. For her. But not for me. I knew why I had stayed; I packed up next morning. Her doctor tells me she had a few good months; he even thought for a while she was making it. Unless, God knows, he fell in love with her too.

He almost smiles; it is gone.

Look, I'll say it. It's really all I came to say. Barbiturates kill by suffocation. And the signal is a kind of sighing—the diaphragm is paralyzed.

With more difficulty.

And I'd noticed it when we'd begun to argue. . . . I know, it usually does subside, but if not—each second can be most precious, why waste them arguing? What can be so important to gamble her life to get?

The tower lights, fierce, implacable.

. . . My innocence, you see? To get that back you kill most easily. . . . No, don't; I want it . . . just the way it was.

He looks up.

And all those stars, still so fixed, so fortunate! And her precious seconds squirming in my hand like bugs; and I heard. Those deep, unnatural breaths, like the footfalls of my coming peace—and knew . . . I wanted them. How is that possible—I loved that girl!

Slight pause.

And the name . . . yes, the name . . .

Louise appears, young, in her lab costume.

. . . in whose name do you ever turn your back . . .

He looks out at the audience.

. . . but in your own? In Quentin's name! Always in your own blood-covered name you turn your back!

Holga appears on the highest level.

HOLGA: But no one is innocent they did not kill!
QUENTIN: But love, is love enough? What love, what wave of pity will ever reach this knowledge—I know how to kill. . . . I know, I know . . . she was doomed in any case, but will that cure? Or is it possible . . .

He turns toward the tower, moves toward it as toward a terrible God.

. . . that this is not bizarre . . . to anyone? And I am not alone, and no man lives who would not rather be the sole survivor of this place than all its finest victims? What is the cure? Who can be innocent again on this mountain of skulls? I tell you what I know! My brothers died here . . .

He looks down at the fallen Maggie.

. . . but my brothers built this place; our hearts have cut these stones! And what's the cure!

Father and Mother and Dan appear, and Lou and Mickey; all his people are in light now.

. . . No, not love; I loved them all, all! And gave them willingly to failure and to death that I might live, as they gave me and gave each other, with a word, a look, a truth, a lie— and all in love!

HOLGA: Hello!

QUENTIN: But what will defend her?

He cries up to her.

That woman hopes!

She stands unperturbed, resolute.

Or is that . . .

Struck—to the Listener:

. . . exactly why she hopes, because she knows? What burning cities taught her and the death of love taught me—that we are very dangerous!

Staring, seeing his vision.

And that, that's why I wake each morning like a boy—even now, even now! I swear to you, there's something in me that could dare to love this world again! . . . Is the knowing all? To know, and even happily that we meet unblessed; not in some garden of wax fruit and painted trees, that lie of Eden, but after, after the Fall, after many, many deaths. Is the knowing all? And the wish to kill is never killed, but with some gift of courage one may look into its face when it appears, and with a stroke of love—as to an idiot in the house—forgive it; again and again . . . forever?

He is evidently interrupted by the Listener, glances at his watch.

. . . Yes, I don't want to be late. Thanks for making time for me. . . . No, it's not certainty, I don't feel that. But it does seem feasible . . . not to be afraid. Perhaps it's all one has. I'll tell her that. . . . Yes, she will, she'll know what I mean. Well, see you again some time. Good luck, and thanks.

He turns upstage. He hesitates; all his people face him. He walks past Louise, pausing; but she turns her face away. He goes on and pauses beside Mother, who lowers her head in un-comprehended sorrow, and gestures as though he touched her chin and she looks up at him and dares a smile, and he smiles back. He pauses at his dejected Father and Dan, and with a look he magically makes them stand. Felice is about to raise her hand in blessing—he shakes her hand, aborting her enslave-ment. Mickey and Lou are standing together; he looks at them and neither of them is looking at him, but they move in behind him. Now he arrives at Maggie; she rises from the floor webbed in with demons, trying to awake. And with his life following him he climbs toward Holga, who raises her arm as though seeing him, and speaks with great love.

HOLGA: Hello!

He comes to a halt a few yards from her. A whispering goes up from all his people. He straightens against it and walks toward her, holding out his hand.

QUENTIN: Hello.

The darkness takes them all.

CURTAIN

INCIDENT AT VICHY

THE CHARACTERS

LEBEAU, a painter
BAYARD, an electrician
MARCHAND, a businessman
POLICE GUARD
MONCEAU, an actor
GYPSY
WAITER
BOY
MAJOR
FIRST DETECTIVE
OLD JEW
SECOND DETECTIVE
LEDUC, a doctor
POLICE CAPTAIN
VON BERG, a Prince
PROFESSOR HOFFMAN
FERRAND, a café proprietor
FOUR PRISONERS

Vichy, France, 1942. A place of detention.

At the right a corridor leads to a turning and an unseen door to the street. Across the back is a structure with two grimy window panes in it—perhaps an office, in any case a private room with a door opening from it at the left.

A long bench stands in front of this room, facing a large empty area whose former use is unclear but which suggests a warehouse, perhaps, an armory, or part of a railroad station not used by the public. Two small boxes stand apart on either side of the bench.

When light begins to rise, six men and a boy of fifteen are discovered on the bench in attitudes expressive of their personalities and functions, frozen there like members of a small orchestra at the moment before they begin to play.

As normal light comes on, their positions flow out of the frieze. It appears that they do not know one another and are sitting like people thrown together in a public place, mutually curious but self-occupied. However, they are anxious and frightened and tend to make themselves small and unobtrusive. Only one, Marchand, a fairly well-dressed businessman, keeps glancing at his watch and bits of paper and calling cards he keeps in his pockets, and seems normally impatient.

Now, out of hunger and great anxiety, Lebeau, a bearded, unkempt man of twenty-five, lets out a dramatized blow of air and leans forward to rest his head on his hands. Others glance at him, then away. He is charged with the energy of fear, and it makes him seem aggressive.

LEBEAU: Cup of coffee would be nice. Even a sip.

No one responds. He turns to Bayard beside him; Bayard is his age, poorly but cleanly dressed, with a certain muscular austerity in his manner. Lebeau speaks in a private undertone.

You wouldn't have any idea what's going on, would you?
BAYARD, *shaking his head:* I was walking down the street.
LEBEAU: Me too. Something told me— Don't go outside today.

133

So I went out. Weeks go by and I don't open my door. Today I go out. And I had no reason, I wasn't even going anywhere. *Looks left and right to the others. To Bayard:* They get picked up the same way?

BAYARD—*shrugs:* I've only been here a couple of minutes my-self—just before they brought you in.

LEBEAU—*looks to the others:* Does anybody know anything?

They shrug and shake their heads. Lebeau looks at the walls, the room; then he speaks to Bayard.

This isn't a police station, is it?

BAYARD: Doesn't seem so. There's always a desk. It's just some building they're using, I guess.

LEBEAU, *glancing about uneasily, curiously:* It's painted like a police station, though. There must be an international police paint, they're always the same color everywhere. Like dead clams, and a little yellow mixed in.

Pause. He glances at the other silent men, and tries to silence himself like them. But it's impossible, and he speaks to Bayard with a nervous smile.

You begin wishing you'd committed a crime, you know? Something definite.

BAYARD—*he is not amused, but not unsympathetic:* Try to take it easy. It's no good getting excited. We'll find out soon.

LEBEAU: It's just that I haven't eaten since three o'clock yester-day afternoon. Everything gets more vivid when you're hungry—you ever notice that?

BAYARD: I'd give you something, but I forgot my lunch this morning. Matter of fact, I was just turning back to get it when they came up alongside me. Whyn't you try to sit back and relax?

LEBEAU: I'm nervous. . . . I mean I'm nervous anyway. *With a faint, frightened laugh:* I was even nervous before the war.

His little smile vanishes. He shifts in his seat. The others wait with subdued anxiety. He notices the good clothes and secure manner of Marchand, who is at the head of the line, nearest the door. He leans forward to attract him.

Excuse me.

Marchand does not turn to him. He gives a short, sharp, low whistle. Marchand, already offended, turns slowly to him.

Is that the way they picked you up? On the street?

Marchand turns forward again without answering.

Sir?

Marchand still does not turn back to him.

Well, Jesus, pardon me for living.

MARCHAND: It's perfectly obvious they're making a routine identity check.

LEBEAU: Oh.

MARCHAND: With so many strangers pouring into Vichy this past year there're probably a lot of spies and God knows what. It's just a document check, that's all.

LEBEAU—*turns to Bayard, hopefully:* You think so?

BAYARD—*shrugs; obviously he feels there is something more to it:* I don't know.

MARCHAND, *to Bayard:* Why? There are thousands of people running around with false papers, we all know that. You can't permit such things in wartime.

The others glance uneasily at Marchand, whose sense of security is thereby confined to him alone.

Especially now with the Germans starting to take over down here you have to expect things to be more strict, it's inevitable.

A pause. Lebeau once again turns to him.

LEBEAU: You don't get any . . . special flavor, huh?

MARCHAND: What flavor?

LEBEAU, *glancing at the others:* Well like . . . some racial . . . implication?

MARCHAND: I don't see anything to fear if your papers are all right. *He turns front, concluding the conversation.*

Again silence. But Lebeau can't contain his anxiety. He studies Bayard's profile, then turns to the man on his other side and studies his. Then, turning back to Bayard, he speaks quietly.

LEBEAU: Listen, you are . . . Peruvian, aren't you?

BAYARD: What's the matter with you, asking questions like that in here? *He turns forward.*

LEBEAU: What am I supposed to do, sit here like a dumb beast?

BAYARD, *laying a calming hand on his knee:* Friend, it's no good getting hysterical.

LEBEAU: I think we've had it. I think all the Peruvians have had it in Vichy. *Suppressing a shout:* In 1939 I had an American visa. Before the invasion. I actually had it in my hand. . . .

BAYARD: Calm down—this may all be routine.

Slight pause. Then . . .

LEBEAU: Listen . . .

He leans in and whispers into Bayard's ear. Bayard glances toward Marchand, then shrugs to Lebeau.

BAYARD: I don't know, maybe; maybe he's not.

LEBEAU, *desperately attempting familiarity:* What about you?

BAYARD: Will you stop asking idiotic questions? You're making yourself ridiculous.

LEBEAU: But I am ridiculous, aren't you? In 1939 we were packed for America. Suddenly my mother wouldn't leave the furniture. I'm here because of a brass bed and some fourth-rate crockery. And a stubborn, ignorant woman.

BAYARD: Yes, but it's not all that simple. You should try to think of why things happen. It helps to know the meaning of one's suffering.

LEBEAU: What meaning? If my mother—

BAYARD: It's not your mother. The monopolies got control of Germany. Big business is out to make slaves of everyone, that's why you're here.

LEBEAU: Well I'm not a philosopher, but I know my mother, and that's why I'm here. You're like people who look at my paintings—"What does this mean, what does that mean?" *Look* at it, don't ask what it means; you're not God, you can't tell what anything means. I'm walking down the street before, a car pulls up beside me, a man gets out and measures my nose, my ears, my mouth, the next thing I'm sitting in a police station—or whatever the hell this is here—and in the

middle of Europe, the highest peak of civilization! And you
know what it means? After the Romans and the Greeks and
the Renaissance, and you know what this means?

BAYARD: You're talking utter confusion.

LEBEAU, *in terror:* Because I'm utterly confused! *He suddenly
springs up and shouts:* Goddamnit, I want some coffee!

*The Police Guard appears at the end of the corridor, a revolver
on his hip; he strolls down the corridor and meets Lebeau, who
has come halfway up. Lebeau halts, returns to his place on the
bench, and sits. The Guard starts to turn to go up the corridor
when Marchand raises his hand.*

MARCHAND: Excuse me, officer, is there a telephone one can
use? I have an appointment at eleven o'clock and it's
quite . . .

*The Guard simply walks up the corridor, turns the corner, and
disappears. Lebeau looks toward Marchand and shakes his
head, laughing silently.*

LEBEAU, *to Bayard, sotto:* Isn't it wonderful? The man is probably
on his way to work in a German coal mine and he's worried
about breaking an appointment. And people want realistic
painting, you see what I mean? *Slight pause.* Did they measure your nose? Could you at least tell me that?

BAYARD: No, they just stopped me and asked for my papers. I
showed them and they took me in.

MONCEAU, *leaning forward to address Marchand:* I agree with
you, sir.

*Marchand turns to him. Monceau is a bright-eyed, cheerful
man of twenty-eight. His clothes were elegant, now frayed. He
holds a gray felt hat on his knee, his posture rather elegant.*

Vichy must be full of counterfeit papers. I think as soon as
they start, it shouldn't take long. *To Lebeau:* Try to settle
down.

LEBEAU, *to Monceau:* Did they measure your nose?

MONCEAU, *disapprovingly:* I think it'd be best if we all kept
quiet.

LEBEAU: What is it, my clothes? How do you know, I might be
the greatest painter in France.

MONCEAU: For your sake, I hope you are.

LEBEAU: What a crew! I mean the animosity!

Pause.

MARCHAND, *leaning forward to see Monceau:* You would think, though, that with the manpower shortage they'd economize on personnel. In the car that stopped me there was a driver, two French detectives, and a German official of some kind. They could easily have put a notice in the paper—everyone would have come here to present his documents. This way it's a whole morning wasted. Aside from the embarrassment.

LEBEAU: I'm not embarrassed, I'm scared to death. *To Bayard:* You embarrassed?

BAYARD: Look, if you can't be serious just leave me alone.

Pause. Lebeau leans forward to see the man sitting on the far side of Marchand. He points.

LEBEAU: Gypsy?

GYPSY, *drawing closer a copper pot at his feet:* Gypsy.

LEBEAU, *to Monceau:* Gypsies never have papers. Why'd they bother him?

MONCEAU: In his case it might be some other reason. He probably stole that pot.

GYPSY: No. On the sidewalk. *He raises the pot from between his feet.* I fix, make nice. I sit down to fix. Come police. Pfft!

MARCHAND: But of course they'll tell you anything. . . . *To Gypsy, laughing familiarly:* Right?

Gypsy laughs and turns away to his own gloom.

LEBEAU: That's a hell of a thing to say to him. I mean, would you say that to a man with pressed pants?

MARCHAND: They don't mind. In fact, they're proud of stealing. *To Gypsy:* Aren't you?

Gypsy glances at him, shrugs.

I've got a place in the country where they come every summer. I like them, personally—especially the music. *With a broad grin he sings toward the Gypsy and laughs.* We often listen to them around their campfires. But they'll steal the eyes out of your head. *To Gypsy:* Right?

Gypsy shrugs and kisses the air contemptuously. Marchand laughs with brutal familiarity.

LEBEAU: Why shouldn't he steal? How'd you get *your* money?

MARCHAND: I happen to be in business.

LEBEAU: So what have you got against stealing?

BAYARD: Are you trying to provoke somebody? Is that it?

LEBEAU: Another businessman.

BAYARD: I happen to be an electrician. But a certain amount of solidarity wouldn't hurt right now.

LEBEAU: How about some solidarity with Gypsies? Just because they don't work nine to five?

WAITER—*a small man, middle-aged, still wearing his apron:* I know this one. I've made him go away a hundred times. He and his wife stand outside the café with a baby, and they beg. It's not even their baby.

LEBEAU: So what? They've still got a little imagination.

WAITER: Yes, but they keep whining to the customers through the shrubbery. People don't like it.

LEBEAU: You know—you all remind me of my father. Always worshiped the hard-working Germans. And now you hear it all over France—we have to learn how to work like the Germans. Good God, don't you ever read history? Whenever a people starts to work hard, watch out, they're going to kill somebody.

BAYARD: That depends on how production is organized. If it's for private profit, yes, but—

LEBEAU: What are you talking about, when did the Russians start getting dangerous? When they learned how to work. Look at the Germans—for a thousand years peaceful, disorganized people—they start working and they're on everybody's back. Nobody's afraid of the Africans, are they? Because they don't work. Read the Bible—work is a curse, you're not supposed to worship work.

MARCHAND: And how do you propose to produce anything?

LEBEAU: Well that's the problem.

Marchand and Bayard laugh.

What are you laughing at? *That is the problem!* Yes! To work without making work a god! What kind of crew is this?

The office door opens and the Major comes out. He is twenty-eight, a wan but well-built man; there is something ill about him. He walks with a slight limp, passing the line of men as he goes toward the corridor.

WAITER: Good morning, Major.
MAJOR—*startled, nods to the Waiter:* Oh. Good morning.

He continues up the corridor, where he summons the Guard around the corner—the Guard appears and they talk unheard.

MARCHAND, *sotto:* You know him?
WAITER, *proudly:* I serve him breakfast every morning. Tell you the truth, he's really not a bad fellow. Regular Army, see, not one of these S.S. bums. Got wounded somewhere, so they stuck him back here. Only came about a month ago, but he and I—

The Major comes back down the corridor. The Guard returns to his post out of sight at the corridor's end. As the Major passes Marchand . . .

MARCHAND, *leaping up and going to the Major:* Excuse me, sir.

The Major slowly turns his face to Marchand. Marchand affects to laugh deferentially.

I hate to trouble you, but I would be much obliged if I could use a telephone for one minute. In fact, it's business connected to the food supply. I am the manager of . . .

He starts to take out a business card, but the Major has turned away and walks to the door. But there he stops and turns back.

MAJOR: I'm not in charge of this procedure. You will have to wait for the Captain of Police. *He goes into the office.*
MARCHAND: I beg your pardon.

The door has been closed on his line. He goes back to his place and sits, glaring at the Waiter.

WAITER: He's not a really bad fellow.

They all look at him, eager for some clue.

He even comes at night sometimes, plays a beautiful piano.

Gives himself French lessons out of a book. Always has a few nice words to say, too.

LEBEAU: Does he know that you're a . . . Peruvian?

BAYARD, *instantly:* Don't discuss that here, for God's sake! What's the matter with you?

LEBEAU: Can't I find out what's going on? If it's a general identity check it's one thing, but if—

From the end of the corridor enter First Detective with the Old Jew, a man in his seventies, bearded, carrying a large sackcloth bundle; then the Second Detective, holding the arm of Leduc; then the Police Captain, uniformed, with Von Berg; and finally the Professor in civilian clothes.

The First Detective directs the Old Jew to sit, and he does, beside the Gypsy. The Second Detective directs Von Berg to sit beside the Old Jew. Only now does the Second Detective release his hold on Leduc and indicate that he is to sit beside Von Berg.

SECOND DETECTIVE, *to Leduc:* Don't you give me any more trouble now.

The door opens and the Major enters. Instantly Leduc is on his feet, approaching the Major.

LEDUC: Sir, I must ask the reason for this. I am a combat officer, captain in the French Army. There is no authority to arrest me in French territory. The Occupation has not revoked French law in southern France.

The Second Detective, infuriated, throws Leduc back into his seat. He returns to the Professor.

SECOND DETECTIVE, *to Major, of Leduc:* Speechmaker.

PROFESSOR, *doubtfully:* You think you two can carry on now?

SECOND DETECTIVE: We got the idea, Professor. *To the Major:* There's certain neighborhoods they head for when they run away from Paris or wherever they come from. I can get you as many as you can handle.

FIRST DETECTIVE: It's a question of knowing the neighborhoods, you see. In my opinion you've got at least a couple thousand in Vichy on false papers.

PROFESSOR: You go ahead, then.

As the Second Detective turns to go with the First Detective, the Police Captain calls him.

CAPTAIN: Saint-Père.

SECOND DETECTIVE: Yes sir.

The Captain walks downstage with the Detective.

CAPTAIN: Try to avoid taking anybody out of a crowd. Just cruise around the way we did before, and take them one at a time. There are all kinds of rumors. We don't want to alarm people.

SECOND DETECTIVE: Right, sir.

The Captain gestures, and both Detectives leave up the corridor.

CAPTAIN: I am just about to order coffee. Will you gentlemen have some?

PROFESSOR: Please.

WAITER, *timidly:* And a croissant for the Major.

The Major glances quickly at the Waiter and barely smiles. The Captain, who has thrown a mystified look at the Waiter, goes into the office.

MARCHAND, *to the Professor:* I believe I am first, sir.

PROFESSOR: Yes, this way.

He goes into the office, followed by the eager Marchand.

MARCHAND, *going in:* Thank you. I'm in a dreadful hurry. . . . I was on my way to the Ministry of Supply, in fact. . . .

His voice is lost within. As the Major reaches the door, Leduc, who has been in a fever of calculation, calls to him.

LEDUC: Amiens.

MAJOR—*he halts at the door, turns to Leduc, who is at the far end of the line:* What about Amiens?

LEDUC, *suppressing his nervousness:* June ninth, 'forty. I was in the Sixteenth Artillery, facing you. I recognize your insignia, which of course I could hardly forget.

MAJOR: That was a bad day for you fellows.

LEDUC: Yes. And evidently for you.

MAJOR—*glances down at his leg:* Can't complain.

The Major goes into the office, shuts the door. A pause.

LEDUC, *to all:* What's this all about?

WAITER, *to all:* I told you he wasn't a bad guy. You'll see.

MONCEAU, *to Leduc:* It seems they're checking on identification papers.

Leduc receives the news, and obviously grows cautious and quietly alarmed. He examines their faces.

LEDUC: What's the procedure?

MONCEAU: They've just started—that businessman was the first.

LEBEAU, *to Leduc and Von Berg:* They measure your noses?

LEDUC, *sharply alarmed:* Measure noses?

LEBEAU, *putting thumb and forefinger against the bridge and tip of his nose:* Ya, they measured my nose, right on the street. I tell you what I think . . . *To Bayard:* With your permission.

BAYARD: I don't mind you talking as long as you're serious.

LEBEAU: I think it's to carry stones. It just occurred to me—last Monday a girl I know came up from Marseille—the road is full of detours. They probably need labor. She said there was a crowd of people just carrying stones. Lot of them Jews, she thought; hundreds.

LEDUC: I never heard of forced labor in the Vichy Zone. Is that going on here?

BAYARD: Where do you come from?

LEDUC—*slight pause—he decides whether to reveal:* I live in the country. I don't get into town very often. There's been no forced-labor decree, has there?

BAYARD, *to all:* Now, listen. *Everyone turns to his straightforward, certain tone.* I'm going to tell you something, but I don't want anybody quoting me. Is that understood?

They nod. He glances at the door. He turns to Lebeau.

You hear what I said?

LEBEAU: Don't make me out some kind of an idiot. Christ's sake, I know it's serious!

BAYARD, *to the others:* I work in the railroad yards. A thirty-car freight train pulled in yesterday. The engineer is Polish, so I couldn't talk to him, but one of the switchmen says he heard people inside.

LEDUC: Inside the cars?

BAYARD: Yes. It came from Toulouse. I heard there's been a

quiet roundup of Jews in Toulouse the last couple of weeks. And what's a Polish engineer doing on a train in southern France? You understand?

LEDUC: Concentration camp?

MONCEAU: Why? A lot of people have been volunteering for work in Germany. That's no secret. They're doubling the ration for anybody who goes.

BAYARD, *quietly:* The cars are locked on the outside. *Slight pause.* And they stink. You can smell the stench a hundred yards away. Babies are crying inside. You can hear them. And women. They don't lock volunteers in that way. I never heard of it.

A long pause.

LEDUC: But I've never heard of them applying the Racial Laws down here. It's still French territory, regardless of the Occupation—they've made a big point of that.

Pause.

BAYARD: The Gypsy bothers me.

LEBEAU: Why?

BAYARD: They're in the same category of the Racial Laws. Inferior.

Leduc and Lebeau slowly turn to look at the Gypsy.

LEBEAU, *turning back quickly to Bayard:* Unless he really stole that pot.

BAYARD: Well, yes, if he stole the pot then of course he—

LEBEAU, *quickly, to the Gypsy:* Hey, listen. *He gives a soft, sharp whistle. The Gypsy turns to him.* You steal that pot?

The Gypsy's face is inscrutable. Lebeau is embarrassed to press this, and more desperate.

You did, didn't you?

GYPSY: No steal, no.

LEBEAU: Look, I've got nothing against stealing. *Indicating the others:* I'm not one of these types. I've slept in parked cars, under bridges—I mean, to me all property is theft anyway so I've got no prejudice against you.

GYPSY: No steal.

LEBEAU: Look . . . I mean you're a Gypsy, so how else can you live, right?

WAITER: He steals everything.

LEBEAU, *to Bayard:* You hear? He's probably in for stealing, that's all.

VON BERG: Excuse me . . .

They turn to him.

Have you all been arrested for being Jewish?

They are silent, suspicious and surprised.

I'm terribly sorry. I had no idea.

BAYARD: I said nothing about being Jewish. As far as I know, nobody here is Jewish.

VON BERG: I'm terribly sorry.

Silence. The moment lengthens. In his embarrassment he laughs nervously.

It's only that I . . . I was buying a newspaper and this gentleman came out of a car and told me I must have my documents checked. I . . . I had no idea.

Silence. Hope is rising in them.

LEBEAU, *to Bayard:* So what'd they grab *him* for?

BAYARD—*looks at Von Berg for a moment, then addresses all:* I don't understand it, but take my advice. If anything like that happens and you find yourself on that train . . . there are four bolts halfway up the doors on the inside. Try to pick up a nail or a screwdriver, even a sharp stone—you can chisel the wood out around those bolts and the doors will open. I warn you, don't believe anything they tell you—I heard they're working Jews to death in the Polish camps.

MONCEAU: I happen to have a cousin; they sent him to Auschwitz; that's in Poland, you know. I have several letters from him saying he's fine. They've even taught him bricklaying.

BAYARD: Look, friend, I'm telling you what I heard from people who know. *Hesitates.* People who make it their business to know, you understand? Don't listen to any stories about re-settlement, or that they're going to teach you a trade or something. If you're on that train get out before it gets where it's going.

Pause.

LEDUC: I've heard the same thing.

They turn to him and he turns to Bayard.

How would one find tools, you have any idea?

MONCEAU: This is so typical! We're in the French Zone, nobody has said one word to us, and we're already on a train for a concentration camp where we'll be dead in a year.

LEDUC: But if the engineer is a Pole . . .

MONCEAU: So he's a Pole, what does that prove?

BAYARD: All I'm saying is that if you have some kind of tool . . .

LEDUC: I think what this man says should be taken seriously.

MONCEAU: In my opinion you're hysterical. After all, they were picking up Jews in Germany for years before the war, they've been doing it in Paris since they came in—are you telling me all those people are dead? Is that really conceivable to you? War is war, but you still have to keep a certain sense of proportion. I mean Germans are still *people.*

LEDUC: I don't speak this way because they're Germans.

BAYARD: It's that they're Fascists.

LEDUC: Excuse me, no. It's exactly because they are people that I speak this way.

BAYARD: I don't agree with *that.*

MONCEAU—*looks at Leduc for an instant:* You must have had a peculiar life, is all I can say. I happen to have played in Germany; I know the German people.

LEDUC: I studied in Germany for five years, and in Austria and I—

VON BERG, *happily:* In Austria! Where?

LEDUC—*again he hesitates, then reveals:* The Psychoanalytic Institute in Vienna.

VON BERG: Imagine!

MONCEAU: You're a psychiatrist. *To the others:* No wonder he's so pessimistic!

VON BERG: Where did you live? I am Viennese.

LEDUC: Excuse me, but perhaps it would be wiser not to speak in . . . detail.

VON BERG, *glancing about as though he had committed a gaffe:* I'm terribly sorry . . . yes, of course. *Slight pause.* I was only curious if you knew Baron Kessler. He was very interested in the medical school.

LEDUC, *with an odd coolness:* No, I was never in that circle.

VON BERG: Oh, but he is extremely democratic. He . . . *shyly:* He is my cousin, you see. . . .

LEBEAU: You're a nobleman?

VON BERG: Yes.

LEDUC: What is your name?

VON BERG: Wilhelm Johann Von Berg.

MONCEAU, *astonished, impressed:* The prince?

VON BERG: Yes . . . forgive me, have we met?

MONCEAU, *excited by the honor:* Oh, no. But naturally I've heard your name. I believe it's one of the oldest houses in Austria.

VON BERG: Oh, that's of no importance any more.

LEBEAU, *turning to Bayard—bursting with hope:* Now, what the hell would they want with an Austrian prince?

Bayard looks at Von Berg, mystified.

I mean . . . *Turning back to Von Berg:* You're Catholic, right?

VON BERG: Yes.

LEDUC: But is your title on your papers?

VON BERG: Oh, yes, my passport.

Pause. They sit silent, on the edge of hope, but bewildered.

BAYARD: Were you . . . political or something?

VON BERG: No, no, I never had any interest in that direction. *Slight pause.* Of course, there is this resentment toward the nobility. That might explain it.

LEDUC: In the Nazis? Resentment?

VON BERG, *surprised:* Yes, certainly.

LEDUC, *with no evident viewpoint but with a neutral but pressing interest in drawing the nobleman out:* Really. I've never been aware of that.

VON BERG: Oh, I assure you.

LEDUC: But on what ground?

VON BERG—*laughs, embarrassed to have to even suggest he is offended:* You're not asking that seriously.

LEDUC: Don't be offended, I'm simply ignorant of that situation. I suppose I have taken for granted that the aristocracy is . . . always behind a reactionary regime.

VON BERG: Oh, there are some, certainly. But for the most part they never took responsibility, in any case.

LEDUC: That interests me. So you still take seriously the . . . the title and . . .

VON BERG: It is not a "title"; it is my name, my family. Just as you have a name, and a family. And you are not inclined to dishonor them, I presume.

LEDUC: I see. And by responsibility, you mean, I suppose, that—

VON BERG: Oh, I don't know; whatever that means. *He glances at his watch.*

Pause.

LEDUC: Please forgive me, I didn't mean to pry into your affairs. *Pause.* I'd never thought about it, and it's obvious now—they *would* want to destroy whatever power you have.

VON BERG: Oh, no, I have no power. And if I did it would be a day's work for them to destroy it. That's not the issue.

Pause.

LEDUC, *fascinated—he is drawn to some truth in Von Berg:* What is it, then? Believe me, I'm not being critical. Quite the contrary . . .

VON BERG: But these are obvious answers! *He laughs.* I have a certain . . . standing. My name is a thousand years old, and they know the danger if someone like me is perhaps . . . not vulgar enough.

LEDUC: And by vulgar you mean . . .

VON BERG: Well, don't you think Nazism . . . whatever else it may be . . . is an outburst of vulgarity? An ocean of vulgarity?

BAYARD: I'm afraid it's a lot more than that, my friend.

VON BERG, *polite, to Bayard:* I am sure it is, yes.

BAYARD: You make it sound like they have bad table manners, that's all.

VON BERG: They certainly do, yes. Nothing angers them more than a sign of any . . . refinement. It is decadent, you see.

BAYARD: What kind of statement is that? You mean you left Austria because of their table manners?

VON BERG: Table manners, yes; and their adoration of dreadful art; and grocery clerks in uniform telling the orchestra what music it may not play. Vulgarity can be enough to send a man out of his country, yes, I think so.

BAYARD: In other words, if they had good taste in art, and elegant table manners, and let the orchestra play whatever it liked, they'd be all right with you.

VON BERG: But how would that be possible? Can people with respect for art go about hounding Jews? Making a prison of Europe, pushing themselves forward as a race of policemen and brutes? Is that possible for artistic people?

MONCEAU: I'd like to agree with you, Prince von Berg, but I have to say that the German audiences—I've played there—no audience is as sensitive to the smallest nuance of a performance; they sit in the theater with respect, like in a church. And nobody listens to music like a German. Don't you think so? It's a passion with them.

Pause.

VON BERG, *appalled at the truth:* I'm afraid that is true, yes. *Pause.* I don't know what to say. *He is depressed, deeply at a loss.*

LEDUC: Perhaps it isn't those people who are doing this.

VON BERG: I'm afraid I know many cultivated people who . . . did become Nazis. Yes, they did. Art is perhaps no defense against this. It's curious how one takes certain ideas for granted. Until this moment I had thought of art as a . . . *To Bayard:* You may be right—I don't understand very much about it. Actually, I'm essentially a musician—in an amateur way, of course, and politics has never . . .

The office door opens and Marchand appears, backing out, talking to someone within. He is putting a leather document-wallet into his breast pocket, while with the other hand he holds a white pass.

MARCHAND: That's perfectly all right, I understand perfectly. Good day, gentlemen. *Holding up the pass to them:* I show the pass at the door? Thank you.

Shutting the door, he turns and hurries past the line of prisoners, and, as he passes the Boy . . .

BOY: What'd they ask you, sir?

Marchand turns up the corridor without glancing at the Boy, and as he approaches the end the Guard, hearing him, appears there. He hands the pass to the Guard and goes out. The Guard moves around the turning of the corridor and disappears.

LEBEAU, *half mystified, half hopeful:* I could have sworn he was a Jew! *To Bayard:* Didn't you think so?

Slight pause.

BAYARD—*clearly he did think so:* You have papers, don't you?
LEBEAU: Oh sure, I have good papers. *He takes rumpled documents out of his pants pocket.*
BAYARD: Well, just insist they're valid. Maybe that's what he did.
LEBEAU: I wish you'd take a look at them, will you?
BAYARD: I'm no expert.
LEBEAU: I'd like your opinion, though. You seem to know what's going on. How they look to you?

Bayard quickly hides the papers as the office door opens. The Professor appears and indicates the Gypsy.

PROFESSOR: Next. You. Come with me.

The Gypsy gets up and starts toward him. The Professor indicates the pot in the Gypsy's hand.

You can leave that.

The Gypsy hesitates, glances at the pot.

I said leave it there.

The Gypsy puts the pot down on the bench unwillingly.

GYPSY: Fix. No steal.
PROFESSOR: Go in.
GYPSY, *indicating the pot, warning the others:* That's mine.

The Gypsy goes into the office. The Professor follows him in and shuts the door. Bayard takes the pot, bends the handle off, puts it in his pocket, and sets the pot back where it was.

LEBEAU, *turning back to Bayard, indicating his papers:* What do you think?

BAYARD—*holds a paper up to the light, turns it over, gives it back to Lebeau:* Look good far as I can tell.

MONCEAU: That man did seem Jewish to me. Didn't he to you, Doctor?

LEDUC: I have no idea. Jews are not a race, you know. They can look like anybody.

LEBEAU, *with the joy of near-certainty:* He just probably had good papers. Because I know people have papers, I mean all you have to do is look at them and you know they're phony. But I mean if you have good papers, right?

Monceau has meanwhile taken out his papers and is examining them. The Boy does the same with his. Lebeau turns to Leduc.

That's true, though. My father looks like an Englishman. The trouble is I took after my mother.

BOY, *to Bayard, offering his papers:* Could you look at mine?

BAYARD: I'm no expert, kid. Anyway, don't sit there looking at them like that.

Monceau puts his away, as the Boy does. A pause. They wait.

MONCEAU: I think it's a question of one's credibility—that man just now did carry himself with a certain confidence. . . .

The Old Jew begins to pitch forward onto the floor. Von Berg catches him and with the Boy helps him back onto the seat.

LEBEAU, *with heightened nervousness:* Christ, you'd think they'd shave off their beards. I mean, to walk around with a beard like that in a country like this!

Monceau looks at his beard, and Lebeau touches it.

Well, I just don't waste time shaving, but . . .

VON BERG, *to the Old Jew:* Are you all right, sir?

Leduc bends over Von Berg's lap and feels the Old Jew's pulse. Pause. He lets his hand go, and looks toward Lebeau.

LEDUC: Were you serious? They actually measured your nose?

LEBEAU: With his fingers. That civilian. They called him "professor." *Pause. Then, to Bayard:* I think you're right; it's all a question of your papers. That businessman certainly looked Jewish. . . .

MONCEAU: I'm not so sure now.

LEBEAU, *angrily:* A minute ago you were sure, now suddenly . . . !

MONCEAU: Well, even if he wasn't—it only means it really is a general checkup. On the whole population.

LEBEAU: Hey, that's right too! *Slight pause.* Actually, I'm often taken for a gentile myself. Not that I give a damn but most of the time, I . . . *To Von Berg:* How about you, they measure your nose?

VON BERG: No, they told me to get into the car, that was all.

LEBEAU: Because actually yours looks bigger than mine.

BAYARD: Will you cut that out! Just cut it out, will you?

LEBEAU: Can't I try to find out what I'm in for?

BAYARD: Did you ever think of anything beside yourself? Just because you're an artist? You people demoralize everybody!

LEBEAU, *with unconcealed terror:* What the hell am I supposed to think of? Who're you thinking of?

The office door opens. The Police Captain appears, and gestures toward Bayard.

CAPTAIN: Come inside here.

Bayard, trying hard to keep his knees from shaking, stands. Ferrand, a café proprietor, comes hurrying down the corridor with a tray of coffee things covered with a large napkin. He has an apron on.

Ah, at last!

FERRAND: Sorry, Captain, but for you I had to make some fresh.

CAPTAIN, *as he goes into the office behind Ferrand:* Put it on my desk.

The door is closed. Bayard sits, wipes his face. Pause.

MONCEAU, *to Bayard, quietly:* Would you mind if I made a suggestion?

Bayard turns to him, already defensive.

You looked terribly uncertain of yourself when you stood up just now.

BAYARD, *taking offense:* Me uncertain? You've got the wrong man.

MONCEAU: Please, I'm not criticizing you.

BAYARD: Naturally I'm a little nervous, facing a room full of Fascists like this.

MONCEAU: But that's why one must seem especially self-confident. I'm quite sure that's what got that businessman through so quickly. I've had similar experiences on trains, and even in Paris when they stopped me several times. The important thing is not to look like a victim. Or even to feel like one. They can be very stupid, but they do have a sense for victims; they know when someone has nothing to hide.

LEDUC: But how does one avoid feeling like a victim?

MONCEAU: One must create one's own reality in this world. I'm an actor, we do this all the time. The audience, you know, is very sadistic; it looks for your first sign of weakness. So you must try to think of something that makes you feel self-assured; anything at all. Like the day, perhaps, when your father gave you a compliment, or a teacher was amazed at your cleverness . . . Any thought—*to Bayard*—that makes you feel . . . valuable. After all, you are trying to create an illusion; to make them believe you are who your papers say you are.

LEDUC: That's true, we must not play the part they have written for us. That's very wise. You must have great courage.

MONCEAU: I'm afraid not. But I have talent instead. *To Bayard:* One must show them the face of a man who is right, not a man who is suspect and wrong. They sense the difference.

BAYARD: My friend, you're in a bad way if you have to put on an act to feel your rightness. The bourgeoisie sold France; they let in the Nazis to destroy the French working class. Remember the causes of this war and you've got *real* confidence.

LEDUC: Excepting that the causes of this war keep changing so often.

BAYARD: Not if you understand the economic and political forces.

LEDUC: Still, when Germany attacked us the Communists refused to support France. They pronounced it an imperialist

war. Until the Nazis turned against Russia; then in one afternoon it all changed into a sacred battle against tyranny.
What confidence can one feel from an understanding that
turns upside down in an afternoon?

BAYARD: My friend, without the Red Army standing up to
them right now you could forget France for a thousand
years!

LEDUC: I agree. But that does not require an understanding of
political and economic forces—it is simply faith in the Red
Army.

BAYARD: It is faith in the future; and the future is Socialist. And
that is what *I* take in there with *me*.

To the others:

I warn you—I've had experience with these types. You'd
better ram a viewpoint up your spine or you'll break in half.

LEDUC: I understand. You mean it's important not to feel
alone, is that it?

BAYARD: None of us is alone. We're members of history. Some
of us don't know it, but you'd better learn it for your own
preservation.

LEDUC: That we are . . . symbols.

BAYARD, *uncertain whether to agree:* Yes. Why not? Symbols, yes.

LEDUC: And you feel that helps you. Believe me, I am genuinely interested.

BAYARD: It helps me because it's the truth. What am I to them
personally? Do they know me? You react personally to this,
they'll turn you into an idiot. You can't make sense of this
on a personal basis.

LEDUC: I agree. *Personally:* But the difficulty is—what can one
be if not oneself? For example, the thought of torture or
something of that sort . . .

BAYARD, *struggling to live his conviction:* Well, it frightens
me—of course. But they can't torture the future; it's out of
their hands. Man was not made to be the slave of Big Business. Whatever they do, something inside me is laughing.
Because they can't win. Impossible. *He has stiffened himself
against his rising fear.*

LEDUC: So that in a sense . . . you aren't here. You personally.

BAYARD: In a sense. Why, what's wrong with that?

LEDUC: Nothing; it may be the best way to hold on to oneself. It's only that ordinarily one tries to experience life, to be in spirit where one's body is. For some of us it's difficult to shift gears and go into reverse. But that's not a problem for you.

BAYARD, *solicitously:* You think a man can ever be himself in this society? When millions go hungry and a few live like kings, and whole races are slaves to the stock market—how can you be yourself in such a world? I put in ten hours a day for a few francs, I see people who never bend their backs and they own the planet. . . . How can my spirit be where my body is? I'd have to be an ape.

VON BERG: Then where is your spirit?

BAYARD: In the future. In the day when the working class is master of the world. *That's* my confidence . . . *To Monceau:* Not some borrowed personality.

VON BERG, *wide-eyed, genuinely asking:* But don't you think . . . excuse me. Are not most of the Nazis . . . of the working class?

BAYARD: Well, naturally, with enough propaganda you can confuse anybody.

VON BERG: I see. *Slight pause.* But in that case, how can one have such confidence in them?

BAYARD: Who do you have confidence in, the aristocracy?

VON BERG: Very little. But in certain aristocrats, yes. And in certain common people.

BAYARD: Are you telling me that history is a question of "certain people"? Are we sitting here because we are "certain people"? Is any of us an individual to them? Class interest makes history, not individuals.

VON BERG: Yes. That seems to be the trouble.

BAYARD: Facts are not trouble. A human being has to glory in the facts.

VON BERG, *with a deep, anxious out-reaching to Bayard:* But the facts . . . Dear sir, what if the facts are dreadful? And will always be dreadful?

BAYARD: So is childbirth, so is . . .

VON BERG: But a child comes of it. What if nothing comes of the facts but endless, endless disaster? Believe me, I am happy to meet a man who is not cynical; any faith is precious these days. But to give your faith to a . . . a class of people is impossible, simply impossible—ninety-nine per cent of the Nazis are ordinary working-class people!

BAYARD: I concede it *is* possible to propagandize . . .

VON BERG, *with an untoward anxiety, as though the settlement of this issue is intimate with him:* But what can *not* be propagandized? Isn't that the . . . the only point? A few individuals. Don't you think so?

BAYARD: You're an intelligent man, Prince. Are you seriously telling me that five, ten, a thousand, ten thousand decent people of integrity are all that stand between us and the end of everything? You mean this whole world is going to hang on that thread?

VON BERG, *struck:* I'm afraid it does sound impossible.

BAYARD: If I thought that, I wouldn't have the strength to walk through the door, I wouldn't know how to put one foot in front of the other.

VON BERG—*slight pause:* Yes. I hadn't really considered it that way. But . . . you really think the working class will . . .

BAYARD: They will destroy Fascism because it is against their interest.

VON BERG—*nods:* But in that case, isn't it even more of a mystery?

BAYARD: I see no mystery.

VON BERG: But they adore Hitler.

BAYARD: How can you say that? Hitler is the creation of the capitalist class.

VON BERG, *in terrible mourning and anxiety:* But they adore him! My own cook, my gardeners, the people who work in my forests, the chauffeur, the gamekeeper—they are *Nazis*! I saw it coming over them, the love for this creature—my housekeeper dreams of him in her bed, she'd serve my breakfast like a god had slept with her; in a dream slicing my toast! I saw this adoration in my own house! That, that is the dreadful fact. *Controlling himself:* I beg your pardon, but it disturbs me. I admire your faith; all faith to some degree is beautiful. And when I know that yours is based on something so untrue—it's terribly disturbing. *Quietly:* In any case, I cannot glory in the facts; there is no reassurance there. They adore him, the salt of the earth. . . . *Staring:* Adore him.

There is a burst of laughter from within the office. He glances there, as they all do.

Strange; if I did not know that some of them in there were French, I'd have said they laugh like Germans. I suppose vulgarity has no nation, after all.

The door opens. Mr. Ferrand comes out, laughing; within, the laughter is subsiding. He waves within, closing the door. His smile drops. And as he goes past the Waiter, he glances at the door, then quickly leans over and whispers hurriedly into his ear. They all watch. Now Ferrand starts away. The Waiter reaches out and grasps his apron.

WAITER: Ferrand!

FERRAND, *brushing the Waiter's hand off his apron:* What can I do? I told you fifty times to get out of this city! Didn't I? *Starting to weep:* Didn't I?

He hurries up the corridor, wiping his tears with his apron. They all watch the Waiter, who sits there staring.

BAYARD: What? Tell me. Come on, I'm next, what'd he say?

WAITER—*whispers, staring ahead in shock:* It's not to work.

LEDUC, *leaning over toward him to hear:* What?

WAITER: They have furnaces.

BAYARD: What furnaces? . . . Talk! What is it?

WAITER: He heard the detectives; they came in for coffee just before. People get burned up in furnaces. It's not to work. They burn you up in Poland.

Silence. A long moment passes.

MONCEAU: That is the most fantastic idiocy I ever heard in my life!

LEBEAU, *to the Waiter:* As long as you have regular French papers, though . . . There's nothing about Jew on *my* papers.

WAITER, *in a loud whisper:* They're going to look at your penis.

The Boy stands up as though with an electric shock. The door of the office opens; the Police Captain appears and beckons to Bayard. The Boy quickly sits.

CAPTAIN: You can come now.

Bayard stands, assuming an artificial and almost absurd posture of confidence. But approaching the Captain he achieves an authority.

BAYARD: I'm a master electrician with the railroad, Captain. You may have seen me there. I'm classified First Priority War Worker.

CAPTAIN: Inside.

BAYARD: You can check with Transport Minister Duquesne.

CAPTAIN: You telling me my business?

BAYARD: No, but we can all use advice from time to time.

CAPTAIN: Inside.

BAYARD: Right.

Without hesitation Bayard walks into the office, the Captain following and closing the door.

A long silence. Monceau, after a moment, smooths out a rough place on the felt of his hat. Lebeau looks at his papers, slowly rubbing his beard with the back of his hand, staring in terror. The Old Jew draws his bundle deeper under his feet. Leduc takes out a nearly empty pack of cigarettes, starts to take one for himself, then silently stands, crosses the line of men, and offers it to them. Lebeau takes one.

They light up. Faintly, from the next-door building, an accordion is heard playing a popular tune.

LEBEAU: Leave it to a cop to play now.

WAITER: No, that's the boss's son, Maurice. They're starting to serve lunch.

Leduc, who has returned to his position as the last man on the bench, cranes around the corner of the corridor, observes, and sits back.

LEDUC, *quietly:* There's only one guard at the door. Three men could take him.

Pause. No one responds. Then . . .

VON BERG, *apologetically:* I'm afraid I'd only get in your way. I have no strength in my hands.

MONCEAU, *to Leduc:* You actually believe that, Doctor? About the furnaces?

LEDUC—*he thinks; then:* I believe it is possible, yes. Come, we can do something.

MONCEAU: But what good are dead Jews to them? They want free labor. It's senseless. You can say whatever you like, but the Germans are not illogical; there's no conceivable advantage for them in such a thing.

LEDUC: You can be sitting here and still speak of advantages? Is there a rational explanation for your sitting here? But you are sitting here, aren't you?

MONCEAU: But an atrocity like that is . . . beyond any belief.

VON BERG: That is exactly the point.

MONCEAU: *You* don't believe it. Prince, you can't tell me you believe such a thing.

VON BERG: I find it the most believable atrocity I have heard.

LEBEAU: But why?

Slight pause.

VON BERG: Because it *is* so inconceivably vile. That is their power. To do the inconceivable; it paralyzes the rest of us. But if that is its purpose it is not the cause. Many times I used to ask my friends—if you love your country why is it necessary to hate other countries? To be a good German why must you despise everything that is not German? Until I realized the answer. They do these things not because they are German but because they are nothing. It is the hallmark of the age—the less you exist the more important it is to make a clear impression. I can see them discussing it as a kind of . . . truthfulness. After all, what *is* self-restraint but hypocrisy? If you despise Jews the most honest thing is to burn them up. And the fact that it costs money, and uses up trains and personnel—this only guarantees the integrity, the purity, the existence of their feelings. They would even tell you that only a Jew would think of the cost. They are poets, they are striving for a new nobility, the nobility of the totally vulgar. I believe in this fire; it would prove for all time that they exist, yes, and that they were sincere. You must not calculate these people with some nineteenth-century arithmetic of loss and gain. Their motives are musical, and people are merely sounds they play. And in my opinion, win or lose this war, they have pointed the way to the future. What one used to conceive a human being to be will have no room on this earth. I would try anything to get out.

A pause.

MONCEAU: But they arrested you. That German professor is an expert. There is nothing Jewish about you. . . .

VON BERG: I have an accent. I noticed he reacted when I started to speak. It is an Austrian inflection. He may think I am another refugee.

The door opens. The Professor comes out, and indicates the Waiter.

PROFESSOR: Next. You.

The Waiter makes himself small, pressing up against Lebeau.

Don't be alarmed, it's only to check your papers.

The Waiter suddenly bends over and runs away—around the corner and up the corridor. The Guard appears at the end, collars him, and walks him back down the corridor.

WAITER, *to the Guard:* Felix, you know me. Felix, my wife will go crazy. Felix . . .

PROFESSOR: Take him in the office.

The Police Captain appears in the office doorway.

GUARD: There's nobody at the door.

CAPTAIN—*grabs the Waiter from the Guard:* Get in here, you Jew son-of-a-bitch. . . .

He throws the Waiter into the office; the Waiter collides with the Major, who is just coming out to see what the disturbance is. The Major grips his thigh in pain, pushing the Waiter clear. The Waiter slides to the Major's feet, weeping pleadingly. The Captain strides over and violently jerks him to his feet and pushes him into the office, going in after him.

From within, unseen:

You want trouble? You want trouble?

The Waiter is heard crying out; there is the sound of blows struck. Quiet. The Professor starts toward the door. The Major takes his arm and leads him down to the extreme forward edge of the stage, out of hearing of the prisoners.

MAJOR: Wouldn't it be much simpler if they were just asked whether they . . .

Impatiently, without replying, the Professor goes over to the line of prisoners.

PROFESSOR: Will any of you admit right now that you are carrying forged identification papers?

Silence.

So. In short, you are all bona fide Frenchmen.

Silence. He goes over to the Old Jew, bends into his face.

Are there any Jews among you?

Silence. Then he returns to the Major.

There's the problem, Major; either we go house by house investigating everyone's biography, or we make this inspection.

MAJOR: That electrician fellow just now, though—I thought he made a point there. In fact, only this morning in the hospital, while I was waiting my turn for X-ray, another officer, a German officer, a captain, in fact—his bathrobe happened to fall open . . .

PROFESSOR: It is entirely possible.

MAJOR: It was unmistakable, Professor.

PROFESSOR: Let us be clear, Major; the Race Institute does not claim that circumcision is conclusive proof of Jewish blood. The Race Institute recognizes that a small proportion of gentiles . . .

MAJOR: I don't see any reason not to say it, Professor—I happen to be, myself.

PROFESSOR: Very well, but I certainly would never mistake you for a Jew. Any more than you could mistake a pig for a horse. Science is not capricious, Major; my degree is in racial anthropology. In any case, we can certainly separate the gentiles by this kind of examination.

He has taken the Major's arm to lead him back to the office.

MAJOR: Excuse me. I'll be back in a few minutes. *Moving to leave:* You can carry on without me.

PROFESSOR: Major; you have your orders; you are in command of this operation. I must insist you take your place beside me.

MAJOR: I think some mistake has been made. I am a line officer, I have no experience with things of this kind. My training is engineering and artillery.

Slight pause.

PROFESSOR—*he speaks more quietly, his eyes ablaze:* We'd better be candid, Major. Are you refusing this assignment?

MAJOR, *registering the threat he feels:* I'm in pain today, Professor. They are still removing fragments. In fact, I understood I was only to . . . hold this desk down until an S.S. officer took over. I'm more or less on loan, you see, from the regular Army.

PROFESSOR—*takes his arm, draws him down to the edge of the stage again:* But the Army is not exempt from carrying out the Racial Program. My orders come from the top. And my report will go to the top. You understand me.

MAJOR—*his resistance seems to fall:* I do, yes.

PROFESSOR: Look now, if you wish to be relieved, I can easily telephone General von—

MAJOR: No—no, that's all right. I . . . I'll be back in a few minutes.

PROFESSOR: This is bizarre, Major—how long am I supposed to wait for you?

MAJOR, *holding back an outburst of resentment:* I need a walk. I am not used to sitting in an office. I see nothing bizarre in it, I am a line officer, and this kind of business takes a little getting used to. *Through his teeth:* What do you find bizarre in it?

PROFESSOR: Very well.

Slight pause.

MAJOR: I'll be back in ten minutes. You can carry on.

PROFESSOR: I will not continue without you, Major. The Army's responsibility is quite as great as mine here.

MAJOR: I won't be long.

The Professor turns abruptly and strides into the office, slamming the door shut. Very much wanting to get out, the Major goes up the corridor. Leduc stands as he passes.

LEDUC: Major . . .

The Major limps past him without turning, up the corridor and out. Silence.

BOY: Mister?

Leduc turns to him.

I'd try it with you.

LEDUC, *to Monceau and Lebeau:* What about you two?

LEBEAU: Whatever you say, but I'm so hungry I wouldn't do you much good.

LEDUC: You can walk up to him and start an argument. Distract his attention. Then we—

MONCEAU: You're both crazy, they'll shoot you down.

LEDUC: Some of us might make it. There's only one man at the door. This neighborhood is full of alleyways—you could disappear in twenty yards.

MONCEAU: How long would you be free—an hour? And when they catch you they'll really tear you apart.

BOY: Please! I have to get out. I was on my way to the pawnshop. *Takes out a ring.* It's my mother's wedding ring, it's all that's left. She's waiting for the money. They have nothing in the house to eat.

MONCEAU: You take my advice, boy; don't do anything, they'll let you go.

LEDUC: Like the electrician?

MONCEAU: He was obviously a Communist. And the waiter irritated the Captain.

LEBEAU: Look, I'll try it with you but don't expect too much; I'm weak as a chicken, I haven't eaten since yesterday.

LEDUC, *to Monceau:* It would be better with another man. The boy is very light. If you and the boy rush him I'll get his gun away.

VON BERG, *to Leduc, looking at his hands:* Forgive me.

Monceau springs up, goes to a box, and sits.

MONCEAU: I am not going to risk my life for nothing. That businessman had a Jewish face. *To Lebeau:* You said so yourself.

LEBEAU, *to Leduc, appeasingly:* I did. I thought so. Look, if your papers are good, maybe that's it.

LEDUC, *to Lebeau and Monceau:* You know yourself the Germans have been moving into the Southern Zone; you see they are picking up Jews; a man has just told you that you are marked for destruction. . . .

MONCEAU—*indicates Von Berg:* They took him in. Nobody's explained it.

VON BERG: My accent . . .

MONCEAU: My dear Prince, only an idiot could mistake you for anything but an Austrian of the upper class. I took you for nobility the minute you walked in.

LEDUC: But if it's a general checkup why would they be looking at penises?

MONCEAU: There's no evidence of that!

LEDUC: The waiter's boss . . .

MONCEAU, *suppressing a nervous shout:* He overheard two French detectives who can't possibly know anything about what happens in Poland. And if they do that kind of thing, it's not the end either—I had Jew stamped on my passport in Paris and I was playing Cyrano at the same time.

VON BERG: Really! Cyrano!

LEBEAU: Then why'd you leave Paris?

MONCEAU: It was an absolutely idiotic accident. I was rooming with another actor, a gentile. And he kept warning me to get out. But naturally one doesn't just give up a role like that. But one night I let myself be influenced by him. He pointed out that I had a number of books which were on the forbidden list—of Communist literature—I mean things like Sinclair Lewis, and Thomas Mann, and even a few things by Friedrich Engels, which everybody was reading at one time. And I decided I might as well get rid of them. So we made bundles and I lived on the fifth floor of a walkup and we'd take turns going down to the street and just leaving them on benches or in doorways or anywhere at all. It was after midnight, and I was just dropping a bundle into the gutter near the Opéra, when I noticed a man standing in a doorway watching me. At that moment I realized that I had stamped my name and address in every one of those books.

VON BERG: Hah! What did you do?

MONCEAU: Started walking, and kept right on down here to the Unoccupied Zone. *An outcry of remorse:* But in my opinion, if I'd done nothing at all I might still be working!

LEDUC, *with higher urgency, but deeply sympathetic; to Monceau:* Listen to me for one moment. I beg you. There is only one man guarding that door; we may never get another chance like this again.

LEBEAU: That's another thing; if it was all that serious, wouldn't they be guarding us more heavily? I mean, that's a point.

LEDUC: That is exactly the point. They are relying on us.

MONCEAU: Relying on us!

LEDUC: Yes. To project our own reasonable ideas into their heads. It is reasonable that a light guard means the thing is not important. They rely on our own logic to immobilize ourselves. But you have just told us how you went all over Paris advertising the fact that you owned forbidden books.

MONCEAU: But I didn't do it purposely.

LEDUC: May I guess that you could no longer bear the tension of remaining in Paris? But that you wanted to keep your role in Cyrano and had to find some absolute compulsion to save your own life? It was your unconscious mind that saved you. Do you understand? You cannot wager your life on a purely rational analysis of this situation. Listen to your feelings; you must certainly *feel* the danger here. . . .

MONCEAU, *in high anxiety:* I played in Germany. That audience could not burn up actors in a furnace. *Turning to Von Berg:* Prince, you cannot tell me you believe that!

VON BERG, *after a pause:* I supported a small orchestra. When the Germans came into Austria three of the players prepared to escape. I convinced them no harm would come to them; I brought them to my castle; we all lived together. The oboist was twenty, twenty-one—the heart stopped when he played certain tones. They came for him in the garden. They took him out of his chair. The instrument lay on the lawn like a dead bone. I made certain inquiries; he is dead now. And it was even more terrible—they came and sat down and listened until the rehearsal was over. And *then* they took him. It is as though they wished to take him at exactly the moment when he was most beautiful. I know how you feel—but I tell you nothing any longer is forbidden. Nothing. *Tears are in his eyes; he turns to Leduc.* I ask you to forgive me, Doctor.

Pause.

BOY: Will they let you go?

VON BERG, *with a guilty glance at the Boy:* I suppose. If this is all to catch Jews they will let me go.

BOY: Would you take this ring? And bring it back to my mother?

He stretches his hand out with the ring. Von Berg does not touch it.

Number Nine Rue Charlot. Top floor. Hirsch. Sarah Hirsch. She has long brown hair . . . be sure it's her. She has a little beauty mark on this cheek. There are two other families in the apartment, so be sure it's her.

Von Berg looks into the Boy's face. Silence. Then he turns to Leduc.

VON BERG: Come. Tell me what to do. I'll try to help you. *To Leduc:* Doctor?

LEDUC: I'm afraid it's hopeless.

VON BERG: Why?

LEDUC—*stares ahead, then looks at Lebeau:* He's weak with hunger, and the boy's like a feather. I wanted to get away, not just slaughtered. *Pause. With bitter irony:* I live in the country, you see; I haven't talked to anybody in so long, I'm afraid I came in here with the wrong assumptions.

MONCEAU: If you're trying to bait me, Doctor, forget it.

LEDUC: Would you mind telling me, are you religious?

MONCEAU: Not at all.

LEDUC: Then why do you feel this desire to be sacrificed?

MONCEAU: I ask you to stop talking to me.

LEDUC: But you are making a gift of yourself. You are the only able-bodied man here, aside from me, and yet you feel no impulse to do something? I don't understand your air of confidence.

Pause.

MONCEAU: I refuse to play a part I do not fit. Everyone is playing the victim these days; hopeless, hysterical, they always assume the worst. I have papers; I will present them with the single idea that they must be honored. I think that is exactly what saved that businessman. You accuse us of acting the part the Germans created for us; I think you're the one who's doing that by acting so desperate.

LEDUC: And if, despite your act, they throw you into a freight car?

MONCEAU: I don't think they will.

LEDUC: But if they do. You certainly have enough imagination to visualize that.

MONCEAU: In that case, I will have done my best. I know what failure is; it took me a long time to make good; I haven't the personality for leading roles; everyone said I was crazy to stay in the profession. But I did, and I imposed my idea on others.

LEDUC: In other words, you will create yourself.

MONCEAU: Every actor creates himself.

LEDUC: But when they tell you to open your fly.

Monceau is silent, furious.

Please don't stop now; I'm very interested. How do you regard that moment?

Monceau is silent.

Believe me, I am only trying to understand this. I am incapable of penetrating such passivity; I ask you what is in your mind when you face the command to open your fly. I am being as impersonal, as scientific as I know how to be—I believe I am going to be murdered. What do you believe will happen when they point to that spot between your legs?

Pause.

MONCEAU: I have nothing to say to you.

LEBEAU: I'll tell you what I'll feel. *Indicates Von Berg.* I'll wish I was him.

LEDUC: To be someone else.

LEBEAU, *exhausted:* Yes. To have been arrested by mistake. God—to see them relaxing when they realize I am innocent.

LEDUC: You feel guilty, then.

LEBEAU—*he has gradually become closer to exhaustion:* A little, I guess. Not for anything I've done but . . . I don't know why.

LEDUC: For being a Jew, perhaps?

LEBEAU: I'm not ashamed of being a Jew.

LEDUC: Then why feel guilty?

LEBEAU: I don't know. Maybe it's that they keep saying such terrible things about us, and you can't answer. And after years and years of it, you . . . I wouldn't say you believe it, but . . . you do, a little. It's a funny thing—I used to say to my mother and father just what you're saying. We could have gone to America a month before the invasion. But they wouldn't leave Paris. She had this brass bed, and carpets, and draperies and all kinds of junk. Like him with his Cyrano. And I told them, "You're doing just what they want you to do!" But, see, people won't believe they can be killed. Not them with their brass bed and their carpets and their faces. . . .

LEDUC: But do you believe it? It seems to me you don't believe it yourself.

LEBEAU: I believe it. They only caught me this morning because I . . . I always used to walk in the morning before I sat down to work. And I wanted to do it again. I knew I shouldn't go outside. But you get tired of believing in the truth. You get tired of seeing things clearly. *Pause.* I always collected my illusions in the morning. I could never paint what I saw, only what I imagined. And this morning, danger or no danger, I just had to get out, to walk around, to see something real, something else but the inside of my head . . . and I hardly turned the corner and that motherless son-of-a-bitch of a scientist got out of the car with his fingers going for my nose. . . . *Pause.* I believe I can die. But you can get so tired . . .

LEDUC: That it's not too bad.

LEBEAU: Almost, yes.

LEDUC, *glancing at them all:* So that one way or the other, with illusions or without them, exhausted or fresh—we have been trained to die. The Jew and the gentile both.

MONCEAU: You're still trying to bait me, Doctor, but if you want to commit suicide do it alone, don't involve others. The fact is there are laws and every government enforces its laws; and I want it understood that I have nothing to do with any of this talk.

LEDUC, *angering now:* Every government does not have laws condemning people because of their race.

MONCEAU: I beg your pardon. The Russians condemn the middle class, the English have condemned the Indians, Africans, and anybody else they could lay their hands on, the French, the Italians . . . every nation has condemned somebody because of his race, including the Americans and what they do to Negroes. The vast majority of mankind is condemned because of its race. What do you advise all these people—suicide?

LEDUC: What do you advise?

MONCEAU, *seeking and finding conviction:* I go on the assumption that if I obey the law with dignity I will live in peace. I may not like the law, but evidently the majority does, or they would overthrow it. And I'm speaking now of the French majority, who outnumber the Germans in this town fifty to one. These are French police, don't forget, not German. And if by some miracle you did knock out that guard you would find yourself in a city where not one person in a thousand would help you. And it's got nothing to do with being Jewish or not Jewish. It is what the world is, so why don't you stop insulting others with romantic challenges!

LEDUC: In short, because the world is indifferent you will wait calmly and with great dignity—to open your fly.

MONCEAU—*frightened and furious, he stands:* I'll tell you what I think; I think it's people like you who brought this on us. People who give Jews a reputation for subversion, and this Talmudic analysis, and this everlasting, niggling discontent.

LEDUC: Then I will tell you that I was wrong before; you didn't advertise your name on those forbidden books in order to

find a reason to leave Paris and save yourself. It was in order
to get yourself caught and be put out of your misery. Your
heart is conquered territory, mister.

MONCEAU: If we meet again you will pay for that remark.

LEDUC: Conquered territory! *He leans forward, his head in his
hands.*

BOY, *reaching over to hand the ring to Von Berg:* Will you do it?
Number Nine Rue Charlot?

VON BERG, *deeply affected:* I will try.

He takes the ring. The Boy immediately stands.

LEDUC: Where are you going?

*The Boy, terrified but desperate, moves on the balls of his feet to
the corridor and peeks around the corner. Leduc stands, tries to
draw him back.*

You can't; it'll take three men to . . .

*The boy shakes loose and walks rapidly up the hallway. Leduc
hesitates, then goes after him.*

Wait! Wait a minute! I'm coming.

*The Major enters the corridor at its far end. The Boy halts,
Leduc now beside him. For a moment they stand facing him.
Then they turn and come down the corridor and sit, the Major
following them. He touches Leduc's sleeve, and Leduc stands
and follows him downstage.*

MAJOR—*he is "high"—with drink and a flow of emotion:* That's
impossible. Don't try it. There are sentries on both corners.
Glancing toward the office door: Captain, I would only like to
say that . . . this is all as inconceivable to me as it is to you.
Can you believe that?

LEDUC: I'd believe it if you shot yourself. And better yet, if you
took a few of them with you.

MAJOR, *wiping his mouth with the back of his hand:* We would
all be replaced by tomorrow morning, wouldn't we?

LEDUC: We might get out alive, though; you could see to that.

MAJOR: They'd find you soon.

LEDUC: Not me.

MAJOR, *with a manic amusement, yet deeply questioning:* Why do you deserve to live more than I do?

LEDUC: Because I am incapable of doing what you are doing. I am better for the world than you.

MAJOR: It means nothing to you that I have feelings about this?

LEDUC: Nothing whatever, unless you get us out of here.

MAJOR: And then what? Then what?

LEDUC: I will remember a decent German, an honorable German.

MAJOR: Will that make a difference?

LEDUC: I will love you as long as I live. Will anyone do that now?

MAJOR: That means so much to you—that someone love you?

LEDUC: That I be worthy of someone's love, yes. And respect.

MAJOR: It's amazing; you don't understand anything. Nothing of that kind is left, don't you understand that yet?

LEDUC: It is left in me.

MAJOR, *more loudly, a fury rising in him:* There are no persons any more, don't you see that? There will never be persons again. What do I care if you love me? Are you out of your mind? What am I, a dog that I must be loved? You—*turning to all of them*—goddamned Jews!

The door opens; the Professor and the Police Captain appear.

Like dogs, Jew-dogs. Look at him—*indicating the Old Jew* —with his paws folded. Look what happens when I yell at him. Dog! He doesn't move. Does he move? Do you see him moving? *He strides to the Professor and takes him by the arm.* But we move, don't we? We measure your noses, don't we, Herr Professor, and we look at your cocks, we keep moving continually!

PROFESSOR, *with a gesture to draw him aside:* Major . . .

MAJOR: Hands off, you civilian bastard.

PROFESSOR: I think . . .

MAJOR, *drawing his revolver:* Not a word!

PROFESSOR: You're drunk.

The Major fires into the ceiling. The prisoners tense in shock.

MAJOR: Everything stops now.

He goes in thought, revolver cocked in his hand, and sits beside Lebeau.

Now it is all stopped.

His hands are shaking. He sniffs in his running nose. He crosses his legs to control them, and looks at Leduc, who is still standing.

Now you tell me. You tell me. Now nothing is moving. You tell me. Go ahead now.

LEDUC: What shall I tell you?

MAJOR: Tell me how . . . how there can be persons any more. I have you at the end of this revolver—*indicates the Professor*—he has me—and somebody has him—and somebody has somebody else. Now tell me.

LEDUC: I told you.

MAJOR: I won't repeat it. I am a man of honor. What do you make of that? I will not tell them what you advised me to do. What do you say—damned decent of me, isn't it . . . not to repeat your advice?

Leduc is silent. The Major gets up, comes to Leduc. Pause.

You are a combat veteran.

LEDUC: Yes.

MAJOR: No record of subversive activities against the German authority.

LEDUC: No.

MAJOR: If you were released, and the others were kept . . . would you refuse?

Leduc starts to turn away. The Major nudges him with the pistol, forcing him face to face.

Would you refuse?

LEDUC: No.

MAJOR: And walk out of that door with a light heart?

LEDUC—*he is looking at the floor now:* I don't know. *He starts to put his trembling hands into his pockets.*

MAJOR: Don't hide your hands. I am trying to understand why you are better for the world than me. Why do you hide your hands? Would you go out that door with a light heart, run to your woman, drink a toast to your skin? . . . Why are you better than anybody else?

LEDUC: I have no duty to make a gift of myself to your sadism.

MAJOR: But I do? To others' sadism? Of myself? I have that duty and you do not? To make a gift of myself?

LEDUC—*looks at the Professor and the Police Captain, glances back at the Major:* I have nothing to say.

MAJOR: That's better.

He suddenly gives Leduc an almost comradely push and nearly laughs. He puts his gun away, turns swaying to the Professor and with a victorious shout:

Next!

The Major brushes past the Professor into the office. Lebeau has not moved.

PROFESSOR: This way.

Lebeau stands up, starts sleepily toward the corridor, turns about, and moves into the office, the Professor following him.

CAPTAIN, *to Leduc:* Get back there.

Leduc returns to his seat. The Captain goes into the office; the door shuts. Pause.

MONCEAU: You happy now? You got him furious. You happy?

The door opens; the Captain appears, beckoning to Monceau.

CAPTAIN: Next.

Monceau gets up at once; taking papers out of his jacket, he fixes a smile on his face and walks with erect elegance to the Captain and with a slight bow, his voice cheerful:

MONCEAU: Good morning, Captain.

He goes right into the office; the Captain follows, and shuts the door. Pause.

BOY: Number Nine Rue Charlot. Please.

VON BERG: I'll give it to her.

BOY: I'm a minor. I'm not even fifteen. Does it apply to minors?

Captain opens the door, beckons to the Boy.

BOY, *standing:* I'm a minor. I'm not fifteen until February . . .
CAPTAIN: Inside.
BOY, *halting before the Captain:* I could get my birth certificate for you.
CAPTAIN, *prodding him along:* Inside, inside.

They go in. The door shuts. The accordion is heard again from next door. The Old Jew begins to rock back and forth slightly, praying softly. Von Berg, his hand trembling as it passes down his cheek, stares at the Old Jew, then turns to Leduc on his other side. The three are alone now.

VON BERG: Does he realize what is happening?
LEDUC, *with an edgy note of impatience:* As much as anyone can, I suppose.
VON BERG: He seems to be watching it all from the stars. *Slight pause.* I wish we could have met under other circumstances. There are a great many things I'd like to have asked you.
LEDUC, *rapidly, sensing the imminent summons:* I'd appreciate it if you'd do me a favor.
VON BERG: Certainly.
LEDUC: Will you go and tell my wife?
VON BERG: Where is she?
LEDUC: Take the main highway north two kilometers. You'll see a small forest on the left and a dirt road leading into it. Go about a kilometer until you see the river. Follow the river to a small mill. They are in the tool shed behind the wheel.
VON BERG, *distressed:* And . . . what shall I say?
LEDUC: That I've been arrested. And that there may be a possibility I can . . . *Breaks off.* No, tell her the truth.
VON BERG, *alarmed:* What do you mean?
LEDUC: The furnaces. Tell her that.
VON BERG: But actually . . . that's only a rumor, isn't it?
LEDUC—*turns to him—sharply:* I don't regard it as a rumor. It should be known. I never heard of it before. It must be known. Just take her aside—there's no need for the children to hear it, but tell her.

VON BERG: It's only that it would be difficult for me. To tell such a thing to a woman.

LEDUC: If it's happening you can find a way to say it, can't you?

VON BERG—*hesitates; he senses Leduc's resentment:* Very well. I'll tell her. It's only that I have no great . . . facility with women. But I'll do as you say. *Pause. He glances to the door.* They're taking longer with that boy. Maybe he *is* too young, you suppose?

Leduc does not answer. Von Berg seems suddenly hopeful.

They would stick to the rules, you know. . . . In fact, with the shortage of physicians you suppose they—

He breaks off.

I'm sorry if I said anything to offend you.

LEDUC, *struggling with his anger:* That's all right.

Slight pause. His voice is trembling with anger.

It's just that you keep finding these little shreds of hope and it's a little difficult.

VON BERG: Yes, I see. I beg your pardon. I understand.

Pause. Leduc glances at the door; he is shifting about in high tension.

Would you like to talk of something else, perhaps? Are you interested in . . . in music?

LEDUC, *desperately trying to control himself:* It's really quite simple. It's that you'll survive, you see.

VON BERG: But I can't help that, can I?

LEDUC: That only makes it worse! I'm sorry, one isn't always in control of one's emotions.

VON BERG: Doctor, I can promise you—it will not be easy for me to walk out of here. You don't know me.

LEDUC—*he tries not to reply; then:* I'm afraid it will only be difficult because it is so easy.

VON BERG: I think that's unfair.

LEDUC: Well, it doesn't matter.

VON BERG: It does to me. I . . . I can tell you that I was very close to suicide in Austria. Actually, that is why I left. When they murdered my musicians—not that alone, but when I told the story to many of my friends there was hardly any reaction. That was almost worse. Do you understand such indifference?

LEDUC—*he seems on the verge of an outbreak:* You have a curious idea of human nature. It's astounding you can go on with it in these times.

VON BERG, *with hand on heart:* But what is left if one gives up one's ideals? What *is* there?

LEDUC: Who are you talking about? You? Or me?

VON BERG: I'm terribly sorry. . . . I understand.

LEDUC: Why don't you just stop talking. I can't listen to anything. *Slight pause.* Forgive me. I do appreciate your feeling. *Slight pause.* I see it too clearly, perhaps—I know the violence inside these people's heads. It's difficult to listen to amelioration, even if it's well-meant.

VON BERG: I had no intention of ameliorating—

LEDUC: I think you do. And you must; you will survive, you will have to ameliorate it; just a little, just enough. It's no reflection on you. *Slight pause.* But, you see, this is why one gets so furious. Because all this suffering is so pointless—it can never be a lesson, it can never have a meaning. And that is why it will be repeated again and again forever.

VON BERG: Because it cannot be shared?

LEDUC: Yes. Because it cannot be shared. It is total, absolute, waste.

He leans forward suddenly, trying to collect himself against his terror. He glances at the door.

How strange—one can even become impatient.

A groan as he shakes his head with wonder and anger at himself.

Hm!—what devils they are.

VON BERG, *with an overtone of closeness to Leduc:* You understand now why I left Vienna. They can make death seductive. It is their worst sin. I had dreams at night—Hitler in a great flowing cloak, almost like a gown, almost like a woman. He was beautiful.

LEDUC: Listen—don't mention the furnaces to my wife.

VON BERG: I'm glad you say that, I feel very relieved, there's really no point . . .

LEDUC, *in a higher agony as he realizes:* No, it's . . . it's . . . You see there was no reason for me to be caught here. We have a good hideout. They'd never have found us. But she has an exposed nerve in one tooth and I thought I might find some codeine. Just say I was arrested.

VON BERG: Does she have sufficient money?

LEDUC: You could help her that way if you like. Thank you.

VON BERG: The children are small?

LEDUC: Two and three.

VON BERG: How dreadful. How dreadful. *He looks with a glance of fury at the door.* Do you suppose if I offered him something? I can get hold of a good deal of money. I know so little about people—I'm afraid he's rather an idealist. It could infuriate him more.

LEDUC: You might try to feel him out. I don't know what to tell you.

VON BERG: How upside down everything is—to find oneself wishing for a money-loving cynic!

LEDUC: It's perfectly natural. We have learned the price of idealism.

VON BERG: And yet can one wish for a world without ideals? That's what's so depressing—one doesn't know what to wish for.

LEDUC, *in anger:* You see, I knew it when I walked down the road, I knew it was senseless! For a goddamned toothache! So what, so she doesn't sleep for a couple of weeks! It was perfectly clear I shouldn't be taking the chance.

VON BERG: Yes, but if one loves someone . . .

LEDUC: We are not in love any more. It's just too difficult to separate in these times.

VON BERG: Oh, how terrible.

LEDUC, *more softly, realizing a new idea:* Listen . . . about the furnaces . . . don't mention that to her. Not a word, please. *With great self-contempt:* God, at a time like this—to think of taking vengeance on her! What scum we are! *He almost sways in despair.*

Pause. Von Berg turns to Leduc; tears are in his eyes.

VON BERG: There is nothing, is that it? For you there is
nothing?

LEDUC, *flying out at him suddenly:* Well what do you propose?
Excuse me, but what in hell are you talking about?

*The door opens. The Professor comes out and beckons to the Old
Jew. He seems upset, by an argument he had in the office, possibly.*

Next.

The Old Jew does not turn to him.

You hear me, why do you sit there?

*He strides to the Old Jew and lifts him to his feet brusquely. The
man reaches down to pick up his bundle, but the Professor tries
to push it back to the floor.*

Leave that.

With a wordless little cry, the Old Jew clings to his bundle.

Leave it!

*The Professor strikes at the Old Jew's hand, but he only holds on
tighter, uttering his wordless little cries. The Police Captain
comes out as the Professor pulls at the bundle.*

Let go of that!

*The bundle rips open. A white cloud of feathers blows up out of
it. For an instant everything stops as the Professor looks in surprise at the feathers floating down. The Major appears in the
doorway as the feathers settle.*

CAPTAIN: Come on.

*The Captain and the Professor lift the Old Jew and carry him
past the Major into the office. The Major with deadened eyes
glances at the feathers and limps in, closing the door behind him.*

*Leduc and Von Berg stare at the feathers, some of which have
fallen on them. They silently brush them off. Leduc picks the last
one off his jacket, opens his fingers, and lets it fall to the floor.*

*Silence. Suddenly a short burst of laughter is heard from the
office.*

VON BERG, *with great difficulty, not looking at Leduc:* I would like to be able to part with your friendship. Is that possible?

Pause.

LEDUC: Prince, in my position one gets the habit of looking at oneself quite impersonally. It is not you I am angry with. In one part of my mind it is not even this Nazi. I am only angry that I should have been born before the day when man has accepted his own nature; that he is *not* reasonable, that he is full of murder, that his ideals are only the little tax he pays for the right to hate and kill with a clear conscience. I am only angry that, knowing this, I still deluded myself. That there was not time to truly make part of myself what I know, and to teach others the truth.

VON BERG, *angered, above his anxiety:* There are ideals, Doctor, of another kind. There are people who would find it easier to die than stain one finger with this murder. They exist. I swear it to you. People for whom everything is *not* permitted, foolish people and ineffectual, but they do exist and will not dishonor their tradition. *Desperately:* I ask your friendship.

Again laughter is heard from within the office. This time it is louder. Leduc slowly turns to Von Berg.

LEDUC: I owe you the truth, Prince; you won't believe it now, but I wish you would think about it and what it means. I have never analyzed a gentile who did not have, somewhere hidden in his mind, a dislike if not a hatred for the Jews.

VON BERG, *clapping his ears shut, springing up:* That is impossible, it is not true of me!

LEDUC, *standing, coming to him, a wild pity in his voice:* Until you know it is true of you you will destroy whatever truth can come of this atrocity. Part of knowing who we are is knowing we are not someone else. And Jew is only the name we give to that stranger, that agony we cannot feel, that death we look at like a cold abstraction. Each man has his Jew; it is the other. And the Jews have their Jews. And now, now above all, you must see that you have yours—the man whose death leaves you relieved that you are not him, despite your decency. And that is why there is nothing and will be nothing—until you face your own complicity with this . . . your own humanity.

VON BERG: I deny that. I deny that absolutely. I have never in my life said a word against your people. Is that your implication? That I have something to do with this monstrousness! I have put a pistol to my head! To my head!

Laughter is heard again.

LEDUC, *hopelessly:* I'm sorry; it doesn't really matter.

VON BERG: It matters very much to me. Very much to me!

LEDUC, *in a level tone full of mourning; and yet behind it a howling horror:* Prince, you asked me before if I knew your cousin, Baron Kessler.

Von Berg looks at him, already with anxiety.

Baron Kessler is a Nazi. He helped to remove all the Jewish doctors from the medical school.

Von Berg is struck; his eyes glance about.

You were aware of that, weren't you?

Half-hysterical laughter comes from the office.

You must have heard that at some time or another, didn't you?

VON BERG, *stunned, inward-seeing:* Yes. I heard it. I . . . had forgotten it. You see, he was . . .

LEDUC: . . . Your cousin. I understand.

They are quite joined; and Leduc is mourning for the Prince as much as for himself, despite his anger.

And in any case, it is only a small part of Baron Kessler to you. I understand it. But it is all of Baron Kessler to me. When you said his name it was with love; and I'm sure he must be a man of some kindness, with whom you can see eye to eye in many things. But when I hear that name I see a knife. You see now why I say there is nothing, and will be nothing, when even you cannot really put yourself in my place? Even you! And that is why your thoughts of suicide do not move me. It's not your guilt I want, it's your responsibility—that might have helped. Yes, if you had understood that Baron Kessler was in part, in some part, in some small and frightful part—doing your will. You might have done something then, with your standing, and your name and your decency, aside from shooting yourself!

VON BERG, *in full horror, his face upthrust, calling:* What can ever save us? *He covers his face with his hands.*

The door opens. The Professor comes out.

PROFESSOR, *beckoning to the Prince:* Next.

Von Berg does not turn, but holds Leduc in his horrified, beseeching gaze. The Professor approaches the Prince.

Come!

The Professor reaches down to take Von Berg's arm. Von Berg angrily brushes away his abhorrent hand.

VON BERG: *Hände weg!*

The Professor retracts his hand, immobilized, surprised, and for a moment has no strength against his own recognition of authority. Von Berg turns back to Leduc, who glances up at him and smiles with warmth, then turns away.

Von Berg turns toward the door and, reaching into his breast pocket for a wallet of papers, goes into the office. The Professor follows and closes the door.

Alone, Leduc sits motionless. Now he begins the movements of the trapped; he swallows with difficulty, crosses and recrosses his legs. Now he is still again and bends over and cranes around the corner of the corridor to look for the guard. A movement of his foot stirs up feathers. The accordion is heard outside. He angrily kicks a feather off his foot. Now he makes a decision; he quickly reaches into his pocket, takes out a clasp knife, opens the blade, and begins to get to his feet, starting for the corridor.

The door opens and Von Berg comes out. In his hand is a white pass. The door shuts behind him. He is looking at the pass as he goes by Leduc, and suddenly turns, walks back, and thrusts the pass into Leduc's hand.

VON BERG, *in a strangely angered whisper, motioning him out:* Take it! Go!

Von Berg sits quickly on the bench, taking out the wedding ring. Leduc stares at him, a horrified look on his face. Von Berg hands him the ring.

Number Nine Rue Charlot. Go.

LEDUC, *in a desperate whisper:* What will happen to you?

VON BERG, *angrily waving him away:* Go, go!

Leduc backs away, his hands springing to cover his eyes in the awareness of his own guilt.

LEDUC—*a plea in his voice:* I wasn't asking you to do this! You don't owe me this!

VON BERG: Go!

Leduc, his eyes wide in awe and terror, suddenly turns and strides up the corridor. At the end of it the Guard appears, hearing his footsteps. He gives the Guard the pass and disappears.

A long pause. The door opens. The Professor appears.

PROFESSOR: Ne— *He breaks off. Looks about, then, to Von Berg:* Where's your pass?

Von Berg stares ahead. The Professor calls into the office.

Man escaped!

He runs up the corridor, calling.

Man escaped! Man escaped!

The Police Captain rushes out of the office. Voices are heard outside calling orders. The accordion stops. The Major hurries out of the office. The Police Captain rushes past him.

CAPTAIN: What? *Glancing back at Von Berg, he realizes and rushes up the corridor, calling:* Who let him out! Find that man! What happened?

The voices outside are swept away by a siren going off. The Major has gone to the opening of the corridor, following the Police Captain. For a moment he remains looking up the corridor. All that can be heard now is the siren moving off in pursuit. It dies away, leaving the Major's rapid and excited breaths, angry breaths, incredulous breaths.

Now he turns slowly to Von Berg, who is staring straight ahead. Von Berg turns and faces him. Then he gets to his feet. The moment lengthens, and lengthens yet. A look of anguish and fury is stiffening the Major's face; he is closing his fists. They stand there, forever incomprehensible to one another, looking into each other's eyes.

At the head of the corridor four new men, prisoners, appear. Herded by the Detectives, they enter the detention room and sit on the bench, glancing about at the ceiling, the walls, the feathers on the floor, and the two men who are staring at each other so strangely.

CURTAIN

THE PRICE

THE CHARACTERS

VICTOR FRANZ
ESTHER FRANZ
GREGORY SOLOMON
WALTER FRANZ

ACT ONE

New York.

Two windows are seen at the back of the stage. Daylight filters through their sooty panes, which have been X'd out with fresh whitewash to prepare for the demolition of the building.

Now daylight seeps through a skylight in the ceiling, grayed by the grimy panes. The light from above first strikes an overstuffed armchair in center stage. It has a faded rose slipcover. Beside it on its right, a small table with a filigreed radio of the Twenties on it and old newspapers; behind it a bridge lamp. At its left an old wind-up Victrola and a pile of records on a low table. A white cleaning cloth and a mop and pail are nearby.

The room is progressively seen. The area around the armchair alone appears to be lived-in, with other chairs and a couch related to it. Outside this area, to the sides and back limits of the room and up the walls, is the chaos of ten rooms of furniture squeezed into this one.

There are four couches and three settees strewn at random over the floor; armchairs, wingbacks, a divan, occasional chairs. On the floor and stacked against the three walls up to the ceiling are bu-reaus, armoires, a tall secretary, a breakfront, a long, elaborately carved serving table, end tables, a library table, desks, glass-front bookcases, bow-front glass cabinets, and so forth. Several long rolled-up rugs and some shorter ones. A long sculling oar, bed-steads, trunks. And overhead one large and one smaller crystal chandelier hang from ropes, not connected to electric wires. Twelve dining-room chairs stand in a row along a dining-room table at left.

There is a rich heaviness, something almost Germanic, about the furniture, a weight of time upon the bulging fronts and curv-ing chests marshalled against the walls. The room is monstrously crowded and dense, and it is difficult to decide if the stuff is im-pressive or merely over-heavy and ugly.

An uncovered harp, its gilt chipped, stands alone downstage, right. At the back, behind a rather make-shift drape, long since faded, can be seen a small sink, a hotplate, and an old icebox. Up right, a door to the bedroom. Down left, a door to the corridor and stairway, which are unseen.

We are in the attic of a Manhattan brownstone soon to be torn down.

From the down-left door, Police Sergeant Victor Franz enters in uniform. He halts inside the room, glances about, walks at random a few feet, then comes to a halt. Without expression, yet somehow stilled by some emanation from the room, he lets his gaze move from point to point, piece to piece, absorbing its sphinxlike presence.

He moves to the harp with a certain solemnity, as toward a coffin, and, halting before it, reaches out and plucks a string. He turns and crosses to the dining-room table and removes his gun belt and jacket, hanging them on a chair which he has taken off the table, where it had been set upside down along with two others.

He looks at his watch, waiting for time to pass. Then his eye falls on the pile of records in front of the phonograph. He raises the lid of the machine, sees a record already on the turntable, cranks, and sets the tone arm on the record. Gallagher and Shean sing. He smiles at the corniness.

With the record going he moves to the long sculling oar which stands propped against furniture and touches it. Now he recalls something, reaches in behind a chest, and takes out a fencing foil and mask. He snaps the foil in the air, his gaze held by memory. He puts the foil and mask on the table, goes through two or three records on the pile, and sees a title that makes him smile widely. He replaces the Gallagher and Shean record with this. It is a Laughing Record—two men trying unsuccessfully to get out a whole sentence through their wild hysteria.

He smiles. Broader. Chuckles. Then really laughs. It gets into him; he laughs more fully. Now he bends over with laughter, taking an unsteady step as helplessness rises in him.

Esther, his wife, enters from the down-left door. His back is to her. A half-smile is already on her face as she looks about to see who is laughing with him. She starts toward him, and he hears her heels and turns.

ESTHER: What in the world is that?
VICTOR, *surprised:* Hi! *He lifts the tone arm, smiling, a little embarrassed.*

ESTHER: Sounded like a party in here!

He gives her a peck.

Of the record: What *is* that?

VICTOR, *trying not to disapprove openly:* Where'd you get a drink?

ESTHER: I told you. I went for my checkup. *She laughs with a knowing abandonment of good sense.*

VICTOR: Boy, you and that doctor. I thought he told you not to drink.

ESTHER—*laughs:* I had one! One doesn't hurt me. Everything's normal anyway. He sent you his best. *She looks about.*

VICTOR: Well, that's nice. The dealer's due in a few minutes, if you want to take anything.

ESTHER, *looking around with a sigh:* Oh, dear God—here it is again.

VICTOR: The old lady did a nice job.

ESTHER: Ya—I never saw it so clean. *Indicating the room:* Make you feel funny?

VICTOR—*shrugs:* No, not really—she didn't recognize me, imagine?

ESTHER: Dear boy, it's a hundred and fifty years. *Shaking her head as she stares about:* Huh.

VICTOR: What?

ESTHER: Time.

VICTOR: I know.

ESTHER: There's something different about it.

VICTOR: No, it's all the way it was. *Indicating one side of the room:* I had my desk on that side and my cot. The rest is the same.

ESTHER: Maybe it's that it always used to seem so pretentious to me, and kind of bourgeois. But it does have a certain character. I think some of it's in style again. It's surprising.

VICTOR: Well, you want to take anything?

ESTHER, *looking about, hesitates:* I don't know if I want it around. It's all so massive . . . where would we put any of it? That chest is lovely. *She goes to it.*

VICTOR: That was mine. *Indicating one across the room:* The one over there was Walter's. They're a pair.

ESTHER, *comparing:* Oh ya! Did you get hold of him?

VICTOR—*rather glances away, as though this had been an issue:*
I called again this morning—he was in consultation.

ESTHER: Was he in the office?

VICTOR: Ya. The nurse went and talked to him for a minute—it
doesn't matter. As long as he's notified so I can go ahead.

She suppresses comment, picks up a lamp.

That's probably real porcelain. Maybe it'd go in the bedroom.

ESTHER, *putting the lamp down:* Why don't I meet you somewhere? The whole thing depresses me.

VICTOR: Why? It won't take long. Relax. Come on, sit down;
the dealer'll be here any minute.

ESTHER, *sitting on a couch:* There's just something so damned
rotten about it. I can't help it; it always was. The whole thing
is infuriating.

VICTOR: Well, don't get worked up. We'll sell it and that'll be
the end of it. I picked up the tickets, by the way.

ESTHER: Oh, good. *Laying her head back:* Boy, I hope it's a
good picture.

VICTOR: Better be. Great, not good. Two-fifty apiece.

ESTHER, *with sudden protest:* I don't care! I want to go somewhere. *She aborts further response, looking around.* God, what's
it all about? When I was coming up the stairs just now, and
all the doors hanging open . . . It doesn't seem possible . . .

VICTOR: They tear down old buildings every day in the week,
kid.

ESTHER: I know, but it makes you feel a hundred years old. I
hate empty rooms. *She muses.* What was that screwball's name?
—rented the front parlor, remember?—repaired saxophones?

VICTOR, *smiling:* Oh—Saltzman. *Extending his hand sideways:*
With the one eye went out that way.

ESTHER: Ya! Every time I came down the stairs, there he was
waiting for me with his four red hands! How'd he ever get
all those beautiful girls?

VICTOR—*laughs:* God knows. He must've smelled good.

She laughs, and he does.

He'd actually come running up here sometimes; middle of
the afternoon—"Victor, come down quick, I got extras!"

ESTHER: And you did, too!

VICTOR: Why not? If it was free, you took it.

ESTHER, *blushing:* You never told me that.

VICTOR: No, that was before you. Mostly.

ESTHER: You dog.

VICTOR: So what? It was the Depression.

She laughs at the non sequitur.

No, really—I think people were friendlier; lot more daytime screwing in those days. Like the McLoughlin sisters—remember, with the typing service in the front bedroom? *He laughs.* My father used to say, "In that typing service it's two dollars a copy."

She laughs. It subsides.

ESTHER: And they're probably all dead.

VICTOR: I guess Saltzman would be—he was well along. Although—*He shakes his head, laughs softly in surprise.* Jeeze, he wasn't either. I think he was about . . . my age now. Huh!

Caught by the impact of time, they stare for a moment in silence.

ESTHER—*gets up, goes to the harp:* Well, where's your dealer?

VICTOR, *glancing at his watch:* It's twenty to six. He should be here soon.

She plucks the harp.

That should be worth something.

ESTHER: I think a lot of it is. But you're going to have to bargain, you know. You can't just take what they say . . .

VICTOR, *with an edge of protest: I* can bargain; don't worry, I'm not giving it away.

ESTHER: Because they *expect* to bargain.

VICTOR: Don't get depressed already, will you? We didn't even start. *I* intend to bargain, I know the score with these guys.

ESTHER—*withholds further argument, goes to the phonograph; firing up some slight gaiety:* What's this record?

VICTOR: It's a Laughing Record. It was a big thing in the Twenties.

ESTHER, *curiously:* You remember it?

VICTOR: Very vaguely. I was only five or six. Used to play them at parties. You know—see who could keep a straight face. Or maybe they just sat around laughing; I don't know.

ESTHER: That's a wonderful idea!

Their relation is quite balanced, so to speak; he turns to her.

VICTOR: You look good.

She looks at him, an embarrassed smile.

I mean it.—I *said* I'm going to bargain, why do you . . . ?

ESTHER: I believe you.—This is the suit.

VICTOR: Oh, is that it! And how much? Turn around.

ESTHER, *turning:* Forty-five, imagine? He said nobody'd buy it, it was too simple.

VICTOR, *seizing the agreement:* Boy, women are dumb; that is really handsome. See, I don't mind if you get something for your money, but half the stuff they sell is such crap . . . *Going to her:* By the way, look at this collar. Isn't this one of the ones you just bought?

ESTHER, *examining it:* No, that's an older one.

VICTOR: Well, even so. *Turning up a heel:* Ought to write to Consumers Union about these heels. Three weeks—look at them!

ESTHER: Well, you don't walk straight.—You're not going in uniform, I hope.

VICTOR: I could've murdered that guy! I'd just changed, and McGowan was trying to fingerprint some bum and he didn't want to be printed; so he swings out his arm just as I'm going by, right into my container.

ESTHER, *as though this symbolized:* Oh, God . . .

VICTOR: I gave it to that quick cleaner, he'll try to have it by six.

ESTHER: Was there cream and sugar in the coffee?

VICTOR: Ya.

ESTHER: He'll never have it by six.

VICTOR, *assuagingly:* He's going to try.

ESTHER: Oh, forget it.

Slight pause. Seriously disconsolate, she looks around at random.

VICTOR: Well, it's only a movie . . .

ESTHER: But we go out so rarely—why must everybody know your salary? I want an evening! I want to sit down in a restaurant without some drunken ex-cop coming over to the table to talk about old times.

VICTOR: It happened twice. After all these years, Esther, it would seem to me . . .

ESTHER: I know it's unimportant—but like that man in the museum; he really did—he thought you were the sculptor.

VICTOR: So I'm a sculptor.

ESTHER, *bridling:* Well, it was nice, that's all! You really do, Vic—you look distinguished in a suit. Why not? *Laying her head back on the couch:* I should've taken down the name of that scotch.

VICTOR: All scotch is chemically the same.

ESTHER: I know; but some is better.

VICTOR, *looking at his watch:* Look at that, will you? Five-thirty sharp, he tells me. People say anything. *He moves with a heightened restlessness, trying to down his irritation with her mood. His eye falls on a partly opened drawer of a chest, and he opens it and takes out an ice skate.* Look at that, they're still good! *He tests the edge with his fingernail; she merely glances at him.* They're even sharp. We ought to skate again sometime. *He sees her unremitting moodiness.* Esther, I said I would bargain!—You see?—you don't know how to drink; it only depresses you.

ESTHER: Well, it's the kind of depression I enjoy!

VICTOR: Hot diggity dog.

ESTHER: I have an idea.

VICTOR: What?

ESTHER: Why don't you leave me? Just send me enough for coffee and cigarettes.

VICTOR: Then you'd *never* have to get out of bed.

ESTHER: I'd get out. Once in a while.

VICTOR: I got a better idea. Why don't you go off for a couple of weeks with your doctor? Seriously. It might change your viewpoint.

ESTHER: I wish I could.

VICTOR: Well, do it. He's got a suit. You could even take the dog—especially the dog. *She laughs.* It's not funny. Every time you go out for one of those walks in the rain I hold my breath what's going to come back with you.

ESTHER, *laughing:* Oh, go on, you love her.

VICTOR: I love her! You get plastered, you bring home strange animals, and I "love" them! I do not love that goddamned dog!

She laughs with affection, as well as with a certain feminine defiance.

ESTHER: Well, I want her!

VICTOR—*pause:* It won't be solved by a dog, Esther. You're an intelligent, capable woman, and you can't lay around all day. Even something part-time, it would give you a place to go.

ESTHER: I don't need a place to go. *Slight pause.* I'm not quite used to Richard not being there, that's all.

VICTOR: He's gone, kid. He's a grown man; you've got to do something with yourself.

ESTHER: I can't go to the same place day after day. I never could and I never will. Did you *ask* to speak to your brother?

VICTOR: I asked the nurse. Yes. He couldn't break away.

ESTHER: That son of a bitch. It's sickening.

VICTOR: Well, what are you going to do? He never had that kind of feeling.

ESTHER: What feeling? To come to the phone after sixteen years? It's common decency. *With sudden intimate sympathy:* You're furious, aren't you?

VICTOR: Only at myself. Calling him again and again all week like an idiot . . . To hell with him, I'll handle it alone. It's just as well.

ESTHER: What about his share?

He shifts; pressed and annoyed.

I don't want to be a pest—but I think there could be some money here, Vic.

He is silent.

You're going to raise that with him, aren't you?

VICTOR, *with a formed decision:* I've been thinking about it.

He's got a right to his half, why should he give up anything?

ESTHER: I thought you'd decided to put it to him?

VICTOR: I've changed my mind. I don't really feel he owes me
anything, I can't put on an act.

ESTHER: But how many Cadillacs can he drive?

VICTOR: That's why he's got Cadillacs. People who love money
don't give it away.

ESTHER: I don't know why you keep putting it like charity.
There's such a thing as a moral debt. Vic, you made his
whole career possible. What law said that only he could study
medicine—?

VICTOR: Esther, please—let's not get back on that, will you?

ESTHER: I'm not back on anything—you were even the better
student. That's a real debt, and he ought to be made to face
it. He could never have finished medical school if you hadn't
taken care of Pop. I mean we ought to start talking the way
people talk! There could be some real money here.

VICTOR: I doubt that. There are no antiques or—

ESTHER: Just because it's ours why must it be worthless?

VICTOR: Now what's that for?

ESTHER: Because that's the way we think! We do!

VICTOR, *sharply:* The man won't even come to the phone, how
am I going to—?

ESTHER: Then you write him a letter, bang on his door. This
belongs to you!

VICTOR, *surprised, seeing how deadly earnest she is:* What are
you so excited about?

ESTHER: Well, for one thing it might help you make up your
mind to take your retirement.

A slight pause.

VICTOR, *rather secretively, unwillingly:* It's not the money been
stopping me.

ESTHER: Then what is it?

He is silent.

I just thought that with a little cushion you could take a
month or two until something occurs to you that you want
to do.

VICTOR: It's all I think about right now, I don't have to quit to think.

ESTHER: But nothing seems to come of it.

VICTOR: Is it that easy? I'm going to be fifty. You don't just start a whole new career. I don't understand why it's so urgent all of a sudden.

ESTHER—*laughs:* All of a sudden! It's all I've been talking about since you became eligible—I've been saying the same thing for three years!

VICTOR: Well, it's not three years—

ESTHER: It'll be three years in March! It's *three years.* If you'd gone back to school then you'd almost have your Master's by now; you might have had a chance to get into something you'd love to do. Isn't that true? Why can't you make a move?

VICTOR—*pause. He is almost ashamed:* I'll tell you the truth. I'm not sure the whole thing wasn't a little unreal. I'd be fifty-three, fifty-four by the time I could start doing anything.

ESTHER: But you always knew that.

VICTOR: It's different when you're right on top of it. I'm not sure it makes any sense now.

ESTHER, *moving away, the despair in her voice:* Well . . . this is exactly what I tried to tell you a thousand times. It makes the same sense it ever made. But you might have twenty more years, and that's still a long time. Could do a lot of interesting things in that time. *Slight pause.* You're so young, Vic.

VICTOR: I am?

ESTHER: Sure! I'm not, but you are. God, all the girls goggle at you, what do you want?

VICTOR—*laughs emptily:* It's hard to discuss it, Es, because I don't understand it.

ESTHER: Well, why not talk about what you don't understand? Why do you expect yourself to be an authority?

VICTOR: Well, one of us is got to stay afloat, kid.

ESTHER: You want me to pretend everything is great? I'm bewildered and I'm going to act bewildered! *It flies out as though long suppressed:* I've asked you fifty times to write a letter to Walter—

VICTOR, *like a repeated story:* What's this with Walter again? What's Walter going to—?

ESTHER: He is an important scientist, and that hospital's building a whole new research division. I saw it in the paper, it's his hospital.

VICTOR: Esther, the man hasn't called me in sixteen years.

ESTHER: But neither have you called him!

He looks at her in surprise.

Well, you haven't. That's also a fact.

VICTOR, *as though the idea were new and incredible:* What would I call him for?

ESTHER: Because, he's your brother, he's influential, and he could help— Yes, that's how people do, Vic! Those articles he wrote had a real idealism, there was a genuine human quality. I mean people do change, you know.

VICTOR, *turning away:* I'm sorry, I don't need Walter.

ESTHER: I'm not saying you have to approve of him; he's a selfish bastard, but he just might be able to put you on the track of something. I don't see the humiliation.

VICTOR, *pressed, irritated:* I don't understand why it's all such an emergency.

ESTHER: Because I don't know where in hell I am, Victor! *To her surprise, she has ended nearly screaming. He is silent. She retracts.* I'll do anything if I know why, but all these years we've been saying, once we get the pension we're going to start to live. . . . It's like pushing against a door for twenty-five years and suddenly it opens . . . and we stand there. Sometimes I wonder, maybe I misunderstood you, maybe you like the department.

VICTOR: I've hated every minute of it.

ESTHER: I did everything wrong! I swear, I think if I demanded more it would have helped you more.

VICTOR: That's not true. You've been a terrific wife—

ESTHER: I don't think so. But the security meant so much to you I tried to fit into that; but I was wrong. God—just before coming here, I looked around at the apartment to see if we could use any of this—and it's all so ugly. It's worn and shabby and tasteless. And I have good taste! I know I do!

It's that everything was always temporary with us. It's like
we never were anything, we were always about-to-be. I think
back to the war when any idiot was making so much money
—that's when you should have quit, and I knew it, I knew it!

VICTOR: That's when I wanted to quit.

ESTHER: I only had one drink, Victor, so don't—

VICTOR: Don't change the whole story, kid. I wanted to quit,
and you got scared.

ESTHER: Because you said there was going to be a Depression
after the war.

VICTOR: Well, go to the library, look up the papers around
1945, see what they were saying!

ESTHER: I don't care! *She turns away—from her own irration-
ality.*

VICTOR: I swear, Es, sometimes you make it sound like we've
had no life at all.

ESTHER: God—my mother was so right! I can never believe
what I see. I knew you'd never get out if you didn't during
the war—I saw it happening, and I said nothing. You know
what the goddamned trouble is?

VICTOR, *glancing at his watch, as he senses the end of her revolt:*
What's the goddamned trouble?

ESTHER: We can never keep our minds on money! We worry
about it, we talk about it, but we can't seem to *want* it. I do,
but you don't. I really do, Vic. I want it. Vic? *I want money!*

VICTOR: Congratulations.

ESTHER: You go to hell!

VICTOR: I wish you'd stop comparing yourself to other people,
Esther! That's all you're doing lately.

ESTHER: Well, I can't help it!

VICTOR: Then you've got to be a failure, kid, because there's
always going to be somebody up ahead of you. What happened? I have a certain nature; just as you do—I didn't
change—

ESTHER: But you have changed. You've been walking around
like a zombie ever since the retirement came up. You've gotten so vague—

VICTOR: Well, it's a decision. And I'd like to feel a little more
certain about it. . . . Actually, I've even started to fill out
the forms a couple of times.

ESTHER, *alerted:* And?

VICTOR, *with difficulty—he cannot understand it himself:* I suppose there's some kind of finality about it that . . . *He breaks off.*

ESTHER: But what else did you expect?

VICTOR: It's stupid; I admit it. But you look at that goddamned form and you can't help it. You sign your name to twenty-eight years and you ask yourself, Is that all? Is that it? And it is, of course. The trouble is, when I think of starting something new, that number comes up—five oh—and the steam goes out. But I'll do something. I will! *With a greater closeness to her now:* I don't know what it is; every time I think about it all—it's almost frightening.

ESTHER: What?

VICTOR: Well, like when I walked in here before . . . *He looks around.* This whole thing—it hit me like some kind of craziness. Piling up all this stuff here like it was made of gold. *He half-laughs, almost embarrassed.* I brought up every stick; damn near saved the carpet tacks. *He turns to the center chair.* That whole way I was with him—it's inconceivable to me now.

ESTHER, *with regret over her sympathy:* Well . . . you loved him.

VICTOR: I know, but it's all words. What was he? A busted businessman like thousands of others, and I acted like some kind of a mountain crashed. I tell you the truth, every now and then the whole thing is like a story somebody told me. You ever feel that way?

ESTHER: All day, every day.

VICTOR: Oh, come on—

ESTHER: It's the truth. The first time I walked up those stairs I was nineteen years old. And when you opened that box with your first uniform in it—remember that? When you put it on the first time?—how we laughed? If anything happened you said you'd call a cop! *They both laugh.* It was like a masquerade. And we were right. That's when we were right.

VICTOR, *pained by her pain:* You know, Esther, every once in a while you try to sound childish and it—

ESTHER: I mean to be! I'm sick of the— Oh, forget it, I want a drink. *She goes for her purse.*

VICTOR, *surprised:* What's that, the great adventure? Where are you going all of a sudden?

ESTHER: I can't stand it in here, I'm going for a walk.

VICTOR: Now you cut out this nonsense!

ESTHER: I am not an alcoholic!

VICTOR: You've had a good life compared to an awful lot of people! You trying to turn into a goddamned teenager or something?

ESTHER, *indicating the furniture:* Don't talk childishness to me, Victor—not in this room! You let it lay here all these years because you can't have a simple conversation with your own brother, and I'm childish? You're still eighteen years old with that man! I mean I'm stuck, but I admit it!

VICTOR, *hurt:* Okay. Go ahead.

ESTHER—*she can't quite leave:* You got a receipt? I'll get your suit. *He doesn't move. She makes it rational:* I just want to get out of here.

VICTOR—*takes out a receipt and gives it to her. His voice is cold:* It's right off Seventh. The address is on it. *He moves from her.*

ESTHER: I'm coming back right away.

VICTOR, *freeing her to her irresponsibility:* Do as you please, kid. I mean it.

ESTHER: You were grinding your teeth again last night. Did you know that?

VICTOR: Oh! No wonder my ear hurts.

ESTHER: I wish I had a tape recorder. I mean it, it's gruesome; sounds like a lot of rocks coming down a mountain. I wish you could hear it, you wouldn't take this self-sufficient attitude.

He is silent, alarmed, hurt. He moves upstage as though looking at the furniture.

VICTOR: It's okay. I think I get the message.

ESTHER, *afraid—she tries to smile and goes back toward him:* Like what?

VICTOR—*moves a chair and does a knee bend and draws out the chassis of an immense old radio:* What other message is there?

Slight pause.

ESTHER, *to retrieve the contact:* What's that?

VICTOR: Oh, one of my old radios that I made. Mama mia, look at those tubes.

ESTHER, *more wondering than she feels about radios:* Would that work?

VICTOR: No, you need a storage battery. . . . *Recalling, he suddenly looks up at the ceiling.*

ESTHER, *looking up:* What?

VICTOR: One of my batteries exploded, went right through there someplace. *He points.* There! See where the plaster is different?

ESTHER, *striving for some spark between them:* Is this the one you got Tokyo on?

VICTOR, *not relenting, his voice dead:* Ya, this is the monster.

ESTHER, *with a warmth:* Why don't you take it?

VICTOR: Ah, it's useless.

ESTHER: Didn't you once say you had a lab up here? Or did I dream that?

VICTOR: Sure, I took it apart when Pop and I moved up here. Walter had that wall, and I had this. We did some great tricks up here.

She is fastened on him.

He avoids her eyes and moves waywardly. I'll be frank with you, kid—I look at my life and the whole thing is incomprehensible to me. I know all the reasons and all the reasons and all the reasons, and it ends up—nothing. *He goes to the harp, touches it.*

It's strange, you know? I forgot all about it—we'd work up here all night sometimes, and it was often full of music. My mother'd play for hours down in the library. Which is peculiar, because a harp is so soft. But it penetrates, I guess.

ESTHER: You're dear. You are, Vic. *She starts toward him, but he thwarts her by looking at his watch.*

VICTOR: I'll have to call another man. Come on, let's get out of here. *With a hollow, exhausted attempt at joy:* We'll get my suit and act rich!

ESTHER: Vic, I didn't mean that I—

VICTOR: Forget it. Wait, let me put these away before somebody walks off with them. *He takes up the foil and mask.*

ESTHER: Can you still do it?

VICTOR, *his sadness, his distance clinging to him:* Oh no, you gotta be in shape for this. It's all in the thighs—

ESTHER: Well, let me see, I never saw you do it!

VICTOR, *giving the inch:* All right, but I can't get down far enough any more. *He takes position, feet at right angles, bouncing himself down to a difficult crouch.*

ESTHER: Maybe you could take it up again.

VICTOR: Oh no, it's a lot of work, it's the toughest sport there is. *Resuming position:* Okay, just stand there.

ESTHER: Me?

VICTOR: Don't be afraid. *Snapping the tip:* It's a beautiful foil, see how alive it is? I beat Princeton with this. *He laughs tiredly and makes a tramping lunge from yards away; the button touches her stomach.*

ESTHER, *springing back:* God! Victor!

VICTOR: What?

ESTHER: You looked beautiful.

He laughs, surprised and half-embarrassed—when both of them are turned to the door by a loud, sustained coughing out in the corridor. The coughing increases.

Enter Gregory Solomon. In brief, a phenomenon; a man nearly ninety but still straight-backed and the air of his massiveness still with him. He has perfected a way of leaning on his cane without appearing weak.

He wears a worn fur-felt black fedora, its brim turned down on the right side like Jimmy Walker's—although much dustier—and a shapeless topcoat. His frayed tie has a thick knot, askew under a curled-up collar tab. His vest is wrinkled, his trousers baggy. A large diamond ring is on his left index finger. Tucked under his arm, a wrung-out leather portfolio. He hasn't shaved today.

Still coughing, catching his breath, trying to brush his cigar ashes off his lapel in a hopeless attempt at businesslike decorum, he is nodding at Esther and Victor and has one hand raised in a promise to speak quite soon. Nor has he failed to glance with some suspicion at the foil in Victor's hand.

VICTOR: Can I get you a glass of water?

Solomon gestures an imperious negative, trying to stop coughing.

ESTHER: Why don't you sit down?

Solomon gestures thanks, sits in the center armchair, the cough subsiding.

You sure you don't want some water?

SOLOMON, *in a Russian-Yiddish accent:* Water I don't need; a little blood I could use. Thank you. *He takes deep breaths, his attention on Victor, who now puts down the foil.* Oh boy. That's some stairs.

ESTHER: You all right now?

SOLOMON: Another couple steps you'll be in heaven. Ah—excuse me, Officer, I am looking for a party. The name is . . . *He fingers in his vest.*

VICTOR: Franz.

SOLOMON: That's it, Franz.

VICTOR: That's me.

Solomon looks incredulous.

Victor Franz.

SOLOMON: So it's a policeman!

VICTOR, *grinning:* Uh huh.

SOLOMON: What do you know! *Including Esther:* You see? There's only one beauty to this lousy business, you meet all kinda people. But I never dealt with a policeman. *Reaching over to shake hands:* I'm very happy to meet you. My name is Solomon, Gregory Solomon.

VICTOR, *shaking hands:* This is my wife.

ESTHER: How do you do.

SOLOMON, *nodding appreciatively to Esther:* Very nice. *To Victor:* That's a nice-looking woman. *He extends his hands to her.* How do you do, darling. Beautiful suit.

ESTHER—*laughs:* The fact is, I just bought it!

SOLOMON: You got good taste. Congratulations, wear it in good health. *He lets go her hand.*

ESTHER: I'll go to the cleaner, dear. I'll be back soon. *With a step toward the door—to Solomon:* Will you be very long?

SOLOMON, *glancing around at the furniture as at an antagonist:*

With furniture you never know, can be short, can be long, can be medium.

ESTHER: Well, you give him a good price now, you hear?

SOLOMON: Ah ha! *Waving her out:* Look, you go to the cleaner, and we'll take care everything one hundred per cent.

ESTHER: Because there's some very beautiful stuff here. I know it, but he doesn't.

SOLOMON: I'm not sixty-two years in the business by taking advantage. Go, enjoy the cleaner.

She and Victor laugh.

ESTHER, *shaking her finger at him:* I hope I'm going to like you!

SOLOMON: Sweetheart, all the girls like me, what can I do?

ESTHER, *still smiling—to Victor as she goes to the door:* You be careful.

VICTOR, *nodding:* See you later.

She goes.

SOLOMON: I like her, she's suspicious.

VICTOR, *laughing in surprise:* What do you mean by that?

SOLOMON: Well, a girl who believes everything, how you gonna trust her?

Victor laughs appreciatively.

I had a wife . . . *He breaks off with a wave of the hand.* Well, what's the difference? Tell me, if you don't mind, how did you get my name?

VICTOR: In the phone book.

SOLOMON: You don't say! The phone book.

VICTOR: Why?

SOLOMON, *cryptically:* No-no, that's fine, that's fine.

VICTOR: The ad said you're a registered appraiser.

SOLOMON: Oh yes. I am registered, I am licensed, I am even vaccinated.

Victor laughs.

Don't laugh, the only thing you can do today without a license is you'll go up the elevator and jump out the window. But I don't have to tell you, you're a policeman, you know this world. *Hoping for contact:* I'm right?

VICTOR, *reserved:* I suppose.

SOLOMON, *surveying the furniture, one hand on his thigh, the other on the chair arm in a naturally elegant position:* So. *He glances about again, and with an uncertain smile:* That's a lot of furniture. This is all for sale?

VICTOR: Well, ya.

SOLOMON: Fine, fine. I just like to be sure where we are. *With a weak attempt at a charming laugh:* Frankly, in this neighborhood I never expected such a load. It's very surprising.

VICTOR: But I said it was a whole houseful.

SOLOMON, *with a leaven of unsureness:* Look, don't worry about it, we'll handle everything very nice. *He gets up from the chair and goes to one of the pair of chiffoniers which he is obviously impressed with. He looks up at the chandeliers. Then straight at Victor:* I'm not mixing in, Officer, but if you wouldn't mind—what is your connection? How do you come to this?

VICTOR: It was my family.

SOLOMON: You don't say. Looks like it's standing here a long time, no?

VICTOR: Well, the old man moved everything up here after the '29 crash. My uncles took over the house and they let him keep this floor.

SOLOMON, *as though to emphasize that he believes it: I* see. *He walks to the harp.*

VICTOR: Can you give me an estimate now, or do you have to—?

SOLOMON, *running a hand over the harp frame:* No-no, I'll give you right away, I don't waste a minute, I'm very busy. *He plucks a string, listens. Then bends down and runs a hand over the sounding board:* He passed away, your father?

VICTOR: Oh, long time ago—about sixteen years.

SOLOMON, *standing erect:* It's standing here sixteen years?

VICTOR: Well, we never got around to doing anything about it, but they're tearing the building down, so . . . It was very good stuff, you know—they had quite a little money.

SOLOMON: Very good, yes . . . I can see. *He leaves the harp with an estimating glance.* I was also very good; now I'm not so good. Time, you know, is a terrible thing. *He is a distance from the harp and indicates it.* That sounding board is cracked, you know. But don't worry about it, it's still a nice object. *He goes to an armoire and strokes the veneer.* It's a funny thing—an armoire like this, thirty years you couldn't give it away; it was a regular measles. Today all of a sudden, they want it again. Go figure it out. *He goes to one of the chests.*

VICTOR, *pleased:* Well, give me a good price and we'll make a deal.

SOLOMON: Definitely. You see, I don't lie to you. *He is pointing to the chest.* For instance, a chiffonier like this I wouldn't have to keep it a week. *Indicating the other chest:* That's a pair, you know.

VICTOR: I know.

SOLOMON: That's a nice chair, too. *He sits on a dining-room chair, rocking to test its tightness.* I like the chairs.

VICTOR: There's more stuff in the bedroom, if you want to look.

SOLOMON: Oh? *He goes toward the bedroom.* What've you got here? *He looks into the bedroom, up and down.* I like the bed. That's a very nice carved bed. That I can sell. That's your parents' bed?

VICTOR: Yes. They may have bought that in Europe, if I'm not mistaken. They used to travel a good deal.

SOLOMON: Very handsome, very nice. I like it. *He starts to return to the center chair, eyes roving the furniture.* Looks a very nice family.

VICTOR: By the way, that dining-room table opens up. Probably seat about twelve people.

SOLOMON, *looking at the table:* I know that. Yes. In a pinch even fourteen. *He picks up the foil.* What's this? I thought you were stabbing your wife when I came in.

VICTOR, *laughing:* No, I just found it. I used to fence years ago.

SOLOMON: You went to college?

VICTOR: Couple of years, ya.

SOLOMON: That's very interesting.

VICTOR: It's the old story.

SOLOMON: No, listen— What happens to people is always the main element to me. Because when do they call me? It's either a divorce or somebody died. So it's always a new story. I mean it's the same, but it's different. *He sits in the center chair.*

VICTOR: You pick up the pieces.

SOLOMON: That's very good, yes. I pick up the pieces. It's a little bit like you, I suppose. You must have some stories, I betcha.

VICTOR: Not very often.

SOLOMON: What are you, a traffic cop, or something . . . ?

VICTOR: I'm out in Rockaway most of the time, the airports.

SOLOMON: That's Siberia, no?

VICTOR, *laughing:* I like it better that way.

SOLOMON: You keep your nose clean.

VICTOR, *smiling:* That's it. *Indicating the furniture:* So what do you say?

SOLOMON: What I say? *Taking out two cigars as he glances about:* You like a cigar?

VICTOR: Thanks, I gave it up long time ago. So what's the story here?

SOLOMON: I can see you are a very factual person.

VICTOR: You hit it.

SOLOMON: Couldn't be better. So tell me, you got some kind of paper here? To show ownership?

VICTOR: Well, no, I don't. But . . . *He half-laughs.* I'm the owner, that's all.

SOLOMON: In other words, there's no brothers, no sisters.

VICTOR: I have a brother, yes.

SOLOMON: Ah hah. You're friendly with him. Not that I'm mixing in, but I don't have to tell you the average family they love each other like crazy, but the minute the parents die is all of a sudden a question who is going to get what and you're covered with cats and dogs—

VICTOR: There's no such problem here.

SOLOMON: Unless we're gonna talk about a few pieces, then it wouldn't bother me, but to take the whole load without a paper is a—

VICTOR: All right, I'll get you some kind of statement from him; don't worry about it.

SOLOMON: That's definite; because even from high-class people you wouldn't believe the shenanigans—lawyers, college professors, television personalities—five hundred dollars they'll pay a lawyer to fight over a bookcase it's worth fifty cents—because you see, everybody wants to be number one, so . . .

VICTOR: I said I'd get you a statement. *He indicates the room.*
  Now what's the story?

SOLOMON: All right, so I'll tell you the story. *He looks at the
  dining-room table and points to it.* For instance, you mention
  the dining-room table. That's what they call Spanish Jacobean. Cost maybe twelve, thirteen hundred dollars. I would
  say—1921, '22. I'm right?

VICTOR: Probably, ya.

SOLOMON—*clears his throat:* I see you're an intelligent man, so
  before I'll say another word, I ask you to remember—with
  used furniture you cannot be emotional.

VICTOR—*laughs:* I haven't opened my mouth!

SOLOMON: I mean you're a policeman, I'm a furniture dealer,
  we both know this world. Anything Spanish Jacobean you'll
  sell quicker a case of tuberculosis.

VICTOR: Why? That table's in beautiful condition.

SOLOMON: Officer, you're talking reality; you cannot talk reality with used furniture. They don't like that style; not only
  they don't like it, they hate it. The same thing with that
  buffet there and that . . . *He starts to point elsewhere.*

VICTOR: You only want to take a few pieces, is that the ticket?

SOLOMON: Please, Officer, we're already talking too fast—

VICTOR: No-no, you're not going to walk off with the gravy
  and leave me with the bones. All or nothing or let's forget it.
  I told you on the phone it was a whole houseful.

SOLOMON: What're you in such a hurry? Talk a little bit, we'll
  see what happens. In a day they didn't build Rome. *He cal-
  culates worriedly for a moment, glancing again at the pieces
  he wants. He gets up, goes and touches the harp.* You see, what
  I had in mind—I would give you such a knockout price for
  these few pieces that you—

VICTOR: That's *out.*

SOLOMON, *quickly:* Out.

VICTOR: I'm not running a department store. They're tearing
  the building down.

SOLOMON: Couldn't be better! We understand each other,
  so—*with his charm*—so there's no reason to be emotional.
  He goes to the records. These records go? *He picks up one.*

VICTOR: I might keep three or four.

SOLOMON, *reading a label:* Look at that! Gallagher and Shean!

VICTOR, *with only half a laugh:* You're not going to start playing them now!

SOLOMON: Who needs to play? I was on the same bill with Gallagher and Shean maybe fifty theaters.

VICTOR, *surprised:* You were an actor?

SOLOMON: An actor! An acrobat; my whole family was acrobats. *Expanding with this first opening:* You never heard "The Five Solomons"—may they rest in peace? I was the one on the bottom.

VICTOR: Funny—I never heard of a Jewish acrobat.

SOLOMON: What's the matter with Jacob, he wasn't a wrestler? —wrestled with the Angel?

Victor laughs.

Jews been acrobats since the beginning of the world. I was a horse them days: drink, women, anything—on-the-go, on-the-go, nothing ever stopped me. Only life. Yes, my boy. *Almost lovingly putting down the record:* What do you know, Gallagher and Shean.

VICTOR, *more intimately now, despite himself; but with no less persistence in keeping to the business:* So where are we?

SOLOMON—*glancing off, he turns back to Victor with a deeply concerned look:* Tell me, what's with crime now? It's up, hey?

VICTOR: Yeah, it's up, it's up. Look, Mr. Solomon, let me make one thing clear, heh? I'm not sociable.

SOLOMON: You're not.

VICTOR: No, I'm not; I'm not a businessman, I'm not good at conversations. So let's get to a price, and finish. Okay?

SOLOMON: You don't want we should be buddies.

VICTOR: That's exactly it.

SOLOMON: So we wouldn't be buddies! *He sighs.* But just so you'll know me a little better—I'm going to show you something. *He takes out a leather folder which he flips open and hands to Victor.* There's my discharge from the British navy. You see? "His Majesty's Service."

VICTOR, *looking at the document:* Huh! What were you doing in the British Navy?

SOLOMON: Forget the British Navy. What does it say the date of birth?

VICTOR: "Eighteen . . ." *Amazed, he looks up at Solomon.* You're almost ninety?

SOLOMON: Yes, my boy. I left Russia sixty-five years ago, I was twenty-four years old. And I smoked all my life. I drinked, and I loved every woman who would let me. So what do I need to steal from you?

VICTOR: Since when do people need a reason to steal?

SOLOMON: I never saw such a man in my life!

VICTOR: Oh yes you did. Now you going to give me a figure or—?

SOLOMON—*he is actually frightened because he can't get a hook into Victor and fears losing the good pieces:* How can I give you a figure? You don't trust one word I say!

VICTOR, *with a strained laugh:* I never saw you before, what're you asking me to trust you?!

SOLOMON, *with a gesture of disgust:* But how am I going to start to talk to you? I'm sorry; here you can't be a policeman. If you want to do business a little bit you gotta believe or you can't do it. I'm . . . I'm . . . Look, forget it. *He gets up and goes to his portfolio.*

VICTOR, *astonished:* What are you doing?

SOLOMON: I can't work this way. I'm too old every time I open my mouth you should practically call me a thief.

VICTOR: Who called you a thief?

SOLOMON, *moving toward the door:* No—I don't need it. I don't want it in my shop. *Wagging a finger into Victor's face:* And don't forget it—I never gave you a price, and look what you did to me. You see? I never gave you a price!

VICTOR, *angering:* Well, what did you come here for, to do me a favor? What are you talking about?

SOLOMON: Mister, I pity you! What is the matter with you people! You're worse than my daughter! Nothing in the world you believe, nothing you respect—how can you live? You think that's such a smart thing? That's so hard, what you're doing? Let me give you a piece of advice—it's not that you can't believe nothing, that's not so hard—it's that you still got to believe it. *That's* hard. And if you can't do that, my friend—you're a dead man! *He starts toward the door.*

VICTOR, *chastened despite himself:* Oh, Solomon, come on, will you?

SOLOMON: No-no. You got a certain problem with this furniture but you don't want to listen so how can I talk?

VICTOR: I'm listening! For Christ's sake, what do you want me to do, get down on my knees?

SOLOMON, *putting down his portfolio and taking out a wrinkled tape measure from his jacket pocket:* Okay, come here. I realize you are a factual person, but some facts are funny. *He stretches the tape measure across the depth of a piece.* What does that read? *Then turns to Victor, showing him.*

VICTOR—*comes to him, reads:* Forty inches. So?

SOLOMON: My boy, the bedroom doors in a modern apartment house are thirty, thirty-two inches maximum. So you can't get this in—

VICTOR: What about the old houses?

SOLOMON, *with a desperation growing:* All I'm trying to tell you is that my possibilities are smaller!

VICTOR: Well, can't I ask a question?

SOLOMON: I'm giving you architectural facts! Listen—*Wiping his face, he seizes on the library table, going to it.* You got there, for instance, a library table. That's a solid beauty. But go find me a modern apartment with a library. If they would build old hotels, I could sell this, but they only build new hotels. People don't live like this no more. This stuff is from another world. So I'm trying to give you a modern viewpoint. Because the price of used furniture is nothing but a viewpoint, and if you wouldn't understand the viewpoint is impossible to understand the price.

VICTOR: So what's the viewpoint—that it's all worth nothing?

SOLOMON: That's what you said, I didn't say that. The chairs is worth something, the chiffoniers, the bed, the harp—

VICTOR—*turns away from him:* Okay, let's forget it, I'm not giving you the cream—

SOLOMON: What're you jumping!

VICTOR, *turning to him:* Good God, are you going to make me an offer or not?

SOLOMON, *walking away with a hand at his temple:* Boy, oh boy, oh boy. You must've arrested a million people by now.

VICTOR: Nineteen in twenty-eight years.

SOLOMON: So what are you so hard on me?

VICTOR: Because you talk about everything but money and I don't know what the hell you're up to.

SOLOMON, *raising a finger:* We will now talk money. *He returns to the center chair.*

VICTOR: Great. I mean you can't blame me—every time you open your mouth the price seems to go down.

SOLOMON, *sitting:* My boy, the price didn't change since I walked in.

VICTOR, *laughing:* That's even better! So what's the price?

Solomon glances about, his wit failed, a sunk look coming over his face.

What's going on? What's bothering you?

SOLOMON: I'm sorry, I shouldn't have come. I thought it would be a few pieces but . . . *Sunk, he presses his fingers into his eyes.* It's too much for me.

VICTOR: Well, what'd you come for? I told you it was the whole house.

SOLOMON, *protesting:* You called me so I came! What should I do, lay down and die? *Striving again to save it:* Look, I want very much to make you an offer, the only question is . . . *He breaks off as though fearful of saying something.*

VICTOR: This is a hell of a note.

SOLOMON: Listen, it's a terrible temptation to me! But . . . *As though throwing himself on Victor's understanding:* You see, I'll tell you the truth; you must have looked in a very old phone book; a couple of years ago already I cleaned out my store. Except a few English andirons I got left, I sell when I need a few dollars. I figured I was eighty, eighty-five, it was time already. But I waited—and nothing happened—I even moved out of my apartment. I'm living in the back of the store with a hotplate. But nothing happened. I'm still practically a hundred per cent—not a hundred, but I feel very well. And I figured maybe you got a couple nice pieces—not that the rest can't be sold, but it could take a year, year and half. For me that's a big bet. *In conflict, he looks around.* The trouble is I love to work; I love it, but—*Giving up:* I don't know what to tell you.

VICTOR: All right, let's forget it then.

SOLOMON, *standing:* What're you jumping?

VICTOR: Well, are you in or out!

SOLOMON: How do I know where I am! You see, it's also this particular furniture—the average person he'll take one look, it'll make him very nervous.

VICTOR: Solomon, you're starting again.

SOLOMON: I'm not bargaining with you!

VICTOR: Why'll it make him nervous?

SOLOMON: Because he knows it's never gonna break.

VICTOR, *not in bad humor, but clinging to his senses:* Oh come on, will you? Have a little mercy.

SOLOMON: My boy, you don't know the psychology! If it wouldn't break there is no more possibilities. For instance, you take—*crosses to table*—this table . . . Listen! *He bangs the table.* You can't move it. A man sits down to such a table he knows not only he's married, he's got to stay married—there is no more possibilities.

Victor laughs.

You're laughing, I'm telling you the factual situation. What is the key word today? Disposable. The more you can throw it away the more it's beautiful. The car, the furniture, the wife, the children—everything has to be disposable. Because you see the main thing today is—shopping. Years ago a person, he was unhappy, didn't know what to do with himself—he'd go to church, start a revolution—*something*. Today you're unhappy? Can't figure it out? What is the salvation? Go shopping.

VICTOR, *laughing:* You're terrific, I have to give you credit.

SOLOMON: I'm telling you the truth! If they would close the stores for six months in this country there would be from coast to coast a regular massacre. With this kind of furniture the shopping is over, it's finished, there's no more possibilities, you *got* it, you see? So you got a problem here.

VICTOR, *laughing:* Solomon, you are one of the greatest. But I'm way ahead of you, it's not going to work.

SOLOMON, *offended:* What "work"? I don't know how much time I got. What is so terrible if I say that? The trouble is, you're such a young fella you don't understand these things—

VICTOR: I understand very well, I know what you're up against. I'm not so young.

SOLOMON, *scoffing:* What are you, forty? Forty-five?

VICTOR: I'm going to be fifty.

SOLOMON: Fifty! You're a baby boy!

VICTOR: Some baby.

SOLOMON: My God, if I was fifty . . . ! I got married I was seventy-five.

VICTOR: Go on.

SOLOMON: What are you talking? She's still living by Eighth Avenue over there. See, that's why I like to stay liquid, because I don't want her to get her hands on this. . . . Birds she loves. She's living there with maybe a hundred birds. She gives you a plate of soup it's got feathers. I didn't work all my life for them birds.

VICTOR: I appreciate your problems, Mr. Solomon, but I don't have to pay for them. *He stands.* I've got no more time.

SOLOMON, *holding up a restraining hand—desperately:* I'm going to buy it! *He has shocked himself, and glances around at the towering masses of furniture.* I mean I'll . . . *He moves, looking at the stuff.* I'll have to live, that's all, I'll make up my mind! I'll buy it.

VICTOR—*he is affected as Solomon's fear comes through to him:* We're talking about everything now.

SOLOMON, *angrily:* Everything, everything! *Going to his portfolio:* I'll figure it up, I'll give you a very nice price, and you'll be a happy man.

VICTOR, *sitting again:* That I doubt.

Solomon takes a hard-boiled egg out of the portfolio.

What's this now, lunch?

SOLOMON: You give me such an argument, I'm hungry! I'm not supposed to get too hungry.

VICTOR: Brother!

SOLOMON—*cracks the shell on his diamond ring:* You want me to starve to death? I'm going to be very quick here.

VICTOR: Boy—I picked a number!

SOLOMON: There wouldn't be a little salt, I suppose.

VICTOR: I'm not going running for salt now!

SOLOMON: Please, don't be blue. I'm going to knock you off your feet with the price, you'll see. *He swallows the egg. He now faces the furniture, and, half to himself, pad and pencil poised:* I'm going to go here like an IBM. *He starts estimating on his pad.*

VICTOR: That's all right, take it easy. As long as you're serious.

SOLOMON: Thank you. *He touches the hated buffet:* Ay, yi, yi. All right, well . . . *He jots down a figure. He goes to the next piece, jots down another figure. He goes to another piece, jots down a figure.*

VICTOR, *after a moment:* You really got married at seventy-five?

SOLOMON: What's so terrible?

VICTOR: No, I think it's terrific. But what was the point?

SOLOMON: What's the point at twenty-five? You can't die twenty-six?

VICTOR, *laughing softly:* I guess so, ya.

SOLOMON: It's the same like secondhand furniture, you see; the whole thing is a viewpoint. It's a mental world. *He jots down another figure for another piece.* Seventy-five I got married, fifty-one, and twenty-two.

VICTOR: You're kidding.

SOLOMON: I wish! *He works, jotting his estimate of each piece on the pad, opening drawers, touching everything. Peering into a dark recess, he takes out a pencil flashlight, switches it on, and begins to probe with the beam.*

VICTOR—*he has gradually turned to watch Solomon, who goes on working:* Cut the kidding now—how old are you?

SOLOMON, *sliding out a drawer:* I'm eighty-nine. It's such an accomplishment?

VICTOR: You're a hell of a guy.

SOLOMON, *smiling with the encouragement and turning to Victor:* You know, it's a funny thing. It's so long since I took on such a load like this—you forget what kind of life it puts into you. To take out a pencil again . . . it's a regular injection. Frankly, my telephone you could use for a ladle, it wouldn't interfere with nothing. I want to thank you. *He points at Victor.* I'm going to take good care of you, I mean it. I can open that?

VICTOR: Sure, anything.

SOLOMON, *going to an armoire:* Some of them had a mirror . . . *He opens the armoire, and a rolled-up fur rug falls out. It is about three by five.* What's this?

VICTOR: God knows. I guess it's a rug.

SOLOMON, *holding it up:* No-no—that's a lap robe. Like for a car.

VICTOR: Say, that's right, ya. When they went driving. God, I haven't seen that in—

SOLOMON: You had a chauffeur?

VICTOR: Ya, we had a chauffeur.

> *Their eyes meet. Solomon looks at him as though Victor were coming into focus. Victor turns away. Now Solomon turns back to the armoire.*

SOLOMON: Look at that! *He takes down an opera hat from the shelf within.* My God! *He puts it on, looks into the interior mirror.* What a world! *He turns to Victor:* He must've been some sporty guy!

VICTOR, *smiling:* You look pretty good!

SOLOMON: And from all this he could go so broke?

VICTOR: Why not? Sure. Took five weeks. Less.

SOLOMON: You don't say. And he couldn't make a comeback?

VICTOR: Well some men don't bounce, you know.

SOLOMON—*grunts:* Hmm! So what did he do?

VICTOR: Nothing. Just sat here. Listened to the radio.

SOLOMON: But what did he do? What—?

VICTOR: Well, now and then he was making change at the Automat. Toward the end he was delivering telegrams.

SOLOMON, *with grief and wonder:* You don't say. And how much he had?

VICTOR: Oh . . . couple of million, I guess.

SOLOMON: My God. What was the matter with him?

VICTOR: Well, my mother died around the same time. I guess that didn't help. Some men just don't bounce, that's all.

SOLOMON: Listen, I can tell you bounces. I went busted 1932; then 1923 they also knocked me out; the panic of 1904, 1898 . . . But to lay down like *that* . . .

VICTOR: Well, you're different. He believed in it.

SOLOMON: What he believed?

VICTOR: The system, the whole thing. He thought it was his fault, I guess. You—you come in with your song and dance, it's all a gag. You're a hundred and fifty years old, you tell your jokes, people fall in love with you, and you walk away with their furniture.

SOLOMON: That's not nice.

VICTOR: Don't shame me, will ya?—What do you say? You don't need to look any more, you know what I've got here.

Solomon is clearly at the end of his delaying resources. He looks about slowly; the furniture seems to loom over him like a threat or a promise. His eyes climb up to the edges of the ceiling, his hands grasping one another.

What are you afraid of? It'll keep you busy.

Solomon looks at him, wanting even more reassurance.

SOLOMON: You don't think it's foolish?

VICTOR: Who knows what's foolish? You enjoy it—

SOLOMON: Listen, I love it—

VICTOR:—so take it. You plan too much, you end up with nothing.

SOLOMON, *intimately:* I would like to tell you something. The last few months, I don't know what it is—she comes to me. You see, I had a daughter, she should rest in peace, she took her own life, a suicide. . . .

VICTOR: When was this?

SOLOMON: It was . . . 1916—the latter part. But very beautiful, a lovely face, with large eyes—she was pure like the morning. And lately, I don't know what it is—I see her clear like I see you. And every night practically, I lay down to go to sleep, so she sits there. And you can't help it, you ask yourself—what happened? What *happened*? Maybe I could have said something to her . . . maybe I *did* say something . . . it's all . . . *He looks at the furniture.* It's not that I'll die, you can't be afraid of that. But . . . I'll tell you the truth—a minute ago I mentioned I had three wives . . . *Slight pause. His fear rises.* Just this minute I realize I had four. Isn't that terrible? The first time was nineteen, in Lithuania. See, that's what I mean—it's impossible to know what is important. Here I'm sitting with you . . . and . . . and . . . *He looks around at the furniture.* What for? Not that I don't want it, I want it, but . . . You see, all my life I was a terrible fighter—you could never take nothing from me; I pushed, I pulled, I struggled in six different countries, I nearly got killed a couple times, and it's . . . It's like now I'm sitting here talking to you and I tell you it's a dream, it's a dream! You see, you can't imagine it because—

VICTOR: I know what you're talking about. But it's not a dream —it's that you've got to make decisions before you know what's involved, but you're stuck with the results anyway. Like I was very good in science—I loved it. But I had to drop out to feed the old man. And I figured I'd go on the Force temporarily, just to get us through the Depression, then go back to school. But the war came, we had the kid, and you turn around and you've racked up fifteen years on the pension. And what you started out to do is a million miles away. Not that I regret it all—we brought up a terrific boy, for one thing; nobody's ever going to take that guy. But it's like you were saying—it's impossible to know what's important. We always agreed, we stay out of the rat race and live our own life. That was important. But you shovel the crap out the window, it comes back in under the door—it all ends up she wants, she wants. And I can't really blame her— there's just no respect for anything but money.

SOLOMON: What've you got against money?

VICTOR: Nothing, I just didn't want to lay down my life for it. But I think I laid it down another way, and I'm not even sure any more what I was trying to accomplish. I look back now, and all I can see is a long, brainless walk in the street. I guess it's the old story; do anything, but just be sure you win. Like my brother; years ago I was living up here with the old man, and he used to contribute five dollars a month. A *month*! And a successful surgeon. But the few times he'd come around, the expression on the old man's face—you'd think God walked in. The respect, you know what I mean? The respect! And why not? Why not?

SOLOMON: Well, sure, he had the power.

VICTOR: Now you said it—if you got that you got it all. You're even lovable! *He laughs.* Well, what do you say? Give me the price.

SOLOMON—*slight pause:* I'll give you eleven hundred dollars.

VICTOR—*slight pause:* For everything?

SOLOMON, *in a breathless way:* Everything.

Slight pause. Victor looks around at the furniture.

I want it so I'm giving you a good price. Believe me, you will never do better. I want it; I made up my mind.

Victor continues staring at the stuff. Solomon takes out a common envelope and removes a wad of bills.

Here . . . I'll pay you now. *He readies a bill to start counting it out.*

VICTOR: It's that I have to split it, see—

SOLOMON: All right . . . so I'll make out a receipt for you and I'll put down six hundred dollars.

VICTOR: No-no . . . *He gets up and moves at random, looking at the furniture.*

SOLOMON: Why not? He took from you so take from him. If you want, I'll put down four hundred.

VICTOR: No, I don't want to do that. *Slight pause.* I'll call you tomorrow.

SOLOMON, *smiling:* All right; with God's help if I'm there tomorrow I'll answer the phone. If I wouldn't be . . . *Slight pause.* Then I wouldn't be.

VICTOR, *annoyed, but wanting to believe:* Don't start that again, will you?

SOLOMON: Look, you convinced me, so I want it. So what should I do?

VICTOR: *I* convinced *you?*

SOLOMON, *very distressed:* Absolutely you convinced me. You saw it—the minute I looked at it I was going to walk out!

VICTOR, *cutting him off, angered at his own indecision:* Ah, the hell with it. *He holds out his hand.* Give it to me.

SOLOMON, *wanting Victor's good will:* Please, don't be blue.

VICTOR: Oh, it all stinks. *Jabbing forth his hand:* Come on.

SOLOMON, *with a bill raised over Victor's hand—protesting:* What stinks? You should be happy. Now you can buy her a nice coat, take her to Florida, maybe—

VICTOR, *nodding ironically:* Right, right! We'll all be happy now. Give it to me.

Solomon shakes his head and counts bills into his hand. Victor turns his head and looks at the piled walls of furniture.

SOLOMON: There's one hundred; two hundred; three hundred; four hundred . . . Take my advice, buy her a nice fur coat your troubles'll be over—

VICTOR: I know all about it. Come on.

SOLOMON: So you got there four, so I'm giving you . . . five, six, seven . . . I mean it's already in the Bible, the rat race. The minute she laid her hand on the apple, that's it.

VICTOR: I never read the Bible. Come on.

SOLOMON: If you'll read it you'll see—there's always a rat race, you can't stay out of it. So you got there seven, so now I'm giving you . . .

A man appears in the doorway. In his mid-fifties, well-barbered; hatless, in a camel's-hair coat, very healthy complexion. A look of sharp intelligence on his face.

Victor, seeing past Solomon, starts slightly with shock, withdrawing his hand from the next bill which Solomon is about to lay in it.

VICTOR, *suddenly flushed, his voice oddly high and boyish:* Walter!

WALTER—*enters the room, coming to Victor with extended hand and with a reserve of warmth but a stiff smile:* How are you, kid?

Solomon has moved out of their line of sight.

VICTOR—*shifts the money to his left hand as he shakes:* God, I never expected you.

WALTER, *of the money—half-humorously:* Sorry I'm late. What are you doing?

VICTOR, *fighting a treason to himself, thus taking on a strained humorous air:* I . . . I just sold it.

WALTER: Good! How much?

VICTOR, *as though absolutely certain now he has been had:* Ah . . . eleven hundred.

WALTER, *in a dead voice shorn of comment:* Oh. Well, good. *He turns rather deliberately—but not overly so—to Solomon:* For everything?

SOLOMON—*comes to Walter, his hand extended; with an ener-*

gized voice that braves everything: I'm very happy to meet you, Doctor! My name is Gregory Solomon.

WALTER—*the look on his face is rather amused, but his reserve has possibilities of accusation:* How do you do?

He shakes Solomon's hand, as Victor raises his hand to smooth down his hair, a look of near-alarm for himself on his face.

CURTAIN

ACT TWO

*The action is continuous. As the curtain rises Walter is just re-
leasing Solomon's hand and turning about to face Victor. His
posture is reserved, stiffened by traditional control over a nearly
fierce curiosity. His grin is disciplined and rather hard, but his
eyes are warm and combative.*

WALTER: How's Esther?

VICTOR: Fine. Should be here any minute.

WALTER: Here? Good! And what's Richard doing?

VICTOR: He's at M.I.T.

WALTER: No kidding! M.I.T.!

VICTOR, *nodding:* They gave him a full scholarship.

WALTER, *dispelling his surprise:* What do you know. *With a
wider smile, and embarrassed warmth:* You're proud.

VICTOR: I guess so. They put him in the Honors Program.

WALTER: Really. That's wonderful.—You don't mind my coming, do you?

VICTOR: No! I called you a couple of times.

WALTER: Yes, my nurse told me. What's Richard interested in?

VICTOR: Science. So far, anyway. *With security:* How're yours?

WALTER—*moving, he breaks the confrontation:* I suppose Jean
turned out best—but I don't think you ever saw her.

VICTOR: I never did, no.

WALTER: The *Times* gave her quite a spread last fall. Pretty fair
designer.

VICTOR: Oh? That's great. And the boys? They in school?

WALTER: They often are. *Abruptly laughs, refusing his own embarrassment:* I hardly see them, Vic. With all the unsolved
mysteries in the world they're investigating the guitar. But
what the hell . . . I've given up worrying about them. *He
walks past Solomon, glancing at the furniture:* I'd forgotten
how much he had up here. There's your radio!

VICTOR, *smiling with him:* I know, I saw it.

WALTER, *looking down at the radio, then upward to the ceiling
through which the battery once exploded. Both laugh. Then he
glances with open feeling at Victor:* Long time.

VICTOR, *fending off the common emotion:* Yes. How's Dorothy?

WALTER, *cryptically:* She's all right, I guess. *He moves, glancing at the things, but again with suddenness turns back.* Looking forward to seeing Esther again. She still writing poetry?

VICTOR: No, not for years now.

SOLOMON: He's got a very nice wife. We met.

WALTER, *surprised; as though at something intrusive:* Oh? *He turns back to the furniture.* Well. Same old junk, isn't it?

VICTOR, *downing a greater protest:* I wouldn't say that. Some of it isn't bad.

SOLOMON: One or two very nice things, Doctor. We came to a very nice agreement.

VICTOR, *with an implied rebuke:* I never thought you'd show up; I guess we'd better start all over again—

WALTER: Oh, no-no, I don't want to foul up your deal.

SOLOMON: Excuse me, Doctor—better you should take what you want now than we'll argue later. What did you want?

WALTER, *surprised, turning to Victor:* Oh, I didn't want anything. I came by to say hello, that's all.

VICTOR: I see. *Fending off Walter's apparent gesture with an over-quick movement toward the oar:* I found your oar, if you want it.

WALTER: Oar?

Victor draws it out from behind furniture. A curved-blade sweep.

Hah! *He receives the oar, looks up its length, and laughs, hefting it.* I must have been out of my mind!

SOLOMON: Excuse me, Doctor; if you want the oar—

WALTER, *standing the oar before Solomon, whom he leaves holding on to it:* Don't get excited, I don't want it.

SOLOMON: No. I was going to say—a personal thing like this I have no objection.

WALTER, *half-laughing:* That's very generous of you.

VICTOR, *apologizing for Solomon:* I threw in everything—I never thought you'd get here.

WALTER, *with a strained over-agreeableness:* Sure, that's all right. What are you taking?

VICTOR: Nothing, really. Esther might want a lamp or something like that.

SOLOMON: He's not interested, you see; he's a modern person, what are you going to do?

WALTER: You're not taking the harp?

VICTOR, *with a certain guilt:* Well, nobody plays . . . You take it, if you like.

SOLOMON: You'll excuse me, Doctor—the harp, please, that's another story . . .

WALTER—*laughs—archly amused and put out:* You don't mind if I make a suggestion, do you?

SOLOMON: Doctor, please, don't be offended, I only—

WALTER: Well, why do you interrupt? Relax, we're only talking. We haven't seen each other for a long time.

SOLOMON: Couldn't be better; I'm very sorry. *He sits, nervously pulling his cheek.*

WALTER, *touching the harp:* Kind of a pity—this was Grandpa's wedding present, you know.

VICTOR, *looking with surprise at the harp:* Say—that's right!

WALTER, *to Solomon:* What are you giving him for this?

SOLOMON: I didn't itemize—one price for everything. Maybe three hundred dollars. That sounding board is cracked, you know.

VICTOR, *to Walter:* You want it?

SOLOMON: Please, Victor, I hope you're not going to take that away from me. *To Walter:* Look, Doctor, I'm not trying to fool you. The harp is the heart and soul of the deal. I realize it was your mother's harp, but like I tried to tell—*to Victor*—you before—*to Walter*—with used furniture you cannot be emotional.

WALTER: I guess it doesn't matter. *To Victor:* Actually, I was wondering if he kept any of Mother's evening gowns, did he?

VICTOR: I haven't really gone through it all—

SOLOMON, *raising a finger, eagerly:* Wait, wait, I think I can help you. *He goes to an armoire he had earlier looked into, and opens it.*

WALTER, *moving toward the armoire:* She had some spectacular—

SOLOMON, *drawing out the bottom of a gown elaborately embroidered in gold:* Is this what you mean?

WALTER: Yes, that's the stuff!

Solomon blows dust off and hands him the bottom of the gown.

Isn't that beautiful! Say, I think she wore this at my wedding! *He takes it out of the closet, holds it up.* Sure! You remember this?

VICTOR: What do you want with it?

WALTER, *drawing out another gown off the rack:* Look at this one! Isn't that something? I thought Jeannie might make something new out of the material, I'd like her to wear something of Mother's.

VICTOR—*a new, surprising idea:* Oh! Fine, that's a nice idea.

SOLOMON: Take, take—they're beautiful.

WALTER, *suddenly glancing about as he lays the gowns across a chair:* What happened to the piano?

VICTOR: Oh, we sold that while I was still in school. We lived on it for a long time.

WALTER, *very interestedly:* I never knew that.

VICTOR: Sure. And the silver.

WALTER: Of course! Stupid of me not to remember that. *He half-sits against the back of a couch. His interest is avid, and his energy immense.* I suppose you know—you've gotten to look a great deal like Dad.

VICTOR: *I* do?

WALTER: It's very striking. And your voice is very much like his.

VICTOR: I know. It has that sound to me, sometimes.

SOLOMON: So, gentlemen . . . *He moves the money in his hand.*

VICTOR, *indicating Solomon:* Maybe we'd better settle this now.

WALTER: Yes, go ahead! *He walks off, looking at the furniture.*

SOLOMON, *indicating the money Victor holds:* You got there seven—

WALTER, *oblivious of Solomon; unable, so to speak, to settle for the status quo:* Wonderful to see you looking so well.

VICTOR—*the new interruption seems odd; observing more than speaking:* You do too, you look great.

WALTER: I ski a lot; and I ride nearly every morning. . . . You know, I started to call you a dozen times this year—*He breaks off. Indicating Solomon:* Finish up, I'll talk to you later.

SOLOMON: So now I'm going to give you—*A bill is poised over Victor's hand.*

VICTOR, *to Walter:* That price all right with you?

WALTER: Oh, I don't want to interfere. It's just that I dealt with these fellows when I split up Dorothy's and my stuff last year, and I found—

VICTOR, *from an earlier impression:* You're not divorced, are you?

WALTER, *with a nervous shot of laughter:* Yes!

Esther enters on his line; she is carrying a suit in a plastic wrapper.

ESTHER, *surprised:* Walter! For heaven's sake!

WALTER, *eagerly jumping up, coming to her, shaking her hand:* How are you, Esther!

ESTHER, *between her disapproval and fascinated surprise:* What are *you* doing here?

WALTER: You've hardly changed!

ESTHER, *with a charged laugh, conflicted with herself:* Oh, go on now! *She hangs the suit on a chest handle.*

WALTER, *to Victor:* You son of a gun, she looks twenty-five!

VICTOR, *watching for Esther's reaction:* I know!

ESTHER, *flattered, and offended, too:* Oh stop it, Walter! *She sits.*

WALTER: But you do, honestly; you look marvelous.

SOLOMON: It's that suit, you see? What did I tell you, it's a very beautiful suit.

Victor laughs a little as Esther looks conflicted by Solomon's compliment.

ESTHER, *with mock-affront—to Victor:* What are you laughing at? It is. *She is about to laugh.*

VICTOR: You looked so surprised, that's all.

ESTHER: Well, I'm not used to walking into all these compliments! *She bursts out laughing.*

WALTER, *suddenly recalling—eagerly:* Say! I'm sorry I didn't know I'd be seeing you when I left the house this morning— I'd have brought you some lovely Indian bracelets. I got a whole boxful from Bombay.

ESTHER, *still not focused on Walter, sizing him up:* How do you come to—?

WALTER: I operated on this big textile guy and he keeps sending me things. He sent me this coat, in fact.

ESTHER: I was noticing it. That's gorgeous material.

WALTER: Isn't it? Two gallstones.

ESTHER, *her impression lingering for the instant:* How's Dorothy?—Did I hear you saying you were—?

WALTER, *very seriously:* We're divorced, ya. Last winter.

ESTHER: I'm sorry to hear that.

WALTER: It was coming a long time. We're both much better off—we're almost friendly now. *He laughs.*

ESTHER: Oh, stop that, you dog.

WALTER, *with naive excitement:* It's true!

ESTHER: Look, I'm for the woman, so don't hand me that. *To Victor—seeing the money in his hand:* Have you settled everything?

VICTOR: Just about, I guess.

WALTER: I was just telling Victor—*to Victor:* when we split things up I—*to Solomon:* you ever hear of Spitzer and Fox?

SOLOMON: Thirty years I know Spitzer and Fox. Bert Fox worked for me maybe ten, twelve years.

WALTER: They did my appraisal.

SOLOMON: They're good boys. Spitzer is not as good as Fox, but between the two you're in good hands.

WALTER: Yes. That's why I—

SOLOMON: Spitzer is vice president of the Appraisers' Association.

WALTER: I see. The point I'm making—

SOLOMON: I used to be president.

WALTER: Really.

SOLOMON: Oh yes. I made it all ethical.

WALTER, *trying to keep a straight face—and Victor as well:* Did you?

Victor suddenly bursts out laughing, which sets off Walter and Esther, and a warmth springs up among them.

SOLOMON, *smiling, but insistent:* What's so funny? Listen, before me was a jungle—you wouldn't laugh so much. I put in all the rates, what we charge, you know—I made it a profession, like doctors, lawyers—used to be it was a regular snakepit. But today, you got nothing to worry—all the members are hundred per cent ethical.

WALTER: Well, that was a good deed, Mr. Solomon—but I think you can do a little better on this furniture.

ESTHER, *to Victor, who has money in his hand:* How much has
   he offered?

VICTOR, *embarrassed, but braving it quite well:* Eleven hundred.

ESTHER, *distressed; with a transcendent protest:* Oh, I think that's
   . . . isn't that very low? *She looks to Walter's confirmation.*

WALTER, *familiarly:* Come on, Solomon. He's been risking his
   life for you every day; be generous—

SOLOMON, *to Esther:* That's a real brother! Wonderful. *To Walter:* But you can call anybody you like—Spitzer and Fox, Joe
   Brody, Paul Cavallo, Morris White—I know them all and I
   know what they'll tell you.

VICTOR, *striving to retain some assurance; to Esther:* See, the
   point he was making about it—

SOLOMON, *to Esther, raising his finger:* Listen to him because
   he—

VICTOR, *to Solomon:* Hold it one second, will you? *To Esther
   and Walter:* Not that I'm saying it's true, but he claims a lot
   of it is too big to get into the new apartments.

ESTHER, *half-laughing:* You believe that?

WALTER: I don't know, Esther, Spitzer and Fox said the same
   thing.

ESTHER: Walter, the city is full of big, old apartments!

SOLOMON: Darling, why don't you leave it to the boys?

ESTHER, *suppressing an outburst:* I wish you wouldn't order me
   around, Mr. Solomon! *To Walter, protesting:* Those two bu-
   reaus alone are worth a couple of hundred dollars!

WALTER, *delicately:* Maybe I oughtn't interfere—

ESTHER: Why? *Of Solomon:* Don't let him bulldoze you—

SOLOMON: My dear girl, you're talking without a basis—

ESTHER, *slashing:* I don't like this kind of dealing, Mr. Solomon! I just don't like it! *She is near tears. A pause. She turns
   back to Walter:* This money is very important to us, Walter.

WALTER, *chastised:* Yes. I . . . I'm sorry, Esther. *He looks about.*
   Well . . . if it was mine—

ESTHER: Why? It's yours as much as Victor's.

WALTER: Oh no, dear—I wouldn't take anything from this.

   Pause.

VICTOR: No, Walter, you get half.

WALTER: I wouldn't think of it, kid. I came by to say hello, that's all.

Pause.

ESTHER—*she is very moved:* That's terrific, Walter. It's . . . Really, I . . .

VICTOR: Well, we'll talk about it.

WALTER: No-no, Vic, you've earned it. It's yours.

VICTOR, *rejecting the implication:* Why have I earned it? You take your share.

WALTER: Why don't we discuss it later? *To Solomon:* In my opinion—

SOLOMON, *to Victor:* So now you don't even have to split. *To Victor and Walter:* You're lucky they're tearing the building down—you got together, finally.

WALTER: I would have said a minimum of three thousand dollars.

ESTHER: That's exactly what I had in mind! *To Solomon:* I was going to say thirty-five hundred dollars.

WALTER, *to Victor; tactfully:* In that neighborhood.

Silence. Solomon sits there holding back comment, not looking at Victor, blinking with protest. Victor thinks for a moment; then turns to Solomon, and there is a wide discouragement in his voice.

VICTOR: Well? What do you say?

SOLOMON, *spreading out his hands helplessly, outraged:* What can I say? It's ridiculous. Why does he give you three thousand? What's the matter with five thousand, ten thousand?

WALTER, *to Victor, without criticism:* You should've gotten a couple of other estimates, you see, that's always the—

VICTOR: I've been calling you all week for just that reason, Walter, and you never came to the phone.

WALTER, *blushing:* Why would that stop you from—?

VICTOR: I didn't think I had the right to do it alone—the nurse gave you my messages, didn't she?

WALTER: I've been terribly tied up—and I had no intention of taking anything for myself, so I assumed—

VICTOR: But how was I supposed to know that?

WALTER, *with open self-reproach:* Yes. Well, I . . . I beg your pardon. *He decides to stop there.*

SOLOMON: Excuse me, Doctor, but I can't understand you; first it's a lot of junk—

ESTHER: Nobody called it a lot of junk!

SOLOMON: He called it a lot of junk, Esther, when he walked in here.

Esther turns to Walter, puzzled and angry.

WALTER, *reacting to her look; to Solomon:* Now just a minute—

SOLOMON: No, please. *Indicating Victor:* This is a factual man, so let's be factual.

ESTHER: Well, that's an awfully strange thing to say, Walter.

WALTER, *intimately:* I didn't mean it in that sense, Esther—

SOLOMON: Doctor, please. You said junk.

WALTER, *sharply—and there is an over-meaning of much greater anger in his tone:* I didn't mean it in that sense, Mr. Solomon! *He controls himself—and, half to Esther:* When you've been brought up with things, you tend to be sick of them. . . . *To Esther:* That's all I meant.

SOLOMON: My dear man, if it was Louis Seize, Biedermeier, something like that, you wouldn't get sick.

WALTER, *pointing to a piece, and weakened by knowing he is exaggerating:* Well, there happens to be a piece right over there in Biedermeier style!

SOLOMON: Biedermeier "style"! *He picks up his hat.* I got a hat it's in Borsalino style but it's not a Borsalino. *To Victor:* I mean he don't have to charge me to make an impression.

WALTER, *striving for an air of amusement:* Now what's that supposed to mean?

VICTOR, *with a refusal to dump Solomon:* Well, what basis *do* you go on, Walter?

WALTER, *reddening but smiling:* I don't know . . . it's a feeling, that's all.

ESTHER—*there is ridicule:* Well, on what basis do you take eleven hundred, dear?

VICTOR, *angered; his manly leadership is suddenly in front:* I simply felt it was probably more or less right!

ESTHER, *as a refrain:* Oh God, here we go again. All right, throw it away—

SOLOMON, *indicating Victor:* Please, Esther, he's not throwing nothing away. This man is no fool! *To Walter as well:* Excuse me, but this is not right to do to him!

WALTER, *bridling, but retaining his smile:* You going to teach me what's right now?

ESTHER, *to Victor, expanding Walter's protest:* Really! I *mean.*

VICTOR—*obeying her protest for want of a certainty of his own, he touches Solomon's shoulder:* Mr. Solomon . . . why don't you sit down in the bedroom for a few minutes and let us talk?

SOLOMON: Certainly, whatever you say. *He gets up.* Only please, you made a very nice deal, you got no right to be ashamed. . . . *To Esther:* Excuse me, I don't want to be personal.

ESTHER—*laughs angrily:* He's fantastic!

VICTOR, *trying to get him moving again:* Whyn't you go inside?

SOLOMON: I'm going; I only want you to understand, Victor, that if it was a different kind of man—*turning to Esther:* I would say to you that he's got the money in his hand, so the deal is concluded.

WALTER: He can't conclude any deal without me, Solomon, I'm half owner here.

SOLOMON, *to Victor:* You see? What did I ask you the first thing I walked in here? "Who is the owner?"

WALTER: Why do you confuse everything? I'm not making any claim, I merely—

SOLOMON: Then how do you come to interfere? He's got the money; I know the law!

WALTER, *angering:* Now you stop being foolish! Just stop it! I've got the best lawyers in New York, so go inside and sit down.

VICTOR, *as he turns back to escort Solomon:* Take it easy, Walter, come on, cut it out.

ESTHER, *striving to keep a light, amused tone:* Why? He's perfectly right.

VICTOR, *with a hard glance at her, moving upstage with Solomon:* Here, you better hold onto this money.

SOLOMON: No, that's yours; you hold . . .

He sways. Victor grasps his arm. Walter gets up.

WALTER: You all right?

SOLOMON—*dizzy, he grasps his head:* Yes, yes, I'm . . .

WALTER, *coming to him:* Let me look at you. *He takes Solomon's wrists, looks into his face.*

SOLOMON: I'm only a little tired, I didn't take my nap today.

WALTER: Come in here, lie down for a moment. *He starts Solomon toward the bedroom.*

SOLOMON: Don't worry about me, I'm . . . *He halts and points back at his portfolio, leaning on a chest.* Please, Doctor, if you wouldn't mind—I got a Hershey's in there.

Walter hesitates to do his errand.

Helps me.

Walter unwillingly goes to the portfolio and reaches into it.

I'm a very healthy person, but a nap, you see, I have to have a . . .

Walter takes out an orange.

Not the orange—on the bottom is a Hershey's.

Walter takes out a Hershey bar.

That's a boy.

WALTER—*returns to him and helps him to the bedroom:* All right, come on . . . easy does it . . .

SOLOMON, *as he goes into the bedroom:* I'm all right, don't worry. You're very nice people.

Solomon and Walter exit into the bedroom. Victor glances at the money in his hand, then puts it on a table, setting the foil on it.

ESTHER: Why are you being so apologetic?

VICTOR: About what?

ESTHER: That old man. Was that his first offer?

VICTOR: Why do you believe Walter? He was obviously pulling a number out of a hat.

ESTHER: Well, I agree with him. Did you try to get him to go higher?

VICTOR: I don't know how to bargain and I'm not going to start now.

ESTHER: I wish you wouldn't be above everything, Victor, we're not twenty years old. We need this money.

He is silent.

You hear me?

VICTOR: I've made a deal, and that's it. You know, you take a tone sometimes—like I'm some kind of an incompetent.

ESTHER—*gets up, moves restlessly:* Well anyway, you'll get the whole amount.—God, he's certainly changed. It's amazing.

VICTOR, *without assent:* Seems so, ya.

ESTHER, *wanting him to join her:* He's so human! And he laughs!

VICTOR: I've seen him laugh.

ESTHER, *with a grin of trepidation:* Am I hearing something or is that my imagination?

VICTOR: I want to think about it.

ESTHER, *quietly:* You're not taking his share?

VICTOR: I said I would like to think . . .

Assuming he will refuse Walter's share, she really doesn't know what to do or where to move, so she goes for her purse with a quick stride.

VICTOR, *getting up:* Where you going?

ESTHER, *turning back on him:* I want to know. Are you or aren't you taking his share?

VICTOR: Esther, I've been calling him all week; doesn't even bother to come to the phone, walks in here and smiles and I'm supposed to fall into his arms? I can't behave as though nothing ever happened, and you're not going to either! Now just take it easy, we're not dying of hunger.

ESTHER: I don't understand what you think you're upholding!

VICTOR, *outraged:* Where have you been?!

ESTHER: But he's doing exactly what you thought he should do! What do you *want*?

VICTOR: Certain things have happened, haven't they? I can't turn around this fast, kid. He's only been here ten minutes, I've got twenty-eight years to shake off my back. . . . Now sit down, I want you here. *He sits.*

She remains standing, uncertain of what to do.

Please. You can wait a few minutes for your drink.

ESTHER, *in despair:* Vic, it's all blowing away.

VICTOR, *to diminish the entire prize:* Half of eleven hundred dollars is five-fifty, dear.

ESTHER: I'm not talking about money.

Voices are heard from the bedroom.

He's obviously making a gesture, why can't you open yourself a little? *She lays her head back.* My mother was right—I can never believe anything I see. But I'm going to. That's all I'm going to do. What I see.

A chair scrapes in the bedroom.

VICTOR: Wipe your cheek, will you?

Walter enters from the bedroom.

How is he?

WALTER: I think he'll be all right. *Warmly:* God, what a pirate! *He sits.* He's eighty-nine!

ESTHER: I don't believe it!

VICTOR: He is. He showed me his—

WALTER, *laughing:* Oh, he show you that too?

VICTOR, *smiling:* Ya, the British Navy.

ESTHER: *He* was in the British Navy?

VICTOR, *building on Walter's support:* He's got a discharge. He's not altogether phony.

WALTER: I wouldn't go that far. A guy that age, though, still driving like that . . . *As though admitting Victor was not foolish:* There *is* something wonderful about it.

VICTOR, *understating: I* think so.

ESTHER: What do you think we ought to do, Walter?

WALTER—*slight pause. He is trying to modify what he believes is his overpowering force so as not to appear to be taking over. He is faintly smiling toward Victor:* There is a way to get a good deal more out of it. I suppose you know that, though.

VICTOR: Look, I'm not married to this guy. If you want to call another dealer we can compare.

WALTER: You don't have to do that; he's a registered appraiser.— You see, instead of selling it, you could make it a charitable contribution.

VICTOR: I don't understand.

WALTER: It's perfectly simple. He puts a value on it—let's say twenty-five thousand dollars, and—

ESTHER, *fascinated with a laugh:* Are you kidding?

WALTER: It's done all the time. It's a dream world but it's legal. He estimates its highest retail value, which could be put at some such figure. Then I donate it to the Salvation Army. I'd have to take ownership, you see, because my tax rate is much higher than yours so it would make more sense if I took the deduction. I pay around fifty per cent tax, so if I make a twenty-five-thousand-dollar contribution I'd be saving around twelve thousand in taxes. Which we could split however you wanted to. Let's say we split it in half, I'd give you six thousand dollars. *A pause.* It's really the only sensible way to do it, Vic.

ESTHER—*glances at Victor, but he remains silent:* Would it be costing you anything?

WALTER: On the contrary—it's found money to me. *To Victor:* I mentioned it to him just now.

VICTOR, *as though this had been the question:* What'd he say?

WALTER: It's up to you. We'd pay him an appraisal fee—fifty, sixty bucks.

VICTOR: Is he willing to do that?

WALTER: Well, of course he'd rather buy it outright, but what the hell—

ESTHER: Well, that's not his decision, is it?

VICTOR: No . . . it's just that I feel I did come to an agreement with him and I—

WALTER: Personally, I wouldn't let that bother me. He'd be making fifty bucks for filling out a piece of paper.

ESTHER: That's not bad for an afternoon.

Pause.

VICTOR: I'd like to think about it.

ESTHER: There's not much time, though, if you want to deal with *him*.

VICTOR, *cornered:* I'd like a few minutes, that's all.

WALTER, *to Esther:* Sure . . . let him think it over. *To Victor:* It's perfectly legal, if that's what's bothering you. I almost did it with my stuff but I finally decided to keep it. *He laughs.*

In fact, my own apartment is so loaded up it doesn't look too different from this.

ESTHER: Well, maybe you'll get married again.

WALTER: I doubt that very much, Esther.—I often feel I never should have.

ESTHER, *scoffing:* Why!

WALTER: Seriously. I'm in a strange business, you know. There's too much to learn and far too little time to learn it. And there's a price you have to pay for that. I tried awfully hard to kid myself but there's simply no time for people. Not the way a woman expects, if she's any kind of woman. *He laughs.* But I'm doing pretty well alone!

VICTOR: How would I list an amount like that on my income tax?

WALTER: Well . . . call it a gift.

Victor is silent, obviously in conflict. Walter sees the emotion.

Not that it is, but you could list it as such. It's allowed.

VICTOR: I see. I was just curious how it—

WALTER: Just enter it as a gift. There's no problem.

With the first sting of a vague resentment, Walter turns his eyes away. Esther raises her eyebrows, staring at the floor. Walter lifts the foil off the table—clearly changing the subject.

You still fence?

VICTOR, *almost gratefully pursuing this diversion:* No, you got to join a club and all that. And I work weekends often. I just found it here.

WALTER, *as though to warm the mood:* Mother used to love to watch him do this.

ESTHER, *surprised, pleased:* Really?

WALTER: Sure, she used to come to all his matches.

ESTHER, *to Victor, somehow charmed:* You never told me that.

WALTER: Of course; she's the one made him take it up. *He laughs to Victor.* She thought it was elegant!

VICTOR: Hey, that's right!

WALTER, *laughing at the memory:* He did look pretty good too! *He spreads his jacket away from his chest.* I've still got the wounds! *To Victor, who laughs:* Especially with those French gauntlets she—

VICTOR, *recalling:* Say . . . ! *Looking around with an enlivened need:* I wonder where the hell . . . *He suddenly moves
toward a bureau.* Wait, I think they used to be in . . .

ESTHER, *to Walter: French* gauntlets?

WALTER: She brought them from Paris. Gorgeously embroidered. He looked like one of the musketeers.

*Out of the drawer where he earlier found the ice skate, Victor
takes a pair of emblazoned gauntlets.*

VICTOR: Here they are! What do you know!

ESTHER, *reaching her hand out:* Aren't they beautiful!

He hands her one.

VICTOR: God, I'd forgotten all about them. *He slips one on his
hand.*

WALTER: Christmas, 1929.

VICTOR, *moving his hand in the gauntlet:* Look at that, they're
still soft . . . *To Walter—a little shy in asking:* How do you
remember all this stuff?

WALTER: Why not? Don't you?

ESTHER: He doesn't remember your mother very well.

VICTOR: I remember her. *Looking at the gauntlet:* It's just her
face; somehow I can never *see* her.

WALTER, *warmly:* That's amazing, Vic. *To Esther:* She adored
him.

ESTHER, *pleased:* Did she?

WALTER: Victor? If it started to rain she'd run all the way to
school with his galoshes. Her Victor—my God! By the time
he could light a match he was already Louis Pasteur.

VICTOR: It's odd . . . like the harp! I can almost hear the
music . . . But I can never see her face. Somehow. *For a
moment, silence, as he looks across at the harp.*

WALTER: What's the problem?

*Pause. Victor's eyes are swollen with feeling. He turns and looks
up at Walter, who suddenly is embarrassed and oddly anxious.*

SOLOMON—*enters from the bedroom. He looks quite distressed.
He is in his vest, his tie is open. Without coming downstage:*
Please, Doctor, if you wouldn't mind I would like to . . . *He
breaks off, indicating the bedroom.*

WALTER: What is it?

SOLOMON: Just for one minute, please.

Walter stands. Solomon glances at Victor and Esther and returns to the bedroom.

WALTER: I'll be right back. *He goes rather quickly up and into the bedroom.*

A pause. Victor is sitting in silence, unable to face her.

ESTHER, *with delicacy and pity, sensing his conflicting feelings:* Why can't you take him as he is?

He glances at her.

Well you can't expect him to go into an apology, Vic—he probably sees it all differently, anyway.

He is silent. She comes to him.

I know it's difficult, but he is trying to make a gesture, I think.

VICTOR: I guess he is, yes.

ESTHER: You know what would be lovely? If we could take a few weeks and go to like . . . out-of-the-way places . . . just to really break it up and see all the things that people do. You've been around such mean, petty people for so long and little ugly tricks. I'm serious—it's not romantic. We're much too suspicious of everything.

VICTOR, *staring ahead:* Strange guy.

ESTHER: Why?

VICTOR: Well, to walk in that way—as though nothing ever happened.

ESTHER: Why not? What can be done about it?

VICTOR—*slight pause:* I feel I have to say something.

ESTHER, *with a slight trepidation, less than she feels:* What can you say?

VICTOR: You feel I ought to just take the money and shut up, heh?

ESTHER: But what's the point of going backwards?

VICTOR, *with a self-bracing tension:* I'm not going to take this money unless I talk to him.

ESTHER, *frightened:* You can't bear the thought that he's decent.

He looks at her sharply.

That's all it is, dear. I'm sorry, I have to say it.

VICTOR, *without raising his voice:* I can't bear that he's *decent*!

ESTHER: You throw this away, you've got to explain it to me. You can't go on blaming everything on him or the system or God knows what else! You're free and you can't make a move, Victor, and that's what's driving me crazy! *Silence. Quietly:* Now take this money.

He is silent, staring at her.

You take this money! Or I'm washed up. You hear me? If you're stuck it doesn't mean I have to be. Now that's it.

Movements are heard within the bedroom. She straightens. Victor smooths down his hair with a slow, preparatory motion of his hand, like one adjusting himself for combat.

WALTER—*enters from the bedroom, smiling, shaking his head. Indicating the bedroom:* Boy—we got a tiger here. What is this between you, did you know him before?

VICTOR: No. Why? What'd he say?

WALTER: He's still trying to buy it outright. *He laughs.* He talks like you added five years by calling him up.

VICTOR: Well, what's the difference, I don't mind.

WALTER, *registering the distant rebuke:* No, that's fine, that's all right. *He sits. Slight pause.* We don't understand each other, do we?

VICTOR, *with a certain thrust, matching Walter's smile:* I am a little confused, Walter . . . yes.

WALTER: Why is that?

Victor doesn't answer at once.

Come on, we'll all be dead soon!

VICTOR: All right, I'll give you one example. When I called you Monday and Tuesday and again this morning—

WALTER: I've explained that.

VICTOR: But I don't make phone calls to pass the time. Your

nurse sounded like I was a pest of some kind . . . it was humiliating.

WALTER—*oddly, he is over-upset:* I'm terribly sorry, she shouldn't have done that.

VICTOR: I know, Walter, but I can't imagine she takes that tone all by herself.

WALTER, *aware now of the depth of resentment in Victor:* Oh no—she's often that way. I've never referred to you like that.

Victor is silent, not convinced.

Believe me, will you? I'm terribly sorry. I'm overwhelmed with work, that's all it is.

VICTOR: Well, you asked me, so I'm telling you.

WALTER: Yes! You should! But don't misinterpret that. *Slight pause. His tension has increased. He braves a smile.* Now about this tax thing. He'd be willing to make the appraisal twenty-five thousand. *With difficulty:* If you'd like, I'd be perfectly willing for you to have the whole amount I'd be saving.

Slight pause.

ESTHER: Twelve thousand?

WALTER: Whatever it comes to.

Pause. Esther slowly looks to Victor.

You must be near retirement now, aren't you?

ESTHER, *excitedly:* He's past it. But he's trying to decide what to do.

WALTER: Oh. *To Victor—near open embarrassment now:* It would come in handy, then, wouldn't it?

Victor glances at him as a substitute for a reply.

I don't need it, that's all, Vic. Actually, I've been about to call you for quite some time now.

VICTOR: What for?

WALTER—*suddenly, with a strange quick laugh, he reaches and touches Victor's knee:* Don't be suspicious!

VICTOR, *grinning:* I'm just trying to figure it out, Walter.

WALTER: Yes, good. All right. *Slight pause.* I thought it was time we got to know one another. That's all.

Slight pause.

VICTOR: You know, Walter, I tried to call you a couple of times before this about the furniture—must be three years ago.

WALTER: I was sick.

VICTOR, *surprised:* Oh . . . Because I left a lot of messages.

WALTER: I was quite sick. I was hospitalized.

ESTHER: What happened?

WALTER—*slight pause. As though he were not quite sure whether to say it:* I broke down.

Slight pause.

VICTOR: I had no idea.

WALTER: Actually, I'm only beginning to catch up with things. I was out of commission for nearly three years. *With a thrust of success:* But I'm almost thankful for it now—I've never been happier!

ESTHER: You seem altogether different!

WALTER: I think I am, Esther. I live differently, I think differently. All I have now is a small apartment. And I got rid of the nursing homes—

VICTOR: What nursing homes?

WALTER, *with a removed self-amusement:* Oh, I owned three nursing homes. There's big money in the aged, you know. Helpless, desperate children trying to dump their parents— nothing like it. I even pulled out of the market. Fifty per cent of my time now is in City hospitals. And I tell you, I'm alive. For the first time. I do medicine, and that's it. *Attempting an intimate grin:* Not that I don't soak the rich occasionally, but only enough to live, really. *It is as though this was his mission here, and he waits for Victor's comment.*

VICTOR: Well, that must be great.

WALTER, *seizing on this minute encouragement:* Vic, I wish we could talk for weeks, there's so much I want to tell you. . . . *It is not rolling quite the way he would wish and he must pick examples of his new feelings out of the air.* I never had friends—you probably know that. But I do now, I have good friends. *He moves, sitting nearer Victor, his enthusiasm flowing.* It all happens so gradually. You start out wanting to be the best, and there's no question that you do need a certain fanaticism; there's so much to know and so little time. Until you've eliminated everything extraneous—*he smiles* —including people. And of course the time comes when you realize that you haven't merely been specializing in something—something has been specializing in you. You become a kind of instrument, an instrument that cuts money out of people, or fame out of the world. And it finally makes you stupid. Power can do that. You get to think that because you can frighten people they love you. Even that you love them.—And the whole thing comes down to fear. One night I found myself in the middle of my living room, dead drunk with a knife in my hand, getting ready to kill my wife.

ESTHER: Good Lord!

WALTER: Oh ya—and I nearly made it too! *He laughs.* But there's one virtue in going nuts—provided you survive, of course. You get to see the terror—not the screaming kind, but the slow, daily fear you call ambition, and cautiousness, and piling up the money. And really, what I wanted to tell you for some time now—is that you helped me to understand that in myself.

VICTOR: Me?

WALTER: Yes. *He grins warmly, embarrassed.* Because of what you did. I could never understand it, Vic—after all, you *were* the better student. And to stay with a job like that through all those years seemed . . . *He breaks off momentarily, the uncertainty of Victor's reception widening his smile.* You see, it never dawned on me until I got sick—that you'd made a choice.

VICTOR: A choice, how?

WALTER: You wanted a real life. And that's an expensive thing; it costs. *He has found his theme now; sees he has at last touched something in Victor. A breath of confidence comes through now.* I know I may sound terribly naive, but I'm still unused to talking about anything that matters. Frankly, I didn't answer your calls this week because I was afraid. I've struggled so long for a concept of myself and I'm not sure I can make it believable to you. But I'd like to. *He sees permission to go on in Victor's perplexed eyes:* You see, I got to a certain point where . . . I dreaded my own work; I finally couldn't cut. There are times, as you know, when if you leave someone alone he might live a year or two; while if you go in you might kill him. And the decision is often . . . not quite, but almost . . . arbitrary. But the odds are acceptable, provided you think the right thoughts. Or don't think at all, which I managed to do till then. *Slight pause. He is no longer smiling; instead, a near-embarrassment is on him.* I ran into a cluster of misjudgments. It can happen, but it never had to me, not one on top of the other. And they had one thing in common; they'd all been diagnosed by other men as inoperable. And quite suddenly the . . . the whole prospect of my own motives opened up. Why had I taken risks that very competent men had declined? And the quick answer, of course, is—to pull off the impossible. Shame the competition. But suddenly I saw something else. And it was terror. In dead center, directing my brains, my hands, my ambition —for thirty years.

Slight pause.

VICTOR: Terror of what?

Pause.

WALTER, *his gaze direct on Victor now:* Of it ever happening to me—*he glances at the center chair*—as it happened to him. Overnight, for no reason, to find yourself degraded and thrown-down. *With the faintest hint of impatience and challenge:* You know what I'm talking about, don't you?

Victor turns away slightly, refusing commitment.

Isn't that why you turned your back on it all?

VICTOR, *sensing the relevancy to himself now:* Partly. Not altogether, though.

WALTER: Vic, we were both running from the same thing. I thought I wanted to be tops, but what it was was untouchable. I ended in a swamp of success and bankbooks, you on civil service. The difference is that you haven't hurt other people to defend yourself. And I've learned to respect that, Vic; you simply tried to make yourself useful.

ESTHER: That's wonderful—to come to such an understanding with yourself.

WALTER: Esther, it's a strange thing; in the hospital, for the first time since we were boys, I began to feel . . . like a brother. In the sense that we shared something. *To Victor:* And I feel I would know how to be friends now.

VICTOR—*slight pause; he is unsure:* Well fine. I'm glad of that.

WALTER—*sees the reserve but feels he has made headway and presses on a bit more urgently:* You see, that's why you're still so married. That's a very rare thing. And why your boy's in such good shape. You've lived a real life. *To Esther:* But you know that better than I.

ESTHER: I don't know what I know, Walter.

WALTER: Don't doubt it, dear—believe me, you're fortunate people. *To Victor:* You know that, don't you?

VICTOR, *without looking at Esther:* I think so.

ESTHER: It's not quite as easy as you make it, Walter.

WALTER—*hesitates, then throws himself into it:* Look, I've had a wild idea—it'll probably seem absurd to you, but I wish you'd think about it before you dismiss it. I gather you haven't decided what to do with yourself now? You're retiring . . . ?

VICTOR: I'll decide one of these days, I'm still thinking.

WALTER, *nervously:* Could I suggest something?

VICTOR: Sure, go ahead.

WALTER: We've been interviewing people for the new wing. For the administrative side. Kind of liaison people between the scientists and the board. And it occurred to me several times that you might fit in there.

Slight pause.

ESTHER, *with a release of expectation:* That would be wonderful!

VICTOR—*slight pause. He glances at her with suppression, but his voice betrays excitement:* What could I do there, though?

WALTER, *sensing Victor's interest:* It's kind of fluid at the moment, but there's a place for people with a certain amount of science who—

VICTOR: I have no degree, you know.

WALTER: But you've had analytic chemistry, and a lot of math and physics, if I recall. If you thought you needed it you could take some courses in the evenings. I think you have enough background.—How would you feel about that?

VICTOR, *digging in against the temptation:* Well . . . I'd like to know more about it, sure.

ESTHER, *as though to press him to accept:* It'd be great if he could work in science, it's really the only thing he ever wanted.

WALTER: I know; it's a pity he never went on with it. *Turning to Victor:* It'd be perfectly simple, Vic, I'm chairman of the committee. I could set it all up—

Solomon enters. They turn to him, surprised. He seems about to say something, but in fear changes his mind.

SOLOMON: Excuse me, go right ahead. *He goes nervously to his portfolio, reaching into it—which was not his original intention.* I'm sorry to disturb you. *He takes out an orange and starts back to the bedroom, then halts, addressing Walter:* About the harp. If you'll make me a straight out-and-out sale, I would be willing to go another fifty dollars. So it's eleven fifty, and between the two of you nobody has to do any favors.

WALTER: Well, you're getting warmer.

SOLOMON: I'm a fair person! So you don't have to bother with the appraisal and deductions, all right? *Before Walter can answer:* But don't rush, I'll wait. I'm at your service. *He goes quickly and worriedly into the bedroom.*

ESTHER, *starting to laugh; to Victor:* Where did you *find* him?

WALTER: —that wonderful? He "made it all ethical"!

Esther bursts out laughing, and Walter with her, and Victor manages to join. As it begins to subside, Walter turns to him.

What do you say, Vic? Will you come by?

The laughter is gone. The smile is just fading on Victor's face. He looks at nothing, as though deciding. The pause lengthens, and lengthens still. Now it begins to seem he may not speak at all. No one knows how to break into his puzzling silence. At last he turns to Walter with a rather quick movement of his head as though he had made up his mind to take the step.

VICTOR: I'm not sure I know what you want, Walter.

Walter looks shocked, astonished, almost unbelieving. But Victor's gaze is steady on him.

ESTHER, *with a tone of the conciliator shrouding her shock and protest:* I don't think that's being very fair, is it?

VICTOR: Why is it unfair? We're talking about some pretty big steps here. *To Walter:* Not that I don't appreciate it, Walter, but certain things have happened, haven't they? *With a half laugh:* It just seems odd to suddenly be talking about—

WALTER, *downing his resentment:* I'd hoped we could take one step at a time, that's all. It's very complicated between us, I think, and it seemed to me we might just try to—

VICTOR: I know, but you can understand it would be a little confusing.

WALTER—*unwillingly, anger peaks his voice:* What do you find confusing?

VICTOR—*considers for a moment, but he cannot go back:* You must have some idea, don't you?

WALTER: This is a little astonishing, Victor. After all these years you can't expect to settle everything in one conversation, can you? I simply felt that with a little good will we . . . we . . . *He sees Victor's adamant poise.* Oh, the hell with it. *He goes abruptly and snatches up his coat and one of the evening gowns.* Get what you can from the old man, I don't want any of it. *He goes and extends his hand to Esther, forcing a smile.* I'm sorry, Esther. It was nice seeing you anyway.

Sickened, she accepts his hand.

Maybe I'll see you again, Vic. Good luck. *He starts for the door. There are tears in his eyes.*

ESTHER, *before she can think:* Walter?

Walter halts and turns to her questioningly. She looks to Victor helplessly. But he cannot think either.

WALTER: I don't accept this resentment, Victor. It simply baffles me. I don't understand it. I just want you to know how I feel.

ESTHER, *assuaging:* It's not resentment, Walter.

VICTOR: The whole thing is a little fantastic to me, that's all. I haven't cracked a book in twenty-five years, how do I walk into a research laboratory?

ESTHER: But Walter feels that you have enough background—

VICTOR, *almost laughing over his quite concealed anger at her:* I know less chemistry than most high-school kids, Esther. *To*

Walter: And physics, yet! Good God, Walter. *He laughs.* Where you been?

WALTER: I'm sure you could make a place for yourself—

VICTOR: What place? Running papers from one office to another?

WALTER: You're not serious.

VICTOR: Why? Sooner or later my being your brother is not going to mean very much, is it? I've been walking a beat for twenty-eight years, I'm not qualified for anything technical. What's this all about?

WALTER: Why do you keep asking what it's about? I've been perfectly open with you, Victor!

VICTOR: I don't think you have.

WALTER: Why! What do you think I'm—?

VICTOR: Well, when you say what you said a few minutes ago, I—

WALTER: What did I say?!

VICTOR, *with a resolutely cool smile:* What a pity it was that I didn't go on with science.

WALTER, *puzzled:* What's wrong with that?

VICTOR, *laughing:* Oh, Walter, come on, now!

WALTER: But I feel that. I've always felt that.

VICTOR, *smiling still, and pointing at the center chair; a new reverberation sounds in his voice:* There used to be a man in that chair, staring into space. Don't you remember that?

WALTER: Very well, yes. I sent him money every month.

VICTOR: You sent him five dollars every month.

WALTER: I could afford five dollars. But what's that got to do with you?

VICTOR: What it's got to do with me!

WALTER: Yes, I don't see that.

VICTOR: Where did you imagine the rest of his living was coming from?

WALTER: Victor, that was your decision, not mine.

VICTOR: My decision!

WALTER: We had a long talk in this room once, Victor.

VICTOR, *not recalling:* What talk?

WALTER, *astonished:* Victor! We came to a complete understanding—just after you moved up here with Dad. I told you then that I was going to finish my schooling come hell or high water, and I advised you to do the same. In fact, I

warned you not to allow him to strangle your life. *To Esther:*
And if I'm not mistaken I told you the same at your wedding, Esther.

VICTOR, *with an incredulous laugh:* Who the hell was supposed
to keep him alive, Walter?

WALTER, *with a strange fear, more than anger:* Why did anybody have to? He wasn't sick. He was perfectly fit to go to
work.

VICTOR: Work? In 1936? With no skill, no money?

WALTER—*outburst:* Then he could have gone on welfare! Who
was he, some exiled royalty? What did a hundred and fifty
million other people do in 1936? He'd have survived, Victor.
Good God, you must know that by now, don't you?!

Slight pause.

VICTOR—*suddenly at the edge of fury, and caught by Walter's
voicing his own opinion, he turns to Esther:* I've had enough
of this, Esther; it's the same old thing all over again, let's get
out of here. *He starts rapidly upstage toward the bedroom.*

WALTER, *quickly:* Vic! Please! *He catches Victor, who frees his
arm.* I'm not running him down. I loved him in many ways—

ESTHER, *as though conceding her earlier position:* Vic, listen—
maybe you *ought* to talk about it.

VICTOR: It's all pointless! The whole thing doesn't matter to
me! *He turns to go to the bedroom.*

WALTER: He exploited you!

Victor halts, turns to him, his anger full in his face.

Doesn't that matter to you?

VICTOR: Let's get one thing straight, Walter—I am nobody's
victim.

WALTER: But that's exactly what I've tried to tell you. I'm not
trying to condescend.

VICTOR: Of course you are. Would you be saying any of this if
I'd made a pile of money somewhere? *Dead stop.* I'm sorry,
Walter, I can't take that. I made no choice; the icebox was
empty and the man was sitting there with his mouth open.
Slight pause. I didn't start this, Walter, and the whole thing
doesn't interest me, but when you talk about making choices,
and I should have gone on with science, I have to say

something.—Just because you want things a certain way doesn't make them that way. *He has ended at a point distant from Walter.*

A slight pause.

WALTER, *with affront mixed into his trepidation:* All right then . . . How do *you* see it?

VICTOR: Look, you've been sick, Walter, why upset yourself with all this?

WALTER: It's important to me!

VICTOR, *trying to smile—and in a friendly way:* But why? It's all over the dam. *He starts toward the bedroom again.*

ESTHER: I think he's come to you in good faith, Victor.

He turns to her angrily, but she braves his look.

I don't see why you can't consider his offer.

VICTOR: I said I'd consider it.

ESTHER, *restraining a cry:* You know you're turning it down! *In a certain fear of him, but persisting:* I mean what's so dreadful about telling the truth, can it be any worse than this?

VICTOR: What "truth?" What are you—?

Solomon suddenly appears from the bedroom.

ESTHER: For God's sake, *now* what?

SOLOMON: I just didn't want you to think I wouldn't make the appraisal; I will, I'll do it—

ESTHER, *pointing to the bedroom:* Will you please leave us alone!

SOLOMON, *suddenly, his underlying emotion coming through; indicating Victor:* What do you want from him! He's a policeman! I'm a dealer, he's a doctor, and he's a policeman, so what's the good you'll tear him to pieces?!

ESTHER: Well, one of us has got to leave this room, Victor.

SOLOMON: Please, Esther, let me . . . *Going quickly to Walter:* Doctor, listen to me, take my advice—stop it. What can come of this? In the first place, if you take the deduction how do you know in two, three years they wouldn't come back to you, whereby they disallow it? I don't have to tell you, the Federal Government is not reliable. I understand very well you want to be sweet to him—*to Esther*—but can

be two, three years before you'll know how sweet they're
going to allow him. *To Victor and Walter:* In other words,
what I'm trying to bring out, my boys, is that—

ESTHER: —you want the furniture.

SOLOMON, *shouting at her:* Esther, if I didn't want it I wouldn't
buy it! But what can they settle here? It's still up to the
Federal Government, don't you see? If they can't settle
nothing they should stop it right now! *With a look of warning and alarm in his eyes:* Now please—do what I tell you!
I'm not a fool! *He walks out into the bedroom, shaking.*

WALTER, *after a moment:* I guess he's got a point, Vic. Why
don't you just sell it to him; maybe then we can sit down and
talk sometime. *Glancing at the furniture:* It isn't really a very
conducive atmosphere.—Can I call you?

VICTOR: Sure.

ESTHER: You're both fantastic. *She tries to laugh.* We're giving
this furniture away because nobody's able to say the simplest
things. You're incredible, the both of you.

WALTER, *a little shamed:* It isn't that easy, Esther.

ESTHER: Oh, what the hell—I'll say it. When he went to you,
Walter, for the five hundred he needed to get his degree—

VICTOR: Esther! There's no—

ESTHER: It's one of the things standing between you, isn't it?
Maybe Walter can clear it up. I mean . . . Good God, is
there never to be an end? *To Walter, without pause:* Because
it stunned him, Walter. He'll never say it, but—*she takes the
plunge*—he hadn't the slightest doubt you'd lend it to him.
So when you turned him down—

VICTOR, *as though it wearies him:* Esther, he was just starting
out—

ESTHER, *in effect, taking her separate road:* Not the way you
told me! Please let me finish! *To Walter:* You already had the
house in Rye, you were perfectly well established, weren't you?

VICTOR: So what? He didn't feel he could—

WALTER, *with a certain dread, quietly:* No, no, I . . . I could
have spared the money . . . *He sits slowly.* Please, Vic—sit
down, it'll only take a moment.

VICTOR: I just don't see any point in—

WALTER: No—no; maybe it's just as well to talk now. We've
never talked about this. I think perhaps we have to. *Slight*

pause. Toward Esther: It *was* despicable; but I don't think I can leave it quite that way. *Slight pause.* Two or three days afterward—*to Victor*—after you came to see me, I phoned to offer you the money. Did you know that?

Slight pause.

VICTOR: Where'd you phone?
WALTER: Here. I spoke to Dad.

Slight pause. Victor sits.

I saw that I'd acted badly, and I—
VICTOR: You didn't act badly—
WALTER, *with a sudden flight of his voice:* It was frightful! *He gathers himself against his past.* We'll have another talk, won't we? I wasn't prepared to go into all this. . . .

Victor is expressionless.

In any case . . . when I called here he told me you'd joined the Force. And I said—he mustn't permit you to do a thing like that. I said—you had a fine mind and with a little luck you could amount to something in science. That it was a terrible waste. Etcetera. And his answer was—"Victor wants to help me. I can't stop him."

Pause.

VICTOR: You told him you were ready to give me the money?
WALTER: Victor, you remember the . . . the helplessness in his voice. At that time? With Mother recently gone and everything shot out from under him?
VICTOR, *persisting:* Let me understand that, Walter; did you tell—?
WALTER, *in anguish, but hewing to himself:* There are conversations, aren't there, and looking back it's impossible to explain why you said or didn't say certain things? I'm not defending it, but I would like to be understood, if that's possible. You all seemed to need each other more, Vic—more than I needed them. I was never able to feel your kind of . . . faith in him; that . . . confidence. His selfishness—which was perfectly normal—was always obvious to me, but you never seemed to notice it. To the point where I used to blame

myself for a lack of feeling. You understand? So when he said that you wanted to help him, I felt somehow that it'd be wrong for me to try to break it up between you. It seemed like interfering.

VICTOR: I see.—Because he never mentioned you'd offered the money.

WALTER: All I'm trying to convey is that . . . I was never indifferent; that's the whole point. I did call here to offer the loan, but he made it impossible, don't you see?

VICTOR: I understand.

WALTER, *eagerly:* Do you?

VICTOR: Yes.

WALTER, *sensing the unsaid:* Please say what you think. It's absurd to go on this way. What do you want to say?

VICTOR—*slight pause:* I think it was all . . . very convenient for you.

WALTER, *appalled:* That's all?

VICTOR: I think so. If you thought Dad meant so much to me—and I guess he did in a certain way—why would five hundred bucks break us apart? I'd have gone on supporting him; it would have let me finish school, that's all.—It doesn't make any sense, Walter.

WALTER, *with a hint of hysteria in his tone:* What makes sense?

VICTOR: You didn't give me the money because you didn't want to.

WALTER, *hurt and quietly enraged—slight pause:* It's that simple.

VICTOR: That's what it comes to, doesn't it? Not that you had any obligation, but if you want to help somebody you do it, if you don't you don't. *He sees Walter's growing frustration and Esther's impatience.* Well, why is that so astonishing? We do what we want to do, don't we? *Walter doesn't reply. Victor's anxiety rises.* I don't understand what you're bringing this all up for.

WALTER: You don't feel the need to heal anything.

VICTOR: I wouldn't mind that, but how does this heal anything?

ESTHER: I think he's been perfectly clear, Victor. He's asking your friendship.

VICTOR: By offering me a job and twelve thousand dollars?

WALTER: Why not? What else can I offer you?

VICTOR: But why do you have to offer me anything?

Walter is silent, morally checked.

It sounds like I have to be saved, or something.

WALTER: I simply felt that there was work you could do that you'd enjoy and I—

VICTOR: Walter, I haven't got the education, what are you talking about? You can't walk in with one splash and wash out twenty-eight years. There's a price people pay. I've paid it, it's all gone, I haven't got it any more. Just like you paid, didn't you? You've got no wife, you've lost your family, you're rattling around all over the place? Can you go home and start all over again from scratch? This is where we are; now, right here, now. And as long as we're talking, I have to tell you that this is not what you say in front of a man's wife.

WALTER, *glancing at Esther, certainty shattered:* What have I said . . . ?

VICTOR, *trying to laugh:* We don't need to be saved, Walter! I've done a job that has to be done and I think I've done it straight. You talk about being out of the rat race, in my opinion, you're in it as deep as you ever were. Maybe more.

ESTHER—*stands:* I want to go, Victor.

VICTOR: Please, Esther, he's said certain things and I don't think I can leave it this way.

ESTHER, *angrily:* Well, what's the difference?

VICTOR, *suppressing an outburst:* Because for some reason you don't understand *anything* any more! *He is trembling as he turns to Walter.* What are you trying to tell me—that it was all unnecessary? Is that it?

Walter is silent.

Well, correct me, is that the message? Because that's all I get out of this.

WALTER, *toward Esther:* I guess it's impossible—

VICTOR, *the more strongly because Walter seems about to be allied with Esther:* What's impossible? . . . What do you *want*, Walter!

WALTER—*in the pause is the admission that he indeed has not leveled yet. And there is fear in his voice:* I wanted to be of some use. I've learned some painful things, but it isn't enough to know; I wanted to act on what I know.

VICTOR: Act—in what way?

WALTER, *knowing it may be a red flag, but his honor is up:* I feel . . . I could be of help. Why live, only to repeat the same mistakes again and again? I didn't want to let the chance go by, as I let it go before.

Victor is unconvinced.

And I must say, if this is as far as you can go with me, then you're only defeating yourself.

VICTOR: Like I did before.

Walter is silent.

Is that what you mean?

WALTER—*hesitates, then with frightened but desperate acceptance of combat:* All right, yes; that's what I meant.

VICTOR: Well, that's what I thought.—See, there's one thing about the cops—you get to learn how to listen to people, because if you don't hear right sometimes you end up with a knife in your back. In other words, I dreamed up the whole problem.

WALTER, *casting aside his caution, his character at issue:* Victor, my five hundred dollars was not what kept you from your degree! You could have left Pop and gone right on—he was perfectly fit.

VICTOR: And twelve million unemployed, what was that, my neurosis? I hypnotized myself every night to scrounge the outer leaves of lettuce from the Greek restaurant on the corner? The good parts we cut out of rotten grapefruit . . . ?

WALTER: I'm not trying to deny—

VICTOR, *leaning into Walter's face:* We were eating garbage here, buster!

ESTHER: But what is the point of—

VICTOR, *to Esther:* What are you trying to do, turn it all into a dream? *To Walter:* And perfectly fit! What about the inside of his head? The man was ashamed to go into the street!

ESTHER: But Victor, he's gone now.

VICTOR, *with a cry—he senses the weakness of his position:* Don't tell me he's gone now! *He is wracked, terribly alone before her.* He was here then, wasn't he? And a system broke down, did I invent that?

ESTHER: No, dear, but it's all different now.

VICTOR: What's different now? We're a goddamned army holding this city down and when it blows again you'll be thankful
for a roof over your head! *To Walter:* How can you say that
to me? I could have left him with your five dollars a month?
I'm sorry, you can't brainwash me—if you got a hook in
your mouth don't try to stick it into mine. You want to make
up for things, you don't come around to make fools out of
people. I didn't invent my life. Not altogether. You had a
responsibility here and you walked on it. . . . You can go.
I'll send you your half.

*He is across the room from Walter, his face turned away. A long
pause.*

WALTER: If you can reach beyond anger, I'd like to tell you
something. Vic? *Victor does not move.* I know I should have
said this many years ago. But I did try. When you came to
me I told you—remember I said, "Ask Dad for money"? I
did say that.

Pause.

VICTOR: What are you talking about?

WALTER: He had nearly four thousand dollars.

ESTHER: When?

WALTER: When they were eating garbage here.

Pause.

VICTOR: How do you know that?

WALTER: He'd asked me to invest it for him.

VICTOR: Invest it.

WALTER: Yes. Not long before he sent you to me for the loan.

Victor is silent.

That's why I never sent him more than I did. And if I'd had
the strength of my convictions I wouldn't have sent him that!

*Victor sits down in silence. A shame is flooding into him which
he struggles with. He looks at nobody.*

VICTOR, *as though still absorbing the fact:* He actually had it? In
the bank?

WALTER: Vic, that's what he was living on, basically, till he died. What we gave him wasn't enough; you know that.

VICTOR: But he had those jobs—

WALTER: Meant very little. He lived on his money, believe me. I told him at the time, if he would send you through I'd contribute properly. But here he's got you running from job to job to feed him—I'm damned if I'd sacrifice when he was holding out on you. You can understand that, can't you?

Victor turns to the center chair and, shaking his head, exhales a blow of anger and astonishment.

Kid, there's no point getting angry now. You know how terrified he was that he'd never earn anything any more. And there was just no reassuring him.

VICTOR, *with protest—it is still nearly incredible:* But he saw I was supporting him, didn't he?

WALTER: For how long, though?

VICTOR, *angering:* What do you mean, how long? He could see I wasn't walking out—

WALTER: I know, but he was sure you would sooner or later.

ESTHER: He was waiting for him to walk out.

WALTER—*fearing to inflame Victor, he undercuts the obvious answer:* Well . . . you could say that, yes.

ESTHER: I knew it! God, when do I believe what I see!

WALTER: He was terrified, dear, and . . . *To Victor:* I don't mean that he wasn't grateful to you, but he really couldn't understand it. I may as well say it, Vic—I myself never imagined you'd go that far.

Victor looks at him. Walter speaks with delicacy in the face of a possible explosion.

Well, you must certainly see now how extreme a thing it was, to stick with him like that? And at such cost to you?

Victor is silent.

ESTHER, *with sorrow:* He sees it.

WALTER, *to erase it all, to achieve the reconciliation:* We could work together, Vic. I know we could. And I'd love to try it. What do you say?

There is a long pause. Victor now glances at Esther to see her expression. He sees she wants him to. He is on the verge of throwing it all up. Finally he turns to Walter, a new note of awareness in his voice.

VICTOR: Why didn't you tell me he had that kind of money?

WALTER: But I did when you came to me for the loan.

VICTOR: To "ask Dad"?

WALTER: Yes!

VICTOR: But would I have come to you if I had the faintest idea he had four thousand dollars under his ass? It was meaningless to say that to me.

WALTER: Now just a second . . . *He starts to indicate the harp.*

VICTOR: Cut it out, Walter! I'm sorry, but it's kind of insulting. I'm not five years old! What am I supposed to make of this? You knew he had that kind of money, and came here many times, you sat here, the two of you, watching me walking around in this suit? And now you expect me to—?

WALTER, *sharply:* You certainly knew he had *something*, Victor!

VICTOR: What do you want here? What do you want here!

WALTER: Well, all I can tell you is that *I* wouldn't sit around eating garbage with *that* staring me in the face! *He points at the harp.* Even then it was worth a couple of hundred, maybe more! Your degree was right there. Right there, if nothing else.

Victor is silent, trembling.

But if you want to go on with this fantasy, it's all right with me. God knows, I've had a few of my own.

He starts for his coat.

VICTOR: Fantasy.

WALTER: It's a fantasy, Victor. Your father was penniless and your brother a son of a bitch, and you play no part at all. I said to ask him because you could see in front of your face that he had some money. You knew it then and you certainly know it now.

VICTOR: You mean if he had a few dollars left, that—?

ESTHER: What do you mean, a few dollars?

VICTOR, *trying to retract:* I didn't know he—

ESTHER: But you knew he had something?

VICTOR, *caught; as though in a dream where nothing is explicable:* I didn't say that.

ESTHER: Then what are you saying?

VICTOR, *pointing at Walter:* Don't you have anything to say to *him*?

ESTHER: I want to understand what you're saying! You knew he had money left?

VICTOR: Not four thousand dol—

ESTHER: But enough to make out?

VICTOR, *crying out in anger and for release:* I couldn't nail him to the wall, could I? He said he had nothing!

ESTHER, *stating and asking:* But you knew better.

VICTOR: I don't know what I knew! *He has called this out, and his voice and words surprise him. He sits staring, cornered by what he senses in himself.*

ESTHER: It's a farce. It's all a goddamned farce!

VICTOR: Don't. Don't say that.

ESTHER: Farce! To stick us into a furnished room so you could send him part of your pay? Even after we were married, to go on sending him money? Put off having children, live like mice—and all the time you knew he . . . ? Victor, I'm trying to understand you. Victor?—Victor!

VICTOR, *roaring out, agonized:* Stop it! Silence. *Then:* Jesus, you can't leave everything out like this. The man was a beaten dog, ashamed to walk in the street, how do you demand his last buck—?

ESTHER: You're still saying that? The man had *four thousand dollars*!

He is silent.

It was all an act! Beaten dog!—he was a calculating liar! And in your heart you knew it!

He is struck silent by the fact, which is still ungraspable.

No wonder you're paralyzed—you haven't believed a word you've said all these years. We've been lying away our existence all these years; down the sewer, day after day after day . . . to protect a miserable cheap manipulator. No wonder it all seemed like a dream to me—it *was*; a god-damned nightmare. I knew it was all unreal, I knew it and I let it go by. Well, I can't any more, kid. I can't watch it another day. *I'm* not ready to die. *She moves toward her purse.*

She sits. Pause.

VICTOR—*not going to her; he can't. He is standing yards from her.* This isn't true either.

ESTHER: We are dying, that's what's true!

VICTOR: I'll tell you what happened. You want to hear it? *She catches the lack of advocacy in his tone, the simplicity. He moves from her, gathering himself, and glances at the center chair, then at Walter.* I did tell him what you'd said to me. I faced him with it. *He doesn't go on; his eyes go to the chair.* Not that I "faced" him, I just told him—"Walter said to ask you." *He stops; his stare is on the center chair, caught by memory; in effect, the last line was addressed to the chair.*

WALTER: And what happened?

Pause.

VICTOR, *quietly:* He laughed. I didn't know what to make of it. Tell you the truth—*to Esther*—I don't think a week has gone by that I haven't seen that laugh. Like it was some kind of a wild joke—because we *were* eating garbage here. *He breaks off.* I didn't know what I was supposed to do. And I went out. I went—*he sits, staring*—over to Bryant Park behind the public library. *Slight pause.* The grass was covered with men. Like a battlefield; a big open-air flophouse. And not bums—some of them still had shined shoes and good hats, busted businessmen, lawyers, skilled mechanics. Which I'd seen a hundred times. But suddenly—you know?—I *saw* it. *Slight pause.* There was no mercy. Anywhere. *Glancing at the chair at the end of the table:* One day you're the head of the house, at the head of the table, and suddenly you're shit. Overnight. And I tried to figure out that laugh.—How could he be holding out on me when he loved me?

ESTHER: Loved . . .

VICTOR, *his voice swelling with protest:* He loved me, Esther!

He just didn't want to end up on the grass! It's not that you don't love somebody, it's that you've got to survive. We know what that feels like, don't we!

She can't answer, feeling the barb.

We do what we have to do. *With a wide gesture including her and Walter and himself:* What else are we talking about here? If he did have something left it was—

ESTHER: "*If*" he had—

VICTOR: What does that change! I know I'm talking like a fool, but what does that change? He couldn't believe in anybody anymore, and it was unbearable to me! *The unlooked-for return of his old feelings seems to anger him. Of Walter:* He'd kicked him in the face; my mother—*he glances toward Walter as he speaks; there is hardly a pause*—the night he told us he was bankrupt, my mother . . . It was right on this couch. She was all dressed up—for some affair, I think. Her hair was piled up—and long earrings? And he had his tuxedo on . . . and made us all sit down; and he told us it was all gone. And she vomited. *Slight pause. His horror and pity twist in his voice.* All over his arms. His hands. Just kept on vomiting, like thirty-five years coming up. And he sat there. Stinking like a sewer. And a look came onto his face. I'd never seen a man look like that. He was sitting there, letting it dry on his hands. *Pause. He turns to Esther.* What's the difference what you know? Do *you* do everything you know?

She avoids his eyes, his mourning shared.

Not that I excuse it; it was idiotic, nobody has to tell me that. But you're brought up to believe in one another, you're filled full of that crap—you can't help trying to keep it going, that's all. I thought if I stuck with him, if he could see that somebody was still . . . *He breaks off; the reason strangely has fallen loose. He sits.* I can't explain it; I wanted to . . . stop it from falling apart. I . . . *He breaks off again, staring.*

Pause.

WALTER, *quietly:* It won't work, Vic.

Victor looks at him, then Esther does.

You see it yourself, don't you? It's not that at all. You see that, don't you?

VICTOR, *quietly, avidly:* What?

WALTER, *with his driving need:* Is it really that something fell apart? Were we really brought up to believe in one another? We were brought up to succeed, weren't we? Why else would he respect me so and not you? What fell apart? What was here to fall apart?

Victor looks away at the burgeoning vision.

Was there ever any love here? When he needed her, she vomited. And when you needed him, he laughed. What was unbearable is not that it all fell apart, it was that there was never anything here.

Victor turns back to him, fear on his face.

ESTHER, *as though she herself were somehow moving under the rays of judgment:* But who . . . who can ever face that, Walter?

WALTER, *to her:* You have to! *To Victor:* What you saw behind the library was not that there was no mercy in the world, kid. It's that there was no love in this house. There was no loyalty. There was nothing here but a straight financial arrangement. That's what was unbearable. And you proceeded to wipe out what you saw.

VICTOR, *with terrible anxiety:* Wipe out—

WALTER: Vic, I've been in this box. I wasted thirty years protecting myself from that catastrophe. *He indicates the chair:* And I only got out alive when I saw that there was no catastrophe, there had never been. They were never lovers—she said a hundred times that her marriage destroyed her musical career. I saw that nothing fell here, Vic—and he doesn't follow me any more with that vomit on his hands. I don't look high and low for some betrayal any more; my days belong to *me* now, I'm not afraid to risk believing someone. All I ever wanted was simply to do science, but I invented an efficient, disaster-proof, money-maker. You—*to Esther, with a warm smile:* He could never stand the sight of blood. He was shy, he was sensitive . . . *To Victor:* And what do you do? March straight into the most violent profession there is.

We invent ourselves, Vic, to wipe out what we know. You invent a life of self-sacrifice, a life of duty; but what never existed here cannot be upheld. You were not upholding something, you were denying what you knew they were. And denying yourself. And that's all that is standing between us now—an illusion, Vic. That I kicked them in the face and you must uphold them against me. But I only saw then what you see now—there was nothing here to betray. I am not your enemy. It is all an illusion and if you could walk through it, we could meet . . . *His reconciliation is on him.* You see why I said before, that in the hospital—when it struck me so that we . . . we're brothers. It was only two seemingly different roads out of the same trap. It's almost as though—*he smiles warmly, uncertain still*—we're like two halves of the same guy. As though we can't quite move ahead—alone. You ever feel that?

Victor is silent.

Vic?

Pause.

VICTOR: Walter, I'll tell you—there are days when I can't remember what I've got against you. *He laughs emptily, in suffering.* It hangs in me like a rock. And I see myself in a store window, and my hair going, I'm walking the streets—and I can't remember why. And you can go crazy trying to figure it out when all the reasons disappear—when you can't even hate any more.

WALTER: Because it's unreal, Vic, and underneath you know it is.

VICTOR: Then give me something real.

WALTER: What can I give you?

VICTOR: I'm not blaming you now, I'm asking you. I can understand you walking out. I've wished a thousand times I'd done the same thing. But, to come here through all those years knowing what you knew and saying nothing . . . ?

WALTER: And if I said—Victor, if I said that I did have some wish to hold you back? What would that give you now?

VICTOR: Is that what you wanted? Walter, tell me the truth.

WALTER: I wanted the freedom to do my work. Does that

mean I stole your life? *Crying out and standing:* You made those choices, Victor! And that's what you have to face!

VICTOR: But, what do you face? You're not turning me into a walking fifty-year-old mistake—we have to go home when you leave, we have to look at each other. What do *you* face?

WALTER: I have offered you everything I know how to!

VICTOR: I would know if you'd come to give me something! I would know that!

WALTER, *crossing for his coat:* You don't want the truth, you want a monster!

VICTOR: You came for the old handshake, didn't you! The okay!

Walter halts in the doorway.

And you end up with the respect, the career, the money, and the best of all, the thing that nobody else can tell you so you can believe it—that you're one hell of a guy and never harmed anybody in your life! Well, you won't get it, not till I get mine!

WALTER: And you? You never had any hatred for me? Never a wish to see me destroyed? To destroy me, to destroy me with this saintly self-sacrifice, this mockery of sacrifice? What will you give me, Victor?

VICTOR: I don't have it to give you. Not any more. And you don't have it to give me. And there's nothing to give—I see that now. I just didn't want him to end up on the grass. And he didn't. That's all it was, and I don't need anything more. I couldn't work with you, Walter. I can't. I don't trust you.

WALTER: Vengeance. Down to the end. *To Esther:* He is sacrificing his life to vengeance.

ESTHER: Nothing was sacrificed.

WALTER, *to Victor:* To prove with your failure what a treacherous son of a bitch I am!—to hang yourself in my doorway!

ESTHER: Leave him, Walter—please, don't say any more!

WALTER—*humiliated by her. He is furious. He takes an unplanned step toward the door:* You quit; both of you. *To Victor as well:* You lay down and quit, and that's the long and short of all your ideology. It is all envy!

Solomon enters, apprehensive, looks from one to the other.

And to this moment you haven't the guts to face it! But your failure does not give you moral authority! Not with me! I *worked* for what I made and there are people walking around today who'd have been dead if I hadn't. Yes. *Moving toward the door, he points at the center chair.* He was smarter than all of us—he saw what you wanted and he gave it to you! *He suddenly reaches out and grabs Solomon's face and laughs.* Go ahead, you old mutt—rob them blind, they love it! *Letting go, he turns to Victor.* You will never, never again make me ashamed! *He strides toward the doorway. A gown lies on the dining table, spread out, and he is halted in surprise at the sight of it.*

Suddenly Walter sweeps it up in his hands and rushes at Victor, flinging the gown at him with an outcry. Victor backs up at his wild approach.

VICTOR: Walter!

The flicker of a humiliated smile passes across Walter's face. He wants to disappear into air. He turns, hardly glancing at Victor, makes for the door, and, straightening, goes out.

VICTOR—*starts hesitantly to the door:* Maybe he oughtn't go into the street like that—
SOLOMON, *stopping him with his hand:* Let him go.

Victor turns to Solomon uncertainly.

What can you do?
ESTHER: Whatever you see, huh.

Solomon turns to her, questioningly.

You believe what you see.
SOLOMON, *thinking she was rebuking him:* What then?
ESTHER: No—it's wonderful. Maybe that's why you're still going.

Victor turns to her. She stares at the doorway.

I was nineteen years old when I first walked up those stairs— if that's believable. And he had a brother, who was the cleverest, most wonderful young doctor . . . in the world. As he'd be soon. Somehow, some way. *She turns to the center chair.* And a rather sweet, inoffensive gentleman, always waiting for the news to come on. . . . And next week, men we never saw or heard of will come and smash it all apart and take it all away.—So many times I thought—the one thing he wanted most was to talk to his brother, and that if they could— But he's come and he's gone. And I still feel it—isn't that terrible? It always seems to me that one little step more and some crazy kind of forgiveness will come and lift up everyone. When do you stop being so . . . foolish?

SOLOMON: I had a daughter, should rest in peace, she took her own life. That's nearly fifty years. And every night I lay down to sleep, she's sitting there. I see her clear like I see you. But if it was a miracle and she came to life, what would I say to her? *He turns back to Victor, paying out.* So you got there seven; so I'm giving you eight, nine, ten, eleven—*he searches, finds a fifty*—and there's a fifty for the harp. Now you'll excuse me—I got a lot of work here tonight. *He gets his pad and pencil and begins carefully listing each piece.*

VICTOR—*folds the money:* We could still make the picture, if you like.

ESTHER: Okay.

He goes to his suit and begins to rip the plastic wrapper off.

Don't bother.

He looks at her.

She turns to Solomon. Good-bye, Mr. Solomon.

SOLOMON—*looks up from his pad:* Good-bye, dear. I like that suit, that's very nice. *He returns to his work.*

ESTHER: Thank you. *She walks out with her life.*

VICTOR—*buckles on his gun belt, pulls up his tie:* When will you be taking it away?

SOLOMON: With God's help if I'll live, first thing in the morning.

VICTOR, *of the suit:* I'll be back for this later, then. And there's my foil, and the mask, and the gauntlets. *Puts on his uniform jacket.*

SOLOMON, *continuing his work:* Don't worry, I wouldn't touch it.

VICTOR, *extending his hand:* I'm glad to have met you, Solomon.

SOLOMON: Likewise. And I want to thank you.

VICTOR: What for?

SOLOMON, *with a glance at the furniture:* Well . . . who would ever believe I would start such a thing again . . . ? *He cuts himself off.* But go, go, I got a lot of work here.

VICTOR, *starting to the door, putting his cap on:* Good luck with it.

SOLOMON: Good luck you can never know till the last minute, my boy.

VICTOR, *smiling:* Right. Yes. *With a last look around at the room.* Well . . . bye-bye.

SOLOMON, *as Victor goes out:* Bye-bye, bye-bye.

He is alone. He has the pad and pencil in his hand, and he takes the pencil to start work again. But he looks about, and the challenge of it all oppresses him and he is afraid and worried. His hand goes to his cheek, he pulls his flesh in fear, his eyes circling the room.

His eye falls on the phonograph. He goes, inspects it, winds it up, sets the tone arm on the record, and flicks the starting lever. The Laughing Record plays. As the two comedians begin their routine, his depressed expression gives way to surprise. Now he smiles. He chuckles, and remembers. Now a laugh escapes, and he nods his head in recollection. He is laughing now, and shakes his head back and forth as though to say, "It still works!" And the laughter, of the record and his own, increase and combine. He holds his head, unable to stop laughing, and sits in the center chair. He leans back sprawling in the chair, laughing with tears in his eyes, howling helplessly to the air.

SLOW CURTAIN

FAME

MEYER RUBIN *enters from left glancing behind him as though escaping from someone. But as he crosses a* WOMAN *enters from right, and as they pass each other she slows on seeing his face, halts, and then runs after him, plucking his sleeve.*

MEYER *is a bearded man of forty, hatless, wearing wrinkled slacks and a wornout sports jacket and a tieless shirt.*

WOMAN: Please, oh please just one second! (*He halts.*) Are you . . . ?

MEYER: Ya. Where is it? (*He takes out a pen.*)

WOMAN: I knew the minute I saw you!

MEYER: Well that's the way it goes dear. Where is it?

WOMAN: I just bought the *Life* magazine with your picture on the cover. (*Holding it for him to sign.*) Would you mind here?

MEYER: Just hold it still.

WOMAN: Could you put "To Doris"? You're my favorite playwright now. I mean the wisdom! Honestly. I saw both your plays the same week.

MEYER (*edging away*): That's nice. I'm glad.

WOMAN: You know what my husband calls you? The King of Broadway!

MEYER: Thanks very much, thank you, thank you . . .

He hurries out. She walks off treasuring the magazine.

MEYER *re-enters from right, approaching a bar which is now lighting up. Nobody there but him. He sits on a stool and holds his head in his hands.* CHARLEY, *a Chinese, enters and comes around the bar and faces him.*

CHARLEY: So? (*Meyer drops his hands.*) Get it all signed?

MEYER: The cab drivers wave to me.

CHARLEY (*enthralled*): Yeah?

MEYER: I feel like a prize fighter. One jumped out and shook my hand. "Hi, Meyer! How ya doin!" (*Charley laughs, loves it.*) Five women came out of Korvette's and I had to sign all their packages. Another one right out front here.

CHARLEY: You got everything settled?

MEYER: Yup. One contract had sixty-three pages. I had to initial each page.

CHARLEY: Wonderful. (*To savor it.*) How much you getting?

MEYER: Well on that play I get six hundred thousand over ten years. On the other one I get seven hundred and fifty thousand.

CHARLEY: Plus your royalties every week.

MEYER: That's right, ya.

CHARLEY: How much is the royalties?

MEYER: On both plays? About ten thousand a week.

CHARLEY: Not counting London.

MEYER: No, just New York. London's about three thousand a week.

CHARLEY: For both.

MEYER: Yeah, both. The pound is down.

CHARLEY: Why don't you buy something?

MEYER: I stopped by a jewelry store on Madison Avenue just now. Thought I'd get my mother a string of pearls. You know, pearls are only about three, four thousand dollars?

CHARLEY: Yeah?

MEYER: Ya, I thought it'd be more. It's funny, I realized suddenly, if I wanted I could buy that whole store.

CHARLEY: You want a jewelry store?

MEYER: No, it's just that it occurred to me. Coming down Fifty-sixth street . . . there were seventeen cars parked on that street; I could have bought all of them.

CHARLEY: That's right, yeah.

MEYER: Or a bus. I could buy the Madison Avenue bus.

CHARLEY (*reaches and touches a loose button on Meyer's cuff*): Button's coming off.

MEYER: Oh. Pull it. I'll sew it later. (*Charley pulls the button and gives it to Meyer.*)

CHARLEY (*pointing to another button on his waist*): There's another one.

MEYER: No, that's got a couple of days yet.

CHARLEY: Whyn't you buy a new jacket?

MEYER: Why? I just got this last Spring.

CHARLEY: I mean if you want to buy something.

MEYER: Well I bought a new typewriter.

CHARLEY: But you can't wear it though.

MEYER: That's true. (*He sits looking morose.*)

CHARLEY: Take a little scotch.

MEYER: Good. All right.

CHARLEY (*fixing the drink*): Looks to me like you're in a constant state of tension, Meyer.

MEYER (*denying it*): I'll buy something.

CHARLEY: Aside from that. Used to come in here, have a few nice eggrolls, nice scotch and soda—relax. You used to be a very nice eater.

MEYER: I still eat nice.

CHARLEY: Not as nice as you used to eat. Nowadays you take half the time with your dinners.

MEYER: Well, I used to like to sit and watch people. But it's hard when everybody's looking at you.

CHARLEY: Why? Sit back and enjoy it.

MEYER: I'm trying to do that. I just realized the other night—I don't seem to see anything anymore; I seem to be constantly waiting to be recognized. It's awful. And the worst thing is that everybody's so damned nice to me.

CHARLEY: What's the matter with that?

MEYER: It's unreal, Charley. I have to keep reminding myself that up to this year very few people liked me. In fact, practically nobody. I used to tell a joke or a story, nobody laughed; now I ask somebody what time it is and I'm witty, they die laughing.

CHARLEY: I think after a while you get more accustomed.

MEYER: I hope so. I feel like I'm carrying some kind of a dummy around. He signs autographs, gets his hand shaken, delivers opinions about everything—and I stand there and watch. Disturbing.

CHARLEY: I got an idea—shave off your beard. All your photographs got the beard in.

MEYER: Yeah, but then nobody'll recognize me. (*He shoots a laugh, self-aware.*)

CHARLEY (*laughs*): I wish I was famous. Must be a big advantage with the girls, heh?

MEYER: Superficially. Which is not nothing. But it seems to

invigorate their ambition. Getting into bed with a famous man corrupts the intimacy. It's like three in bed—you, her, and your fame.

CHARLEY: You got the only troubles I wish I had.

MEYER: I'm not complaining. But it's very strange.

Enter ABE DORFMAN *and* WIFE. ABE *is very well dressed, in overcoat and pearl grey hat. His wife wears a mink wrap. He is implicitly pompous and overwhelmingly successful.*

ABE: We get a table or is it too early?

CHARLEY: No, we servin' dinner. This way, please.

CHARLEY *starts to lead them upstage but* ABE *sees* MEYER *and stops. Goes over to him.*

ABE: I beg your pardon. You aren't Meyer Rubin by any chance?

MEYER (*takes an instant before tiredly turning to Abe*): Ya, I am.

ABE: You're kidding.

MEYER: (*Sighs, turns away.*)

ABE: You're Meyer Rubin?

MEYER: Well if there's any doubt let's forget it.

ABE: From Washington Heights.

MEYER: M hm. (*Turns away to get a peanut off the bar.*)

ABE: Remember me?

MEYER (*the reversal surprises him as he turns back*): Do I know you?

ABE (*with a half-offended grin*): You don't remember me?

MEYER: Who are you?

ABE: Who am I!

MEYER: Well, if you don't like "Who are you?" then, how are you?

ABE (*as though the memory door will spring open*): I'm Abe Dorfman. (*He expects a vast reunion, apparently.*)

MEYER (*embarrassed*): Dorman.

ABE (*nodding*): Abe Dorfman.

MEYER: Abe Dorfman.

ABE: Ya. (*Waits for the recognition.*)

MEYER (*with uncertainty now—Dorfman's certainty convinces him the man is legitimate*): Gee, I'm afraid I . . .

ABE: We sat next to each other in English for three years in high school.

MEYER: Really?

ABE: Sure. I knew you right through that beard.

MEYER: Well, it's nice to see you anyway. How are you?

ABE: You remember me now, don't you?

MEYER (*touching Abe's arm for forgiveness*): I don't, but I've got a terrible memory . . . .

ABE: You don't remember Abe Dorfman with the curly red hair? (*With which he removes his hat, revealing a totally bald head.*)

MEYER (*indicating his head, laughs lightly*): Not anymore . . .

ABE (*glancing up*): Well, I mean though, in those days. . . .

MEYER: Well, what's the difference, I'm glad to see you anyway.

ABE (*insisting*): But we sat next to each other every day for three years!

MEYER: Look, I believe you. . . .

ABE: It's not a question of believing me—you sit next to a person every day for three years, it . . .

MEYER: Ya, but you probably changed a lot.

ABE: I didn't change *that* much.

MEYER: Well maybe it is coming back a little . . . You sat . . . next to me.

ABE: Well you sat next to me, too, I mean . . .

MEYER: Yeah, I mean we sat next to each other.

ABE: Ya, side by side. You were here and I was there. You were always borrowing everything.

CHARLEY: That sounds right.

MEYER: Ya, that must've been me. Well, I'm sorry, forgive me. . . . You look very well.

ABE: I feel well.

MEYER: You look well.

ABE: You look tired.

MEYER: I am. I'm pretty tired. (*He self-consciously adjusts his collar.*) I was just going out for a little walk. (*To explain away his raggedness.*)

ABE: A walk won't do it, you ought to try to get away a little. I always get away. Florida, Europe, West Indies—just get away. Don't you ever get away?

MEYER: Yeah, I get away. (*Putting out his hand to dismiss him.*) Well, it was nice to have seen you, Abe.

ABE (*smiling*): You remember me now, don't you?

MEYER: It'll probably come back but . . . what's the difference?

ABE: What do you mean, what's the difference? You sit next to somebody for three years. . . .

MEYER: Well don't be offended, I don't remember anything—that's why I make everything up. (*To deflect his deadly line.*) What do you do?

ABE (*it is extremely important and inflating*): I'm in shoulder pads.

MEYER: . . . Really! Shoulder pads.

ABE: Yes. You know . . . (*touching his own*) like for coats and dresses. . . .

MEYER: Oh, I see. Ya. I never knew there was a whole separate industry of shoulder pads.

ABE: Well certainly. We're on the American Stock Exchange. Acme International. We're the largest in the country. The world, in fact.

MEYER (*relieved, somehow*): You don't say. That's marvellous.

ABE: I'm Vice President.

MEYER: Huh.

ABE: You've heard of Acme, haven't you?

MEYER (*afraid not to*): Well now that I think about it, ya—I think I did hear something . . .

ABE: I'm in charge of everything East of the Mississippi.

MEYER: Boy, I bet that's a lot of shoulder pads.

ABE (*with humor*): You're damned tootin.

MEYER: Well, I'm certainly glad to hear that.

ABE: Oh ya, I've done very well. *Very* well.

MEYER: Well that's wonderful, Abe. I'm very glad to hear it. —You know, I think it's beginning to come back. You were always very well-prepared with your homework.

ABE: Sure! And you would borrow it.

MEYER: Right, right.

ABE: Every morning first thing—"Where's the homework?"

MEYER: Right! But you were a lot smaller then . . . Naturally you were smaller, but I mean—than me.

ABE (*overwhelmingly*): *I* was smaller than *you*?

MEYER: No?

ABE (*offended*): I was never smaller than you.

MEYER (*dismissing it*): Well. Good luck, then Abe.

ABE: Likewise. (*With an over-sympathetic condescension. Shakes hands.*) What do *you* do?

MEYER: (*It strangles his breathing. Slips his hand away. He sniffs to stall; turns away to get a peanut; glances a worried smile at Abe . . .*)

ABE: It's okay, I don't want to be nosey. . . .

MEYER: No-no, that's okay. I . . . write.

ABE (*eyebrows up, faint smile of amusement*): You write.

MEYER: Yeah, like. . . . You know, I'm a writer.

ABE: Huh! You mean like . . . ? What kind? What do you write?

MEYER (*as though an axe had been slipped into his hand which he would half-like to drop*): Well . . . all kinds. Stories, sometimes. . . .

ABE: Don't say. (*Still smiling with amusement.*) Get any published?

MEYER: Well ya . . . I've published . . . uh . . . quite a few.

ABE: Don't say. —We don't get much time for reading. We see the big hits though. Even off-Broadway. We don't read too much. My wife to some degree, but I . . . You do that for a living or you . . . ?

MEYER: Ya, for a living. I . . . I do it for a living.

ABE: You make out? I mean can you . . . ?

MEYER: Ya, I make out. —Look, don't let me keep you . . .

ABE: I like you to meet my wife. Honey, come here. Estelle? (*She comes over.*) Want you to meet Meyer Rubin; sat next to each other in English.

WIFE: Oh! How do you do?

MEYER: Hi. (*They shake hands. She is impressed.*)

WIFE: You really sat next to each other?

ABE: We better eat, Darling. (*To Meyer.*) If you ever need anything . . . you know, tide you over or something . . . come by and see me. (*Hands him a card. Wife is shocked, appalled.*) We're leaving for the Caribbean but we'll be back in a couple of weeks.

MEYER: Thanks.

ABE (*wife looks at him in distress*): Just in case . . . you know. (*Taking her arm.*) Whyn't you write plays? There's the real money.

MEYER: I have.

ABE: Plays?

WIFE (*trying to lead him away*): Darling, maybe we. . . .

MEYER: Ya, I mostly write plays.

ABE (*with that grin*): Ever get any on?

WIFE: Abe, dear. . . .

ABE: Hold it a second, he's an old friend. (*To Meyer.*) Get any on?

MEYER: Ya, I get them on.

ABE: Any I would have heard of?

MEYER: Well. . . . I've got one in the Martin Beck.

ABE (*a shock beginning to show on his face*): No kidding.

MEYER: Ya. And the one next door is mine. "Mostly Florence."

WIFE (*trying to insinuate the horror*): We're seeing it tonight, dear.

ABE (*a totally estranged look, a look of both interior shock and sheer unfamiliarity takes over*): Are you. . . . "*Meyer Rubin*"?

MEYER: Uh huh.

ABE: Well, I'm . . . (*Holds out his hand with the most remote and respectful formality.*) I'm very happy to meet you.

MEYER (*shaking hands*): Ha.

ABE: Well, this is certainly an . . . an honor. I really. . . . (*He breaks off and takes his wife's arm and starts walking.*)

WIFE: We've got a table dear . . .

But he walks her out. CHARLEY *and* MEYER *are left staring after them.*

MEYER: Now you see what I mean, heh?

CHARLEY (*turning to him—not understanding*): See what?

MEYER: Give me another drink, will you?

CHARLEY *goes behind the bar.* MEYER *leans on one hand in morose silence, staring ahead.*

BLACKOUT

THE REASON WHY

A veranda in sunlight. Two porch rockers face front, in one of them CHARLES *is seated, idly staring ahead smoking his pipe. A bird's chirping turns his head upward toward the branches of an invisible tree, and he watches the bird for a long moment until the song is stilled. Then he sighs contentedly and lets his eyes rove the horizon.*

His WIFE*'s voice is heard from off as through a nearby window.*

WIFE: How about some more coffee?

CHARLES: Thanks, dear, I've had enough. —What a morning.

WIFE: You going swimming?

CHARLES: Too cool, isn't it? You going?

WIFE: I think so. Soon as I clean up in here.

CHARLES (*looking up at the sky*): The moon is still out.

WIFE: I know, I saw it.

CHARLES: I will never understand how that works. (*Looks toward the ground, right.*) All your flowers are so beautiful.

WIFE: That rain was marvellous.

CHARLES: Just beautiful. You sure have the touch. And the grass is so lush. I love that deep green color. —Great day to be a cow.

WIFE (*laughs contentedly*): You want me to go for the paper?

CHARLES: Would you? I'd just like to sit here for a while.

WIFE: Sure. We need some groceries anyway. —That's a beautiful haircut.

CHARLES: Yes. (*He turns to the source of her voice, touching his hair, smiling.*)

WIFE: What was that bird before?

CHARLES: Redwing. (*Looks up at the tree.*) He's still up there. (*He looks ahead again. Pause.*) How motionless everything is.

WIFE: You notice the light? It's so pure.

CHARLES: Yes. It's like the first day of the world. God, I love the Fall. The sun is just exactly warm enough. (*Slight pause.*) I guess the end of the year for me is September; somehow life begins again around October.

WIFE: Okay, I'm off. I'll leave the coffee plugged in.

CHARLES: Fine.

WIFE: You need anything from town?

CHARLES: No.

WIFE: Bye!

CHARLES: Thanks, dear!

(*He stares about in silence—at the sky, the earth.* ROGER *appears to his left. He is carrying a pair of binoculars.*)

See anything?

ROGER: These are terrific. (*He sits in the other rocker, raising the glasses, looking out front.*)

CHARLES: Got them in the Virgin Islands. Much cheaper there.

ROGER: They really focus. Terrific. (*He hefts them.*) And so light.

CHARLES: Where'd you walk?

ROGER (*points front, up and to the right*): Just to the top of the pasture.

CHARLES: Isn't that a gorgeous view from up there?

ROGER: Marvellous, just marvellous. (*Looking about.*) I haven't seen a more beautiful landscape anywhere in the world.

CHARLES: It's always changing too. In all these years I've never been bored with it; always some new detail.

ROGER: And this air! (*Inhales.*) God—it's hard to believe the world can be so messed up. Just beautiful.

(*They look front in silence. The silence deepens. A kind of reverence, almost a sadness creeps into them as they absorb the perfection before them.*)

CHARLES (*pointing front suddenly*): Look! Out there! Quick!

ROGER (*looking at random*): What.

CHARLES: No, next to the stone fence. (*He leaps up and goes behind Roger and points out over the latter's shoulder.*) The top of the pasture; see it out there?

ROGER (*slight pause, his eyes fixed on something now*): What the hell is that?

CHARLES (*lowering his hand*): Woodchuck.

ROGER (*disbelieving*): No! (*He raises the glasses.*)

CHARLES: It is; that's the way they are around here.

ROGER (*watching through the glasses*): Say, it is too! He is a big boy. Huh! God, he's got *shoulders*.

CHARLES: Let me see. (*Roger hands him the glasses.*) Oh yeah— that's the papa.

ROGER: I've never seen them anywhere near that big; he's like a fox terrier.

CHARLES: Can you see? He's sitting up. (*Quickly handing back the glasses.*) Look at him sitting up.

ROGER (*looks out through the glasses*): Unbelievable. He's damn near as big as a raccoon.

CHARLES (*returns to his rocker, watching the woodchuck; and sits*): I wonder if I could hit him.

ROGER (*lowering the glasses*): From here?

CHARLES: Probably not, huh? How far would you say that was?

ROGER: That? —Three, three hundred and fifty yards.

CHARLES (*uncertainly*): Well I've hit a few up there—maybe a little further down, though.

ROGER: Well yes, but not way up there. That's a long shot.

CHARLES: Two summers ago I got forty-two in that field.

ROGER: Forty-two! What for?

CHARLES: We had the vegetable garden then. You put in all that work and one morning you come out and it's like a lawn mower ran over it. It's infuriating.

ROGER (*raises the glasses*): He's still up there.

CHARLES: Oh, they'll go on feeding for half an hour, this time of day.

ROGER: They're rodents, aren't they?

CHARLES: I'm not sure of that. They're vegetarians. The head is like a rat but the tail is kind of short and bushy. I think they're related to the rabbits. Whatever the hell that is.

ROGER (*incredulously*): *Forty-two?*

CHARLES: Oh, at least. I kept hoping they'd get the message and move back into the woods there. But they kept right on coming. We finally had to give up the garden. —You ever hunt?

ROGER: Years ago. Birds. But I never really liked it. They're so beautiful, it breaks your heart.

CHARLES: I know. It's awful. And I don't care what they say, there's an area in every hunter that's absolutely stupid. (*Pointing front.*) Look—he's sitting up again.

ROGER: He is monstrous. —I'm not sure about the stupidity, though. I've known some pretty intelligent guys loved to hunt.

CHARLES: I suppose. But like two summers ago when I was after them—it almost got to where I couldn't think of anything else. Every time I'd walk out of the house I'd be looking around for them. (*Roger laughs.*) Honestly. And if none showed up I'd even be disappointed! (*They both laugh.*) It gets to be a real addiction. You see one come out of his hole; you don't move; he crawls away from the hole; he sits up; you tiptoe into the house, get the gun, load it, come out, close the screen door softly, sight him—and wham. It was a lot of fun, but after a while it got to be quite strange. You begin to feel . . . I don't know what to call it. Some kind of emptiness. You feel emptied out, afterwards. (*Roger smiles.*) It occurred to me a couple of times that it must be like that in a war.

ROGER: Sounds like it, yes . . . in a way.

CHARLES: Did you ever hit anybody?

ROGER: Twice, yes.

CHARLES: Could you see them go down?

ROGER: Sure. It was on the desert. A man stands out sharply on desert.

CHARLES: Did it feel like that?

ROGER: Well of course you're in danger yourself so that kind of justifies it. But it's true—there is a certain hangover afterwards. —Why'd you stop?

CHARLES: Actually, it's very interesting. As I say, when I started out I only intended to kill three or four and maybe scare the others away. But then it got up to six, and ten, and twenty—it was only a limited war in the beginning, you know? (*They both laugh.*) But I began to get involved. It surprised me. I even began to feel a real hatred. I'd come out, take a look, and there they were—a whole field full of those bastards again. And it was getting expensive, one of those bullets costs fifteen cents, and you don't always hit with one shot. And the hawks—Christ, there were always two or three hawks up there with those hooked beaks; I was in league with the hawks. It got depressing. —And the truth is, for what it cost to kill them we could have bought all the tomatoes we'd eat in a year. (*Roger laughs.*) Seriously—it kept reminding me of war. For what it costs to kill these days, we could put a tractor on every farm in the world and send all their kids to the University of Texas.

ROGER (*he laughs and raises the glasses*): I think he's come down a little closer.

CHARLES: He has, ya.

ROGER (*lowers the glasses*): I know what you mean. These goddamned wars—they make everything seem so senseless.

CHARLES: There's an endless feeling of depression. It never goes away.

ROGER: I feel that too. I never did before.

(*A pause.* ROGER *raises the glasses again.* CHARLES *stares out at the field. The pause lengthens.*)

CHARLES: You want to take a shot at him? (*Roger looks at Charles in surprise, and laughs.*) Well if you'd like to—you'd probably never hit him anyway.

ROGER: I'd never reach him from here.

CHARLES: Wait a minute.

(CHARLES *goes into the house.* ROGER *idles. Now he swats an insect on his cheek.* CHARLES *returns with a rifle into which he is pressing two cartridges.*)

ROGER: Telescopic sight?

CHARLES: It's terrific. Take a look. (*Roger takes the gun and examines the sight.*) I bought it used. Sixty-five bucks. That's seven power.

ROGER: What's the caliber?

CHARLES: 222. It's quite a large cartridge but there's no kick. It's nice and light.

ROGER: It is, ya. (*Roger raises the gun, moving it along the horizon, then holds it still.*)

CHARLES: Handle nice?

ROGER: Beautiful. —There he is! Boy, this really brings it up close. —It has the head of a rat.

CHARLES: Maybe they are rats.

ROGER: They're quite ugly.

CHARLES: I know. I hate them.

(*They both laugh.* ROGER *lowers the rifle,* CHARLES *takes it and aims. Silence.* ROGER *now raises the binoculars.*)

Can you hit anything standing up?

ROGER: Fairly well.

CHARLES (*sitting in the rocker*): I'm no good unless I rest my arm on something. (*He crosses his legs, props one elbow on his thigh, and sights the gun.*)

ROGER: You correct for the wind?

CHARLES: No wind now, is there?

ROGER: No, it seems perfectly still. That's at least three hundred and fifty yards, Charles.

CHARLES: I think I could reach him.

ROGER (*raising the glasses*): That's impossible.

CHARLES (*with only half-certainty*): I think I could.

(*He throws the bolt.* ROGER *starts to lower his glasses when the rifle fires.* ROGER *quickly—rather avidly—raises the glasses again.*)

ROGER: He's running away.

CHARLES (*throwing the bolt back, and forth again*): Was I high or low?

ROGER: I had the glasses down. He's stopped. Can you see? (*Charles is aiming again.*) He's sitting up looking around. You see him? (*Charles has the rifle held to a point.*) He's starting to run!

(CHARLES, *holding his breath, tracks the animal, the rifle slowly moving. He fires. Puts the gun down, looking front.* ROGER *is looking through the glasses.*)

I'll be goddamned. Oh dear.

CHARLES (*eagerly*): Can you see him?

ROGER: You got him. (*Still with the glasses raised; with amazed admiration.*) By God, you really got him. He's dead as Kelcey's ass.

CHARLES (*reaching for the binoculars*): Let me see!

(*He looks out through the glasses. Now* ROGER *turns to him, a half laugh of wonder and surprise coming from his mouth.*)

ROGER: What the hell'd you do that for?

CHARLES (*lowering the glasses, he laughs, but with a certain embarrassment*): I don't know. —Come on, let's take a look.

(They get up and walk together.)

ROGER: I'd never have believed it.

CHARLES: I told you, it's a hell of a rifle.

ROGER (*taking the gun from him and examining it as they walk*): It sure is; I'd have bet a hundred to one you could never . . .

CHARLES (*proudly*): The trajectory is very flat. And it's got terrific power. The only trouble is, it's a little awkward to load, but if you can get something in the sight you've *got* it.

ROGER: It's amazing.

(They have been walking along a maze-like path which leads them all over the stage until they arrive at a point, center, where they halt looking down at the ground.)

Poor thing.

CHARLES: Yes. Right through the head, you see?

ROGER: Yes. Look at those claws. (*He kneebends and with one finger pantomimes lifting the animal's paw.*)

CHARLES: They live in the ground. See?—it hasn't got a rat's tail.

ROGER (*He pantomimes grasping the tail and stands holding the animal before him*): He certainly was big. Heavy! —What do you do with him?

CHARLES: Just leave him. The hawks'll come.

ROGER (*He drops the animal, looks down at it for a moment. And turns to Charles, smiling with great curiosity, his brows drawn together with a certain bewilderment*): Why'd you do that?

CHARLES: I don't know. I probably won't anymore, though.

(From the back of the theatre the WIFE's voice is heard calling.)

WIFE: Charles? Yoo hoo!

CHARLES (*waving toward the audience*): Here we are, darling! Here!

(Now he whistles loudly through his fingers, waving out front to draw her attention.)

BLACKOUT

THE CREATION OF THE
WORLD AND OTHER
BUSINESS

THE CHARACTERS

GOD
ADAM
EVE
LUCIFER
RAPHAEL
AZRAEL } Angels
CHEMUEL
CAIN
ABEL

ACT ONE

Music.

A night sky full of stars. Day spreads its pristine light, forming shadows in the contrasting sunlight. It is Paradise, the ultimate Garden—which is to say that it is all an impression of color rather than terrestrial details of plants and vines. Only one such feature stands apart; from the left, reaching out like an inverted, finger-spread hand, is a tree branch with golden leaves, from which hangs —an apple.

God appears on his throne above the acting level. He is deep in thought as he tries to visualize the inevitable future.

Now, as light spreads, the caw of a crow sounds, the dawn-welcoming chatter of monkeys, the hee-hawing ass, the lion's echo-ing roar, seals barking, pigs grunting, the loon's sudden laughter —all at once in free cacophony.

And as they subside and day is full, one of the shadows moves— a man, Adam, who reaches up above his head and plucks a fig and, propped up against a rock, crosses his legs and idly chews. He is in every way a man and naked, but his skin is imprinted with striped and speckled shadows, an animated congealment of light and color and darkness.

God emerges behind and to one side of him. He looks about, at the weather, up at the sky. Then He turns and looks down at Adam, who gradually feels His presence, and with only the slight-est start of surprise. . . .

ADAM: Oh! Good morning, God!

GOD: Good morning, Adam. Beautiful day.

ADAM: Oh, perfect, Lord. But they all are.

GOD: I've turned up the breeze a little. . . .

ADAM: I just noticed that. *Holds up a hand to feel it.* This is exactly right now. Thanks, Lord.

GOD: I'm very pleased with the way you keep the garden. I see you've pruned the peach tree.

ADAM: I had to, Lord. An injured branch was crying all night. Are we going to name more things today?

GOD: I have something else to discuss with you this morning, but I don't see why we couldn't name a few things first. *He points.* What would you call that?

ADAM: That? I'd call that a lion.

GOD: Lion. Well, that sounds all right. And that?

ADAM: That? Ahhh . . . lamb?

GOD, *trying the word:* Lamb.

ADAM: I don't know what it is today—everything seems to start with L.

GOD: I must say that *looks* like a lamb. And that?

ADAM: L, L, L . . . That should be—ah . . . labbit?

GOD, *cocking His head doubtfully:* Labbit doesn't seem—

ADAM, *quickly:* You're right, that's wrong. See, I was rushing.

GOD: Slow down, we have all the time in the world.

ADAM: Actually, that looks like something that should begin with an R. . . . Rabbit!

GOD: Rabbit sounds much better.

ADAM, *happily:* Rabbit, rabbit!—oh, sure, that's much better.

GOD: How about that?

ADAM: I've been wondering about that. I have a feeling it should have a name that goes up and down, like . . . ka . . . ka . . .

GOD: Yes? Go on. . . . *Ka* what?

ADAM, *undulantly:* Ca-ter-pill-ar.

GOD: What an amazing creature you've turned out to be; I would never have thought of "Caterpillar" in a million years. That'll be enough for today. I imagine you've noticed by this time that all the animals live in pairs—there are male and female?

ADAM: I'm so glad you mentioned that.

GOD: Oh, it disturbs you?

ADAM: Oh no, Lord, nothing disturbs me.

GOD: I'm glad to see that you've settled for perfection.

ADAM: It just seemed odd that, of all the creatures, only I am alone. But I'm sure you have your reasons.

GOD: Actually, Adam—and I know this won't shake your confidence—but now and then I do something and, quite frankly, it's only afterwards that I discover the reasons. Which, of course, is just as well. In your case it was extremely experimental. I had just finished the chimpanzee and had some clay left over. And I—well, just played around with it, and by golly there you were, the spitting image of me. In fact, that is probably why I feel such a special closeness to you: you sprang out of my instinct rather than some design. And that is probably why it never occurred to me to give you a wife, you see.

ADAM: Oh, I see. What would it look like? Or don't you know yet?

GOD: Supposing I improvise something and see how it strikes you.

ADAM: All right. But would I have to—like, talk to it all the time?

GOD: What in the world gave you an idea like that?

ADAM: Well, these lions and monkeys and mice—they're all constantly talking to each other. And I so enjoy lying on my back and just listening to the lilacs budding.

GOD: You mean you'd rather remain alone?

ADAM: I don't know! I've never had anybody.

GOD: Well, neither have I, so I'm afraid I can't help you there. Why don't we just try it and see what happens?

ADAM: Of course, Lord, anything you say.

GOD: Lie down, then, and I'll put you to sleep.

ADAM: Yes, Lord.

He lies down. God feels his rib cage.

GOD: I'll take out a bottom rib. This one here. You'll never know the difference.

ADAM, *starting up:* Is that—fairly definite?

GOD: Oh, don't worry, I shouldn't have put it in in the first place, but I wanted to be extra sure. Now close your eyes.

ADAM, *lying back nervously:* Yes, sir. . . . *Starts up again.* Is this also going to be experimental, or—I mean how long are we going to keep her?

GOD: Now look, son, you don't have to hang around her every minute. If it gets too much, you just walk off by yourself.

ADAM: Oh, good. *Starts lying down, then sits up nervously.* I just wondered.

GOD: Sleep, Adam! *He ceremonially lowers his hands on Adam's rib. Something stirs on the periphery, rising from the ground. Music.*

> This is now bone of thy bones,
> And flesh of thy flesh;
> She shall be called . . . Woman,
> Because she was taken out of Man.

Wake up, Adam. *Adam opens his eyes and sits up. Eve moves out of the darkness, and they look at each other. Her skin too is covered with shadow-marks. God walks around her, inspecting her.* Hmmmm. Very nice. *To Adam:* What do you say? *Music dies off.*

ADAM, *nervously:* Well . . . she certainly is *different.*

GOD: Is that all?

ADAM: Oh, Lord, she's perfect! *But he is still uneasy.*

GOD: I think so too.

ADAM: Me too.

GOD: Huh! I don't know how I do it! What would you like to call her?

ADAM: Eve.

GOD: Eve! Lovely name. *Takes her hand.* Now dear, you will notice many different kinds of animals in this garden. Each has its inborn rule. The bee will not eat meat; the elephant will not sing and fish have no interest in flowers.—Those are apples on that tree; you will not eat them.

EVE: Why?

ADAM: That's the rule!

GOD: Be patient, Adam, she's very new. *To Eve:* Perhaps the day will come when I can give you a fuller explanation; for the moment, we'll put it this way. That is the Tree of Knowledge, Knowledge of Good and Evil. All that you have here springs from my love for you; out of love for me you will not eat of that tree or you will surely die. Not right away, but sometime. Now tell me, Eve—when you look at that tree, what do you think of?

EVE, *looks up at the tree:* . . . God?

ADAM: She got it!

GOD: That's exactly the point, dear. *Takes both their hands.* Now be glad of one another. And remember—if you eat of that tree you shall surely die. Not right away, but sometime. If you stay clear of it, everything will go on just as it is, forever. Eve?

EVE: Yes, Lord.

GOD: Adam?

ADAM: Yes, Lord.

GOD: It is all yours, my children, till the end of time.

He walks away and vanishes. Adam and Eve turn from God and face each other. They smile tentatively. Examine each other's hands, breasts. He sniffs her. Sniffs closer.

ADAM: You smell differently than I do.

EVE: You do too.

He kisses her lips. Then she kisses his. They smile. He gives a little wave.

ADAM: Well . . . maybe I'll see you again sometime. I feel like lying down over there.

EVE: I do too!

ADAM, *halting:* You do?

She stretches out.

EVE: I think I have the same thoughts you do.

ADAM, *deciding to test this:* Are you a little thirsty?

EVE: Mmhm.

ADAM: Me too. And a little hungry?

EVE: Mmhm.

ADAM: Well, that's nice. Here, want a fig?

EVE: I just felt like a fig! *They chew.*

ADAM: We can go swimming later, if you like.

EVE: Fine! That's just what I was thinking. *They lie in silence.*

ADAM: Beautiful, isn't it?

EVE: Oh, ya. Is it all right to ask—

ADAM: What?

EVE: —what you do all day?

ADAM: Well, up till recently I've been naming things. But that's practically over now. See that up there? *She looks up.* I named that a pomegranate.

EVE: Pomewhat?

ADAM: Pomegranate.

EVE: That doesn't look like a pomegranate.

ADAM: Of course it's a pomegranate. *He fetches her one.* Here, eat one, you'll see. As you're spitting out the seeds it feels

like "pomegranate, pomegranate, pomegranate." *She bites
into it. As she spits out seeds.* Granate, granate, granate. . . .

EVE, *chewing, spitting out seeds:* Say . . . you're right, you're
right.

ADAM: That's better.

EVE—*she suddenly plucks something out of his hair and holds it
between her fingers:* What's this?

ADAM: That? That's a prndn. *He scratches himself.* It's one of
the first things I named.

EVE: This you named a prndn?

ADAM, *with a tingle of alarm:* Now look, woman, once a thing
is named, it's *named.*

EVE, *hurt, surprised:* Oh.

ADAM—*conviction failing, he turns back to her:* Why? What
should I call it?

EVE: Well, to *me*, this is a louse.

ADAM: Saaay! No wonder I woke up full of L's this morning!
With a happy laugh, she eats the louse. Isn't it marvelous how
we both have exactly the same thoughts, pretty near!

EVE, *chewing:* Yes. *He stares ahead, considering for a moment,
then, to show off, he spreads his arms and stands on one foot.* So
what do you do all day?

ADAM: Sometimes I do this. Or this. *He rolls onto his head and
does a headstand. She watches for a moment. His headstand
collapses.* Why? Do you have something in mind?

EVE: I think I do, but I don't know what it is. Say, that bush!

ADAM: What about it?

EVE: I just saw it growing!

ADAM: Oh, sure. Listen . . . do you hear?

EVE: Yes. What is that sound?

ADAM: That's the sound of sunset.

EVE: And that crackling?

ADAM: A shadow is moving across dry leaves.

EVE: What is that piping sound?

ADAM: Two trout are talking in the river.

EVE, *looking upward:* Something has exhaled.

ADAM: God is sighing.

EVE: Something is rising and falling.

ADAM: That's the footsteps of an angel walking through the
vines. Come, I'll show you the pool.

EVE, *getting up:* I was just thinking that!

ADAM: Good for you! I'll teach you to ride my alligators! *With a comradely arm over her shoulder he walks her out, as angels Chemuel, Azrael, and Raphael enter on the platform.*

CHEMUEL: Did you ever see anything so sweet?

RAPHAEL: Look at him putting a plum in her mouth! How lovely!

God enters on the platform.

CHEMUEL: She's adorable! Lord, you've done it again. *God, however, has left the group and stands in deep thought, apart.* Everybody! Halllllll-elujah!

ANGELS, *singing Handel:* Hallelujah, hallelujah . . .

A full-blown orchestra and mighty chorus erupt from the air in accompaniment.

GOD, *motioning them out:* Excuse me! A little later, perhaps. I'd like a few words with Lucifer.

CHEMUEL, *kissing God's hand, as they leave:* Congratulations, Lord!

RAPHAEL: We'll bring the full chorus tonight!

Alone, God looks down at the earth, as Lucifer enters.

GOD: All right, go ahead, say it.

LUCIFER: Nothing for me to say, Lord. *He points below.* You see it as well as I.

GOD, *looking down, shaking His head:* What did I do wrong?

LUCIFER: Why look at it that way? They're beautiful, they help each other, they praise You every few minutes—

GOD: Lucifer, they don't multiply.

LUCIFER: Maybe give them a few more years. . . .

GOD: But there's no sign of anything. Look at them—the middle of a perfect, moonlit night, and they're playing handball.

LUCIFER: Well, You wanted them innocent.

GOD: Every once in a while, though, he does seem to get aroused.

LUCIFER: Aroused, yes, but what's the good if he doesn't get it in the right place? And when he does, she walks off to pick a flower or something.

GOD: I can't figure that out. *Pause. They stare down.*

LUCIFER: Of course, You could always—*He breaks off.*

GOD: What?

LUCIFER: Look, I don't want to mix in, and then You'll say I'm criticizing everything—

GOD: I don't know why I stand for your superciliousness.

LUCIFER: At least I don't bore You like the rest of these spirits.

GOD: Sometimes I'd just as soon you did. What have you got in mind?

LUCIFER: Now, remember, You asked me.

GOD: What have you got in mind!

LUCIFER: You see? You're mad already.

GOD, *roaring furiously:* I am not mad!

LUCIFER: All right, all right. You could take her back and restring her insides. Reroute everything, so wherever he goes in it connects to the egg.

GOD: No-no-no, I don't want to fool with that. She's perfect now; I'm not tearing her apart again. Out of the question.

LUCIFER: Well, then, You've only got one other choice. You've got to thin out the innocence down there. *God turns to him suspiciously.* See? You're giving me that look again; whatever I say, You turn it into some kind of a plot. Like when You made that fish with the fur on. Throw him in the ocean, and all the angels run around screaming hosannas. *I* come and tell You the thing's drowned, and You're insulted.

GOD: Yes. But I—I've stopped making fish with fur any more.

LUCIFER: But before I can penetrate with a fact I've got to go through hell.

GOD—*He suddenly points down:* He's putting his arm around her. *Lucifer looks down.* Lucifer! *They both stretch over the edge to see better.* Lucifer!! *Suddenly His expression changes to incredulity, then anger, and He throws up His hands in futile protest.* Where in the world does he get those stupid ideas!

LUCIFER, *still looking down:* Now he's going to sleep.

GOD: Oh, dear, dear, dear, dear. *He sits disconsolately.*

LUCIFER: Lord, the problem down there is that You've made it all so perfect. Everything they look at is not only good, it's equally good. The sun is good, rats are good, fleas are good, the moon, lions, athlete's foot—every single thing is just as good as every other thing. Because, naturally, You created everything, so everything's as attractive as everything else.

GOD: What's so terrible about perfection? Except that you can't stand it?

LUCIFER: Well, simply—if You want him to go into her, into the right place, and stay there long enough, You'll have to make that part better.

GOD: I am not remaking that woman.

LUCIFER: It's not necessary. All I'm saying is that sex has to be made not just good, but—well, terrific. Right now he'd just as soon pick his nose. In other words, You've got to rivet his attention on that one place.

GOD: How would I do that?

LUCIFER: Well, let's look at it. What is the one thing that makes him stop whatever he's doing and pay strict attention?

GOD: What?

LUCIFER: You, Lord. Soon as You appear, he, so to speak, comes erect. Give sex that same sort of holiness in his mind, the same sort of hope that is never discouraged and never really fulfilled, the same fear of being unacceptable. Make him feel toward sex as he feels toward You, and You're in— *unbeschreiblich*! Between such high promise and deadly terror, he won't be able to think of anything else.

Pause.

GOD: How?

LUCIFER: Well . . . *He hesitates a long moment, until God slowly turns to him with a suspicious look.* All right, look— there's no way around it, I simply have to talk about those apples.

GOD, *stamps His foot and stands, strides up and down, trying to control His temper:* Lucifer!

LUCIFER: I refuse to believe that man's only way to demonstrate his love for God is to refuse to eat some fruit! That kind of game is simply unworthy of my father!

GOD, *angered:* Really now!

LUCIFER: Forgive me, sir, but I am useless to you if I don't speak my mind. May I tell you why *I* think You planted that tree in the garden? *God is silent, but consenting, even if unwillingly.* Objectively speaking, it *is* senseless. You wanted

Adam's praise for everything You made, absolutely innocent of any doubt about Your goodness. Why, then, plant a fruit which can only make him wise, sophisticated, and analytical? May I continue? *God half-willingly nods.* He certainly will begin to question everything if he eats an apple, but why is that necessarily bad? *God looks surprised, angering.* He'll not only marvel that the flower blooms, he will ask why and discover chlorophyll—and bless You for chlorophyll. He'll not only praise You that food makes him strong, he will discover his bile duct and praise You for his pancreas. He may lose his innocence, but the more he learns of Your secrets, the more reasons he will have to praise You. And that is why, quite without consciously knowing it, You planted that tree there. It was Your fantastic inner urge to magnify Your glory to the last degree. In six words, Lord, You wanted full credit for everything.

GOD: He must never eat those apples.

LUCIFER: Then why have You tempted him? What is the point?

GOD: I wanted him to wake each morning, look at that tree, and say, "For God's sake I won't eat these apples." Not even one.

LUCIFER: Fine. But with that same absence of curiosity he is not investigating Eve.

GOD: But the other animals manage.

LUCIFER: Their females go into heat, and the balloon goes up. But Eve is ready almost any time, and that means no time. It's part of that whole dreadful uniformity down there.

GOD: They are my children; I don't want them to know evil.

LUCIFER: Why call it evil? One apple, and he'll know the difference between good and better. And once he knows that, he'll be all over her. *He looks down.* Look, he's kissing a tree. You see? The damned fool has no means of discriminating.

GOD, *looking down:* Well, he should kiss trees too.

LUCIFER: Fine. If that's the way You feel, You've got Adam and Eve, and it'll be a thousand years before you're a grandfather. *He stands.* Think it over. I'd be glad to go down and—*God gives him a look.* I'm only trying to help!

GOD: Lucifer, I'm way ahead of you.

LUCIFER: Lord, that's inevitable.

GOD: Stay away from that tree.

LUCIFER, *with a certain evasiveness:* Whatever You say, sir. May I go now?

GOD, *after a pause:* Don't have the illusion that I am in conflict about this; I mean, don't decide to go down there and do Me a favor, or something. I know perfectly well why I put that tree there.

LUCIFER, *surprised:* Really!

GOD: Yes, really. I am in perfect control over my unconscious, friend. It was not to tempt Adam; it's I who was tempted. I finished him and I saw he was beautiful, and for a moment I loved him beyond anything I had ever made—and I thought, maybe I should let him see through the rose petal to its chemistry, the formation of amino acids to the secrets of life. His simple praise for surfaces made me impatient to show him the physics of My art, which would raise him to a god.

LUCIFER: Why'd You change Your mind?

GOD: Because I thought of what became of you. The one angel who really understands biology and physics, the one I loved before all the rest and took such care to teach—and you can't take a breath without thinking how to overthrow Me and take over the universe!

LUCIFER: Lord, I only wanted them to know more, the more to praise You!

GOD: The more they know, the less they will need Me, Lucifer; you know that as well as I! And that's all you're after, to grind away their respect for Me. "Give them an apple!" If it weren't for the Law of the Conservation of Energy I would destroy you! Don't go near that tree or those dear people— not in any form, you hear? They are innocent, and innocent they will remain till I turn out the lights forever!

God goes out. Lucifer is alone.

LUCIFER: Now what is He *really* saying? He put it there to tempt *Himself*! Therefore He's not of one mind about in- nocence; and how could He be when innocence blinds Adam to half the wonders He has made? I will help the Lord. Yes, that's the only way to put it; I'm His helper. I open up the marvels He dares not show, and thereby mag- nify His glory. In short, I disobey what He says and carry out what He means, and if that's evil, it's only to do good. Strange—I never felt so close to my creator as I do right now! Once Adam eats, he'll multiply, and Lucifer completes the lovely world of God! Oh, praise the Lord who gave me all this insight! My fight with Him is over! Now evil be my good, and Eve and Adam multiply in blessed sin! Make way, dumb stars, the world of man begins!

He exits as light rises on Paradise, where Eve is bent over from the waist, examining a—to us invisible—turtle. Adam enters. His attention is caught by her raised buttocks, and he approaches, halts, and stares—then looks off, puzzled by an idea he can't quite form in his mind. Giving it up, he asks . . .

ADAM: You want to play volleyball?

Lucifer enters.

LUCIFER: Good evening.
ADAM: Good evening. *He nervously nudges Eve, who now stands up. Something in Lucifer moves something in her.*
EVE: Oh!

Lucifer exchanges a deep glance with her, then moves, glancing about, and then turns back to Adam.

LUCIFER: Had enough?
EVE: Enough of what?
LUCIFER: You don't imagine, do you, that God intended you to lie around like this forever?
ADAM: We're going swimming later.
LUCIFER: Swimming! What about making something of yourselves?
ADAM: Making some . . . ?
LUCIFER, *with a quick glance about for God:* I'm a little short of time, Adam. By the way, my name is Lucifer. The archangel?
ADAM, *impressed:* Ohhh! I'm very pleased to meet you. This is my wife, Eve.
EVE: How do you do?
LUCIFER, *taking her hand with a little pressure:* Awfully nice to meet you, Eve. Tell me, you ever hold your breath?
ADAM: Oh, sure, she does that a lot. Show him, Eve. *She inhales*

and holds it. She can do that till she turns blue. *Eve lets out the air.*

EVE: I can really turn blue if I want to.

LUCIFER: And why does that happen?

ADAM: Because God makes it.

LUCIFER: But how, dear?

ADAM: How should she know?

LUCIFER: But God *wants* her to know.

ADAM: But why didn't He tell us?

LUCIFER: He's trying to tell you; that's why I've come; I am the Explainer. Adam, the fact is that God gives His most important commands through His silences. For example, there is nothing He feels more passionate about than that you begin to multiply.

EVE: Really?

LUCIFER: Of course. That's why that tree is there.

EVE: We multiply with the tree?

LUCIFER: No, but if you eat the fruit you'll know how. He just can't bring Himself to say it, you see.

EVE: Is that so!

ADAM: Now, wait a minute, excuse me. We're not even supposed to *think* about that tree.

EVE: Say, that's right. In fact, lately, that's practically all I do is go around not thinking about it.

LUCIFER: Oh, you find that's getting difficult?

EVE: No, but it takes up so much time.

ADAM: It's because we'll die if we eat those things. *Lucifer reaches up, takes the apple.* You better watch out, they're not good for you—Don't! *Lucifer bites into the apple, chews. They watch him, wide-eyed.* Oh, I know why, it's that you're an angel!

LUCIFER: You could be too.

ADAM, *worried:* Angels?

LUCIFER: Absolutely. Now listen carefully, because this is fairly deep and I may have to leave any minute. You know by now why the Lord put you in this lovely garden.

ADAM: To praise everything.

LUCIFER: Right. Now what if I told you that there are a number of things you've been leaving out?

ADAM, *shocked:* Oh, no! I praise absolutely everything.

LUCIFER, *pointing to his penis:* And what about this thing here? Do you praise Him for that?

ADAM, *looking down at himself:* Well, not in particular, but I include it in.

LUCIFER: But how can you when you don't know what it's for?

EVE: He pees that way.

LUCIFER: Pees! That is so incidental it's not even worth mentioning. *To Adam:* You have no idea, do you?

ADAM: Well . . . ahh . . .

LUCIFER: Yes?

ADAM: I'm only guessing, but sometimes it makes me feel—

LUCIFER: Feel what?

ADAM: Well . . . kind of sporty?

LUCIFER: Adam! God has made you in His image, given you His body. How dare you refuse to understand the very best part of it? Now you will eat this apple.

ADAM: Angel, please—I really don't feel I should.

LUCIFER, *holding the apple to Adam's tightly shut lips:* You must! Could I make this offer without God's permission?

EVE: Say, that's right!

LUCIFER: Of course it's right! I mean nothing happens He doesn't want to happen—*n'est-ce pas?* Now, you take one bite, and I promise you will understand everything. Adam, open your mouth and you will become—*he glances quickly about, lowers his voice*—like God.

ADAM: Like *God!* You should never say a thing like that!

LUCIFER: You're not even living like animals!

ADAM: I don't want to hear any more! He said it in plain Hebrew, don't eat those apples, and that's it! I'm going swimming. Eve?

EVE, *extending her hand to Lucifer:* Very nice to have met you.

LUCIFER, *slowly running his eyes from her feet to her face:* Likewise.

A strange sensation emanates from his eyes, and she slowly looks down at her body.

ADAM: Eve?

She unwillingly breaks from Lucifer, and they leave. Lucifer looks at the apple in his hand and takes a big bite. He stands there chewing thoughtfully. Offstage a splash is heard. A pause. Eve returns, glancing behind her, and hurries to Lucifer.

EVE: There's only one thing I wonder if you could tell me.

LUCIFER: I love questions, my dear. What is it?

EVE—*she looks down at herself, pointing:* Why has he got that thing and I don't?

LUCIFER: Isn't it funny? I knew you were going to ask that question.

EVE: Well, I mean, is it going to grow on later?

LUCIFER: Never.

EVE: Why?

LUCIFER, *offering her his apple:* Take a bite, Eve, and everything will clear up.

EVE—*she accepts the apple, looks at it:* It smells all right.

LUCIFER: Of course. It *is* all right.

EVE: Maybe just a little bite.

LUCIFER: Better make it medium. You have an awful lot to learn, dear.

EVE: Well . . . here goes! *She bites and chews, her eyes widening, her body moving sinuously. A dread sound fills the air. She approaches him.*

LUCIFER, *retreating:* 'Fraid I've got to leave, dear.

EVE: You going *now*?

LUCIFER: Oh, yes, right now! But I'll be around.

He hurries off, glancing behind with trepidation. She stands there staring. She feels her body, her breasts, her face, awakening to herself. She starts her hand down to her genitals and inhales a surprised breath. Adam enters. The sound goes silent.

ADAM: Where were you? Come on, the water's perfect! . . . Eve? *She turns to him.* What's the matter? *She sensuously touches his arm and puts it around her.* What are you doing? *She smashes her lips against his.* What is this? *She holds her apple before his face.*

EVE: Eat it.

ADAM: Eve!

EVE: It's marvelous! Please, a bite, a bite!

ADAM: But God said—

EVE: I'm God.

ADAM: You're what?

EVE: He is in me! He'll be in you! I never felt like this! I am the best thing that ever happened! Look at me! Adam, don't you see me?

ADAM: Well, sure, I—

EVE: You're not looking at me!

ADAM: Of course I'm looking at you!

EVE: But you're not *seeing* me! You don't see anything!

ADAM: Why? I see the trees, the sky—

EVE: You wouldn't see anything else if you were seeing me.

ADAM: How's that possible?

EVE: Say "Ahh."

ADAM: Ahh.

She suddenly pushes the apple into his mouth.

EVE: Chew! Swallow!

He chews. The dread sound again. She watches. He looks down at his penis. Then to her. Then up at her face, astonished. He starts to reach for her.

VOICE OF GOD, *echoing through the theater on the PA system:* WHERE ART THOU! *They both retract, glancing desperately around. They rush about, trying to hide from each other.* WHERE ART THOU!

ADAM: Here, quick! Put something on! *He hands her a leaf, which she holds in front of her.* Gee, you know you look even better with that leaf on—

EVE, *looking off:* He's coming!

They disappear. God enters.

GOD: Where art thou?

ADAM, *still unseen:* Here, Lord. *God turns, looking around. Adam emerges. He is wearing a large leaf. Nervously apologizing.* I heard Thy voice in the garden and I was afraid, because I was naked; and I hid myself. *Eve emerges.*

GOD: Who told thee that thou wast naked?

ADAM: Who told me?

GOD: Who told thee! You didn't know you were naked!

ADAM, *appalled, looking down at himself:* Say, that's right.

GOD, *mimicking him:* "Say, that's right." You ate the apple!

ADAM: She made me.

EVE: I couldn't help it. A snake came. *To Adam:* Wasn't he a snake?

ADAM: Like a snake, ya.

GOD: That son of a . . . *Calling out:* Lucifer, I get my hands on you . . . !

EVE: But why'd You put the tree here if You . . . ?

GOD: *You're* questioning *Me*! Who the hell do you think you are? I put the tree here so there would be at least one thing you shouldn't think about! So, unlike the animals, you should exercise a little self-control.

EVE: Oh!

GOD: "Oh," she says. I'll give you an "Oh" that you'll wish you'd never been born! But first I'm going to fix it between you and snakes. Serpent, because thou hast done this,

> Thou art cursed above all cattle,
> And above every beast of the field;
> And I will put enmity between thee and woman—
> That means all women will hate snakes.
> Or almost all.

You see? It's already impossible to make an absolute state-ment around here! You bad girl, look what you did to Me!

EVE, *covering her face:* I'm ashamed.

GOD: Ashamed! You don't know the half of it.

> I will greatly multiply thy sorrow and thy conception;
> In sorrow thou shalt bring forth children—

EVE: Oh God!

GOD: And thy desire shall be to thy husband
> And he shall rule over thee.

No more equals, you hear? He's the boss forever. Pull up your leaf.

He turns to Adam. And as for you, schmuck!

> Cursed is the ground for thy sake,
> In sorrow shalt thou eat of it all the days of thy life.
> Thorns and thistles shall it bring forth to thee;
> No more going around just picking up lunch.
> In the sweat of thy face shalt thou eat bread,
> Till thou return unto the ground;
> Yes, my friend, now there is time and age and death,
> No more living forever. You got it?

    For dust thou art.

    And unto dust shalt thou return.

ADAM—*he sobs:* What am I doing? What's this water?

GOD: You're weeping, my son, those are your first tears;

    There will be more before you're finished.

    Now you have become as one of us,

    A little lower than the angels,

    Because now you know good and evil.

    Adam and Eve? Get out of the Garden.

ADAM: Out where?

GOD, *pointing:* There!

ADAM: But that's a desert!

GOD: Right! It wasn't good enough for you here? Go and see
how you make out on your own.

ADAM: God. Dear God, isn't there any way we can get back in?
I don't want to be ashamed, I don't want to be so full of
sadness. It was so wonderful here, we were both so innocent!

GOD: Out! You know too much to live in Eden.

ADAM: But I am ignorant!

GOD: Knowing you are ignorant is too much to know.

    The lion and the elephant, the spider and the mouse—

    They will remain, but they know My perfection

    Without knowing it. You ate what I forbade,

    You yearned for what you were not

    And thus laid a judgment on My work.

    I Am What I Am What I Am, but it was not enough;

    The warmth in the sand, the coolness of water,

    The coming and going of day and night—

    It was not enough to live in these things.

    You had to have power, and power is in you now,

    But not Eden any more. Listen, Adam. Listen, Eve.

    Can you hear the coming of night?

ADAM—*surprised, he raises his hand:* Why . . . no!

GOD: Can you hear the sound of shadows on the leaves?

EVE, *with immense loss and wonder:* No!

God turns his back on them, hurt, erect.

EVE: Where is the voice of the trout talking in the river?

ADAM: Where are the footsteps of angels walking through the
vines?

On the verge of weeping, they are turning to catch the sounds they knew, deaf to the world. Light is playing on them as instruments are heard playing a lugubrious tune. They dejectedly leave Paradise.

A sad bassoon solo emerges, played by Raphael. God, hands behind his back, turns to Raphael, Chemuel, and Azrael, who enter together.

GOD: That is the most depressing instrument I have ever heard.

RAPHAEL, *the bassoonist, protesting:* But You invented it, Lord.

GOD: I can't imagine how I could have thought of such a thing.

CHEMUEL: It was just after Eve ate the apple. You were very down. And You said, "I think I will invent the bassoon."

GOD: Well, put it away, Raphael.

AZRAEL: Look at Adam and Eve down there. All they do any more is screw.

CHEMUEL: Maybe we ought to talk about something cheerful.

GOD: Do that, yes.

Pause. The angels think.

CHEMUEL: I think the Rocky Mountains are the best yet! *God turns to him, pained.* I mean the way they go up.

RAPHAEL: And then the way they go down.

GOD: I'm afraid that Lucifer was the only one of you who knew how to carry on a conversation.

AZRAEL, *a fierce fellow, deep-throated:* I would like to kill Adam and Eve.

GOD: That's natural, Azrael, as the Angel of Death, but I'm not ready for that yet.

AZRAEL: They like to swim; I could drown them. Or push them over a cliff—

GOD, *pained:* Don't say those things, stop it.

AZRAEL: I have to say, Lord, I warned You at the time: You mustn't make a creature that looks like You, or You'll *never* let me kill him.

CHEMUEL: It was such a pleasure with the lions and the gorillas.

GOD: Yes, but—*He looks down at the earth*—when they're good it makes me feel so marvelous.

AZRAEL: But how often are they good?

GOD: I know, but when they praise My name and all that.

There's nothing like it. When they send up those hallelujahs from Notre Dame—

AZRAEL: Notre Dame!

RAPHAEL: Lord, Notre Dame isn't for six thousand years.

GOD: I know, but I'm looking forward. *He stands, shocked, His eye caught by something below.* Look at that! How do they think up such positions?

AZRAEL: I don't understand why You let them go on offending You like this. You called back other mistakes—the fish with fur who drowned—

CHEMUEL: And the beetle who hiccupped whenever it snowed.

AZRAEL: Why don't You let me go down and wipe them out?

GOD: They are the only ones who need Me.

CHEMUEL: Sure! Give them a chance.

GOD: I'll never forget the first time I realized what I meant to them. It was the first time Adam laid her down and went into her. She closed her eyes, and she began to breathe so deeply I thought she'd faint, or die, or explode. And suddenly she cried out, "Oh dear God!" I have never heard My name so genuinely praised.

AZRAEL: I find the whole spectacle disgusting.

GOD: I know. It's the worst thing that ever happened. *He is in conflict, staring.* It can't go on this way; I must have it out with Lucifer.

ALL: Lucifer!

GOD, *energetically:* I have never before been in conflict with Myself. Look at it; My poor, empty Eden; the ripened peach falls uneaten to the ground, and My two idiotic darlings roam the desert scrounging for a crust. It has definitely gone wrong. And not one of you has an idea worth talking about. Clear away; I must decide.

CHEMUEL: Decide what, Lord?

GOD: I don't know yet, but a decision is definitely rising in Me. And that was the one thing Lucifer always knew—the issue. Go. *Chemuel throws up his hands.*

ALL, *singing:* Hallelujah, hallelujah . . .

The angels are walking out.

GOD: One more.

ALL: Hallelujah!

They go. God is alone. He concentrates. Lucifer appears.

LUCIFER, *wary, looking for cues to God's attitude:* Thank You, Father. I have been waiting. I am ready to face my ordeal.

GOD: Lucifer, I have been struggling to keep from destroying you. The Law of the Conservation of Energy does not protect an angel from being broken into small pieces and sprinkled over the Atlantic Ocean.

LUCIFER: Wouldn't that just spread him around, though?

GOD: What restrains me is a feeling that somewhere in the universe a stupendous event has occurred. For an instant it made Me terribly happy. I thought it might be the icecaps, but they're not really working out.

LUCIFER: Trouble?

GOD: There is a definite leak.

LUCIFER: Can You repair it?

GOD: I've decided to let them run. It will mean a collection of large lakes across North America, and some in Europe.

LUCIFER: Oh, Father, surely You planned it that way.

GOD: I see now that I probably did; but frankly I wasn't thinking of the lakes; I simply felt there should be icecaps on both poles. But that's the way it is—one thing always leads to another.

LUCIFER: Then you must already know the fantastic news I've brought You.

GOD, *staring for his thought:* I undoubtedly do. *At a loss:* Happy news.

LUCIFER: Glorious.

GOD: I knew it! In the very midst of all my disappointments I suddenly felt a sort of . . . hopeful silence.

LUCIFER: The silent seed of Adam squirming into Eve's ovarian tube.

GOD, *striking His forehead:* Aaaaah! Of course! And the ovum?

LUCIFER: Has been fertilized.

GOD: And has attached itself . . .

LUCIFER: To the womb. It is holding on nicely.

GOD: Then so far—

LUCIFER: So good. I can't see any reason to worry.

GOD, *clapping His hands:* My first upright pregnancy! *Worried:* Maybe she ought to lie down more.

LUCIFER: Lord, she could stand on her head and not lose it.

GOD: And how is she feeling?

LUCIFER: I thought I'd ask You about that. She is slightly nauseated in the mornings.

GOD: That is partly disgust with herself. At least I hope so. But it is also the blood supply diverting to the womb.

LUCIFER: I never thought of that! In any case, it works.

GOD: How utterly, utterly superb.

LUCIFER: Oh, dear Father, ever since my interview with Eve I've been terrified You'd never speak to me again. And now when I so want to thank You properly, all metaphor, simile, and image scatter before this victory of ours. *God becomes alert.* Like the firm cheek of Heaven, the wall of her womb nuzzles the bud of the first son of man.

GOD: Say that again?

LUCIFER: Like the firm—

GOD: No, before that.

Slight pause.

LUCIFER: But surely it was all according to plan?

GOD, *peering at him:* According to . . . ?

LUCIFER: It was supposed to happen through me. Of course, I am perfectly aware that I merely acted as Your agent.

GOD: Not on your life! They would have made it in Paradise, clean and innocent, and with My blessing instead of My curse!

LUCIFER: But the fact is, they were not making it!

GOD: They might have by accident!

LUCIFER: Father, I can't believe a technicality is more important than this service to Your cause!

GOD: Technicality! I am going to condemn you, Lucifer.

LUCIFER: Dear God, for what? For making You a grandfather?

GOD: I forbade that apple! Nobody violates a Commandment, I don't care how good it comes out!

LUCIFER: You mean the letter of the law is more important than the survival of the human race? *God is silent. A smile breaks onto Lucifer's face.* This is a test, isn't it? You're testing me? *God is inscrutable.* That's all right, don't answer. Now I will confess myself and prove that I finally understand my part in the Plan.

GOD: What Plan? What are you talking about?

LUCIFER: Your hidden Plan for operating the world. All my life, sir, I've had the feeling that I was somehow . . . a *useless* angel. I look at Azrael, so serious and grave, perfect for the Angel of Death. And our sweet Chemuel—exactly right for the Angel of Mercy. But when I tried to examine *my* character, I could never find any. Gorgeous profile, superb intelligence, but what was Lucifer *for*? Am I boring You?

GOD: Not at all.

LUCIFER, *worried:* How do you mean that? *God simply looks at him.* Good, good—don't make it easy for me. I will now explain about the apple. You see, I'd gone down there to help you, but she took one bite and that innocent stare erupted with such carnal appetite that I began to wonder, was it possible I had actually done something—*He breaks off.*

GOD: Evil?

LUCIFER: Oh, that terrible word! But now I will face it! *The desperate yet joyful confession.* Father, I've *always* had certain impulses that mystified me. If I saw my brother angels soaring upwards, my immediate impulse was to go down. A raspberry cane bends to the right, I'd find myself leaning left. Others praise the forehead, I am drawn to the ass. Holes—I don't want to leave anything out—I adore holes. Every hole is precious to me. I'll go even further—in excrement, decay, the intestine of the world is my stinking desire. You ever hear anything so straightforwardly disgusting? I tell you I have felt so worthless, I was often ready to cut my throat. But Eve is pregnant now, and I see the incredible, hidden truth.

GOD: Which is?

LUCIFER: How can I be rotten? How else but through my disobedience was Eve made pregnant with mankind? How dare I hate myself? Not only am I not rotten—I am God's corrective symmetry, that festering embrace which keeps His world from impotent virtue. And once I saw that, I saw Your purpose working through me and I nearly wept with self-respect. And I fell in love—with both of us. *Slight pause. God is motionless.* Well, that's—the general idea, right?

GOD: Lucifer, you are a degenerate! You are a cosmic pervert!

LUCIFER: But God in Heaven, who made me this way?

God whacks him across the face; Lucifer falls to his knees.

GOD: Don't you ever, ever say that.

LUCIFER: Adonoi elohaenu, adonoi echaud. Father, I know Your anger is necessary, but my love stands fast!

GOD: Love! The only love you know is for yourself! You think I haven't seen you standing before a mirror whole years at a time!

LUCIFER: I have, Lord, admiring Your handiwork.

GOD: How can you lie like this and not even blush!

LUCIFER: All right! *He stands up.* Now I will tell You the Truth! *At the pinnacle:* Lord, I am ready to take my place beside the throne.

GOD: Beside the *what*?

LUCIFER: Why, the throne, Lord. At Your right hand. If not the right, then the left. I can suggest a title: Minister of Excremental Matters. I can walk with a limp, now watch this. *He walks, throwing one leg out spastically.*

GOD: What is this?

LUCIFER: And I do a tic, You see? *He does a wild tic as he walks crazily.*

GOD: What are you doing?

LUCIFER: I'll stutter, too. *Horribly:* Whoo, wha—munnnn—

GOD: What is this?

LUCIFER: I'll wear a hunch back and masturbate incessantly, eternal witness that God loves absolutely everything He made! What a *lesson*! But before You answer—the point, the far-reaching ultimate, is that this will change the future. Do you remember the future, Lord?

GOD: Of course I remember the future.

LUCIFER: It is a disaster; it is one ghastly war after another down through the centuries.

GOD: You can never change the future. The past, yes, but not the future.

LUCIFER: How do you change the past?

GOD: Why, the past is always changing—nobody remembers anything. But the future can no more be turned away than the light flowing off the moon.

LUCIFER: Unless we stood together, Lord, You immaculate on Your throne, absolutely good, and I beside You, perfectly evil. Father and son, the two inseparable buddies. *God is caught by it.* There could never, never be war! You see it, I can see You see it! If good and evil stand as one, what'll they have to fight about? What army could ever mobilize if on all the flags was written: "For God and Country and the Stinking Devil"? Without absolute righteousness there can never be a war! We will flummox the generals! Father, you are a handshake away from a second Paradise! Peace on earth to the end of time. *God is peering, feverish.* And that, sir, is your entire plan for me as I see it.

GOD: In other words, I would no longer be absolutely right.

LUCIFER: Just in public, sir. Privately, of course—*a gesture connecting them*—we know what's what.

GOD: We do.

LUCIFER: Oh, Lord, I have no thought of . . . actually—

GOD: Sharing power.

LUCIFER: God forbid. I'm speaking purely of the image.

GOD: But in reality . . .

LUCIFER: Nothing's changed. You're good, and I'm bad. It's just that to the public—

GOD: We will appear to be—

LUCIFER: Yes.

GOD: Equal.

LUCIFER: Not morally equal. Just equally real. Because if I'm sitting beside You in Heaven—

GOD: Then I must love you.

LUCIFER: Exactly. And if God can love the Devil, He can love absolutely anybody.

GOD: *That's* certainly true, yes.

LUCIFER: So people would never come to hate themselves, and there's the end of guilt. Another Eden, and everybody innocent again.

Pause.

GOD: Operationally speaking—

LUCIFER: Yes.

GOD: Yes *sir.*

LUCIFER: Yes sir. Excuse me.

GOD: In cases of lying, cheating, fornication, murder, and so on—you mean they are no longer to be judged?

LUCIFER: Oh, on the contrary! Between the two of us *no one* will escape the judgment of Heaven. I'll judge the bad people, and you judge the good.

GOD: But who would try to be good if it's just as good to be bad?

LUCIFER: And will the bad be good for fear of your judgment? So you may as well let them be bad and the good be good, and either way they'll all love God because they'll know that God . . . loves . . . me. Sir, I am ready to take my place. Between the two of us we'll have mankind mousetrapped.

GOD: Yes. *Slight pause.* There is only one problem.

LUCIFER: But basically that's the Plan, isn't it?

GOD: There is a problem.

LUCIFER: What's that?

GOD, *looking straight at him:* I don't love you.

LUCIFER, *shocked—he can hardly speak:* You can't mean that.

GOD: Afraid I do.

LUCIFER: Well. *He gives a deflated laugh.* This is certainly a surprise.

GOD: I see that. And it is fundamentally why we can never sit together. Nothing is real to you. Except your appetite for distinction and power. I've been waiting for some slightest sign of repentance for what you did to Paradise, but there's nothing, is there? Instead, I'm to join you in a cosmic comedy where good and evil are the same. It doesn't occur to you that I am unable to share the bench with the very incarnation of all I despise?

LUCIFER: I can't believe You'd let Your feelings stand in the way of peace.

GOD: But that is why I am perfect—I *am* my feelings.

LUCIFER: You don't think that's a limitation?

GOD: It certainly is. I am perfectly limited. Where evil begins, I end. When good loves evil, it is no longer good, and if God could love the Devil, then God has died. And that is precisely what you're after, isn't it?!

LUCIFER: I am after peace! Between us and mankind!

GOD: Then let there be war! Better ten thousand years of war

than I should rule one instant with the help of unrighteousness!

LUCIFER: Lord God, I am holding out my hand!

GOD, *rising:*

> Go to Hell! Now thou art fallen in all thy beauty.
> As the rain doth fall and green the grass
> And the fish out of water suffocates,
> So dost thy fall prove that there are consequences.
> Now die in Heaven, Lucifer, and live in Hell
> That man may ever know how good and evil separate!

LUCIFER: Lord? *He is upright, stern.* You will not take my
hand?

GOD: Never! Never, never, never!

LUCIFER: Then I will take the world. *He exits.*

GOD, *calling:* And if you ever do, I will burn it, I will flood it
out, I will leave it a dead rock spinning in silence! For I am
the Lord, and the Lord is good and only good!

ANGELS' VOICES, *singing loudly and sharply:* Blessed is the Lord
my God, Glory, glory, glory!

God sits, cleaved by doubt. He turns His head, looking about.

GOD: Why do I miss him? *He stares ahead.* How strange.

CURTAIN

ACT TWO

Darkness. The sound of a high wind. It dies off. A starry sky.

In the starlight, Adam and Eve are discovered asleep, but apart. He snores contentedly, she lies in silence on her back, her very pregnant belly arching up.

Lucifer, in black now, rises from the ground. He scans the sky for any sign of God, then looks down at the two people. In deep thought he walks to the periphery and sits, his chin on his fist, staring.

Overhead a bird begins to sing. He looks up.

LUCIFER: Oh, shut up. *The birdsong effloresces gloriously.* Will you get out of here? Go! Glorify the Lord some place else! *Flapping of wings. He follows the bird's flight overhead with his gaze.* Idiot. *Depressed, he stares ahead.* Everything I see throws up the same irrational lesson. The hungriest bird sings best. What a system! That deprivation should make music—is anarchy! And what is greatness in God's world? A peaceful snake lies dozing in the sun with no more dignity than a long worm; but let him arch his head to strike—and there, by God, is a *snake!* Yes! I have reasoned, pleaded, argued, when only murder in this world makes majesty—God's included. Was He ever Godlier, ever more my king than when He murdered my hopes? And will I ever be more than a ridiculous angel—*he turns to Adam and Eve*—until I murder His? *He stands, goes to Eve, looks down at her.* Where is His dearest hope in all the world—but in that belly? *He suddenly raises his foot to stomp her, then retracts.* No. N-no. Let her do it. Make her do it. *He looks skyward.* Oh, the shock, the shock! If she refused the Lord the fruit of man because He made the world unreasonable! *He inspires himself, slowly sinks to the ground, and insinuates into Eve's ear:* This is a dream. *He ceremoniously lifts his hand and with his middle finger touches her forehead.* I enter the floor of thy skull. *He bends and kisses her belly.* Now, woman, help me save the world from the anarchy of God. *She inhales sensuously, and her knee rises, her cloak falling away, exposing a bare thigh.*

316

Your time has come, dear woman. *He slides his hand along her thigh.*

EVE, *exhaling pleasurably:* Aaaaaahhh!

LUCIFER: Sssh! Don't wake up; the only safe place to have this conversation is inside your head. Am I clear in your mind? Do you remember me?

EVE: Oh, yes! When our fingers touched around the apple—

LUCIFER: Flesh to naked flesh!

EVE: And I awoke and saw myself! How beautiful I was! *She opens her eyes.*

LUCIFER: What in the world has happened to you? How'd you get so ugly?

EVE, *covering her face:* I can't stand myself!

LUCIFER: When I think how you looked in Paradise—*she weeps* —Why did you let yourself go?

EVE: Can you help me, angel? Something's got into my belly, and it keeps getting bigger.

LUCIFER: No idea what it is?

EVE: Well . . . I *have* been eating a lot of clams lately.

LUCIFER: Clams.

EVE: Sometimes it even squirms. *Lucifer looks away in thought.* Isn't that it?

LUCIFER, *turning back to her:* Like to have it out?

EVE, *clapping her hands:* Could I?

LUCIFER: But are you sure you won't change your mind afterwards?

EVE: No! I want to be as I was. Please, angel, take thy power and drive it out.

LUCIFER: Lie back, dear.

EVE: Oh, thank you, angel, I will adore you forever!

LUCIFER, *starting to spread her knees:* I certainly hope so. Now just try to relax. . . .

EVE, *on her back, facing the sky, her arms stretched upward:* Oh, won't the Lord be happy when He sees me looking good again! *Lucifer removes his hands, instantly turning away to think. She, on her back, can't see what he is doing.* Is anything happening?

LUCIFER, *drawing her upright:* Woman, I don't want you hating me in the morning; now listen, and I will waken your mind as once I awakened your body in Paradise.

EVE: By the way, I've been wanting to ask you: did you ever come to me again—*after* Paradise?

LUCIFER, *evasively:* Why do you ask?

EVE: Near twilight, once, I was lying on my stomach, looking at my face in a pool; and suddenly a strange kind of weight pressed down on my back, and it pressed and pressed until we seemed to go tumbling out like dragonflies above the water. And in my ear a voice kept whispering. "This is God's will, darling. . . ."

LUCIFER: Which it was, at the time.

EVE, *marveling:* It was you!

LUCIFER: All me. About nine months ago.

EVE, *gleefully:* Oh, angel, that was glorious! Come, make me beautiful again! *She starts to lie back; he stops her.*

LUCIFER: You will have it out, Eve, but it's important there be no recriminations afterwards, so I'm going to tell you the truth. I have been thrown out of Heaven.

EVE: How's that possible? You're an *angel*!

LUCIFER: Dear girl, we are dealing with a spirit to whom nothing is sacred.

EVE: But why? What did you do?

LUCIFER: What He could not do. *He breaks off.*

EVE: What?

LUCIFER, *taking the plunge:* I caused you to multiply.

EVE: You mean—*she looks down at her belly*—I'm multiplying?

LUCIFER: What you have in your belly . . . is a man.

EVE: A man! *Overjoyed, she rolls back onto the ground.* In me!

LUCIFER: Remember what you said! You want it out!

EVE, *sitting up:* How is God feeling about me? Does He know?

LUCIFER: All right, then. Yes, He knows and He is ecstatic!

EVE: Oh, praise the Lord!

LUCIFER, *furiously:* Quadruple hallelujahs!

EVE: Glory to Him in the highest!

LUCIFER: Precisely. *Jabbing his finger at her:* And now I'll bet your agony begins!

EVE, *with a shock of pain:* Aaaahhhhh!

LUCIFER: Why'd you stop praising Him? *She yells in pain.* Where's the hallelujah!?

EVE: What is happening to me?

LUCIFER: What're you complaining about? You praise God, and this is what you get for it!

EVE: But why?

LUCIFER: Don't you remember Him cursing you out of Paradise?

EVE: And this—

LUCIFER: Is it, honey.

EVE, *pointing to the sleeping Adam:* But he ate the apple too!

LUCIFER: Right. And he looks better than ever.

EVE, *furiously pounding her hands on the ground:* WHY?

LUCIFER, *grabbing her face, driving his point home:* Because this is the justice of the world He made, and only you can change that world!

EVE: Angel . . . it's getting worse.

LUCIFER: Oh, it'll get worse than this, dear.

EVE: It can't get worse!

LUCIFER: Oh, yes, it can, because He's perfect, and when He makes something worse, it's *perfectly* worse!

EVE: Oh God, what have I done!

LUCIFER: You multiplied with my help, not with His, and your agony is His bureaucratic revenge. Now listen to me—

EVE: I can't stand any more! *Lashing about on the ground.* Where's a rock, I'll kill him! *With clawed hands she starts for Adam.*

LUCIFER: He is as innocent as you!

EVE, *bursting into helpless tears:* This is not *right*!

LUCIFER: Oh, woman, to hear that word at last from other lips than mine! It is not right, no—it is chaos. Eve, you are the only voice of reason God's insane world can ever have, for in you alone His chaos shows its claws. *In poena veritas*—the only truth is pain. Now mount it and take your power.

EVE: What power? I'm a grain of dust.

LUCIFER: He is pacing up and down in Heaven waiting for this child. You have in your belly the crown of God.

EVE: The crown . . . ?

LUCIFER: His highest honor is your gratitude for the agony He is giving you. He is a maniac! *He takes her hand.* You can refuse. You must deny this crown to chaos. Kill it. *He is behind her, his lips to her ear, his hand on her belly.*

Let the serpent in again, and we'll murder him,
And so teach the Lord His first humility.

He slips around in front of her, starting to press her back to the ground.

Crown His vengeance on thee not with life
But with a death; a lump of failure
Lay before the Lord a teaching, woman—

EVE, *in conflict, resisting his pressure to lie down: I* teach God?

LUCIFER:

Teach God, yes!—that if men must be born
Only in the pain of unearned sin,
Then there will be no men at all!
Open to me!

He tries to spread her legs. She reaches uncertainly to his face, while trying to fend his hands off.

EVE: Angel, I'm afraid!

LUCIFER: Hold still! *He is on top of her to pin her down.*

EVE: I don't think I can do that!

LUCIFER: Open up, you bitch! *He violently tries to spread her knees; she breaks free, skittering away on the ground.*

EVE: I can't! I mustn't! I won't! *Sexually infuriated, he starts again for her.* I want him! *Adam turns over. Lucifer springs out of her line of sight so that she is looking around at empty space, holding her belly. In short, she has only now awakened in the dream's hangover. Day is dawning.* Where am I? *The baaing of sheep is heard.*

LUCIFER:

The dream ends here, a dark rehearsal of the coming day;
This day you must decide—to crown unreason with thy gift of life,
Or with a tiny death teach justice. *He bends and kisses her.*
I understand thee, woman—I alone.
Call any time at all.

Intimately, pointing into her face: You know what I mean.

Adams sits up. Lucifer goes. Day dawns. Adam stares at Eve, as she sits there. Now she brings her body forward and wipes her eyes.

ADAM: What a night! I don't think I slept five minutes. *She gives him a look.* Did you?

EVE, *after a slight pause, guiltily:* I slept very well, yes.

Disturbed, inward, she gets up, begins gathering pieces of wood for the fire. The baaing of sheep is heard.

ADAM, *looking around:* Say! *She stops moving, looks at him.* The wind! It finally stopped! See? I told you I'd find a place that's not windy!

A blast of howling wind makes them both huddle into their clothes. It dies off. She gets out some figs, places them in a bowl.

EVE: There's your figs.

ADAM: Could it be, you suppose, that everywhere but in Paradise it's just naturally windy? *He bites into a fig.*

EVE: I just don't know, Adam.

ADAM—*he spits out sand:* They're sandy.

EVE: Well, it's windy.

He leans his head on his fist disconsolately.

ADAM: What a way to live! At least if I knew how long it was going to last—

EVE: I still don't understand what's so wrong about digging a hole. We could sit in it and keep out of the wind. Like the groundhogs.

ADAM: I wish you'd stop trying to change the rules! We're not groundhogs. If He meant us to live in holes, He would have given us claws.

EVE: But if He meant us to live in a windstorm, He'd have put our eyes in our armpits. *Another blast of wind; then it dies.*

ADAM: Aren't you eating anything?

EVE: I don't feel like it.

ADAM: You know something? You don't look so green today.

EVE, *faintly hopeful, a little surprised at his interest:* I don't?

ADAM: All your color came back. What happened? *He slides over to her, looking quizzically and somewhat excitedly into her face.* You look beautiful, Eve.

EVE—*she laughs nervously:* Well, I can't imagine why!

ADAM, *pushing her back, starting to open her cloak:* It's amazing! I haven't seen you look this way since Paradise! *His hand on her swollen belly stops him.* Oh, excuse me.

EVE, *grasping his hand:* That's all right!

ADAM, *getting up, sliding his hand out of hers:* I forgot that thing. *He stands, looks around.* What a funny morning!

EVE: Why do you always look around like that?

ADAM, *after a slight pause:* I miss God.

EVE, *looking down in sorrow:* I'm sorry, Adam. *Sheep are heard again.*

ADAM, *looking off:* It is just that I'm never really sure what to do next. That grass is giving out; we'll have to move this afternoon.

EVE: I don't think I can walk very far.

ADAM: Goddamn clams . . .

EVE: I'm always out of breath, Adam. This thing has gotten very heavy.

ADAM: Does it still move?

EVE: It's doing it now. Would you like to feel it?

ADAM, *touching her belly:* Huh!

EVE: It's almost like a little foot pressing.

ADAM: A foot! No. *He presses his stomach.* I have the same thing sometimes.

EVE, *with sudden hope:* You too? Let me feel it! *She feels his stomach.* I don't feel anything.

ADAM: Well, it stopped. I can't remember—did He say to kill clams before eating?

EVE: But they squash so.

ADAM: I'm not sure we're supposed to eat live things. I can't remember half the things He said any more.

EVE, *tentatively, with some trepidation:* Can I talk to you about that? I'm not sure any more it is those clams.

ADAM: Don't worry, it's the clams. Sits down and eats maybe fifty clams, and suddenly it's not the clams.

EVE: Well, I *like* clams. Especially lately.

ADAM: I like eggs.

EVE: Adam, dear, there's something I feel I should tell you.

ADAM: I had three delicious eggs last— *He breaks off, recalling.* No, no, that was a dream!

EVE, *startled:* You dreamed?

ADAM: Why, did you?

EVE, *quickly:* Tell me yours first.

ADAM: I . . . was in Paradise. Huh! Remember those breakfasts there?

EVE: I wasn't there long enough for breakfast. I was born just before lunch. And I never even got that.

ADAM: Pity you missed it. What a dream! Everything was just the way it used to be. I woke up, and there He was—

EVE: God.

ADAM: Yes. And He brought a tray—and about six beautifully scrambled eggs.

EVE, *with guilt and hunger:* Ohhhh!

ADAM: And no sand whatsoever. I guess it was Sunday because there was also a little tray of warm croissants.

EVE, *sadly charmed:* And then?

ADAM: Same as always—I named a few things. And then we took a nice nap. And angels were playing some soft music. *He hums, trying to recall the tune.* How perfect it all was!

EVE: Until I showed up.

ADAM: Yes. *He looks about with a heightened longing, and, seeing this, she weeps.*

EVE: I don't know why He made me!

ADAM: Well, don't cry, maybe we'll find out some day. I'll round up the sheep. *He starts out.*

EVE—*trying not to call him, she does:* Adam!

ADAM, *halting:* You'll just have to walk. That thing might go away if you get some exercise. *He moves to go.*

EVE: An angel came.

ADAM: When?

EVE: Last night.

ADAM—*happily astounded, he rushes to her:* Which one?

EVE, *fearfully:* It was, ah . . .

ADAM: Chemuel?

EVE: No, not Chemuel.

ADAM: Raphael? Michael?

EVE, *holding her forehead:* No.

ADAM: Well, what'd he look like? Short or tall?

EVE: Quite tall.

ADAM: It wasn't God, was it?

EVE: Oh, not God.

ADAM: What'd he want?

EVE: I—I can't remember it clearly.

ADAM: Was it about getting back into Paradise?

EVE: Well, no. . . .

ADAM: About what we're supposed to do next?

EVE: Not exactly. . . .

ADAM: Why didn't you wake me up?

EVE: I couldn't move!

ADAM: You mean God sends an angel down, and you can't even remember what he said?

EVE: It was about this—*she touches her belly*—thing.

ADAM, *disbelieving; in fact, with disappointment:* About that?

EVE—*she looks up at him:* Would you sit down, Adam? I think I know what we're supposed to do now. *He senses something strange, sits on his heels.* He came through the mist. Like the mist on the sea. Smoke rose from his hair, and his hands smoked.

Lucifer materializes; motionless, he stands in his terrible beauty at the periphery.

ADAM, *with wonder:* Ahhh!

EVE: And he said—*She breaks off in fear as she feels the attraction of the Evil One.*

ADAM: What?

A blast of wind. They huddle. It dies. She has remained staring ahead. Now she turns to him.

EVE: That angel opened my eyes, Adam. I see it all very clearly now—with you the Lord was only somewhat disappointed, but with me He was furious. *Lucifer gravely nods.* And his curse is entirely on me. It is the reason why you've hardly changed out here in the world; but I bleed, and now I am ugly and swollen up like a frog. And I never dream of Paradise, but you do almost every night, and you seem to expect to find it over every hill. And that is right—I think now that you belong in Eden. But not me. And as long as I am with you, you will never find it again. *Slight pause.* Adam, I haven't the power to move from this place, and this is the proof that I must stay here, and you—go back to Paradise.

ADAM, *in conflict with his wishes:* Alone?

EVE: He would lead you there if you walked away alone. You are thirsting for Eden, and the Lord knows that.

ADAM: But so are you.

EVE: Eden is not in me any more.

Lucifer seems to expand with joy.

ADAM: Eve!

EVE: I disgust Him! I am abominable to Him!

ADAM: But the Lord said we are to cleave to one another. I don't think I'm *supposed* to go.

EVE, *bursting into tears, as much with pity for him as with her own indignation:* But you don't like me any more either!

ADAM, *pointing at her belly:* That thing—that thing is what I cannot bear! It turns my stomach! I can't seem to get near you any more! Every time I turn around I'm bumping into it! *She cries louder, turns to find herself face to face with Lucifer.* I don't understand you. Do you *like* that thing?

EVE, *turning back to him from the tempting angel:* I—I don't know!

ADAM: Because if it moves it's alive, and if it's alive we could just hit it! *She gasps, holding her belly.* There, you see? You like it! And this is why I don't know where I am any more! I told you when it started, if you jumped up and down—

EVE: I did jump!

ADAM: You did not jump. You went like that. *He makes a few measly hops.*

EVE: I jumped as hard as I could!

ADAM: I think you're taking *care* of that thing! *Jealously.* You know what's in there, don't you?

EVE, *crying out:* I love thee, husband, and I know this thing will be thy curse!

ADAM: Woman, you will tell me what is in thy belly!

EVE, *clapping her hands over her eyes:* It is a death!

Pause.

ADAM: Whose death?

Pause. Eve lowers her hands, staring ahead.

EVE: Its own.

Pause.

ADAM: Who told thee?

EVE: Lucifer.

ADAM: You're seeing Lucifer again?

EVE: I screamed, but you didn't hear me!

ADAM: Well, I was sleeping!

EVE: You're always sleeping! Every time that son of a bitch comes around, you're someplace else! I would never have touched that apple in the first place if you hadn't left me alone with him!

ADAM: Well, I was *swimming*!

EVE: If you're not swimming, you're sleeping!

ADAM: You mean I can't turn my back for a minute on my own *wife*?

EVE: I couldn't help it, it was like a dream!

ADAM: I don't know how a decent woman can dream about the Devil.

EVE: Adam—he's not all bad.

ADAM: He's not all . . . ! *Light dawns in his head.* Ohhhh! No wonder you looked so juicy when you woke up! I want to know what's so good about him!

EVE, *clapping her hands to her ears:* I can't stand any more!

ADAM, *furiously:* God said I am thy master, woman, and you are going to tell me what went on here! No wonder I haven't been able to get near you. There's been something strange about you for months!

EVE: There is a man in my belly, Adam.

ADAM, *chilled with astonishment, wonder, fear:* A man!

EVE: He told me.

Long pause.

ADAM: How could a man fit in there?

EVE: Well . . . small. To start off with. Like the baby monkeys and the little zebras—

ADAM: Zebras! He's got you turning us into animals now? No human being has been born except grown-up! I may be confused about a lot of things, but I know facts!

EVE: But it's what God said—we were to go forth and multiply.

ADAM, *striking his chest indignantly:* If we're going to multiply, it'll be through me! Same as it always was! What am I going to do with you? After everything he did to us with his god-damned lies, you still—

EVE: Husband, he told me to do with it exactly what you have told me to do with it.

ADAM, *struck:* What I . . . ?

EVE: He told me it is a man and he told me to kill it. What the Devil hath spoken, thou hast likewise spoken.

Silence. Neither moves. One sheep baas, like a sinister snarl. A sudden surge of wind, which quickly dies.

ADAM, *tortured:* But I had no idea it was a man when I said that.

EVE, *holding her belly, with a long gaze beyond them both:* Adam . . . I believe I am meant to bring out this man—alone.

ADAM, *furiously, yet unable to face her directly:* Are you putting me with that monster?

EVE: But why do you all want him dead!

ADAM: I forbid you to say that again! I am not Lucifer! *A heartbroken cry escapes him.* Eve! *He sinks to his knees. He curls up in ignominy, then prostrates himself before her, flat out on the ground, pressing his lips to her foot.* Forgive me! *He weeps. Wind blasts. It dies.*

EVE—*a new thought interrupts her far-off gaze, and she looks at his prostrate body:* Will you dig us a hole?

ADAM—*he joyously scrambles up and kisses her hand:* A hole!

EVE: It needn't be too big—

ADAM: What do you mean? I'll dig you the biggest hole you ever saw in your life! Woman . . . *With a cry of gratitude he sweeps her into his arms.* Woman, thou art my salvation!

EVE: Oh, my darling, that's so good to hear!

ADAM: How I thirst for thee! My doe, my rabbit . . .

EVE: My five-pointed buck, my thundering bull!

ADAM, *covering his crotch:* Oh, Eve, thy forgiveness hath swelled me like a ripened ear of corn.

EVE: Oh, how sweet. Then I will forgive thee endlessly.

Lucifer shows alarm and rising anger.

ADAM: Say, now, the Lord will probably expect me to think of a name for him. Or do you want to? *He indicates her belly.*

EVE: No, you. You're so good at names.

ADAM—*he thinks, paces:* Well, let's see . . .

EVE: I'll be quiet. *She watches him with pleasure.* It ought to be something clear and clean and—something for a *handsome* man.

ADAM: Y'know, when I saw the first giraffe—it may not fit, but it went through my mind at the time.

EVE: What?

ADAM: Frank?

EVE: Don't you think that's a little too, ah . . . ?

{ ADAM: I guess so, yes. Maybe it ought to begin with A.
{ EVE, *simultaneously:* . . . to begin with an A.

    They point at each other and laugh.

{ ADAM: I mean because he's the first.
{ EVE: He's the first.

    They laugh again.

{ EVE: Isn't it marvelous that we both have the same thoughts . . .
{ ADAM: Both have the same thoughts.

EVE, *in the clear:* . . . again!

ADAM, *lifting his arms thankfully:* What a God we have!

EVE: How perfectly excellent is the Lord!

    Lucifer throws up his hands and goes into darkness, holding his head.

ADAM, *suddenly looking down at the ground, astonished:* Eve?

EVE: What, my darling?

ADAM: Is this grass growing?

EVE, *looking about quickly at the ground:* I believe it is!

ADAM, *looking front:* Look at the pasture! It's up to their bellies!

EVE: Adam, the wind . . . !

    They look up and around. There is silence.

ADAM: Woman, we must have done something right! *He looks upward.* I think He loves us again.

EVE—*her hands shoot up, open-palmed, her eyes wide with terror:* Sssh!

ADAM: Could it possibly be . . .

EVE, *a hand moving toward her belly:* Ssh, sh!

ADAM: . . . that the curse is *over? She grips her belly. She suddenly rushes right and is stopped by a wild, curling cry of a high-screaming French horn. He is oblivious to the sound.* What are you doing? *She turns and rushes upstage; he is starting after her, and she is stopped short by a whining blow on a timpani and a simultaneous snarling trumpet blast. He nearly catches her, but she gets away and is rushing left and is stopped by a pair of cacophonic flutes. He catches her now.* Eve! *She wrenches free of him—and she shows terror of him; and for an instant they are two yards apart, he uncomprehending, she in deadly fear of him. Protesting:* It's Adam. I am thy husband!

She rushes to a point and halts, crying upwards.

EVE: *Chemuuuuu-ellll!* Merciful sweet angel, take me out of myself! *She is seized by her agony and rolls over and over along the ground, as a massive cacophonic music flares up. Adam is put off, unmanned, afraid to touch her. She slams her hands on the ground as she writhes on her back.* God! Oh, God!

ADAM: Maybe it'll get better.

EVE: It will get worse. And when it gets worse it—*she sits up, recalling*—will get perfectly worse. . . . *A contraction.* Oh, God! *Stretching on her side, hands outstretched:* I call on any angel whatsoever!

ADAM, *calling upward:* Chemuel, come! Bring mercy!

EVE: Help me, demon! Come to me, Lucifer!

ADAM, *clapping his ears shut:* Aiiiii!

EVE, *as though whipped, submissively begging:* Take out this agony! Demon, I am awake! Still me, angel! Take him out of my flesh!

ADAM, *falling to his knees:* God in Heaven, she is out of her mind!

EVE: I am *in* my mind—He never gave me a chance!

ADAM: Lord, give her a chance!

EVE: No, He loves this! God, if this is Thy pleasure, then I owe Thee nothing any more, and I call, I call, I call for—*A seizure; with each call she pounds the earth.* God. Oh, God. Oh, God. God—damn—you—God!

ADAM, *curled up in terror:* Aiiii!

Lucifer appears at the periphery.

EVE: Still me, demon . . . take this out! Don't waste another minute! Not a minute more! He is bursting me! Kill him! Kill him!

Lucifer takes a step toward her and is halted by trumpets: a single melodious chord. She faints. Adam tries to rise and, seeing her, he faints too. God enters. A step behind Him are Azrael, Angel of Death, and Chemuel, Angel of Mercy.

GOD, *standing over her, looking down:* Now bend, Azrael, and blow thy cold death across her lip. *Azrael bends and exhales over her face. Eve shudders as with icy cold and gasps in air, still asleep.* That's enough. Chemuel, in thy compassion, drive anguish to the corner of her mind, and seal it up. *Chemuel kneels, kisses her once. Eve exhales with relief. God walks a few yards away and sits.* Go away, Death. *Azrael stands fast.* Go, Azrael. And wait her need. *Azrael exits unwillingly.* Chemuel, in thy mercy, deliver Eve. *Chemuel reaches, lays his hand on her swollen belly, and with a short pull removes the swelling; clutching it to his breast, he starts to lean to kiss her again.* That's enough. *Chemuel hesitates, glancing up at God.* Go, Chemuel, and wait her need. *Chemuel stands and goes out.* Now in thy slumber let us reason together. *Adam and Eve sit up, their eyes shut in sleep.* Behold the stranger thine agony hath made. *A youth of sixteen appears, his eyes shut, his arms drawn in close to his body, his hands clasping his forward-tilted head. He moves waywardly, like a windblown leaf, and as he at last approaches Eve, he halts some feet away as God speaks again.* Here is the first life of thy life, woman. And it is fitting that the first letter stand before his name. But seeing that in thy extremity thou hast already offered his life to Lucifer; and seeing, Adam, that in your ignorance you have likewise threatened him with murder—*He loses his calm*—all of which amazes Me and sets My teeth on edge—*He breaks off, gritting His teeth*—I am nevertheless mindful that this child—*He turns to the youth*—is innocent. So we shall try again. And rather than call him Abel, who was in jeopardy, he shall be Cain, for his life's sake. *He stands.* Now Cain is born!

Cain lies down, coiled beside Eve. She sits up, opens her eyes, and looks down at Cain.

EVE, *joyfully surprised:* Ahhh!
ADAM, *waking quickly, seeing Cain:* What's that?
EVE: It is . . .
GOD: Cain. Thy son.

Both gasp, surprised by His presence.

EVE—*she suddenly feels her flat belly and with a cry prostrates before God:* I see I have been favored of Thee, O Lord!
GOD, *indicating the inert Cain:* Here is thine innocence returned to thee, which thou so lightly cast away in Eden. Now protect him from the worm of thine own evil, which this day hath uncovered in thee. Look in My face, woman.
EVE, *covering her eyes:* I dare not, for I doubted Thy goodness!
GOD: And will you doubt Me any more?
EVE: Never, never, never!
GOD: Then lift up thine eyes.

She slowly dares to face Him on her knees.

EVE: I have gotten a man from the Lord.
GOD: Thou art the mother of mankind.
EVE: And generations unknown to me shall spring from my loins. *He extends His hand. She rests hers on it and rises.*
              I am the river abounding in fish,
              I am the summer sun arousing the bee,
              As the rising moon is held in her place
              By Thine everlasting mind, so am I held
              In Thine esteem.
GOD: Eve, you are my favorite girl!

An angelic waltz strikes up. God sweeps Eve in a glorious dance all over the stage. Adam, happiness on his face, makes light and abortive attempts to cut in. God and Eve exit, dancing, Adam trailing behind and calling.

ADAM: Eve! Look at Him dance! *Laughing, bursting with joy, he waltzes out after them.*

Lucifer, alone with Cain coiled up nearby, looks off toward the party and shakes his head.

LUCIFER: You've got to hand it to Him. *He turns front, staring.* What a system! *Now he looks down at Cain.* So this is Cain. *He crouches over Cain.* With the kiss of Lucifer begin thy life; let my nature coil around thine own. And on thy shoulders may I climb the throne. *He bends and kisses him.*

CURTAIN

ACT THREE

The family discovered asleep. A primitive shelter is suggested, hanging skins, and a cooking area in one corner. God is seated on a rock. He is thoughtfully watching them. He shakes his head, baffled, then raises a hand.

GOD: Azrael! *Azrael lights up behind the left screen.* Angel of Death, I have work for you today. The time has come when the human race will spread across the earth. But these people have all but forgotten God. They eat to live and live to eat. By what law shall the multitudes be governed when even now my name is hardly mentioned any more? *Stands, looking down at the people.* Therefore, when this dawn comes, you will blow visions of death into their dreams. But be careful not to kill anybody; you are only to remind them that they cannot live forever. And having seen death, I hope they'll think of God again, and begin to face their terrible responsibilities. *Azrael starts to raise his arms.* Not yet!—wait till dawn. I want them to remember what they've dreamed when they awake. *To the people:* Dear people, I shall be watching every move you make today. *He exits. Lucifer comes up out of the trap. Looks about, notices a golden bowl and picks it up.*

LUCIFER: Every time I come up here they've got more junk. What a race—a little prosperity and they don't even need the Devil.

EVE, *awakening:* What spirit art thou?

LUCIFER: It's me, honey.

EVE: Why don't you just go to hell and stay there?

LUCIFER: Darling, I'm terribly worried about your soul! A beautiful, intelligent woman like you can't waste her life just cooking and doing the house. You simply have no idea what you're missing!

EVE: I have absolutely everything I ever dreamed of, Angel. . . .

LUCIFER: But don't you want to broaden your horizons?

EVE: No! *She lies back down.*

LUCIFER: Whatever you say, darling. Sweet dreams, pretty girl. *Comes away from her.* For all the bad I've done I might as well have stayed in heaven. Only bad trouble will make them call to me for help. I'll break them apart!—or they'll turn the whole earth into this smug suburb of Heaven. Now let's see—Cain is jealous of his brother; suppose we start from there. . . . *He leaps to Cain when the light of dawn glows and Azrael appears behind the screen. Lucifer hides to observe him. Sotto:* Azrael? What's this about? *Azrael raises his caped arms menacingly.* My God, is somebody going to die? *Azrael blows three loud, short breaths. The people instantly groan. Azrael vanishes. Lucifer comes down to the people.* Groaning! Did he blow dreams into them?

ADAM—*sits up:* What a dream! *She turns to him expectantly.* I think I saw . . . something die.

EVE, *against her fear:* Maybe a sheep.

ADAM: No. It had a face.

LUCIFER: But none of them is old or sick—how do they die?

EVE: A *person's* face?

ADAM: Yes. And there was blood.

EVE: Blood!

LUCIFER: Blood?—Is he setting them up for a murder?—Of course! What better way to make them guilty and put the fear of God back into them! What a mistake I nearly made— I've got to keep them out of trouble, not get them into it.

CAIN, *sitting up:* What a dream!

ADAM AND EVE: What!

CAIN: I think I saw something die.

LUCIFER: And here's my opening at last! I'll stop this killing and they'll love me for it, and hate the Lord who has to have a death and their remorse! Oh, this is beautiful! But which one kills, and who's supposed to die? *He continuously moves around the periphery and sometimes in among them, searchingly, awaiting his opening.*

ABEL, *sitting up:* What a dream!

ADAM: That's enough. Eve, make breakfast.

ABEL: I was flying across the sky. . . .

EVE: But that's a wonderful dream!

ABEL: And then I fell. . . . *Mystified:* And an angel kissed me.

CAIN, *instantly—an exhale of recognition, his finger raised:* Ohhhhh! *All turn to him as he points to Abel.* I remember now. He died. *Eve gasps.*

EVE: Don't say that! *She gets up and goes to Abel and, holding his head in her arms, kisses him. Adam moves her aside, and he kisses him.*

LUCIFER: It's Abel dies? But who kills him?

CAIN, *kisses Abel:* I saw thee on the ground, thy face crushed, and a blood-covered flail . . . rolling away.

ADAM: All right, now wait a minute.

CAIN, *turning to Adam:* How is it that he dies in my sleep? *Turning to Abel:* You haven't done anything, have you?

ABEL, *to Eve:* The minute anything happens he always blames me!

EVE: You two stop fighting.

ADAM: Now pay attention. Nobody ever dreamed of death before, so I don't want to hear any arguments of any kind whatsoever today.

LUCIFER: Good man! *To Eve:* Brighten it up.

EVE: I'll make a nice breakfast!

CAIN: Father. *Adam turns to him, sensing his strange intensity.* When you decided to leave Paradise, did God . . . ?

EVE: What's Paradise got to do with this?

CAIN: I wish we could talk about it, Mother! Didn't God give you any instructions when you left? I mean, how do we know we're saying the right prayers. Or maybe we don't pray enough.

ADAM: Oh, no. I'm sure He'd let us know if we were doing something wrong.

CAIN: But maybe that's what the dream was for.

ADAM, *struck by this:* Say!

CAIN: Because lately when I'm out in the fields chopping weeds—it suddenly seems so strange . . .

EVE, *impatiently:* What, dear?

CAIN: Did God order you to make me the farmer and Abel to tend the sheep?

ADAM: You can't expect Him to go into those kind of details, Cain. He just felt it was time we went out in the world and multiplied, that's all.

CAIN: Father, I've never understood why you couldn't have stayed in the Garden and multiplied.

EVE: In the *Garden*!

ADAM: Oh, no, boy—

EVE: That's not something you do in the *Garden*, darling.

CAIN: Well, what did He say, exactly, when you left?

ADAM: He said to get out—

EVE: Not "Get out!"

ADAM, *quickly:* No, no, not "Get out!"

EVE: I think he's overtired.

CAIN: I am not overtired! Why do you always make everything ridiculous? I'm not talking about sheep or farming; I'm talking about what God wants us to *do*!

ABEL: If you think He wants me to farm, I'll be glad to switch.

CAIN, *to Adam with a laugh:* He's going to farm!

ADAM, *laughing:* God help us!

ABEL, *protesting:* Why!

CAIN: With your sense of responsibility, we'd be eating thistle soup!

EVE, *touching Abel:* He's just more imaginative.

LUCIFER: Will you just shut up?

CAIN: Imaginative!

ABEL: Have I ever lost a sheep?

CAIN: How *could* you lose them? They always end up in my corn.

ABEL: Cain, that only happened once!

CAIN, *with raw indignation:* Go out there and sweat the way I do and tell me it only happened once!

EVE: He's just younger!

CAIN: And I'm older, and I'll be damned if I plant another crop until he fences those sheep!

LUCIFER: Stop this!

EVE, *to Adam:* Stop this!

CAIN: Why must you always take his side?

EVE: But how can he build a fence?

CAIN: The same way I plant a crop, Mother! By bending his back! Abel, I'm warning you, if you ever again—

ADAM: Boys, boys!

ABEL, *turning away:* If he wants a fence, I think he should build it.

CAIN: *I* should build it! Are the corn eating the sheep or the sheep eating the corn?

ABEL: It's not natural for me to build a fence.

CAIN: Not natural! You've been talking to God lately?

ABEL: I don't know anything about God. But it's the nature of sheep to move around, and it's the nature of corn to stay in one place. So the fence should fence the thing that stays in one place and not the thing that moves around.

ADAM: That's logical, Cain.

CAIN: In other words, the work belongs to me and the whole wide world belongs to him!

ADAM, *at a loss:* No, that's not fair either.

ABEL, *angering, to Adam:* Well, I can't fence the mountains, can I? I can't fence the rivers where they go to drink. *To Cain:* I know you work harder, Cain, but I didn't decide that. I've even thought sometimes that it is unfair, and maybe we should change places for a while—

CAIN: You wouldn't last a week.

ABEL, *crying out:* Then what am I supposed to do? *Cain is close, staring into his face, a tortured expression in his eyes which puzzles Abel.* Why is he looking like that? *Suddenly Cain embraces Abel, hugging him close.*

ADAM: Attaboy!

EVE, *puzzled and alarmed:* Cain?

CAIN—*he lets Abel go and moves a few steps, staring:* I don't know what's happening to me.

ADAM: Abel, shake his hand. Go on, make up. You're both sorry.

ABEL, *holding out his hand:* Cain?

LUCIFER, *victoriously to Heaven:* Why don't you give up?

Cain has just raised his hand to approach Abel when a large snake is dropped in their midst from Heaven. Eve screams. Lucifer rushes and flings it out of sight.

LUCIFER: Scat! Get out of here!

EVE: It flew in and flew out!

ADAM: A flying snake?

Instantly the high howling of several coyotes is heard, and the family turns in all directions, as though toward an invading force.

LUCIFER, *off to one side, looking up to Heaven:* Father, this is low!

ADAM, *looking about at the air:* Something is happening. *To Eve, who is staring about:* I think . . . I'd better tell them. *She covers her eyes in trepidation.* Eve? Maybe we're supposed to, now.

EVE, *lowering her hands:* All right. Then maybe everything will be as it was again.

ADAM: Boys? Maybe you'd better sit down, boys.

ABEL: Tell what, Pa?

They all sit except Eve, who remains standing, staring about apprehensively.

ADAM: About the question of leaving Paradise—I don't want you to think that we tried to mislead you or anything like that.

EVE, *pleadingly to Cain:* It's just everything was going so good, you see?

ADAM, *with a glance around at the air:* But it looks like something is happening, so maybe we better get this settled.

ABEL: What, Pa?

ADAM: We . . . didn't exactly *decide* to go, y'see. We were ah—*he blinks away a tear*—told to leave.

CAIN: *Told?*

ABEL: Why, Pa?

ADAM, *fumbling:* Why? Well . . . *He turns helplessly to Eve.* Why?

EVE: We just didn't fit in, you see. I mean if a person doesn't fit in—

ADAM: If we're going to tell it, we better tell it.

EVE: But the way you're telling it, it sounds like it was all my fault!

ADAM: I didn't say anything yet!

EVE: Well, when are you going to say it?

ADAM, *setting himself:* Well—as we told you before, I was alone with God for a long time, and then—

ABEL: He made Mama.

ADAM: Right.

ABEL, *with a big smile:* And you liked her right away, heh?

CAIN: Of course he did.

ADAM: She was gorgeous. Of course, there wasn't much choice. *He laughs.*

EVE: Ha. Ha. Ha.

ADAM: Well, anyway, I believe I mentioned there was this tree—with an apple—

ABEL: Of good and evil.

ADAM: Right.

CAIN: Which you're never allowed to eat under any circumstances.

ADAM: Right. Well, the thing is, you see—we ate it.

ABEL—*thrilled and scared, he laughs:* You ate it!

CAIN: I thought you said you—

ADAM: No, we ate it.

ABEL, *more scared now:* Not Mama, though.

ADAM: Mama too.

Cain goes to a lyre and, turning his back on them, he plays. They watch him for a moment, aware of his intense feeling.

ABEL, *avidly:* And then what happened?

Cain strums as loud as he can, then stops.

ADAM, *with a worried glance at Cain:* Well, the next thing—I looked at her, y'see. And there was something funny. I didn't know what it was. And then I realized. She was naked.

Cain now turns to them.

CAIN AND ABEL: Mama?

EVE: Well, *he* was too.

CAIN—*shocked, he drops the lyre:* Mama!

LUCIFER, *holding his head:* Ohhh!

EVE: We didn't know it, darling!

CAIN: How could you not know you were naked?

EVE: Well, we were like children; like you, like Abel. You remember, when Abel was a baby and ran around—

CAIN, *outraged, accusing:* But you weren't a baby!

EVE, *to Adam, at a loss:* Aren't you going to say anything?

ABEL, *explaining for Adam:* Well, they were like animals.

CAIN, *pained, horrified:* Don't you say a thing like that!

ADAM, *to Cain:* Well, I told you—I could smell water?

ABEL: Sure! And they could hear the trout talking.

CAIN: But you never said you were actually . . . *animals.*

ADAM: Now just a minute, Cain. That was the way God wanted
it—

CAIN: I can't believe that! God could never have wanted my
mother going around without any clothes on!

ADAM, *angrily, standing:* You mean *I* wouldn't let her put her
clothes on?

EVE, *going to him:* Darling, we were innocent!

CAIN, *furiously:* You were naked and innocent? Don't you understand that that's why He threw you out?

EVE: But He loved us most when we were naked. He only got
mad when we knew we were. *Slight pause.*

CAIN, *swept by this truth:* No wonder we dreamed of death!

EVE: Why?

CAIN: We've been saying all the wrong prayers. We shouldn't
be thanking God—we should be begging His forgiveness.
We've been living as though we were innocent. We've been
living as though we were blessed!

EVE: But we are, darling.

CAIN: We are cursed, Mother!

EVE, *furiously to Adam:* You should never have told him!

CAIN: Why did you lie to us?

ADAM: Now just a minute . . .

CAIN, *accusingly:* I always *knew* there was something you
weren't saying!

ADAM: Just a minute! *Slight pause.* We didn't want to frighten
you, that's all. But maybe now you're old enough to
understand.—He did curse us when He threw us out. And
part of the curse is that we will have to die.

CAIN: *We're* going to die?

ABEL: Like the sheep, you mean?

ADAM: Sheep, birds, everything.

CAIN: You and Mama, too? You mean we wouldn't see you any
more?

EVE: Don't worry about it, darling. I'm sure we have a long,
long time yet.

CAIN: You mean before He got angry you would never die?

ADAM: Far as I know—yes.

CAIN: Oh, my God—then He must have been absolutely furious with you.

EVE: I'm sure He's forgiven us, dear, or we wouldn't have you and everything so wonderful—

CAIN, *sinking to his knees:* Listen to me! I tell you we have been warned. Now we must do what has never been done.

EVE: Do what?

CAIN: We must give this day—not to the animals or the crops; this day we must give to God. I tell you—*he looks upward tenderly*—if we will open up our sins to Him and cleanse ourselves, he might show his face and tell us we are supposed to live. Father, Mother, Abel—come and pray with me.

ADAM, *to Eve:* Well—a prayer wouldn't hurt.

EVE, *recalling:* Maybe he's right. Maybe it'll all be sweet again. *Going to her knees:* What should we pray, darling?

Cain faces Heaven. Adam goes to his knees. And finally Abel.

CAIN: Almighty God, seeing that our parents were thrown out of Paradise for their transgressions against Thee, we, Cain and Abel, beseech Thy forgiveness. Let this family live, let us be innocent again! Now each one, give up the sin.

Adam and Eve shut their eyes and concentrate. Abel watches them, then leans over to Eve.

ABEL, *with a glance at the praying Cain:* Does this mean I'm building a fence?

CAIN, *eyes shut:* It seems to me that when a person dies in his brother's dream he ought to pray!

ADAM: I saw it too, Abel—you were dead. I think you'd better pray.

Pause. All heads are lowered. Lucifer stands up. He comes down to them and sits next to Abel.

ABEL, *softly:* Mother!

EVE: Sssh!

ABEL: Someone has come.

ADAM: I don't see anybody.

A slight pause. They contemplate, but Abel is glancing apprehensively toward Lucifer.

ABEL: Who are thou?

The family turns quickly to him, astonished, Lucifer being invisible to all but Abel.

LUCIFER: I am what you fear in your heart is true—your brother is dangerous. Tell him you'll build the fence. *Abel reacts in refusal.* This man is inconsolable!

ABEL: Why?

LUCIFER: She loves you best, Abel.

ABEL: But Cain is loved!

EVE: How sweet! *To Adam:* Did you hear?

LUCIFER: Cain has her respect, but her love has gone to you. Tell him you'll build it if you care to live! This man is murderous. *Now Abel turns with new eyes to Cain.*

ABEL: About the fence—

CAIN: Yes?

ABEL: You're right. It's not the corn that eat the sheep but the sheep that eat the corn—

LUCIFER: Attaboy!

EVE, *to Adam, happily:* Listen!

ABEL: So I will build the fence around the sheep.

EVE, *to Adam:* Do you hear!

ADAM: Marvelous.

CAIN: Where would you build it?

ABEL: Well—anywhere out of the way. In the valley?

CAIN: I need the valley.

ABEL: Oh . . . On the hillside?

CAIN: I'll need the hillside. I'm planning to set out quite a large vineyard this spring.

ABEL: Where would you suggest, then?

CAIN: There is very rich pasture across the mountain.

ABEL: That's . . . pretty far away, though, isn't it?

CAIN: I don't think it's all that far.

LUCIFER: Agree! Agree!

ABEL, *swallowing his resentment:* All right, Cain.

LUCIFER: I know how you feel, son, but lying is better than dying.

EVE, *affected by Abel's anguish:* Cain, dear, I want you to tell him you didn't mean that before—

LUCIFER: Abel, shut her up—

EVE, *to Cain, insistently:* You won't make him go so far away to pasture, will you?

LUCIFER: She is killing you, word by loving word!

ABEL: I don't mind, Mother. In fact—

LUCIFER: I *like* long walks.

ABEL: I *like* long walks.

EVE: But you *agreed* to build the fence! *To Cain:* Why must you humiliate him?

Cain slams his hands down on the ground and springs up furiously, goes to a big rock and picks it up.

LUCIFER, *to Abel:* Watch out! Don't turn your back on him! *Abel quickly turns to watch his brother.*

EVE: What are you doing?

Cain places the boulder on top of another.

CAIN: What has never been done. It has come to me to make an offering to the Lord.

LUCIFER, *shaking a fist at Heaven:* Don't you ever give up?

EVE, *vastly relieved:* That's a wonderful idea!

ADAM: Say, now! That sounds very good, Cain.

EVE: You think He'll come?

ADAM: He might. The way Cain loves Him, He might just stop by. *To Cain, with his expertise:* Take the best of thy corn and the first of thy wheat, and a little parsley—He always rather liked parsley.

Cain finds a flat stone and sets it on top of the altar he is constructing. Eve immediately takes a broom and starts sweeping the area.

EVE: What about some grapes?

ADAM, *calling to Cain:* Grapes too!

CAIN: The grapes aren't too good this year—

EVE: You'd better not, then.

ADAM, *all excited:* Don't listen to her; it doesn't matter if they're not too good, it's the feeling behind it. Because He's fair,

Cain, you'll see. And here's another thing. We've got to praise Him more. We haven't been praising Him enough.

EVE: Praise God! Praise the Lord!

ADAM: Will you wait! *To Cain:* Hurry up, get the stuff. *Cain rushes back to load a tray with his crops.*

EVE, *clasping her hands together feverishly:* He's going to come! I feel it, I tell you I feel it!

ADAM, *supervising Cain, calling:* I'd throw in a few onions. *To Eve:* Loved a good onion.

EVE: It's going to be like it was again! *She rushes to Abel.* Push back your hair, darling. Adam, there's dirt on your cheek. *Adam brushes it off. Abel fixes his hair. Cain turns to them now with a tray loaded with vegetables and fruit. Silence for an instant; then Eve suddenly is swept forward to him.* Would you mind, darling? *She picks an apple off the tray.* No apples. *She hides the apple in her clothes.*

CAIN, *in tension:* Is it all right, Pa?

Adam comes forward, inspects the tray. Silence.

ADAM: This looks absolutely beautiful, Cain. Now, when you see His face, regard the right eye. Because that's the one He loves you with. The left one squints, y'see, because that's the one He judges with. So watch the right eye and don't be frightened.

CAIN: I love Him, Father.

ADAM: I know that, Cain, and now you will know His love for thee. *He kisses Cain, who turns and tensely starts for the altar.*

EVE: Cain!

He halts. She comes to him, elevated within. She kisses the offering. Then she kisses him. He turns again to the altar. Abel steps before him. They stare at one another. Now Cain leans and kisses him. Then he carefully sets the offering on the altar and steps back. All go to their knees before the altar, as—

EVE, *to Adam, tentatively:* I think Abel ought to make an offering too.

Abel sits up, and Adam considers this. Cain remains bowed. Lucifer cries out, rushing about before Abel.

LUCIFER: Don't! Under no circumstances must you get into this competition!

CAIN: It was my idea, Mother. Can't he do it another time?

EVE: It was just a suggestion. You don't have to get angry.

ABEL, *struck by his vision:* Maybe He would come because of me. . . .

LUCIFER: What are *you* guilty about? Just because your mother loves you best? Lie back and enjoy it.

ABEL: But it is not fair to Cain, and I can't bear that any more! I want God to bring us peace!

LUCIFER: And what if it turns out God also loves you best? Is *that* fair to Cain?

ABEL: But—Cain would have to accept *that*!

LUCIFER: Boy, even with God's help, nobody can be Number One and good at the same time. Don't compete!

ABEL: Get thee behind me! *He draws his knife and rushes upstage.*

EVE, *to Adam:* He's going to do it! *Calling to Abel, who is exiting:* Pick a nice fat lamb, darling!

LUCIFER, *as he rushes upstage after Abel:* Abel! Don't call down God!

Cain is still on his knees, staring ahead. Eve feels his anguish.

EVE: He'll come now, dear, and He'll bless you both, as I do. *But Cain refuses to turn to her; she sees his hurt.* I love thee, Cain, I always loved thee from the hour of thy conception!

LUCIFER, *looks to Heaven:* What a genius that old fart is—with one dream of death he's got them all guilty! By God, I'll free them now or never—with the truth! *He exits.*

Abel enters, holding before him a slab of wood loaded with the flesh and entrails of a lamb, his hands dripping blood. Adam instantly goes to him, smears his own hand, and snaps the blood into the air toward the sky.

ADAM: The blood is the life, and the life is the Lord's.

EVE—*she looks up at the sky:*

> Now, Maker, show Thyself and spread Thy peace
> On all of us, my Abel and my Cain.

She and Adam kiss Abel from his right and left. He sets his offering on the altar. The deep bellow of a bull is heard.

ALL: Aiee!

The bellowing resounds again, and now a figure rises behind the altar, a man with the head of a bull. At the right they all prostrate themselves on the ground.

LUCIFER:
A second time I come with thine awakening, Mankind!
Nobody's guilty any more!
And for your progeny now and forever
I declare one massive, eternal, continuous parole!
From here on out there is no sin or innocence
But only Man. *He flings off his mask.*
Now claim thy birthright! *He leaps, stands away from the altar, welcoming arms outflung.*
Total freedom!
EVE, *leaps up:* Thank God!
ADAM, *springing to his feet:* That's the Devil!
LUCIFER: There are two Gods, Adam—in Heaven, God; and God on earth is me!
ADAM: Slaughter him! *He starts for Lucifer, and the boys stand. Eve throws herself before Lucifer to shield him.* Woman!
EVE: I believe this angel!
ADAM: This is the enemy!
EVE: I won't deny it any more—this spirit makes me happy!
ADAM, *to the altar:* Lord, show Thy face, my wife is going to Hell!
EVE: Adam! *She raises her hand gently toward him.*
Where has all our old contentment gone?
You were so long in Paradise
With God, that all your dreams go there,
But the only home I ever had is on this dust,
This windy world,
And here I am condemned. I know God rules in Heaven,
But in the name of peace, I have to speak the truth:
Except for one short dance—*she nearly weeps*—
God never showed me any kindness.
ADAM: Woman!

EVE:
> I see it, husband!
> This God is mine—I know it!
> For only this one frees me of my sin.

ADAM: There is one God!

EVE: No—two! One for me and one for—*A strange light blossoms around the altar, and, seeing it, she breaks off and like the others backs away. Lucifer rushes down to her.*

LUCIFER: Let's end this war! Dance with me, woman. Show God your love and end this stupid war!

A wild music explodes, then diminishes as Lucifer pulls her to himself, and in conflict she breaks and with arms spread calls to Abel.

EVE: Abel! Cain! *Rushing to them, grabbing them:* Love! Love, my darlings!

ADAM: I forbid this! God's coming!

EVE—*clamping both their heads to her, she calls out to Adam and Heaven:* Is God not pleased if peace comes in? *She springs from them and then turns back invitingly to them.* Let hate go out and love come in!

LUCIFER:
> Now save yourselves with music and the truth!
> Be what you are and as you are.
> Give God to Adam, boys—and I will give you Eve!

The music flies up: Eve begins to dance—awkwardly at first, and Lucifer grabs her, awakens her again, and her body loosens, writhes; then she flies to Abel, who is embarrassed but quickly learns, and now she flies to Cain, who is stiff at first, but Lucifer helps him loosen up, and finally she is whirling among the three of them, kissing them in turn, her hands flowing over their bodies and theirs over hers—and suddenly Cain explodes into a prancing step, flapping his arms like a giant mating bird. Eve is astonished, innocently laughs, but in a sweep he pulls her down and climbs onto her. The truth is out—fuck her, Cain, and save the world! *Adam rushes to separate them. Lucifer grabs him.* Shame! How can you be so selfish! *And with Cain on his stunned but compliant mother and Abel trying to hold out till Cain is done—God appears behind the altar.*

Adam roars a gigantic, horrified roar. Silence. Cain rolls off Eve and sits looking up at the Presence. Eve sits up. Adam prostrates himself.

ADAM: Glory to God in the highest!

LUCIFER: Good morning, sir. *With an ironic gesture toward the crew.* May I introduce you to mankind? I don't believe I need labor the point—to the naked eye how pious and God-fearing they were; but with a moment's instruction and the right kind of music, a bear would blush at their morality. Dear Father, what are we fighting about? Truly, Lord, what is Man beyond his appetite? *Extends his hand.* Come, make peace; share Heaven—I the God of what-they-are, and you in charge of their improvement. In you let them find their hopes, in me their pleasure, and shut the gates of Hell forever. Sir, I am ready to take my place.

Striving against anger, God turns his head to each of the people in turn. Then He looks down at the offerings and picks out an onion.

GOD: Peace, children, on this first Sabbath. Whose is this?

LUCIFER: You'll accept those offerings when the filth in their hearts stinks to Heaven!

GOD: Whose is this?

CAIN, *with uncertainty:* That was mine, Lord.

GOD: Do you want me to taste it?

LUCIFER: You saw him on his mother!

GOD: Cain?

CAIN, *his eyes averted:* If it please Thee.

GOD: Why?

CAIN: It's . . . my *onion*, sir.

GOD: Then you still have respect for an onion?

CAIN: Lord, it's my work, my labor; it is the best of all I've made.

GOD, *with angry eyes:* And were you not the best that I had made?

Cain looks up, aware, and lowers his eyes in shame. God bites the onion, chews it.

GOD: That . . . is a good onion, Cain. *Cain falls to his knees weeping.* And this is Abel's meat?

ABEL: It's mine, sir, yes.

GOD: Mutton.

EVE: Oh, no, sir—lamb.

GOD—*He glances at her, then with high interest leans and inhales the delicious scent:* Ohhh, yes.

ABEL, *encouraged:* My youngest, fattest lamb, Lord. I hope it will please Thee.

EVE: I usually sprinkle it with salt and pepper first. . . .

GOD: You might try rubbing a bud of garlic over it.

EVE: Oh, I will!

ADAM: Do that next time, definitely.

EVE: Oh, yes, Adam!

Now God picks up a piece of meat. All grow tense. Abel raises his head to watch. God puts the meat in His mouth and chews, His eyes opening wider with the taste.

GOD: What in the world do you feed your flock?

ABEL, *joyously:* I find the sweetest grass, sir!

CAIN: And corn. *God turns to him. Abel, tense, turns to him.*

GOD, *understanding:* Oh, yes. I see. *He turns slowly to Abel.* Abel? Rise. *Abel springs to his feet.* Young man, this is undoubtedly the sweetest, most delicious, delicate, and profoundly *satisfying* piece of meat I have ever tasted since the world began.

Adam, filled with glory, comes to Abel and shakes his hand.

ADAM: Boy, this is our proudest moment.

EVE—*unable to hold back, she starts for Abel:* Darling! *She grabs Abel's face, kisses him on the lips, and turns up to God.* There is one God now and forever, there is no other on earth or in Heaven!

GOD: And don't you forget it, either. *Turning to Lucifer, who is staring at the ground:* I seem to have forgotten what you were saying. What was that all about, fallen angel?

LUCIFER, *bitterly:* About the truth, sir—my mistake. But this isn't over yet!

GOD, *steps down from the altar:* Come, children, and walk a little way with me, and we shall talk a while together of life and earth and Heaven. Come, Adam. *He takes Adam by the hand.* Eve? *She comes to him, enthralled, and gives him her hand.* Abel? Cain?

CAIN: Lord, there's still my corn. You haven't tasted my corn.

GOD: Oh, I can see it's all very nice. You have done quite well, Cain. Keep it up. *With which He walks into light with Adam, and Abel following behind.*

EVE, *beckoning:* Cain? *Seeing his shock:* Darling, he loved your vegetables. Come.

Cain seems to hardly hear her and takes a few dead steps following her. She goes, and he comes to a halt. Lucifer starts for him, then halts as he sees his strange expression.

LUCIFER: Now control yourself, boy. Cain?

CAIN: He never even tasted my corn.

LUCIFER: You mustn't get excited.

CAIN, *with the undercurrent of dangerous laughter:* But do you know what goes into an ear of corn? I planted twice this year; the floods washed my seeds away the first time. *His eyes fall on a flask beside the altar.* And my wine. *Going to the flask:* I was going to offer . . . *He suddenly kicks down the altar.*

LUCIFER: Listen to me—*For good measure Cain sends all the food flying with another kick.* We've got to get serious!

CAIN: Cain, serious? That's all over, Devil, now Cain starts to *live! He starts throwing everyone out of the shelter.*

LUCIFER: What's this, now?

CAIN: This is my house! Mine! *He faces Lucifer.* No one enters here but Cain any more. They have God, and I have this farm—and before I'm finished, my fences will stretch out to cover the earth!

LUCIFER: Adam will never agree to leave this house—

CAIN: Oh, he'll agree, all right—*he strides to his flail and brandishes it*—once I explain it to him! *He whips the flail with a whoosh, and, holding it up:* There's the only wisdom I will ever need again! *A deep hum sounds in the earth, like a dynamo.*

LUCIFER: Listen! *Cain freezes.* He has set a moaning in the earth. *Daylight changes to night; stars appear.* Look! *Both look up at the night sky.*

He is giving you a night at noon,
Darkening your mind to kill for him!

*Frightened, Cain turns from the sky to the flail in his hand
and throws it down guiltily.*

Don't let him use you. Go away. Hide yourself.

CAIN: I, hide? I was the one who thought of the offerings;
from me this Sabbath came! Let them hide! I want nothing
from anyone any more!

LUCIFER: But God wants a murder from you.

CAIN, *astonished:* God . . . wants . . . ?

LUCIFER: He has designed your vengeance, boy. He's boiling
your blood in his hand.

CAIN: But why?

LUCIFER:

So He may stand above your crime, the blameless God,
The only assurance of Mankind, and His power is safe.
Come now,
We'll hide you till this anger's gone.

*He leads Cain a few yards; Cain moves as though being car-
ried, staring into Lucifer's face.*

ABEL'S VOICE, *calling from a distance:* Cain? Where are you?
Come on!

Cain swerves about toward the voice.

LUCIFER: Don't stop!

CAIN—*a cry, as though from his bowel, to the sky:* How is Abel
the favorite of God?

LUCIFER:

God has no favorites! *He grasps Cain's astounded face.*
Man's a mirror to Him, Cain,
In which He looks to see His praise.

CAIN: But I have praised Him! And Abel only played His
flute!

LUCIFER: So where is good and where is evil?
God wants power, not morals!

ABEL'S VOICE, *closer now, calling:* Cain! We're all waiting for
you!

LUCIFER, *grabbing for him:* Come!

CAIN: I have to face him first! *He breaks from Lucifer, facing in the direction of Abel's voice.*

LUCIFER:

> Then face him with indifference.
> Kill love, Cain, kill whatever in you cares;
> Murder now is but another sort of praise to God!
> Don't praise Him with a death!

ABEL, *closer yet:* Cain?

CAIN:

> His voice is like silver, like his life,
> And mine is the voice of the ox, the driven beast!

LUCIFER: Indifference, Cain!

Abel enters.

ABEL: Aren't you coming? God is sitting by the river, telling all about Paradise—come on! *Cain stares front.*

LUCIFER, *facing front:* I swear this, Cain—if man will not kill man, God is unnecessary! Walk away and you're free! *Cain starts to walk away.*

ABEL: Brother! God wants you there!

CAIN, *halting:* Wants *me?*

LUCIFER: Swallow it and walk!

ABEL: Of course—he loves you, Cain. He was just saying how you do everything He wants.

CAIN: Then, by God, I order you out of here and your mother and father, and never come back!

ABEL: Brother!—I've as much right here as you. *He moves toward Cain.*

CAIN: Are you even so sure of his blessing that you come to me?

ABEL: You'll not hurt me, Cain.

CAIN: Why? Am I thy servant? *He sweeps up his flail.* Am I thy fool? Run from me!

ABEL: *Astonished at the flail, he starts to back away.* Brother! God loves us both!

CAIN: You are dead to me, Abel—run!

ABEL, *halts:* I will not! Come to the Lord!

CAIN, *moving toward him, raising the flail:* Run for your life!

ABEL: Brother, let God calm you!

CAIN, *whirling about, flail raised, he calls to the air:* Save us, Lord . . . !

ABEL, *rushing to him:* Come to Him!

CAIN—*he turns on Abel, calling to God:* Now save us! *He strikes at Abel, who dodges and runs.*

ABEL, *screaming:* Mother!

CAIN—*pursuing him, he strikes Abel down:* Save us! *He strikes him again on the ground.* Save us!

LUCIFER: Cain! How can you love God so!

GOD, *calling from off:* Cain! Where art thou!

Cain flings the flail away like an alien thing that somehow got into his hand. God enters rapidly, behind Him Eve and Adam.

GOD: Where is thy brother?

Cain is silent.

EVE: Where is Abel?

ADAM: Where is he?

GOD: Where is Abel, thy brother?

CAIN, *with a new, dead indifference:* I know not. Am I my brother's keeper?

GOD: The voice of thy brother's blood crieth unto me from the ground.

EVE—*seeing the corpse, like a sigh at first:* Ahhh.

ADAM, *wide-eyed:* Ohhh. *The sigh repeatedly emanating from her, she halts, looking down at the corpse. Adam comes and faces it.* Ohhhh.

EVE—*she goes down beside the corpse, keening.* Abel? Wake, my darling!

ADAM: Abel? *Calls.* Abel!

GOD: What hast thou done!

CAIN, *with a bitter, hard grin, plus a certain intimate, familiar tone:* What had to be done. As the Lord surely knew when I laid before Him the fruit of my sweat—for which there was only Thy contempt.

GOD: But why contempt? Didn't I approve of your offering?

CAIN: As I would "approve" my ox. Abel's lamb was not "approved," it was adored, like his life!

GOD, *indignantly:* But I *like* lamb! *Cain is dumbfounded.* I don't deny it, I like lamb better than onions.

LUCIFER: Surely there can be no accounting for taste.

CAIN: And this is Your justice?

GOD: Justice!

CAIN, *with a bitter laugh:* Yes, justice! Justice!

GOD: When have I ever spoken that word?

CAIN: You mean our worth and value are a question of *taste?*

GOD, *incredulously:* But Cain, there are eagles and sparrows, lions and mice—is every bird to be an eagle? Are there to be no mice? Let a man do well, and he shall be accepted.

CAIN: I have done well and I am humiliated!

GOD: You hated Abel before this day, so you cannot say you have done well.

EVE, *rising from the corpse:* You argue with *Him? She rushes to tear at Cain, Adam holding her back.* Kill him! He's a murderer! *Weeping, held by Adam, she calls:* Take his life!

GOD: Surely you repent this, Cain.

CAIN: When God repents His injustice, I will repent my own!

LUCIFER: Why should he repent? Who sent death down here? You did! *He points to God.* There is the murderer!

ADAM: Watch your mouth!

LUCIFER: He arranged it all from beginning to end! *Eve stops weeping, straightens, astonished, turns to God.* Do You deny Azrael was here this morning while they slept? *To Eve:* Ask him!

EVE: You sent the Angel of Death?

Pause.

GOD: Yes.

EVE: Lord God . . . did you want this?

Pause.

GOD: Eve . . . soon the multitudes will spring from this first family and cover the earth. How will the thousands be shepherded as I have shepherded thee? Only if the eye of God opens in the heart of every man; only if each himself will choose the way of life, not death. For otherwise you go as beasts, locked up in the darkness of their nature. *Slight pause.* I saw that Cain was pious, yet in him I saw envy too. And so I thought—if Cain was so enraged that he lift his hand against his brother, but then, remembering his love for Abel and for me, even in his fury lay down his arms? *To Cain:* Man!—you would have risen like a planet before the generations, the victory of God, first brother and the first to reject a murder. Oh, Cain, how I hoped for thee!

ADAM, *to Eve:* Do you understand? He was trying to help us. *She stands rigid, wide-eyed.* Eve, you must beg his pardon.

EVE, *turning to God:* But why must my child have died? You could have tested me, or Adam or Abel—we could *never* have killed.

GOD: Woman, a moment ago you commanded me to take Cain's life.

EVE: But I . . . I was *angry.*

GOD: Cain was also angry. *She turns away, rejecting.* Do you understand me? *Beginning to anger.* Then am I a wanton murderer? Speak! What am I to you?

ADAM: Eve! Tell him you understand!

EVE: I do not understand . . . why we *can't just live*!

GOD: Because without God you'll murder each other!

EVE, *furiously:* And with God? With God?

GOD: Then do you want the Devil? Tell me now before the multitudes arrive. Who do you want!

ADAM: You, Lord, you!

GOD: Why? Your innocent son is dead; why!

ADAM: Because . . . how do I know?—maybe for someone, somewhere, even this . . . is good? Right?

GOD, *outraged:* You are all worthless! The mother blames God, the father blames no one, and the son knows no blame at all. *To Lucifer:* Angel, you have won the world—and I hereby give it over to your ministry.

ADAM: *Him!*

GOD: This is the chaos you want, and him you shall have—the God who judges nothing, the God of infinite permission. I shall continue to do the hurricanes, the gorillas, and all that, but I see now that your hearts' desire is anarchy and I wash my hands. I do not want to be God . . . any more! *He starts away.*

LUCIFER, *dashing after Him:* Lord! You don't mean—not me all by myself!

GOD: That's what you've been after, isn't it?

LUCIFER: No, no—with You! It's out of the question for me to run the world alone.

GOD: But what do you need Me for?

LUCIFER: But I can't—I can't *make* anything!

GOD: Really! But you're such a superb critic.

LUCIFER: But they're two entirely different things!

GOD: Perhaps once you're in charge you'll become more creative. *He starts away again; Eve rushes to Him.*

EVE: Wait, Lord, please!

GOD: Oh, woman, for thy torment especially I am most deeply sorry. Good-bye, dear Eve. *He starts away.*

EVE: But what do we do about Cain?

Now He halts, turns, alert.

LUCIFER, *to God:* Very well, I take the world! *To Eve:* Tell Him to go!

EVE, *to Lucifer:* But what about Cain?

LUCIFER: There'll be no more talk about Cain. The boy simply got caught in a rotten situation, and no emotions are called for.

GOD: She seems to have a question—

LUCIFER: She is free! She has no further questions! *To Eve:* Tell Him to go back to His hurricanes.

EVE, *to Lucifer:* But He murdered my son.

GOD: But what is the question?

EVE: HE MURDERED MY SON!

GOD: And what is the *question*, woman!

LUCIFER: You've got your freedom! Stop here!

EVE, *to Lucifer:* But how—*turning to Cain's adamant face:* How do I hand him his breakfast tomorrow? How do I call him to dinner? "Come, mankiller, I have meat for thee"?

CAIN, *holding his ground, his profile to her eyes:* It was not my fault!

EVE, *crying out to God:* How can we live with him!

GOD: But what did you say to me a moment ago—"Why can't we just live?" Why can't you do it? Take your unrepentant son and start living.

LUCIFER: Why not? Will blaming Cain bring Abel back?

EVE: But shouldn't he . . . shouldn't he repent?

LUCIFER: You mean a few appropriate words will console you?

EVE: Not words, but . . . *To Cain:* Don't you feel you've done *anything*?

LUCIFER: What's the difference what he feels?

EVE, *with high anxiety:* You mean nothing has *happened?*

LUCIFER: There is no consolation, woman! Unless you want the lie of God, the false tears of a killer repenting!

EVE: But why must they be false? If he loved his brother, maybe now he feels . . . *She breaks off, backing a step from Lucifer, and turns to God:* Is this . . . why he can't be God?

GOD, *quickly:* Why can't he be God?

LUCIFER: I can and I will be—I am the truth!

EVE: But you . . . *In fear:* you don't . . .

ADAM: He doesn't love us!

EVE: Yes!

GOD: And that is why, whatever you do, it's all the same to him—it's only his power this angel loves!

ADAM AND EVE, *rushing to God:* Father, save us!

GOD: Oh, my children, I thought you'd never understand!

LUCIFER, *with a furious, bitter irony, as God approaches the beseeching people:* And here He comes again—Father Guilt is back! *Rushing to Cain:* Cain, help me! You're the one free, guiltless man. Tell God you have no need for Him! Speak out your freedom and save the world!

CAIN—*he has been staring in silence; now he turns his dead eyes to Lucifer:* Angel, none of this seems to matter, you know? One way or the other. Why don't you let it all go?

With a near-sob Lucifer claps his hands over his ears, then, straightening, he comes to a salute before God.

LUCIFER: You have my salute! You have gorgeously prearranged this *entire* dialogue, and it all comes out the way You want—but You have solved absolutely nothing!

GOD, *lifting His eyes from the kneeling Adam and Eve:* Except, angel, that you will never be God. And not because I forbid it, but because they will never—at least not for very long—believe it. For I made them not of dust alone, but dust and love; and by dust alone they will not, cannot long be governed. *Lucifer bursts into sobbing tears.* Why do you weep, angel? They love, and with love, kill brothers. Take heart, I see now that our war goes on.

ADAM AND EVE: No, Lord!

Lucifer looks at God now, clear-eyed, expectant.

GOD: It does go on. For love, I see, is not enough; though the Devil himself cry peace, you'll find your war. Now I want to know what is in your heart. Tell me, man, what do you feel?

CAIN: I am thirsty.

GOD, *after a slight pause:* So in thy thirst will I sentence thee, Cain—to live. And in this loneliness shalt thou walk forever in the populous cities, a fugitive and a vagabond all the days of thy life. And whoever looks on thee will point and say, "There is the man who murdered his brother."

CAIN, *coming alive:* Better kill me now! They will stone me wherever I go!

GOD: No. I declare to all the generations: Whoever slayeth Cain, vengeance shall be taken on him sevenfold. For I will set a mark upon thee, Cain, that will keep thee from harm.

CAIN: What mark?

GOD, *holding two index fingers pointed toward Cain's face:* Come to me, my son. *Terrified, Cain comes up to His fingers, and He comes around behind Cain, who is facing front, and presses his cheeks, forming a smile which Cain cannot relax. God lowers His fingers.*

CAIN, *smiling:* What is the mark?

GOD: That smile is.

CAIN: But they will know that I killed my brother!

GOD: Yes, they will know, and you will smile forever with agony in your eyes—the sundered mark of Cain who killed for pride and power in the name of love.

Smiling, his eyes desperate, Cain turns to Eve. She cries out and hides her face in her hands. He tears at his cheeks, but his smile remains. He lowers his hands—a smiling man with astonished, terrifying eyes.

GOD: Adam? Eve? Now the way of life is revealed before you, and the way of death. Seek Me only in your hearts, you will never see My face again.

Lucifer, who has been staring off, swerves about. The people come alert, startled. God turns and walks upstage.

ADAM, *rushing a half-step behind God:* What'd you say? Lord, I don't understand . . . *God continues, moving into light. Adam halts, calling.* Did you say *never?*

EVE: What does that mean? Almighty God! *She starts to run up toward Him, but He disappears among the stars. Adam, above her now, turns down to Lucifer.*

ADAM: Angel! *He comes down to Lucifer, his finger rising toward the angel.* Did he mean that you are . . . ?

Lucifer turns from the vanished God to Adam, his face twisted with puzzlement.

ADAM AND EVE, *with a heartbroken, lost cry:* Who is God?

LUCIFER: Does it really matter? Why don't you have a nice breakfast together—the three of you—and forget the whole thing? After all, whoever God is, we have to be sensible. *He walks away, glancing back to Eve.* And whenever you'd like to start the dancing—just call.

EVE: Don't ever come back!

LUCIFER, *pointing insinuatingly at her:* You know exactly what I mean.

Lucifer walks into darkness. Adam and Eve turn to Cain.

ADAM: He condemned you to wander the earth. You'll have to go.

CAIN: But he let me live; there was some forgiveness in that. There's too much work here for one man, Father.

EVE: How can you ask forgiveness? *Indicating Abel.* You can't even weep for him. You are still full of hate!

CAIN: And your hate, Mother? *She turns away.* How will I weep? You never loved Cain!

ADAM: Spare one another . . . !

EVE, *turning to the corpse:* I loved him more. *To Cain:* Yes, more than you. And God was *not* fair. To me, either. *Indicating Abel.* And I still don't understand why he had to die, or who or what rules this world. But this boy was innocent—that I know. And you killed him, and with him any claim to justice you ever had.

CAIN: I am not to blame!

EVE: Are you telling me that nothing *happened* here? I will not sit with you as though nothing happened!

ADAM: Ask her pardon! *Cain turns away from both.* Cain, we are surrounded by the beasts! And God's not coming any more —*Cain starts away.* Boy, we are all that's left responsible!—

ask her pardon! *Cain, adamant, the smile fixed on his face, walks out.* Call to him. Pardon him. In God's name cry mercy, Eve, there is no other!

With his arm around her he has drawn her to the periphery, where she stands, her mouth open, struggling to speak. But she cannot, and she breaks into weeping. As though in her name, Adam calls toward the departed Cain: Mercy!

The roars, songs, and cries of the animals fill the air. Adam looks up and about, and to the world, a clear-eyed prayer: Mercy!

CURTAIN

UP FROM PARADISE

A Musical

BOOK & LYRICS BY
ARTHUR MILLER

MUSIC BY
STANLEY SILVERMAN

CHARACTERS

GOD, *Bass Baritone*

ADAM, *Baritone*

EVE, *Mezzo Soprano (low A to high B)*

LUCIFER, *Tenor (or High Baritone)*

CHEMUEL (Angel of Mercy), *Tenor*

URIEL (Angel of Philosophy), *High Baritone*

AZRAEL (Angel of Death), *Bass*

CAIN, *Baritone*

ABEL, *Tenor*

ACT ONE

OVERTURE

(*Three* ANGELS *enter as* GOD *unfurls a sky drop, creating heaven.*)

AZRAEL: In the beginning, God created heaven, and all the
hosts of angels.

ANGELS (*sing*):
> THE LORD IS A HAMMER OF LIGHT
> THE LORD IS PERFECTLY ADORABLE
> GOD IS TALL
> AND OFTEN SHORT
> THE LORD IS PERFECTLY ADORABLE.

CHEMUEL: He also created the world, and all the creatures in it.

AZRAEL: And every kind of music.

ANGELS (*sing*):
> GOD IS ROUGH, AND ALSO SMOOTH
> HE IS NOISE AND SILENCE
> GOD IS PERFECTLY ADORABLE
> HE IS NOISE AND SILENCE
> HAL . . . LE . . . LU . . .

AZRAEL: All this is perfectly possible.

ANGELS (*whispered*):
> THE LORD IS A HAMMER OF LIGHT
> THE LORD IS

   (*sung loud*)

> PERFECTLY ADORABLE

CHEMUEL:
> THE LORD IS VERY WIDE

AZRAEL:
> HE IS OFTEN VERY NARROW

URIEL:
> THE LORD IS TOTALLY ADORABLE

ANGELS:
> TOTALLY, TOTALLY ADORABLE
> ADORABLE, ADORABLE

UTTERLY ADOR–ABLE
ADORABLE (*fading*) ADORABLE . . . Adorable . . .

(*Paradise, the Garden. ADAM enters.*)

URIEL: It is also possible that in the Beginning, Man created God and all his attributes. But either way, there can be no question that they used to talk to each other frequently.

GOD: Adam, I'd like you to try that again.

ADAM: Sure. (*He balances on one leg.*)

AZRAEL: About what they spoke it is not hard to guess, for the world was altogether new, and each day revealed another aspect of its perfection and its beauty.

GOD: Now before you answer, think carefully. Was this easier when you had the tail?

ADAM (*falls onto both feet*): I think I balance better. (*Looking behind.*) But I like the way this looks. More like you.

GOD: Well, now! I hadn't thought of that. Run along, Adam. But here . . . don't forget the teeth. (*GOD hands him a joined pair of boar's teeth which ADAM looks at unhappily.*)

ADAM: Could I say something, Lord . . .

GOD: Now look here, son, you have to give them time to work in.

ADAM: But watch what happens . . . (*puts them in, pointing at the tip of one near his eye*) they stick me in the eye.

GOD: Open. (*Takes out the teeth, looks at them, then turns to ADAM . . .*) Well, perhaps the time has come to simply admit it.

ADAM: What's that father?

GOD: You are perfect.

ADAM (*rubbing the healing wound on his coccyx*): I'm glad to hear that.

GOD: Yes, I think you are finished at last. Now run along.

CHEMUEL: And when the world was finished and the Lord had taken his rest, he would often venture into the Garden where Adam dwelt, there to take pleasure in his own image—this man into whom he had blown the breath of life.

URIEL: And Adam too was always pleased to turn from his thoughts and see *his* image taking form in the limpid air of Paradise. They were, in fact, so entirely pleased with one another that they found it hard sometimes to remember where one began and the other left off.

ADAM: Oh! Good morning, God!

GOD: Good morning, Adam. Beautiful day.

ADAM: Oh, perfect, Lord. But they all are.

GOD: I've turned up the breeze a little . . .

ADAM: I just noticed that. (*Holds up a hand to feel it.*) This is exactly right now. Thanks, Lord.

GOD: I'm very pleased with the way you tend the garden. How do you keep it all so perfect?

ADAM: Well, when I do have a problem, I just ask myself—"How would God handle this?" And it clears right up. Are we going to name more things, Lord?

GOD (*pleased*): You'd like that.

ADAM: Oh, Lord—naming things is the best part of my day.

GOD: Well, now . . . I don't see why we couldn't name a few things. (*He points.*) What would you call that? (*Silent pause.*)

ADAM: I'd call that a lion.

GOD: Lion. Well, that sounds all right. And that?

ADAM: I'd call that a lamb.

GOD (*doubtfully*): Lamb?

ADAM: Lamb.

GOD (*brightening*): Lamb sounds all right!

ANGELS (*sing*):
> HOW FINE IT IS TO NAME THINGS WITH THE
> LORD

ADAM:
> I TRY TO GUESS RIGHT
> BUT WHEN I GUESS WRONG
> HE HOLDS HIS BREATH
> AND THE UNIVERSE STOPS
> TILL I GET THE RIGHT NAME—
> AND HE STARTS BREATHING AGAIN.
>
> HOW FINE IT IS
> HOW FINE IT IS, HOW FINE IT IS . . . ETC.
>   . . . ETC.
>   . . . TO NAME THINGS WITH THE LORD!

ANGELS:
> HOW FINE IT IS TO NAME THINGS WITH THE
> LORD.

GOD:
>   NOW WHAT WOULD YOU CALL THAT?

ADAM:
>   I'D CALL THAT A LION.

GOD:
>   AND WHAT WOULD YOU CALL THAT?

ADAM:
>   I'D CALL THAT A LAMB.

GOD:
>   AND WHAT WOULD YOU CALL THAT?

GOD:	ADAM:
AND THAT?	I'D CALL IT LIZARD.
AND THAT?	I'D CALL IT LEOPARD.
AND THAT?	I'D CALL IT RABBIT.
ETC.	ANOTHER RABBIT.
AND THAT?	THAT?

GOD AND ANGELS:

AND THAT?	I'D CALL IT TURTLE.
AND THAT?	I'D CALL IT BEAVER.
AND THAT?	I'D CALL IT WOODCHUCK.
ETC.	I'D CALL IT LLAMA.
	TIGER!
	CAMEL!
	HIPPO!
	(*exhausted*)

ANGELS (*ecstatic*):
>   HOW FINE IT IS,
>   HOW FINE IT IS TO NAME THINGS WITH THE
>   LORD!

ALL:
>   HOW FINE IT IS TO NAME THINGS WITH THE
>   LORD!
>   HOW FINE IT IS, HOW FINE IT IS, ETC.
>   TO NAME THINGS WITH THE LORD,
>   TO NAME THINGS WITH THE LORD,

ADAM:
>   WHAT'S THAT!

GOD: I think that will be enough for now. (*ANGELS exit.*)

ADAM: Are you leaving?

GOD: What's the matter, Adam?

ADAM: I don't know.

ADAM (*sings*):

WHEN THE NIGHT STARTS TO FALL
EVERY CREATURE GOES TO REST,
THE FOX IN HIS HOLE
AND THE EAGLE TO HIS NEST.
WE'RE ALL GOOD COMPANIONS,
WE'RE TOGETHER ALL DAY . . .

BUT A LION LIKES A LION
AND A LYNX LIKES A LYNX
BETTER THAN THEY LIKE ME

GOD (*spoken*): But they do like you, Adam.

ADAM (*sings*):

YES, BUT NOT QUITE AS MUCH
AS THEY LIKE THEM.

SO WHEN NIGHT STARTS TO FALL
I AM FILLED WITH A STRANGE KIND OF
    WISHING . . .

GOD (*spoken*): For what?

ADAM (*sings*):

I DON'T KNOW. I DON'T KNOW.
I DON'T KNOW.

GOD: Adam?

ADAM: Yes, Lord.

GOD: Lie down.

ADAM: Lie. . . ?

GOD (*with a magical movement of his open hand before ADAM's eyes*): Down. (*ADAM goes back down on his back.*) I'll take out a bottom rib.

ADAM (*ADAM sits up abruptly, protectively pressing his rib.*): A what?

GOD (*motioning him down again*): You'll never know the difference. I only put it in to be extra sure.

ADAM (*starting up again*): Could I ask. . . ?

GOD: Ssssh!—sleep, Adam.

(*ANGELS enter.*)

ANGELS (*sing*):
> BONE . . .

GOD (*sings as* EVE *materializes . . .*):
> THIS IS NOW BONE OF THY BONES,
> AND FLESH OF THY FLESH:
> SHE SHALL BE CALLED WOMAN
> BECAUSE SHE WAS TAKEN OUT OF MAN.

(*EVE approaches.*)

GOD: Wake up, Adam.

ADAM: Oh, God! What is it?

GOD: —Adam, I have made you a wife!

ADAM: It's *my wife*?

GOD: I don't know why I never thought of it before. Except that I live alone and I suppose I took for granted that you would, too. How does she strike you?

ADAM: Oh, Lord, she's perfect!

GOD: I don't know how I do it.

CHEMUEL:
> BEHOLD THY WOMAN THAT GOD HATH
>   MIRACULOUSLY DEVISED
> THAT ADAM MAY NOT WASTE HIMSELF IN
>   LONELINESS
> HALLELUJAH.

(*ANGELS sing "Hallelujahs" in harmony. ADAM joins them, making a barbershop quartet.*)

GOD: You'll have to think of a name. This one's important so take your time.

ADAM (*instantly*): Eve.

GOD: Why that's a lovely name! (*ANGELS sing Hallelujahs softly underneath. GOD takes EVE's hand, and with an extended embrace toward ADAM, moves to a point.*) Here is the Garden I have made; here you will live forever. See the four rivers flowing through it, Adam? (*He points at each river in turn as ADAM says their names.*)

ADAM: The Pishon, the Gihon, the Tigris and the Euphrates.

GOD: Their crystal waters will keep your garden green forever. There is the currant bush, excellent for jam; there is thyme, there is rosemary, the feathery dill; that is the peach, the

plum and the pear, and there you have all the sweet figs you
can possibly desire . . .

ADAM: But not too many.

GOD: That's true, my dear—not too many figs.

EVE: Why? (*ANGELS cut off abruptly.*)

ADAM: That's the rule!

GOD: Be patient, Adam, she's very new. (*ANGELS resume singing
Hallelujahs softly.*) That is the tree of Knowledge, my dear,
Knowledge of Good and Evil. But everything is perfect in
this garden, nothing can ever be improved. You will live here
forever in the center of my mind, in the purest light of my
perfect love. Only one obligation have I laid upon you both
—don't eat that apple. (*ANGELS crescendo and cadence.*)

ANGELS:

    HUMMMMMMMMMMMMMMMMMM

AZRAEL:

    SO RESOLVE EACH MORNING WHEN YOU
        OPEN YOUR EYES
    THAT FOR LOVE OF YOUR FATHER YOU WILL
    REFUSE THE TEMPTATION OF THAT LOVELY
        TREE
    IN THE CENTER OF YOUR MIND KEEP THE
        LORD.

ANGELS:

    IN THE CENTER OF YOUR MIND KEEP THE
        LORD.

GOD:

    SO RENEW YOUR VOW TO ME.

ANGELS & GOD:

    EACH DAY.

AZRAEL:

    IN THE CENTER OF YOUR MIND, KEEP THE
        LORD.

ADAM & EVE:

    IN THE CENTER OF YOUR MIND, KEEP THE
        LORD.

GOD:

    SO RESOLVE EACH MORNING WHEN YOU
        OPEN YOUR EYES
    THAT FOR LOVE OF YOUR FATHER YOU WILL

> REFUSE THE TEMPTATION OF THAT LOVELY
> TREE
> IN THE CENTER OF YOUR MIND, KEEP THE
> LORD.
> IN THE CENTER OF YOUR MIND, KEEP THE
> LORD . . .

ADAM:

> IN THE CENTER OF YOUR MIND, KEEP THE
> LORD.
> IN THE CENTER OF YOUR MIND, KEEP THE
> LORD.

ADAM, EVE & GOD:

> IN THE CENTER OF YOUR MIND, KEEP THE
> LORD.
> IN THE CENTER OF YOUR MIND, KEEP THE
> LORD.
> IN THE CENTER OF YOUR MIND . . .

ALL:

> KEEP THE LORD
> IN THE CENTER OF YOUR MIND, KEEP THE
> LORD.

(*Repeats to climax.*)

KEEP THE LORD!

(*GOD, CHEMUEL and URIEL exit. During exit ANGELS chant "IN THE CENTER OF YOUR MIND." . . .*)

AZRAEL: And so it came to pass that the man taught the woman all that he knew. Until the time came when she knew what he knew and he knew everything she knew, so neither had a secret to keep from the other. And thus they were perfectly innocent. (*AZRAEL exits.*)

ADAM (*sings*):

> IT'S JUST LIKE I WAS YOU

EVE:

> AND I WAS PRACTICALLY YOU.

BOTH:

> LIKE WE'RE BOTH THE SAME PERSON
> WITH DIFFERENT NAMES
> I CAN HARDLY TELL THE DIFFERENCE AT ALL.

ADAM:

IF YOU TRIP OVER A ROCK OR A HOLE
I'M THE ONE WHO FALLS.
IT'S JUST LIKE I WAS YOU.

EVE:

AND I WAS PRACTICALLY YOU.

BOTH:

IT'S LIKE WE'RE BOTH THE SAME PERSON
NEITHER BETTER NOR WORSE THAN
THE VERY SAME PERSON WITH
DIFFERENT, BUT EQUALLY BEAUTIFUL NAMES.

EVE:

IF A SPECK OF DUST FALLS INTO YOUR EYES,
TEARS WELL UP IN MINE.
IT'S JUST LIKE I WAS YOU.

ADAM:

AND I WAS PRACTICALLY YOU.

BOTH:

IT'S LIKE WE'RE BOTH THE SAME PERSON
NEITHER BETTER NOR WORSE THAN
THE VERY SAME PERSON WITH
DIFFERENT, BUT EQUALLY BEAUTIFUL NAMES.
HALLELUJAH, HALLELUJAH.

(*LUCIFER, GOD and ANGELS enter.*)

LUCIFER: Did you ever see anything so *sweet?*

CHEMUEL: Congratulations, Lord.

GOD: Excuse me . . . a little later perhaps. I'd like a few words
with Lucifer. (*ANGELS exit.*) All right. Go ahead. Say it.

LUCIFER: I expected something beautiful. (*GOD looks outraged.*)
But she is . . . she is . . . (*shakes his head.*) For the first time
in my life, I have no words.

GOD: The idea came so suddenly—maybe that's it; not a muscle
had to be revised.

LUCIFER: Well, that's the difference between you and me. I'd
think about it, plan every detail and end up with nothing.
You plunge right in and you can't do anything wrong. Sincerely, father, I think that woman is your masterpiece.

GOD: She might be, yes.

LUCIFER: So—what now?

GOD: I think I'll just rest for a while.

LUCIFER: And when do you plan to finish them?

GOD: Finish them?

LUCIFER: I mean when do they eat the apple?

GOD: Eat the apple! I forbade that!

LUCIFER: I know that, sir, but I assumed it was to make sure that they ate it. But Father, with the intellectual potential you've given them, it's inevitable their curiosity will drive them to it. In fact, forbidding apples seemed to me your most brilliant stroke. They might ignore the figs, oranges and pears, but really, Father, those apples? (*GOD, in thought, walks past him.*) It seemed so obvious, I mean . . . what *is* the point? (*GOD turns to him, unable to speak.*) You mean you've given a magnificent brain like that to a couple of . . . *gardeners?*

GOD (*in defensive irritation*): Gardening is not all that simple!

LUCIFER: But I never dreamed it was that complicated.

GOD: It can be if you do it right!

LUCIFER: I'm trying to get the picture, Father—you mean that to transplant the tulips and mow the lawn you invented a race of gods?

GOD: They are not gods and must never be.

LUCIFER: Angels, then.

GOD: Not angels at all.

LUCIFER: Not animals either.

GOD: Not quite animals, no.

LUCIFER: Then what are they?

GOD: They are what I would be if I were not God.

LUCIFER: Well, now, that's deep. But—forgive me, Lord—what would the point of that be?

GOD: To a mind like yours, that ought to be obvious.

LUCIFER: Praise?

GOD: In a sense, yes.

LUCIFER: But surely the Angels praise you sufficiently.

GOD: Of course, but they have no alternative.

LUCIFER: But what alternative has Man?

GOD: He can always eat apples.

LUCIFER: Aaaahhh!—

GOD: Yes.

LUCIFER: In other words, this is the only race that has the power to disobey the Lord.

GOD: And the love and devotion to keep them from doing it.

LUCIFER: That is breathtaking. That is not only praise, it's excrutiating. In other words, to praise you, they must exercise a certain discipline . . .

GOD: They must love the Lord, period. Not automatically, like angels; not in the hope of personal advancement, like you; but perfectly, by lovingly doing my will . . .

LUCIFER: When they might do otherwise. It's beautiful. But could I just dot a couple of i's? This is purely theoretical, but if by some absolutely accidental accident . . .

GOD: They will not eat!

LUCIFER: No question. But if they did, I can see where they'd end up praising you even more than they can now . . . But . . .

GOD: This is it.

LUCIFER: Well, there you go. I tell you how I went wrong. When I saw you planting the tree of Knowledge I thought "something's up." Then when I laid eyes on Adam, I was almost sure. But with this woman I was convinced that you had decided to rule the earth—with a brand new race of gods. That is the only word for those two people, Lord— with the bone and blood of beasts and the soul and knowingness of gods—what a fitting crown for all creation! . . . But this is it.

GOD (*even more deeply conflicted*): This is it.

LUCIFER (*nods; slight pause*): I even thought that you might want me to teach some elementary physics, chemistry, languages . . .

GOD: Let's clear up one thing now, Angel! (*ANGELS enter listening to the commotion.*)

LUCIFER (*apprehensively*): Yes sir.

GOD: Whatever my pupose, it was not to provide you with two simpletons before whom you could parade your superior intellect. You were never in this picture. Do we have that straight?

LUCIFER: This is it.

GOD: This is it!

(*ANGELS sing* "*Hallelujah.*")

LUCIFER: My job is to speak the unspeakable, Lord and as angry as you are it is your will. If Adam must remain so utterly ignorant why do you tempt him with that fruit?

GOD (*sings*):

> I WANTED HIM TO WAKE EACH MORNING
> AND OF HIS OWN FREE WILL DECLARE
> "FOR GOD'S SAKE I WILL NOT EAT THAT
> APPLE."

LUCIFER (*sings*):

> BUT IF SOMETHING LEADS TO GOOD CAN IT
> BE BAD?
> WITH ONE SMALL BITE HIS CURIOSITY
> WILL BRING HIM TO INVESTIGATE HIS LIFE.
> TO BE SURE HE'LL LOSE HIS CHILDISH
> INNOCENCE.
> HE'LL BECOME MORE ANALYTICAL AND WISE:
> BUT HIS LOVE FOR GOD WILL DEEPEN IN THE
> END,
> HIS LOVE MUST DEEPEN WITH HIS WISDOM.
> RIGHT NOW HE ONLY MARVELS AT THE
> ARTISTRY OF GOD
> WHO PAINTS THE COLORS OF THE SPRING
> AND FALL.
> BUT SUPPOSING HE DISCOVERS
> CHLOROPHYLL, DEAR LORD.
> YOU'LL ALSO AMAZE HIM AS A SCIENTIST.
> AND HE'LL PRAISE YOU MORE FOR
> CHLOROPHYLL
> AND FOR DISCOVERING HIS PANCREAS
> THAN FOR PAINTING THE SPRING AND THE
> FALL.

GOD:

> I LOVE MY CHILDREN, THEY ARE PERFECT
> NOW,
> I CAN'T BEAR THEM EVER TO KNOW EVIL.
> THEY MUST LIVE FOREVER IN THE CENTER OF
> MY MIND.

LUCIFER:
> AND THAT IS WHY I THINK THAT TREE IS
>   THERE
> YOU WOULD LIKE THEM TO APPRECIATE:

(*Spoken.*) To sum it all up, Dad, you secretly wanted full credit for everything . . .

> WHAT A GENIUS YOU ARE.

GOD: Lucifer, I'm very ahead of you.

LUCIFER: It's inevitable, Lord! May I go now? (*Tag chord.*)

GOD: Mmmm . . . now listen, my son, and with extreme care. You will not go near that tree or those dear people—not in any form, do you hear? They are innocent, and innocent they will remain till I turn out the lights forever! (*GOD exits.*)

LUCIFER: Now what is He really saying? Makes a pair of boring, simpleminded yokels, yet He hangs above their heads, an arm's-length away, the secret of all knowledge, the living seed of godhood. Why? (*Skeptically wrinkling his nose.*) To prove their innocent devotion? But what is proved if they are never truly tempted? All things come from God. Therefore, if a thing that can be done is left undone, it must be God's will that it should be done—why else would He devise the possibility? Therefore, in some ultimate sense He does want it done. —Then why forbid it so strenuously? Because . . . (*His eyes widen.*) He wants it done—dangerously. —Oh God!—this is all a test for Lucifer! He must have some incredibly high position in mind for me, and He wants to see if I'll do His will even at the risk of His anger! Oh praise the Lord who gave me all this insight. My argument with Him is over! When this is done, the mangod rises on the earth; and Lucifer to God has proved his worth! (*Softly, with infinite pleasure.*) Strange!—I never felt so close to my Creator as I do right now!

(*ADAM and EVE in the garden, both staring heavenward. A beat. Now a new mood from her—she glances at the tree.*)

EVE: I think I understand absolutely everything now, except one . . .

ADAM (*glancing at the tree—worriedly*): I know.

EVE: It looks so lusciously red. I mean why would He. . . ?

ADAM (*longingly*): I *wish* He'd come by again.

EVE: Could you ask Him to explain it more slowly?

ADAM: There's another reason I'd love to see Him—I keep getting a terrific feeling that I could name something.

EVE: Is there anything left?

ADAM: I'm not sure. But whenever I'd get a name there was always something that it fit.

EVE: What's the name?

ADAM: Today.

EVE: Today! What could be a Today?

ADAM (*inhales*): I think it's . . . sort of . . . all this. (*Gestures.*)

EVE: All what?

ADAM: Well, like . . . before it got dark I think it was . . . Yesterday.

EVE: Oh, I see. And after it gets dark again?

ADAM: Tomorrow. So everything between them is today.

EVE: Isn't that marvelous!—We won't have to point anymore! (*Trying it out.*) Now let's see . . . what I'm going to do Tomorrow, is . . .

ADAM: Sssssshhh!—you can't—He hasn't okayed it yet.

EVE: But He is always crazy about your names, isn't He?

ADAM: Yeah, but I can't just decide all by myself that this is Today!

EVE: I disagree—to me this is Today.

ADAM: Please don't do this.

EVE (*challengingly, calling upward*): Today, Yesterday and Tomorrow!

ADAM: She doesn't mean it!

EVE: What are you so frightened about!—they're beautiful names!

ADAM: Because He's supposed to be *here* when I name. Otherwise it's just me making them up, and that's not even polite—I mean I say them, but they really come from *Him*.

(*LUCIFER appears.*)

LUCIFER: Then why did He always look so surprised when you came up with Platypus and Sloth and Virginia Creeper!

ADAM: Yeah, but . . . you can't mean that I've really and truly all by myself . . .

LUCIFER: Why not?

ADAM (*peering into* LUCIFER's *face as through fog*): Who are you? Why do I see you through a fog?

LUCIFER: It's not a fog—Just hard to know whether I'm coming or going.

ADAM: What's your name? Lucifer?

LUCIFER: Uh huh.

ADAM (*astonished, points at him*): Your name is *Lucifer*?

LUCIFER: Why the surprise?

ADAM (*to* EVE *too*): But I just this minute made it up! I could feel it in my mouth suddenly, like a goldfish!—And you're an angel, I suppose?

LUCIFER: I am the Archangel.

ADAM: *I* named the *Archangel*?

EVE: Listen!—since you probably see Him a lot . . .

LUCIFER: Constantly.

EVE: We can't seem to keep it straight why we are not supposed to . . . you know, the apples there.

LUCIFER (*as though surprised*): Oh. But (*to* ADAM) haven't you explained it to her?

EVE: He really doesn't follow it either.

LUCIFER: But how's that possible?—he invented it!

ADAM: *Me!*

LUCIFER: But why would God bother making a fruit as lovely as that and forbid your eating it?

EVE: No wonder I always thought it was some kind of mistake! I knew you had it all wrong! He's probably even insulted that we're refusing to eat it.

LUCIFER: I suggest you start eating now, and I'm sure the Lord will gradually forgive you. (*Swings apple in front of her.*) There you are dear.

EVE (*picks the apple, cups it*): Mmm! (*To* ADAM.) Want to smell it?

ADAM: He said we would die!

LUCIFER: But He loves you—you've confused everything.

EVE: Here, Darling—(*Holds it under his nose.*)

ADAM (*smells it, bewildered, tempted*): But why would I have made up such a thing?

LUCIFER: I mean, forbidding her to touch it or smell it or even admit that it's there.

ADAM: It does seem a little odd. (*EVE bites.* ADAM *looks into her*

totally absorbed expression, then . . .) I better go feed the
trout.

EVE: Adam! (*He halts. She come to him, inhales and blows out.*)
Whah. . . !!

ADAM (*feels her head*): She seems all right!—What's it like?

EVE: It's ah . . . well ah . . . like sort of a sweet quince.

ADAM (*enviously, grabs the apple*): A sweet quince! (*Immediately
bites, savors, gives to* LUCIFER *to bite.* LUCIFER *turns and walks.*)
You leaving?

LUCIFER: See you again sometime. Goodbye dear Eve.

ADAM: Why did you come?

LUCIFER: Introduce myself. Look around. Sort of felt the call,
you know? Ta-ta. (*He exits.*)

ADAM: You all right?

EVE: Ya, I'm ah . . .

ADAM: Me too. And I'll tell you something that I . . .

EVE: Right, but you just . . .

ADAM: Couldn't.

EVE: But now.

ADAM: Yes. It's that you . . . have never been . . . exactly . . .

EVE: Well, neither were you . . . you mean clear.

ADAM: That's what I'm saying—it's like . . .

EVE: It's like I always saw you through the water. And now
. . . And now we sort of . . .

ADAM & EVE: CAME OUT!

ADAM (*sings*):
　　MY GOD, I'M ME!
　　I USED TO THINK SOMETIMES THAT I WAS YOU—
　　I'M NOT . . . I'M ABSOLUTELY ME!

EVE:
　　YOU'RE YOU, ADAM, YOU'RE YOU, ADAM
　　YOU'RE YOU, ADAM, YOU ADAM, YOU!
　　ADAM, YOU'RE YOU.

ADAM:
　　I EVEN HAD MYSELF MIXED UP WITH TREES
　　AND ROCKS AND FISH AND WHATEVER I WAS
　　　　LOOKING AT
　　LIKE FROGS AND CHIMPANZEES.

EVE:
　　I WAS SURE MIXED UP BEFORE

WITH FAWNS AND RAINBOW TROUT
BUT I AM ABSOLUTELY NOTHING ELSE BUT
   ME!

EVE:
   I'M ME

ADAM:
   I SEE

EVE:
   I'M REALLY ME

ADAM:
   I SUDDENLY SEE YOU

EVE:
   I LOOK!

ADAM:
   NOT AT ALL LIKE ME!

EVE:
   NO-NO-NO-NO, I'M ME. I'M WONDERFUL

ADAM:
   IMAGINE THAT . . . YOU'RE YOU!

EVE:
   I'M ME.

BOTH:
   IMAGINE THAT . . . WE'RE US!

(*LUCIFER dances across stage swiftly and exits.*)

LUCIFER:
   BUT IF SOMETHING LEADS TO GOOD CAN IT
   BE BAD?

(*Pause. Music hangs there softly. Apart, they look at each other.*)

ADAM (*singing*):
   I'M LONELY. I'VE NEVER BEEN SO GODAWFUL
   LONELY.

EVE:
   ME TOO—HOLD ME.

ADAM:
   YOU HOLD ME.

BOTH:
   I'M SCARED.

(*They embrace, go to the ground.*)

CHEMUEL: And they fell to the ground and made love that they might be one again as they had been in their innocence.

GOD (*eagerly, from off*): Children?

EVE (*looking off*): He's coming!

ADAM: Put something on!

(*GOD enters from platform.*)

GOD: Where art thou?

ADAM: Here, Lord. (*GOD turns, looking around. ADAM emerges, nervously apologizing.*) I heard Thy voice in the garden and I was afraid, because I was naked, and I hid myself.

GOD: Who told thee that thou wast naked?

ADAM: Who told me?

GOD: Who told thee! You didn't know you were naked! You ate of the Tree of Knowledge!

ADAM: She made me.

EVE: I couldn't help it. A snake came. (*To ADAM*) Wasn't he a snake?

ADAM: Like a snake, ya.

GOD: You have spoiled everything!

EVE (*covering her face*): I feel ashamed.

GOD: Ashamed? My purest darling, ashamed?!

GOD (*sings*):
> I WILL GREATLY MULTIPLY THY SORROWS IN
>   THY CONCEPTION
> IN SORROW THOU SHALT BRING FORTH
>   CHILDREN
>
> AND THY DESIRE SHALL BE TO THY HUSBAND,
> AND HE SHALL RULE OVER THEE

ADAM: Don't worry, Lord. I'll see to it that it will never happen again.

GOD:
> CURSED IS THE GROUND FOR THY SAKE NOW
> IN THE SWEAT OF THY FACE SHALT THOU EAT
>   BREAD.
> YES, MY CHILDREN
> NOW THERE IS TIME, AND AGE, AND DEATH.

YES, THE DAYS OF THY LIFE ARE NUMBERED
NOW
FOR DUST THOU ART
AND UNTO DUST SHALT THOU RETURN.

ADAM: But why!

GOD: —I am the Lord!—and you will never be with all your knowing! Get out of the Garden!

ADAM: Out!

EVE: Father, there's only sand out there!

GOD: Daughter—get out!

ADAM: Is there any way we can get back in?

GOD: Out! You know too much to live in Eden.

ADAM: But I am ignorant.

GOD: Knowing you are ignorant is too much to know.

EVE: I'm so sorry.

ADAM: Goodbye, Father.

GOD: Stay together. Take care of each other. And don't forget— . . . I'm always watching you! (*ADAM & EVE exit.*)

AZRAEL: One thing is certain here—whether God created Man or Man imagined God . . . Paradise was empty for them both. The green and rolling lawns, the banks of flowers, the dark cascading wisteria, upreaching elm, the perfect thrust of tulip, the cedar's canopy—all stood in a fixed and useless . . . silence.

GOD: . . . Why?

LUCIFER: My Lord . . .

GOD: Lucifer!? . . . Been quite a day.

LUCIFER: Yes, sir! They're out on the desert now, you know.

GOD: Yes, I know. It's rather pitiful.

LUCIFER: Not for long, though. I'll be going down in a couple days to kick things off with a few tips on building a house . . .

GOD: Oh?

LUCIFER: Sure . . . show them how to dig a well and so on . . . with the potential you put into them it'll all be coming up roses in no time.

GOD: Awfully good of you, but I . . .

LUCIFER: Anything I can do to help.

GOD: . . . Tell me, my son—how do you see yourself now? As my emissary? Ambassador?

LUCIFER: Candidly? . . . I think we're talking a second throne at the top of the world. There's no rush, but if you're asking . . .

GOD: And who will occupy this throne?

LUCIFER: Strictly your option, Dad. Not that I haven't given it some thought. I have. And I'm ready. I mean I just am.

GOD: And your responsibilities?

LUCIFER: Broadly? I'll see to it that nobody can escape the Government of Heaven. I mean take your muggers, your rapists, your second story heisters—you're never going to have time for those types. So how are they supposed to end up—atheists, God help us? You have to have somebody to accept the ones who you have to condemn.

GOD: And that will be you.

LUCIFER: I'm still roughing it in, but—yes, it would definitely be me.

GOD: In other words, no one would ever be judged.

LUCIFER: No, on the contrary—*everyone* gets judged, it's just that I'll judge the bad ones and you judge the good.

GOD: But how will you judge the bad ones?

LUCIFER: Basically? I'd tell them they couldn't help it and just forget the whole thing.

GOD: But who would try to be good anymore if it's just as good to be bad?

LUCIFER: But that's the whole beauty!—they don't have to be good as long as they keep being members—But don't misunderstand, they're going to love you, Father, because they'll know that you love me, the god who lets them do anything. It's watertight, guarantee your power forever!—May I requisition a throne?

GOD: There is a problem.

LUCIFER: What problem is that, sir?

GOD: I don't love you.

LUCIFER: You can't mean that.

GOD: As seriously as you mean my destruction.

LUCIFER: Destruction! I am trying to make you feasible.

GOD: By enthroning evil at my side? When God can love evil God has died—as you damned well know! Lucifer, I condemn you to everlasting darkness!

LUCIFER: Wait!—what's the hurry! Please, listen—without me, you'll be eternally at war with the nature of man!

GOD: Then let there be war! Better ten thousand years of war than I rule one instant with the help of unrighteousness! (*Music.*)

LUCIFER: Lord God, I am holding out my hand!

GOD: Go to hell! (*Thunder music.*)
  Now in thy beauty fallen
  Be thou to man the proof,
  That God will never love evil
  Between us man must choose.

LUCIFER: Lord? (*Threateningly.*) You will not take my hand?

GOD: Never, never, never!

LUCIFER: Then I will take the world! (*He exits.*)

GOD (*calling after him*): And if you ever do, I will burn it, I will flood it out, I will leave it a dead rock spinning in silence! For the Lord is good and only Good!

ANGELS (*sing*):
  HALLELUJAH!
  HALLELUJAH!

GOD: Why do I miss him? How strange. (*He walks to the edge of the stage, looks down deeply troubled.*)

(*Music. The desert. ADAM and EVE are wandering. She is visibly pregnant. LUCIFER is wandering as well.*)

LUCIFER (*sings*):
  I'M LONELY? GODAWFUL . . .

ADAM:
  LONELY.

LUCIFER:
  LONELY.

EVE:
  ME TOO.

LUCIFER:
  BUT IF SOMETHING . . .

EVE:
  IF A SPECK OF DUST . . .
  HOLD ME.

LUCIFER & ADAM:
    YOU HOLD ME.
ADAM:
    HE HELD HIS BREATH
    AND THE UNIVERSE STOPPED
    TIL I GOT THE RIGHT NAME
    AND HE . . .
LUCIFER:
    LONELY.
EVE:
    ME TOO.

    (*Lights up on* GOD.)

GOD:
    LONELY IS MY HOUSE
    MY SON, MY CHILDREN GONE
LUCIFER:
    LONELY IS MY LIFE.
ADAM & EVE:
    LONELY IS OUR LIFE.
ALL:
    LONELY, NEVER BEEN SO
    GODAWFUL LONELY.
    LONELY.

    (GOD *and* LUCIFER *exit.*)

EVE: Wait! Adam! I can't go on. (*ADAM halts, looks back at her, and sits to catch his breath. She crawls over to him, sits close to him, he puts an arm around her.*) What a desert!

ADAM (*nods*): Big. (*A lion roars nearby.*)

EVE (*screams*): Ah! (*She huddles against ADAM in fear.*)

ADAM (*looking around*): I can't get over it—I named every one of those animals and now they're trying to eat us. (*Holds up a finger.*)

EVE: This is much too much, Adam—really. We couldn't help it.

ADAM: Not in his opinion. He said it in plain Hebrew—"don't eat that apple . . ."

EVE (*breaks into tears*): You're blaming me again!

ADAM (*pointing to her belly*): That thing—that thing is what I can't bear. It turns my stomach. I can't seem to get near you anymore. Everytime I turn around I'm bumping into it. I don't understand you. Do you like that thing?

EVE: I—I don't know.

ADAM: Because if it moves, it's alive, and if it's alive, we could just hit it! (*EVE moves back.*) See! See what I mean! You like it, don't you? And that's why I don't know where I am anymore! I told you when it started, if you jumped up and down—

EVE: I did jump.

ADAM: You did not jump. You went like that . . .

EVE: I jumped as hard as I could! (*She whimpers.*)

ADAM: Don't cry again, please! It's probably something you ate. Let's get going, come on. (*He pulls her hand.*)

EVE: Adam. It's moving. Feel this.

ADAM: Oh, I get that all the time. (*Pulls her hand again.*)

EVE (*holding back*): How do you know he'll let us back in?

ADAM: Don't worry—once we find it, we'll sit down just on the other side of the hedge there, right next to the gate. He'll know we came back and He'll come out and once He sees us, we're in.

EVE: But if He's still mad . . .

ADAM: Listen, I know God. This whole thing is just to teach us a lesson so that when we get back to Paradise we'll appreciate it, that's all. (*Starts to pull her by the hand.*)

EVE: How do we know it's that way? (*Points downstage left.*)

ADAM: Because we just came from that way and it wasn't there. (*Points upstage right.*)

EVE: No, we came from that way. (*Points upstage right, but then she is unsure.*) No,—wait a minute.

ADAM (*pointing, where she had*): No, I think I was wrong. (*He moves, pointing around in a circle, and she is doing the same in a different direction.*) My God, I'm all turned around!

EVE (*crying out in deep fear, utterly lost*): We're never going to get out of here! (*In moving on the line she has stubbed her toe on something soft in the darkness and she screams and runs back to ADAM.*)

ADAM: Who's there?

LUCIFER (*barely glancing toward them in his humiliation*): Me.

EVE (*excited—not knowing whether to fear or be happy*): It's Lucifer!

ADAM (*grabbing her*): Don't go near him!

LUCIFER (*exhausted, hanging his head*): Don't worry, I'm harmless. He threw me out, too. By the time He's finished the only one who'll be left up there is the Angel of Death. (*EVE carefully approaches.*)

EVE: You wouldn't know the way back to the Garden, would you?

LUCIFER: You're standing on it.

ADAM: Where?

LUCIFER: He ripped it up root and branch.

EVE (*horrified*): Adam!

ADAM: I can't believe it! I had just transplanted my strawberries!

LUCIFER: Look, people—make up your minds to it—we are dealing with a spirit to whom nothing is sacred.

ADAM: The Garden is right there—I can see it!—in the center of my mind.

LUCIFER: It's gone forever, Adam.

ADAM: He couldn't have destroyed it, He wouldn't do that!

LUCIFER: Well, (*turning to go*) . . . I hope you both survive.

EVE: Maybe he knows where there's water!—Angel, wait! (*To ADAM.*) Well, there's nothing wrong in just asking!

ADAM: Would you . . . know where there's any water?

LUCIFER: You're kneeling on it. Just dig down about the length of your arm, there's water there. Well . . . see you!

EVE (*to ADAM*): Maybe . . . maybe we should all stay together.

ADAM: Now just a minute . . .

EVE: But he knows so much and we don't know anything.

ADAM: Now just a minute!

LUCIFER: No, Eve, I understand him, he's perfectly right, he has reason not to trust me . . . (*ADAM chortles balefully, LUCIFER mimics him.*) and he still loves God. You have to respect that. Bye.

ADAM: Wait!—All right. There is one question I want to ask you. I have an idea but I don't know how to do it. Whereby we could stay out of the wind and it would be like all around us.

LUCIFER: A house.

ADAM: I'll do the names, you just tell me what I've got in mind.

LUCIFER: Fine. When God ripped up the garden, some of the poplars landed about two thousand cubits out that way. If you'd like to, go out and bring back about eight and sink four corner posts, take four more and join the top corners of the poles, then get some reeds and lay them over the top, and weave them together on the sides.

ADAM: Yeah, well, that was my idea. Come on, dear, we'll get some poles . . . What's the matter?

LUCIFER: She's pregnant.

EVE: Something's moving.

ADAM: It's those goddamned clams!

EVE: It is not the clams!

ADAM: How does he know you're pregnant?

EVE: Because he's an angel and he knows! Because he feels for people and doesn't go around just yelling at me and telling me not to do this and not to do that!

LUCIFER: Eve, dear, easy does it . . .

ADAM: What is this! What is this!

EVE: Will you build that house or am I going to have it here like an animal?

ADAM: I'm going. I'm going. Wait! I'm not so sure I want to leave her alone with you.

LUCIFER: Whatever you say.

ADAM: All right! (*Turns to leave.*) Eve, close your shirt. And remember . . . He sees everything!

LUCIFER: I bet I know what you'd give anything to have right now.

EVE: What?

LUCIFER: A good wash.

EVE: Oh, if I . . .

LUCIFER (*with a magic gesture toward the ground*): Here's water. (*EVE is surprised.*) I'm an angel, Honey. (*She is tempted but turns quickly toward where ADAM went. She turns back to him, conflicted. He leans into her face, smiling, but his eyes are devilishly certain—he strokes her hair.*) Oh, come on, dear, you know me. And I know you—better than anybody ever will.

EVE: I'm all swollen up like a frog.

LUCIFER: That's his vengeance on you, Honey. We can fix that in a minute.

LUCIFER (*sings*):

HOW LOVELY IS EVE . . . WHEN EVE IS ALONE.
WHEN GOD IS AWAY AND ADAM'S OFF
THINKING

HOW ALIVE IS HER FLESH IN THE SHINE OF
THE WATER.
FOR EVE'S NOT ASHAMED AND SHE NEEDN'T
ATONE
WHEN EVE IS ALONE.

THE MAN IS ENSLAVED TO THE PAST AND THE
FUTURE,
AND GOD TAKES REVENGE ON HER BEAUTY:
BETWEEN PARADISE LOST AND EDEN
REGAINED
STANDS THE WOMAN ALONE,
THE WOMAN ALONE WITH THE TRUTH OF
CREATION
THE WOMAN ALONE WITH THE TRUTH.

(*She gasps suddenly with the first surge of pain and grasps her belly.*)

HOW LOVELY IS EVE WHEN EVE IS ALONE
WHEN GOD IS AWAY AND ADAM'S OFF
THINKING
HOW ALIVE IS HER FLESH IN THE SHINE OF
THE WATER:
FOR EVE'S NOT ASHAMED AND SHE NEEDN'T
ATONE
WHEN EVE IS ALONE.

EVE (*astonished, but also with resentment*): It's hurting!

LUCIFER: Well this is how He designed it, dear,—you're supposed to thank Him.

EVE: (*another surge*): It's getting worse.

LUCIFER: It'll get much worse than this.

EVE: It can't.

LUCIFER: Sure can—remember, He's Perfect!—and what He makes worse is perfectly worse. (*Into her face.*) This'll go on for hours!

EVE (*staggers back*): No!

LUCIFER: Oh yes,—days, weeks!

EVE (*another surge*): Oww! (*Desperately, imploring him.*) Oh, angel, angel, you've got to help me. Do something!

LUCIFER: I could, but God wouldn't like it.

EVE: I don't care what He'd like, it's got to stop!

LUCIFER (*getting down in front of her*): You're sure now! This is your decision!

EVE: Anything, anything—but make it stop!

LUCIFER (*grasping her*): Want to kill it?

EVE: Kill?

LUCIFER: I could show you how. If you kill what our Father desires most, then you'll face Him as one god to another, and the world is as you want it. What do you say?

EVE: Ow!

(*ADAM enters.*)

ADAM: Eve! What're you doing! EVE!!! (*ADAM tries to pull her from LUCIFER.*)

LUCIFER: Kill it!

EVE: Help me! Oh, God, you never gave me a chance!

ADAM (*She screams.*): Lord, give her a chance!

LUCIFER: Kill it.

ADAM: Hold still—I'll hit it. (*He raises his fist. She screams again.*) Lord help me! I can't do it!

EVE: Lucifer, save me!

ADAM: Are you out of your mind? What're you calling *him* for?

EVE: Don't waste another minute! He is bursting me!

LUCIFER: Kill it!

ADAM: Wait! God may not like this.

LUCIFER: Kill it! Kill it!

EVE: I musn't!

LUCIFER (*furiously*): *Woman . . .*

EVE (*as though transported*): I want it!

(*Music: A melodious chord—GOD's chord. Both of them instantly look about.*)

ADAM (*pointing into distance*): Eve! LOOK! Suddenly there's a pasture full of sheep!

(*ANGELS enter.*)

URIEL: Seeing the desert turn green, she fainted, and seeing this, Adam fainted too. (*ADAM faints.*) And in the mind of the woman the sky trembled like a harp and Lucifer saw the

Lord descending; at his left Chemuel the Angel of Mercy, and on the other side Azrael, the Angel of Death. And the devil fled.

(*LUCIFER hurries off as* GOD *enters.*)

GOD: Now death's angel bend, that she may feel how close she is to dying; blow icy air across her lips, Azrael. (*AZRAEL blows on her face,* EVE *shudders.*) That's enough! Chemuel, in thy compassion, deliver Eve.

URIEL: And the Angel of Mercy brought out the first child of woman.

GOD: Behold the stranger thine agony hath made! (*ANGELS exit.*)

EVE (*opening her eyes, looking at an imaginary infant on ground*): Ahhh!

ADAM (*opening his eyes*): What's that?

GOD: It is thy son, Adam. You must give him a name.

ADAM: You know when I saw the first giraffe—it may not fit, but it went through my head at the time.

GOD: What?

ADAM: Frank.

GOD: Don't you think that's a little too . . . ah . . .

EVE: Cain. His name is Cain.

GOD: Now Cain is born!

EVE: I see I have been favored of Thee, O Lord!

GOD: Look in my face, Woman.

EVE (*covering her eyes*): I dare not, for I doubted Thy goodness!

GOD: And will you doubt Me anymore?

EVE: Never, never, never!

GOD (*She slowly dares to face him on her knees.*): Then lift up thine eyes.

EVE: I have gotten a man from the Lord.

GOD: Thou art the mother of mankind. (*He extends his hand. She rests hers on it and rises.*)

EVE (*sings*):

    I AM THE RIVER ABOUNDING IN FISH
    I AM THE SUMMER SUN AROUSING THE BEE,
    AS THE RISING MOON IS HELD IN ITS PLACE

BY THINE EVERLASTING MIND, SO AM I HELD
IN THINE ESTEEM.

GOD: Eve, you are my favorite girl!

(*A waltz strikes up.* GOD *and* EVE *face each other swaying to it.* ADAM *counting the beat trying to think of a name for it.* GOD *and* EVE *move out together dancing. Now the dance grows less stately, more generously joyous, celebratory,* ADAM *joining in. At one of* GOD's *turns . . .*)

ADAM: Eve, look at him dance!

(*They dance off.* CAIN *enters, looking about at the new world. Lucifer enters. They look at each other.*)

LUCIFER: So this is Cain.

(*Music sweeps to swirling climax.*)

END ACT ONE

ACT TWO

MUSICAL ENTR'ACTE ending with the ANGELS *singing a forceful hallelujah. Since they seem to be in above average voice, they indulge in a display of their musical gifts, purely for their own amusement.*

ANGELS:

    I.
    LOOK AT THE SEA,
    WHAT A BLUE BLUE SEA:
    LOOK AT THE SKY,
    WHAT A BLUE BLUE SKY:
    LOOK ON THE LAND,
    WHAT A GREEN GREEN LAND,
            AND ALL OF THAT MADE FOR ME.

    II.
    LOOK ON THE CLOUDS,
    THOSE WHITE WHITE CLOUDS:
    LOOK AT THE RAIN,
    WHAT A SILVERY RAIN;
    LOOK IN MY SOUL,
    WHAT A JOYFUL SOUL,
            AND ALL OF THAT MADE FOR ME.

    III.
    NO STAR GETS LOST
    IN DARK OF NIGHT,
    AND THE MOON GOES BY
    ON TIME, JUST RIGHT.

    THE SUN COMES UP
    WHEN I NEED THE LIGHT
    AND GOES BACK DOWN
    ON TIME, JUST RIGHT.

    IV.
    THE SEA IS MINE
    THAT BLUE BLUE SEA,

THE SKY'S ALL MINE
THAT BLUE BLUE SKY
MY SOUL IS MINE
OH MY JOYFUL SOUL
          'CAUSE ALL OF THAT'S MADE FOR ME.
          'CAUSE ALL OF THAT'S MADE FOR ME.

(*III and IV repeat.*)

(*A dining table and chairs.* ANGELS *are concluding "All Of That Made For Me" as* LUCIFER *enters. He is unkempt, dejected, and sits to one side with a depressed air.*)

LUCIFER (*to* ANGELS): Oh, shut up. Get out of here! Go glorify the Lord someplace else! (ANGELS *exit. He shakes his head, staring front.*) Amazing how every creature is happy, they all know why they're alive—excepting me. (*Sudden cry upwards.*) Why did you make me?—merely as a bad example! A . . . a . . . (*Breaks off.*) Here I go again, demanding a logical answer from that oaf! Oh, how I would love to take God's place and make the world reasonable! My misfortune is so clear to me—it's that the only creatures capable of worship are human beings. When you think of their taste, what more needs be said? (*Sees off.*) And here they come now, the first fine family. (CAIN *enters, begins setting table.*) It hasn't rained in weeks, your whole crop'll dry up soon—can't you at least show a little logical resentment?

CAIN (*bows his head, then looks upward*): Thank you, Lord, for all this sunshine. (*He resumes setting table.*)

LUCIFER: —But why do I keep expecting logic from them, when their God throws them out of Paradise with the most ferocious curse, and they end up happier and more prosperous than ever! (ABEL *enters.*) And now this Abel idiot. The world's original hard worker. Hopelessly happy . . . (*Sees off.*) Ah yes, and now the lords of creation in person, Mr. and Mrs. Chicken-fat, Sir and Lady Smug, the Walking Reasons For it All, crowning glory of the universe with as much spiritual curiosity as a clam has feathers! (ADAM *and* EVE *enter. She begins distributing food.* MUSICAL *introduction.*) And with this material I'm trying to do evil! (LUCIFER *exits.* FAMILY *seated at table.*)

EVE (*singing*):
    CAIN AND ABEL
    YOU AND I
    SHEEP IN THE PASTURE
    GOD IN THE SKY
    DID YOU EVER IMAGINE
    IT COULD BE AS GOOD
    AS GOOD AS PARADISE?

ADAM:
    I DREAMED OF SONS
    AND GOAT'S MILK
    I THOUGHT OF FIELDS
    WAVING LIKE SILK
    BUT I NEVER IMAGINED
    IT COULD BE AS GOOD
    AS GOOD AS PARADISE

EVE:
    LOOK AT THE CHILDREN

ADAM:
    TASTE THAT MILK

CAIN:
    WIND IN THE BARLEY

ALL:
    WAVING LIKE SILK

ADAM & EVE (*sung as a canon*):

ADAM & EVE:	BOYS:
DID YOU EVER IMAGINE	EVEN MAMA AND PAPA
THINGS COULD BE SO FINE	ARE AMAZED AT THE VINES
SHEEP IN THE PASTURE	WIND IN THE BARLEY
WIND IN THE BARLEY	
	WAVING LIKE SILK
	SHEEP IN THE PASTURE
WAVING LIKE SILK	

WARMTH OF THE   WARMTH OF THE
  SUN   SUN
COOL OF THE FALL   COOL OF THE FALL

(*Adam*) PARADISE   (*All*) PARADISE

WHO COULD EVER   BET THEY NEVER
                                 IMAGINED
                               IT COULD BE AS
                                 GOOD

IMAGINE IT WOULD
  BE AS GOOD

AS GOOD AS P-A-R-A-   AS GOOD AS P-A-R-A-
  D-I-S-E   D-I-S-E

EVE: ABEL:

DOESN'T IT SEEM   P-A-R-A-D . . .
  LIKE AGES
  AGO . . .

ADAM:

LOST IN THE
  WINDSTORM
RAIN AND   . . . D-I-S-E . . .
  SNOW . . .

CAIN:

GOOD GROWING WEATHER

ABEL:

NOTHING'S BETTER

CAIN:

WEEDED THE VINES

ABEL:

THE FLOCK IS FINE

ADAM:

REAL NICE MILK

EVE:

BARLEY . . .

ALL:

. . . WAVING LIKE SILK
AND IT SEEMS LIKE AGES AGO
AGO

AGES AGO
AGES AGO
CAIN:
AGES AGO
ALL (*joyfully*):
AGES AGO-O-O-O-O-O-O!
EVE: Eat!

(*Lights down on* FAMILY *eating.* GOD *enters. The* ANGELS *follow, playing an instrumental version of their Hallelujah.* GOD *has heard all this before and is clearly not pleased by their incessant adoration. He turns front, troubled.*)

CHEMUEL: The Lord seems troubled by a foreboding.

GOD: They're all so deliciously happy down there. Can it possibly be that—they don't need me anymore?

URIEL: Why don't we talk about something cheerful?

GOD: Like what?

AZRAEL: I would like to go down and kill Adam and Eve.

GOD: Really? Kill them?

AZRAEL: They like to swim—I could drown them . . . actually.

GOD (*with a sigh*): My dear Spirits, I'm afraid I have to say it —Lucifer was the only one of you who could carry on a conversation.

CHEMUEL (*to cheer him up*): I'm just thinking, Lord—how wonderfully peaceful it all was before there were people.

GOD: Before!—oh! That was a different story.

AZRAEL: It was so pleasant, it all went so smooth . . .

GOD: Yes . . .

(*The* ANGELS *play a mysterious, primeval introduction on their instruments.*)

GOD:
ARCHIPELAGOS AND CONTINENTS
I SHIFTED WITH EASE,
WHOLE HEMISPHERES I LIFTED
AND FIT THEM AS I PLEASED.

MOUNTAINS FROM AFRICA
I TRANSFERRED TO FRANCE,

THE UNIVERSE WAS LEAPING
IN A MOLECULAR DANCE.

BUT ALL THROUGH CREATION
EVERY RULE WAS OBEYED
TILL MANKIND ARRIVED
TO DISTURB WHAT I MADE

THE SUN FED THE PLANKTON
AND THE PLANKTON FED THE CLAM,
THE SHARK ATE THE GULL
WHO STOLE THE CLAM FROM ITS SHELL
AND THE SHARK WAS DEVOURED
IN HIS TIME AS WELL . . .

THE GREEN EARTH WAS BLACKENED
BY THE HEAT OF FALLING STARS
VOLCANOES ERUPTING
ACCORDING TO PLAN,
IT WAS SO PEACEFUL
BEFORE THERE WAS MAN.

NO FLORA, NO FAUNA
EVER STOOD IN MY WAY,
I PULLED STARS FROM THE SKY
IF THEY DARED DISOBEY

EACH NIGHT BROUGHT ITS MORNING
AND EACH MORNING BROUGHT A DAY
FROM PLANKTON TO CLAM
IT ALL PROPERLY RAN.
IT WAS SO PEACEFUL
BEFORE THERE WAS MAN.

(*ANGELS play a hot dixieland chorus.*)

FROM PLANKTON TO CLAM
IT ALL PROPERLY RAN.
IT WAS SO PEACEFUL
BEFORE THERE WAS MAN.

ABEL: How'd you like that lamb, Ma? (*The FAMILY moans in appreciation of the meal.*)

EVE: Oh, darling your lamb is always marvelous.

CAIN: You didn't like my spinach?

EVE: I loved it, Darling,—but I was a little full.

CAIN: You know, I don't *have* to raise spinach, I could raise something else.

EVE (*just slightly irritated*): I'll have it cold for lunch!

ADAM: Boys? (*He prepares to say Grace and* ABEL *and* EVE *likewise* . . .) Thank thee, Lord, for a really great meal . . . (*He sees* CAIN *not joining in.*) Cain?—we're saying Grace.

CAIN: Maybe you are, Father, but maybe you're not.

EVE: What's this now?

CAIN: I'm sorry, Mother, but I've decided not to do anything I don't believe anymore. (*To* ADAM.) I mean you made this whole thing up yourself, didn't you? God never told you to say Grace—especially *after* a meal.

ADAM: Why not, after?

ABEL: We're too hungry, before.

CAIN: A little suffering won't hurt anybody, you know. It might even show God that we're more than a lot of overstuffed trout.

ADAM: Now wait, Boy—I know God—

CAIN: Well maybe, but I'll tell you the truth; I'm not even sure anymore that we're even saying the right prayers. I mean you made them all up too, didn't you?

EVE: I assure you, darling, nobody ends up with a farm like this by saying the wrong prayers.

CAIN: You mean the whole thing comes down to what we can *get*? Is that why He made you? (*They are abashed, silent.*) I swear, sometimes I . . . I get frightened. Like when I'm out in the field, and suddenly I don't know why I'm digging in the ground, or why I do anything. And it's like we're all going to—like disappear suddenly, because we didn't do what we were supposed to.

ADAM: Like what?

CAIN: I don't know!—I still can't understand why—when you had the Lord with you to tell you what to do, and eveything was so perfect—why did you leave the Garden?

EVE: What's the Garden got to do with. . . ?

CAIN: Because I've never been able to understand . . .

EVE (*clearing dishes*): But we've explained it a hundred times, Darling . . .

ABEL: They just decided to go out and see the world.

CAIN: But what about God—He just agreed?

ADAM: One hundred percent.

CAIN: He . . . he wasn't ever . . . angry with you, was He?

EVE (*a look of alarm at* ADAM *as she scoffs at the idea*): Angry!

ADAM (*stalling*): *God?*

CAIN: Never, huh?

ADAM (*hedging*): Well, I'm not saying He couldn't get a little . . .

EVE: . . . Thoughtful. He *could* get . . .

ADAM: Right!—and sometimes *very* thoughtful. But with that kind of perfection all around . . . He cheered up quick.

ABEL: Say! Maybe he'd rather tend the sheep? Is that it? . . . 'cause I'd be glad to switch.

CAIN: He's going to farm!

ADAM: God help us!

ABEL: Why!

CAIN: With your sense of responsibility, we'd be eating thistle soup! (ADAM *and* CAIN *laugh.*)

EVE: He's just imaginative.

CAIN: Imaginative?!!! He lays on his back all day playing that stupid flute and everything falls into his lap. And you call that imaginative? (CAIN *leaves* FAMILY *and comes downstage.*)

ABEL (*sings to* CAIN):
ANY ANSWER I WANT
I JUST CLOSE MY EYES
AND IT COMES TO ME

WHEN I WANT A NEW TUNE
I JUST LISTEN,
AND IT COMES TO ME.

WHEN A SHEEP GETS LOST
THEN I STAND STOCK STILL
I CLOSE MY EYES LET MY SPIRIT FILL
AND IT COMES TO ME

ANY QUESTION AT ALL
I CAN ANSWER
IT MAY TAKE A WHILE
BUT IT COMES TO ME.

IF I DON'T HAVE A THOUGHT
I PRETEND IT'S THERE
AND IT COMES TO ME

LIKE A BIRD IN A TREE
IF I WHISTLE
IT COMES DOWN TO ME

SOMETIMES I FIND MYSELF WISHING
FOR SOMETHING
REALLY HARD TO UNDERSTAND
BUT THE MINUTE A MYSTERY APPEARS
I CLOSE MY EYES, AND IT CLEARS.

ALL ALONE IN THE HILLS,
IN THAT SILENCE
I CAN CALL THE STARS
AND THEY COME TO ME

(*Interlude:* ABEL *tries to teach* CAIN *how to play the flute or to whistle.* CAIN *tries and fails.*)

WHEN A SHEEP GETS LOST
THEN I STAND STOCK STILL
I CLOSE MY EYES LET MY SPIRIT FILL
AND IT COMES TO ME

ANY QUESTION GOD SENDS
TO MY BROTHER
FOR THE ANSWERING
HE COMES TO ME
COME TO ME

ABEL: Have I ever lost a sheep?

CAIN: How *could* you lose them? They always end up in my corn.

ABEL: Cain, that only happened once!

CAIN: Go out there and sweat the way I do and tell me it only happened once!

EVE: He's younger!

CAIN: And I'm older, and I'll be damned if I plant another crop until he fences those sheep!

EVE: But how can he build a fence?

CAIN: By bending over same as I do! He won't break in half!

ADAM: Cain . . .

CAIN: Why must she always take his side? (*Touches her face.*) There are *four* people in this world, Mother!

ABEL: It's not natural for me to build a fence.

CAIN: Not natural! You've been talking to God lately?

ABEL: I don't know anything about God. But it's the nature of sheep to move around, and it's the nature of corn to stay in one place. So the fence should fence the thing that stays in one place and not the thing that moves around.

ADAM: That's logical, Cain. (*Music begins.*)

CAIN (*fed up*): In other words, the work belongs to me and the whole wide world belongs to him.

ADAM (*at a loss*): No, that's not fair either.

ABEL (*sings*):
> CAN I FENCE THE MOUNTAINS, BROTHER?
> THE RIVERS WHERE THEY GO TO DRINK?
> I KNOW YOU WORK HARDER, BUT DID I
>   DECIDE THAT?

I'd be glad to change places . . .

CAIN (*concerned*): You wouldn't last a week.

ABEL:
> THEN WHAT AM I SUPPOSED TO DO!
> I LOVE YOU, CAIN, I WANT TO BE FRIENDS!

CAIN (*warming towards ABEL*):
> I KNOW THAT ABEL, I KNOW . . .

ABEL:
> THEN TELL ME, WHAT TO DO!

CAIN (*takes ABEL into his confidence, not wanting ADAM and EVE to overhear*):
> I DON'T KNOW WHAT IS HAPPENING TO ME:
> I FEEL LIKE A STRANGER IN MY FAMILY
> I TRY TO PRAY FOR A PEACEFUL HEART
> BUT NO ANSWER COMES FROM THE SKY.
>
> I GET A TERRIBLE FEELING SOMETIMES
> THAT WE'RE NOT OBEYING SOME LAW OF GOD
> THAT WE'RE NOT LIVING AS HE MEANT US TO,

I GET A TERRIBLE FEELING SOMETIMES,
I GET A TERRIBLE FEELING
I GET A TERRIBLE . . . FEELING.

(*CAIN returns to family table.*)

OH MY GOD WHAT IS HAPPENING TO ME;
I SIT LIKE A STRANGER WITH MY FAMILY,
I WALK LIKE A STRANGER IN MY OWN LAND
WHAT A TERRIBLE FEELING,
A TERRIBLE . . . FEELING.

(*All seated.*)

CAIN: Father! I want an answer. When you decided to leave the Garden, did God agree or what?

EVE: Agree!—He was enthusiastic! (*To ADAM.*) Say something.

CAIN: Why do I have a feeling that we're not doing something that we should be doing?

EVE: Now listen, everything this family does is exactly right. (*To ADAM.*) You just going to sit there?

ADAM: All right, now wait a minute. You're both big boys now, I'm going to tell you what happened.

EVE: And don't make it all my fault.

ADAM: I didn't say anything yet.

EVE: So say it.

ADAM: The thing is . . .

EVE: . . . We didn't fit in, that's all, I mean if a person doesn't fit in . . . (*The FAMILY freezes, listening to ADAM.*)

ADAM (*setting himself*): Well, as we told you before, I was alone with God for a long time, and then . . .

ABEL: He made Mama.

ADAM: Right.

ABEL (*big smile*): And you liked her right away, huh?

CAIN: Of course he did.

ADAM: She was gorgeous. Of course there wasn't much choice . . . (*He laughs.*)

EVE: Ha, ha, ha.

ADAM: Well, anyway, I believe I mentioned there was this tree —with an apple.

ABEL: Of good and evil.

ADAM: Right.

CAIN: Which you're never allowed to eat under any circumstances.

ADAM: Right. Well, the thing is, you see . . . we ate it.

ABEL: You ate it!

CAIN: I thought you said you . . .

ADAM: No. We ate it.

ABEL (*more scared now*): Not mama, though.

ADAM: Mama, too.

CAIN: And then what happened?

ADAM: They may be old enough to understand. He cursed us when he threw us out. And part of the curse is that we will have to die.

CAIN: We're going to die?

ABEL: Like the sheep, you mean?

ADAM: Sheep, birds, everything.

CAIN: You and Mama, too? You mean we wouldn't see you anymore?

EVE: Don't worry about it, darling. I'm sure we have a long, long time yet.

CAIN: You mean before he got angry, you would never die?

ADAM: As far as I know, yes.

CAIN: No wonder I felt something was wrong!

ADAM: What's wrong?

CAIN: We've been going around all these years thanking God!

ADAM: Well yes, of course.

CAIN: But we should have been begging his forgiveness! God is furious with us . . .

EVE: Now let's just stop right there . . .

CAIN: You've been lying to us long enough, Mother—now *I* have something to say!

ADAM: That's no way to talk to your mother, Cain!

ABEL: I think you ought to take that back, y'know?

CAIN: It has come to me.

ADAM: What's that, boy?

CAIN (*staring wildly; he feels he is being controlled from without*): I will make an offering to the Lord.

ABEL: What's an offering?

CAIN: I will set before him the best of my crop and He . . . (*He hardly dares say it aloud, he looks upward.*) He will come down from Heaven to receive it . . . and to forgive us at last! (*He goes to the table, making it into an altar, bringing his things to it, while the* FAMILY *is watching with alarm. He goes to his knees.*) Come everybody—pray with me!

EVE: For what?

CAIN (*furiously*): For God to come down and tell us what we should be doing, for once!

ADAM (*getting her to her knees*): Come on, dear . . . a little prayer wouldn't hurt.

EVE: He's not coming down *here*, is he?

ADAM: Who knows?—the way Cain loves him, he might just stop by! (*Getting down to his knees and craning his neck to see the offering.*) Did you throw in a little parsley? He always rather liked parsley.

EVE (*to Abel*): Push back your hair, darling. (*She sees an apple and reaching over . . .*) For God's sake . . . you put an apple? (*She throws the apple away, bends down in prayer: sotto voce to* ADAM.) You had to go and tell him.

ADAM: You had to go and eat it . . .

ABEL (*catching the excitement*): Could I make an offering too?

EVE: Of course you can—

CAIN: It was my idea.

ABEL: Please, Pa!

CAIN: I thought of it and I would like to do it alone! He never thought of God in his life.

(*LUCIFER enters.*)

LUCIFER: Cain, Cain.

EVE: We'll make a special point of telling Him it was all your idea!

LUCIFER (*heard only by* CAIN): Don't be frightened, I'm an angel—

EVE (*to* ABEL): Why don't you offer God one of your nice lamb chops, darling? (*ABEL gets plate.*)

LUCIFER: I know what's hidden in your heart.

EVE (*chants*):
    NOW MAKER, SHOW THY FACE
    AND BLESS MY ABEL'S WORK— AND CAIN'S

ADAM (*chants*):
    BUT PLEASE, LORD—BLESS BOTH THE SAME . . .
    SO WE CAN HAVE SOME PEACE AGAIN—

(*ADAM, EVE and ABEL continue praying and chanting. CAIN listens, as in a daydream.*)

LUCIFER: Now try to remember, let your mind roll back— remember how it was before Abel was born? Just Mama and Papa—and you? You—and them? Wherever you looked you saw them, wherever you were they knew. Them and you. You and them. So clean, so sweet, so simple. And now, now, Cain . . . (*CAIN lowers his head.*) who listens, who sees, who cares? You might as well not be around, they'd hardly know you were gone. Why does one who works the hardest and worries most about God always end up with the rotten end of the stick? Because God doesn't care about justice. But you know that, don't you—you know it Cain! (*Chants, mocking the FAMILY's prayer . . .*)
      THEN WHY DO YOU GO ON KISSING HIS ASS

(*The ANGELS appear and pick up the family chant. As the FAMILY remembers the old chant, it builds to a climax.*)

ANGELS AND FAMILY (*sing*):
      IN THE CENTER OF YOUR MIND KEEP THE
         LORD.

(*A chord. The FAMILY is in a state of suspension, as in a miracle.*)

EVE (*sings*):
      I FEEL A HAPPINESS
      LIFTING ME UP—
ADAM AND ABEL:
      ALL LOVE, ALL LOVE, ALL LOVE.
EVE:
      OUR TROUBLES ARE VANISHING
      FROM THIS DAY—
ADAM, ABEL AND CHEMUEL:
      ALL LOVE, ALL LOVE, ALL LOVE.
EVE:
      IT'S GOING TO BE
      LIKE THE GARDEN WAS . . .
ADAM, ABEL, CAIN AND ANGELS:
      ALL LOVE, ALL LOVE, ALL LOVE.

EVE AND ANGELS (*responsively*):
> NOW THAT HE'S TOLD US
> THE WAY TO GO—
> ALL LOVE, ALL LOVE, ALL LOVE.
>
> I FEEL A HAPPINESS
> LIFTING ME UP—
> ALL LOVE, ALL LOVE, ALL LOVE.
>
> WITH MY MEN BESIDE ME,
> EACH OF THEM BLESS'D—
> ALL LOVE, ALL LOVE, ALL LOVE.
>
> AND I'LL NEVER FEAR
> WHAT I FEARED BEFORE—
> ALL LOVE, ALL LOVE, ALL LOVE.

(GOD *begins to materialize upstage.*)

> WE HAVE PLEASED THE LORD
> WE'VE ALL PASSED HIS TEST—
> ALL LOVE, ALL LOVE, ALL LOVE.
>
> NOW THE HOUSE AND THE LAND
> IN THE PALM OF HIS HAND,
> ALL LOVE, ALL LOVE, ALL LOVE.
>
> WITH MY MEN BESIDE ME
> AND THE LORD ABOVE ME
> ALL LOVE, ALL LOVE, ALL LOVE
>
> IT'S GOING TO BE
> LIKE THE GARDEN WAS—
> ALL LOVE, ALL LOVE, ALL LOVE.

(*Lights up on* GOD. *He appears as a vision in the Garden.*)

> NOW THAT HE'S TOLD US
> THE WAY TO GO—
> ALL LOVE, ALL LOVE, ALL LOVE.

(GOD *looks down at the "offerings." Then he turns to* ABEL *who feels it and looks to him.* ADAM & EVE *remain with heads bowed. The* ANGELS *exit.*)

ADAM: From the first sons of man to Heaven.

GOD: These offerings I receive. (*He very, very slowly reaches out his hand down to the "altar." The* FAMILY *straighten in tension.*) Whose is this?

CAIN: Mine, Lord, may it please thee.

GOD (*He looks deeply into* CAIN's *eyes. Then he tastes it—slowly*): This is good spinach. And this . . . is Abel's mutton?

EVE: Oh no, Lord: baby lamb!

GOD (*He tastes it, smells it as he chews. He looks into* CAIN's *face for a long moment, then turns to* ABEL): My son . . . (*with no greater emphasis than he praised* CAIN's *spinach*) that is also good. (*To* ABEL.) In all truth, my son, it is the sweetest, perhaps the most satisfying piece of meat I have tasted since the world began. (ABEL, *swelling with pride, stands facing* GOD.) I will not deny it, you have pleased me mightily in thine offering.

EVE (*rushing to kiss* ABEL): Darling!

ADAM (*leaps to* ABEL, *grasping his hand*): Boy, this is our proudest moment! (*But* CAIN *is shocked; and they go silent sensing his feelings, and seeing that* GOD *has turned down to him.*)

GOD: You have done well, Cain—why are you angry? (CAIN, *striving to contain himself glances toward* ABEL *and the proud parents and back to* GOD, *unable to speak.*) If a man does well, shall he not be accepted?

CAIN (*barely audible, suppressing his hurt*): Yes, Lord.

GOD: Sin waits at the door, my son, but do well and you shall rule over it.

CAIN: I will . . . I will try.

(*LUCIFER appears.*)

GOD: I had a feeling you'd be coming along about now.

LUCIFER: Oh yes, I have come to watch Cain kill his brother.

GOD: He musn't, he won't, he loves him!

LUCIFER: I catch the uncertainty . . . so I will make you a final offer. Let me rule beside you, and I will talk to Cain. Ten minutes with me and Cain will be boasting about his little brother's lamb chops, grateful that God so much as tasted his spinach. Incidentally, why *were* you so terribly unjust to Cain.

GOD: Unjust? I told him the truth. I must tell them the truth!

LUCIFER: That you love lamb far better than spinach.

GOD: I love everything—but not in the same way.

LUCIFER: You do get deeper and deeper . . . Well, sir, do you employ me? . . . And mind you, once brother kills brother it's only a matter of time till they murder each other down to the last man . . . Your proudest creation gone to guts and blood. Shall I go to work on Cain for you?

GOD (*in higher tension*): No. I will wager everything on his brotherly love.

LUCIFER: And if you lose? You'll bet again?

GOD (*with sadness*): If I must, yes!

LUCIFER (*fierce irony*): Oh yes, and again!

GOD (*defiantly*): Yes!

LUCIFER: . . . Until there is no one left on earth to kill.

GOD: They are free! It is for them to choose to love or die. I will not swindle them into staying alive. My love has made this world; now let their love keep it or they deserve oblivion!

LUCIFER: It's murder now, I'll see to it! Make the deal!

GOD (*resolved*): No. I will let his love contend with thee, and forever . . . if need be.

CAIN (*standing with plate*): Lord? There's also my corn. You haven't tasted my corn.

GOD: Oh, I can see it's all very nice. You have done very well, my boy, keep it up. (*LUCIFER exits.*) Come now children, and walk a little way with me, and we shall talk a while together of life, and earth, and heaven. Come Adam, Eve? Abel? Cain? (*He exits with ABEL.*)

EVE (*beckoning CAIN*): Come!

CAIN: Mother . . .

EVE (*barely concealing her irritation, impatience*): Why do you look like that, Darling? He loved your vegetables. Come on! (*He doesn't move. EVE looks to ADAM.*)

ADAM: I'm not going to pretend that I think he was fair, boy. But I tell you, I think this could be one of his mysteries, y'know?—that he likes to slide across the floor at a person. When it happens to me, see,—what I do is to watch it coming, I see it getting closer; maybe it curls around behind me, but I don't even turn, I just stand there like any other Tuesday.— And pretty soon, either it just goes away by itself, or it stays there and I forget about it. (*CAIN doesn't understand.*)

EVE: Now what is this, what is the name for this kind of behaviour—*God is here!* Is this the time for a tantrum?

CAIN: Go ahead . . . you don't need me! (*ADAM exits.*)

EVE: You are disgracing this family in the eyes of God. Cain, darling, why do you take everything so personally? Next time he'll probably like your vegetables the best. (*Referring to ABEL.*) I mean, God certainly knows he's never had a serious thought in his head, so he probably figured he'll encourage him to be like you. Now come on, dear . . . he's waiting by the river, telling all about Paradise. (*He does not respond.*) I am sick and tired of this attitude, Cain! I do not deserve this from you. All right then, don't come . . . stay here . . . and be an ungrateful, snivelling snot! (*ABEL enters. To ABEL:*) Leave him, let him enjoy pitying himself! (*LUCIFER enters.*)

LUCIFER: Now break God's heart.

ABEL: Come, brother—God loves you! He was just saying how you do everything he wants, and Mama said . . .

CAIN: DON'T . . . don't, don't speak.

ABEL: You can't tell me not . . .

LUCIFER: Break it! Break it!

CAIN: Go and tell God and your father and mother never to come back! This is my house now, and the farm, and my fences will stretch out to cover the earth! Now get off my land!

ABEL: *Your* land?!! (*CAIN grabs ABEL. Struggling to break CAIN's grasp:*) Lord!!!!! SAVE ME!!!! (*CAIN breaks ABEL's neck. The body goes limp and slumps down CAIN's leg.*)

LUCIFER (*sings*):
> NOW NOTHING'S LEFT OF GOD
> AND EVERYTHING IS REAL;
> REJOICE, YOUR EYES ARE OPEN
> YOU MAY DO WHATEVER YOU FEEL.
>
> A MAN CAN NEVER LOVE ANOTHER
> AS MUCH AS HE LOVES HIMSELF,
> BE IT SON OR FATHER OR MOTHER,
> THE HEART OF MAN IS STEEL.
>
> SO NOTHING'S LEFT OF GOD
> AND EVERYTHING IS REAL,
> REJOICE, YOUR EYES ARE OPEN
> THE WHOLE WORLD IS REVEALED.

FOR MAN LOVES ONLY POWER
TAKE HEART, IT'S SOMETHING TO TRUST
NO LOVE OR FAITH CAN DEFEND YOU,
—EACH MAN WILL KILL WHEN HE MUST.

(*dance*)

SO NOTHING'S LEFT OF GOD
AND EVERYTHING IS REAL
REJOICE, YOUR EYES ARE OPEN
YOU MAY DO WHATEVER YOU FEEL.

(*GOD, ADAM and EVE enter.*)

GOD: Where is Abel?
CAIN: I know not.
ADAM: Where is he? (*ADAM and EVE see ABEL's body.*)
CAIN: Am I my brother's keeper?
GOD: Abel is dead. (*Music begins. ADAM aproaches CAIN.*)
LUCIFER (*to ADAM and EVE*): God's injustice killed him. Don't
    blame this boy. (*ADAM and EVE kneel over body.*)
GOD (*sings to CAIN who stares off defiantly*):
    MAN, I SAW YOU RISING LIKE A PLANET
    BEFORE THE GENERATIONS:
    FIRST BROTHER IN THE WORLD
    AND FIRST TO REJECT MURDER.
    CAIN. . . .

(*Hearing his name, CAIN turns to GOD.*)

    ALL MY HOPES FOR MAN
    I PLACED IN THEE.

(*Musical interlude. Enter AZRAEL, the Angel of Death.*)

A fugitive and a vagabond shalt thou live all the days of thine
unforgiven life. Go . . . into the world.

(*Music continues. CAIN exits. At the same time AZRAEL leads
ABEL off in the opposite direction. Following this, GOD begins to
exit, but pauses to hear the outcome of the following.*)

LUCIFER: Adam?
ADAM: Get out.

LUCIFER: I'll be back when you're feeling better. Ta-ta. (*GOD completes his exit and* LUCIFER *exits.*)

URIEL: The first funeral was that of a very young man. Now they had learned to fear, to love, to hate and to adore—had passed through every mood and motion of the human spirit, but not yet consolation—that bargaining with death, that reasoning with silence.

(*URIEL exits. ADAM & EVE have come to a point, halted, and stand in silence, staring at this new experience of death. The spell is broken by the baa-ing of sheep and the tinkling of goat's bells. They turn slightly in awareness of these sounds of life.*)

ADAM: We'd better get something to eat. Come . . . make the fire. (*He takes her hand. She faces him, and with a dead smile . . .*) I'll draw some water.

EVE: No more Cain to draw the water; no more Abel to close in the sheep . . .

ADAM (*points at her belly*): Well, I'll take it easy when that one's ready to help me.

EVE (*her hand on her belly*): I don't know how I can put another in this world.

ADAM: It's almost dark, I've got to bring the sheep in. —Go on Eve—a nice fire, something to eat . . . (*backing away from her*) Go ahead woman, we've got a lot to do . . . (*She turns and takes a step obeying him, and almost falls. He catches her in his arms.*)

EVE (*at the peak of anxiety*): Oh, Adam, I'm afraid! I don't know how to start again!

ADAM: Look at the night, listen to it. . . ! (*Sings.*)
GOD IS WHERE HE ALWAYS WAS
IN PARADISE. IN THE GARDEN.
AND HE'S WEEPING NOW
THERE ARE TEARS IN HIS EYES.
FOR WHAT WE'VE DONE TO HIS WORLD.

I KNOW HE WANTS US
TO PRAISE HIS MORNINGS
I KNOW HE WANTS US
TO PRAISE HIS NIGHTS.

    I KNOW HE WANTS US
    TO SEIZE EACH DAY
    AND MAKE THINGS GROW
    WHERE THEY DIDN'T BEFORE.

    I KNOW HE WANTS US
    TO TEND THE GARDEN
    I KNOW HE WANTS US
    TO LIVE IN HOPE.

    I KNOW HE WANTS US
    TO MEET OUR DANGERS
ADAM AND EVE:
    HAND IN HAND
    AS WE DID BEFORE

    WITH HEARTBREAK AND HOPE
    WE TURN TO THE SKY
    THAT IS PAVED WITH HIS LOVE.

    WITH HEARTBREAK AND HOPE
    WE BEND TO THE EARTH
FULL COMPANY (*entering*):
    WE WERE MADE FOR HIS LOVE.

    AND SO I WANT US
    TO PRAISE OUR MORNINGS
    AND SO I WANT US
    TO PRAISE OUR NIGHTS

    AND SO I WANT US
    TO SEIZE EACH DAY
    AND MAKE THINGS GROW
    AS WE DID BEFORE.

                    CURTAIN

THE AMERICAN CLOCK

A Vaudeville

BASED IN PART ON STUDS TERKEL'S *HARD TIMES*

CHARACTERS

THEODORE K. QUINN
LEE BAUM
ROSE BAUM, Lee's mother
MOE BAUM, Lee's father
ARTHUR A. ROBERTSON
CLARENCE, a shoeshine man
FRANK, the Baums' chauffeur
FANNY MARGOLIES, Rose's sister
GRANDPA, Rose's father
DR. ROSMAN
JESSE LIVERMORE ⎫
WILLIAM DURANT ⎬ Financiers
ARTHUR CLAYTON ⎭
TONY, a speakeasy owner
DIANA MORGAN
HENRY TAYLOR, a farmer
IRENE, a middle-aged black woman
BANKS, a black veteran
JOE, a boyhood friend of Lee's
MRS. TAYLOR, Henry's wife
HARRIET TAYLOR, their daughter
BREWSTER ⎫
CHARLEY ⎬ Farmers
JUDGE BRADLEY
FRANK HOWARD, an auctioneer
MISS FOWLER, Quinn's secretary
GRAHAM, a *New York Times* reporter

SIDNEY MARGOLIES, Fanny's son

DORIS GROSS, the landlady's daughter

RALPH
RUDY } Students

ISABEL, a prostitute

ISAAC, a black café proprietor

RYAN, a federal relief supervisor

MATTHEW R. BUSH

GRACE
KAPUSH
DUGAN } People at the relief office
TOLAND
LUCY

EDIE, a comic-strip artist

LUCILLE, Rose's niece

STANISLAUS, a seaman

BASEBALL PLAYER

WAITER

THIEF

FARMERS

BIDDERS

SHERIFF

DEPUTIES

MARATHON DANCERS

WELFARE WORKER

SOLDIERS

ACT ONE

The set is a flexible area for actors. The actors are seated in a choral area onstage and return to it when their scenes are over. The few pieces of furniture required should be openly carried on by the actors. An impression of a surrounding vastness should be given, as though the whole country were really the setting, even as the intimacy of certain scenes is provided for. The background can be sky, clouds, space itself, or an impression of the geography of the United States.

A small jazz band onstage plays "Million-Dollar Baby" as a baseball pitcher enters, tossing a ball from hand to glove. QUINN *begins to whistle "Million-Dollar Baby" from the balcony. Now he sings, and the rest of the company joins in, gradually coming onstage. All are singing by the end of the verse. All form in positions onstage. The band remains onstage throughout the play.*

ROSE: By the summer of 1929 . . .

LEE: I think it's fair to say that nearly every American . . .

MOE: Firmly believed that he was going to get . . .

COMPANY: Richer and richer . . .

MOE: Every year.

ROBERTSON: The country knelt to a golden calf in a blanket of red, white, and blue. (*He walks to Clarence's shoeshine box.*) How you making out, Clarence?

CLARENCE: Mr. Robertson, I like you to lay another ten dollars on that General Electric. You do that for me?

ROBERTSON: How much stock you own, Clarence?

CLARENCE: Well, this ten ought to buy me a thousand dollars' worth, so altogether I guess I got me about hundred thousand dollars in stock.

ROBERTSON: And how much cash you got home?

CLARENCE: Oh, I guess about forty, forty-five dollars.

ROBERTSON (*slight pause*): All right, Clarence, let me tell you something. But I want you to promise me not to repeat it to anyone.

CLARENCE: I never repeat a tip you give me, Mr. Robertson.

417

ROBERTSON: This isn't quite a tip, this is what you might call an untip. Take all your stock, and sell it.

CLARENCE: Sell! Why, just this morning in the paper Mr. Andrew Mellon say the market's got to keep goin' up. *Got* to!

ROBERTSON: I have great respect for Andrew Mellon, Clarence, know him well, but he's up to his eyebrows in this game— he's got to say that. You sell, Clarence, believe me.

CLARENCE (*drawing himself up*): I never like to criticize a customer, Mr. Robertson, but I don't think a man in your position ought to be carryin' on that kind of talk! Now you take this ten, sir, put it on General Electric for Clarence.

ROBERTSON: I tell you something funny, Clarence.

CLARENCE: What's that, sir?

ROBERTSON: You sound like every banker in the United States.

CLARENCE: Well, I should hope so!

ROBERTSON: Yeah, well . . . bye-bye.

He exits. CLARENCE *exits with his shoeshine box. The company exits singing and humming "Million-Dollar Baby";* QUINN *sings the final line.*

Light rises on ROSE *at the piano, dressed for an evening out. Two valises stand center stage.*

ROSE (*playing piano under speech*): Now sing, darling, but don't forget to breathe—and then you'll do your homework.

LEE (*starts singing "I Can't Give You Anything But Love," then speaks over music*): Up to '29 it was the age of belief. How could Lindbergh fly the Atlantic in that tiny little plane? He believed. How could Babe Ruth keep smashing those homers? He believed. Charley Paddock, "The World's Fastest Human," raced a racehorse . . . and won! Because he believed. What I believed at fourteen was that my mother's hair was supposed to flow down over her shoulders. And one afternoon she came into the apartment . . .

ROSE, *at piano, sings a line of "I Can't Give You Anything But Love."*

. . . and it was short!

ROSE *and* LEE *sing the last line together.*

ROSE (*continuing to play, speaking over music*): I personally think with all the problems there was never such a glorious time for anybody who loved to play or sing or listen or dance to music. It seems to me every week there was another marvelous song. What's the matter with you?

LEE *can only shake his head—"nothing."*

Oh, for God's sake! Nobody going to bother with long hair anymore. All I was doing was winding it up and winding it down . . .

LEE: It's *okay*! I just didn't think it would ever . . . happen.

ROSE: But why can't there be something new!

LEE: But why didn't you *tell* me!

ROSE: Because you would do exactly what you're doing now— carrying on like I was some kind of I-don't-know-what! Now stop being an idiot and *sing*!

LEE *starts singing "On the Sunny Side of the Street."*

You're not breathing, dear.

MOE *enters carrying a telephone, joins in song.* LEE *continues singing under dialogue.*

ROSE: Rudy Vallee is turning green.

FRANK *enters in a chauffeur's uniform.*

MOE (*into phone*): Trafalgar five, seven-seven-one-one. (*Pause.*) Herb? I'm just thinking, maybe I ought to pick up another five hundred shares of General Electric. (*Pause.*) Good. (*He hangs up.*)

FRANK: Car's ready, Mr. Baum.

FRANK *chimes in with* LEE *on the last line of "Sunny Side of the Street." Then* LEE *sits on the floor, working on his crystal set.*

ROSE (*to* FRANK): You'll drop us at the theatre and then take my father and sister to Brooklyn and come back for us after the show. And don't get lost, please.

FRANK: No, I know Brooklyn.

He exits with the baggage. FANNY *enters—Rose's sister.*

FANNY (*apprehensively*): Rose . . . listen . . . Papa really doesn't want to move in with us.

A slow turn with rising eyebrows from MOE; ROSE *is likewise alarmed.*

ROSE (*to* FANNY): Don't be silly, he's been with us six months.

FANNY (*fearfully, voice lowered*): I'm telling you . . . he is not happy about it.

MOE (*resoundingly understating the irony*): He's not happy.

FANNY (*to* MOE): Well, you know how he loves space, and this apartment is so roomy.

MOE (*to* LEE): He bought himself a grave, you know. It's going to be in the cemetery on the aisle. So he'll have a little more room to move around, . . .

ROSE: Oh, stop it.

MOE: . . . get in and out quicker.

FANNY (*innocently*): Out of a grave?

ROSE: He's kidding you, for God's sake!

FANNY: Oh! (*To* ROSE): I think he's afraid my house'll be too small; you know, with Sidney and us and the one bathroom. And what is he going to do with himself in Brooklyn? He never liked the country.

ROSE: Fanny, dear, make up your mind—he's going to *love* it with you.

MOE: Tell you, Fanny—maybe we should *all* move over to your house and he could live here with an eleven-room apartment for himself, and we'll send the maid every day to do his laundry . . .

FANNY: He's brushing his hair, Rose, but I know he's not happy. I think what it is, he still misses Mama, you see.

MOE: Now *that's* serious—a man his age still misses his mother . . .

FANNY: No, *our* mother—*Mama.* (*To* ROSE, *almost laughing, pointing at* MOE): He thought Papa misses his own mother!

ROSE: No, he didn't, he's kidding you!

FANNY: Oh, you . . . ! (*She swipes at* MOE.)

ROSE (*walking her to the doorway*): Go hurry him up. I don't want to miss the first scene of this show; it's Gershwin, it's supposed to be wonderful.

FANNY: See, what it is, something is always happening here . . .

MOE (*into phone*): Trafalgar five, seven-seven-one-one.

FANNY: . . . I mean with the stock market and the business. . . . Papa just loves all this!

GRANDPA *appears, in a suit, with a cane; very neat, proper— and very sorry for himself. Comes to a halt, already hurt.*

MOE (*to* GRANDPA): See you again soon, Charley!

FANNY (*deferentially*): You ready, Papa?

MOE (*on phone*): Herb? . . . Maybe I ought to get rid of my Worthington Pump. Oh . . . thousand shares? And remind me to talk to you about gold, will you? (*Pause.*) Good. (*He hangs up.*)

FANNY (*with* ROSE, *getting* GRANDPA *into his coat*): Rose'll come every few days, Papa . . .

ROSE: Sunday we'll all come out and spend the day.

GRANDPA: Brooklyn is full of tomatoes.

FANNY: No, they're starting to put up big apartment houses now; it's practically not the country anymore. (*In a tone of happy reassurance*): On some streets there's hardly a tree! (*To* ROSE, *of her diamond bracelet*): I'm looking at that bracelet! Is it new?

ROSE: For my birthday.

FANNY: It's gorgeous.

ROSE: He gave exactly the same one to his mother.

FANNY: She must be overjoyed.

ROSE (*with a cutting smile, to* MOE): Why not?

GRANDPA (*making a sudden despairing announcement*): Well? So I'm going! (*With a sharp tap of his cane on the floor, he starts off.*)

LEE: Bye-bye, Grandpa!

GRANDPA (*goes to* LEE, *offers his cheek, gets his kiss, then pinches Lee's cheek*): You be a good boy. (*He strides past* ROSE, *huffily snatches his hat out of her hand, and exits.*)

MOE: There goes the boarder. I lived to see it!

ROSE (*to* LEE): Want to come and ride with us?

LEE: I think I'll stay and work on my radio.

ROSE: Good, and go to bed early. I'll bring home all the music from the show, and we'll sing it tomorrow. (*She kisses* LEE.) Good night, darling. (*She swings out in her furs.*)

MOE (*to* LEE): Whyn't you get a haircut?

LEE: I did, but it grew back, I think.

MOE (*realizing Lee's size*): Should you talk to your mother about college or something?

LEE: Oh, no, not for a couple of years.

MOE: Oh. Okay, good. (*He laughs and goes out, perfectly at one with the world.*)

ROBERTSON *appears, walks over to the couch, and lies down.* DR. ROSMAN *appears and sits in a chair behind Robertson's head.*

ROBERTSON: Where'd I leave off yesterday?

DR. ROSMAN: Your mother had scalded the cat.

Pause.

ROBERTSON: There's something else, Doctor. I feel a conflict about saying it . . .

DR. ROSMAN: That's what we're here for.

ROBERTSON: I don't mean in the usual sense. It has to do with money.

DR. ROSMAN: Yes?

ROBERTSON: Your money.

DR. ROSMAN (*turns down to him, alarmed*): What about it?

ROBERTSON (*hesitates*): I think you ought to get out of the market.

DR. ROSMAN: Out of the market!

ROBERTSON: Sell everything.

DR. ROSMAN (*pauses, raises his head to think, then speaks carefully*): Could you talk about the basis for this idea? When was the first time you had this thought?

ROBERTSON: About four months ago. Around the middle of May.

DR. ROSMAN: Can you recall what suggested it?

ROBERTSON: One of my companies manufactures kitchen utensils.

DR. ROSMAN: The one in Indiana?

ROBERTSON: Yes. In the middle of May all our orders stopped.

DR. ROSMAN: Completely?

ROBERTSON: Dead stop. It's now the end of August, and they haven't resumed.

DR. ROSMAN: How is that possible? The stock keeps going up.

ROBERTSON: Thirty points in less than two months. This is what I've been trying to tell you for a long time now, Doctor—the market represents nothing but a state of mind. (*He sits up.*) On the other hand, I must face the possibility that this is merely my personal fantasy . . .

DR. ROSMAN: Yes, your fear of approaching disaster.

ROBERTSON: But I've had meetings at the Morgan Bank all week, and it's the same in almost every industry—it's not just my companies. The warehouses are overflowing, we can't move the goods, that's an objective fact.

DR. ROSMAN: Have you told your thoughts to your colleagues?

ROBERTSON: They won't listen. Maybe they can't afford to—we've been tossing the whole country onto a crap table in a game where nobody is ever supposed to lose! . . . I sold off a lot two years ago, but when the market opens tomorrow I'm cashing in the rest. I feel guilty for it, but I can't see any other way.

DR. ROSMAN: Why does selling make you feel guilty?

ROBERTSON: Dumping twelve million dollars in securities could start a slide. It could wipe out thousands of widows and old people. . . . I've even played with the idea of making a public announcement.

DR. ROSMAN: That you're dumping twelve million dollars? That could start a slide all by itself, couldn't it?

ROBERTSON: But it would warn the little people.

DR. ROSMAN: Yes, but selling out quietly might not disturb the market quite so much. You *could* be wrong, too.

ROBERTSON: I suppose so. Yes. . . . Maybe I'll just sell and shut up. You're right. I could be mistaken.

DR. ROSMAN (*relieved*): You probably are—but I think I'll sell out anyway.

ROBERTSON: Fine, Doctor. (*He stands, straightens his jacket.*) And one more thing. This is going to sound absolutely nuts, but . . . when you get your cash, don't keep it. Buy gold.

DR. ROSMAN: You can't be serious.

ROBERTSON: Gold bars, Doctor. The dollar may disappear with the rest of it. (*He extends his hand.*) Well, good luck.

DR. ROSMAN: Your hand is shaking.

ROBERTSON: Why not? Ask any two great bankers in the United States and they'd say that Arthur A. Robertson had lost his mind. (*Pause.*) Gold bars, Doctor . . . and don't put them in the bank. In the basement. Take care, now. (*He exits.*)

A bar. People in evening dress seated morosely at tables. An atmosphere of shock and even embarrassment.

LIVERMORE: About Randolph Morgan. Could you actually see him falling?

TONY: Oh, yeah. It was still that blue light, just before it gets dark? And I don't know why, something made me look up. And there's a man flyin' spread-eagle, falling through the air. He was right on top of me, like a giant! (*He looks down.*) And I look. I couldn't believe it. It's Randolph!

LIVERMORE: Poor, poor man.

DURANT: Damned fool.

LIVERMORE: I don't know—I think there is a certain gallantry . . . When you lose other people's money as well as your own, there can be no other way out.

DURANT: There's always a way out. The door.

TONY: Little more brandy, Mr. Durant?

LIVERMORE (*raising his cup*): To Randolph Morgan.

DURANT *raises his cup.*

TONY: Amen here. And I want to say something else—everybody should get down on their knees and thank John D. Rockefeller.

LIVERMORE: Now you're talking.

TONY: Honest to God, Mr. Livermore, didn't that shoot a thrill in you? I mean, there's a *man*—to come out like that with the whole market falling to pieces and say, "I and my sons are buying six million dollars in common stocks." I mean, that's a bullfighter.

LIVERMORE: He'll turn it all around, too.

TONY: Sure he'll turn it around, because the man's a capitalist, he knows how to put up a battle. You wait, tomorrow morning it'll all be shootin' up again like Roman candles!

Enter WAITER, *who whispers in Tony's ear.*

Sure, sure, bring her in.

WAITER *hurries out.* TONY *turns to the two financiers.*

My God, it's Randolph's sister. . . . She don't know yet.

Enter DIANA, *a young woman of elegant ease.*

How do you do, Miss Morgan, come in, come in. Here, I got a nice table for you.

DIANA (*all bright Southern belle*): Thank you!

TONY: Can I bring you nice steak? Little drink?

DIANA: I believe I'll wait for Mr. Robertson.

TONY: Sure. Make yourself at home.

DIANA: Are you the . . . *famous* Tony?

TONY: That's right, miss.

DIANA: I certainly am thrilled to meet you. I've read all about this marvelous place. (*She looks around avidly.*) Are all these people literary?

TONY: Well, not all, Miss Morgan.

DIANA: But this is the speakeasy F. Scott Fitzgerald frequents, isn't it?

TONY: Oh, yeah, but tonight is very quiet with the stock market and all, people stayin' home a lot the last couple days.

DIANA: Is that gentleman a writer?

TONY: No, miss, that's Jake the Barber, he's in the liquor business.

DIANA: And these?

She points to DURANT *and* LIVERMORE. DURANT, *having overheard, stands.*

TONY: Mr. Durant, Miss Morgan. Mr. Livermore, Miss Morgan.

DIANA (*in a Southern accent, to the audience*): The name of Jesse Livermore was uttered in my family like the name of a genius! A Shakespeare, a Dante of corporate finance.

CLAYTON, *at the bar, picks up a phone.*

LEE (*looking on from choral area*): And William Durant . . . he had a car named after him, the Durant Six.

MOE (*beside* LEE): A *car?* Durant had control of General Motors, for God's sake.

DIANA: Not *the* Jesse Livermore?

LIVERMORE: Afraid so, yes!

DIANA: Well, I declare! And sitting here just like two ordinary millionaires!

LEE: Ah, yes, the Great Men. The fabled High Priests of the neverending Boom.

DIANA: This is certainly a banner evening for me! . . . I suppose you know Durham quite well.

LIVERMORE: Durham? I don't believe I've ever been there.

DIANA: But your big Philip Morris plant is there. You do still own Philip Morris, don't you?

LIVERMORE: Oh, yes, but to bet on a horse there's no need to ride him. I never mix in business. I am only interested in stocks.

DIANA: Well, that's sort of miraculous, isn't it, to own a place like that and never've seen it! My brother's in brokerage—Randolph Morgan?

LIVERMORE: I dealt with Randolph when I bought the controlling shares in IBM. Fine fellow.

DIANA: But I don't understand why he'd be spending the night in his office. The market's closed at night, isn't it?

Both men shift uneasily.

DURANT: Oh, yes, but there's an avalanche of selling orders from all over the country, and they're working round the clock to tally them up. The truth is, there's not a price on anything at the moment. In fact, Mr. Clayton over there at the end of the bar is waiting for the latest estimates.

DIANA: I'm sure something will be done, won't there? (*She laughs.*) They've cut off our telephone!

LIVERMORE: How's that?

DIANA: It seems that Daddy's lived on loans the last few months and his credit stopped. I had no idea! (*She laughs.*) I feel like a figure in a dream. I sat down in the dining car the other day, absolutely famished, and realized I had only forty cents! I am surviving on chocolate bars! (*Her charm barely hides her anxiety.*) Whatever has become of all the money?

LIVERMORE: You mustn't worry, Miss Morgan, there'll soon be plenty of money. Money is like a shy bird: the slightest rustle in the trees and it flies for cover. But money cannot bear soli-

tude for long, it must come out and feed. And that is why
we must all speak positively and show our confidence.

ROSE (*from choral area*): And they were nothing but pick-
pockets in a crowd of innocent pilgrims.

LIVERMORE: With Rockefeller's announcement this morning
the climb has probably begun already.

ROBERTSON (*from choral area*): Yes, but they also believed.

TAYLOR (*from choral area*): *What* did they believe?

IRENE and BANKS (*from choral area, echoing* TAYLOR): Yeah,
what did they believe?

ROBERTSON: Why, the most important thing of all—that talk
makes facts!

DURANT: If I were you, Miss Morgan, I would prepare myself
for the worst.

LIVERMORE: Now, Bill, there is no good in that kind of talk.

ROBERTSON: And they ended up believing it themselves!

DURANT: It's far more dreamlike than you imagine, Miss
Morgan.

MOE: There they are, chatting away, while the gentleman at the
end of the bar . . .

DURANT: . . . That gentleman . . . who has just put down
the telephone is undoubtedly steeling himself to tell me that
I have lost control of General Motors.

DIANA: What!

CLAYTON, *at the bar, has indeed put down the phone, has
straightened his vest, and is now crossing to their table.*

DURANT (*watching him approach*): If I were you, I'd muster all
the strength I have, Miss Morgan. Yes, Clayton?

CLAYTON: If we could talk privately, sir . . .

DURANT: Am I through?

CLAYTON: If you could borrow for two or three weeks . . .

DURANT: From whom?

CLAYTON: I don't know, sir.

DURANT (*standing*): Good night, Miss Morgan.

She is looking up at him, astonished.

How old are you?

DIANA: Nineteen.

DURANT: I hope you will look things in the face, young lady. Shun paper. Paper is the plague. Good luck to you. (*He turns to go.*)

LIVERMORE: We have to talk, Bill . . .

DURANT: Nothing to say, Jesse. Go to bed, old boy. It's long past midnight.

MOE (*trying to recall*): Say . . . didn't Durant end up managing a bowling alley in Toledo, Ohio?

CLAYTON (*nods*): Dead broke.

LIVERMORE (*turns to* CLAYTON, *adopting a tone of casual challenge*): Clayton . . . what's Philip Morris going to open at, can they tell?

CLAYTON: Below twenty. No higher. If we can find buyers at all.

LIVERMORE (*his smile gone*): But Rockefeller. Rockefeller . . .

CLAYTON: It doesn't seem to have had any effect, sir.

LIVERMORE *stands. Pause.*

I should get back to the office, sir, if I may.

LIVERMORE *is silent.*

I'm very sorry, Mr. Livermore.

CLAYTON *exits.* DIANA *is moved by the excruciating look coming onto Livermore's face.*

DIANA: Mr. Livermore? . . .

ROBERTSON (*entering*): Sorry I'm late, Diana. How was the trip? (*Her expression turns him to* LIVERMORE. *He goes to him.*) Bad, Jesse?

LIVERMORE: I am wiped out, Arthur.

ROBERTSON (*trying for lightness*): Come on, now, Jesse, a man like you has always got ten million put away somewhere.

LIVERMORE: No, no. I always felt that if you couldn't have *real* money, might as well not have any. Is it true what I've heard, that you sold out in time?

ROBERTSON: Yes, Jesse. I told you I would.

LIVERMORE (*slight pause*): Arthur, can you lend me five thousand dollars?

ROBERTSON: Certainly. (*He sits, removes one shoe. To audience*): Five weeks ago, on his yacht in Oyster Bay, he told me he had four hundred and eighty million dollars in common stocks.

LIVERMORE: What the hell are you doing?

ROBERTSON *removes a layer of five thousand-dollar bills from the shoe and hands* LIVERMORE *one as he stands.* LIVERMORE *stares down at Robertson's shoes.*

By God. Don't you believe in anything?

ROBERTSON: Not much.

LIVERMORE: Well, I suppose I understand that. (*He folds the bill.*) But I can't say that I admire it. (*He pockets the bill, looks down again at Robertson's shoes, and shakes his head.*) Well, I guess it's your country now. (*He turns like a blind man and goes out.*)

ROBERTSON: Not long after, Jesse Livermore sat down to a good breakfast in the Sherry-Netherland Hotel and, calling for an envelope, addressed it to Arthur Robertson, inserted a note for five thousand dollars, went into the washroom, and shot himself.

DIANA (*staring after* LIVERMORE, *then turning to* ROBERTSON): Is Randolph ruined too?

ROBERTSON (*taking her hand*): Diana . . . Randolph is dead. (*Pause.*) He . . . he fell from his window.

DIANA *stands, astonished.* IRENE *sings "'Tain't Nobody's Biz-ness" from choral area. Fadeout.*

ROSE (*calling as she enters*): Lee? Darling?

LEE (*takes a bike from prop area and rides on, halting before her*): How do you like it, Ma!

ROSE: What a beautiful bike!

LEE: It's a Columbia Racer! I just bought it from Georgie Rosen for twelve dollars.

ROSE: Where'd you get twelve dollars?

LEE: I emptied my savings account. But it's worth way more! . . .

ROSE: Well, I should say! Listen, darling, you know how to get to Third Avenue and Nineteenth Street, don't you?

LEE: Sure, in ten minutes.

ROSE (*taking a diamond bracelet from her bag*): This is my diamond bracelet. (*She reaches into the bag and brings out a card.*) And this is Mr. Sanders' card and the address. He's expecting you; just give it to him, and he'll give you a receipt.

LEE: Is he going to fix it?

ROSE: No, dear. It's a pawnshop. Go. I'll explain sometime.

LEE: Can't I have an idea? What's a pawnshop?

ROSE: Where you leave something temporarily and they lend you money on it, with interest. I'm going to leave it the rest of the month, till the market goes up again. I showed it to him on Friday, and we're getting a nice loan on it.

LEE: But how do you get it back?

ROSE: You just pay back the loan plus interest. But things'll pick up in a month or two. Go on, darling, and be careful! I'm so glad you bought that bike. . . . It's gorgeous!

LEE (*mounting his bike*): Does Papa know?

ROSE: Yes, dear. Papa knows . . .

She starts out as JOEY *hurries on.*

JOEY: Oh, hiya, Mrs. Baum.

ROSE: Hello, Joey. . . . Did you get thin?

JOEY: Me? (*He touches his stomach defensively.*) No, I'm okay. (*To* LEE *as well, as he takes an eight-by-ten photo out of an envelope*): See what I just got?

ROSE *and* LEE *look at the photo.*

ROSE (*impressed*): Where did you get that!

LEE: How'd you get it autographed?

JOEY: I just wrote to the White House.

LEE (*running his finger over the signature*): Boy . . . look at that, huh? "Herbert Hoover"!

ROSE: What a human thing for him to do! What did you write him?

JOEY: Just wished him success . . . you know, against the Depression.

ROSE (*wondrously*): Look at that! You're going to end up a politician, Joey. (*She returns to studying the photo.*)

JOEY: I might. I like it a lot.

LEE: But what about dentistry?

JOEY: Well, either one.

ROSE: Get going, darling.

She exits, already preoccupied with the real problem. LEE *mounts his bike.*

LEE: You want to shoot some baskets later?

JOEY: What about now?

LEE (*embarrassed*): No . . . I've got something to do for my mother. Meet you on the court in an hour. (*He starts off.*)

JOEY (*stopping him*): Wait, I'll go with you, let me on! (*He starts to mount the crossbar.*)

LEE: I can't, Joey.

JOEY (*sensing some forbidden area, surprised*): Oh!

LEE: See you on the court.

LEE *rides off.* JOEY *examines the autograph and mouths silently,* "Herbert Hoover . . ." *He shakes his head proudly and walks off.*

ROBERTSON (*from choral area*): To me . . . it's beginning to look like Germany in 1922, and I'm having real worries about the banks. There are times when I walk around with as much as twenty-five, thirty thousand dollars in my shoes.

FRANK *enters in a chauffeur's uniform, a lap robe folded over his arm.* MOE *enters, stylishly dressed in a fur-collared overcoat, as though on a street.*

FRANK: Morning, Mr. Baum. Got the car nice and warmed up for you this morning, sir. And I had the lap robe drycleaned.

MOE (*showing* FRANK *a bill*): What is that, Frank?

FRANK: Oh. Looks like the garage bill.

MOE: What's that about tires on there?

FRANK: Oh, yes, sir, this is the bill for the new tires last week.

MOE: And what happened to those tires we bought six weeks ago?

FRANK: Those weren't very good, sir, they wore out quick— and I want to be the first to admit that!

MOE: But twenty dollars apiece and they last six weeks?

FRANK: That's just what I'm telling you, sir—they were just no good. But these ones are going to be a whole lot better, though.

MOE: Tell you what, Frank . . .

FRANK: Yes, sir—what I mean, I'm giving you my personal guarantee on this set, Mr. Baum.

MOE: I never paid no attention to these things, but maybe you heard of the market crash? The whole thing practically floated into the ocean, y'know.

FRANK: Oh, yes, sir, I certainly heard about it.

MOE: I'm glad you heard about it, because I heard a *lot* about it. In fact, what you cleared from selling my tires over the last ten years . . .

FRANK: Oh, no, sir! Mr. Baum!

MOE: Frank, lookin' back over the last ten years, I never heard of that amount of tires in my whole life since I first come over from Europe a baby at the age of six. That is a lot of tires, Frank; so I tell ya what we're gonna do now, you're going to drive her over to the Pierce Arrow showroom and leave her there, and then come to my office and we'll settle up.

FRANK: But how are you going to get around!

MOE: I'm a happy man in a taxi, Frank.

FRANK: Well, I'm sure going to be sorry to leave you people.

MOE: Everything comes to an end, Frank, it was great while it lasted. No hard feelings. (*He shakes Frank's hand.*) Bye-bye.

FRANK: But what . . . what am I supposed to do now?

MOE: You got in-laws?

FRANK: But I never got along with them.

MOE: You should've. (*He hurries off, calling*): Taxi!

FRANK (*cap in hand, throws down lap robe and walks off aimlessly*): Damn!

IRENE *enters with a pram filled with junk and sings a few lines of "'Tain't Nobody's Bizness," unaccompanied. She picks up robe and admiringly inspects it. Then:*

IRENE: You got fired, you walked away to nothing; no unemployment insurance, no Social Security—just the in-laws and fresh air. (*She tosses the robe in with her junk.*)

Fadeout.

ROSE: Still . . . it was very nice in a certain way. On our block in Brooklyn a lot of married children had to move back with the parents, and you heard babies crying in houses that didn't have a baby in twenty years. But of course the doubling up could also drive you crazy . . .

With hardly a pause, she turns to GRANDPA, *who is arriving center with canes and hatboxes. He drops the whole load on the floor.*

What are *you* doing?

GRANDPA (*delivering a final verdict*): There's no room for these in my closet . . .

ROSE: For a few *canes?*

GRANDPA: And what about my hats? You shouldn't have bought such a small house, Rose.

ROSE (*of the canes*): I'll put them in the front-hall closet.

GRANDPA: No, people step on them. And where will I put my hats?

ROSE (*trying not to explode*): Papa, what do you want from me? We are doing what we can do!

GRANDPA: One bedroom for so many people is not right! You had three bathrooms in the apartment, and you used to look out the window, there was the whole New York. Here . . . listen to that street out there, it's a Brooklyn cemetery. And this barber here is *very* bad—look what he did to me. (*He shows her.*)

ROSE: Why? It's beautiful. (*She brushes some hairs straight.*) It's just a little uneven . . .

GRANDPA (*pushing her hand away*): I don't understand, Rose— why does he declare bankruptcy if he's going to turn around and pay his debts?

ROSE: For his reputation.

GRANDPA: His reputation! He'll have the reputation of a fool! The reason to go bankrupt is *not* to pay your debts!

ROSE (*uncertain herself*): He wanted to be honorable.

GRANDPA: But that's the whole beauty of it! He should've asked me. When I went bankrupt I didn't pay *nobody!*

ROSE (*deciding*): I've got to tell you something, Papa. From now on, I wish you . . .

GRANDPA (*helping her fold a bed sheet*): And you'll have to talk to Lee—he throws himself around in his bed all night, wakes me up ten times, and he leaves his socks on the floor. . . . Two people in that bedroom is too much, Rose.

ROSE: I don't want Moe to get aggravated, Papa.

He is reached, slightly glances at her.

He might try to start a new business, so he's nervous, so please, don't complain, Papa. Please?

GRANDPA: What did I say?

ROSE: Nothing. (*Suddenly she embraces him guiltily.*) Maybe I can find an umbrella stand someplace.

GRANDPA: I was reading about this Hitler . . .

ROSE: Who?

GRANDPA: . . . He's chasing all the radicals out of Germany. He wouldn't be so bad if he wasn't against the Jews. But he won't last six months. . . . The Germans are not fools. When I used to take Mama to Baden-Baden this time of year . . .

ROSE: How beautiful she was.

GRANDPA: . . . one time we were sitting on the train ready to leave for Berlin. And suddenly a man gallops up calling out my name. So I says, "Yes, that's me!" And through the window he hands me my gold watch and chain: "You left it in your room, mein Herr." Such a thing could only happen in Germany. This Hitler is finished.

ROSE (*of the canes*): Please. . . . Put them back in your closet, heh? (*He starts to object.*) I don't want Moe to get mad, Papa! (*She cuts the rebellion short and loads him with his canes and hatboxes.*)

GRANDPA (*muttering*): Man don't even know how to go bankrupt.

He exits. LEE *appears on his bike—but dressed now for winter. He dismounts and parks the bike just as* ROSE *lies back in the chair.*

LEE: Ma! Guess what!

ROSE: What?

LEE: Remember I emptied my bank account for the bike?

ROSE: So?

LEE: The bank has just been closed by the government! It's broke! There's a whole mob of people in the street yelling where's their money! They've got cops and everything! There is no more money in the bank!

ROSE: You're a genius!

LEE: Imagine! . . . I could have lost my twelve dollars! . . . Wow!

ROSE: That's wonderful. (*She removes a pearl choker.*)

LEE: Oh, Ma, wasn't that Papa's wedding present?

ROSE: I hate to, but . . .

LEE: What about Papa's business! Can't he . . .

ROSE: He put too much capital in the stock market, dear—it made more there than in his business. So now . . . it's not there anymore.

A THIEF *swiftly appears and rides off on the bike.*

But we'll be all right. Go. You can have a jelly sandwich when you come back.

LEE *stuffs the pearls into his pants as he approaches where the bike was; he looks in all directions, his bones chilling. He runs in all directions and finally comes to a halt, breathless, stark horror in his face. As though sensing trouble,* ROSE *walks over to him.*

Where's your bike?

He can't speak.

They stole your bike?

He is immobile.

May he choke on his next meal. . . . Oh, my darling, my darling, what an awful thing.

He sobs once but holds it back. She, facing him, tries to smile.

So now you're going to have to walk to the hockshop like everybody else. Come, have your jelly sandwich.

LEE: No, I'd like to see if I can trot there—it'd be good for my track. By the way, I've almost decided to go to Cornell, I think. Cornell or Brown.

ROSE (*with an empty congratulatory exclamation*): Oh! . . . Well, there's still months to decide.

ROSE *and* LEE *join the company as they stand up to sing the Iowa Hymn, Verse 1: "We gather together to ask the Lord's blessing, He chastens and hastens His will to make known: The wicked oppressing now cease from distressing, Sing praises to His name: He forgets not His own." The hymn music continues under the following.*

ROBERTSON: Till then, probably most people didn't think of it as a system.

TAYLOR: It was more like nature.

MRS. TAYLOR: Like weather; had to expect bad weather, but it always got good again if you waited. And so we waited. And it didn't change. (*She is watching* TAYLOR *as he adopts a mood of despair and slowly sits on his heels.*) And we waited some more and it never changed. You couldn't hardly believe that the day would come when the land wouldn't give. Land always gives. But there it lay, miles and miles of it, and there was us wanting to work it, and couldn't. It was like a spell on Iowa. We was all there, and the land was there waitin', and we wasn't able to move. (*The hymn ends.*) Amen.

BREWSTER, *followed by* FARMERS, *comes front and calls to the crowd in the audience's direction.*

BREWSTER: Just sit tight, folks, be startin' in a few minutes.

FARMER I (*hitting his heels together*): Looks like snow up there.

FARMER 2 (*laughs*): Even the weather ain't workin'.

Low laughter in the crowd.

BREWSTER (*heading over to* TAYLOR): You be catchin' cold sitting on the ground like that, won't you, Henry?

TAYLOR: Tired out. Never slept a wink all night. Not a wink.

MRS. TAYLOR *appears carrying a big coffeepot, accompanied by* HARRIET, *her fifteen-year-old daughter, who has a coffee mug hanging from each of her fingers.*

MRS. TAYLOR: You'll have to share the cups, but it's something hot anyway.

BREWSTER: Oh, that smells good, lemme take that, ma'am.

She gives the coffeepot to BREWSTER *and comes over to* TAYLOR. HARRIET *hands out the cups.*

MRS. TAYLOR (*sotto voce, irritated and ashamed*): You can't be sitting on the ground like that, now come on! (*She starts him to his feet.*) It's a auction—anybody's got a right to come to a auction.

TAYLOR: There must be a thousand men along the road—they never told me they'd bring a thousand men!

MRS. TAYLOR: Well, I suppose that's the way they do it.

TAYLOR: They got guns in those trucks!

MRS. TAYLOR (*frightened herself*): Well, it's too late to stop 'em now. So might as well go around and talk to people that come to help you.

CHARLEY (*rushing on*): Brewster! Where's Brewster!

BREWSTER (*stepping forward from the crowd*): What's up, Charley?

CHARLEY (*pointing off*): Judge Bradley! He's gettin' out of the car with the auctioneer!

Silence. All look to BREWSTER.

BREWSTER: Well . . . I don't see what that changes. (*Turning to all*): I guess we're gonna do what we come here to do. That right?

The crowd quietly agrees: "Right," "Stick to it, Larry," "No use quittin' now," etc. Enter JUDGE BRADLEY, *sixty, and* MR. FRANK HOWARD, *the auctioneer. The silence spreads.*

JUDGE BRADLEY: Good morning, gentlemen. (*He looks around. There is no reply.*) I want to say a few words to you before Mr. Howard starts the auction. (*He walks up onto a raised platform.*) I have decided to come here personally this morning in order to emphasize the gravity of the situation that has developed in the state. We are on the verge of anarchy in Iowa, and that is not going to help anybody. Now, you are all property owners, so you—

BREWSTER: Used to be, Judge, used to be!

JUDGE BRADLEY: Brewster, I will not waste words; there are forty armed deputies out there. (*Slight pause.*) I would like to make only one point clear—I have levied a deficiency judgment on this farm. Mr. Taylor has failed to pay what he owes on his equipment and some of his cattle. A contract is sacred. The National Bank has the right to collect on its loans. Now then, Mr. Howard will begin the auction. But he has discretionary power to decline any unreasonable bid.

I ask you again, obey the law. Once law and order go down, no man is safe. Mr. Howard?

MR. HOWARD (*with a clipboard in hand, climbs onto the platform*): Well, now, let's see. We have here one John Deere tractor and combine, three years old, beautiful condition.

Three BIDDERS *enter, and the crowd turns to look at them with hostility as they come to a halt.*

I ask for bids on the tractor and combine.

BREWSTER: Ten cents!

MR. HOWARD: I have ten cents. (*His finger raised, he points from man to man in the crowd.*) I have ten cents, I have ten cents . . .

He is pointing toward the BIDDERS, *but they are looking around at the crowd in fear.*

BIDDER 1: Five hundred.

JUDGE BRADLEY (*calling*): Sheriff, get over here and protect these men!

The SHERIFF *and four* DEPUTIES *enter and edge their way in around the three* BIDDERS. *The deputies carry shotguns.*

MR. HOWARD: Do I hear five hundred dollars? Do I hear five . . .

BIDDER 1: Five hundred!

MR. HOWARD: Do I hear six hundred?

BIDDER 2: Six hundred!

MR. HOWARD: Do I hear seven hundred?

BIDDER 3: Seven hundred!

Disciplined and quick, the FARMERS *grab the* DEPUTIES *and disarm them; a shotgun goes off harmlessly.*

JUDGE BRADLEY: Brewster! Great God, what are you doing!

BREWSTER *has pinned the Judge's arms behind him, and another man lowers a noose around his neck.*

BREWSTER (*to* DEPUTIES): You come any closer and we're gonna string him up! You all get back on that road or we string up the Judge! So help me Christ, he goes up if any one of you deputies interferes with this auction! Now, let me just clear up one thing for you, Judge Bradley . . .

TAYLOR: Let him go, Brewster—I don't care anymore, let them take it!

BREWSTER: Just sit tight, Henry, nobody's takin' anything. That is all over, Judge. Mr. Howard, just to save time, why don't you take a bid on the whole place? Do that, please?

MR. HOWARD (*turns to the crowd, his voice shaking*): I . . . I'll hear bids on . . . everything. Tractor and combine, pair of mules and wagon, twenty-six cows, eight heifers, farm and outbuildings, assorted tools . . . and so forth. Do I hear . . .

BREWSTER: One dollar.

MR. HOWARD (*rapidly*): I hear one dollar. One dollar, one dollar? . . . (*He looks around.*) Sold for one dollar.

BREWSTER (*handing him a dollar*): Now, will you just sign that receipt, please?

MR. HOWARD *scribbles and hands him a receipt.* BREWSTER *leaps off the platform, goes to* TAYLOR, *and gives him the receipt.*

Henry? Whyn't you go along now and get to milkin'. Let's go, boys.

He waves to the crowd, and his men follow him out. JUDGE BRADLEY, *removing the noose, comes down off the platform and goes over to* TAYLOR, *who is staring down at the receipt.*

JUDGE BRADLEY: Henry Taylor? You are nothing but a thief!

TAYLOR *cringes under the accusation. The* JUDGE *points to the receipt.*

That is a crime against every law of God and man! And this isn't the end of it, either! (*He turns and stalks out.*)

HARRIET: Should we milk 'em, Papa?

MRS. TAYLOR: Of course we milk 'em—they're ours. (*But she needs Taylor's compliance.*) Henry?

TAYLOR (*staring at the receipt*): It's like I stole my own place.

Near tears, humiliated, TAYLOR *moves into darkness with his wife. The* FARMERS *disperse.*

ROBERTSON (*from choral area*): Nobody knows how many

people are leaving their hometowns, their farms and cities, and hitting the road. Hundreds of thousands, maybe millions of internal refugees, Americans transformed into strangers.

BANKS *enters in army cap, uniform jacket and jeans, carrying his little bundle of clothes and a cooking pot.*

BANKS:
I still hear that train.
Still hear that long low whistle.
Still hear that train, yeah.

He imitates train whistle: Whoo-ooo! *He sings the first verse of "How Long," then speaks over music, which continues.*

Nineteen twenty-nine was pretty hard. My family had a little old cotton farm, McGehee, Arkansas. But a man had to be on the road—leave his wife, his mother—just to try to get a little money to live on. But God help me, I couldn't get anything, and I was too ashamed to send them a picture, all dirty and ragged and hadn't shaved. Write a postcard: "Dear Mother, doin' wonderful and hope you're all fine." And me sleepin' on a Los Angeles sidewalk under a newspaper. And my ma'd say, "Oh, my son's in Los Angeles, he's doin' pretty fair." (*He grins.*) Yeah . . . "all the way on the Santa Fe." So hungry and weak I begin to see snakes through the smoke, and a white hobo named Callahan got a scissors on me, wrapped me 'tween his legs—otherwise I'd have fell off into a cornfield there. But except for Callahan there was no friendships in the hobo jungle. Everybody else was worried and sad-lookin', and they was evil to each other. I still hear that long low whistle . . . *whoo-ooo!*

BANKS *sings the second verse of "How Long." Then the music changes into "The Joint is Jumpin'":* MARATHON DANCERS *enter, half asleep, some about to drop. They dance. Fadeout.*

Light comes up on MOE *in an armchair.* LEE *enters with college catalogues.*

MOE: When you say three hundred dollars tuition . . . Lee!
LEE: That's for Columbia. Some of these others are cheaper.

MOE: That's for the four years.

LEE: Well, no, that's one year.

MOE: Ah. (*He lies back in the chair and closes his eyes.*)

LEE (*flipping a page of a catalogue*): Minnesota here is a hundred and fifty, for instance. And Ohio State is about the same, I think. (*He turns to* MOE, *awaiting his reaction.*) Pa?

MOE *is asleep.*

He always got drowsy when the news got bad. And now the mystery of the marked house began. Practically every day you'd see the stranger coming down the street, poor and ragged, and he'd go past house after house, but at our driveway he'd make a turn right up to the back porch and ask for something to eat. Why us?

TAYLOR *appears at one side of the stage in mackinaw, farm shoes, and peaked hunter's cap, a creased paper bag under his arm. Looking front, he seems gaunt, out of his element; now he rings the doorbell. Nothing happens. Then* LEE *goes to the "door."*

LEE: Yes?

TAYLOR (*shyly, still an amateur at the routine*): Ah . . . sorry to be botherin' you on a Sunday and all.

ROSE (*enters in housedress and apron, wiping her hands on a dish towel*): Who is that, dear? (*She comes to the door.*)

LEE: This is my mother.

TAYLOR: How-de-do, ma'am, my name is Taylor, and I'm just passing by, wondering if you folks have any work around the place . . .

MOE (*waking up suddenly*): Hey! The bell rang! (*He sees the conclave.*) Oh . . .

ROSE (*ironically*): Another one looking for work!

TAYLOR: I could paint the place or fix the roof, electrical, plumbing, masonry, gardening . . . I always had my own farm, and we do all that, don't you know. I'd work cheap . . .

ROSE: Well, we don't need any kind of . . .

MOE: Where you from?

TAYLOR: State of Iowa.

LEE (*as though it's the moon*): Iowa!

TAYLOR: I wouldn't hardly charge if I could have my meals, don't you know.

MOE (*beginning to locate* TAYLOR *in space*): Whereabouts in Iowa?

ROSE: My sister's husband comes from Cleveland.

MOE: No, no, Cleveland is nowhere near. (*To* TAYLOR): Whereabouts?

TAYLOR: You know Styles?

MOE: I only know the stores in the big towns.

TAYLOR (*giving a grateful chuckle*): Well! I never expected to meet a . . .

> *He suddenly gets dizzy, breaks off, and reaches for some support.* LEE *holds his arm, and he goes down like an elevator and sits there.*

ROSE: What's the matter!

MOE: Mister?

LEE: I'll get water! (*He rushes out.*)

ROSE: Is it your heart?

TAYLOR: 'Scuse me . . . I'm awful sorry . . .

> *He gets on his hands and knees as* LEE *enters with a glass of water and hands it to him. He drinks half of it, returns the glass.*

Thank you, sonny.

ROSE (*looks to* MOE, *sees his agreement, gestures within*): He better sit down.

MOE: You want to sit down?

> TAYLOR *looks at him helplessly.*

Come, sit down.

> LEE *and* MOE *help him to a chair, and he sits.*

ROSE (*bending over to look into his face*): You got some kind of heart?

TAYLOR (*embarrassed, and afraid for himself now*): Would you be able to give me something to eat?

> *The three stare at him; he looks up at their shocked astonishment and weeps.*

ROSE: You're *hungry*?

TAYLOR: Yes, ma'am.

ROSE *looks at* MOE *whether to believe this.*

MOE (*unnerved*): Better get him something.

ROSE (*hurrying out immediately*): Oh, my God in heaven!

MOE (*now with a suspicious, even accusatory edge*): What're you doing, just going around? . . .

TAYLOR: Well, no, I come east when I lost the farm. . . . They was supposed to be hiring in New Jersey, pickers for the celery? But I only got two days. . . . I been to the Salvation Army four, five times, but they only give me a bun and a cup of coffee yesterday . . .

LEE: You haven't eaten since *yesterday?*

TAYLOR: Well, I generally don't need too much . . .

ROSE (*entering with a tray, bowl of soup, and bread*): I was just making it, so I didn't put in the potatoes yet . . .

TAYLOR: Oh, beets?

ROSE: That's what you call borscht.

TAYLOR (*obediently*): Yes, ma'am.

He wastes no time, spoons it up. They all watch him: their first hungry man.

MOE (*skeptically*): How do you come to lose a farm?

TAYLOR: I suppose you read about the Farmers' Uprisin' in the state couple months ago?

LEE: I did.

MOE (*to* LEE): What uprising?

LEE: They nearly lynched a judge for auctioning off their farms. (*To* TAYLOR, *impressed*): Were you in *that?*

TAYLOR: Well, it's all over now, but I don't believe they'll be auctioning any more farms for a while, though. Been just terrible out there.

ROSE (*shaking her head*): All I thought they were all Republicans in Iowa.

TAYLOR: Well, I guess they all are.

LEE: Is that what they mean by radical, though?

TAYLOR: Well . . . it's like they say—people in Iowa are practical. They'll even go radical if it seems like it's practical. But as soon as it stops being practical they stop being radical.

MOE: Well, you probably all learned your lesson now.

LEE: Why! He was taking their homes away, that judge!

MOE: So you go in a court and lynch him?

LEE: But . . . but it's all *wrong*, Pa!

ROSE: Shh! Don't argue . . .

LEE (*to* ROSE): But *you* think it's wrong, don't you? Suppose they came and threw us out of *this* house?

ROSE: I refuse to think about it. (*To* TAYLOR): So where do you sleep?

MOE (*instantly*): Excuse me. We are not interested in where you sleep, Mr. . . . what's your name?

TAYLOR: Taylor. I'd be satisfied with just my meals if I could live in the basement . . .

MOE (*to* TAYLOR, *but half addressing* ROSE): There is no room for another human being in this house, y'understand? Including the basement. (*He takes out two or three bills.*)

TAYLOR: I wasn't asking for charity . . .

MOE: I'm going to loan you a dollar, and I hope you're going to start a whole new life. Here . . . (*He hands* TAYLOR *the bill, escorting him to the door.*) And pay me back, but don't rush. (*He holds out his hand.*) Glad to have met you, and good luck.

TAYLOR: Thanks for the soup, Mrs. . . .

ROSE: Our name is Baum. You have children?

TAYLOR: One's fifteen, one's nine. (*He thoughtfully folds the dollar bill.*)

GRANDPA *enters, eating a plum.*

ROSE: Take care of yourself, and write a letter to your wife.

TAYLOR: Yes, I will. (*To* MOE): Goodbye, sir . . .

MOE (*grinning, tipping his finger at* TAYLOR): Stay away from rope.

TAYLOR: Oh, yeah, I will . . . (*He exits.*)

LEE (*goes out on the periphery and calls to him as he walks away*): Goodbye, Mr. Taylor!

TAYLOR (*turns back, waves*): Bye, sonny!

He leaves. LEE *stares after him, absorbing it all.*

GRANDPA: Who was that?

MOE: He's a farmer from Iowa. He tried to lynch a judge, so she wanted him to live in the cellar.

GRANDPA: What is a farmer doing here?

ROSE: He went broke, he lost everything.

GRANDPA: Oh. Well, he should borrow.

MOE (*snaps his fingers to* LEE): I'll run down the street and tell him! He got me hungry. (*To* ROSE): I'm going down the corner and get a chocolate soda. . . . What do you say, Lee?

LEE: I don't feel like it.

MOE: Don't be sad. Life is tough, what're you going to do? Sometimes it's not as tough as other times, that's all. But it's always tough. Come, have a soda.

LEE: Not now, Pa, thanks. (*He turns away.*)

MOE (*straightens, silently refusing blame*): Be back right away. (*He strolls across the stage, softly, tonelessly whistling, and exits.*)

GRANDPA, *chewing, the plum pit in his hand, looks around for a place to put it.* ROSE *sees the inevitable and holds out her hand.*

ROSE (*disgusted*): Oh, give it to me.

GRANDPA *drops the pit into her palm, and she goes out with it and the soup plate.*

LEE (*still trying to digest*): That man was starving, Grandpa.

GRANDPA: No, no, he was hungry but not starving.

LEE: He was, he almost fainted.

GRANDPA: No, that's not starving. In Europe they starve, but here not. Anyway, couple weeks they're going to figure out what to do, and you can forget the whole thing. . . . God makes one person at a time, boy—worry about yourself.

Fadeout.

ROBERTSON: His name is Theodore K. Quinn.

Music begins—"My Baby Just Cares for Me"—and QUINN, *with boater and cane, sings and dances through Robertson's speech.*

The greatest Irish soft-shoe dancer ever to serve on a board of directors. They know him at Lindy's, they love him at Twenty-one. High up on top of the American heap sits Ted Quinn, hardly forty years of age in 1932 . . .

QUINN (*continues singing, then breaks off and picks up the phone*):
Ted Quinn. Come over, Arthur, I've got to see you. But
come to the twenty-ninth floor. . . . I've got a new office.

ROBERTSON (*looking around, as at a striking office*): All this
yours?

QUINN: Yup. You are standing on the apex, the pinnacle of
human evolution. From that window you can reach out and
touch the moustache of Almighty God.

ROBERTSON (*moved, gripping Quinn's hand*): Ted! *Ted!!*

QUINN: Jesus, don't say it that way, will ya?

ROBERTSON: President of General Electric!

QUINN: I'm not sure I want it, Arthur.

ROBERTSON *laughs sarcastically.*

I'm not, goddammit! I never expected Swope to pick me
—never!

ROBERTSON: Oh, go on, you've been angling for the presidency
the last five years.

QUINN: No! I swear not. I just didn't want anybody else to get
it . . .

ROBERTSON *laughs.*

Well, that's not the same thing! . . . Seriously, Arthur, I'm
scared. I don't know what to do. (*He looks around.*) Now
that I'm standing here, now that they're about to paint
my name on the door . . . and the *Times* sending a
reporter . . .

ROBERTSON (*seriously*): What the hell's got into you?

QUINN (*searching in himself*): I don't know. . . . It's almost
like shame.

ROBERTSON: For *what?* It's that damned upbringing of yours,
that anarchist father . . .

QUINN: The truth is, I've never been comfortable with some of
the things we've done.

ROBERTSON: But why suddenly after all these years . . .

QUINN: It's different taking orders and being the man who
gives them.

ROBERTSON: I don't know what the hell you are talking about.

Pause. For QUINN *it is both a confession and something he must bring out into the open. But he sustains his humor.*

QUINN: I had a very unsettling experience about eighteen months ago, Arthur. Got a call from my Philadelphia district manager that Frigidaire was dropping the price on their boxes. So I told him to cut ours. And in a matter of weeks they cut, we cut, they cut, we cut, till I finally went down there myself. Because I was damned if I was going to get beat in Philadelphia . . . and I finally cut our price right down to our cost of production. Well—ting-a-ling-a-ling, phone call from New York: "What the hell is going on down there?" Gotta get down to Wall Street and have a meeting with the money boys. . . . So there we are, about ten of us, and I look across the blinding glare of that teakwood table, and lo and behold, who is facing me but Georgy Fairchild, head of sales for Frigidaire. Old friends, Georgy and I, go way back together, but he *is* Frigidaire, y'know—what the hell is he doing in a GE meeting? . . . Well, turns out that both companies are owned by the same money. And the word is that Georgy and Quinn are going to cut out this nonsense and get those prices up to where they belong. (*He laughs.*) Well, I tell you, I was absolutely flabbergasted. Here I've been fightin' Georgy from Bangkok to the Bronx, layin' awake nights thinkin' how to outfox him—hell, we were like Grant and Lee with thousands of soldiers out to destroy each other, and it's suddenly like all these years I'd been shellin' my own men! (*He laughs.*) It was farcical.

ROBERTSON: It's amazing. You're probably the world's greatest salesman, and you haven't an ounce of objectivity . . .

QUINN: Objectivity! Arthur, if I'm that great a salesman—which I'm far from denying—it's because I believe; I believe deeply in the creative force of competition.

ROBERTSON: Exactly, and GE is the fastest-growing company in the world because. . . .

QUINN (loves *this point*): . . . because we've had the capital to buy up one independent business after another. . . . It's haunting me, Arthur—thousands of small businesses are going under every week now, and we're getting bigger and bigger every day. What's going to become of the independent person in this country once everybody's sucking off the same tit? How can there be an America without Americans—people not beholden to some enormous enterprise that'll run their souls?

ROBERTSON: Am I hearing what I think?

QUINN *is silent.*

Ted? You'd actually resign?

QUINN: If I did, would it make any point to you at all? If I made a statement that . . .

ROBERTSON: What statement can you possibly make that won't call for a return to the horse and buggy? The America you love is cold stone dead in the parlor, Ted. This is a corporate country; you can't go back to small personal enterprise again.

QUINN: A corporate country! . . . Jesus, Arthur, what a prospect!

MISS FOWLER *enters.*

MISS FOWLER: The gentleman from the *Times* is waiting, Mr. Quinn . . . unless you'd like to make it tomorrow or . . .

QUINN (*slight pause*): No, no—it has to be now or never. Ask him in.

She exits.

Tell me the truth, Arthur, do I move your mind at all?

ROBERTSON: Of course I see your point. But you can't buck the inevitable.

GRAHAM *enters with* MISS FOWLER.

MISS FOWLER: Mr. Graham.

QUINN (*shakes hands, grinning*): Glad to meet you. . . . My friend Mr. Robertson.

GRAHAM (*recognizing the name*): Oh, yes, how do you do?

ROBERTSON: Nice to meet you. (*To* QUINN, *escaping*): I'll see you later . . .

QUINN: No, stay . . . I'll only be a few minutes . . .

ROBERTSON: I ought to get back to my office.

QUINN (*laughs*): I'm still the president, Arthur—stay! I want to feel the support of your opposition.

ROBERTSON *laughs with* QUINN, *glancing uneasily at* GRAHAM, *who doesn't know what's going on.*

I'll have to be quick, Mr. Graham. Will you sit down?

GRAHAM: I have a few questions about your earlier life and background. I understand your father was one of the early labor organizers in Chicago.

QUINN: Mr. Graham, I am resigning.

GRAHAM: Beg your pardon?

QUINN: Resigning, I said.

GRAHAM: From the presidency? I don't understand.

QUINN: I don't believe in giant business, or giant government, or giant anything. And the laugh is . . . no man has done more to make GE the giant it is today.

GRAHAM: Well, now! (*He laughs.*) I think this takes us off the financial section and onto the front page! But tell me, how does a man with your ideas rise so high in a great corporation like this? How did you get into GE?

QUINN: Well, it's a long story, but I love to tell it. I started out studying law at night and working as a clerk in a factory that manufactured bulbs for auto headlights. Y'see, in those days they had forty or fifty makes of car and all different specifications for the lightbulbs. Now, say you got an order for five thousand lamps. The manufacturing process was not too accurate, so you had to make eight or nine thousand to come out with five thousand perfect ones. Result, though, was that we had hundreds of thousands of perfectly good lamps left over at the end of the year. So . . . one night on my own time I went through the records and did some simple calculations and came up with a new average. My figure showed that to get five thousand good bulbs we only had to make sixty-two hundred instead of eight thousand. Result was, that company saved a hundred and thirty thousand dollars in one year. So the boss and I became very friendly, and one day he says, "I'm selling out to General Electric," but he couldn't tell whether they'd be keeping me on. So he says to me, "Ted, tell you what we do. They're coming out from Wall Street"—these bankers, y'see—"and I'm going to let you pick them up at the depot." Figuring I'd be the first to meet them and might draw their attention and they'd rehire me, y'see. Well, I was just this hick-town kid, y'know, about to meet these great big juicy Wall Street bankers—I tell you, I hardly slept all night tryin' to figure how to make an impression. And just toward dawn . . . it was during breakfast—and I suddenly thought of that wall. See, the factory had this brick wall a block long; no windows, two stories high, just a tremendous wall of bricks. And it went through my mind that one of them might ask me how many bricks were in that wall. 'Cause I could answer any question about the company except that. So I got over to the plant as quick as I could, multiplied the vertical and horizontal bricks, and got the number. Well . . . these three bankers arrive, and I get them into the boss's limousine, and we ride. Nobody asks me anything! Three of them in those big fur-lined coats, and not one goddamn syllable. . . . Anyway, we round the corner, and doesn't one of them turn to me and say, "Mr. Quinn, how many bricks you suppose is in that wall!" And by God, I told him! Well, he wouldn't believe it, got out and counted himself—and it broke the ice, y'see, and one thing and another they made me manager of the plant. And that's how I got into GE.

GRAHAM (*astonished*): What are your plans? Will you join another company or . . .

QUINN: No. I've been tickling the idea I might set up an advisory service for small business. Say a fella has a concept, I could teach him how to develop and market it . . . 'cause I *know* all that, and maybe I could help (*to the audience*) to keep those individuals coming. Because with this terrible Depression you hear it everywhere now—an individual man is not worth a bag of peanuts. I don't know the answers, Mr. Graham, but I sure as hell know the question: How do you keep everything that's big from swallowing everything that's small? 'Cause when that happens—God Almighty—it's not going to be much fun!

GRAHAM: Well . . . thanks very much. Good day. Good day, Mr. Robertson. I must say . . . ! (*With a broken laugh and a shake of the head, he hurries out.*)

QUINN: He was not massively overwhelmed, was he?

ROBERTSON: He heard the gentle clip-clop of the horse and buggy coming down the road.

QUINN: All right, then, damn it, maybe what you ought to be looking into, Arthur, is horseshoes!

ROBERTSON: Well, you never did do things in a small way! This is unquestionably the world record for the shortest presidency in corporate history. (*He exits.*)

Alone, QUINN *stares around in a moment of surprise and fright at what he's actually done. Soft-shoe music steals up, and he insinuates himself into it, dancing in a kind of uncertain mood that changes to release and joy, and at the climax he sings the last lines of "My Baby Just Cares for Me." As the lyrics end, the phone rings. He picks up the receiver, never losing the beat, and simply lets it drop, and dances off.*

ROSE *comes downstage, staring front, a book in her hand.*

ROSE: Who would believe it? You look out the window in the middle of a fine October day, and there's a dozen college graduates with advanced degrees playing ball in the street like children. And it gets harder and harder to remember when life seemed to have so much purpose, when you couldn't wait for the morning!

LEE *enters, takes a college catalogue off the prop table, and approaches her, turning the pages.*

LEE: At Cornell there's no tuition fee at all if you enroll in bacteriology.

ROSE: Free *tuition*!

LEE: Maybe they're short of bacteriologists.

ROSE: Would you like that?

LEE (*stares, tries to see himself as a bacteriologist, sighs*): Bacteriology?

ROSE (*wrinkling her nose*): Must be awful. Is anything else free?

LEE: It's the only one I've seen.

ROSE: I've got to finish this before tomorrow. I'm overdue fourteen cents on it.

LEE: What is it?

ROSE: *Coronet* by Manuel Komroff. It's about this royal crown that gets stolen and lost and found again and lost again for generations. It's supposed to be literature, but I don't know, it's very enjoyable. (*She goes back to her book.*)

LEE (*closes the catalogue, looks at her*): Ma?

ROSE (*still reading*): Hm?

LEE (*gently breaking the ice*): I guess it's too late to apply for this year anyway. Don't you think so?

ROSE (*turns to him*): I imagine so, dear . . . for this year.

LEE: Okay, Ma . . .

ROSE: I feel so terrible—all those years we were throwing money around, and now when you need it—

LEE (*relieved, now that he knows*): That's okay. I think maybe I'll try looking for a job. But I'm not sure whether to look under "Help Wanted, Male" or "Boy Wanted."

ROSE: Boy! (*Their gazes meet. She sees his apprehension.*) Don't be frightened, darling—you're going to be wonderful! (*She hides her feeling in the book.*)

Fadeout. Light comes up on FANNY, *standing on the first-level balcony. She calls to* SIDNEY, *who is playing the piano and singing "Once in a While."*

FANNY: Sidney?

He continues singing.

Sidney?

He continues singing.

Sidney?

He continues singing.

I have to talk to you, Sidney.

He continues singing.

Stop that for a minute!

SIDNEY (*stops singing*): Ma, look . . . it's only July. If I was still in high school it would still be my summer vacation.

FANNY: And if I was the Queen of Rumania I would have free rent. You graduated, Sidney, this is not summer vacation.

SIDNEY: Mama, it's useless to go to employment agencies—there's grown men there, engineers, college graduates. They're willing to take anything. If I could write one hit song like this, just one—we wouldn't have to worry again. Let me have July, just July—see if I can do it. Because that man was serious—he's a good friend of the waiter who works where Bing Crosby's manager eats. He could give him any song I write, and if Crosby just sang it one time . . .

FANNY: I want to talk to you about Doris.

SIDNEY: What Doris?

FANNY: Doris! Doris from downstairs. I've been talking to her mother. She likes you, Sidney.

SIDNEY: Who?

FANNY: Her mother! Mrs. Gross. She's crazy about you.

SIDNEY (*not comprehending*): Oh.

FANNY: She says all Doris does is talk about you.

SIDNEY (*worried*): What is she talking about me for?

FANNY: No, nice things. She likes you.

SIDNEY (*amused, laughs incredulously*): Doris? She's thirteen.

FANNY: She'll be fourteen in December. Now listen to me.

SIDNEY: What, Ma?

FANNY: It's all up to you, Sidney, I want you to make up your own mind. But Papa's never going to get off his back again, and after Lucille's wedding we can forget about *her* salary. Mrs. Gross says—being she's a widow, y'know? And with her goiter and everything . . .

SIDNEY: What?

FANNY: If you like Doris—only if you like her—and you would agree to get married—when she's eighteen, about, or seventeen, even—if you would agree to it now, we could have this apartment rent-free. Starting next month.

SIDNEY (*impressed, even astounded*): Forever?

FANNY: Of course. You would be the husband, it would be your house. You'd move downstairs, with that grand piano and the tile shower . . . I even think if you'd agree she'd throw in the three months' back rent that we owe. I wouldn't even be surprised you could take over the bakery.

SIDNEY: The bakery! For God's sake, Mama, I'm a composer!

FANNY: Now listen to me . . .

DORIS *enters and sits on the floor weaving a cat's cradle of string.*

SIDNEY: But how can I be a baker!

FANNY: Sidney, dear, did you ever once look at that girl?

SIDNEY: Why should I look at her!

FANNY (*taking him to the "window"*): Because she's a beauty. I wouldn't have mentioned it otherwise. Look. Look at that nose. Look at her hands. You see those beautiful little white hands? You don't find hands like that everywhere.

SIDNEY: But Ma, listen—if you just leave me alone for July, and if I write one hit song . . . I know I can do it, Mama.

FANNY: Okay. Sidney, we're behind a hundred and eighty dollars. August first we're out on the street. So write a hit, dear. I only hope that four, five years from now you don't accidentally run into Doris Gross somewhere and fall in love with her—after we all died from exposure!

SIDNEY: But Ma, even if I agreed—supposing next year or the year after I meet some other girl and I really like her . . .

FANNY: All right, and supposing you marry *that* girl and a year after you meet another girl you like better—what are you going to do, get married every year? . . . But I only wanted you to know the situation. I'll close the door, everything'll be quiet. Write a big hit, Sidney! (*She exits.*)

SIDNEY *begins to sing "Once in a While"*; DORIS *echoes him timorously. They trade a few lines,* SIDNEY *hesitant and surprised. Then:*

DORIS (*fully confident, ending the song*): ". . . nearest your heart."

SIDNEY (*sits on his heels beside her as she weaves the string*): Gee, you're really terrific at that, Doris.

He stands, she stands, and they shyly walk off together as he slips his hand into hers.

ROBERTSON (*from choral area*): I guess the most shocking thing is what I see from the window of my Riverside Drive apartment. It's Calcutta on the Hudson, thousands of people living in cardboard boxes right next to that beautiful drive. It is like an army encampment down the length of Manhattan Island. At night you see their campfires flickering, and some nights I go down and walk among them. Remarkable, the humor they still have, but of course people still blame themselves rather than the government. But there's never been a society that hasn't had a clock running on it, and you can't help wondering—how long? How long will they stand for this? So now Roosevelt's got in I'm thinking—boy, he'd better move. He'd better move fast. . . . And you can't help it; first thing every night when I get home, I go to the window and look down at those fires, the flames reflecting off the river through the night.

Lights come up on MOE *and* ROSE. MOE, *in a business suit and hat, is just giving her a peck.*

ROSE: Goodbye, darling. This is going to be a good day—I know it!

MOE (*without much conviction*): I think you're right. G'bye. (*He walks, gradually comes to a halt. Much uncertainty and tension as he glances back toward his house and then looks down to think.*)

LEE *enters, and* ROSE *gives him a farewell kiss. He wears a mackinaw. She hands him a lunch bag.*

ROSE: Don't squeeze it, I put in some cookies. . . . And listen—it doesn't mean you can *never* go to college.

LEE: Oh, I don't mind Ma. Anyway, I like it around machines. I'm lucky I got the job!

ROSE: All the years we had so much, and now when you need it—

LEE (*cutting her off*): See ya!

He leaves her; she exits. He walks and is startled by MOE *standing there.*

I thought you left a long time ago!

MOE: I'll walk you a way.

He doesn't bother explaining, simply walks beside LEE, *but at a much slower pace than* LEE *took before.* LEE *feels his unusual tension but can only glance over at him with growing apprehension and puzzlement. Finally* MOE *speaks.*

Good job?

LEE: It's okay. I couldn't believe they picked me!

MOE (*nodding*): Good.

> *They walk on in silence, weaving all over the stage, the tension growing as* LEE *keeps glancing at* MOE, *who continuously stares down and ahead as they proceed. At last* MOE *halts and takes a deep breath.*

How much money've you got, Lee?

LEE (*completely taken aback*): . . . money have I got?

MOE (*indicating Lee's pockets*): I mean right now.

LEE: Oh! Well, about . . . (*he takes out change*) . . . thirty-five cents. I'm okay.

MOE: . . . Could I have a quarter? . . . So I can get downtown.

LEE (*pauses an instant, astonished*): Oh, sure, Pa! (*He quickly searches his pockets again.*)

MOE: You got your lunch—I'll need a hotdog later.

LEE (*handing him a quarter*): It's okay. I have a dollar in my drawer. . . . Should I . . . (*He starts to go back.*)

MOE: No, don't go back. (*He proceeds to walk again.*) Don't, ah . . . mention it, heh?

LEE: Oh, no!

MOE: She worries.

LEE: I know. (*To audience*): We went down to the subway together, and it was hard to look at one another. So we pretended that nothing had happened. (*They come to a halt and sit, as though on a subway.*) But something had. . . . It was like I'd started to support my *father*! And why that should have made me feel so happy, I don't know, but it did! And to cheer him up I began to talk, and before I knew it I was inventing a fantastic future! I said I'd be going to college in no more than a year, at most two; and that I'd straighten out my mind and become an A student; and then I'd not only get a job on a newspaper, but I'd have my own column, no less! By the time we got to Forty-second Street, the Depression was practically over! (*He laughs.*) And in a funny way it *was*— (*He touches his breast*) —in here . . . even though I knew we had a long bad time ahead of us. And so, like most people, I waited with that crazy kind of expectation that comes when there is no hope, waited for the dream to come back from wherever it had gone to hide.

A voice from the theatre sings the end of "In New York City, You Really Got to Know Your Line," or similar song.

END OF ACT ONE

ACT TWO

ROSE, *at the piano, has her hands suspended over the keyboard as the band pianist plays. She starts singing "He Loves and She Loves," then breaks off.*

ROSE: But this piano is not leaving this house. Jewelry, yes, but nobody hocks this dear, darling piano. (*She "plays" and sings more of the song.*) The crazy ideas people get. Mr. Warsaw on our block, to make a little money he started a racetrack in his kitchen, with cockroaches. Keeps them in matchboxes with their names written on—Alvin, Murray, Irving . . . They bet nickels, dimes. (*She picks up some sheet music.*) Oh, what a show, that *Funny Face.* (*She sings the opening of "'SWonderful."*) The years go by and you don't get to see a show and Brooklyn drifts further and further into the Atlantic; Manhattan becomes a foreign country, and a year can go by without ever going there. (*She sings more of "'SWonderful."*) Wherever you look there's a contest; Kellogg's, Post Toasties, win five thousand, win ten thousand. I guess I ought to try, but the winners are always in Indiana somehow. I only pray to God our health holds up, because one filling and you've got to lower the thermostat for a month. Sing! (*She sings the opening of "Do-Do-Do What You Done-Done-Done Before."*) I must go to the library—I must start taking out some good books again; I must stop getting so stupid. I don't see anything, I don't hear anything except money, money, money . . . (*She "plays" Schumann. Fadeout.*)

ROBERTSON (*from choral area*): Looking back, of course, you can see there were two sides to it—with the banks foreclosing right and left, I picked up some first-class properties for a song. I made more money in the thirties than ever before, or since. But I knew a generation was coming of age who would never feel this sense of opportunity.

LEE: After a lot of jobs and saving, I did get to the university, and it was a quiet island in the stream. Two pairs of socks and a shirt, plus a good shirt and a mackinaw, and maybe a part-time job in the library, and you could live like a king and never see cash. So there was a distinct reluctance to graduate into that world out there . . . where you knew nobody wanted you.

JOE, RALPH, *and* RUDY *gather in graduation caps and gowns.*

Joey! Is it possible?

JOE: What?

LEE: You're a dentist!

RALPH: Well, I hope things are better when you get out, Lee.

LEE: You decide what to do?

RALPH: There's supposed to be a small aircraft plant still working in Louisville . . .

LEE: Too bad you picked propellers for a specialty.

RALPH: Oh, they'll make airplanes again—soon as there's a war.

LEE: How could there be another war?

JOE: Long as there's capitalism, baby.

RALPH: There'll always be war, y'know, according to the Bible. But if not, I'll probably go into the ministry.

LEE: I never knew you were religious.

RALPH: I'm sort of religious. They pay pretty good, you know, and you get your house and a clothing allowance . . .

JOE (*comes to* LEE, *extending his hand in farewell*): Don't forget to read Karl Marx, Lee. And if you're ever in the neighborhood with a toothache, look me up. I'll keep an eye out for your byline.

LEE: Oh, I don't expect a newspaper job—papers are closing all over the place. Drop me a card if you open an office.

JOE: It'll probably be in my girl's father's basement. He promised to dig the floor out deeper so I can stand up . . .

LEE: What about equipment?

JOE: I figure two, three years I'll be able to open, if I can make a down payment on a used drill. Come by, I'll put back those teeth Ohio State knocked out.

LEE: I sure will! . . . So long, Rudy!

RUDY: Oh, you might still be seeing me around next semester.

JOE: You staying on campus?

RUDY: I might for the sake of my root canals. If I just take one university course I'm still entitled to the Health Service— could get my canals finished.

LEE: You mean there's a course in the Lit School you haven't taken?

RUDY: Yeah, I just found out about it. Roman Band Instruments.

JOE (*laughs*): You're kiddin'!

RUDY: No, in the Classics Department. Roman Band Instruments. (*He pulls his cheek back.*) See, I've still got three big ones to go on this side.

Laughter.

Well, if you really face it, where am I running? Chicago's loaded with anthropologists. Here, the university's like my mother—I've got free rent, wash dishes for my meals, get my teeth fixed, and God knows, I might pick up the paper one morning and there's an ad: "Help Wanted: Handsome young college graduate, good teeth, must be thoroughly acquainted with Roman band instruments"!

Laughter. They sing "Love and a Dime" accompanied by Rudy on banjo.

RALPH: I'll keep looking for your byline anyway, Lee.

LEE: No, I doubt it; but I might angle a job on a Mississippi paddleboat when I get out.

RUDY: They still run those?

LEE: Yeah, there's a few. I'd like to retrace Mark Twain's voyages.

RUDY: Well, if you run into Huckleberry Finn—

LEE: I'll give him your regards.

Laughing, RALPH *and* RUDY *start out.*

RALPH: Beat Ohio State, kid!

JOE (*alone with* LEE, *gives him a clenched-fist salute*): So long, Lee.

LEE (*returning the salute*): So long, Joe! (*With fist still clenched, he mimes pulling a whistle, dreamily imagining the Mississippi.*) Toot! Toot!

He moves to a point, taking off his shirt, with which he wipes sweat off his face and neck as in the distance we hear a paddleboat's engines and wheel in water and whistle. LEE *stares out as though from a deck. He is seeing aloud.*

How scary and beautiful the Mississippi is. How do they manage to live? Every town has a bank boarded up, and all those skinny men sitting on the sidewalks with their backs against the storefronts. It's all stopped; like a magic spell. And the anger, the anger . . . when they were handing out meat and beans to the hungry, and the maggots wriggling out of the beef, and that man pointing his rifle at the butcher demanding the fresh meat the government had paid him to hand out . . . How could this have happened, is Marx right? Paper says twelve executives in tobacco made more than thirty thousand farmers who raised it. How long can they accept this? The anger has a smell, it hangs in the air wherever people gather. . . . Fights suddenly break out and simmer down. Is this when revolution comes? And why not? How would Mark Twain write what I have seen? Armed deputies guarding cornfields and whole families sitting beside the road, staring at that food which nobody can buy and is rotting on the stalk. It's insane. (*He exits.*)

ROSE (*from choral area, to audience*): But how can he become a sportswriter if he's a Communist?

> JOE, *carrying a large basket of flowers, crosses downstage to the sound effect of a subway train passing. He sings a verse of "In New York City, You Really Got to Know Your Line." He then breaks upstage and enters Isabel's apartment. She is in bed.*

ISABEL: Hello, honey.

JOE: Could you start calling me Joe? It's less anonymous. (*He starts removing his shoes and top pair of trousers.*)

ISABEL: Whatever you say. You couldn't come later—hey, could you? I was just ready to go to sleep, I had a long night.

JOE: I can't, I gotta catch the girls before they get to the office, they like a flower on the desk. And later I'm too tired.

ISABEL: Ain't that uncomfortable—hey? Two pairs of pants?

JOE: It's freezing cold on that subway platform. The wind's like the Gobi Desert. The only problem is when you go out to pee it takes twice as long.

ISABEL: Sellin' books too—hey?

JOE: No, I'm reading that. Trying not to forget the English language. All I hear all day is shit, fuck, and piss. I keep meaning

to tell you, Isabel, it's so relaxing to talk to you, especially
when you don't understand about seventy percent of what
I'm saying.

ISABEL (*laughs, complimented*): Hey!

JOE (*takes her hand*): In here I feel my sanity coming back, to a
certain extent. Down in the subway all day I really wonder
maybe some kind of lunacy is taking over. People stand there
waiting for the train, talking to themselves. And loud, with
gestures. And the number of men who come up behind me
and feel my ass. (*With a sudden drop in all his confidence*):
What scares me, see, is that I'm getting too nervous to pick
up a drill—if I ever get to practice dentistry at all, I mean.
The city . . . is crazy! A hunchback yesterday suddenly comes
up to me . . . apropos of nothing . . . and he starts yelling, "You will not find one word about democracy in the
Constitution, this is a Christian Republic!" Nobody laughed.
The Nazi swastika is blossoming out all over the toothpaste
ads. And it seems to be getting worse—there's a guy on
Forty-eighth Street and Eighth Avenue selling two hotdogs
for seven cents! What can he make?

ISABEL: Two for *seven*? Jesus.

JOE: I tell you I get the feeling every once in a while that some
bright morning millions of people are going to come pouring out of the buildings and just . . . I don't know
what . . . kill each other? Or only the Jews? Or just maybe
sit down on the sidewalk and cry. (*Now he turns to her and
starts to climb up on the bed beside her.*)

ISABEL (*looking at the book*): It's about families?

JOE: No, it's just called *The Origin of the Family, Private Property, and the State*, by Friedrich Engels. Marxism.

ISABEL: What's that?

JOE (*his head resting on hers, his hand holding her breast*): Well,
it's the idea that all of our relationships are basically ruled
by money.

ISABEL (*nodding, as she well knows*): Oh, right—hey, yeah.

JOE (*raising himself up*): No, it's not what you think . . .

ISABEL: It's a whole book about *that*?

JOE: It's about socialism, where the girls would all have jobs so
they wouldn't have to do this, see.

ISABEL: Oh! But what would the guys do, though?

JOE (*flustered*): Well . . . like for instance if I had money to open an office I would probably get married very soon.

ISABEL: Yeah, but I get married guys. (*Brightly*): And I even get two dentists that you brought me . . . Bernie and Allan? . . . and they've got offices, too.

JOE: You don't understand. . . . He shows that underneath our ideals it's all economics between people, and it shouldn't be.

ISABEL: What should it be?

JOE: Well, you know, like . . . love.

ISABEL: Ohhh! Well that's nice—hey. You think I could read it?

JOE: Sure, try. . . . I'd like your reaction. I like you early, Isabel, you look so fresh. Gives me an illusion.

ISABEL: I'm sorry if I'm tired.

JOE (*kisses her, trying to rouse himself*): Say . . . did Bernie finish the filling?

ISABEL: Yeah, he polished yesterday.

JOE: Open.

She opens her mouth.

Bernie's good. (*Proudly*): I told you, we were in the same class. Say hello when you see him again.

ISABEL: He said he might come after five. He always says to give you his best.

JOE: Give him my best, too.

ISABEL (*readying herself on the bed*): Till you I never had so many dentists.

He lowers onto her. Fadeout.

Lights come up on BANKS, *suspended in a painter's cradle, painting a bridge. He sings a verse of "Backbone and Navel Doin' the Belly Rub," then speaks.*

BANKS: Sometimes you'd get the rumor they be hirin' in New York City so we all went to New York City but they wasn't nothin' in New York City, so we'd head for Lima, Ohio; Detroit, Michigan; Duluth, Minnesota; or go down Baltimore; or Alabama or Decatur, Illinois. But anywhere you'd go was always a jail. I was in a chain gang in Georgia pickin' cotton for four months just for hoboin' on a train. That was 1935 in the summertime, and when they set me free they give me thirty-five cents. Yes, sir, thirty-five cents is what they give me, pickin' cotton four months against my will. (*Pause.*) Yeah, I still hear that train, that long low whistle, *whoo-ooo!*

Fadeout. Lights come up on ROSE, *seated at the piano, playing. Two moving men in work aprons enter, raise her hands from the piano, and push the piano off.*

ROSE (*half to herself, furious*): How stupid it all is. How stupid! (*Prayerfully*): Oh, my dear Lee, wherever you are—believe in something. Anything. But believe. (*She turns and moves off with the piano stool, as though emptied out.*)

Lights come up on LEE, *sitting at an open-air café table under a tree.* ISAAC, *the black proprietor, brings him a watermelon slice.*

ISAAC: You been workin' the river long? I ain't seen you before, have I?

LEE: No, this is my first trip down the river, I'm from New York City—I'm just kind of looking around the country, talking to people.

ISAAC: What you lookin' around *for?*

LEE: Nothing—just trying to figure out what's happening. Ever hear of Mark Twain?

ISAAC: He from round here?

LEE: Well, long time ago, yeah. He was a story writer.

ISAAC: Unh-unh. I ain't seen him around here. You ask at the post office?

LEE: No, but I might. I'm kind of surprised you can get fifteen cents a slice down here these days.

ISAAC: Ohhh—white folks *loves* watermelon. Things as bad as this up North?

LEE: Probably not quite. I sure wouldn't want to be one of you people down here . . . specially with this Depression.

ISAAC: Mister, if I was to tell you the God's honest truth, the main thing about the Depression is that it finally hit the white people. 'Cause us folks never had nothin' else. (*He looks offstage.*) Well, now—here come the big man.

LEE: He trouble?

ISAAC: He's anything he wants to be, mister—he the sheriff.

The SHERIFF *enters, wearing holstered gun, boots, badge, broad-*

brimmed hat, carrying something wrapped under his arm. He silently stares at LEE, *then turns to* ISAAC.

SHERIFF: Isaac?

ISAAC: Yes, sir.

SHERIFF (*after a moment*): Sit down.

ISAAC: Yes, sir.

He sits on a counter stool; he is intensely curious about the Sheriff's calling on him but not frightened. The SHERIFF *seems to be having trouble with Lee's strange presence.*

LEE (*makes a nervous half-apology*): I'm off the boat. (*He indicates offstage.*)

SHERIFF: You don't bother me, boy—relax.

He sits and sets his package down and turns with gravity to ISAAC. LEE *makes himself unobtrusive and observes in silence.*

ISAAC: Looks like rain.

SHERIFF (*preoccupied*): Mm . . . hard to know.

ISAAC: Yeah . . . always is in Louisiana. (*Pause.*) Anything I can do for you, Sheriff?

SHERIFF: Read the papers today?

ISAAC: I couldn't read my name if an air-o-plane wrote it in the sky, Sheriff, you know that.

SHERIFF: My second cousin Allan? The state senator?

ISAAC: Uh-huh?

SHERIFF: The governor just appointed him. He's gonna help run the state police.

ISAAC: Uh-huh?

SHERIFF: He's comin' down to dinner Friday night over to my house. Bringin' his wife and two daughters. I'm gonna try to talk to Allan about a job on the state police. They still paying the *state* police, see.

ISAAC: Uh-huh. Well, that be nice, won't it.

SHERIFF: Isaac, I like you to cook me up some of that magical fried chicken around six o'clock Friday night. Okay? I'll pick it up.

ISAAC (*noncommittal*): Mm.

SHERIFF: That'd be for . . . let's see . . . (*counts on his fingers*) . . . eight people. My brother and his wife comin' over too, 'cause I aim to give Allan a little spread there, get him talkin' real good, y'know.

ISAAC: Mm.

An embarrassed pause.

SHERIFF: What's that gonna cost me for eight people, Isaac?

ISAAC (*at once*): Ten dollars.

SHERIFF: Ten.

ISAAC (*with a little commiseration*): That's right, Sheriff.

SHERIFF (*slight pause; starts to unwrap radio*): Want to show you something here, Isaac. My radio, see?

ISAAC: Uh-huh. (*He runs his hand over it.*) Play?

SHERIFF: Sure! Plays real good. I give twenty-nine ninety-five for that two years ago.

ISAAC (*looks in the back of it*): I plug it in?

SHERIFF: Go right ahead, sure. You sure painted this place up real nice. Like a real restaurant. You oughta thank the Lord, Isaac.

ISAAC (*takes out the wire and plugs it in*): I sure do. The Lord and fried chicken!

SHERIFF: You know, the county ain't paid nobody at all in three months now . . .

ISAAC: Yeah, I know. Where you switch it on?

SHERIFF: Just turn the knob. There you are. (*He turns it on.*) They're still payin' the *state* police, see. And I figure if I can get Allan to put me on—

Radio music. It is very faint.

ISAAC: Cain't hardly hear it.

SHERIFF (*angrily*): Hell, Isaac, gotta get the aerial out! (*Untangling a wire at the back of the set*): You give me eight fried chicken dinners and I let you hold this for collateral, okay? Here we go now.

The SHERIFF *backs away, stretching out the aerial wire, and Roosevelt's voice suddenly comes on strong. The* SHERIFF *holds still, the wire held high.* LEE *is absorbed.*

ROOSEVELT: Clouds of suspicion, tides of ill-will and intolerance gather darkly in many places. In our own land we enjoy, indeed, a fullness of life . . .

SHERIFF: And nice fat chickens, hear? Don't give me any little old scruffy chickens.

ISAAC (*of Roosevelt*): Who's that talkin'?

ROOSEVELT: . . . greater than that of most nations. But the rush of modern civilization itself has raised for us new difficulties . . .

SHERIFF: Sound like somebody up North.

ISAAC: Hush! (*To* LEE): Hey, that's Roosevelt, ain't it?

LEE: Yes.

ISAAC: Sure! That's the President!

SHERIFF: How about it, we got a deal? Or not?

ISAAC *has his head close to the radio, absorbed.* LEE *comes closer, bends over to listen.*

ROOSEVELT: . . . new problems which must be solved if we are to preserve to the United States the political and economic freedom for which Washington and Jefferson planned and fought. We seek not merely to make government a mechanical implement, but to give it the vibrant personal character that is the embodiment of human charity. We are poor indeed if this nation cannot afford to lift from every recess of American life the dark fear of the unemployed that they are not needed in the world. We cannot afford to accumulate a deficit in the books of human fortitude.

SIDNEY *and* DORIS *enter as lights fade on* LEE, ISAAC, *and the* SHERIFF.

SIDNEY: What's the matter? Boy, you can change quicker than . . .

DORIS (*shaking her head, closing her eyes*): I can't help it, it keeps coming back to me.

SIDNEY: How can you let a dope like Francey bother you like this?

DORIS: Because she's spreading it all over the class! And I still don't understand how you could have said a thing like that.

SIDNEY: Hon . . . all I said was that if we ever got married I would probably live downstairs. Does that mean that that's the reason we'd get married? Francey is just jealous!

DORIS (*deeply hurt*): I just wish you hadn't said that.

SIDNEY: You mean you think I'd do a thing like that for an *apartment*? What must you think of me! . . .

DORIS (*sobs*): It's just that I love you so much! . . .

SIDNEY: If I could only sell a song! Or even pass the post office exam. Then I'd have my own money, and all this garbage would stop.

DORIS: . . . I said I love you, why don't *you* say something?

SIDNEY: I love you, I love you, but I tell ya, you know what I think?

DORIS: What?

SIDNEY: Honestly—I think we ought to talk about seeing other people for a while.

DORIS (*uncomprehending*): What other people?

SIDNEY: Going out. You're still a little young, honey . . . and even at my age, it's probably not a good idea for us if we never even went out with somebody else—

DORIS: Well, who . . . do you want to take out?

SIDNEY: Nobody! . . .

DORIS: Then what do you mean?

SIDNEY: Well, it's not that I *want* to.

DORIS: Yeah, but who?

SIDNEY: Well, I don't know . . . like maybe . . . what's-her-name, Margie Ganz's sister . . .

DORIS (*alarmed*): You mean Esther Ganz with the . . . ? (*She cups her hands to indicate big breasts.*)

SIDNEY: Then *not* her!

DORIS (*hurt*): You want to take out *Esther Ganz*?

SIDNEY: I'm not saying *necessarily*! But . . . for instance, you could go out with Georgie.

DORIS: Which Georgie?

SIDNEY: Georgie Krieger.

DORIS: You're putting me with *Georgie Krieger* and *you* go out with *Esther Ganz*?

SIDNEY: It was only an *example*!

DORIS (*with incredulous distaste*): But Georgie *Krieger*! . . .

SIDNEY: Forget Georgie Krieger! Make it . . . all right, *you* pick somebody, then.

DORIS (*stares, reviewing faces*): Well . . . how about Morris?

SIDNEY (*asking the heart-stopping question*): What Morris? You mean Morris from . . .

DORIS: Yeah, Morris from the shoe store.

SIDNEY (*glimpsing quite a different side of her*): *Really?*

DORIS: Well, didn't he go a year to City College?

SIDNEY: No, he did not, he went one semester—and he *still* walks around with a comb in his pocket. . . . I think maybe we just better wait.

DORIS: I don't know, maybe it would be a good idea . . . at least till I'm a little older . . .

SIDNEY: No, we'll wait, we'll think it over.

DORIS: But you know . . .

SIDNEY (*with high anxiety*): *We'll think it over,* hon! . . .

He goes to the piano, plays a progression. She comes to him, then runs her fingers through his hair.

DORIS: Play "Sittin' Around"?

SIDNEY: It's not any good.

DORIS: What do you mean, it's your greatest! Please!

SIDNEY (*sighs, sings*):
You've got me
Sittin' around
Just watching shadows
On the wall;
You've got me
Sittin' around,
And all my hopes beyond recall;

I want to hear
The words of love,
I want to feel
Your lips on mine,
DORIS:
And know
The days and nights
There in your arms.
SIDNEY and DORIS:
Instead I'm . . .

Sittin' around
And all the world
Is passing by,
You've got me

Sittin' around
Like I was only
Born to cry,

When will I know
The words of love,
Your lips on mine—
Instead of

Sittin' around,
Sittin' around,
Sittin' around . . .

Fadeout. A large crowd emerges from darkness as a row of factory-type lights descend, illuminating rows of benches and scattered chairs. This is an emergency welfare office temporarily set up to handle the flood of desperate people. A WELFARE WORKER *hands each applicant a sheet of paper and then wanders off.*

MOE: I don't understand this. I distinctly read in the paper that anybody wants to work can go direct to WPA and they fix you up with a job.

LEE: They changed it. You can only get a WPA job now if you get on relief first.

MOE (*pointing toward the line*): So this is not the WPA.

LEE: I told you, Pa, this is the relief office.

MOE: Like . . . welfare.

LEE: Look, if it embarrasses you—

MOE: Listen, if it has to be done it has to be done. Now let me go over it again—what do I say?

LEE: You refuse to let me live in the house. We don't get along.

MOE: Why can't you live at home?

LEE: If I can live at home, I don't need relief. That's the rule.

MOE: Okay. So I can't stand the sight of you.

LEE: Right.

MOE: So you live with our friend in a rooming house.

LEE: Correct.

MOE: . . . They're gonna believe that?

LEE: Why not? I've got a few clothes over there.

MOE: All this for twenty-two dollars a week?

LEE (*angering*): What am I going to do? Even old-time newspapermen are out of work. . . . See, if I can get on the WPA Writers Project, at least I'd get experience if a real job comes along. I've explained this a dozen times, Pa, there's nothing complicated.

MOE (*unsatisfied*): I'm just trying to get used to it. All right.

They embrace.

We shouldn't look too friendly, huh?

LEE (*laughs*): That's the idea!

MOE: I don't like you, and you can't stand the sight of me.

LEE: That's it! (*He laughs.*)

MOE (*to the air, with mock outrage*): So he laughs.

They move into the crowd and find seats in front of RYAN, *the supervisor, at a desk.*

RYAN: Matthew R. Bush!

A very dignified man of forty-five rises, crosses, and follows RYAN *out.*

MOE: Looks like a butler.

LEE: Probably was.

MOE (*shakes his head mournfully*): Hmm!

ROBERTSON (*from choral area*): I did a lot of walking back in those days, and the contrasts were startling. Along the West Side of Manhattan you had eight or ten of the world's greatest ocean liners tied up—I recall the SS *Manhattan*, the *Berengaria*, the *United States*—most of them would never sail again. But at the same time they were putting up the Empire State Building, highest in the world. But with whole streets and avenues of empty stores who would ever rent space in it?

A baby held by GRACE, *a young woman in the back, cries.* MOE *turns to look, then stares ahead.*

MOE: Lee, what'll you do if they give you a pick-and-shovel job?

LEE: I'll take it.

MOE: You'll dig holes in the streets?

LEE: It's no disgrace, Dad.

ROBERTSON: It was incredible to me how long it was lasting. I would never, never have believed we could not recover before this. The years were passing, a whole generation was withering in the best years of its life . . .

The people in the crowd start talking: KAPUSH, *Slavonic, in his late sixties, with a moustache;* DUGAN, *an Irishman;* IRENE, *a middle-aged black woman;* TOLAND, *a cabbie.*

KAPUSH (*with ferocious frustration*): What can you expect from a country that puts a frankfurter on the Supreme Court? Felix the Frankfurter. Look it up.

DUGAN (*from another part of the room*): Get back in the clock, ya cuckoo!

KAPUSH (*turning his body around angrily to face* DUGAN *and jarring* IRENE, *sitting next to him*): Who's talkin' to me!

IRENE: Hey, now, don't mess with me, mister!

DUGAN: Tell him, tell him!

RYAN *rushes in. He is pale, his vest is loaded with pens and pencils, and a sheaf of papers is in his hand. A tired man.*

RYAN: We gonna have another riot, folks? Is that what we're gonna have? Mr. Kapush, I told you three days running now, if you live in Bronx, you've got to apply in Bronx.

KAPUSH: It's all right, I'll wait.

RYAN (*as he passes* DUGAN): Leave him alone, will you? He's a little upset in his mind.

DUGAN: He's a fascist. I seen him down Union Square plenty of times.

IRENE *slams her walking stick down on the table.*

RYAN: Oh, Jesus . . . here we go again.

IRENE: Gettin' on to ten o'clock, Mr. Ryan.

RYAN: I've done the best I can, Irene . . .

IRENE: That's what the good Lord said when he made the jack-ass, but he decided to knuckle down and try harder. People been thrown out on the sidewalk, mattresses, pots and pans, and everything else they own. Right on A Hundred and Thirty-eighth Street. They goin' back in their apartments today or we goin' raise us some real hell.

RYAN: I've got no more appropriations for you till the first of the month, and that's it, Irene.

IRENE: Mr. Ryan, you ain't talkin' to me, you talkin' to Local

Forty-five of the Workers Alliance, and you know what that mean.

DUGAN (*laughs*): Communist Party.

IRENE: That's right, mister, and they don't mess. So why don't you get on your phone and call Washington. And while you're at it, you can remind Mr. Roosevelt that I done swang One Hundred and Thirty-ninth Street for him in the last election, and if he want it swung again he better get crackin'!

RYAN: Holy Jesus.

He hurries away, but LEE *tries to delay him.*

LEE: I was told to bring my father.

RYAN: What?

LEE: Yesterday. You told me to—

RYAN: Get off my back, will ya? (*He hurries out.*)

DUGAN: This country's gonna end up on the top of the trees throwin' coconuts at each other.

MOE (*quietly to* LEE): I hope I can get out by eleven, I got an appointment with a buyer.

TOLAND (*next to* MOE, *with a* Daily News *open in his hands*): Boy, oh, boy, looka this—Helen Hayes gonna put on forty pounds to play Victoria Regina.

MOE: Who's that?

TOLAND: Queen of England.

MOE: She was so fat?

TOLAND: Victoria? Horse. I picked up Helen Hayes when I had my cab. Very small girl. And Adolphe Menjou once—he was small too. I even had Al Smith once, way back before he was governor. He was real small.

MOE: Maybe your cab was large.

TOLAND: What do you mean? I had a regular Ford.

MOE: You lost it?

TOLAND: What're you gonna do? The town is walkin'. I paid five hundred dollars for a new Ford, including bumpers and a spare. But thank God, at least I got into the housing project. It's nice and reasonable.

MOE: What do you pay?

TOLAND: Nineteen fifty a month. It sounds like a lot, but we got three nice rooms—providin' I get a little help here. What's your line?

MOE: I sell on commission right now. I used to have my own business.

TOLAND: Used-ta. Whoever you talk to, "I used-ta." If they don't do something, I tell ya, one of these days this used-ta be a country.

KAPUSH (*exploding*): Ignorance, ignorance! People don't know facts. Greatest public library system in the entire world and nobody goes in but Jews.

MOE (*glancing at him*): Ah-ha.

LEE: What're you, Iroquois?

DUGAN: He's a fascist. I seen him talking on Union Square.

IRENE: Solidarity, folks, black and white together, that's what we gotta have. Join the Workers Alliance, ten cents a month, and you git yourself some solidarity.

KAPUSH: I challenge anybody to find the word democracy in the Constitution. This is a republic! *Demos* is the Greek word for mob.

DUGAN (*imitating the bird*): *Cuckoo!*

KAPUSH: Come to get my money and the bank is closed up! Four thousand dollars up the flue. Thirteen years in hardware, savin' by the week.

DUGAN: Mental diarrhea.

KAPUSH: Mobocracy. Gimme, gimme, gimme, all they know.

DUGAN: So what're *you* doing here?

KAPUSH: Roosevelt was sworn in on a Dutch Bible! (*Silence.*) Anybody know that? (*To* IRENE): Betcha didn't know that, did you?

IRENE: You givin' me a headache, mister . . .

KAPUSH: I got nothin' against colored. Colored never took my store away. Here's my bankbook, see that? Bank of the United States. See that? Four thousand six hundred and ten dollars and thirty-one cents, right? Who's got that money? Savin' thirteen years, by the week. *Who's got my money?*

He has risen to his feet. His fury has turned the moment silent. MATTHEW BUSH *enters and sways.* RYAN *enters.*

RYAN (*calls*): Arthur Clayton!

CLAYTON (*starts toward* RYAN *from the crowd and indicates* BUSH): I think there's something the matter with—

BUSH *collapses on the floor. For a moment no one moves. Then* IRENE *goes to him, bends over him.*

IRENE: Hey. Hey, mister.

LEE *helps him up and sits him in the chair.*

RYAN (*calling*): Myrna, call the ambulance!

IRENE *lightly slaps Bush's cheeks.*

LEE: You all right?
RYAN (*looking around*): Clayton?
CLAYTON: I'm Clayton.
RYAN (*Clayton's form in his hand*): You're not eligible for relief; you've got furniture and valuables, don't you?
CLAYTON: But nothing I could realize anything on.
RYAN: Why not?
IRENE: This man's starvin', Mr. Ryan.
RYAN: What're you, a medical doctor now, Irene? I called the ambulance! Now don't start makin' an issue, will you? (*To* CLAYTON): Is this your address? Gramercy Park South?
CLAYTON (*embarrassed*): That doesn't mean a thing. I haven't really eaten in a few days, actually . . .
RYAN: Where do you get that kind of rent?
CLAYTON: I haven't paid my rent in over eight months . . .
RYAN (*starting away*): Forget it, mister, you got valuables and furniture; you can't—
CLAYTON: I'm very good at figures, I was in brokerage. I thought if I could get anything that required . . . say statistics . . .
IRENE: Grace? You got anything in that bottle?

GRACE, *in a rear row with a baby in her arms, reaches forward with a baby bottle that has an inch of milk at the bottom. She hands the bottle to* IRENE.

GRACE: Ain't much left there . . .
IRENE (*takes nipple off bottle*): Okay, now, open your mouth, mister.

BUSH *gulps the milk.*

There, look at that, see? Man's starvin'!

MOE (*stands, reaching into his pocket*): Here . . . look . . . for God's sake. (*He takes out change and picks out a dime.*) Why don't you send down, get him a bottle of milk?

IRENE (*calls toward a young woman in the back*): Lucy?

LUCY (*coming forward*): Here I am, Irene.

IRENE: Go down the corner, bring back a bottle of milk.

MOE *gives her the dime, and* LUCY *hurries out.*

And a couple of straws, honey! You in bad shape, mister— why'd you wait so long to get on relief?

BUSH: Well . . . I just don't like the idea, you know.

IRENE: Yeah, I know—you a real bourgeoisie. Let me tell you something—

BUSH: I'm a chemist.

IRENE: I believe it, too—you so educated you sooner die than say brother. Now lemme tell you people. (*Addressing the crowd*): Time has come to say brother. My husband pass away and leave me with three small children. No money, no work— I's about ready to stick my head in the cookin' stove. Then the city marshal come and take my chest of drawers, bed, and table, and leave me sittin' on a old orange crate in the middle of the room. And it come over me, mister, come over me to get mean. And I got real mean. Go down in the street and start yellin' and howlin' like a real mean woman. And the people crowd around the marshal truck, and 'fore you know it that marshal turn himself around and go on back downtown empty-handed. And that's when I see it. I see the solidarity, and I start to preach it up and down. 'Cause I got me a stick, and when I start poundin' time with this stick, a whole lot of people starts to march, keepin' time. We shall not be moved, yeah, we shall in no wise be disturbed. Some days I goes to court with my briefcase, raise hell with the judges. Ever time I goes into court the cops commence to holler, "Here comes that old lawyer woman!" But all I got in here is some old newspaper and a bag of cayenne pepper. Case any cop start musclin' me around—that hot pepper, that's hot cayenne pepper. And if the judge happen to be Catholic I got my rosary layin' in there, and I kind of let that crucifix hang out so's they think I'm Catholic too. (*She draws a rosary out of her bag and lets it hang over the side.*)

LUCY (*enters with milk*): Irene!

IRENE: Give it here, Lucy. Now drink it slow, mister. Slow, slow . . .

BUSH *is drinking in sips. People now go back into themselves, read papers, stare ahead.*

RYAN: Lee Baum!

LEE (*hurries to* MOE): Here! Okay, Dad, let's go.

LEE *and* MOE *go to Ryan's desk.*

RYAN: This your father?

MOE: Yes.

RYAN (*to* MOE): Where's he living now?

LEE: I don't live at home because—

RYAN: Let *him* answer. Where's he living, Mr. Baum?

MOE: Well, he . . . he rents a room someplace.

RYAN: You gonna sit there and tell me you won't let him in the house?

MOE (*with great difficulty*): I won't let him in, no.

RYAN: You mean you're the kind of man, if he rang the bell and you opened the door and saw him, you wouldn't let him inside?

MOE: Well, naturally, if he just wants to come in the house—

LEE: I don't want to live there—

RYAN: I don't care what *you* want, fella. (*To* MOE): You will let him into the house, right?

MOE (*stiffening*): . . . I can't stand the sight of him.

RYAN: Why? I saw you both sitting here talking together the last two hours.

MOE: We weren't talking. . . . We were arguing, fighting! . . .

RYAN: Fighting about what?

MOE (*despite himself, growing indignant*): Who can remember? We were fighting, we're always fighting! . . .

RYAN: Look, Mr. Baum . . . you're employed, aren't you?

MOE: I'm employed? Sure I'm employed. Here. (*He holds up the folded* Times.) See? Read it yourself. R. H. Macy, right? Ladies' full-length slip, genuine Japanese silk, hand-embroidered with lace top and trimmings, two ninety-eight. My boss makes four cents on these, I make a tenth of a cent. That's how I'm employed!

RYAN: You'll let him in the house. (*He starts to move.*)

MOE: I will not let him in the house! He . . . he don't believe in anything!

LEE and RYAN *look at* MOE *in surprise.* MOE *himself is caught off balance by his genuine outburst and rushes out.* RYAN *glances at* LEE, *stamps a requisition form, and hands it to him, convinced.* RYAN *exits.*

LEE moves slowly, staring at the form. The welfare clients exit, the row of overhead lights flies out.

Lights come up on ROBERTSON.

ROBERTSON: Then and now, you have to wonder what really held it all together, and maybe it was simply the Future: the people were still not ready to give it up. Like a God, it was always worshiped among us, and they could not yet turn their backs on it. Maybe it's that simple. Because from any objective viewpoint, I don't understand why it held.

The people from the relief office form a line as on a subway platform. JOE *comes behind the line singing and offering flowers from a basket. There is the sound of an approaching train, its windows flashing light.* JOE *throws himself under it: a squeal of brakes. The crowd sings "In New York City, You Really Got to Know Your Line," one by one taking the lyrics, ending in a chorus. Fadeout.*

Lights come up on EDIE. LEE *is in spotlight.*

LEE (*to audience*): Any girl with an apartment of her own was beautiful. She was one of the dialogue writers for the *Superman* comic strip. (*To her*): Edie, can I sleep here tonight?

EDIE: Oh, hi, Lee—yeah, sure. Let me finish and I'll put a sheet on the couch. If you have any laundry, throw it in the sink. I'm going to wash later.

He stands behind her as she works.

This is going to be a terrific sequence.

LEE: It's amazing to me how you can keep your mind on it.

EDIE: He's also a great teacher of class consciousness.

LEE: Superman?

EDIE: He stands for justice!

LEE: Oh! You mean under capitalism you can't . . .

EDIE: Sure! The implications are terrific. (*She works lovingly for a moment.*)

LEE: Y'know, you're beautiful when you talk about politics, your face lights up.

EDIE (*smiling*): Don't be such a bourgeois horse's ass. I'll get your sheet. (*She starts up.*)

LEE: Could I sleep in your bed tonight? I don't know what it is lately—I'm always lonely. Are you?

EDIE: Sometimes. But a person doesn't have to go to bed with people to be connected to mankind.

LEE: You're right. I'm ashamed of myself.

EDIE: Why don't you join the Party?

LEE: I guess I don't want to ruin my chances; I want to be a sportswriter.

EDIE: You could write for the *Worker* sports page.

LEE: The *Daily Worker* sports page?

EDIE: Then help improve it! Why are you so defeatist, hundreds of people are joining the Party every week.

LEE: I don't know why, maybe I'm too skeptical—or cynical. Like . . . when I was in Flint, Michigan, during the sit-down strike. Thought I'd write a feature story . . . all those thousands of men barricaded in the GM plant, the wives hoisting food up to the windows in baskets. It was like the French Revolution. But then I got to talk to them as individuals, and the prejudice! The ignorance! . . . In the Ford plant there was damn near a race war because some of the Negro workers didn't want to join the strike. . . . It was murderous.

EDIE: Well, they're still backward, I know that.

LEE: No, they're normal. I really wonder if there's going to be time to save this country from itself. You ever wonder that? You do, don't you.

EDIE (*fighting the temptation to give way*): You really want my answer?

LEE: Yes.

EDIE: We're picketing the Italian consulate tomorrow, to protest Mussolini sending Italian troops to the Spanish Civil War. Come! *Do* something! You love Hemingway so much, read what he just said—"One man alone is no fucking good." As decadent as he is, even *he's* learning.

LEE: Really, your face gets so beautiful when you . . .

EDIE: Anyone can be beautiful if what they believe is beautiful! I believe in my comrades. I believe in the Soviet Union. I believe in the working class and the peace of the whole world when socialism comes . . .

LEE: Boy, you really are wonderful. Look, now that I'm on relief can I take you out to dinner? I'll pay, I mean.

EDIE (*smiles*): Why must you pay for me, just because I'm a woman?

LEE: Right! I forgot about that.

EDIE (*working*): I've got to finish this panel. . . . I'll make up the couch in a minute. . . . What about the Writer's Project, you getting on?

LEE: I think so; they're putting people on to write a WPA Guide, it's going to be a detailed history of every section of the country. I might get sent up to the Lake Champlain district. Imagine? They're interviewing direct descendants of the soldiers who fought the Battle of Fort Ticonderoga. Ethan Allen and the Green Mountain Boys?

EDIE: Oh, yes! They beat the British up there.

LEE: It's a wonderful project; 'cause people really don't know their own history.

EDIE (*with longing and certainty*): When there's socialism everyone will.

LEE (*leaning over to look at her work*): Why don't you have Superman get laid? Or married even.

EDIE: He's much too busy.

He comes closer to kiss her; she starts to respond, then rejects.

What are you *doing*?

LEE: When you say the word "socialism" your face gets so beautiful . . .

EDIE: You're totally cynical, aren't you.

LEE: Why!

EDIE: You pretend to have a serious conversation when all you want is to jump into my bed; it's the same attitude you have to the auto workers . . .

LEE: I can't see the connection between the auto workers and . . . !

EDIE (*once again on firm ground*): Everything is connected! I have to ask you to leave!

LEE: Edie!

EDIE: You are not a good person! (*She bursts into tears and rushes off.*)

LEE (*alone, full of remorse*): She's right, too! (*He exits.*)

GRANDPA *enters from choral area, sits with his newspaper, and is immediately immersed. Then Rose's niece* LUCILLE, *her sister* FANNY, *and* DORIS, *who wears a bathrobe, carry folding chairs and seat themselves around a table.* LUCILLE *deals cards. Now* ROSE *begins speaking within the choral area, and as she speaks, she moves onto the stage proper.*

ROSE: That endless Brooklyn July! That little wooden house baking in the heat. (*She enters the stage.*) I never smelled an owl, but in July the smell of that attic crept down the stairs, and to me it smelled as dry and dusty as an owl. (*She surveys the women staring at their cards.*) From Coney Island to Brooklyn Bridge, how many thousands of women waited out the afternoons dreaming at their cards and praying for luck? Ah, luck, luck . . .

DORIS: Sidney's finishing a beautiful new song, Aunt Rose.

ROSE (*sitting at the table, taking up her hand of cards*): Maybe this one'll be lucky for you. Why are you always in a bathrobe?

DORIS: I'm only half a block away.

ROSE: But you're so young! Why don't you get dressed and leave the block once in a while?

FANNY (*smugly*): All my girls love it home, too.

ROSE: It's you, isn't it?

FANNY (*brushing dandruff off her bosom and nervously examining her cards*): I'm trying to make up my mind.

ROSE: Concentrate. Forget your dandruff for a minute.

FANNY: It wasn't dandruff, it was a thread.

ROSE: Her dandruff is threads. It's an obsession.

LUCILLE: I didn't tell you; this spring she actually called me and my sisters to come and spend the day cleaning her house.

FANNY: What's so terrible! We used to have the most marvelous times the four of us cleaning the house . . . (*Suddenly*): It's turning into an oven in here.

LUCILLE: I'm going to faint.

ROSE: Don't faint, all the windows are open in the back of the house. We're supposed to be away.

FANNY: But there's no draft. . . . For Papa's sake . . .

LUCILLE: Why couldn't you be away and you left a window open? . . . Just don't answer the door.

ROSE: I don't want to take the chance. This one is a professional collector, I've seen him do it; if a window's open he tries to listen. They're merciless. . . . I sent Stanislaus for lemons, we'll have cold lemonade. Play.

FANNY: I can't believe they'd actually evict you, Rose.

ROSE: You can't? Wake up, Fanny. It's a bank—may they choke after the fortune of money we kept in there all those years! Ask them for two hundred dollars now and they . . . (*Tears start to her eyes.*)

FANNY: Rose, dear, come on—something'll happen, you'll see. Moe's got to find something soon, a man so well known.

LUCILLE: Couldn't he ask his mother for a little?

ROSE: His mother says there's a Depression going on. Meantime you can go blind from the diamonds on her fingers. Which he gave her! The rottenness of people! I tell you, the next time I start believing in anybody or anything I hope my tongue is cut out!

DORIS: Maybe Lee should come back and help out?

ROSE: Never! Lee is going to think his own thoughts and face the facts. He's got nothing to learn from us. Let him help himself.

LUCILLE: But to take up Communism—

ROSE: Lucille, what do you know about it? What does anybody know about it? The newspapers? The newspapers said the stock market will never come down again.

LUCILLE: But they're against God, Aunt Rose.

ROSE: I'm overjoyed you got so religious, Lucille, but please for God's sake don't tell me about it again!

FANNY (*rises, starts to leave*): I'll be right down.

ROSE: Now she's going to pee on her finger for luck.

FANNY: All right! So I won't go! (*She returns to her chair.*) And I wasn't going to pee on my finger!

ROSE: So what're we playing—cards or statues?

DORIS *sits looking at her cards, full of confusion.*

GRANDPA (*putting down his paper*): Why do they need this election?

ROSE: What do you mean, why they need this election?

GRANDPA: But everybody knows Roosevelt is going to win again. I still think he's too radical, but to go through another election is a terrible waste of money.

ROSE: What are you talking about, Papa—it's four years, they have to have an election.

GRANDPA: Why! If they decided to make him king . . .

ROSE: King!

FANNY (*pointing at* GRANDPA, *agreeing and laughing*): Believe me!

GRANDPA: If he was king he wouldn't have to waste all his time making these ridiculous election speeches, and maybe he could start to improve things!

ROSE: If I had a stamp I'd write him a letter.

GRANDPA: He could be another Kaiser Franz Joseph. Then after he dies you can have all the elections you want.

ROSE (*to* DORIS): Are you playing cards or hatching an egg?

DORIS (*startled*): Oh, it's my turn? (*She turns a card.*) All right; here!

ROSE: Hallelujah.

She plays a card. It is LUCILLE*'s turn; she plays.*

Did you lose weight?

LUCILLE: I've been trying. I'm thinking of going back to the carnival.

DORIS *quickly throws an anxious look toward* GRANDPA, *who is oblivious, reading.*

FANNY (*indicating* GRANDPA *secretively*): You better not mention . . .

LUCILLE: He doesn't have to know, and anyway I would never dance anymore; I'd only assist the magician and tell a few jokes. They're talking about starting up again in Jersey.

ROSE: Herby can't find anything.

LUCILLE: He's going out of his mind, Aunt Rose.

ROSE: God Almighty. So what's it going to be, Fanny?

FANNY (*feeling rushed, studying her cards*): One second! Just let me figure it out.

ROSE: When they passed around the brains this family was out to lunch.

FANNY: It's so hot in here I can't think!

ROSE: Play! I can't open the window. I'm not going to face that man again. He has merciless eyes.

STANISLAUS, *a middle-aged seaman in T-shirt and dungarees, enters through the front door.*

You come in the front door? The mortgage man could come today!

STANISLAUS: I forgot! I didn't see anybody on the street, though. (*He lifts bag of lemons.*) Fresh lemonade coming up on deck. I starched all the napkins. (*He exits.*)

ROSE: Starched all the napkins . . . they're cracking like matzos. I feel like doing a fortune. (*She takes out another deck of cards, lays out a fortune.*)

LUCILLE: I don't know, Aunt Rose, is it so smart to let this man live with you?

DORIS: I would never dare! How can you sleep at night with a strange man in the cellar?

FANNY: Nooo! Stanislaus is a gentleman. (*To* ROSE): I think he's a little bit a fairy, isn't he?

ROSE: I hope!

They all laugh.

For God's sake, Fanny, play the queen of clubs!

FANNY: How did you know I had the queen of clubs!

ROSE: Because I'm smart, I voted for Herbert Hoover. I see what's been played, dear, so I figure what's left.

FANNY (*to* GRANDPA, *who continues reading*): She's a marvel, she's got Grandma's head.

ROSE: Huh! Look at this fortune.

FANNY: Here, I'm playing. (*She plays a card.*)

ROSE (*continuing to lay out the fortune*): I always feed the vagrants on the porch, but Stanislaus, when I hand him a plate of soup he says he wants to wash the windows before he eats. *Before!* That I never heard. I nearly fell over. Go ahead, Doris, it's you.

DORIS (*desperately trying to be quick*): I know just what to do, wait a minute.

The women freeze, study their cards; ROSE *now faces front. She is quickly isolated in light.*

ROSE: When I went to school we had to sit like soldiers, with backs straight and our hands clasped on the desk; things were supposed to be upright. When the navy came up the Hudson River, you cried it was so beautiful. You even cried when they shot the Czar of Russia. He was also beautiful. President Warren Gamaliel Harding, another beauty. Mayor James J. Walker smiled like an angel, what a nose, and those tiny feet. Richard Whitney, president of the Stock Exchange, a handsome, upright man. I could name a hundred from the rotogravure! Who could know that these upright handsome men would either turn out to be crooks who would land in jail or ignoramuses? What is left to believe? The bathroom. I lock myself in and hold on to the faucets so I shouldn't scream. At my husband, my mother-in-law, at God knows what until they take me away . . . (*Returning to the fortune, and with deep anxiety*): What the hell did I lay out here? What is this?

Light returns to normal.

DORIS: "Gray's Elegy in a Country Churchyard."

ROSE: What?

FANNY (*touching her arm worriedly*): Why don't you lie down, Rose? . . .

ROSE: Lie down? . . . Why? (*To* DORIS): What Gray's "Elegy"? What are you . . .

STANISLAUS *enters rapidly, wearing a waist-length white starched waiter's jacket, a tray expertly on his shoulder, with glasses and rolled napkins.* ROSE *shows alarm as she lays a card down on the fortune.*

STANISLAUS: It's a braw bricht moonlicht nicht tonicht—that's Scotch.

FANNY: How does he get those napkins to stand up!

ROSE (*under terrific tension, tears her gaze from the cards she laid out*): What's the jacket suddenly?

The women watch her tensely.

STANISLAUS (*saluting*): SS *Manhattan*. Captain's steward at your service.

ROSE: Will you stop this nightmare? Take the jacket off. What're you talking about, captain's steward? Who are you?

STANISLAUS: I was captain's personal steward, but they're not sailing the *Manhattan* anymore. Served J. Pierpont Morgan, John D. Rockefeller, Enrico Caruso, lousy tipper, Lionel—

ROSE (*very suspiciously*): Bring in the cookies, please.

He picks up the pitcher to pour the lemonade.

Thank you, I'll pour it. Go, please.

She doesn't look at him; he goes out. In the silence she picks up the pitcher, tilts it, but her hand is shaking, and FANNY *takes the pitcher.*

FANNY: Rose, dear, come upstairs . . .

ROSE: How does he look to you?

FANNY: Why? He looks very nice.

LUCILLE: He certainly keeps the house beautiful, Aunt Rose, it's like a ship.

ROSE: He's a liar, though; anything comes into his head, he says; what am I believing him for? What the hell got into me? You can tell he's full of shit, and he comes to the door, a perfect stranger, and I let him sleep in the cellar!

LUCILLE: *Shhh!*

STANISLAUS *enters with a plate of cookies, in T-shirt again, determinedly.*

ROSE: Listen, Stanislaus . . . (*She stands.*)

STANISLAUS (*senses his imminent dismissal*): I go down to the ship chandler store tomorrow, get some special white paint, paint the whole outside the house. I got plenty of credit, don't cost you.

ROSE: I thought it over, you understand?

STANISLAUS (*with a desperate smile*): I borrow big ladder from the hardware store. And I gonna make nice curtains for the cellar windows. Taste the lemonade, I learn that in Spanish submarine. Excuse me, gotta clean out the icebox. (*He gets himself out.*)

FANNY: I think he's very sweet, Rose. . . . Here . . . (*She offers a glass of lemonade.*)

LUCILLE: Don't worry about that mortgage man, Aunt Rose, it's after five, they don't come after five . . .

ROSE (*caught in her uncertainty*): He seems sweet to you?

GRANDPA (*putting the paper down*): What Lee ought to do . . . Rosie?

ROSE: Hah?

GRANDPA: Lee should go to Russia.

The sisters and LUCILLE *turn to him in surprise.*

ROSE (*incredulous, frightened*): To Russia?

GRANDPA: In Russia they need everything; whereas here, y'see, they don't need anything, so therefore, there's no work.

ROSE (*with an edge of hysteria*): Five minutes ago Roosevelt is too radical, and now you're sending Lee to Russia?

GRANDPA: That's different. Look what it says here . . . a hundred thousand American people applying for jobs in Russia. Look, it says it. So if Lee would go over there and open up a nice chain of clothing stores—

ROSE: Papa! You're such a big anti-Communist . . . and you don't know the government owns everything in Russia?

GRANDPA: Yeah, but not the *stores*.

ROSE: Of course the stores!

GRANDPA: The *stores* they own?

ROSE: Yes!

GRANDPA: Them bastards.

ROSE (*to* LUCILLE): I'll go out of my mind here . . .

DORIS: So who wrote it?

ROSE: Wrote what?

DORIS: "Gray's Elegy in a Country Churchyard." It was a fifteen-dollar question on the radio yesterday, but you were out. I ran to call you.

ROSE (*suppressing a scream*): Who wrote Gray's "Elegy in a Country Churchyard"?

DORIS: By the time I got back to the radio it was another question.

ROSE: Doris, darling . . . (*Slowly*): Gray's "Elegy in a—

FANNY *laughs.*

What are you laughing at, do you know?
FANNY (*pleasantly*): How would I know?
LUCILLE: Is it Gray?

ROSE *looks at her, an enormous sadness in her eyes. With a certain timidity,* LUCILLE *goes on:*

Well, it says "Gray's Elegy," right?
DORIS: How could it be Gray? That's the title!

ROSE *is staring ahead in an agony of despair.*

FANNY: What's the matter, Rose?
DORIS: Well, what'd I say?
FANNY: Rose, what's the matter?
LUCILLE: You all right?
FANNY (*really alarmed, turning Rose's face to her*): What is the matter!

ROSE *bursts into tears.* FANNY *gets up and embraces her, almost crying herself.*

Oh, Rosie, please . . . don't. It'll get better, something's got to happen . . .

A sound from the front door galvanizes them. A man calls from off: "Hello?"

DORIS (*pointing*): There's some—
ROSE (*her hands flying up in fury*): Sssh! (*Whispering*): I'll go upstairs. I'm not home.

She starts to go; MOE *enters.*

DORIS (*laughing*): It's Uncle Moe!
MOE: What's the excitement?
ROSE (*going to him*): Oh, thank God, I thought it was the mortgage man. You're home early.

He stands watching her.

FANNY: Let's go, come on.

They begin to clear table of tray, lemonade, glasses, etc.

MOE (*looking into Rose's face*): You crying?

LUCILLE: How's it in the city?

ROSE: Go out the back, huh?

MOE: The city is murder.

FANNY: Will you get your bills together? I'm going downtown tomorrow. I'll save you the postage.

ROSE: Take a shower. Why are you so pale?

LUCILLE: Bye-bye, Uncle Moe.

MOE: Bye, girls.

DORIS (*as she exits with* FANNY *and* LUCILLE): I must ask him how he made that lemonade . . .

They are gone, MOE *is staring at some vision, quite calm, but absorbed.*

ROSE: You . . . sell anything? . . . No, heh?

He shakes his head negatively—but that is not what he is thinking about.

Here . . . (*She gets a glass from the table.*) Come drink, it's cold.

He takes it but doesn't drink.

MOE: You're hysterical every night.

ROSE: No, I'm all right. It's just all so stupid, and every once in a while I can't . . . I can't . . . (*She is holding her head.*)

MOE: The thing is . . . You listening to me?

ROSE: What? (*Suddenly aware of her father's pressure on* MOE, *she turns and goes quickly to him.*) Go on the back porch, Papa, huh? It's shady there now . . . (*She hands him a glass of lemonade.*)

GRANDPA: But the man'll see me.

ROSE: It's all right, he won't come so late, and Moe is here. Go . . .

GRANDPA starts to go.

. . . and why don't you put on your other glasses, they're much cooler.

GRANDPA is gone. She returns to MOE.

Yes, dear. What. What's going to be?

MOE: We are going to be all right.

ROSE: Why?

MOE: Because we are. So this nervousness every night is unnecessary, and I wish to God—

ROSE (*indicating the table and the cards spread out*): It's just a fortune. I . . . I started to do a fortune, and I saw . . . a young man. The death of a young man.

MOE (*struck*): You don't say.

ROSE (*sensing*): Why?

He turns front, amazed, frightened.

Why'd you say that?

MOE: Nothing . . .

ROSE: Is Lee . . .

MOE: Will you cut that out—

ROSE: Tell me!

MOE: I saw a terrible thing on the subway. Somebody jumped in front of a train.

ROSE: Aaaahhh—again! My God! You saw him?

MOE: No, a few minutes before I got there. Seems he was a very young man. One of the policemen was holding a great big basket of flowers. Seems he was trying to sell flowers.

ROSE: I saw it! (*Her spine tingling, she points down at the cards.*) Look, it's there! That's death! I'm going to write Lee to come home immediately. I want you to put in that you want him home.

MOE: I have nothing for him, Rose; how can I make him come home?

ROSE (*screaming and weeping*): Then go to your mother and stand up like a man to her . . . instead of this goddamned fool! (*She weeps.*)

MOE (*stung, nearly beaten, not facing her*): This can't . . . it can't go on forever, Rose, a country can't just die!

She goes on weeping; he cries out in pain.

Will you stop? I'm trying! God Almighty, I am trying!

The doorbell rings. They start with shock. GRANDPA *enters, hurrying, pointing.*

GRANDPA: Rose—
ROSE: *Ssssh!*

The bell rings again. MOE *presses stiffened fingers against his temple, his eyes averted in humiliation.* ROSE *whispers:*

God in heaven . . . make him go away!

The bell rings again. MOE*'s head is bent, his hand quivering as it grips his forehead.*

Oh, dear God, give our new President the strength, and the wisdom . . .

Door knock, a little more insistent.

. . . give Mr. Roosevelt the way to help us . . .

Door knock.

Oh, my God, help our dear country . . . and the people! . . .

Door knock. Fadeout.

Lights come up on company as the distant sound of a fight crowd is heard and a clanging bell signals the end of a round. SIDNEY *enters in a guard's uniform; he is watching* LEE, *who enters smoking a cigar stub, wearing a raincoat, finishing some notes on a pad, his hat tipped back on his head.*

SIDNEY: Good fight tonight, Mr. Baum.
LEE (*hardly glancing at him*): Huh? Yeah, pretty good.

SIDNEY *looks on, amused, as* LEE *slowly passes before him, scribbling away.*

As BANKS *speaks,* SOLDIERS *appear and repeat italicized words after him.*

BANKS: When the *war* came I was so *glad* when I got in the *army*. A man could be *killed* anytime at all on those trains, but with that uniform on I said, "Now I am safe."
SIDNEY: Hey!
LEE: Huh? (*Now he recognizes* SIDNEY.) Sidney!

SIDNEY: Boy, you're some cousin. I'm looking straight at you and no recognito! I'm chief of security here.

BANKS: I felt proud to salute and look around and see all the *good soldiers* of the United States. I was a good *soldier too*, and got five battle stars.

Other SOLDIERS *repeat, "Five, five, five."*

LEE: You still on the block?

SIDNEY: Sure. Say, you know who'd have loved to have seen you again? Lou Charney.

LEE: Charney?

RALPH: Hundred yard dash—you and him used to trot to school together . . .

LEE: Oh, Lou, sure! How is he!

SIDNEY: He's dead. Got it in Italy.

BANKS: Yeah, I seen all kinds of war—including the kind they calls . . .

COMPANY: . . . peace.

Four soldiers sing the beginning of "We're in the Money."

SIDNEY: And you knew Georgie Rosen got killed, didn't you?

LEE: Georgie Rosen.

RALPH: Little Georgie.

SIDNEY: Sold you his racing bike.

RALPH: That got stolen.

LEE: Yes, yes! God—Georgie too.

COMPANY (*whispering*): Korea.

RALPH: Lot of wars on that block.

One actor sings the first verse of "The Times They Are A-Changin'."

SIDNEY: Oh, yeah—Lou Charney's kid was in *Vietnam.*

The company says "Vietnam" with SIDNEY.

Still and all, it's a great country, huh?

LEE: Why do you say that?

SIDNEY: Well, all the crime and divorce and whatnot. But one thing about people like us, you live though the worst, you know the difference between bad and *bad.*

BANKS: One time I was hoboin' through that high country—
the Dakotas, Montana—I come to the monument for General Custer's last stand, Little Big Horn. And I wrote my
name on it, yes, sir. For the memories; just for the note; so
my name will be up there forever. Yes, sir . . .

SIDNEY: But I look back at it all now, and I don't know about
you, but it seems it was friendlier. Am I right?

LEE: I'm not sure it was friendlier. Maybe people just cared
more.

SIDNEY (*with* IRENE *singing "I Want to Be Happy" under his
speech*): Like the songs, I mean—you listen to a thirties song,
and most of them are so happy, and still—you could cry.

BANKS: But I still hear that train sometimes; still hear that long
low whistle. Yes, sir, I still hear that train . . . *whoo-ooo!*

LEE: You still writing songs?

SIDNEY: Sure! I had a couple published.

RALPH: Still waiting for the big break?

SIDNEY: I got a new one now, though—love you to hear it. I'm
calling it "A Moon of My Own." I don't know what happened, I'm sitting on the back porch and suddenly it came
to me—"A Moon of My Own." I ran in and told Doris, she
could hardly sleep all night.

DORIS *quietly sings under the following speeches: ". . . and
know the days and nights there in your arms. Instead I'm sittin' around . . ."*

LEE: How's Doris, are you still . . .

SIDNEY: Oh, very much so. In fact, we were just saying we're
practically the only ones we know didn't get divorced.

LEE: Did I hear your mother died?

SIDNEY: Yep, Fanny's gone. I was sorry to hear about Aunt
Rose, and Moe.

LEE (*over "Life Is Just a Bowl of Cherries" music*): After all these
years I still can't settle with myself about my mother. In her
own crazy way she was so much like the country.

ROSE *sings the first line of "Life Is Just a Bowl of Cherries."
Through the rest of Lee's speech, she sings the next four lines.*

There was nothing she believed that she didn't also believe
the opposite. (ROSE *sings.*) She'd sit down on the subway

next to a black man (ROSE *sings*) and in a couple of minutes
she had him asking her advice (ROSE *sings*) about the most
intimate things in his life. (ROSE *sings*.) Then, maybe a
day later—

LEE and ROSE: "Did you hear! They say the colored are moving in!"

LEE: Or she'd lament her fate as a woman—

ROSE and LEE: "I was born twenty years too soon!"

ROSE: They treat a woman like a cow, fill her up with a baby
and lock her in for the rest of her life.

LEE: But then she'd warn me, "Watch out for women—when
they're not stupid, they're full of deceit." I'd come home
and give her a real bath of radical idealism, and she was ready
to storm the barricades; by evening she'd fallen in love again
with the Prince of Wales. She was so like the country; money
obsessed her, but what she really longed for was some kind
of height where she could stand and see out and around and
breathe in the air of her own free life. With all her defeats
she believed to the end that the world was meant to be better. . . . I don't know; all I know for sure is that whenever
I think of her, I always end up—with this headful of life!

ROSE (*calls, in a ghostly, remote way*): Sing!

Alternating lines, LEE *and* ROSE *sing "Life Is Just a Bowl of
Cherries." The whole company takes up the song in a soft, long-
lost tonality.* ROBERTSON *moves forward, the music continuing
underneath.*

ROBERTSON: There were moments when the word "revolution" was not rhetorical.

TED QUINN *steps forward.*

QUINN: Roosevelt saved them; came up at the right minute
and pulled the miracle.

ROBERTSON: Up to a point; but what really got us out of it was
the war.

QUINN: Roosevelt gave them back their belief in the country.
The government belonged to them again!

ROBERTSON: Well, I'll give you that.

QUINN: Of course you will, you're not a damned fool. The return of that belief is what saved the United States, no more, no less!

ROBERTSON: I think that's putting it a little too . . .

QUINN (*cutting him off and throwing up his hands*): That's it! . . . God, how I love that music!

He breaks into his soft-shoe dance as the singing grows louder. He gestures for the audience to join in, and the company does so as well as the chorus swells . . .

END

THE POOSIDIN'S RESIGNATION

FRAGMENT

(*At the back of the stage two gigantic barred gates hang shut, the gates of a furnace whose flames we can see within. To the left and right stand the symbols of the Religion: elements of a tank, a rocket, gigantic aspects of great trucks, the upthrust wing of a bomber.*

Music underlies the following silent action.

On the left is a Crowd of Parents and their Sons. Some have Daughters as well. Some hold onto the hand of a Son, some stand proudly with them, a few have brought food in baskets for the Sons to eat. They are orderly, waiting, their main attention focused across the stage, past the mouth of the furnace toward the Priests' Area.

Three Priests, assisted by Acolytes, listen to the heartbeats of three Youths, laying them down to do various tests, causing them to run in place, open mouths, take blood samples, etc.

Soldiers with rifles stand on the periphery, on guard.

Now the Chief Priest appears. He is middle-aged, carries an open, thick book. He is flanked by his Assistants. He walks with pious authority, and as he approaches the Priests' Area, the three Youths are prodded to their feet and stand straight in a line before him.)

CHIEF PRIEST: Adondi nyla donda dadoola. Adondi nyla karash. Adondi nyla forever. Do you?
YOUTHS: Do!
CHIEF PRIEST: Adondi nyla freedom. Adondi nyla security.
YOUTHS: Do!
CHIEF PRIEST: Flemmmm!

(*He gestures toward the furnace. The gates swing open. The Youths are started toward it by two Soldiers. Two pairs of Parents and one Mother alone come out of the crowd and join the Youths. The three Mothers kiss the Youths. The Fathers stand manfully and shake their sons' hands. The three Youths move*

499

toward the furnace when one of them halts, turns back to his Mother in an attitude of pleading. His Mother is outraged.)

MOTHER: Adondi nyla donda dadoola!

(She points toward the furnace where the other two Youths wait. Her son glances fearfully toward them and back to her.)

Shame nyla! Shame! Shame nyla!

(She pushes him in a gesture of disgust, and he goes with head hanging to join the other two. They take his hands and the three walk into the furnace, disappearing into the fire.

MUSIC: *A strong upsurge of patriotic, aggressive sound.*
CHORUS: *The Parents and Youths celebrating the burning of the three Youths. This lasts fifteen seconds.)*

CHORUS: Forever! Freedom! Nyla dadoola, dadooli, dadoolum! Security! Nyla! All of it is beautiful, tiful, tiful!

Silence.

(Another Mother steps out of the crowd with her son. She is ecstatic as she moves with him toward the Priests' Area.)

MOTHER *(singing)*: I give him, my only child, my only son.
   Take my boy, my one and only!
CHIEF PRIEST *(blessing her)*: Surely this is ramadala, surely this is haugenbaum,
   Surely this is ochen rizhni, surely this
   Is glorious!
CHORUS: Glory! Us! Us! Glory! Gloryous. Us. Us.

(They press their Sons toward the Priests' Area, kissing them in quick farewell, waving to them.)

Glory, glory, glory, glory, Us! Us! Us!

(The Priests are quickly processing the new Youths who are undressed and sent toward the furnace where they stand in a military line, in ranks, facing the fire, ready to enter.)

CHORUS *(praising the undressed ranks, their music is lyrical and full of elevated feeling as they wave goodbye)*:
   Save us, our sons, oh save us soon,

CHIEF PRIEST: Nyla dadoola the country, the god,
CHORUS: The country, the god, the name,
CHIEF PRIEST: Save with thy kilibili, save with thy kil.
ALL: Save, save, save, save!

(*Suddenly a Man rushes out of the Chorus to the ranks, pulls out his Son and embracing him turns in fright and anger to the Chorus and Chief Priest.*)

ALL: Rawrah! rawrah!
MAN: I love him.
ALL: Rawrah!
MAN:

I have been through the fire, myself.
I don't understand.
I don't understand. Why the fire?
Why the kilibil? Why the nyla?
Why the dadooli? I cannot. I cannot!
ALL: Rawrah backalack! Backalack rawrah!
MAN: But why? Why? Why?
WOMAN WHO GAVE ONLY SON: Why! I gave my only, why not you?
ALL: Clap! Clap-clap!
WOMAN WHO . . . : Why moon, why stars, why, why, why—?

(*Lyrically*)

I know as my boy burns that my womb
Has been Presidentially blessed
When otherwise I was lonely and alone.
Why would these things happen
If this had not been glorious?
MAN: But . . . why?

(*He rushes to the crowd of Parents whose sons have still to be taken.*)

Why? Why? It was not always!
Not always!

(*Soldiers start for him.*)

Say why, say why, say why!

(*Soldiers grab him. A Woman in the crowd steps forward.*)

WOMAN: Why!
A MAN (*Stepping out*): Why!

> (*Others in the crowd cry out and a struggle breaks out between those who pull the Youths toward the furnace and those who pull them away. Suddenly a voice bellows out over the PA system.*)

PA: Leeediesn Ginnymin, the Poosidin of the Firelighted Snakes!

> (*Light goes up—a neon, TV-tube steel blue sheen on an elderly man sitting behind a bare desk on which the Greal Seal shows.*)

POOSIDIN (*a pause*): So's not to stand in the way, lo'n behold—

> (*Slight pause.*)

I ask the prayerful attunshn of my fellow citizens
In this dynasty. Fourscore and seven inspirations
Ago, I, your elected Poosidin, laminated
By incredulous landslide, reverberated
From both slimy coasts, aclimained and rubricked,
I raised the shield before the innocent Chicago
By repulsion of attack on our Navel off Indochinery.
Thus and thus alone, preeminently thus
The fire got lighted up. And thus and thus alone
The God began incinderin' our neares' and deares'.

> (*Slight pause.*)

Now we are engaged in a great Civil War,
Whether this nation or any nation can long endure
Such brutal onlaung, such desecrational onsult
Against indepucinary small fry who want nothing more
Than their own indepundn shoppin' centers,
Their own Swiss, their own baby sinners,
Their own accounts receivable—to live, my fellow
Religionists, to live like younee meenee.
Is all. Okee.

> (*Slight pause. Poosidin-elect steps up beside him.*)

I have tried, I have tried and tired,
To avoid, to aye void, but every great Poosidin
Has his crosspatch to bear, his war. No
Great Poosidin can be great without great unimies.

Every great Poosidin have light his fire
And burn up the younguns. Lookee Wilsm
Addling up the casualties at Chateau Thierry;
Lookee Rosevum hit them Nazos in the clitoris;
Lookee Trumulum firin' up his Nagasaki crematorium;
Lookee Kelody matchin' eyeballs with the Kruschabich—
All great because all in service to the holy,
To that fire. Great nations make great sacrifices,
Great Poosidins know when to strike the Zippo. Okee.

(*Slight pause.*)

Now this fellow asks "Why?" Now let us reason
Together. The reason I'm leavin' is, I'm great.
Now I belong to the pages, to the keeprs of the flame.
I can do no more. I have lit the fire, and God's
Hands I have kept toasty. Nyla dadooli, dadooli
Dadoolum—I step aside, confident
That I have kept this nation's hole;
Now let my successor enter in. Okee. . .

(*Turns to Poosidin-elect.*)

Bring them together; keep the fate,
Make them comfortable. Above all,
Tell 'em why.
POOSIDENT-ELECT (*takes the chair, leans his head back. Two
makeup men paint his face white. He faces front, lit blue*):
Firsh, as your new Poosidin—if I may—
I should like to extress my gratilube for you cowfidunce
In me. I premised in my campaign an honoral
Peace. I feel strongly the respansionality which
You have lorded upon me to put out the fire,
To lay down the kilibili and take up our true hobby,
Which is highwaybuilding and devotional. Our young men
Broil, lamentation smokes families low and high,
And we can say truly—Never ask for whom the Baal dulls,
It dulls for tea. I want that absoloonly clure.

(*Slight pause.*)

Now, as we all know, there are individuals who ask,
Why? Why must the Billy go blowing up the flue?

He has that right, sacredly and unemotionally—
His right to ask respectfully no one humidifies.
So now, pocket the ball and listen;
Put down the ticker tape and dwell;
Close that refrigerator, family father;
Sister, come out now, your hair is dry enough.
Junior, leave off that dribbling
And come home, your typical mother waits
Before my face. As follows.

(*Slight pause.*)

What, my fellow denizens, what is fire—?
We must at long last speak of the trembling fundametals.
Fire is the naturalistic consubstantiation
Of the molecules. Long before men—or ladies,
Antedating the first since Zippo, the initial oyster,
Fish, salad oil or primitive combustion Cadillac—
There it dangled hovering above the wave and the rock,
That holy smog foretelling the five continents,
One of which we officially occupy. Anyone who thinks
    about it
Must find it very moving. And some of us still do.
I believe most of us. Yes, all across this lamb,
Quietly, politely, respectfully, the great majorisy,
Regardless of class or religious affliction,
Small businessmen, little housewives, tiny workers,
Wounded veterans on the golf course uncomplainingly
Losing their balls—all these know in their bones
That a fire that consumes ten men or a hundred
Is not the fire that takes ten thousand,
And the fire that takes ten thousand is not
The fire that smelts the hundreds of thousands,
And that fire, in all deliberation, cometh not
From the hand of man. Those who keep the fate
Know that whatever in this world kills
Enough people has earned the respect of the living.

(*Slight pause.*)

That is my plam; I ask for your prayers
That with the help of Almighty Gog, we will extinguish.

To all doubters I say, with my old dean of men,
Flaunt not audorothy, bleiben zie ruhig,
Keep thy headlights burning, until the enemy
Underlies the firmness of our porpoise
And the everlasting rightness of our claws.
I premise you once again, the very first moment
When we can find our honor, the fire goes out.

(*Light blinks out on him, irising to a pinpoint as on a TV tube, as Chorus of Parents marches about shouting,*)

CHORUS:
Clap. Clap.
Clap-clap-clap.
Clap.
Clap-clap!

THE ARCHBISHOP'S CEILING

CHARACTERS

ADRIAN
MAYA
MARCUS
IRINA
SIGMUND

ACT ONE

Some time ago.

A capital in Europe; the sitting room in the former residence of the archbishop.

Judging by the depth of the casement around the window at right, the walls must be two feet thick. The room has weight and power, its contents chaotic and sensuous. Decoration is early baroque.

The ceiling is first seen: in high relief the Four Winds, cheeks swelling, and cherubim, darkened unevenly by soot and age.

Light is from a few lamps of every style, from a contemporary bridge lamp to something that looks like an electrified hookah, but the impression of a dark, overcrowded room remains; the walls absorb light.

A grand piano, scarved; a large blue vase on the floor under it.

Unhung paintings, immense and dark, leaning against a wall, in heavy gilt frames.

Objects of dull brass not recently polished.

Two or three long, dark carved chests topped with tasseled rose-colored cushions.

A long, desiccated brown leather couch with billowing cushions; a stately carved armchair, bolsters, Oriental camel bags.

*A pink velour settee, old picture magazines piled on its foot and underneath—*Life, Stern, Europeo . . .

A Bauhaus chair in chrome and black leather on one of the smallish Persian rugs.

A wide, ornate rolltop desk, probably out of the twenties, with a stuffed falcon or gamebird on its top.

Contemporary books on shelves, local classics in leather.

A sinuous chaise in faded pink.

Layers of chaos.

At up right a doorway to the living quarters.

At left a pair of heavy doors opening on a dimly lit corridor. More chests here, a few piled-up chairs. This corridor leads upstage into darkness (and the unseen stairway down to the front door). The corridor wall is of large unfaced stones.

ADRIAN *is seated on a couch. He is relaxed, in an attitude of waiting, legs crossed, arms spread wide. Now he glances at the doorway to the living quarters, considers for a moment, then lifts up the couch cushions, looking underneath. He stands and goes to a table lamp, tilts it over to look under its base. He looks about again and peers into the open piano.*

He glances up at the doorway again, the examines the ceiling, his head turned straight up. With another glance at the doorway he proceeds to the window at right and looks behind the drapes.

MAYA *enters from the living quarters with a coffeepot and two cups on a tray.*

ADRIAN: Tremendous view of the city from up here.

MAYA: Yes.

ADRIAN: Like seeing it from a plane. Or a dream. (*He turns and approaches the couch, blows on his hands.*)

MAYA: Would you like one of his sweaters? I'm sorry there's no firewood.

ADRIAN: It's warm enough. He doesn't heat this whole house, does he?

MAYA: It's impossible—only this and the bedroom. But the rest of it's never used.

ADRIAN: I forgot how gloomy it is in here.

MAYA: It's a hard room to light. Wherever you put a lamp it makes the rest seem darker. I think there are too many unre-lated objects—the eye can't rest here. (*She laughs, offers a cup; he takes it.*)

ADRIAN: Thanks, Maya. (*He sits.*) Am I interrupting something?

MAYA: I never do anything. When did you arrive?

ADRIAN: Yesterday morning. I was in Paris.

MAYA: And how long do you stay?

ADRIAN: Maybe tomorrow night—I'll see.

MAYA: So short!

ADRIAN: I had a sudden yen to come look around again, see some of the fellows. And you.

MAYA: They gave a visa so quickly?

ADRIAN: Took two days.

MAYA: How wonderful to be famous.

ADRIAN: I was surprised I got one at all—I've attacked them, you know.

MAYA: In the *New York Times*.

ADRIAN: Oh, you read it.

MAYA: Last fall, I believe.

ADRIAN: What'd you think of it?

MAYA: It was interesting. I partly don't remember. I was surprised you did journalism. (*She sips. He waits; nothing more.*)

ADRIAN: I wonder if they care what anybody writes about them anymore.

MAYA: Yes, they do—very much, I think. But I really don't know. . . . How's your wife?

ADRIAN: Ruth? She's good.

MAYA: I liked her. She had a warm heart. I don't like many women.

ADRIAN: You look different.

MAYA: I'm two years older—and three kilos.

ADRIAN: It becomes you.

MAYA: Too fat.

ADRIAN: No . . . *zaftig*. You look creamy. You changed your hairdo.

MAYA: From *Vogue* magazine.

ADRIAN (*laughs*): That so! It's sporty.

MAYA: What brings you back?

ADRIAN: . . . Your English is a thousand percent better. More colloquial.

MAYA: I recite aloud from *Vogue* magazine.

ADRIAN: You're kidding.

MAYA: Seriously. Is all I read anymore.

ADRIAN: Oh, go on with you.

MAYA: Everything in *Vogue* magazine is true.

ADRIAN: Like the girl in pantyhose leaning on her pink Rolls-Royce.

MAYA: Oh, yes, marvelous. One time there was a completely naked girl in a mink coat (*she extends her foot*) and one foot touching the bubble bath. Fantastic imagination. It is the only modern art that really excites me.

ADRIAN *laughs*.

And their expressions, these girls. Absolutely nothing. Like the goddesses of the Greeks—beautiful, stupid, everlasting. This magazine is classical.

ADRIAN: You're not drinking anymore?

MAYA: Only after nine o'clock.

ADRIAN: Good. You seem more organized.

MAYA: Until nine o'clock.

They laugh. MAYA *sips. Slight pause.* ADRIAN *sips.*

ADRIAN: What's Marcus doing in London?

MAYA: His last novel is coming out there just now.

ADRIAN: That's nice. I hear it was a success here.

MAYA: Very much—you say very much or . . . ?

ADRIAN: Very much so.

MAYA: Very much so—what a language!

ADRIAN: You're doing great. You must practice a lot.

MAYA: Only when the English come to visit Marcus, or the Americans. . . . I have his number in London if you . . .

ADRIAN: I have nothing special to say to him.

Pause.

MAYA: You came back for one day?

ADRIAN: Well, three, really. I was in a symposium at the Sorbonne —about the contemporary novel—and it got so pompous I got an urge to sit down again with writers who had actual troubles. So I thought I'd stop by before I went home.

MAYA: You've seen anyone?

ADRIAN: Yes. (*Slight pause. He reaches for a pack of cigarettes.*)

MAYA (*turning to him quickly, to forgive his not elaborating*): It's all right . . .

ADRIAN: I had dinner with Otto and Sigmund and their wives.

MAYA (*surprised*): Oh! You should have called me.

ADRIAN: I tried three times.

MAYA: But Sigmund knows my number.

ADRIAN: You don't live here anymore?

MAYA: Only when Marcus is away. (*She indicates the bedroom doorway.*) He has that tremendous bathtub . . .

ADRIAN: I remember, yes. When'd you break up?

MAYA: I don't remember—eight or nine months, I think. We are friends. Sigmund didn't tell you?

ADRIAN: Nothing. Maybe 'cause his wife was there.

MAYA: Why? I am friends with Elizabeth. . . . So you have a new novel, I suppose.

ADRIAN (*laughs*): You make it sound like I have one every week.

MAYA: I always think you write so easily.

ADRIAN: I always have. But I just abandoned one that I worked on for two years. I'm still trying to get up off the floor. I forgot how easy you are to talk to.

MAYA: But you seem nervous.

ADRIAN: Just sexual tension.

MAYA: You wanted to make love tonight?

ADRIAN: If it came to it, sure. (*He takes her hand.*) In Paris we were in the middle of a discussion of Marxism and surrealism, and I suddenly got this blinding vision of the inside of your thigh . . .

She laughs, immensely pleased.

. . . so I'm here. (*He leans over and kisses her on the lips. Then he stands.*) Incidentally . . . Ruth and I never married, you know.

MAYA (*surprised*): But didn't you call each other . . .

ADRIAN: We never did, really, but we never bothered to correct people. It just made it easier to travel and live together.

MAYA: And now?

ADRIAN: We're apart together. I want my own fireplace, but with a valid plane ticket on the mantel.

MAYA: Well, that's natural, you're a man.

ADRIAN: In my country I'm a child and a son of a bitch. But I'm toying with the idea of growing up—I may ask her to marry me.

MAYA: Is that necessary?

ADRIAN: You're a smart girl—that's exactly the question.

MAYA: Whether it is necessary.

ADRIAN: Not exactly that—few books are necessary; a writer has to write. It's that it became absurd, suddenly. Here I'm laying out motives, characterizations, secret impulses—the whole psychological chess game—when the truth is I'm not sure anymore that I believe in psychology. That anything we think really determines what we're going to do. Or even what we feel. This interest you?

MAYA: You mean anyone can do anything.

ADRIAN: Almost. Damn near. But the point is a little different. Ruth—when we came back from here two years ago—she went into a terrible depression. She'd had them before, but this time she seemed suicidal.

MAYA: Oh, my God. Why?

ADRIAN: Who knows? There were so many reasons there was no reason. She went back to psychiatry. Other therapies . . . nothing worked. Finally, they gave her a pill. (*Slight pause.*) It was miraculous. Turned her completely around. She's full of energy, purpose, optimism. Looks five years younger.

MAYA: A chemical.

ADRIAN: Yes. She didn't have the psychic energy to pull her stockings up. Now they've just made her assistant to the managing editor of her magazine. Does fifty laps a day in the swimming pool— It plugged her in to some . . . some power. And she lit up.

MAYA: She is happy?

ADRIAN: I don't really know—she doesn't talk about her mind anymore, her soul; she talks about what she does. Which is terrific . . .

MAYA: But boring.

ADRIAN: In a way, maybe—but you can't knock it; I really think it saved her life. But what bothers me is something else. (*Slight pause.*) She knows neither more nor less about herself now than when she was trying to die. The interior landscape has not lit up. What has changed is her reaction to power. Before she feared it, now she enjoys it. Before she fled from it, now she seeks it. She got plugged in, and she's come alive.

MAYA: So you have a problem.

ADRIAN: What problem do you think I have?

MAYA: It is unnecessary to write novels anymore.

ADRIAN: God, you're smart—yes. It made me think of Hamlet. Here we are tracking that marvelous maze of his mind, but isn't that slightly ludicrous when one knows that with the right pill his anxiety would dissolve? Christ, he's got everything to live for, heir to the throne, servants, horses—correctly medicated, he could have made a deal with the king and married Ophelia. Or Socrates—instead of hemlock, a swig of lithium and he'd end up the mayor of Athens and live to a hundred. What is lost? Some wisdom, some knowledge found in suffering. But knowledge is power, that's why it's good—so what is wrong with gaining power without having to suffer at all?

MAYA (*with the faintest color of embarrassment, it seems*): You have some reason to ask me this question?

ADRIAN: Yes.

MAYA: Why?

ADRIAN: You have no pills in this country, but power is very sharply defined here. The government makes it very clear that you must snuggle up to power or you will never be happy. (*Slight pause.*) I'm wondering what that does to people, Maya. Does it smooth them all out when they know they must all plug in or their lights go out, regardless of what they think or their personalities?

MAYA: I have never thought of this question. (*She glances at her watch.*) I am having a brandy, will you? (*She stands.*)

ADRIAN (*laughs*): It's nine o'clock?

MAYA: In one minute. (*She goes upstage, pours.*)

ADRIAN: I'd love one; thanks.

MAYA: But I have another mystery. (*She carefully pours two glasses. He waits. She brings him one, remains standing.*) Cheers.

ADRIAN: Cheers. (*They drink.*) Wow—that's good.

MAYA: I prefer whisky, but he locks it up when he is away. (*She sits apart from him.*) I have known intimately so many writers; they all write books condemning people who wish to be successful and praised, who desire some power in life. But I have never met one writer who did not wish to be praised and successful . . . (*she is smiling*) . . . and even powerful. Why do they condemn others who wish the same for themselves?

ADRIAN: Because they understand them so well.

MAYA: For this reason I love *Vogue* magazine.

He laughs.

I am serious. In this magazine everyone is successful. No one has ever apologized because she was beautiful and happy. I believe this magazine. (*She knocks back the remains of her drink, stands, goes toward the liquor upstage.*) Tell me the truth—why have you come back?

ADRIAN (*slight pause*): You think I could write a book about this country?

MAYA (*brings down the bottle, fills his glass*): No, Adrian.

ADRIAN: I'm too American.

MAYA: No, the Russians cannot either. (*She refills her own glass.*) A big country cannot understand small possibilities. When it is raining in Moscow, the sun is shining in Tashkent. Terrible snow in New York, but it is a beautiful day in Arizona. In a small country, when it rains it rains everywhere. (*She sits beside him.*) Why have you come back?

ADRIAN: I've told you.

MAYA: Such a trip—for three days?

ADRIAN: Why not? I'm rich.

MAYA (*examines his face*): You are writing a book about us.

ADRIAN: I've written it, and abandoned it. I want to write it again.

MAYA: About this country.

ADRIAN: About you.

MAYA: But what do you know about me?

ADRIAN: Practically nothing. But something in me knows everything.

MAYA: I am astonished.

ADRIAN: My visa's good through the week—I'll stay if we could spend a lot of time together. Could we? It'd mean a lot to me.

An instant. She gets up, goes to a drawer, and takes out a new pack of cigarettes.

I promise nobody'll recognize you—the character is blonde and very tall and has a flat chest. What do you say?

MAYA: But why?

ADRIAN: I've become obsessed with this place, it's like some Jerusalem for me.

MAYA: But we are of no consequence . . .

ADRIAN: Neither is Jerusalem, but it always has to be saved. Let me stay here with you till Friday. When is Marcus coming back?

MAYA: I never know—not till spring, probably. Is he also in your book?

ADRIAN: In a way. Don't be mad, I swear you won't be recognized.

MAYA: You want me to talk about him?

ADRIAN: I'd like to understand him, that's all.

MAYA: For example?

ADRIAN: Well . . . let's see. You know, I've run into Marcus in three or four countries the past five years; had long talks together, but when I go over them in my mind I realize he's never said anything at all about himself. I like him, always glad to see him, but he's a total blank. For instance, how does he manage to get a house like this?

MAYA: But why not?

ADRIAN: It belongs to the government, doesn't it?

MAYA: It is the same way he gets everything—his trips abroad, his English suits, his girls . . .

ADRIAN: How?

MAYA: He assumes he deserves them.

ADRIAN: But his money—he seems to have quite a lot.

MAYA (*shrugs, underplaying the fact*): He sells his father's books from time to time. He had a medieval collection . . .

ADRIAN: They don't confiscate such things?

MAYA: Perhaps they haven't thought of it. You are the only person I know who thinks everything in a Socialist country is rational.

ADRIAN: In other words, Marcus is a bit of an operator.

MAYA: Marcus? Marcus is above all naive.

ADRIAN: Naive! You don't mean that.

MAYA: No one but a naive man spends six years in prison, Adrian.

ADRIAN: But in that period they were arresting everybody, weren't they?

MAYA: By no means everybody. Marcus is rather a brave man.

ADRIAN: Huh! I had him all wrong. What do you say, let me bring my bag over.

MAYA: You have your book with you?

ADRIAN: No, it's home.

She seems skeptical.

. . . Why would I carry it with me?

She stares at him with the faintest smile.

What's happening?

MAYA: I don't know—what do you think?

She gets up, cradling her glass, walks thoughtfully to another seat, and sits. He gets up and comes to her.

ADRIAN: What is it?

She shakes her head. She seems overwhelmed by some wider sadness. His tone now is uncertain.

Maya?

MAYA: You've been talking to Allison Wolfe?

ADRIAN: I've talked to him, yes.

She stands, moves, comes to a halt.

MAYA: He is still telling that story?

ADRIAN (*slight pause*): I didn't believe him, Maya.

MAYA: He's a vile gossip.

ADRIAN: He's a writer. All writers are gossips.

MAYA: He is a vile man.

ADRIAN: I didn't believe him.

MAYA: What did he say to you?

ADRIAN: Why go into it?

MAYA: I want to know. Please.

ADRIAN: It was ridiculous, I know that. Allison has a puritan imagination.

MAYA: Tell me what he said.

ADRIAN (*slight pause*): Well . . . that you and Marcus . . . look, it's so stupid . . .

MAYA: That we have orgies here?

ADRIAN: . . . Yes.

MAYA: And we bring in young girls?

He is silent.

Adrian?

ADRIAN: That this house is bugged. And you bring in girls to compromise writers with the government.

Pause.

MAYA: You'd better go, I believe.

He is silent for a moment, observing her. She is full.

I'm tired anyway . . . I was just going to bed when you called.

ADRIAN: Maya, if I believed it, would I have talked as I have in here?

MAYA (*smiling*): I don't know, Adrian—would you? Anyway, you have your passport. Why not?

ADRIAN: You know I understand the situation too well to believe Allison. Resistance is impossible anymore. I know the government's got the intellectuals in its pocket, and the few who aren't have stomach ulcers. (*He comes to her, takes her hand.*) I *was* nervous when I came in, but it was sexual tension—I knew we'd be alone.

Her suspicion remains; she slips her hand out of his.

. . . All right, I did think of it. But that's inevitable, isn't it?

MAYA: Yes, of course. (*She moves away again.*)

ADRIAN: It's hard for anyone to know what to believe in this country, you can understand that.

MAYA: Yes. (*She sits, lonely.*)

ADRIAN (*sits beside her*): Forgive me, will you?

MAYA: It is terrible.

ADRIAN: What do you say we forget it?

She looks at him with uncertainty.

What are you doing now?

Slight pause. She stares front for a moment, then takes a breath as though resolving to carry on. Her tone brightens.

MAYA: I write for the radio.

ADRIAN: No plays anymore?

MAYA: I can't work that hard anymore.

ADRIAN: They wouldn't put them on?

MAYA: Oh, they would—I was never political, Adrian.

ADRIAN: You were, my first time . . .

MAYA: Well, everybody was in those days. But it wasn't really politics.

ADRIAN: What, then?

MAYA: I don't know—some sort of illusion that we could be Communists without having enemies. It was a childishness, dancing around the Maypole. It could never last, life is not like that.

ADRIAN: What do you write?

MAYA: I broadcast little anecdotes, amusing things I notice on the streets, the trams. I am on once a week; they have me on Saturday mornings for breakfast. What is it you want to know?

ADRIAN: I'm not interviewing you, Maya.

MAYA (*stands suddenly, between anger and fear*): Why have you come?

ADRIAN (*stands*): I've told you, Maya—I thought maybe I could grab hold of the feeling again.

MAYA: Of what?

ADRIAN: This country, this situation. It escapes me the minute I cross the border. It's like some goddamned demon that only lives here.

MAYA: But we are only people, what is so strange?

ADRIAN: I'll give you an example. It's an hour from Paris here; we sit down to dinner last night in a restaurant, and two plainclothesmen take the next table. It was blatant. Not the slightest attempt to disguise that they were there to intimidate Sigmund and Otto. They kept staring straight at them.

MAYA: But why did he take you to a restaurant? Elizabeth could have given you dinner.

ADRIAN: . . . I don't understand.

MAYA: But Sigmund knows that will happen if he walks about with a famous American writer.

ADRIAN: You're not justifying it? . . .

MAYA: I have not been appointed to justify or condemn anything. (*She laughs.*) And neither has Sigmund. He is an artist, a very great writer, and that is what he should be doing.

ADRIAN: I can't believe what I'm hearing, Maya.

MAYA (*laughs*): But you must, Adrian. You really must believe it.

ADRIAN: You mean it's perfectly all right for two cops to be . . .

MAYA: But that is their *business*. But it is not Sigmund's business to be taunting the government. Do you go about trying to infuriate your CIA, your FBI?

He is silent.

Of course not. You stay home and write your books. Just as the Russian writers stay home and write theirs . . .

ADRIAN: But Sigmund isn't permitted to write his books . . .

MAYA: My God—don't you understand *anything*?

The sudden force of her outburst is mystifying to him. He looks at her, perplexed. She gathers herself.

I'm very tired, Adrian. Perhaps we can meet again before you leave.

ADRIAN: Okay. (*He looks about.*) I forgot where I put my coat . . .

MAYA: I hung it inside.

She goes upstage and out through the doorway. ADRIAN, *his face taut, looks around at the room, up at the ceiling. She returns, hands him the coat.*

You know your way back to the hotel?

ADRIAN: I'll find it. (*He extends his hand, she takes it.*) I'm not as simple as I seem, Maya.

MAYA: I'm sorry I got excited.

ADRIAN: I understand—you don't want him taking risks.

MAYA: Why should he? Especially when things are improving all the time anyway.

ADRIAN: They aren't arresting anybody? . . .

MAYA: Of course not. Sigmund just can't get himself to admit it, so he does these stupid things. One can live as peacefully as anywhere.

ADRIAN (*putting on his coat*): Still, it's not every country where writers keep a novel manuscript behind their fireplace.

MAYA (*stiffening*): Good night.

ADRIAN (*sees her cooled look; slight pause*): Good night, Maya.

(He crosses the room to the double doors at left, and as he opens one . . .)

MAYA: Adrian?

He turns in the doorway.

You didn't really mean that, I hope.

He is silent. She turns to him.

No one keeps manuscripts behind a fireplace anymore. You know that.

ADRIAN *(looks at her for a moment, with irony)*: . . . Right. *(He stands there, hand on the door handle, looking down at the floor, considering. He smiles, turning back to her.)* Funny how life imitates art; the melodrama kept flattening out my characterizations. It's an interesting problem—whether it matters who anyone is or what anyone thinks, when all that counts anymore—is power.

He goes brusquely into the corridor, walks upstage into darkness. She hesitates, then rushes out, closing the door behind her, and calls up the corridor.

MAYA *(a suppressed call)*: Adrian? *(She waits.)* Adrian!

He reappears from the darkness and stands shaking his head, angry and appalled. She has stiffened herself against her confession.

We can talk out here, it is only in the apartment.

ADRIAN: Jesus Christ, Maya.

MAYA: I want you to come inside for a moment—you should not have mentioned Sigmund's manuscript . . .

ADRIAN *(stunned, a look of disgust—adopting her muffled tone)*: Maya . . . how can you do this?

MAYA *(with an indignant note)*: They never knew he has written a novel, how dare you mention it! Did he give it to you?

ADRIAN: My head is spinning, what the hell is this? . . .

MAYA: Did he give it to you?

ADRIAN *(a flare of open anger)*: How can I tell you anything? . . .

MAYA: Come inside. Say that you have sent it to Paris. Come . . . *(She starts for the door.)*

ADRIAN: How the hell would I send it to Paris?

MAYA: They'll be searching his house now, they'll destroy it! You must say that you sent it today with some friend of yours. (*She pulls him by the sleeve.*)

ADRIAN (*freeing himself*): Wait a minute—you mean they were taping us in bed?

MAYA: I don't know. I don't know when it was installed. Please . . . simply say that you have sent the manuscript to Paris. Come. (*She grasps the door handle.*)

ADRIAN (*stepping back from the door*): That's a crime.

She turns to him with a contemptuous look.

Well, it is, isn't it? Anyway, I didn't say it was his book.

MAYA: It was obviously him. Say you have sent it out! You must! (*She opens the door instantly and enters the room, speaking in a relaxed, normal tone.*) . . . Perhaps you'd better stay until the rain lets up. I might go to bed, but why don't you make yourself comfortable?

ADRIAN (*hesitates in the corridor, then enters the room and stands there in silence, glancing about*): . . . All right. Thanks. (*He stands there, silent, in his fear.*)

MAYA: Yes?

ADRIAN: Incidentally— (*He breaks off. A long hiatus. He is internally positioning himself to the situation.*) . . . that manuscript I mentioned.

MAYA: Yes?

ADRIAN: It's in Paris by now. I . . . gave it to a friend who was leaving this morning.

MAYA: Oh?

ADRIAN: Yes. (*Slight pause. It occurs to him suddenly*): A girl.

MAYA (*as though amused*): You already have girls here?

ADRIAN (*starting to grin*): Well, not really—she's a cousin of mine. Actually, a second cousin. Just happened to meet her on the street. All right if I have another brandy?

MAYA: Of course.

ADRIAN (*pours*): I'll be going in a minute. (*He sits in his coat on the edge of a chair with his glass.*) Just let me digest this. This drink, I mean.

She sits on the edge of another chair a distance away.

Quite an atmosphere in this house. I never realized it before.

MAYA: It's so old. Sixteenth century, I think.

ADRIAN: It's so alive—once you're aware of it.

MAYA: They built very well in those days.

ADRIAN (*directly to her*): Incredible. I really didn't believe it.

MAYA: Please go.

ADRIAN: In one minute. Did I dream it, or did it belong to the archbishop?

MAYA: It was his residence.

ADRIAN (*looks up to the ceiling*): That explains the cherubims . . . (*looks at his drink*) . . . and the antonyms.

She stands.

I'm going. This is . . . (*looks around*) . . . this is what I never got into my book—this doubleness. This density with angels hovering overhead. Like power always with you in a room. Like God, in a way. Just tell me—do you ever get where you've forgotten it?

MAYA: I don't really live here anymore.

ADRIAN: Why? You found this style oppressive?

MAYA: I don't hear the rain. Please.

ADRIAN (*stands facing her*): I'm not sure I should, but I'm filling up with sympathy. I'm sorry as hell, Maya.

She is silent.

I could hire a car—let's meet for lunch and take a drive in the country.

MAYA: All right. I'll pick you up at the hotel. (*She starts past him toward the doors.*)

ADRIAN (*takes her hand as she passes*): Thirty seconds. Please. I want to chat. Just to hear myself. (*He moves her to a chair.*) Half a minute . . . just in case you don't show up.

MAYA (*sitting*): Of course I will.

ADRIAN (*clings to her hand, kneebends before her*): I've never asked you before—you ever been married?

She laughs.

Come on, give me a chat. Were you?

MAYA: Never, no.

ADRIAN: And what were your people—middle class?

MAYA: Workers. They died of flu in the war.

ADRIAN: Who brought you up?

MAYA: The nuns.

ADRIAN (*stands; looks around*): . . . Is it always like a performance? Like we're quoting ourselves?

MAYA (*stands*): Goodnight. (*She goes and opens the door.*)

ADRIAN: My God—you poor girl. (*He takes her into his arms and kisses her.*) Maybe I should say—in all fairness—(*leaving her, he addresses the ceiling*) that the city looks much cleaner than my last time. And there's much more stuff in the shops. And the girls have shaved their legs. In fact—(*he turns to her —she is smiling*) this is the truth—I met my dentist in the hotel this morning. He's crazy about this country! (*With a wild underlay of laughter*): Can't get over the way he can walk the streets any hour of the night, which is impossible in New York. Said he'd never felt so relaxed and free in his whole life! And at that very instant, Sigmund and Otto walked into the lobby, and he congratulated them on having such a fine up-and-coming little civilization! (*He suddenly yells at the top of his lungs.*) Forgive me, I scream in New York sometimes.

She is half smiling, alert to him; he comes to the open doorway and grasps her hands.

Goodnight. And if I never see you again . . .

MAYA: I'll be there, why not?

ADRIAN: How do I know? But just in case—I want you to know that I'll never forget you in that real short skirt you wore last time, and the moment when you slung one leg over the arm of the chair. You have a sublime sluttishness, Maya—don't be mad, it's a gift when it's sublime.

She laughs.

How marvelous to see you laugh—come, walk me downstairs. (*He pulls her through the doorway.*)

MAYA: It's too cold out here . . .

ADRIAN (*shuts the door to the room, draws her away from it*): For old times' sake . . .

MAYA: We'll talk tomorrow.

ADRIAN (*with a wild smile, excited eyes*): You're a government agent?

MAYA: What can I say? Will you believe anything?

ADRIAN (*on the verge of laughter*): My spine is tingling. In my book, Maya—I may as well tell you, I've been struggling with my sanity the last ten minutes—in my book I made you an agent who screws all the writers and blackmails them so they'll give up fighting the government. And I abandoned it because I finally decided it was too melodramatic, the characters got lost in the plot. I invented it and I didn't believe it; and I'm standing here looking at you and *I still don't believe it!*

MAYA: Why should you?

ADRIAN (*instantly, pointing into her face*): That's what you say in the book! (*He grasps her hand passionately in both of his.*) Maya, listen—you've got to help me. I believe in your goodness. I don't care what you've done, I still believe that deep inside you're a rebel and you hate this goddamned government. You've got to tell me—I'll stay through the week—we'll talk, and you're going to tell me what goes on in your body, in your head, in this situation.

MAYA: Wait a minute . . .

ADRIAN (*kissing her hands*): Maya, you've made me believe in my book!

She suddenly turns her head. So does he. Then he sees her apprehension.

You expecting somebody?

Voices are heard now from below. She is listening.

Maya?

MAYA (*mystified*): Perhaps some friends of Marcus.

ADRIAN: He gives out the key?

MAYA: Go, please. Goodnight.

She enters the room. He follows her in.

ADRIAN: You need any help?

A man and woman appear from upstage darkness in the corridor.

MAYA: No—no, I am not afraid . . . (*She moves him to the door.*)

ADRIAN: I'll be glad to stay . . . (*He turns, sees the man, who is just approaching the door, a valise in his hand, wearing a raincoat.*) For Christ's sake—it's Marcus!

MARCUS *is older, fifty-eight. He puts down his valise, spreads out his arms.*

MARCUS: Adrian!

Laughter. A girl, beautiful, very young, stands a step behind him as he and ADRIAN *embrace.*

MAYA (*within the room*): Marcus?

MARCUS (*entering the room*): You're here, Maya! This is marvelous.

He gives her a peck. The girl enters, stands there looking around. He turns to ADRIAN.

A friend of yours is parking my car. He'll be delighted to see you.

ADRIAN: Friend of *mine*?

MARCUS: Sigmund.

MAYA: Sigmund?

ADRIAN: Sigmund's *here*?

MARCUS: He's coming up for a drink. We ran into each other at the airport. (*To* MAYA): Is there food? (*To* ADRIAN): You'll stay, won't you? I'll call some people, we can have a party.

ADRIAN: Party? (*Flustered, he glances at* MAYA.) Well . . . yeah, great!

An understanding outburst of laughter between him and MARCUS.

MAYA: There's only some ham. I'm going home. (*She turns to go upstage to the bedroom.*)

MARCUS (*instantly*): Oh, no, Maya! You mustn't. I was going to call you first thing . . . (*Recalling*): Wait, I have something for you. (*He hurriedly zips open a pocket of his valise, takes out a pair of shoes in tissue.*) I had an hour in Frankfurt. Look, dear . . .

He unwraps the tissue. Her face lights. She half unwillingly takes them.

MAYA: Oh, my God.

MARCUS *laughs. She kicks off a shoe and tries one on.*

MARCUS: Right size?
IRINA (*as* MAYA *puts on the other shoe*): Highly beautiful.

MAYA *takes a few steps, watching her feet, then goes to* MARCUS *and gives him a kiss, then looks into his eyes with a faint smile, her longing and hatred.*

MARCUS (*taking out folds of money*): Here, darling . . . ask Mrs. Andrus to prepare something, will you? (*He hands her money.*) Let's have an evening. (*He starts her toward the bedroom door upstage*—) But come and put something on, it's raining. (*—and comes face to face with the girl.*) Oh, excuse me—this is Irina.

MAYA *barely nods, and goes back to pick up her other shoes.*

ADRIAN: I'll go along with you, Maya— (*He reaches for his coat.*)
MARCUS: No, it's only down the street. Irina, this is my good friend Maya.
IRINA: 'Aloo.

MAYA *silently shakes her hand.*

MARCUS: And here is Adrian Wallach. Very important American writer.

MAYA *exits upstage.*

ADRIAN: How do you do?
IRINA: 'Aloo. I see you Danemark.
ADRIAN: She's going to see me in Denmark?
MARCUS: She's Danish. But she speaks a little English.
IRINA (*with forefinger and thumb barely separated, to* ADRIAN): Very small.
ADRIAN: When do you want to meet in Denmark?

MAYA *enters putting on a raincoat.*

MAYA: Sausages?
MARCUS: And maybe some cheese and bread and some fruit. I'll open wine.
IRINA: I see your book.

ADRIAN (*suddenly, as* MAYA *goes for the door*): Wait! I'll walk her there . . .

MAYA *hesitates at the door.*

MARCUS (*grasping* ADRIAN'*s arm, laughing*): No, no, no, you are our guest; please, it's only two doors down. Maya doesn't mind.

MAYA *starts out to the door.* SIGMUND *appears in the corridor, a heavy man shaking out his raincoat. He is in his late forties. She halts before the doorway.*

MAYA (*questioningly, but with a unique respect*): Sigmund.
SIGMUND: Maya.

He kisses the palm of her hand. For a moment they stand facing each other.

MARCUS: Look who we have here, Sigmund!

MAYA *exits up the corridor as* SIGMUND *enters the room.*

SIGMUND: Oh—my friend! (*He embraces* ADRIAN, *laughing, patting his back.*)
ADRIAN: How's it going, Sigmund? (*He grasps Sigmund's hand.*) What a terrific surprise! How's your cold, did you take my pills?
SIGMUND: Yes, thank you. I take pills, vodka, brandy, whisky— now I have only headache. (*With a nod to* IRINA): *Grüss Gott.*

MARCUS *goes and opens a chest, brings bottles and glasses to the marble table.*

IRINA: *Grüss Gott.*
ADRIAN: Oh, you speak German?
IRINA (*with the gesture*): Very small.
MARCUS: Come, help yourselves. (*He takes a key ring out of his valise.*) I have whisky for you, Adrian.
ADRIAN: I'll drink brandy. How about you, Sigmund?
SIGMUND: For me whisky.
MARCUS (*taking out an address book*): I'll call a couple of people, all right?
ADRIAN: *Girls!*

SIGMUND *sits downstage, takes out a cigarette.*

MARCUS: If you feel like it.

ADRIAN (*glancing at* SIGMUND, *who is lighting up*): Maybe better just us.

MARCUS: Sigmund likes a group. (*He picks up his valise.*)

SIGMUND: What you like.

ADRIAN (*to* MARCUS): Well, okay.

MARCUS (*pointing upstage to* IRINA): Loo?

IRINA: Oh, ja!

MARCUS (*holding* IRINA *by the waist and carrying the valise in his free hand as they move upstage; to* SIGMUND): We can talk in the bedroom in a little while. (*He exits with* IRINA.)

ADRIAN: That's a nice piece of Danish.

SIGMUND *draws on his cigarette.* ADRIAN *gets beside him and taps his shoulder;* SIGMUND *turns up to him.* ADRIAN *points to ceiling, then to his own ear.*

Capeesh?

SIGMUND (*turns front, expressionless*): The police have confiscated my manuscript.

ADRIAN (*his hand flying out to grip Sigmund's shoulder*): No! Oh, Jesus—when?

SIGMUND: Now. Tonight.

ADRIAN (*glancing quickly around, to cover their conversation*): He had a record player . . .

SIGMUND (*with a contemptuous wave toward the ceiling*): No—I don't care.

ADRIAN: The last fifteen, twenty minutes, you mean?

SIGMUND: Tonight. They have take it away.

ADRIAN: My God, Sigmund . . .

SIGMUND *turns to him.*

I mentioned something to Maya, but I had no idea it was really . . . (*He breaks off, pointing to the ceiling.*)

SIGMUND: When, you told Maya?

ADRIAN: In the last fifteen minutes or so.

SIGMUND: No—they came earlier—around six o'clock.

ADRIAN: Nearly stopped my heart . . .

SIGMUND: No, I believe they find out for different reason.

ADRIAN: Why?
SIGMUND: I was so happy.

Pause.

ADRIAN: So they figured you'd finished the book?
SIGMUND: I think so. I worked five years on this novel.
ADRIAN: How would they know you were happy?
SIGMUND (*pause; with a certain projection*): In this city, a man
   my age who is happy, attract attention.
ADRIAN: . . . Listen. When I leave tomorrow you can give
   . . . (*He stops himself and glances upstage to the bedroom
   doorway, taking out a notebook and pencil. As he writes, speak-
   ing in a tone of forced relaxation*): Before I leave you've got
   to give me a tour of the Old Roman bath . . .

He shows the page to SIGMUND, *who reads it and looks up at
him.* SIGMUND *shakes his head negatively.*

(*Horrified*): They've got the only . . . ?

SIGMUND *nods positively and turns away.*

(*Appalled*): Sigmund—why?
SIGMUND: I thought would be safer with . . . (*He holds up a
single finger.*)

Pause. ADRIAN *keeps shaking his head.*

ADRIAN (*sotto*): What are you doing here?
SIGMUND: I met him in the airport by accident.
ADRIAN: What were you doing at the airport?
SIGMUND: To tell my wife. She works there.
ADRIAN: I thought she was a chemist.
SIGMUND: She is wife to me—they don't permit her to be
   chemist. She clean the floor, the windows in the airport.
ADRIAN: Oh, Jesus, Sigmund . . . (*Pause.*) Is there anything
   you can do?
SIGMUND: I try.
ADRIAN: Try what?

SIGMUND *thumbs upstage.*

Could he?

SIGMUND *throws up his chin—tremendous influence.*

Would he?

SIGMUND *mimes holding a telephone to his mouth, then indicates the bedroom doorway.*

Really? To help?
SIGMUND: Is possible.
ADRIAN: Can you figure him out?

SIGMUND *extends a hand and rocks it, an expression of uncertainty on his face.*

ADRIAN: And Maya?
SIGMUND (*for a moment makes no answer*): Woman is always complicated.
ADRIAN: You know that they . . . lie a lot.
SIGMUND: Yes. (*Slight pause. He looks now directly into Adrian's eyes.*) Sometimes not.
ADRIAN: You don't think it's time to seriously consider . . . (*He spreads his arms wide like a plane, lifting them forward in a takeoff, then points in a gesture of flight.*) What I mentioned at dinner?

SIGMUND *emphatically shakes his head no while pointing downward—he'll remain here.*

When we leave here I'd like to discuss whether there's really any point in that anymore.

SIGMUND *turns to him.*

I don't know if it was in your papers, but there's a hearing problem all over the world. Especially among the young. Rock music, traffic—modern life is too loud for the human ear—you understand me. The subtler sounds don't get through much anymore.

SIGMUND *faces front, expressionless.*

On top of that there's a widespread tendency in New York, Paris, London, for people to concentrate almost exclusively on shopping.
SIGMUND: I have no illusion.

ADRIAN: I hope not—shopping and entertainment. Sigmund?

> SIGMUND *turns to him, and* ADRIAN *points into his face, then makes a wide gesture to take in the room, the situation.*

Not entertaining. Not on anybody's mind in those cities.
SIGMUND: I know.
ADRIAN: Boring.
SIGMUND: Yes.
ADRIAN: Same old thing. It's the wrong style.
SIGMUND: I know.
ADRIAN: I meant what I said last night; I'd be happy to support—(*He points at* SIGMUND, *who glances at him.*) Until a connection is made with a university. (*He points to himself.*) Guarantee that.

> SIGMUND *nods negatively and spreads both hands—he will stay here.*

We can talk about it later. I'm going to ask you why. I don't understand the point anymore. Not after this.
SIGMUND: You would also if it was your country.
ADRIAN: I doubt it. I would protect my talent. I saw a movie once where they bricked up a man in a wall.

> MARCUS *enters in a robe, opening a whisky bottle.*

MARCUS: A few friends may turn up. (*He sets the whisky bottle on the marble table. To* ADRIAN): Will you excuse us for a few minutes? Sigmund? (*He indicates the bedroom.*)
SIGMUND: I have told him.

> MARCUS *turns to* ADRIAN *with a certain embarrassment.*

ADRIAN: They wouldn't destroy it, would they?

> MARCUS *seems suddenly put upon, and unable to answer.*

Do you know?
MARCUS (*with a gesture toward the bedroom; to* SIGMUND): Shall we?
SIGMUND (*standing*): I would like Adrian to hear.
ADRIAN (*to* MARCUS): Unless you don't feel . . .
MARCUS (*unwillingly*): No—if he wishes, I have no objection.

SIGMUND *sits.*

ADRIAN: If there's anything I can do you'll tell me, will you?

MARCUS (*to* SIGMUND): Does Maya know?

SIGMUND: She was going out.

MARCUS (*as a muted hope for alliance*): I suppose she might as well. But it won't help her getting excited.

SIGMUND: She will be calm, Maya is not foolish.

ADRIAN: Maybe we ought to get into it, Marcus—they wouldn't destroy the book, would they?

MARCUS (*with a fragile laugh*): That's only one of several questions, Adrian—the first thing is to gather our thoughts. Let me get your drink. (*He stands.*)

ADRIAN: I can wait with the drink. Why don't we get into it?

MARCUS: All right. (*He sits again.*)

ADRIAN: Marcus?

MARCUS *turns to him. He points to the ceiling.*

I know.

MARCUS *removes his gaze from* ADRIAN, *a certain mixture of embarrassment and resentment in his face.*

Which doesn't mean I've drawn any conclusions about anyone. I mean that sincerely.

MARCUS: You understand, Adrian, that the scene here is not as uncomplicated as it may look from outside. You must believe me.

ADRIAN: I have no doubt about that, Marcus. But at the same time I wouldn't want to mislead you . . . (*he glances upward*) . . . or anyone else. If that book is destroyed or not returned to him—for whatever it's worth I intend to publicize what I believe is an act of barbarism. This is not some kind of an issue for me—this man is my brother.

Slight pause. MARCUS *is motionless. Then he turns to* ADRIAN *and gestures to him to continue speaking, to amplify.* ADRIAN *looks astonished.* MARCUS *repeats the gesture even more imperatively.*

For example . . . I've always refused to peddle my books on television, but there's at least two national network shows would be glad to have me, and for this I'd go on.

He stops; MARCUS *gestures to continue.*

Just telling the story of this evening would be hot news from coast to coast—including Washington, D.C., where some congressmen could easily decide we shouldn't sign any more trade bills with this country. And so on and so forth.

MARCUS: It was brandy, wasn't it?

ADRIAN (*still amazed*): . . . Thanks, yes.

MARCUS *goes to get the drinks.* ADRIAN *catches Sigmund's eye, but the latter turns forward thoughtfully.* IRINA *enters, heading for the drinks.* MARCUS *brings* ADRIAN *a brandy as she makes herself a drink. In the continuing silence,* MARCUS *returns to the drink table, makes a whisky, and takes it down to* SIGMUND. ADRIAN *turns toward* IRINA, *upstage.*

So how's everything in Denmark?

IRINA (*with a pleasant laugh*): No, no, not everything.

ADRIAN (*thumbing to the ceiling, to* SIGMUND): *That* ought to keep them busy for a while.

MARCUS (*chuckles, sits with his own drink*): Cheers.

ADRIAN: Cheers.

SIGMUND: Cheers.

They drink. IRINA *brings a drink, sits on the floor beside* MARCUS.

MARCUS: Have you been to London this time?

ADRIAN (*pauses slightly, then glances toward* SIGMUND): . . . No. How was London?

MARCUS: It's difficult there. It seems to be an endless strike.

ADRIAN (*waits a moment*): Yes. (*He decides to continue.*) Last time there my British publisher had emphysema and none of the elevators were working. I never heard so many Englishmen talking about a dictatorship before.

MARCUS: They probably have come to the end of it there. It's too bad, but why should evolution spare the English?

ADRIAN: Evolution toward what—fascism?

MARCUS: Or the Arabs taking over more of the economy.

ADRIAN: I can see the bubble pipes in the House of Commons.

Laughter.

The Honorable Member from Damascus.

Laughter. It dies. ADRIAN *thumbs toward* SIGMUND *and then to the ceiling, addressing* MARCUS.

If they decide to give an answer, would it be tonight?

MARCUS (*turns up his palms*): . . . Relax, Adrian. (*He drinks.*) Please.

ADRIAN (*swallows a glassful of brandy*): This stuff really spins the wheels. (*He inhales.*)

MARCUS: It comes from the mountains.

ADRIAN: I feel like I'm on one.

MARCUS: What's New York like now?

ADRIAN: New York? New York is another room in hell. (*He looks up.*) Of course not as architecturally ornate. In fact, a ceiling like this in New York—I can't imagine it lasting so long without some half-crocked writer climbing up and chopping holes in those cherubim.

MARCUS: The ceiling is nearly four hundred years old, you know.

ADRIAN: That makes it less frightful?

MARCUS: In a sense, maybe—for us it has some reassuring associations. When it was made, this city was the cultural capital of Europe—the world, really, this side of China. A lot of art, science, philosophy poured from this place.

ADRIAN: Painful.

MARCUS (*with a conceding shrug*): But on the other hand, the government spends a lot keeping these in repair. It doesn't do to forget that, you know.

SIGMUND: That is true. They are repairing all the angels. It is very good to be an angel in our country.

MARCUS *smiles.*

Yes, we shall have the most perfect angels in the whole world.

MARCUS *laughs.*

But I believe perhaps every government is loving very much the angels, no, Adrian?

ADRIAN: Oh, no doubt about it. But six months under this

particular kind of art and I'd be ready to cut my throat or somebody else's. What do you say we go to a bar, Marcus?

MARCUS (*to* SIGMUND): *Ezlatchu stau?*

SIGMUND (*sighs, then nods*): *Ezlatchu.*

ADRIAN (*to* MARCUS): Where does that put us?

MARCUS: He doesn't mind staying till we've had something to eat. Afterwards, perhaps.

Pause. Silence.

ADRIAN: Let me in on it, Marcus—are we waiting for something?

MARCUS: No, no, I just thought we'd eat before we talked.

ADRIAN: Oh. All right.

IRINA (*patting her stomach*): I to sandwich?

MARCUS (*patting her head like a child's, laughing*): Maya is bringing very soon.

ADRIAN: She's as sweet as sugar, Marcus, where'd you find her?

MARCUS: Her husband is the head of Danish programming for the BBC. *There's* Maya. (*He crosses to the corridor door.*)

ADRIAN: What does he do, loan her out?

MARCUS (*laughs*): No, no, she just wanted to see the country. (*He exits into the corridor.*)

SIGMUND: And Marcus will show her every inch.

ADRIAN (*bursts out laughing*): Oh Sigmund, Sigmund—what a century! (*Sotto*): What the hell is happening?

Men's shouting voices below, MAYA *yelling loudly.* MARCUS *instantly breaks into a run, disappears up the corridor.* ADRIAN *and* SIGMUND *listen. The shouting continues.* SIGMUND *gets up, goes and listens at the door.*

ADRIAN: What is it?

SIGMUND *opens the door, goes into the corridor, listens.*

Who are they?

A door is heard slamming below, silencing the shouts. Pause.

Sigmund?

SIGMUND *comes back into the room.*

What was it?

SIGMUND: Drunken men. They want to see the traitor to the motherland. Enemy of the working class. (*He sits.*)

Pause.

ADRIAN: . . . Come to my hotel.
SIGMUND: Is not possible. Be calm.
ADRIAN: How'd they know you were here?

SIGMUND shrugs, then indicates the ceiling.

They'd call out hoodlums?

SIGMUND turns up his palms, shrugs.

MARCUS and MAYA appear up the corridor. She carries a large tray covered with a white cloth. He has a handkerchief to his cheekbone. He opens the door for her. IRINA stands and clears the marble table for the tray. MARCUS crosses to the upstage right doorway and exits.

SIGMUND stands. MAYA faces him across the room. Long pause.

What happened?
MAYA (*with a gesture toward the food*): Come, poet.

SIGMUND watches her for a moment more, then goes up to the food. She is staring excitedly into his face.

The dark meat is goose.

SIGMUND turns from her to the food.

Adrian?
ADRIAN: I'm not hungry. Thanks.
MAYA (*takes the plate from SIGMUND and loads it heavily*): Beer?
SIGMUND: I have whisky. You changed your haircut?
MAYA: From *Vogue* magazine. You like it?
SIGMUND: Very.
MAYA (*touching his face*): Very much, you say.
SIGMUND: Very, very much.

He returns to his chair with a loaded plate, sits, and proceeds to eat in silence. She pours herself a brandy, sits near him.

MAYA (*to ADRIAN as she watches SIGMUND admiringly*): He

comes from the peasants, you know. That is why he is so beautiful. And he is sly. Like a snake.

Slight pause. SIGMUND *eats.*

What have you done now? (*She indicates below.*) Why have they come?

SIGMUND *pauses in his eating, not looking at her.*

ADRIAN (*after the pause*): The cops took his manuscript tonight.

She inhales sharply with a gasp, nearly crying out. SIGMUND *continues to eat. She goes to him, embraces his head, mouth pressed to his hair. He draws her hands down, apparently warding off her emotion, and continues eating. She moves and sits further away from him, staring ahead, alarmed and angry.* MARCUS *enters from the bedroom, a bandage stuck to his cheekbone.*

MARCUS (*to* ADRIAN): Have you taken something?
ADRIAN: Not just yet, thanks.

MAYA *rises to confront* MARCUS, *but refusing her look, he passes her, a fixed smile on his face, picks up his drink from the marble table, and comes downstage and stands. First he, then* ADRIAN, *then* MAYA, *turn and watch* SIGMUND *eating. He eats thoroughly.* IRINA *is also eating, off by herself.*

Pause.

MARCUS *goes to his chair, sits, and lights a cigarette.* ADRIAN *watches him.*

It's like some kind of continuous crime.
MAYA: You are so rich, Adrian, so famous—why do you make such boring remarks?
ADRIAN: Because I am a bore.
MARCUS: Oh, now, Maya . . .
MAYA (*sharply, to* MARCUS): Where is it not a continuous crime?
SIGMUND: It is the truth. (*To* ADRIAN): Just so, yes. It is a continuous crime.
MAYA (*to the three*): Stupid. Like children. Stupid!
MARCUS: *Sssh*—take something to eat, dear . . .
ADRIAN: Why are we stupid?

Ignoring his question, she goes up to the table, takes a goose wing, and bites into it. Then she comes down and stands eating. After a moment . . .

MARCUS: It's wonderful to see you again, Adrian. What brought you back?

MAYA: He has been talking to Allison Wolfe.

MARCUS (*smiling, to* ADRIAN): Oh, to Allison.

ADRIAN: Yes.

MARCUS: Is he still going around with that story?

MAYA: Yes.

MARCUS (*slight pause*): Adrian . . . you know, I'm sure, that this house has been a sort of gathering place for writers for many years now. And they've always brought their girlfriends, and quite often met girls here they didn't know before. Our first literary magazine after the war was practically published from this room.

ADRIAN: I know that, Marcus.

MARCUS: Allison happened to be here one night, a month or so ago, when there was a good bit of screwing going on.

ADRIAN: Sorry I missed it.

MARCUS: It *was* fairly spectacular. But believe me—it was a purely spontaneous outburst of good spirits. Totally unexpected, it was just one of those things that happens with enough brandy.

ADRIAN *laughs.*

What I think happened is that—you see, we had a novelist here who was about to emigrate; to put it bluntly, he is paranoid. I can't blame him—he hasn't been able to publish here since the government changed. And I am one of the people he blamed, as though I had anything to say about who is or isn't to be published. But the fact that I live decently and can travel proved to him that I have some secret power with the higher echelons—in effect, that I am some sort of agent.

ADRIAN: Those are understandable suspicions, Marcus.

MARCUS (*with a light laugh*): But why!

MAYA: It is marvelous, Adrian, how understandable everything is for you.

ADRIAN: I didn't say that at all, Maya; I know practically nothing about Marcus, so I could hardly be making an accusation, could I?

MARCUS: Of course not. It's only that the whole idea is so appalling.

ADRIAN: Well, I apologize. But it's so underwater here an outsider is bound to imagine all sorts of nightmares.

MAYA: You have no nightmares in America?

ADRIAN: You know me better than that, Maya—of course we have them, but they're different.

IRINA (*revolving her finger*): Is music?

MARCUS: In a moment, dear.

MAYA: I really must say, Adrian—when you came here the other times it was the Vietnam War, I believe. Did anyone in this country blame you personally for it?

ADRIAN: No, they didn't. But it's not the same thing, Maya.

MAYA: It never is, is it?

ADRIAN: I was arrested twice for protesting the war. Not that that means too much—we had lawyers to defend us, and the networks had it all over the country the next day. So there's no comparison, and maybe I know it better than most people. And that's why I'm not interested in blaming anyone here. This is impossible, Marcus, why don't we find a restaurant, I'm beginning to sound like an idiot.

MARCUS: We can't now, I've invited . . .

ADRIAN: Then why don't you meet us somewhere. Sigmund? What do you say, Maya—where's a good place?

MARCUS: Not tonight, Adrian.

ADRIAN *turns to him, catching a certain obscure decision.* MARCUS *addresses* SIGMUND.

I took the liberty of asking Alexandra to stop by.

SIGMUND *turns his head to him, surprised.* MAYA *turns to* MARCUS *from upstage, the plate in her hand.*

(*To* MAYA): I thought he ought to talk to her. (*To* SIGMUND): I hope you won't mind.

MAYA (*turns to* SIGMUND, *with a certain surprise*): You will talk with Alexandra?

SIGMUND *is silent.*

IRINA (*revolving her finger*): Jazz?

MARCUS: In a moment, dear.

SIGMUND: She is coming?

MARCUS: She said she'd try. I think she will. (*To* ADRIAN): She is a great admirer of Sigmund's.

MAYA *comes down to* ADRIAN *with a plate. She is watching* SIGMUND, *who is facing front.*

MAYA: I think you should have asked if he agrees.

MARCUS: I don't see the harm. She can just join us for a drink, if nothing more.

ADRIAN (*accepting the plate*): Thanks. She a writer?

MAYA: Her father is the Minister of Interior. (*She points at the ceiling.*) He is in charge . . .

ADRIAN: Oh! I see. (*He turns to watch* SIGMUND, *who is facing front.*)

MARCUS: She writes poetry.

MAYA: Yes. (*She glances anxiously to* SIGMUND.) Tremendous . . . (*spreads her arms*) . . . *long* poems. (*She takes a glass and drinks deeply.*)

MARCUS (*on the verge of sharpness*): Nevertheless, I think she has a certain talent.

MAYA: Yes. You think she has a certain talent, Sigmund?

MARCUS: Now, Maya . . . (*He reaches out and lifts the glass from her hand.*)

MAYA: Each year, you see, Adrian—since her father was appointed, this woman's poetry is more and more admired by more and more of our writers. A few years ago only a handful appreciated her, but now practically everybody calls her a master. (*Proudly*): Excepting for Sigmund—until now, anyway. (*She takes the glass from where* MARCUS *placed it.*)

SIGMUND (*pause*): She is not to my taste . . . (*he hesitates*) . . . but perhaps she is a good poet.

MAYA (*slight pause*): But she has very thick legs.

MARCUS *turns to her.*

But that must be said, Marcus . . . (*She laughs.*) We are not yet obliged to overlook a fact of nature. Please say she has thick legs.

MARCUS: I have no interest in her legs.

MAYA: Sigmund, my darling—surely you will say she . . .

MARCUS: Stop that, Maya . . .

MAYA (*suddenly, at the top of her voice*): It is important! (*She turns to* SIGMUND.)

SIGMUND: She has thick legs, yes.

MAYA: Yes. (*She presses his head to her hip.*) Some truths will not change, and certain people, for all our sakes, are appointed never to forget them. How do the Jews say?—If I forget thee, O Jerusalem, may I cut off my hand? . . . (*To* IRINA): You want jazz?

IRINA (*starts to rise, happily*): Jazz!

MAYA (*helping her up*): Come, you poor girl, we have hundreds . . . I mean he does. (*She laughs.*) My God, Marcus, how long I lived here. (*She laughs, nearly weeping.*) I'm going crazy . . .

SIGMUND (*stands*): I must walk. I have eaten too much. (*He buttons his jacket.*)

ADRIAN (*indicating below*): What about those men?

SIGMUND *beckons* ADRIAN *toward the double doors at left. He moves toward the left door, which he opens as* ADRIAN *stands, starts after him, then halts and turns with uncertainty to* MARCUS *and* MAYA, *who look on without expression.* ADRIAN *goes out, shutting the door.* SIGMUND *is standing in the corridor.*

MAYA (*to* IRINA): Come, we have everything. (*She goes and opens an overhead cabinet, revealing hundreds of records.*) From Paris, London, New York, Rio . . . you like conga?

IRINA *reads the labels.* MAYA *turns her head toward the corridor.* MARCUS *now turns as well.*

SIGMUND: Do you understand?

ADRIAN: No.

SIGMUND: I am to be arrested.

ADRIAN: How do you know that?

SIGMUND: Alexandra is the daughter of . . .

ADRIAN: I know—the Minister of . . .

SIGMUND: Marcus would never imagine I would meet with this woman otherwise.

ADRIAN: Why? What's she about?

SIGMUND: She is collecting the dead for her father. She arrange for writers to go before the television and apologize to the government. *Mea culpa*—to kissing their ass.

Slight pause.

ADRIAN: I think you've got to leave the country, Sigmund.

MAYA *crosses the room.*

SIGMUND: Is impossible. We cannot discuss it.

MAYA *enters the corridor, closing the door behind her.*

MAYA: Get out.
SIGMUND (*comes to her, takes her hand gently*): I must talk to Adrian.
MAYA: Get out, get out! (*To* ADRIAN): He must leave the country. (*To* SIGMUND): Finish with it! Tell Marcus.
SIGMUND (*turns her to the door, a hand on her back, and opens the door for her*): Please, Maya.

She enters the room, glancing back at him in terror. He shuts the door.

IRINA (*holding out a record*): Play?

MAYA *looks to* MARCUS, *who turns away. Then she goes and uncovers a record player, turns it on, sets the record on it. During the following the music plays, a jazz piece or conga. First* IRINA *dances by herself, then gets* MARCUS *up and dances with him.* MAYA *sits, drinking.*

Pause.

SIGMUND: You have a pistol?
ADRIAN: . . . A pistol?
SIGMUND: Yes.
ADRIAN: No. Of course not. (*Pause.*) How could I carry a pistol on an airplane?
SIGMUND: Why not? He has one in his valise. I saw it.

Pause.

ADRIAN: What good would a pistol do?

Pause.

SIGMUND: . . . It is very difficult to get pistol in this country.

ADRIAN: This is unreal, Sigmund, you can't be thinking of a . . .

SIGMUND: If you will engage him in conversation, I will excuse myself to the bathroom. He has put his valise in the bedroom. I will take it from the valise.

ADRIAN: And do what with it?

SIGMUND: I will keep it, and he will tell them that I have it. In this case they will not arrest me.

ADRIAN: But why not?

SIGMUND: They will avoid at the present time to shoot me.

ADRIAN: . . . And I'm to do . . . what am I to . . .

SIGMUND: It is nothing; you must only engage him when I am excusing myself to the bathroom. Come . . .

ADRIAN: Let me catch my breath, will you? . . . It's unreal to me, Sigmund, I can't believe you have to do this.

SIGMUND: It is not dangerous, believe me.

ADRIAN: Not for me, but I have a passport. . . . Then this is why Marcus came back?

SIGMUND: I don't know. He has many friend in the government, but . . . I don't know why.

ADRIAN: He's an agent.

SIGMUND: Is possible not.

ADRIAN: Then what is he?

SIGMUND: Marcus is Marcus.

ADRIAN: Please, explain to me. I've got to understand before I go in there.

SIGMUND: It is very complicated between us.

ADRIAN: Like what? Maya?

SIGMUND: Maya also. (*Slight pause.*) When I was young writer, Marcus was the most famous novelist in our country. In Stalin time he has six years in prison. He cannot write. I was not in prison. When he has returned I am very popular, but he was forgotten. It is tragic story.

ADRIAN: You mean he's envious of you.

SIGMUND: This is natural.

ADRIAN: But didn't you say he's protected you . . .

SIGMUND: Yes, of course. Marcus is very complicated man.

ADRIAN: But with all that influence, why can't you sit down and maybe he can think of something for you.

SIGMUND: He has thought of something—he has thought of Alexandra.

ADRIAN: You mean he's trying to destroy you.

SIGMUND: No. Is possible he believes he is trying to help me.

ADRIAN: But subconsciously . . .

SIGMUND: Yes. Come, we must go back.

ADRIAN: Just one more minute. You're convinced he's not an agent.

SIGMUND: My opinion, no.

ADRIAN: But how does he get all these privileges?

SIGMUND: Marcus is lazy. Likewise, he is speaking French, English, German—five, six language. When the foreign writers are coming, he is very gentleman, he makes using salon, he is showing the castles, the restaurants, introduce beautiful girls. When these writers return home they say is no bad problem in this civilized country. He makes very nice impression, and for this they permit him to be lazy. Is not necessary to be agent.

ADRIAN: You don't think it's possible that he learned they were going to arrest you and came back to help you?

SIGMUND *looks at him, surprised.*

That makes as much sense as anything else, Sigmund. Could he have simply wanted to do something decent? Maybe I'm being naive, but if he wanted your back broken, his best bet would be just to sit tight in London and let it happen.

SIGMUND *is silent.*

And as for calling Alexandra—maybe he figured your only chance *is* actually to make peace with the government.

SIGMUND *is silent.*

You grab that gun and you foreclose everything—you're an outlaw. Is it really impossible to sit down with Marcus, man to man? I mean, you're pinning everything on an interpretation, aren't you?

SIGMUND: I know Marcus.

ADRIAN: Sigmund—every conversation I've ever had with him about this country, he's gone out of his way to praise you—your talent and you personally. I can't believe I was taken in;

he genuinely admires your guts, your resistance. Let me call him out here.

SIGMUND *turns, uncertain but alarmed.*

What's to lose? Maybe there's a string he can pull, let's put *his* feet to the fire. Because he's all over Europe lamenting conditions here, he's a big liberal in Europe. I've seen him get girls with those lamentations. Let me call him on it.

SIGMUND (*with a blossoming suspicion in the corners of his eyes*): I will never make speech on the television . . .

ADRIAN (*alarmed*): For Christ's sake, Sigmund, you don't imagine *I* would want that. (*He explodes.*) This is a quagmire, a fucking asylum! . . . But I'm not helping out with any guns. It's suicide, you'll have to do that alone. (*He goes to the door.*)

SIGMUND: Adrian?

ADRIAN: I'm sorry, Sigmund, but that's the way I feel.

SIGMUND: I want my manuscript. If you wish to talk to Marcus, I have nothing to object . . . on this basis.

ADRIAN *looks at him, unsatisfied, angry. He turns and flings the door open, enters the room.*

ADRIAN: Marcus? Can I see you a minute?

MARCUS: Of course. What is it?

ADRIAN: Out here, please . . . if you don't mind?

MARCUS *crosses the room and enters the corridor.* SIGMUND *avoids Marcus's eyes, stands waiting.* MARCUS *turns to* ADRIAN *as he shuts the door.*

MARCUS: Yes?

MAYA *opens the door, enters the corridor, shuts it behind her.* MARCUS *turns up his robe collar.*

ADRIAN (*breaks into an embarrassed grin*): I'm not sure what to say or not say. . . . I'm more of a stranger than I'd thought, Marcus . . .

MARCUS: We're all strangers in this situation—nobody ever learns how to deal with it.

ADRIAN: . . . I take it you have some contacts with the government.

MARCUS: Many of us do; it's a small country.

ADRIAN: I think they ought to know that, ah . . . (*He glances to* SIGMUND, *but* SIGMUND *is not facing in his direction.*) If he's to be arrested, he'll—resist.

MAYA *turns quickly to* SIGMUND, *alarm in her face.*

MARCUS: I don't understand— (*To* SIGMUND, *with a faintly embarrassed grin*): Why couldn't you have said that to me?

SIGMUND, *bereft of an immediate answer, starts to turn to him.*

Well, it doesn't matter. (*He is flushed. He turns back to* ADRIAN.) Yes?

ADRIAN: What I thought was, that . . .

MARCUS: Of course, if we're talking, about some—violent gesture, they will advertise it as the final proof he is insane. Which is what they've claimed all along. But what was your thought?

ADRIAN: I have the feeling that the inevitable is being accepted. They act and you react. I'd like to sit down, the four of us, and see if we can come up with some out that nobody's ever thought of before.

MARCUS: Certainly. But it's a waste of time if you think you can change their program.

ADRIAN: Which is what, exactly?

MARCUS: Obviously—to drive him out of the country. Failing that, to make it impossible for him to function.

ADRIAN: And you think?

MARCUS: There's no question in my mind—he must emigrate. They've taken the work of his last five years, what more do you want?

ADRIAN: There's no one at all you could approach?

MARCUS: With what? What can I offer that they need?

ADRIAN: Like what, for example?

MARCUS: Well, if he agreed to emigrate, conceivably they might let go of the manuscript—providing, of course, that it isn't too politically inflammatory. But that could be dealt with, I think—they badly want him gone.

ADRIAN: There's no one up there who could be made to understand that if they ignored him he would simply be another novelist . . .

MARCUS (*laughing lightly*): But will he ignore *them*? How is it possible? This whole country is inside his skin—that is his greatness—They have a right to be terrified.

ADRIAN: Supposing there were a copy of the manuscript.

MARCUS: But there isn't, so it's pointless talking about it.

ADRIAN: But if there were.

MARCUS: It might have been a consideration.

ADRIAN: . . . If they knew it would be published abroad.

MARCUS: It might slow them down, yes. But they know Sigmund's personality.

ADRIAN: How do you mean?

MARCUS: He's not about to trust another person with his fate—it's a pity; they'd never have found it in this house in a hundred years. The cellar's endless, the gallery upstairs full of junk—to me, this is the saddest part of all. If it had made a splash abroad it might have held their hand for six months, perhaps longer. (*With a regretful glance at* SIGMUND): But . . . so it goes. (*Pause. He blows on his hands.*) It's awfully cold out here, come inside . . . (*He starts for the door.*)

ADRIAN: There's a copy in Paris.

MAYA and SIGMUND turn swiftly to him.

MARCUS: . . . In Paris.

ADRIAN: I sent it off this morning.

MARCUS: *This* morning?

ADRIAN: I ran into a cousin of mine; had no idea she was here. She took it with her to Gallimard—they're my publishers.

A broken smile emerges on Marcus's face. He is filling with a swirl of colors, glancing first at MAYA, *then at* SIGMUND, *then back to* ADRIAN.

MARCUS: Well, then . . . that much is solved. (*He goes to the door.*)

ADRIAN: They should be told, don't you think?

MARCUS (*stands at the door, his hand on the knob, finally turns to all of them*): How terrible. (*Slight pause. To* MAYA *and* SIGMUND): *Such* contempt. (*Slight pause.*) Why? . . . Can you tell me? (*They avoid his gaze. He turns to* ADRIAN.) There's no plane to Paris today. Monday, Wednesday, and Friday. This is Tuesday, Adrian.

SIGMUND: I did not ask him to say that.

MARCUS: But perfectly willing to stand there and hope I'd believe it.

ADRIAN: I'm sorry, Marcus . . .

MARCUS (*laughing*): But Adrian, I couldn't care less.

MAYA (*moving to him*): Help him.

MARCUS: Absolutely not. I am finished with it. No one will ever manipulate me, I will not be in that position.

MAYA: He is a stupid man, he understands nothing!

ADRIAN: Now, hold it a second . . .

MAYA: Get out of here!

ADRIAN: Just hold it a second, goddammit! I'm out of my depth, Marcus, but I've apologized. I'm sorry. But you have to believe it was solely my invention; Sigmund has absolute faith in you.

SIGMUND: You can forgive him, Marcus—he tells you the truth; he believes you are my friend, he said this to me a moment ago.

ADRIAN: I feel he's drowning, Marcus, it was just something to grab for. (*He holds out his hand.*) Forgive me, it just popped out of my mouth.

MARCUS (*silently clasps his hand for an instant, and lets go; to* SIGMUND *and* MAYA *especially*): Come inside. We'll talk.

ADRIAN (*as* MARCUS *turns to the door*): . . . Marcus?

MARCUS *turns to him. He is barely able to continue.*

Don't you think—it would be wiser—a bar or something?

MARCUS: I'm expecting Alexandra.

ADRIAN: Could you leave a note on the door? But it's up to you and Sigmund. (*To* SIGMUND): What do you think?

SIGMUND (*hesitates*): It is for Marcus to decide. (*He looks at* MARCUS.) It is his house.

MARCUS, *expressionless, stands silent.*

MAYA: Darling . . . (*delicately*) . . . it will endure a thousand years. (MARCUS *looks at her.*) . . . I've read it. It is all we ever lived. They must not, must not touch it. Whatever humiliation, whatever is necessary for this book, yes. More than he himself, more than any human being—this book they cannot harm. . . . Francesco's is still open. (*She turns to* ADRIAN.) But I must say to you, Adrian—nothing has ever been found in this house. We have looked everywhere.

ADRIAN: It's entirely up to Marcus. (*To* MARCUS): You feel it's all right to talk in there?

Long pause.

MARCUS (*with resentment*): I think Maya has answered that question, don't you?

ADRIAN: Okay. Then you're not sure.

MARCUS: But you are, apparently.

ADRIAN (*slight pause; to* SIGMUND): I think I ought to leave.

SIGMUND: No, no . . .

ADRIAN: I think I'm only complicating it for you—

SIGMUND: I insist you stay . . .

ADRIAN (*laughs nervously, his arm touching Sigmund's shoulder*): I'm underwater, kid, I can't operate when I'm drowning. (*Without pausing, to* MARCUS): I don't understand why you're offended.

MARCUS: The question has been answered once. There has never been any proof of an installation. But when so many writers congregate here, I've had to assume there might be something. The fact is, I have always warned people to be careful what they say in there—but only to be on the safe side. Is that enough?

SIGMUND: Come! (*To* MARCUS, *heartily, as he begins to press* ADRIAN *toward the door*): Now I will have one big whisky . . .

MARCUS *laughs, starting for the door.*

ADRIAN (*separating himself from* SIGMUND): I'll see you tomorrow, Sigmund.

Silence. They go still.

This is all your marbles, kid. It's too important for anyone to be standing on his dignity. I think I'm missing some of the overtones. (*To* MARCUS): But all I know is that if it were me I'd feel a lot better if I could hear you say what you just said—in there.

MARCUS: What *I* said?

ADRIAN (*slight pause*): That you've always warned people that the government might be listening, in that room.

SIGMUND: Is not necessary . . .

ADRIAN: I think it . . .

SIGMUND: Absolutely not! Please . . . (*He presses* ADRIAN *toward the door and stretches his hand out to* MARCUS.) Come, Marcus, please.

SIGMUND *leads the way into the room, followed by* ADRIAN, *then* MARCUS *and* MAYA. *For an instant they are all awkwardly standing there. Then* SIGMUND *presses his hand against his stomach.*

Excuse me one moment. (*He goes up toward the bedroom doorway.*)

ADRIAN (*suddenly alerted, starts after* SIGMUND): Sigmund . . .

But SIGMUND *is gone.* ADRIAN *is openly conflicted about rushing after him* . . .

MAYA: What is it?

ADRIAN (*blurting, in body-shock*): Level with him. Marcus . . . this is your Hemingway, your Faulkner, for Christ's sake— help him!

SIGMUND *enters from bedroom, a pistol in his hand.* IRINA, *seeing it, strides away from him in fright.*

SIGMUND (*to* MARCUS): Forgive me. I must have it. (*He puts it in his pocket.*)

IRINA (*pointing at his pocket*): Shoot?

SIGMUND: No, no. We are all friend. *Alle gute Freunde hier.*

IRINA: Ah. (*She turns questioningly, to* MARCUS, *then* ADRIAN, MAYA, *and* SIGMUND.)

Pause.

ADRIAN: Marcus?

MARCUS, *at center, turns front, anger mounting in his face.* MAYA *goes and shuts off the record player. Then she turns to him, waiting.*

Will you say it? In here? Please?

END OF ACT ONE

ACT TWO

Positions the same. A tableau, MARCUS *at center, all waiting for him to speak. Finally he moves, glances at* SIGMUND.

MARCUS: They are preparing a trial for you.
MAYA (*clapping her hands together, crying out*): Marcus!

She starts toward him, but he walks from her, turning away in impatience. She halts.

When?

MARCUS *is silent, downing his resentment.*

Do you know when?
MARCUS: I think within the month.
MAYA (*turning to* SIGMUND): My God, my God.
SIGMUND (*after a moment*): And Otto and Peter?
MARCUS: I don't know about them. (*He goes in the silence to his chair, sits.*)

Pause.

ADRIAN: What would they charge him with?
MARCUS: . . . Fantastic. Break off a trip, fly across Europe, and now I'm asked—what am I asked?—to justify myself? Is that it?

Unable to answer, ADRIAN *evades his eyes, then glances to* SIGMUND *for aid; but* SIGMUND *is facing front and now walks to a chair and sits.*

MAYA (*to* MARCUS): No, no, dear . . . (*Of* SIGMUND): It's a shock for him . . .
MARCUS (*rejecting her apology, glances at* ADRIAN): . . . Section Nineteen, I'd imagine. Slandering the state.
ADRIAN: On what grounds?
MARCUS: He's been sending out some devastating letters to the European press; this last one to the United Nations— have you read that?
ADRIAN: Just now in Paris, yes.

MARCUS: What'd you think of it?

ADRIAN (*with a cautious glance at* SIGMUND): It was pretty hot, I guess— What's the penalty for that?

MARCUS: A year. Two, three, five—who knows?

Slight pause.

MAYA: It was good of you to return, dear.

MARCUS *does not respond. She invites Sigmund's gratitude.*

. . . Sigmund?

SIGMUND (*waits an instant*): Yes. Thank you, Marcus.

MARCUS *remains looking front.*

It is definite?

MARCUS: I think it is. And it will affect every writer in the country, if it's allowed to happen.

SIGMUND: How do you know this?

Slight pause.

MARCUS: My publisher had a press reception for me day before yesterday—for my book. A fellow from our London embassy turned up. We chatted for a moment, then I forgot about him, but in the street afterwards, he was suddenly beside me . . . we shared a cab. (*Slight pause. He turns directly to* SIGMUND.) He said he was from the Embassy Press Section.

SIGMUND: Police.

MARCUS (*lowers his eyes in admission*): He was . . . quite violent . . . his way of speaking.

SIGMUND: About me.

Slight pause.

MARCUS: I haven't heard that kind of language . . . since . . . the old days. "You are making a mistake," he said, "if you think we need tolerate this scum any longer . . ."

MAYA: My God, my God . . .

MARCUS: "You can do your friend a favor," he said, "and tell him to get out this month or he will eat his own shit for five or six years."

MAYA *weeps.*

"And as far as a protest in the West, he can wrap it in bacon fat and shove it up his ass." Pounded the seat with his fist. Bloodshot eyes. I thought he was going to hit me for a moment there. . . . It was quite an act.

ADRIAN: An act?

MARCUS: Well, he wasn't speaking for himself, of course. (*Slight pause.*) I started a letter, but I know your feelings about leaving—I felt we had to talk about it face to face.

SIGMUND: Please.

MARCUS (*hesitates, then turns to* ADRIAN): Are you here as a journalist?

ADRIAN: God, no—I just thought I'd stop by . . .

MAYA: He has written a novel about us.

MARCUS (*unguarded*): About us? Really! . . .

ADRIAN: Well, not literally . . .

MARCUS: When is it coming out?

ADRIAN: It won't. I've abandoned it.

MARCUS: Oh! That's too bad. Why?

ADRIAN: I'm not here to write about you, Marcus . . . honestly.

MARCUS *nods, unconvinced.* ADRIAN *addresses* SIGMUND *as well.*

I'll leave now if you think I'm in the way . . .

SIGMUND *doesn't react.*

MARCUS: It's all right. (*Slight pause.*) But if you decide to write something about us . . .

ADRIAN: I've no intention . . .

MARCUS (*smiling*): You never know. We have a tactical disagreement, Sigmund and I. To me, it's really a question of having had different experiences—although there are only seven or eight years between us; things that he finds intolerable are actually—from another viewpoint—improvements over the past . . .

ADRIAN (*indicating* MAYA): I only found out today you were in prison . . .

MARCUS: A camp, actually—we dug coal.

ADRIAN: Six years.

MARCUS: And four months.

ADRIAN: What for?

MARCUS: It's one of those stories which, although long, is not interesting. (*He laughs.*) The point is simple, in any case. We happen to occupy a . . . strategic zone, really—between two hostile ways of life. And no government here is free to do what it would like to do. But some intelligent, sympathetic people are up there now who weren't around in the old times, and to challenge these people, to even insult them, is to indulge in a sort of fantasy . . .

SIGMUND (*pointing to the ceiling*): Marcus, this is reality?

MARCUS: Let me finish . . .

SIGMUND: But is very important—who is fantastic? (*He laughs.*) We are some sort of characters in a poem which they are writing; is not my poem, is their poem . . . and I do not like this poem, it makes me crazy! (*He laughs.*)

ADRIAN: I understand what he means, though . . .

SIGMUND: I not! I am sorry. Excuse me, Marcus—please continue.

MARCUS (*slight pause*): They ought not be forced into political trials again . . .

SIGMUND: *I* am forcing . . . ?

MARCUS: May I finish? It will mean a commitment which they will have to carry through, willingly or not. And that can only mean turning out the lights for all of us, and for a long time to come. It mustn't be allowed to happen, Sigmund. And it need not happen. (*Slight pause.*) I think you have to get out. For all our sakes.

With an ironic shake of his head, SIGMUND *makes a long exhale.*

MARCUS: . . . I've called Alexandra because I think you need a line of communication now. If only to stall things for a time, or whatever you . . .

SIGMUND (*toward* MAYA): I must now communicate with *Alexandra.*

MARCUS: She adores your work, whatever you think of her.

SIGMUND *gives him a sarcastic glance.*

This splendid isolation has to end, Sigmund—it was never real, and now it's impossible.

SIGMUND (*shakes his head*): I will wait for her. I may wait?

MARCUS: I certainly hope you will. (*Slight pause.*) I only ask you to keep in mind that this goes beyond your personal feelings about leaving . . .

SIGMUND: I have never acted for personal feelings.

MARCUS (*insistently*): You've been swept away now and then— that United Nations letter could change nothing except enrage them . . .

SIGMUND: I may not also be enraged?

MAYA: Don't argue about it, please . . .

SIGMUND (*smiling at her*): Perhaps is time we argue . . .

MAYA: Sigmund, we are all too old to be right! (*She picks up a glass.*)

MARCUS: Are you getting drunk?

MAYA: No, I am getting sorry. Is no one to be sorry? I am sorry for both of you. I am sorry for Socialism. I am sorry for Marx and Engels and Lenin— (*She shouts to the air.*) I am sorry! (*To* IRINA, *irritably*): Don't be frightened. (*She pours a drink.*)

Pause.

ADRIAN: I'd like to take back what I asked you before, Marcus.

MARCUS: How can I know what is in this room? How ludicrous can you get?

ADRIAN: I agree. I wouldn't be willing to answer that question in my house either.

SIGMUND: But would not be necessary to ask such question in your house.

ADRIAN: Oh, don't kid yourself . . .

MARCUS: The FBI is everywhere . . .

ADRIAN: Not everywhere, but they get around. The difference with us is that it's illegal.

SIGMUND: *Vive la différence.*

MARCUS: Provided you catch them.

ADRIAN (*laughs*): Right. (*He catches Sigmund's dissatisfaction with him.*) I'm not saying it's the same . . .

SIGMUND (*turns away from* ADRIAN *to* MAYA): Please, Maya, a whisky.

MAYA (*eagerly*): Yes! (*She goes up to the drink table. Silence. She pours a drink, brings it to* SIGMUND.)

ADRIAN: Did this woman say what time she . . .

MARCUS: She's at some embassy dinner. As soon as she can break away. Shouldn't be long. (*Slight pause. He indicates Sigmund's pocket.*) Give me that thing, will you?

SIGMUND *does not respond.*

ADRIAN: Go ahead, Sigmund.

SIGMUND: I . . . keep for few minutes. (*He drinks.*)

Pause.

ADRIAN: I'm exhausted. (*He hangs his head and shakes it.*)

MAYA: You drink too fast.

ADRIAN: No . . . it's the whole thing—it suddenly hit me. (*He squeezes his eyes.*) Mind if I lie down?

MARCUS (*gesturing toward the couch*): Of course.

ADRIAN *goes to the couch.*

What's *your* feeling?

ADRIAN: He's got to get out, I've told him that. (*He lies down.*) They're doing great, what do they need literature for? It's a pain in the ass. (*He throws an arm over his eyes, sighs.*) Christ . . . it's unbelievable. An hour from the Sorbonne.

MAYA (*a long pause; she sits between* SIGMUND *and* MARCUS, *glancing uncomfortably from one to the other*): It was raining in London?

MARCUS: No, surprisingly warm. How's your tooth?

MAYA (*pointing to a front tooth, showing him*): They saved it.

MARCUS: Good. He painted the bathroom.

MAYA: Yes, he came, finally. I paid him. The rest of the money is in the desk.

MARCUS: Thanks, dear. Looks very nice.

Slight pause.

MAYA (*leans her elbow on her knee, her chin on her fist, observes her leg, then glances at* MARCUS): My bird died on Sunday.

MARCUS: Really? Lulu?

MAYA: Yes. I finally found out, though—she was a male. (*To* SIGMUND): And all these years I called him Lulu!

SIGMUND: I can give you one of my rabbits.

MAYA: Oh, my God, no rabbits. (*She sighs.*) No birds, no cats, no dogs . . . Nothing, nothing anymore. (*She drinks.*)

Pause.

ADRIAN (*from the couch*): You ever get mail from your program?

MAYA: Oh, very much. Mostly for recipes, sometimes I teach them to cook.

SIGMUND: She is very comical. She is marvelous actress.

ADRIAN: It's not a political . . . ?

MAYA: No! It's too early in the morning. I hate politics . . . boring, boring, always the same. . . . You know something? You are both very handsome.

SIGMUND *and* MARCUS *look at her and laugh softly.*

You too, Adrian. (*She looks at her glass.*) And this is wonderful whisky.

MARCUS: Not too much, dear.

MAYA: No, no. (*She gets up with her glass, moves toward the window at right.*) There was such a marvelous line—that English poet, what was his name? Very famous . . . you published him in the first or second issue, I think. . . . "The world . . ." (*She presses her forehead.* MARCUS *observes her, and she sees him.*) I'm not drunk, it's only so long ago. Oh, yes! "The world needs a wash and a week's rest."

ADRIAN: Auden.

MAYA: Auden, yes! A wash and week's rest—what a wonderful solution.

ADRIAN: Yeah—last one into the Ganges is a rotten egg.

They laugh.

MARCUS: Every now and then you sound like Brooklyn.

ADRIAN: That's because I come from Philadelphia. How do you know about Brooklyn?

MARCUS: I was in the American army.

ADRIAN (*amazed, sits up*): How do you come to the American army?

MAYA: He was sergeant.

MARCUS: I enlisted in London—we had to get out when the Nazis came. I was translator and interpreter for General McBride, First Army Intelligence.

ADRIAN: Isn't that funny? Every once in a while you come into a kind of—focus, that's very familiar. I've never understood it.

MARCUS: I was in almost three years.

ADRIAN: Huh! (*He laughs.*) I don't know why I'm so glad to hear it . . .

MARCUS: Well, you can place me now—we all want that.

ADRIAN: I guess so. What'd she mean, that you published Auden?

MAYA: Marcus was the editor of the magazine, until they closed it.

ADRIAN (*toward* SIGMUND): I didn't know that.

SIGMUND: Very good editor—Marcus was first editor who accept to publish my story.

MAYA: If it had been in English—or even French or Spanish—our magazine would have been as famous as the *New Yorker*.

MARCUS (*modestly*): Well . . .

MAYA (*to* MARCUS): In my opinion it was better . . . (*To* ADRIAN): But our language even God doesn't read. People would stand on line in the street downstairs, like for bread. People from factories, soldiers from the army, professors . . . It was like some sort of Bible, every week a new prophecy. Pity you missed it . . . It was like living on a ship—every morning there was a different island.

MARCUS (*to* SIGMUND, *with a gesture of communication*): Elizabeth didn't look well, is she all right?

SIGMUND: She was very angry tonight. She is sometimes foolish.

Slight pause.

MAYA: Could he live, in America?

ADRIAN: I'm sure he could. Universities'd be honored to have him.

SIGMUND: I am speaking English like six-years-old child.

ADRIAN: Faculty wives'll be overjoyed to correct you. You'd be a big hit—with all that hair.

SIGMUND (*laughs dryly*): You are not going to Algeria?

MARCUS: On Friday.

ADRIAN: What's in Algeria?

MARCUS: There's a writers' congress—they've asked me to go.

ADRIAN: Communist countries?

MARCUS: Yes. But it's a big one—Arabs, Africans, Latin Americans . . . the lot.

SIGMUND: The French?

MARCUS: Some French, yes—Italians too, I think.

ADRIAN: What do you do at those things?

MAYA (*admiringly*): He represents our country—he lies on the beach with a gin and tonic.

MARCUS (*laughs*): It's too cold for the beach now. (*To* ADRIAN): They're basically ideological discussions.

SIGMUND: Boring, no?

MARCUS: Agony. But there are some interesting people sometimes.

SIGMUND: You can speak of us there?

MARCUS *turns to him, silent, unable to answer.*

No?

MARCUS: We're not on the agenda.

MAYA: It's difficult, dear . . .

SIGMUND: But perhaps privately—to the Italian comrades? . . . French? Perhaps they would be interested for my manuscript.

MARCUS *nods positively but turns up his palms—he'll do what he can.*

(*With the slightest edge of sarcasm*): You will see, perhaps. (*He chucks his head, closes his eyes with his face stretched upward, his hand tapping frustratedly on his chair arm, his foot beating.*) So-so-so-so.

MARCUS (*looking front*): The important thing . . . is to be useful.

SIGMUND (*flatly, without irony*): Yes, always. (*Slight pause.*) Thank you, that you have returned for this, I am grateful.

MARCUS: Whatever you decide, it ought to be soon. Once they move to prosecute . . .

SIGMUND: Yes. I have still some questions—we can take a walk later, perhaps.

MARCUS: All right. I've told you all I know . . .

SIGMUND: . . . About ourselves.

MARCUS (*surprised*): Oh. All right.

Pause.

MAYA: How handsome you all are! I must say . . .

MARCUS *laughs, she persists.*

Really, it's unusual for writers. (*Suddenly, to* IRINA): And she is so lovely . . . *Du bist sehr schön.*

IRINA: *Danke.*

MAYA (*to* MARCUS): Isn't she very young?

MARCUS (*shrugs*): We only met two days ago.

MAYA (*touching his hair*): How marvelous. You are like God, darling—you can always create new people. (*She laughs, and with sudden energy*): Play something, Sigmund! . . . (*She goes to* SIGMUND *to get him up.*) Come . . .

SIGMUND: No, no, no . . .

MAYA (*suddenly bends and kisses the top of his head, her eyes filling with tears*): Don't keep that thing . . .

She reaches for his pocket; he takes her hand and pats it, looking up at her. She stares down at him.

The day he walked in here for the first time . . . (*She glances at* MARCUS.) Do you remember? The snow was half a meter high on his hat—I thought he was a peasant selling potatoes, he bowed the snow all over my typewriter. (*She glances at* ADRIAN.) And he takes out this lump of paper—it was rolled up like a bomb. A story full of colors, like a painting; this boy from the beet fields—a writer! It was a miracle—such prose from a field of beets. That morning—for half an hour —I believed Socialism. For half an hour I . . .

MARCUS (*cutting her off*): What brings you back, Adrian? (*The telephone rings in the bedroom.*) Probably for you.

MAYA: For me? (*She goes toward the bedroom.*) I can't imagine . . . (*She exits.*)

ADRIAN: I don't really know why I came. There's always been something here that I . . .

IRINA (*getting up, pointing to the piano*): I may?

MARCUS: Certainly . . . please.

IRINA *sits at the piano.*

SIGMUND: I think you will write your book again.

ADRIAN: I doubt it—there's a kind of music here that escapes me. I really don't think I dig you people.

IRINA (*testing the piano, she runs a scale; it is badly out of tune, and she makes a face, turning to* MARCUS): Ach . . .

MARCUS (*apologizing*): I'm sorry, it's too old to be tuned anymore . . . but go ahead . . .

MAYA (*entering*): There's no one—they cut off.

SIGMUND *turns completely around to her, alerted.*

MAYA (*to him, reassuringly*): I'm sure they'll call back . . . it was an accident. Good! You play?

IRINA *launches into a fast "Bei Mir Bist Du Schön," the strings whining.*

MAYA: Marvelous! Jitterbug! (*She breaks into a jitterbug with her glass in one hand, lifting her skirt.*) Come on, Adrian! . . . (*She starts for* ADRIAN.)

IRINA (*stops playing and stands up, pushing her fingers into her ears*): Is too, too . . .

MAYA: No, play, play . . .

IRINA (*refusing, laughing, as she descends onto the carpet beside* MARCUS, *shutting her ears*): Please, please, please . . .

MARCUS (*patting* IRINA): I believe she's done concerts . . . serious music. (*He looks at his watch; then, to* SIGMUND): You're not going outside with that thing, are you?

SIGMUND *glances at him.*

It's absurd.

MAYA: It must be the Americans—ever since they started building that hotel the phones keep ringing.

ADRIAN: What hotel?

MAYA: The Hilton . . . three blocks from here. It's disarranged the telephones.

MARCUS: I'd love to read your novel—do you have it with you?

ADRIAN: It's no good.

MARCUS: That's surprising—what's the problem?

ADRIAN (*sits up*): Well . . . I started out with a bizarre, exotic quality. People sort of embalmed in a society of amber. But the longer it got, the less unique it became. I finally wondered if the idea of unfreedom can be sustained in the mind.

MARCUS: You relied on that.

ADRIAN: Yes. But I had to keep injecting melodramatic reminders. The brain tires of unfreedom. It's like a bad back—you simply learn to avoid making certain movements . . . like . . . whatever's in this ceiling; or if nothing is; we still have to live, and talk, and the rest of it. I really thought I knew, but I saw that I didn't; it's been an education tonight. I'd love to ask you something, Marcus—why do you carry a gun?

MARCUS: I don't, normally. I was planning a trip into the mountains in Algeria—still pretty rough up there in places. (*He looks at his watch.*)

MAYA: He fought a battle in Mexico last year. In the Chiapas. Like a cowboy.

MARCUS: Not really—no one was hurt.

ADRIAN: What the hell do you go to those places for?

MARCUS: It interests me—where there is no law, people alone with their customs. I started out to be an anthropologist.

ADRIAN: What happened?

MARCUS: The Nazis, the war. You were too young, I guess.

ADRIAN: I was in the army in the fifties, but after Korea and before Vietnam.

MARCUS: You're a lucky generation, you missed everything.

ADRIAN: I wonder sometimes. History came at us like a rumor. We were never really there.

MARCUS: Is that why you come here?

ADRIAN: Might be part of it. We're always smelling the smoke, but were never quite sure who the devil really is. Drives us nuts.

MARCUS: You don't like ambiguity.

ADRIAN: Oh, sure—providing it's clear. (*He laughs.*) Or maybe it's always clearer in somebody else's country.

MARCUS: I was just about to say—the first time I came to America—a few years after the war . . .

ADRIAN: . . . You're not an American citizen, are you?

MARCUS: Very nearly, but I had a little . . . ambiguity with your Immigration Department. (*He smiles.*)

ADRIAN: You came from the wrong country.

MARCUS: No—it was the right country when I boarded ship for New York. But the Communists took over here while I was on the high seas. A Mr. Donahue, Immigration Inspector, Port of New York, did not approve. He put me in a cage.

ADRIAN: Why!

MARCUS: Suspicion I was a Red agent. Actually, I'd come on an invitation to lecture at Syracuse University. I'd published my first two—or it may have been three novels in Paris by then. I phoned the university—from my cage—and they were appalled, but no one lifted a finger, of course, and I was shipped back to Europe. It was terribly unambiguous, Adrian—you were a fascist country, to me. I was wrong, of course, but so it appeared. Anyway, I decided to come home and have a look here—I stepped off the train directly into the arms of our police.

ADRIAN: As an American spy.

MARCUS (*laughs*): What else?

ADRIAN (*nodding*): I got ya, Marcus.

MARCUS: Yes. (*Slight pause.*) But it's better now.

ADRIAN *glances at* SIGMUND.

It has been, anyway. But one has to be of the generation that can remember. Otherwise, it's as you say—a sort of rumor that has no reality—excepting for oneself.

SIGMUND *drinks deeply from his glass. Slight pause.*

ADRIAN (*stands, and from behind* SIGMUND *looks down at him for an instant*): She's sure to come, huh?

MARCUS: I'm sure she will.

ADRIAN (*strolls to the window at right, stretches his back and arms, looks out of the window*): It's starting to snow. (*Slight pause.*) God, it's a beautiful city. (*He lingers there for a moment, then walks, his hands thrust into his back pockets.*) What do you suppose would happen if I went to the Minister of the Interior tonight—if I lost my mind and knocked on his door and raised hell about this?

MARCUS *turns to him, eyebrows raised.*

I'm serious.

MARCUS: Well . . . what happened when you tried to reason with Johnson or Nixon during Vietnam?

ADRIAN: Right. But of course we could go into the streets, which you can't . . .

SIGMUND: Why not?

ADRIAN (*surprised*): With all their tanks here?

SIGMUND: Yes, even so. (*Pause.*) Is only a question of the fantasy. In this country we have not Las Vegas. The American knows very well is almost impossible to winning money from this slot machine. But he is enjoying to experience hope. He is playing for the hope. For us, is inconceivable. Before such a machine we would experience only despair. For this reason we do not go into the street.

ADRIAN: You're more realistic about power . . .

SIGMUND: This is mistake, Adrian, we are not realistic. We also believe we can escaping power—by telling lies. For this reason, I think you have difficulty to write about us. You cannot imagine how fantastically we lie.

MARCUS: I don't think we're any worse than others . . .

SIGMUND: Oh, certainly, yes—but perhaps is not exactly lying because we do not expect to deceive anyone; the professor lies to the student, the student to the professor—but each knows the other is lying. We must lie, it is our only freedom. To lie is our slot machine—we know we cannot win, but it gives us the feeling of hope. Is like a serious play which no one really believes, but the technique is admirable. Our country is now a theatre, where no one is permitted to walk out and everyone is obliged to applaud.

MARCUS: That is a marvelous description, Sigmund—of the whole world.

SIGMUND: No, I must object—when Adrian speaks to me it is always his personal opinion. But with us, is impossible to speaking so simply, we must always making theatre.

MARCUS: I've been as plain as I know how to be. What is it you don't believe?

SIGMUND (*laughs*): But that is the problem in the theatre—I believe everything but I am convinced of nothing.

MAYA: It's enough.

SIGMUND: Excuse me, Maya—for me is not enough; if I am waking up in New York one morning, I must have concrete reason, not fantastic reason.

MAYA: Darling, they've taken your book . . .

SIGMUND (*with sudden force*): But is my country—is this reason to leave my country!

MAYA: There are people who love you enough to want to keep you from prison. What is fantastic about that?

SIGMUND (*turns to* MARCUS, *with a smile*): You are loving me, Marcus?

MARCUS, *overwhelmed by resentment, turns to* SIGMUND, *silent.*

Then we have not this reason. (*Slight pause.*) Therefore . . . perhaps you have come back for different reason.

MARCUS: I came back to prevent a calamity, a disaster for all of us . . .

SIGMUND: Yes, but is also for them a calamity. If I am in prison the whole world will know they are gangster. This is not intelligent—my book are published in nine country. For them is also disaster.

MARCUS: So this fellow in London? These threats? They're not serious?

SIGMUND: I am sure they wish me to believe so, therefore is very serious.

MARCUS: You don't believe a word I've told you, do you? There was no man at all in London; that conversation never happened? There'll be no arrest? No trial?

SIGMUND (*pause*): I think not.

MARCUS: Then give me back my pistol.

SIGMUND *does not move.* MARCUS *holds out his hand.*

Give it to me, you're in no danger; I've invented the whole thing.

SIGMUND *is motionless.*

Are you simply a thief? Why are you keeping it?

SIGMUND *is silent.*

MAYA: Marcus . . .

MARCUS: I insist he answer me . . . (*To* SIGMUND): Why are you keeping that pistol? (*He laughs.*) But of course you know perfectly well I've told you the truth; it was just too good an opportunity to cover me with your contempt . . . in her eyes and (*pointing toward* ADRIAN) the eyes of the world.

ADRIAN: Now, Marcus, I had no intention . . .

MARCUS: Oh, come now, Adrian, he's been writing this story for you all evening! *New York Times* feature on Socialist decadence.

ADRIAN: Now, wait a minute . . .

MARCUS: But it's so obvious! . . .

ADRIAN: Wait a minute, will you? He has a right to be uneasy.

MARCUS: No more than I do, and for quite the same reason.

ADRIAN: Why!

MARCUS (*laughs*): To whom am *I* talking, Adrian—the *New York Times*, or your novel, or you?

ADRIAN: For Christ's sake, are you serious?

MARCUS (*laughs*): Why not? You may turn out to be as dangerous to me as he believes I am to him. Yes!

ADRIAN *looks astonished.*

Why is it any more absurd? Especially after that last piece of yours, which, you'll pardon me, was stuffed with the most primitive misunderstandings of what it means to live in this country. You haven't a clue, Adrian—you'll forgive me, but I have to say that. So I'm entitled to a bit of uneasiness.

ADRIAN: Marcus, are you asking me to account for myself?

MARCUS: By no means, but why must I?

MAYA: Why don't we all go to the playground and swing with the other children?

MARCUS (*laughs*): Very good, yes.

MAYA (*to* ADRIAN): Why is he so complicated? They allow him this house to store his father's library. These books earn hard currency. To sell them he must have a passport.

MARCUS: Oh, he knows all that, dear—it's hopeless; when did the facts ever change a conviction? It doesn't matter. (*He looks at his watch.*)

ADRIAN: It does, though. It's a terrible thing. It's maddening.

MARCUS (*denigrating*): Well . . .

ADRIAN: It is, you know it is. Christ, you're such old friends, you're writers . . . I never understood the sadness in this country, but I swear, I think it's . . .

MARCUS: Oh, come off it, Adrian—what country isn't sad?

ADRIAN: I think you've accepted something.

MARCUS: And you haven't?

ADRIAN: Goddammit, Marcus, we can still speak for ourselves! And not for some . . . (*He breaks off.*)

MARCUS: Some what?

ADRIAN (*walks away*): . . . Well, never mind.

MARCUS: I've spoken for no one but myself here, Adrian. If there seems to be some . . . unspoken interest . . . well, there is, of course. I am interested in seeing that this country does not fall back into darkness. And if he must sacrifice something for that, I think he should. That's plain enough, isn't it?

ADRIAN: I guess the question is . . . how you feel about that yourself.

MARCUS (*laughs*): But I feel terribly about it. I think it's dreadful. I think there's no question he is our best living writer. Must I go on, or is that enough? (*Silence.*) What change can feelings make? It is a situation which I can tell you—*no one wants* . . . no one. If I flew into an orgasm of self-revelation here it might seem more candid, but it would change nothing . . . except possibly to multiply the confusion.

MAYA (*to* ADRIAN): I think you were saying the same thing before. . . . Tell him.

MARCUS: What?

ADRIAN: Whether it matters anymore, what anyone feels . . . about anything. Whether we're not just some sort of . . . filament that only lights up when it's plugged into whatever power there is.

MAYA: It's interesting.

MARCUS: I don't know—it seems rather childish. When was a man ever conceivable apart from society? Unless you're looking for the angel who wrote each of our blessed names in his book of gold. The collective giveth and the collective taketh away—beyond that . . . (*he looks to the ceiling*) . . . was never anything but a sentimental metaphor; a God which now is simply a form of art. Whose style may still move us, but there was never any mercy in that plaster. The only difference now, it seems to me, is that we've ceased to expect any.

ADRIAN: I know one reason I came. I know it's an awkward question, but—those tanks bivouacked out there in the countryside . . . do they figure at all in your minds?

MAYA: Do you write *every minute?*

ADRIAN: Well, do they? (*To* MARCUS): Are they part of your lives at all?

MARCUS: I don't really know . . .

ADRIAN: Maya? It interests me.

MAYA: It's such a long time, now. And you don't see them unless you drive out there . . .

MARCUS: It's hard to say.

ADRIAN (*of* SIGMUND): Why do you suppose he can't stop thinking about them? I bet there isn't an hour a day when they don't cross his mind.

MAYA: Because he is a genius. When he enters the tram, the conductor refuses to accept his fare. In the grocery store they give him the best oranges. The usher bows in the theatre when she shows him to his seat. (*She goes to* SIGMUND, *touches his hair.*) He is our Sigmund. He is loved, he creates our memories. Therefore, it is only a question of time when he will create the departure of these tanks and they will go home. And then we shall all be ourselves, with nothing overhead but the sky, and he will turn into a monument standing in the park. (*Her eyes fill with tears, she turns up his face.*) Go, darling. Please. There is nothing left for you.

SIGMUND (*touches her face*): Something, perhaps. We shall see.

MAYA *moves right to the window, sips a drink.*

IRINA (*with a swimming gesture, to* MARCUS): I am bathing?

MARCUS: Yes, of course—come, I'll get you a towel. (*He starts to rise.*)

MAYA (*looking out the window*): She'd better wait a little—I used all the hot water. (*With a laugh, to* SIGMUND): I came tonight to take a bath!

MARCUS *laughs.*

ADRIAN: Marcus, when they arrested you . . .

MAYA (*suddenly*): Will you stop writing, for Christ's sake! Isn't there something else to talk about?

MARCUS: Why not—if he's interested?

MAYA: Are we some sick fish in a tank! (*To* ADRIAN): Stop it! (*She gets up, goes to the drink table.*) What the hell do you expect people to *do?* What *is* it?

MARCUS: You've had enough, dear . . .

MAYA (*pouring*): I have not had enough, dear. (*She suddenly slams the glass down on the table.*) Fuck all this diplomacy! (*At* ADRIAN): You're in no position to judge anybody! We have nothing to be ashamed of!

MARCUS (*turning away in disgust*): Oh, for God's sake . . .

MAYA: You know what he brought when he came to me? A bottle of milk!

Perplexed, MARCUS *turns to her.*

I wake up and he's in the kitchen, drinking *milk*! (*She stands before* MARCUS, *awaiting his reaction.*) A grown man!

MARCUS (*to calm her*): Well, they drink a lot of it in the States.

MAYA (*quietly, seeking to explain*): He smelled like a baby, all night.

MARCUS (*stands*): I'll make you some coffee . . .

He starts past her, but she stops him with her hand on his arm, frightened and remorseful. She kisses him.

MAYA: I'm going home. (*She takes his hand, tries to lead him toward* SIGMUND *with imperative force.*) Come, be his friend . . . you are friends, darling . . . (*The telephone in the bedroom rings. She turns up to the entrance in surprise.*) Goddamn that Hilton!

She starts toward the bedroom, but as the telephone rings again, MARCUS *goes up and exits into the bedroom. She comes to* SIGMUND.

Darling . . . (*She points up to the ceiling, speaking softly in desperation.*) I really don't think there is anything there. I would never do that to you, you know that. I think it was only to make himself interesting—he can't write anymore; it left him . . . (*In anguish*): It left him!

SIGMUND: I know.

MAYA: He loves you, he loves you, darling! . . . (*She grips her head.*) My God, I'm sick . . .

She starts upstage as MARCUS *enters. He has a stunned look.*

She halts, seeing him, looks at him questioningly. SIGMUND *turns to look at him, and* ADRIAN. *After a moment . . .*

MARCUS (*turns to* SIGMUND *with a gesture inviting him to go to the phone*): It's Alexandra.

SIGMUND *does not move.*

. . . She wishes to speak to you.

SIGMUND *stands, confounded by Marcus's look, and goes out into the bedroom.* MARCUS *remains there, staring.*

MAYA: What?

MARCUS *is silent, staring.*

ADRIAN: Something happen?

MARCUS *crosses the stage and descends into his chair, his face transfixed by some enigma.*

MAYA (*in fright, starting up toward the bedroom*): Sigmund! . . .

SIGMUND *enters, halts, shakes his head, uttering an almost soundless laugh, his eyes alive to something incredible.*

MARCUS: They're returning his manuscript.

MAYA *claps her hands together, then crosses herself, her face between explosive joy and some terror, rigid, sobered.*

ADRIAN (*grabs* SIGMUND *by the shoulders*): Is it true?

MARCUS: She may be able to bring it when she comes.

ADRIAN: Sigmund! (*He kisses him. They look at each other and laugh.*)

SIGMUND (*half smiling*): You believe it?

ADRIAN (*taken aback*): Don't you?

SIGMUND (*laughs*): I don't know! (*He walks, dumbfounded.*) . . . Yes, I suppose I believe. (*He suddenly laughs.*) Why not! They have made me ridiculous, therefore I must believe it.

MARCUS: Well, the main thing is, you . . .

SIGMUND: Yes, that is the main thing. I must call Elizabeth . . . (*He starts to the bedroom but looks at his watch.*) No . . . she will not yet be home.

ADRIAN (*to all*): What could it mean? (*He laughs, seeing* SIGMUND.) You look punchy. (*He grabs him.*) Wake up! You got it back! . . . Listen, come to Paris with me . . . with the boy and Elizabeth. We'll get you a visa—you can be in New

York in ten days. We'll go to my publisher, I'll break his arm, we'll get you a tremendous advance, and you're on your way.

SIGMUND (*laughing*): Wait, wait . . .

ADRIAN: Say yes! Come on! You can waste the rest of your life in this goddamned country. Jesus, why can't they steal it again tomorrow? (*To the ceiling*): I didn't mean that about the country. But it's infuriating—they play you like a yo-yo.

SIGMUND (*sits; an aura of irony on his voice*): So, Maya . . . you are immortal again.

ADRIAN: Is *she* that character?

MAYA: Of course.

ADRIAN: She sounded terrific.

MAYA: She is the best woman he has ever written—fantastic, complicated personality. (*To* SIGMUND): What is there to keep you now? It is enough, no?

IRINA: Is good?

MARCUS (*patting her*): Yes, very good.

SIGMUND: She is so lucky—she understands nothing. We also understand nothing—but for us is not lucky.

MAYA: We should go to Francesco's later—we should have a party.

SIGMUND (*turns to her with a faint smile*): It is strange, eh? We have such good news and we are sad.

MARCUS: It isn't sadness.

SIGMUND: Perhaps only some sort of humiliation. (*He shakes his head.*) We must admire them—they are very intelligent—they can even create unhappiness with good news.

ADRIAN (*to* MARCUS): What do you suppose happened?

MARCUS: I've no idea.

ADRIAN: It seems like a gesture of some kind. Is it?

MARCUS: I haven't the foggiest.

ADRIAN: Could it be that I was here?

MARCUS: Who knows? Of course they would like to make peace with him, it's a gesture in that sense.

SIGMUND *looks across at him.*

I think you ought to consider it that way.

SIGMUND: It is their contempt; they are laughing.

MARCUS: Not necessarily—some of them have great respect for you.

SIGMUND: No, no, they are laughing.
MAYA: Why are you such children?

SIGMUND *turns to her.*

It is not respect and it is not contempt—it is nothing.
ADRIAN: But it must mean something.
MAYA: Why? They have the power to take it and the power to give it back.
ADRIAN: Well, that's a meaning.
MAYA: You didn't know that before? When it rains you get wet—that is not exactly meaningful (*To the three*): There's nothing to say; it is a terrible embarrassment for geniuses, but there is simply no possible comment to be made.
SIGMUND: How is in Shakespeare? "We are like flies to little boys, they kill us for their sport."
MAYA: They are not killing you at all. Not at all.
SIGMUND: Why are you angry with me? I am not obliged to ask why something happens?
MAYA: Because you can live happily and you don't want to.
ADRIAN: It's not so simple.
MAYA: But for you it is! You are so rich, Adrian, you live so well—why must he be heroic?
ADRIAN: I've never told him to . . .
MAYA: Then tell him to get out! Be simple, be clear to him . . .
ADRIAN: I've been very clear to him . . .
MAYA: Good! (*To* SIGMUND): So the three of us are of the same opinion, you see? Let's have a party at Francesco's . . . call Elizabeth . . . a farewell party. All right?

He looks up at her.

It is all finished, darling!

He smiles, shaking his head. She is frightened and angry.

What? What is it? What more can be said?
SIGMUND (*with a certain laughter*): Is like some sort of theatre, no? Very bad theatre—our emotions have no connection with the event. Myself also—I *must* speak, darling—I do not understand myself. I must confess, I have feeling of gratitude; *before* they have stolen my book I was never grateful. *Now* I am grateful— (*His laughter vanishes.*) I cannot accept

such confusion, Maya, is very bad for my mentality. I must speak! I think we must all speak now! (*He ends looking at* MARCUS; *his anger is open.*)

MARCUS: What can I tell you? I know nothing.

SIGMUND: I am sure not, but we can speculate, perhaps? (*To* MAYA): Please, darling—sit; we must wait for Alexandra, we have nothing to do. Please, Adrian—sit down. . . . I have some idea . . .

ADRIAN *sits.* SIGMUND *continues to* MAYA.

. . . which I would like to discuss before I leave my country.

MAYA *sits slowly, apprehensively. He turns to* MARCUS, *adopting a quiet, calm air.*

Is possible, Marcus—there was some sort of mistake? Perhaps only one police commander has made this decision for himself—to stealing my book? Perhaps the government was also surprised?

MARCUS *considers in silence.*

I am interested your opinion. *I* think so, perhaps—no?

MARCUS: Do you know if they were the Security Police?

SIGMUND: Yes, Security Police.

MARCUS: *They* might, I suppose.

SIGMUND: I think so. But in this case . . . this fellow in London taxi—is possible he was also speaking for himself?

MARCUS: I can't believe that.

SIGMUND: But if he was speaking for government . . . such terrible thing against me—why have they chosen to returning my manuscript? I think is not logical, no?

MARCUS: . . . Unless they had second thoughts, and felt it would make it easier for you to leave.

SIGMUND: Yes. That is very strong idea.

ADRIAN: I think that's it.

SIGMUND: Very good, yes. But at same time, if I have manuscript—you do not object that I . . . ?

MARCUS: Go ahead—it's simply that I know no more than . . .

SIGMUND: You understand is very important to me. . . . I must understand why I am leaving.

MARCUS: Of course. Go ahead.

SIGMUND (*slight pause*): If I have manuscript, I must probably conclude is *not* dangerous for me here, no? I must believe is only some particular antagonistic enemy who wish me to go out. Is possible?

MARCUS: What can I tell you?

SIGMUND (*with nearly an outcry through his furious control*): But you know you are sad! I am sad, Maya is sad—if was some sort of mistake . . . why we are not happy?

MAYA *gets up and strides toward the bedroom.*

Maya?

MAYA (*hardly turning back*): I'm going home . . .

SIGMUND (*leaps up and intercepts her*): No, no—we must have celebration! (*He grips her hands.*)

MAYA: Let me go!

SIGMUND: No! We have tremendous good news, we must have correct emotion!

MAYA (*wrenching her hands free, pointing at his pocket*): Give me that thing . . . Give it to me!

SIGMUND: My God—I had forgotten it. (*He takes out the pistol, looks at it.*)

MAYA: Please. Sigmund. Please! . . .

SIGMUND: I have crazy idea . . .

MAYA (*weeping*): Sigmund . . .

SIGMUND (*moving toward the piano*): One time very long ago, I have read in American detective story . . . that criminal has placed revolver inside piano. (*He sets the pistol on the strings and comes around to the bench.*) Then someone is playing very fortissimo . . . something like Beethoven . . . (*raising his hands over the keyboard*) . . . and he is firing the pistol.

ADRIAN: What the hell are you doing?

SIGMUND (*smashes his hands down on the keyboard*): Ha! Is not true.

ADRIAN (*stands*): What the hell are you doing?

SIGMUND: Wait! I have idea . . . (*He reaches over, takes out the pistol, and cocks it.*)

MAYA: Marcus!

SIGMUND (*replacing the cocked pistol in the piano*): Now we shall see . . .

ADRIAN (*rushing* MAYA *away from the piano*): Watch out!

SIGMUND (*crashes his hands down; the gun explodes, the strings reverberate*): Is true! (*He reaches in and takes up the revolver.*) My God, I am so happy . . . (*He holds up the revolver.*) The truth is alive in our country, Marcus! (*He comes and sits near* MARCUS.) Is unmistakable, no?—when something is true?

He looks at the pistol, puts it in his pocket. MARCUS *turns to him only now.* MAYA *suddenly weeps, sobbing, and makes for the bedroom.*

I cannot permit you to leave, Maya!

She halts, turning to him in terror.

I must insist, darling—is most important evening of my life, and I understand nothing. Why do you weep, why do you go? If I am ridiculous I must understand why? Please . . . sit. Perhaps you can say something.

She sits a distance from him and MARCUS. ADRIAN *remains standing, catching his breath; he leans his head on his hand, as though caught by a rush of sadness, and he shakes his head incredulously, glancing at* MARCUS.

MARCUS: What is it? What *is* it!

SIGMUND: This fellow . . . this fellow in taxi who has threatened me—what was his name?

MARCUS: I don't recall, I only heard it once. Granitz, I think. Or Grodnitz. But I'm sure he didn't know you.

SIGMUND: Grodnitz.

MARCUS: . . . Or Granitz.

ADRIAN: You know him?

SIGMUND: . . . No. (*Slight pause.*) No Granitz. No Grodnitz. (*Slight pause. He takes the pistol out of his pocket, looks at it in his hand, then turns again to* MARCUS.) He exists? Or is imaginary man?

MARCUS *is silent.*

Was *ever* discussion of trial for me? Or is imaginary trial?

MARCUS *is silent.* SIGMUND *looks at the pistol again; then, stretching over to* MARCUS, *he places it in his hand.*

I believe I have no danger, at the moment.

Long pause. No one dares do more than glance at MARCUS, *whose face is filled with his fury. The pause lengthens.* SIGMUND *looks at his watch.*

I will try to call Elizabeth.

MARCUS: The sole function of every other writer is to wish he were you.

SIGMUND *stands and looks to* MAYA, *who avoids his eyes. He exits into the bedroom. After a moment . . .*

ADRIAN (*sotto, to assuage* MARCUS): He's terribly scared . . .

MARCUS (*slight pause; like a final verdict*): I couldn't care less. (*He looks at his watch.*)

ADRIAN (*silent for a moment*): For what it's worth . . . I know he has tremendous feeling for you.

MARCUS: For his monument. To build his monument he has to prove that everyone else is a coward or corrupt. My mistake was to offer him my help—it's a menace to his lonely grandeur. No one is permitted anything but selfishness. He's insane.

ADRIAN: Oh, come on . . .

MARCUS: He's paranoid—these letters to the foreign press are for nothing but to bring on another confrontation. It was too peaceful; they were threatening him with tolerance. He must find evil or he can't be good.

MAYA: Let's not talk about it anymore . . .

MARCUS: I exist too, Maya! I am not dancing around that megalomania again.

Slight pause.

ADRIAN: I can't blame you, but I wish you wouldn't cut out on him yet. Look, I'll stay through the week, maybe I can convince him. Does he have a week?

MARCUS (*slowly turns to* ADRIAN): How would I know?

ADRIAN: All I meant was whether you . . .

MARCUS: I won't have any more of this, Adrian!

Slight pause.

ADRIAN: I believe you—I've told him to get out.
MARCUS: No, you haven't; you've insinuated.
ADRIAN: Christ's sake, you've heard me say . . .
MARCUS: I *have* heard you.

They are facing each other. Slight pause.

You don't believe me, Adrian . . . not really.

ADRIAN *can't answer.*

So it's all over. It's the end of him—I've been there. He will smash his head against the walls, and the rest of us will pay for his grandeur.

Slight pause. ADRIAN *turns front in his conflict.* SIGMUND *enters.* MARCUS *turns away.*

MAYA (*with a forced attempt at cheerfulness*): Did you reach her? Elizabeth?
SIGMUND: She is very happy. (*To* MARCUS): She send you her greetings—she is grateful. (*Slight pause.*) I also.

MARCUS *half turns toward him.* SIGMUND *says no more, goes to his chair and sits.*

ADRIAN: Sigmund? (SIGMUND *glances at him.*) Do you trust me?

SIGMUND *is silent.*

I'm convinced he's told you the truth.

SIGMUND *is silent.*

In all the times we've talked about you, he's never shown anything but a wide-open pride in you, and your work. He's with you. You have to believe that.

SIGMUND *turns, stares at Marcus's profile for a moment, then looks at* MAYA. *She ultimately turns slightly away. He looks down at the floor.*

SIGMUND: I am afraid; that is all. I think I will not be able to write in some other country.
ADRIAN: Oh, that's impossible . . .

SIGMUND: I am not cosmopolitan writer, I am provincial writer. I believe I must hear my language every day, I must walk in these particular streets. I think in New York I will have only some terrible silence. Is like old tree—it is difficult to moving old tree, they most probably die.

ADRIAN: But if they lock you up . . .

SIGMUND: Yes, but that is my fate; I must accept my fate. But to run away because of some sort of rumor—I have only some rumor, no? How will I support this silence that I have brought on myself? This is terrible idea, no? How I can accept to be so ridiculous? Therefore, is reasonable, I believe— that I must absolutely understand who is speaking to me.

ADRIAN (*slight pause, a hesitation*): I'm going to level with you, Sigmund—I think you're being far too . . .

SIGMUND (*a frustrated outburst*): I am not crazy, Adrian! (*All turn to him, fear in their faces. He spreads his arms, with an upward glance.*) Who is commanding me? Who is this voice? *Who is speaking to me?*

MAYA: They. (*An instant's silence; she seems ashamed to look directly at* SIGMUND. *She gestures almost imperceptibly upward.*) It is there.

MARCUS (*in protest*): Maya!

MAYA: Why not! (*To* SIGMUND): They have heard it all.

MARCUS (*To* SIGMUND *and* ADRIAN): It isn't true, there's nothing.

MAYA (*persisting, to* SIGMUND): He has risked everything . . . for you. God knows what will happen for what has been said here.

MARCUS (*to* SIGMUND): There's nothing . . . she can't know . . . (*To* MAYA): You can't know that . . .

MAYA (*her eyes to the ceiling*): Who else have we been speaking to all evening! (*To them all*): Who does not believe it? (*To* MARCUS): It is his life, darling—we must begin to say what we believe. Somewhere, we must begin!

Pause. She sits a distance from SIGMUND; *only after a moment does she turn to face him as she fights down her shame and her fear of him.*

SIGMUND: So.

MAYA (*downing her shame*): Just so, yes. You must go.

SIGMUND: For your sake.

MAYA: Yes.

MARCUS (*softly, facing front*): It isn't true.

MAYA: And yours. For all of us.

SIGMUND: You must . . . deliver me? My departure?

MAYA *stiffens. She cannot speak.*

For your program? His passport? . . .

ADRIAN: Sigmund, it's enough . . .

MAYA: He had no need to return, except he loves you. There was no need. That is also true.

SIGMUND (*his head clamped in his hands*): My God . . . Maya. (*Pause. To* MARCUS): They brought you back to make sure my departure?

ADRIAN (*aborting the violence coming*): Come on, Sigmund, it's enough . . .

SIGMUND (*trying to laugh*): But she is not some sort of whore! I have many years with this woman! . . .

ADRIAN: What more do you *want*!

MARCUS: Her humiliation; she's not yet on her knees to him. We are now to take our places, you see, at the foot of the cross, as he floats upward through the plaster on the wings of his immortal contempt. We lack remorse, it spoils the picture. (*He glares, smiling at* SIGMUND, *who seems on the verge of springing at him.*)

ADRIAN (*to* SIGMUND): Forget it, Sigmund—come on . . . (*To* MARCUS): Maybe you ought to call that Alexandra woman.

MARCUS: She'll be along.

Silence. The moment expands. SIGMUND *stares front, gripping his lower face.* ADRIAN *is glancing at him with apprehension.* MAYA *is looking at no one.*

SIGMUND (*to* MAYA): You can say nothing to me?

MAYA (*slight pause*): You know my feeling.

SIGMUND: I, not. I know your name. Who is this woman?

MARCUS: Don't play that game with him.

SIGMUND: It is a game?

ADRIAN: Come on, fellas . . .

SIGMUND (*irritated, to* ADRIAN): Is interesting to me. (*To* MARCUS): What is your game? What did you mean?

MARCUS: It's called Power. Or Moral Monopoly. The winner takes all the justifications. When you write this, Adrian, I hope you include the fact that they refused him a visa for many years and he was terribly indignant—the right to leave was sacred to civilization. Now he has that right and it's an insult. You can draw your own conclusions.

SIGMUND: And what is the conclusion?

MARCUS: You are a moral blackmailer. We have all humored you, Sigmund, out of some misplaced sense of responsibility to our literature. Or maybe it's only our terror of vanishing altogether. We aren't the Russians—after you and Otto and Peter there aren't a handful to keep the breath of life in this language. We have taken all the responsibility and left you all the freedom to call us morally bankrupt. But now you're free to go, so the responsibility moves to you. Now it's yours. All yours. We have done what was possible; now you will do what is necessary, or turn out our lights. And that is where it stands.

SIGMUND (*slight pause*): This is all?

MARCUS *is silent.*

ADRIAN: What more can be said, Sigmund? What can they give you? It's pointless.

SIGMUND (*turns to* MAYA): What you can give me, Maya? (*She is silent.*) There is nothing? I am only some sort of . . . comical Jesus Christ? Is only my egotism? This is all?

In silence, MAYA *turns to face him.*

You understand what I ask you?

MAYA: Yes.

SIGMUND: You cannot? (*Slight pause. Then he glances toward* MARCUS.) After so many years . . . so many conversations . . . so many hope and disaster—you can only speak for them? (*He gestures toward the ceiling.*) Is terrible, no? Why we have lived?

ADRIAN (*to cut off his mounting anger*): Sigmund . . .

SIGMUND (*swiftly, his eyes blazing*): Why have you come here? What do you want in this country?

ADRIAN (*astonished*): What the hell are you . . .

SIGMUND: You are scientist observing the specimens: this whore? this clever fellow making business with these gangsters?

ADRIAN: For Christ's sake, Sigmund, what can I do!

SIGMUND: They are killing us, Adrian—they have destroyed my friends! You are free man— (*with a gesture toward the ceiling*) why you are obliged to be clever? Why do you come here, Adrian?

MAYA: To save his book.

ADRIAN: That's a lie!

MAYA: But it's exactly what you told me an hour ago. (*She stands. To both* SIGMUND *and* ADRIAN): What is the sin? He has come for his profit, to rescue two years' work, to make more money . . .

ADRIAN: That's a goddamned lie!

MAYA: And for friendship! Oh, yes—his love for you. I believe it! Like ours. Absolutely like ours! Is love not love because there is some profit in it? Who speaks only for his heart? And yes, I speak to them now—this moment, this very moment to them, that they may have mercy on my program, on his passport. Always to them, in some part to them for my profit—here and everywhere in this world! Just as you do.

SIGMUND: I speak for Sigmund.

MAYA: Only Sigmund? Then why can't you speak for Sigmund in America? Because you will not have them in America to hate! And if you cannot hate you cannot write and you will not be Sigmund anymore, but another lousy refugee ordering his chicken soup in broken English—and where is the profit in that? They are your theme, your life, your partner in this dance that cannot stop or you will die of silence! (*She moves toward him. Tenderly*): They are in you, darling. And if you stay . . . it is also for your profit . . . as it is for ours to tell you to go. Who can speak for himself alone?

A heavy brass knocker is heard from below. SIGMUND *lifts his eyes to the ceiling.* MARCUS *stands and faces* SIGMUND, *who now turns to him. Silence.*

SIGMUND: Tell her, please . . . is impossible . . . any transaction. Only to return my property.

MAYA (*with an abjectness, a terror, taking his hand and kissing it*): Darling . . . for my sake. For this little life that I have made . . .

MARCUS (*with anger, disgust*): Stop it! (*He turns to* SIGMUND.)

For your monument. For the bowing ushers in the theatre. For the power . . . the power to bring down everyone.

SIGMUND (*spreads his hands, looks up at the ceiling*): I don't know. (*He turns to* MARCUS.) But I will never leave. Never.

Another knock is heard. MARCUS, *his face set, goes out and up the corridor.* SIGMUND *turns to* MAYA. *She walks away, her face expressionless, and stands at the window staring out.*

Forgive me, Maya.

She doesn't turn to him. He looks to ADRIAN.

Is quite simple. We are ridiculous people now. And when we try to escape it, we are ridiculous too.

ADRIAN: No.

SIGMUND: I think so. But we cannot help ourselves. I must give you . . . certain letters, I wish you to keep them . . . before you leave. (*He sits.*) I have one some years ago from Malraux. Very elegant. *French,* you know? Also Gyula Illyes, Hungarian . . . very wise fellow. Heinrich Böll, Germany, one letter. Kobo Abe, Japan—he also. Nadine Gordimer, South Africa. Also Cortázar, Argentina . . . (*Slight pause.*) My God, eh? So many writers! Like snow . . . like forest . . . these enormous trees everywhere on the earth. Marvelous. (*Slight pause. A welling up in him. He suddenly cries out to* MAYA *across the stage.*) Maya! Forgive me . . . (*He hurries to her.*) I cannot help it.

MAYA: I know. (*She turns to him, reaches out and touches his face.*) Thank you.

SIGMUND (*surprised, he is motionless for an instant, then pulls her into his arms and holds her face*): Oh, my God! Thank you, Maya.

The voices of MARCUS *and* ALEXANDRA *are heard approaching from the darkness up the corridor. The three of them turn toward the door.*

IRINA (*revolving her finger, to* MAYA): Now, music?

CURTAIN

PLAYING FOR TIME

A SCREENPLAY BASED ON
THE BOOK BY FANIA FÉNELON

Fade in on Fania Fénelon singing. Her voice is unheard, we hear only the opening music.

Cut to a sidewalk café in the afternoon. German soldiers relax, accompanied by French girls. We are in German-occupied Paris, 1942.

Cut to the Nazi flag flying over the Arc de Triomphe.

Cut to Fania accompanying herself on the piano in a Parisian ballad warmed with longing and wartime sentiment. The audience, almost all German troops and French girlfriends, is well-behaved and enjoying her homey romanticism, which salts their so-far epic conquests with pathos and a bit of self-pity.

Nothing in her manner betrays her hostility to Nazism and its destruction of France in the recent battles. She hopes they are enjoying their evening, promises to do what she can to help them forget their soldierly duties; but to the knowing eye there is perhaps a little extra irony in a look she casts, a smile she pours onto the upturned face of a nearby officer that suggests her inner turmoil at having to perform for the conqueror. She is radiant here, an outgoing woman who is still young and with a certain heartiness and appetite for enjoyment.

She is roundly applauded now at the number's end, and she bows and backs into darkness.

Cut to a train of freight cars, moving through open French farmland.

Cut to the inside of one freight car. It is packed with people, many of them well-dressed bourgeois, sitting uncomfortably jammed in. The ordinariness of the types is emphasized, but above that their individuation. Moreover, while all are of course deeply uneasy and uncomfortable, there is no open alarm.

A husband is massaging his wife's cramped shoulders.

A mother is working to remove a speck from a teenage daughter's eye.

Worker types survey the mass with suspicion.

A *clocharde*—a beggar woman off a Paris street—wrapped in rags, and rather at home in this situation, surveys the company.

A second mother pulls a young boy away from a neighbor's bag of food.

Chic people try to keep apart; they are soigné, even bored.

Students try to bury themselves in novels.

Two intellectuals scrunched up on the floor are playing chess on a small board.

A boy scout of twelve is doing his knots on a short rope.

An old asthmatic man in a fur-collared coat is urged by his wife to take his pill. He holds it between his fingers, unhappily looking around for water.

Cut to Fania, dressed in a beautiful fur coat and fur hat; her elegant valise is at her feet. She is carrying a net bag, with some fruit and a sausage, bread, and a bottle of water, which she offers the old man. He gratefully accepts it, takes his pill, drinks a sip, and returns her the bottle.

Beside Fania on the straw-covered floor sits Marianne, a girl of twenty, quite well dressed and overweight. Marianne has an unmarked, naive face. She is avidly glancing down at Fania's net bag.

FANIA: Have another piece of sausage, if you like.

MARIANNE: I'm so stupid—I never thought to take anything.

FANIA, *kindly:* Well, I suppose your mother has always done that for you.

MARIANNE: Yes. Just a tiny piece . . . *She breaks off more than a tiny piece.* I still can't believe I'm sitting so close to you! I have every one of your records, I think. Really—all my friends love your style.

Marianne bites her sausage and chews sensually.

FANIA: Do you know why they arrested you?

MARIANNE—*glances about nervously for an interloper:* I think it was because of my boyfriend—he's in the Resistance.

FANIA: Oh!— Mine too.

MARIANNE—*reaches under her coat:* I adore him! Maurice is his name.

She hands a snapshot to Fania who looks at it and smiles admiringly. Then Fania opens her soft leather purse and hands a snapshot to Marianne.

FANIA: He's Robert.

MARIANNE, *looking at photo:* Oh, he's fantastic! —a blond! I love blonds. *They return photos.* In the prison they kept beating me up. . . .

FANIA: Me, too.

MARIANNE: . . . They kept asking where he is, but I don't even know!—They nearly broke this arm. *Glancing around:* But somebody said it's really because we're Jewish that they picked us up. Are you?

FANIA: Half.

MARIANNE: I'm half too. Although it never meant anything to me.

FANIA: Nor me.

They silently stare at the others. Marianne glances down at Fania's food again.

FANIA: You really shouldn't eat so much.

MARIANNE: I can't help it; I never used to until the prison. It made me hungry all the time. I just hope my boyfriend never sees me like this—you wouldn't believe how slim I was only a few months ago. And now I'm bursting out of everything. But my legs are still good. Don't you think? *She extends her leg rather childishly.* I still can't believe I'm sitting next to you! I really have all your records.

Cut to the boy scout, who is now sitting with a compass on his knee, studying the needle. Beside him, his mother is asleep.

FANIA: Can you tell our direction?

BOY SCOUT: South.

A nearby worker overhears.

WORKER: It's probably going to be Munich. They need labor on the farms around there.

SECOND WORKER: I wouldn't mind. I love the outdoors.

A nearby woman adds her wisdom.

WOMAN: They have those tiny little thatched houses down there. I've seen photographs.

FIRST CHESS PLAYER: In my opinion, we'll be machine-gunned right where we sit—and I'm especially sorry for your sake, Madame Fénelon—your music is for me the sound of Paris.

FANIA: Thank you.

MARIANNE, *quietly:* I'm not sure I could do farm work—could you?

FANIA—*shrugs:* Have you ever worked?

MARIANNE—*a little laugh:* Oh no—I never even *met* a worker till the prison. I was in school or at home all my life. *The little laugh again.* And now I don't even know where my parents are. . . . *She verges on a shivering fear with startling rapidity.* Would you mind if we sort of stuck together?

Fania puts an arm around her and Marianne nestles gratefully into Fania's body. A moment passes; Fania reaches into her net bag and gives Marianne a bonbon. Marianne avidly eats it and Fania pats her hair as though, in effect, forgiving her another dietary lapse.

Cut to the boy scout, alert to some change in the compass. He takes it off his knee, shakes it, then sets it back on his knee.

FANIA: Has it changed?

BOY SCOUT: We've turned to the east.

The first chess player turns to the scout, then leans over to read the compass himself. He then resumes his position, a stare of heightened apprehension growing on his face.

SECOND CHESS PLAYER, *reassuringly:* But a compass can't be right with so much metal around it, can it?

Cut to a sudden explosion of indignation from deep in the crowd; people leaping up to escape something under the hay on the floor; yells of disgust and anger. . . . The mother and little boy emerge from within the crowd, he buttoning his pants. . . .

MOTHER: Well, what is he supposed to do!
FIRST MAN: He can use the pail over there!
SECOND MAN: The pail is full.
FIRST MAN, *yelling up to a grill high in a wall of the car:* Hey! Let us empty the pail!

Only the sound of the clanking train returns. Defeated, the deportees rearrange themselves to find dry places on the floor. The train lurches.

Cut to the slop pail, filled with urine, overturning.

Cut to people, with higher disgust, fleeing from the contents and crowding each other even more, some even remaining on their feet.

Cut to Marianne coming out of Fania's embrace. She whispers in Fania's ear, while placing a hand on her own stomach. Fania glances down at her with distress.

FANIA: Try to hold out—they'll *have* to open the doors soon.
MARIANNE: Could I have another sip of water?
FANIA: But only wet your mouth. You've got to try to discipline yourself.

Marianne drinks from the water bottle. Fania, as she is replacing the stopper, happens to catch the thirsty stare of the old asthmatic man. She hesitates, then holds out the bottle, which is taken by the asthmatic's wife. The old man sips; he is weaker than earlier.

Cut to the nearly full water bottle. Superimposed on it is the crowd in its present postures, which are still rather normal for the circumstances—some are standing to avoid the floor, some are alert and energetic.
 The water level in the bottle drops; and the superimposed crowd is losing its energy, with people unconscious, one on top of the other; lips are parched, signs of real distress. . . .

Cut to Fania, asleep sitting up. Marianne awakens, lips parched, tries to get a drop out of the bottle, but it is empty. She looks into Fania's net bag, but it too is empty. Only half alive, Marianne, expressionless, sees a fight starting near her as a man pushes a woman away—and the woman is lowering her dress. . . .

MAN: Do it over there!—this is *my* place!

The woman trips over someone, looks down. . . .

Cut to the old asthmatic man. He's dead. His wife, spiritless and silent, holds his head in her lap.

Cut to the faces of the deportees experiencing the presence of the dead man. Unable to bear it any longer, Fania climbs up to the grill.

FANIA: Halloo! Listen! We've got a dead man in here! Halloo!

Surprisingly now, there is a squeal of brakes. People are thrown against each other, and the train stops. Expectation, fear, hope . . .

Cut to the freight-car doors rolling open. A powerful searchlight bathes the crowd, blinding them. The people try to get to their feet and gather their belongings.

From outside, half a dozen kapos leap into the car—these are prisoners working for the administration—and, armed with truncheons, they pull people out of the car onto the ground. ("Hurry up, everybody out, get moving" . . . etc.) They are brutal, enjoying their power.

Cut to the debarkation area. Under the spectral arc lights the cars are being emptied. Kapos are loading valises onto trolleys, but with a certain care, like porters.

Cut to the train platform. Late at night. Still wearing her fur coat and hat, Fania half unwillingly gives up her valise to a kapo. This kapo eyes Marianne's body and gives her a toothless come-on smile.

Cut to a sudden close-up of Dr. Mengele. This monster, the so-called Angel of Death, is a small, dapper man with a not unattractive face. He is the physician in charge of the selections, and in this shot is simply standing at the edge of the milling crowd, observing the people. Now he nods slightly, an order.

Cut to SS guards pushing the people into a rough line, one behind the other. A dozen or more guard dogs and handlers keep the proceedings lively. Snarls electrify, the air is filled with the whining of eager dogs. But the violence is still controlled.

Dr. Mengele faces the head of the line. With a gesture to right or left, with hardly a second's interval between individuals, he motions people toward several waiting trucks (marked with the Red Cross), or to an area where they stand and wait. Those in the latter are generally stronger, male, and younger.

And so the line moves rapidly toward Mengele's pointing fingers, and the crowd parts to the left and the right.

Cut to Fania, right behind Marianne on line, speaking into her ear.

FANIA: It's going to be all right—you see?—the Red Cross is here.

Cut to people being loaded onto the open-backed "Red Cross" trucks. Babies are passed over the crowd to mothers, the aged are carried aboard with the stronger helping. The air still carries the whining and barking of the dogs, the sounds of hurried commands.

Once again, intermittent close shots individualize the crowd, the types, relationships. The crowd, in fact, is relieved to be aboard and moving to some destination.

Cut to the trucks pulling away. Marianne and Fania, alone on the ground, look up at the packed truck that remains. Kapos raise its tailgate and fasten it.

FANIA: Wait—we're supposed to get on, aren't we?
KAPO: How old are you?
FANIA: I'm twenty-eight, she's twenty.
MARIANNE: I wouldn't mind a walk—may we?
KAPO, *with the very faintest glimmer of humor—he too is exhausted, skinny:* You can walk.

The kapo hurries up ahead and boards the truck. The truck starts to pull away, leaving the two women behind.

Cut to the people on the truck. The camera memorializes the faces we have come to know on the train—the boy scout, the chess players, the boy scout's mother, and so on. The truck moves off into darkness.

Cut to Marianne and Fania as they look around at the dark-ness—shapes of dark buildings surround them. Down the track we hear the activity of the guards and those selected to live.

FANIA: I guess we follow the trucks.

The two move together into the darkness.

Cut to a strange orange glow in the night sky. Is it a massive reflection of bright lights or is it flame? It comes from some half a mile off.

Cut to Fania and Marianne walking, looking up at the glow.

FANIA: There must be some sort of factory.

Out of the darkness a gaunt kapo pops up and starts walking along with them. He puts an arm around Marianne.

KAPO: Listen . . . I'll give you coffee.
FANIA, *pulling the kapo's arm away from Marianne:* This must be some high-class place—a cup of coffee for a woman?
KAPO: That's a lot. *Points arrogantly at Marianne.* See you later, Beauty.

Fania protectively grasps the frightened Marianne's hand and they move on into the dark toward the glow.

Cut to the reception area. Fania and Marianne enter the dimly lit room, perhaps twenty by forty feet. They enter uncertainly, unsure if they're supposed to be here. Five Pol-ish women prisoners, employed here, are lounging around a table. One cleans her nails, another reads a scrap of newspa-per, another is combing her companion's long hair. They are hefty, coarse, peasant types.

FANIA, *after a moment:* Is this where we get our things back?

She asks this question because—as we see now—along one wall of this room and extending out into a corridor which leads deeper into the building are, in neat piles, hundreds and hundreds of valises, stacks of clothes, piles of shoes, bins full of eyeglasses, false teeth, underwear, sweaters, gloves, galoshes, and every other imaginable personal item.

The Polish women turn to Fania and Marianne. One of them beckons silently, and the two approach her.

From the corridor enter two SS women in uniform. One of them is Frau Schmidt, the brutal, stupid German supervisor of the operation. They halt and expressionlessly observe.

The first Polish woman stands up from the table and simply takes Fania's handbag out of her hand. The second Polish woman grabs hold of Fania's fur coat and pulls it off her. Bag and coat go into the hands of the SS women, who admiringly examine them.

FIRST POLISH WOMAN: Your shoes.

Fania and Marianne, both in fear now, remove their shoes, which are carried to Frau Schmidt by the Poles. Frau Schmidt examines the expensive shoes appreciatively.

FIRST POLISH WOMAN: Undress.

Cut to Fania and Marianne, sinking into a stunned astonishment. And now hands working scissors enter the shot. Their hair—Fania has braids which are hard to cut—is almost completely removed, leaving tufts.

Cut to a long number—346,991—being tattooed on an arm. Backing off, we see it is Marianne's arm. She is now in a ludicrously outsized dress and shoes far too large. The same for Fania, who is staring down at her own tattoo. The tattooer is a male kapo, who works with his tongue sticking out the corner of his mouth.

Cut to a hundred or so women being handed dresses, some worn to mere shreds. Others are having their hair shorn as they wait to be tattooed. SS women move about, in charge.

Cut to Frau Schmidt, who is handed the little chess set from the train; she admires it, as well as the boy scout's compass. She sets them on the counter. They are then placed by a Polish woman in a receptacle already loaded with toys, stuffed animals, soccer balls, sports things.

Cut to Fania, nearby, as she recognizes these relics; her eyes flare with terror. She turns toward a nearby window.

Cut to the window. We see the eerie glow in the sky.

Cut to one of the Polish women, all but finished pinning Fania's plaits on her own hair, imitating Fania's sophisticated walk as her sister workers laugh.

Fania, humiliated and angered, touches her bare scalp.

Cut to the work gang, from Fania's point of view. An exhausted woman collapses at the feet of Lagerführerin Maria Mandel, who gestures toward a wheelbarrow. As kapos carry off the woman, one of her arms brushes Mandel's coat. Mandel viciously hits the arm away, brushing off her coat sleeve as the woman is dumped into the wheelbarrow.

POLISH WOMAN: How do I look, Jew-Crap?
FANIA: I'm not Jew-Crap, I'm French!

An uproar of laughter, and out of nowhere a smashing slap knocks Fania reeling to the floor. Over her stands SS Frau Schmidt, a powerhouse, looking down with menace.

Dissolve to dark.

Cut to the quarantine block—this is the barracks; dimly lit by a hanging bulb or two; a corridor between shelves, in effect, where women lie with barely room to turn over. The shelves go to the ceiling.

Fania and Marianne enter the corridor, escorted by a Polish woman, the Blockawa or Block Warden. She gestures for them to take bunks above and turns to leave.

The women in the bunks are cadaverous, barely able to summon interest in these new arrivals.

FANIA: Where are the people we came with? They went off on the trucks . . . ?

The Blockawa grips her arm and leads her to a window and points out.

Cut to the orange sky-glow. But from this closer distance smoke can be seen rising from a tall stack.

Cut to Fania, Marianne, and the Blockawa. The Blockawa points upward through the window.

BLOCKAWA: Your friends. You see? —cooking. You too, pretty soon.

The Blockawa cutely blinks both eyes, grins reassuringly, and walks away.

Cut to Marianne, quietly sobbing as she lies beside Fania on their bunk.

FANIA: Marianne? Listen to me. Come, girl, stop that.
MARIANNE: Why are they doing this? What do they get from it?

Fania glances to her other side where, on the shelf beside her, lies a famished-looking woman who might well be dead.

FANIA, *turning back to Marianne:* I've always had to have an aim in life—something I wanted to do next. That's what we need now if we're ever to get out of here alive.
MARIANNE: What sort of an aim?

Fania looks down into corridor below at the Blockawa, on patrol with a truncheon in her fist.

FANIA: If I ever get out of here alive, I'm going to kill a Polish woman.

Fania lies back, shuts her eyes, hating herself a little.

MARIANNE: I'm so hungry, Fania. Hold me.

Fania, on her back, embraces Marianne; then she turns the other way to look at the woman on her other side; she is skeletal, absolutely still. Cautiously Fania touches her skin and draws her hand away at the cold touch. Then she gives her a little shake. The woman has died.

Now she leans over the edge of the bunk and calls to the Blockawa.

FANIA: There's a dead woman up here.

The Blockawa, club in hand, allows a moment to pass; she slowly looks up at Fania with the interest of a seal, then strolls away.

Cut to a close shot of Fania and Marianne in their bunk. Marianne stares in fright at the corpse, then hides her face in Fania's side.

FANIA: We must have an aim. And I think the aim is to try to remember everything. I'll tell you a story. . . . Once upon a time there was a prince named Jean and he was terribly handsome. And he married a princess named Jeannette and she was terribly beautiful.

Marianne comes out of hiding under Fania's arm—she is childishly interested. . . .

MARIANNE: And?

FANIA: And one day the prince said, "My dear, we must have an aim in life, we must make children," and so they. . . .

As Fania talks, slowly fade to a double exposure of Fania and Marianne. Snow falls over the image of the two women in their bunk: a forest; now spring comes; flowers appear and green grass; brook ice melts—always over the image of Fania and Marianne dragging stones, carrying wood, digging drainage ditches. . . . And finally, once again, in their bunk—now without the dead woman, and they are both asleep, side by side. And both are haggard now, with the half-starved look of the other prisoners.

A voice blares out: "ATTENTION!"

Cut to the barracks. Women start to come obediently out of their bunks into the corridor. The Blockawa yells.

BLOCKAWA: Remain in place! Does anybody know how to sing *Madame Butterfly*!

Astonished silence. The Blockawa is infuriated.

BLOCKAWA: Does anyone know how to sing *Madame Butterfly*!

Cut to Fania, unsure whether to volunteer; she glances at Marianne, who urges her silently to do so. Below in the corridor the Blockawa starts to leave. Fania suddenly lunges and, half hanging out the bunk, waves to the monster woman. . . .

FANIA: I can!

Cut to Fania, entering from exterior darkness into a lighted room. She halts, looking around in total astonishment.

Cut to the musicians' barracks dayroom. Fania, as in a wild dream, sees some twenty-five women, most seated behind music stands, badly but cleanly dressed; some with shaved heads (Jewesses), others still with their hair. Unlike her former barracks, with its faint and few light bulbs, there is brightness here, although it is actually quite bare of furniture.

In the center stands a Bechstein grand, shiny, beautiful. At the sight of the piano, Fania's mouth falls open.

Compared to these women Fania is indeed woebegone —dirty, in ludicrously enormous shoes, a torn and ill-fitting dress.

Elzvieta, an older Pole with a full head of hair, approaches Fania and with a wet cloth wipes her face. Fania regards this kindness incredulously. Now Elzvieta runs her pitying fingers down Fania's cheek.

Etalina, petite, Rumanian, eighteen, brings a lump of bread and puts it in Fania's hand.

ETALINA: I'm Etalina. I saw you in Paris once, at the "Melody." *Fania bites into the bread.* My parents took me there last year for my birthday—I was seventeen.

Michou enters the group—a tiny, determined girl of twenty, a militant communist, terribly pale, with a soft poetic voice. Etalina indicates her (not without a slight air of joking superciliousness toward this wraith).

ETALINA: But she's the one who recognized you. This is Michou.

MICHOU: I saw you yesterday coming out of your barracks and I ran and told our kapo—she promised to audition you—

FANIA: What audition?

ETALINA: For the orchestra—us. *With some awe.* Our conductor is Alma Rosé. *Calls offscreen.* Charlotte, come and meet Fania Fénelon! *To Fania.* She's one of our best players, but she's shy as a deer. She can do Bach solos. . . .

CHARLOTTE—*enters shot. Almost a whisper as she curtsies:* I'm honored to meet you.

FANIA: How do you do, Charlotte. *To Etalina:* Rosé?—there was a string quartet by that name. . . .

MICHOU: Alma is the first violinist's daughter.

FANIA: Then her uncle must be Gustav Mahler—the composer. . . .

ELZVIETA: Yes; she has a fantastic talent.

ETALINA: But not a warm heart, be careful. . . .

Michou touches Etalina to shush her, looking offscreen.

Cut to Alma Rosé, as she makes her entrance—there is instant silence and respect. Now three Blockawas—Polish prisoners acting as police in effect, and all weighty types—appear and look on with belligerent curiosity. They don't approve this coddling of Jews.

Alma comes toward the group. She is thin, extremely Germanic, scrubbed clean, her shabby clothes brushed. Her face shows her determination, even fanatical perfectionism—her only defense here.

ALMA: You are Mademoiselle Fénelon?

FANIA: Yes, Madame.

ALMA: You play the piano?

FANIA: Oh yes, Madame!

The fervor of her voice causes an excited giggle among some of the onlookers.

ALMA: Let me hear something from *Madame Butterfly.*

Alma goes to a chair, sits; others arrange themselves. Fania approaches the fabulous piano; it is all like a dream—she is slogging along in these immense men's shoes, a fuzz of hair on her bald head, her face gaunt from the near-starvation diet—and she sits before the keys and can't help bending over and kissing them. She starts to play "Un bel di". . . .

Cut to Fania's hands. They are crusted with filth, the nails broken. She is stiff and strikes a double note.

Cut to Fania, at the piano. She stops, blows on her fingers. Now she plays and sings. After two bars . . .

Cut to the group. All are glancing at Alma's reaction—she is quickened, eager to claim Fania for her orchestra.

Cut to Fania. In her face and voice, confident now and warm, are the ironic longings for the music's life-giving loveliness. The mood is shattered by the sounds of the scraping of chairs and people suddenly standing. Fania turns, stops playing.

Cut to Lagerführerin Mandel, entering the dayroom; she is chief of the women's section of the entire camp. About twenty-eight, tall, blond, shining with health, beautiful in her black uniform. Musicians, Blockawas, all are standing at rigid attention before her. Fania sees this, and attempts to do likewise—although only half successfully in her state of semi-shock.

MANDEL: At ease.

She comes and examines Fania, head to foot. And to Alma . . .

MANDEL: You will take her.
ALMA: Yes, Frau Mandel, certainly—she is very good.
MANDEL, *facing Fania:* She is wonderful.

There is something competitive in Alma's face.

MANDEL: Do you know any German music?
FANIA—*hesitates, her eyes lowered in trepidation:* Yes . . .
MANDEL: I am Lagerführerin Maria Mandel, in command of all women in this camp.
FANIA—*nods in deference:* I . . . had fogotten to tell Madame Rosé . . . that I really can't join the orchestra . . . unless my friend 346,991 is admitted also—she has a beautiful voice. *Now she meets Mandel's surprised look.* She is in Barracks B. *Mandel is silent; surprised actually.* Without her, I . . . must refuse . . . I'm sorry.

Absolute astonishment strikes the expressions of the other musicians.

Cut to Mandel, who looks at Fania for an additional moment, her mind unreadable.

Cut to the kapos, furious, but more incredulous than anything else.

Cut to Fania and Tchaikowska, a kapo, hurrying down a camp "street" (a corridor between barracks buildings). Fania is urging Tchaikowska to go faster. . . . They turn the corner of a building and come upon about twenty women who are being driven by club-wielding Blockawas. Many of these women are near death, falling down, crawling.

In the background, Mala comes to a halt; with her an SS officer. She is a tall, striking Jewess, wears the Star. But—oddly enough—there is no subservience in her manner but rather a seriousness and confidence. She carries a thick notebook.

Marianne is being pulled and struck by a Blockawa whose pressure she is resisting, trying to get back into the barracks building.

FANIA, *to Tchaikowska, pointing:* That's her! Quick! Marianne. . . !

Fania drops behind the kapo Tchaikowska—who has the authority here and who walks up to the Blockawa.

TCHAIKOWSKA: Mandel wants this one.

Marianne nearly faints into Fania's arms as they start to move away from the surprised Blockawa and the deadened, staggering group of women.

Cut to Marianne, her face still smudged with dirt, deep scratches on her neck. Incredibly enough she is singing to Fania's piano accompaniment in the musicians' barracks.

Cut to Mandel, legs sheathed in silk, her cap off, letting her blond hair fall to her shoulders. She listens. Alma stands a deferential few paces behind her. And in the background, the musicians, all listening.

Fania is playing encouragingly, glancing from time to time up at Marianne to urge her on. Marianne has a fevered look in her eyes, she is singing for her life. The song ends. Silence.

MANDEL, *to Alma:* Get them dressed.

Cut to Marianne, who starts to sway but is held up by Fania.

Cut to a counter; behind it from floor to ceiling is the clothing of the dead.

Blockawas, and the Chief here—Frau Schmidt—stand rigidly at attention. Mandel is holding up a brassiere which she places over Marianne's large breasts. Then she gives it to Marianne. Now she takes a pair of fine silk panties, holds them up for Fania, who accepts them.

MANDEL, *to Frau Schmidt:* Find shoes that fit her.

FRAU SCHMIDT: Of course. *To Fania:* They look very small, what size are they?

FANIA: Four.

FRAU SCHMIDT, *to Mandel:* I doubt very much that we have . . .

MANDEL: Feet must be warm and comfortable or the voice is affected. Find them for my little singer.

Frau Schmidt is irritated but obedient.

Fania and Marianne are thankful to Mandel, but what is the meaning of this incredible insistence?

Mandel exits, leaving Frau Schmidt rummaging in the bin full of women's shoes.

A Blockawa sweeps a woolen coat off the counter and furiously throws it at Fania, who blocks it with her arm.

While Frau Schmidt continues to search, Fania's eye transforms the pile of shoes.

Dissolve to women's legs walking on a railroad station platform. In effect, the shoes come alive on the wearers' feet and move about on a sidewalk.

Cut to Alma, tapping on her podium with her baton, raising her arms to begin a number; the orchestra is ready. Suddenly eyes catch something off-camera and all spring to their feet and at attention.

Mandel enters, followed by her orderly. Mandel is carrying a box full of shoes, four or five pairs.

Cut to Mandel. Her eyes are happy, somehow softened.

MANDEL: Sit down here, Fania.

Fania comes to her from the piano bench, sits before her at her gestured command, Mandel sets the box of shoes down, takes out a pair of fur-lined boots—and kneels before Fania!

Fania is now torn; she dares not turn down these incredible gifts, but at the same time she fears what accepting them may imply for her future. She looks down at the fur boot in Mandel's hand. . . .

Cut to a close shot of the boot. The camera either vivifies this boot, gives it the life of its deceased owner—or actually fills it with a leg, and we see the pair of boots on living legs . . . perhaps walking on a city street.

Cut to Mandel, rising to her feet as Fania stands in the fur boots. She looks up from them to Mandel's pleased face and can't help resolving her conflict by saying . . .

FANIA: *Danke schön*, Frau Lagerführerin.

Cut to Mandel. Her pleasure flows onto her face; there is an element of masterly dominance in her expression, and some sort of affection.

Cut to the entire orchestra, rehearsing. Fania has hands poised over the keyboard; Alma, baton raised, starts the piece—an orchestral number of von Suppé. The sound is not quite horrible, but very nearly. The forty-odd players, apart from some of them being totally inadequate, are distressed by hunger and fear and never quite keep the music together.

Cut to the orchestra. The camera introduces us to the main supporting characters:

Elzvieta, a very good violinist, a rather aristocratic Pole who, as a non-Jew, still has her hair.

Paulette, a woman in her twenties, German-Jewish, an excellent cellist, who is presently pained by the bad playing of her compatriot beside her, who is . . .

Liesle, a bony, timid, near-hysterically frightened mandolin player, trying desperately to keep up with the beat. Belgian.

Charlotte, a violinist, fine player, slim and noble-looking, Belgian, extremely intelligent, poetic face.

Etalina, a wisecracker, small, Rumanian, violinist, a tomboy.

Michou, French, plays the flute, a militant communist. Further in the background of the story are . . .

Giselle, a freckled, very young French girl who can barely play drums at all, but is too young to despair, and thus beats away as loudly as possible.

Berta, a teacher.

Varya, cymbals. A Pole who has her hair.

Katrina, Polish, a very bad guitarist, stubborn, unteachable; has her hair.

Olga, Ukrainian accordionist, a dumbbell who will later take over the orchestra.

Greta, Dutch accordionist, country girl, naive and scared at all times; very poor player.

Esther, a taut, militant Zionist who bears in her intense eyes the vision of Palestine; accordionist.

Tchaikowska, leading kapo.

From time to time, one or more of the secondary characters will emerge on the foreground of this story in order to keep alive and vivid the sense that the "background group" is made of individuals. If this film is to approach even an indication of the vastness of the human disaster involved, the minor characters will have to be kept dramatically alive even in shots where they are only seen and don't have lines.

Cut to Alma, tapping angrily on the podium. . . . the orchestra breaks off.

ALMA: Why is it so loud? This is not band music, we are not playing against the wind—why can you not obey my instructions! *A note of futile and somehow dangerous anxiety on the verge of real anger.* Music is the holiest activity of mankind, you must apply yourselves day and night, you must listen to yourselves, you must aspire to some improvement. . . ! You cannot simply repeat the same mistakes. . . .

She can't go on, and simply walks hurriedly out of the room to recover herself. For a moment, the women keep an abashed silence.

ETALINA: At ease, Philharmonic.

> The women set down their instruments and stand and stretch. . . . Etalina comes to Fania at the piano.

ETALINA: I think you've upset her—your being so good; she suddenly heard what we really sound like.

> Paulette enters the shot and Liesle. Then Giselle.

FANIA: Well it *was* a bit loud. . . .

PAULETTE, *of Liesle:* She can't learn that number—we've got to go loud or she's had it.

LIESLE, *defensively, a whine:* I only studied less than six months in my whole life.

ETALINA: And that's the smartest six months *you* ever spent. *To Fania:* It's not her altogether—it's the maestro herself who's brought on this trouble.

FANIA: Why?

ETALINA: We were simply a marching band when we started— we'd play the prisoners out to their work assignments. But Alma got ambitious, and the first thing you know we're doing these orchestral numbers, giving concerts for the high brass . . . playing Beethoven, for God's sake. She's a victim of her own pride and we're in trouble now.

MARIANNE, *entering the shot:* Do we ever get dinner?

LIESLE—*laughs:* Listen to her. . . !

ETALINA: The slops'll be here any time now, dear.

FANIA: Why trouble, Etalina?

ETALINA: Because once the big shots started coming to hear us they began getting bored hearing the same three numbers.

PAULETTE: We have no other orchestrations. . . .

ETALINA: And no composer ever wrote for this idiotic kind of instrumentation. I mean, piccolos, guitars, flutes, violins, no bass, no horns, no . . .

MICHOU, *to Fania:* You don't orchestrate, do you?

> Obviously Fania doesn't, but her mouth opens and her eyes are inventing. . . .

PAULETTE: I'm really getting worried—we've done practically the same concert at least a dozen times. The Commandant sometimes doesn't even stay to the end.

MARIANNE—*her frightened eyes turn to Fania:* But you do know how to orchestrate, Fania! *Fania looks into her scared face.* And they could play all sorts of things!

FANIA: Actually—*to the women*—I can.

ETALINA AND PAULETTE: *Orchestrate?*

FANIA: Well, yes . . . not professionally, but I . . .

MICHOU: I knew it!

Paulette swerves about and yells to the women.

PAULETTE: She can orchestrate!

Etalina and Paulette instantly take off down the length of the room flanked by a dozen women all cheering and talking . . . and come to Alma's door where Etalina knocks.

Cut to Alma's room. Alma is sitting by a window, baton still in her grip. Etalina and Paulette step into the room.

ETALINA: We thought you'd want to know, Madame—Fania Fénelon knows how to orchestrate.

The importance of this news is evident in Alma's expression. She stands. Fania is brought forward and into the room.

ALMA, *to the others:* Leave us. Leave us, please.

She shuts the door on the women. The last face we see is Marianne's, imploring Fania to press on. Alma gestures to the bed where Fania sits as Alma sits on the chair facing her. Fania looks around at the clean, bare room.

ALMA: Tell me the truth, Fania.

FANIA: Yes, I can—I don't see why not.

ALMA: And I suppose you . . . actually studied?

FANIA, *plunging on:* At the Paris Conservatory.

ALMA: Oh, Fania—what luck! What luck to have you! There's been a terrible pressure on me for some weeks now . . . for something new. . . .

FANIA: So they tell me. . . .

ALMA: I'm so exhausted and rushed that I've simply been unable to, myself. Could you start with. . . ? *She picks up piano music from a table.* I have a piano score for *Carmen.* . . .

FANIA: Well, I suppose, yes, I could do *Carmen.* . . .

ALMA: Or something German . . . here's another von
Suppé. . . .

FANIA: I can't bear von Suppé. . . .

ALMA: I know, but they adore anything by von Suppé and we
must try to please them, Fania. *Their eyes meet. Alma is a
mite defensive, but it comes out with strength.* Well, that is elementary, it seems to me.

FANIA: I suppose. But I prefer to think that I am saving my life
rather than trying to please the SS.

ALMA: And you think you can do one without the other?

Fania shuts up; clearly it is a dilemma, but she is also not
trusting Alma. Now Alma relents.

ALMA: You'll begin immediately.

FANIA: I'll need people to copy the parts . . . and music paper.

ALMA: We can't possibly get music paper. . . .

FANIA: Couldn't you request some?

ALMA: There is a war on, my dear!

Suddenly, in this exclamation is Alma's *own* German indignation.

ALMA: Come—I'll find paper, and you and the girls can draw
the lines yourself. *Fania rises, goes past her to the door.* Fania?
Fania turns to her, a slight smile. I can't help striving for
perfection; I was trained that way, I can't change now.

FANIA: Madame, I'm hardly in a position to criticize you when
I am also trying to please.

ALMA: Exactly—but we are artists, we can't help that; you have
nothing to be ashamed of. *Alma now comes to Fania—and
in a more confessing, intimate tone:* Please try to hurry the
work—they're so very changeable toward us, you see?
Something new and surprising would be—*her fear is outright, open*—a tremendous help. So you'll be quick, Fania?

Cut to Fania. Her eyes are filling with terror and determination. . . .

Cut to the dayroom, that evening. A concert is in full swing,
primarily for Commandant Kramer and Dr. Mengele, but other
officers are here too, including Frau Schmidt and Lagerführerin Mandel, forming an audience of perhaps twenty.

Madame Alma Rosé, face aglow, is apprehensively conducting, pushing the stone uphill.

The camera detects the players' abilities—the few good ones trying to overflow onto the sounds of the shaky ones.

Kramer, Dr. Mengele, and Mandel are naturally seated in the front "row." Mandel is interested; Dr. Mengele, who knows music, is very attentive, also amused; Kramer, a bull-necked killer, is struggling to keep his eyes open.

The number is ending with a flashy run on the piano by Fania. There is applause, more or less perfunctory.

Alma turns and bows as though before a gigantic audience.

ALMA: And now, with your permission, *meine Damen und Herren*—a bit of popular music by our new member, Fania Fénelon.

Mandel alone eagerly applauds.

Fania accompanies herself, singing a smoky, very Parisian ballad. And as she sings . . .

Dissolve to Dr. Mengele, his face superimposed on Fania. Then we see him with finger raised, directing deportees emerging from a freight car to right and left, death or life. *Flames reflect orange light on his face.*

This gives way to . . .

A close up of Mengele. He seems actually attracted to Fania's voice and music.

Cut to Fania, finishing her number—her face is tortured, but she is singing, fully, beautifully, to the finish.

Cut to the audience. Now there is a more heartfelt applause. Fania takes bows, her eyes trying to evade the monsters applauding her.

Cut to Fania, dousing her face with water as though trying to wash herself clean.

Cut to the dormitory. Marianne is drawing out a box from under her bed—she opens it, takes out a package of margarine, starts to dig some out with a finger—and looks up guiltily, her finger nearly in her mouth.

Fania is standing nearby, having discovered her. Fania is still drying herself from the shower.

FANIA: Why do you steal when you know I can't stand margarine?

Marianne starts to put the margarine back in the box, Fania comes and forces it back into her hand. Fania's voice is losing its control.
Other women look up from their beds, still others are entering the dormitory—and gradually all are drawn to this.

FANIA: Anything you want of mine I wish you would simply take, Marianne! *Turning to the other women:* And that goes for everyone—I don't want to keep anything from anyone who wants it. . . . And I hope you'll do the same for me if I'm desperate.

ETALINA: But Fania, we can't very well share everything.

FANIA: I refuse to turn into an animal for a gram of margarine or a potato peel!

PAULETTE: You don't mean share with the Poles too, though.

Fania hesitates . . . glances down the dormitory where half a dozen Polish women stand about—heavy, tough, their contempt evident despite their curiosity of the moment. (Katrina: Beefy, appalling guitarist. Varya: Athlete, shrewd, cymbals.)

ETALINA: Count me out, dear—those are monsters; even here in the same hell as we are, they're just praying every one of us goes to the gas. You share with those bitches, not me.

ELZVIETA—*a delicate, gentle Pole, beautiful head of hair:* We're not all like that.

Slight pause.

PAULETTE: You just have a pet Jew—you like Fania, but you're an anti-Semite, Elzvieta.

ELZVIETA, *timidly:* But I really am not. My father was an actor; we had a lot of Jewish friends in the theater.—I'm really not, Fania. *Glancing at the satiric Etalina.* In my opinion, Etalina —*with a glance toward the Poles*—they think that you people are probably going to be . . . you know . . .

ETALINA: Gassed. —You can say it, dear.

ELZVIETA: Well, the point is that they want to feel superior because they'll probably live to go home, when the war ends . . . being Gentiles. *To Fania.* They're more stupid than evil.

FANIA: Then we should try to teach them.

After the first shock, Etalina laughs. Then another and another until, with glances toward the stolid, suspicious, and bovine Poles, the whole gang are laughing their heads off; and finally the Poles too join in.

GISELLE—*a freckle-faced, red-haired Parisian tomboy:* To hell with this—tell us about Paris—when were you there last? What are they wearing?

Women gather around.

FANIA: I was in Drancy prison almost a year.

PAULETTE: Well, it can't have changed much—where are the skirts now?

FANIA, *indicating:* Oh, to here (*the knee*) but very full—the girls look like flowers.

MARIANNE: The heels are very high—the legs look terrific. You can't buy stockings so they paint their legs. My mother wouldn't let me, though.

PAULETTE: And the hair?—there were some women in a convoy the other day—I think from Holland—curls on top of their heads. . . .

FANIA: In Paris too—piled up top-curls. —Where are those women?

ETALINA: They're burned up by now, I guess. What about songs? —You know any new ones?

FANIA, *to Etalina:* The way you say that, Etalina . . .

ETALINA: That they're burned up?—why not say it? We'll be better prepared for it when our time comes.

GISELLE, *insistently:* Talk about Paris, Fania. . . .

LIESLE: Are they still playing swing?

FANIA: Are you Parisian?

LIESLE: No. But we went there for a vacation just before the war—play us some of the new songs, will you?

OTHERS: That's a great idea. . . . Come on, Fania. . . . Do you know "Stormy Weather"? . . . What was the name of your nightclub? . . . Did you make many records? . . . She's really famous, you know. . . .

The group moves out into the dayroom.

MICHOU: Can you play by ear? . . . Come, sit down. . . .

Fania sits at the piano, Marianne beside her, when . . .

Cut to Shmuel, in prisoner's stripes. He is an electrician, now taping a wire along a wall of the dayroom. He is forty-five, perhaps deranged, perhaps extraordinarily wise, it's hard to say. He's like a little toy animal, large eyes, curly hair, desperately shy. He makes little peeking glances at the assembling women, but there's some air of persistence about him, too.

Cut to Fania, who senses some indecipherable communication from him and lets her gaze linger on him for an instant. Then she breaks away and begins to play the intro for "Stormy Weather."

After the first couple of lines, Marianne interrupts, unable to restrain herself even though she is breaking up Fania's number.

MARIANNE: Could I, Fania? Please?

Fania is quite astonished, looks at her with an embarrassed smile to cover her own resentment.

MARIANNE: I just have such a yen for it suddenly! Do you mind?

Fania, embarrassed, shrugs and obliges, accompanying Marianne, who sings the number—but "appealingly," sentimentally, where Fania sang intelligently, suavely.

Cut to the Polish women. They are identifiable, in part, by the fact they all have hair. They have come out of the dormitory and gather a little apart, and are pleasurably listening.
     And before the music has a chance to die on Marianne's number, Fania picks up another, singing herself.
     Camera pans the women's faces . . . maybe two dozen

clustered around the piano . . . shorn, gaunt captives, yet this music brings up their lust to live and a certain joy. . . .

A chorus of players pick up a lyric and join Fania, singing all together.

Cut to Alma Rosé. Her door opens onto the dayroom, and she is about to protest the noise . . . but her gesture aborts and she stiffly concedes the moment, turns and goes back into her room, shutting the door.

Cut to the next morning, outside in the camp "street." About twenty players form up outside the musicians' barracks. Each wears a bandanna, a uniformlike element, and of course the Jewesses have the yellow Star on their clothing. The Gentiles are indiscriminately mixed in, perhaps four or five of them, identifiable mainly by their hair.

It is gray, just before day, very cold. Fania is in place at one corner of the formation; Alma Rosé appears from the barracks, sees her, and halts.

ALMA: You don't have to do this, you're not in the band.
FANIA: I would like to see it . . . if it's not forbidden.

Alma is surprised, then shrugs, goes around to the head of the formation, raises her baton, and this crazy band, with no horns but with fiddles, flutes, accordion, guitars, and cymbals, goes marching off behind Alma, who marches like a Prussian.

Cut to the camp "square." The band is playing "stirring" march music on a low bandstand. Before them in blocks of five square stand the women prisoners about to go off to work.

Some of them are ill, supported by a neighbor's hand; some are fiercely erect, some old, some teenagers—their shoes don't match, some feet are wrapped in rags, and their clothes are ripped rags.

Cut to a close shot of Fania. Her gaze has moved to a point . . . which is . . .

An angry prisoner.

This woman has caught Fania's eye and mimes spitting at her in contempt.

Cut to Fania, quickly lowering her eyes.

Cut to SS men, some handling attack dogs, ordering the prisoners to march. The whole mass moves across the mud.

SS OFFICER, *a whip against his boot, beating time: Eins, zwei, drei* . . . hup, hup, hup!

Cut to Fania, lifting her eyes, forcing herself to watch. Suddenly up to her ear comes Shmuel. Frightened, surprised, she turns to him swiftly.

SHMUEL, *wild-eyed:* Live!

He quickly limps away, his toolbox on his shoulder.

Cut to the dayroom. Women, lining paper with pencils and straightedges, are spread out around Fania near a window. Outside the gray light of winter afternoon.
    Charlotte, a good violinist, is practicing some distance away—a Bach chaconne.
    Marianne is staring out a window nearby, thinking of food.
    Fania is seated, studying a piano score, pencil poised over a lined sheet on which a few notes have been set down. She is intense—worried?
    Liesle is repeating the same three bars on her accordion, with the same mistakes.

GISELLE, *musing to no one in particular:* Imagine!—painting their legs! I'd love *that*. . . .

Etalina passes behind Fania and, glancing down at the few notes she has written, halts, surprised.

ETALINA: Is that all you've done? *Fania glances up defensively.* Christ, at this rate we'll need another Hundred Years' War to get a score out of you.

Charlotte enters the shot, carrying her violin.

CHARLOTTE: Will you stop bothering her? Orchestrating is tough work even for experts.

Alma comes out of her room, comes over to Fania, and

looks down at the sheet. Then she looks at Fania with real surprise.

ALMA: I have to speak to you.

Alma goes out into her room. Fania stands, as she follows her out, sees . . .
The Polish women, triumphantly laughing (softly, though) and pointing at her and miming her decapitation.

Cut to Alma's room.

ALMA: Then you lied?—you can't orchestrate at all, can you?
FANIA: I'm quite able to do it; I'm sure I can.
ALMA: What is it, then?
FANIA: One of the women this morning—spat at me.
ALMA, *not understanding:* Yes?
FANIA: I hadn't realized . . . how they must hate us.
ALMA: Oh. Yes, of course; what did you expect?
FANIA: Well I . . . I just hadn't thought about it.
ALMA, *now sensing some remote criticism of her own character, is angry:* Perhaps you are too conscientious a person for the orchestra . . .
FANIA: No, no, I didn't mean . . .
ALMA: If you'd be happier back in "B" Barracks . . .
FANIA: Madame, please—I wasn't criticizing you. *Unstrung.* I'm just not used to being hated like that.
ALMA, *decisively:* Fania—there is life or death in this place, there is no room for anything else whatever.—I intend to rehearse that piece tomorrow; I want the parts by morning. If you are able, that is. Are you?
FANIA, *defeated, yet determined:* Yes, Madame.

She walks angrily past Alma out the door.

Cut to the dayroom. Through the window nearby we see darkness of night. Reflection of a big searchlight, which revolves somewhere beyond our line of sight, a rhythm of this flashing light.
Fania at the piano is alone, working out the orchestration. She tries a chord. There is the jarring sound of three rifle shots. She looks up, waits; then silence. Someone probably got killed. She plays the chord again; writes notes.

From outside we hear the hair-raising screeching of someone being destroyed—and the shouts of men killing. Then
silence. Fania is in sharp conflict with herself; she knows she
is walling herself up against all this. Steels herself again. Plays
the chord. Can't continue. Gets up, walks past dormitory
doorway. She looks in.

Cut to the dormitory, at night. The whole orchestra, some
forty, asleep in beds.

Cut to Fania, in the dayroom, passing the dormitory door,
goes into a dark narrow corridor at the end of which is a
door. She opens this door. . . .

Cut to the toilet. On the toilet bowl Marianne is straddling a
man, a kapo still wearing his striped prisoner's hat. In his
hand is gripped two sausages. Marianne turns and sees Fania,
but turns back and continues with the man, who is looking
straight up at Fania.

Cut to the dayroom. Through the window the first light of
dawn. Backing, we find Fania with several pages of completed score under her hand . . . exhausted, but finishing
it. She is fighting self-disgust; at the same time is glad at her
accomplishment. A hand enters the shot, with a piece of
sausage held between forefinger and thumb. Fania looks at it.
    Pull back to Marianne, standing beside Fania, offering the
piece of sausage. Fania stares at it, then up at Marianne.

MARIANNE: Take it—for saving my life. You must be starved,
working all night.

Fania is not looking at her judgmentally but with sorrow
and fear. Marianne sets the piece of sausage on the keyboard.

MARIANNE: I'm not going to live to get out of here anyway.
FANIA: But if you do? Marianne? What if you live?

Marianne is silent, then with a certain stubborn air, walks
away. Fania looks at the sausage. Tries not to eat it. A desperate struggle to refuse this seeming compromise with her
own disgust. Finally she does eat it—and gives way to a look
of almost sensual enjoyment as she carefully lengthens out

the chewing. Then she swallows, stands in intense conflict, her hands clasped to her mouth as she walks about with no escape.

The sudden sound of ear-piercing whistles.

Fania looks out a window, frightened, bewildered.

Three Blockawas, led by their chief, Tchaikowska, come running into the dayroom, buttoning up their coats as they rush past Fania into the dormitory.

Cut to the dormitory. The Blockawas, yelling, *"'Raus, 'raus, schnell . . ."* rip off blankets, push and slap the women out of bed. The women at first are in shock, but quickly obey, start dressing.

Cut to the train platform. Dawn. The band is rushed into a formation before a line of freight cars whose doors are shut. SS men stand waiting, along with kapos preparing to pounce on the luggage.

Commandant Kramer is standing in an open area, beside him Frau Lagerführerin Mandel, in a cape and cap. Kramer signals Alma, who starts the orchestra in a bright march.

Car doors are rolled open; inside a mass of people who are pulled and driven out onto the platform by kapos, their luggage taken.

Cut to a mother, being torn from her child, who is tossed onto a waiting truck. Mother rushes to Frau Mandel to plead with her; Mandel strikes her across the face with a riding crop.

Cut to Fania, by the dayroom window. She sees this, starts to turn away in horror, then forces herself to turn back to the window.

Shmuel suddenly appears outside the window and sees her, glances around, then hurries out of sight.

He enters the dayroom. With a glance of caution behind him he hurriedly limps over to Fania.

SHMUEL: Don't do that.

FANIA: What?

SHMUEL: Turn away. You have to look and see everything, so you can tell him when it is over.

FANIA: Who?

His eyes roll upward, and he dares point upward just a bit with one finger.

FANIA: I don't believe.

A grin breaks onto his face—as though she has decided to play a game with him.

FANIA: Why do you pick me?
SHMUEL: Oh, I always know who to pick!

A crazy kind of joy suffuses his face as he backs out the door.

SHMUEL: Live!

Cut to the smokestack. Dawn. For an instant the stack is in the clear—then it belches a column of smoke.

Cut to the dayroom. Evening. Mengele, Kramer, and Mandel listen to the orchestra, along with their retinues. Fania, accompanying herself, is singing "Un bel di" in an agonized and therefore extraordinarily moving way. She is just finishing. When she does, Mandel stands, applauding—she is excited as a patron, a discoverer of talent, and turns to Kramer, who is also clapping his hands.

MANDEL: Did you ever hear anything more touching, Herr Commandant?
KRAMER: Fantastic. *To Mengele:* But Dr. Mengele's musical opinions are more expert, of course.

Cut to Fania, staring at the ultimate horror—their love for her music.

Cut to the entire dayroom.

MENGELE: I have rarely felt so totally—moved.

And he appears, in fact, to have been deeply stirred.

ALMA: You might thank the Commandant, Fania.

Fania tries to speak, can't and nods instead—gratefully.

FANIA—*finally a whisper: Danke schön,* Herr Commandant.
KRAMER: I must tell you, Mademoiselle Fénelon . . .

FANIA: Excuse me, but my name is really not Fénelon. Fénelon was my mother's name.

MANDEL: What is your name, then?

FANIA: My father's name was Goldstein. I am Fania Goldstein. Excuse me, I didn't mean to interrupt, Herr Commandant.

KRAMER: You must learn to sing German songs.

ALMA: I will see that she learns immediately, Herr Commandant.

KRAMER, *continuing to Fania:* Originally, Mademoiselle, I opposed this idea of an orchestra, but I must say now that with singing of your quality, it is a consolation that feeds the spirit. It strengthens us for this difficult work of ours. *Very* good.

He turns and goes out, followed by his retinue and Mengele. The orchestra is aware that Fania has helped them remain in favor and thus alive.

Mandel turns back at the door and beckons to Fania, who comes to her.

MANDEL: Is there anything you especially need?

FANIA, *out of her conflict, after a struggle:* A . . . toothbrush?

MANDEL—*gestures to Tchaikowska, who approaches:* You will send to Canada for some parcels. *To Fania:* With my compliments.

Mandel exits.

FANIA, *to Tchaikowska:* To *Canada*?!

Cut to a long shot of the smoking chimney.

Cut to a counter set in open air beside anther barracks. Behind it are the black-market girls—sleek, fed, laughing, busy trading with a few desperate-looking women who hand over a slice of bread for a comb or piece of soap. On the counter are perfumes, lotions, soap, and a pile of used toothbrushes. These "Canadians" all have hair—Czechs, Poles, Dutch . . .

FIRST BLACK MARKETEER: Welcome to Canada. So you're the Frenchy singer—what would you like? *Fania picks up a toothbrush. Charlotte accompanies her.* That just came off the last transport—it's practically new and very clean—they were mostly Norwegians. That'll be a good slice of bread.

The black marketeer holds out her hand. Fania takes out a chunk of bread. Charlotte intercepts, returning it to Fania.

CHARLOTTE: I said this is on the Chief!

BLACK MARKETEER, *cheerfully:* What's wrong with trying? *To Fania:* Here's your junk, stupid.

Set aside at one end of the counter are forty tiny packets in soiled and much-used paper. Charlotte and Fania load their arms.

Cut to the high excitement in the dayroom as the girls open their gift packages, which contain, in one case, a bit of butter and a pat of jam which a girl ever so carefully smears on a cracker-sized piece of bread, or an inch of sausage and a chip of chocolate to be savored for a full five minutes, and so forth.

Marianne, suffering, gobbles up her bread and jam in one gulp.

Fania nearby is swallowing. She takes out her tooth-brush.

MARIANNE: You got a toothbrush!—can I see? *She takes it, examines it, reads words on the handle.* From Norway. Looks almost new. *Offering it back:* Nothing like having important friends, right?

Fania's hand stops in air. But then she takes the toothbrush and forces herself to look directly into Marianne's eyes.

MARIANNE: Whoever that belonged to is probably up the chimney now. *Fania is silent.* So why are you superior?

FANIA: If I ever thought I was, I sure don't any more.

Etalina enters the shot . . . addressing all.

ETALINA: I'll say one thing, Fania—I feel a lot safer now that the Chief is so hot for you.

Some of the women laugh, titillated . . . the Poles loudest of all.

ETALINA: Although I wouldn't want to wake up in the morning next to that Nazi bitch's mug.

FANIA: I don't expect to. But it's not her face that disgusts me.

Esther speaks—a shaven Polish Jewess, angular, tight-faced.

ESTHER: Her face doesn't disgust you?

FANIA: No—I'm afraid she's a very beautiful woman, Esther.

ESTHER: That murderer you dare call beautiful?

Others react against Fania—"Shame!" "You toady!" "Just because she favors you!"

FANIA, *overriding:* What disgusts me is that a woman so beautiful can do what she is doing. Don't try to make her ugly, Esther . . . she's beautiful and human. We are the same species. And that is what's so hopeless about this whole thing.

MICHOU: What's the difference that she's human? There's still hope—because when this war is over Europe will be communist—and for that I want to live.

ESTHER: No. To see Palestine—that's why you have to live. You're Jewish women—*that's* your hope: to bring forth Jewish children in Palestine. You have no identity, Fania—and that's why you can call such a monster human and beautiful.

FANIA: I envy you both—you don't feel you have to solve the problem.

ESTHER, *anxiously, aggressively: What* problem! I don't see a problem!

FANIA: She is human, Esther. *Slight pause; she is looking directly into Esther's eyes.* Like you. Like me. You don't think that's a problem?

Fania's eye is caught by Marianne slipping out the dayroom door.

Cut to outside the barracks. While two kapos expectantly watch, Marianne opens a bar of chocolate they have given her and bites into it. They lead her around the corner of the barracks and out of sight. One of them has a bottle half filled with wine.

Cut to Fania, asleep in her bunk. Marianne appears, starts to climb in—she is tipsy—slips and lands on her behind on the floor with a scream. Women awaken.

ETALINA: At least let *us* get some rest, Busy-Ass.

MARIANNE, *to Etalina:* What's it to you? *To Fania:* Say!—your
hair's coming back white!

FANIA: Come to bed, Marianne. . . .

MARIANNE: Oh, screw these idiots. . . .

VOICES: Shut up! Whore! I'm exhausted! She's disgusting!
Somebody throw her out! Shut up!

MARIANNE, *to the whole lot:* Well, it so happens one of them
was a doctor from Vienna. . . .

ETALINA: She just went for a checkup!

MARIANNE: And he thinks we are never going to menstruate
again! *Silence now.* Because of this . . . this fear every day
and night . . . and the food . . . can sterilize . . .

She looks around at their stricken faces. She climbs up,
helped into her bunk by Fania.

Cut to a series of close-ups:

ESTHER, *praying quietly:* Shma Israel, adonai elohaynu . . .

Elzvieta crosses herself and prays quietly.
    Other women are praying.
    Fania is silent, staring, while beside her Marianne lies on
her back asleep and snoring.

Cut to two kapos, carrying Paulette on a stretcher across the
dayroom to the exit door. Paulette, the young cellist, is in high
fever. Alma attempts to explain to the kapos in pidgin . . .

ALMA: Do you understand me? —she is musician, cellist, not
to be gassed. To hospital, you understand? Typhus, you see?
We need her. Well, do you understand or not! *At the door:*
Wait!

Cut to Alma rushing over to Tauber, an SS officer, and Mala.
Mala is the tall, striking Jewess, wearing the Star, but who
appears to show no obsequiousness toward Tauber, the SS
officer beside her. Kapos approach carrying Paulette on a
stretcher.

ALMA: Excuse me, Herr Commandant Tauber—with your
permission, would Mala instruct these men to be sure this
girl is not . . . harmed? She is our cellist and must go to

the hospital—she has high fever, typhus perhaps. I don't know what language they speak. . . .

Without waiting for Tauber's permission, Mala stops the kapos.

MALA: Parl' Italiano? *They shake their heads negatively.* Espagnol? *They shake their heads again.* Russky? *Again.*

KAPO: Romany.

MALA: Ah! *In Rumanian:* Be sure to take her to hospital, not death—she is a musician, they need her.

KAPO: *In Rumanian:* We understand.

They walk off with Paulette. Tauber and staff move off with Mala.

Cut to the dayroom. The orchestra members are clustered at the windows watching this.

MICHOU: Isn't she fantastic?

FANIA, *amazed:* But she's wearing the Star!

MICHOU: Sure—that's Mala, she's their chief interpreter. She's Jewish but she's got them bulldozed.

FANIA: How's it possible?

Alma re-enters the dayroom, goes to her podium, leafs through a score.

MICHOU: She's been here for years—since the camp was built— she escaped once; she and five others were supposed to be gassed, so they'd been stripped, and she got out through an air vent. Ended up stark naked going down a road past the Commandant's house. She's afraid of absolutely nothing, so when he stopped her she demanded some clothes; they got to talking, and he found out she speaks practically every language and made her an interpreter.

LIESLE, *proudly:* She's Belgian, you know—like me.

CHARLOTTE: She was in the Resistance. She even has a lover.

ETALINA: And handsome!

FANIA: Now you're kidding me.

ETALINA: It's true—Edek's his name—a Polish Resistance guy. He's got a job in the Administration.

MICHOU, *starry-eyed:* They're both unbelievable—they've saved people—a few anyway, and helped some. They're afraid of nothing!

ALMA: Fania! *From Alma's viewpoint we see the group turning to her.* Come here now and let us go through your Schubert song. *Fania comes to the piano, sits.* You must try the *ch* sound again—Dr. Mengele has a sensitive ear for the language, and it's his request, you know. Begin . . .

Fania sings a Schubert song with *"lachen"* in the verse, pronouncing it "lacken."

ALMA: No, no, not "lacken"—"la*ch*en . . ."

FANIA, *trying, but . . . :* Lacken.

ALMA: *Lachen! Lachen! Lachen!* Say it!

Alma's face is close to Fania's; Fania looks into Alma's eyes and with a sigh of angry defeat . . .

FANIA: *Lachen.*

ALMA: That's much better. I hope you won't ever be stupid enough to hate a *language*! Now the song once more . . . I want you perfect by Sunday. . . .

Fania, her jaw clenched, forces herself into the song.

Cut to the train platform. It is barely light. Freight-car doors roll open, and the deportees are hustled out. From within the dormitory we hear women yelling and screaming.

Cut to the dormitory. Tchaikowska, burly chief of the barracks, and other Blockawas are pulling Etalina out of her bunk by the ankles, and she lands with a bang on the floor. The other inmates are yelling. . . .

VOICES: Why can't you wake up like everybody else! Why are you always making trouble! and so on . . .

Alma appears on the scene with Fania nearby. Tchaikowska bangs a fist on Etalina's back.

ETALINA: I said I didn't hear you call me!

ALMA—*now she smashes Etalina across the face:* You're a spoiled brat! You will obey, d'you hear?

Alma's face, infuriated.

Cut to Alma's face. She is conducting. Great anxiety about the sounds coming forth. Suddenly she strides from the podium to Etalina. She is near hysteria as she bends over Etalina, who looks up at her in terror.

ALMA: Are you trying to destroy us? That is a B flat; do you know a B flat or don't you? *Etalina is cowering in terror.* I asked if you know B flat or if you do not!

With a blow she knocks Etalina off her chair.

ETALINA, *screaming—she is a teenager, a child:* I want my mother! Mama! Mama!

She collapses in tears. Fania goes to her, holds her.

MICHOU: You'd better get some discipline, Etalina. You're not going to make it on wisecracks.

Alma looks at Fania, a bit guiltily now that her anger has exploded, then goes out into her own room. Fania waits a second, then obediently follows her in and shuts the door.

Cut to Alma's room. Fania is massaging Alma's shoulders and neck as she sits in a chair by the window. Alma moves Fania's fingers to her temples, which she lightly massages. After a moment she has Fania massage her hands, and Fania sits before her doing this.

ALMA: Talk to me, Fania. *Fania keeps silent, wary of expressing herself.* There must be strict discipline. As it is, Dr. Mengele can just bear to listen to us. If we fall below a certain level anything is possible. . . . He's a violently changeable man. *Fania does not respond, only massages.* The truth is, if it weren't for my name they'd have burned them up long ago; my father was first violin with the Berlin Opera, his string quartet played all over the world. . . .

FANIA: I know, Madame.

ALMA: That I, a Rosé, am conducting here is a . . .

FANIA: I realize that, Madame.

ALMA: Why do you resent me? You are a professional, you know what discipline is required; a conductor must be respected.

FANIA: But I think she can be loved, too.

ALMA: You cannot love what you do not respect. In Germany it is a perfectly traditional thing, when a musician is repeatedly wrong . . .

FANIA: To slap?

ALMA: Yes, of course! Furtwängler did so frequently, and his orchestra idolized him. *Fania keeping her silence, simply nods very slightly.* I need your support, Fania. I see that they look up to you. You must back up my demands on them. We will have to constantly raise the level of our playing or I . . . I really don't know how long they will tolerate us. Will you? Will you help me?

FANIA: I . . . I will tell you the truth, Madame—I really don't know how long I can bear this. *She sees resentment in Alma's eyes.* . . . I am trying my best, Madame, and I'll go on trying. But I feel sometimes that pieces of myself are falling away. And believe me, I recognize that your strength is probably what our lives depend on. . . .

ALMA: Then why do you resent me?

FANIA: I don't know! I suppose . . . maybe it's simply that . . . one wants to keep *something* in reserve; we can't . . . we can't really and truly wish to please them. I realize how silly it is to say that, but . . .

ALMA: But you *must* wish to please them, and with all your heart. You are an artist, Fania—you can't purposely do less than your best.

FANIA: But when one looks out the window . . .

ALMA: That is why I have told you *not* to! You have me wrong, Fania—you seem to think that I fail to see. But I *refuse* to see. Yes. And *you* must refuse!

FANIA—*nearly an outcry:* But what . . . *She fears it will sound accusatory* . . . what will be left of me, Madame!

ALMA: Why . . . yourself, the artist will be left. And this is not new, is it? —what did it ever matter, the opinions of your audience? —or whether you approved of their characters? You sang because it was in you to do! And more so now, when your life depends on it! Have you ever married?

FANIA: No, Madame.

ALMA: I was sure you hadn't—you married your art. I did marry . . . *Alma breaks off. She moves, finds herself glancing out the window, but quickly turns away.* . . . Twice. The first time to that . . . *She gestures ironically toward her violin case lying on her cot.* The second time to a man, a violinist, who only wanted my father's name to open the doors for him. But it was my fault—I married him because I pitied myself; I had never had a lover, not even a close friend. There is more than a violin locked in that case, there is a life.

FANIA: I couldn't do that, Madame, I need the friendship of a man.

ALMA—*slight pause:* I understand that, Fania. *She is moved by an impulse to open up.* Once I very nearly loved a man. We met in Amsterdam. The three good months of my life. He warmed me . . . like a coat. I think . . . I could have loved him.

FANIA: Why didn't you?

ALMA: They arrested me . . . as a Jew. It still astonishes me.

FANIA: Because you are so German?

ALMA: Yes. I am. *Slight pause.* In this place, Fania, you will have to be an artist and only an artist. You will have to concentrate on one thing only—to create all the beauty you are capable of. . . .

FANIA, *unable to listen further:* Excuse me, Madame . . .

She quickly pulls open the door and escapes into the day-room; Alma is left with her conflict and her anger. She goes to her violin case on the bed, takes out the instrument. Some emotion has lifted her out of the moment; she walks out of the room.

Cut to the dayroom. Alma enters; the women come quickly out of their torpor, reach for their instruments. Alma halts before them and looks out over them. And with an expression of intense pride which also reprimands and attempts to lead them higher, she plays—and extraordinarily beautifully—the "Meditation" from *Thaïs*, perhaps.

Jew, Gentile, Pole, kapo—Etalina herself and Fania—everyone is captivated, subdued, filled with awe.

As the final crescendo begins, Frau Schmidt and two kapos armed with clubs enter. Everyone leaps up to attention.

FRAU SCHMIDT: Jews to the left, Aryans to the right!

KAPOS: Quick! Hop, hop! Move; quick; five by five!

In the milling around to form two groups, Marianne pushes through and just as the groups make an empty space between them, she pulls an uncomprehending Fania into that space, where they stand alone facing Frau Schmidt.

MARIANNE: She and I are only half.
FRAU SCHMIDT: Half! Half what?
MARIANNE: Half Jewish. Both our mothers were Aryan.

Frau Schmidt's face shows her perplexity as to the regulations in such cases. Alma steps out of the Jewish group and goes to her.

ALMA, *sotto voce, in order not to embarrass her:* Mixed race—are not to be gassed, I'm quite sure, Frau Schmidt. *But Fania overhears and is moved by gratitude and surprise.* But what is this selection for . . . if I may ask?
FRAU SCHMIDT—*her hostility to Alma is quite open:* You belong with the Jews, Madame. *Alma steps back into her group, humiliated but stoic.* Jews! Your hair is getting too long! Haircuts immediately! *To Fania and Marianne:* You two, follow me!

She makes a military about-face and goes out. The two women follow.

Cut to a tiny office in the administration building. The overstuffed noncom is poring over a book of regulations open on a table as Fania and Marianne stand looking on. He lipreads, his finger moving along the lines.
   Now he finds something, nods his head appreciatively as his comprehension gains, then he looks at the women.

SERGEANT: In this case you are allowed to cut off the upper half of the Star of David.

Marianne reacts instantly, ripping a triangle off her coat. (The Star is actually two separate triangles superimposed.) Fania is uncertain, does nothing.

Cut to the dayroom. Much agitation: an impromptu sort of

trial is taking place. Sides are taken with Marianne and Fania alone in the middle.

Fania and Marianne both have half-stars on their dresses. As they are attacked, Marianne reacts with far more anguish than Fania, who, although disturbed, is strong enough to remain apart from any group.

ESTHER: You've behaved like dirty goyim, you've dishonored the Jews in your families.

MARIANNE: But if it's the truth why should I hide it? I *am* only half. . . .

ETALINA: Maybe they'll only be half-gassed.

Laughter. Varya, who is standing with other Poles, steps out of the group.

VARYA: You ashamed to be Jews. You, filth. But you never be Aryan. God always spit on you. We Aryan, never you! *Spits.* Paa!

Her sister Poles guffaw and heavily nod agreement.

ESTHER: For once the Poles are right!

ETALINA: It's disgusting!—cutting the Star of David in half?

MARIANNE: Why not?—if we can avoid the gas?

FANIA: Since when have you all become such Jewish nationalists? Suddenly you're all such highly principled ladies?

ELZVIETA: Bravo! You get up on your high horse with them because you don't dare open your traps with anybody else!

FANIA: I'm sorry; your contempt doesn't impress me. Not when you've accepted every humiliation without one peep. We're just a convenience.

ESTHER: The blood of innocent Jews cries out against your treason!

FANIA: Oh, Esther, why don't you just shut up? I am sick of the Zionists-and-the-Marxists; the Jews-and-the-Gentiles; the Easterners-and-the-Westerners; the Germans-and-the-non-Germans; the French-and-the-non-French. I am sick of it, sick of it, sick of it! I am a woman, not a tribe! And I am humiliated! That is all I know.

She sits on a chair by the window, her face turned from them. After a silence . . .

MARIANNE: You're all just jealous. And anyway, we're just as much betraying the Catholics—our mothers were Catholic, after all.

Fania suddenly gets up and escapes through the door into the dormitory.

Cut to Fania, seated on a lower bunk, is sewing the upper half of her Star back on. Marianne enters and behind her some of the other arguers are approaching in curiosity.

MARIANNE: What are you doing that for? *Fania is silent.* Fania?
FANIA—*glances up at the group with resentment, then continues sewing:* I don't know. I'm doing it. So I'm doing it.

She sews angrily—angry at herself too.

Cut to the barracks "street" outside the dayroom; through windows we see the orchestra and Alma conducting a practice session—phrases are played, then repeated.

The rhythm of a passing beam of the arc light ceaselessly surveys the camp, but here it is only an indirect brightening and darkening.

Coming to the corner of the building, Fania turns into the adjacent street just as a hanging bulb overhead goes out. Shmuel is standing on a short ladder, then descends, leading a wire down with him which he busies himself peeling back to make a fresh connection. Fania hardly looks at him or he at her, this conversation being forbidden.

The music continues in the background from within the dayroom.

SHMUEL: Behind you, in the wall.

Fania leans against the barracks wall; stuck in a joint between boards is a tiny folded piece of paper which she palms.

FANIA—*a whisper:* Thank you.
SHMUEL: Don't try to send an answer—it's too dangerous; just wants you to know he's here . . . your Robert. *She nods once, starts to leave.* Fania? They are gassing twelve thousand a day now. *Her face drains. He goes up the ladder with wire.* Twelve thousand angels fly up every day.
FANIA: Why do you keep telling me these things? What do you want from me!

Shmuel makes the bulb go on, the light flaring on the wild and sweet look in his face. He looks up.

SHMUEL: Look with your eyes—the air is full of angels! You mustn't stop looking, Fania!

He perplexes and unnerves her; she claps hands over her ears and hurries along the barracks wall. As she turns the corner she nearly collides with Tchaikowska, who is enjoying a cigarette. She is standing next to the door to her own room. Fania gives her a nod, starts to pass, when the door opens; a kapo comes out buttoning his shirt.

TCHAIKOWSKA: Two more cigarettes—you took longer this time.
KAPO: I'm broke—give you two more next time.

Marianne comes through this door. She is eating meat off a bone. She sees Fania, is slightly surprised, but goes on eating. The kapo gives her ass a squeeze and walks away.
    Tchaikowska goes into the room.
    Fania sees into the room—Tchaikowska is straightening the rumpled bed in what is obviously her room.

Cut to a barracks street. Fania catches up with Marianne, who is stashing the bone with some slivers of meat still on it in her pocket.

FANIA: At least share some of it with the others—for your own sake, so you don't turn into an animal altogether!
MARIANNE: Jealous?

She walks away, flaunting her swinging backside and enters the dormitory.

Cut to Fania playing the piano with the orchestra. (A light piece—airy, popular music.) The keyboard starts tilting. The orchestra stops, breaking off the music.
    Four kapos are turning the piano on its side, onto a dolly.
    Fania rescues her music and skitters out of the way, astonished and frightened. Alma and the orchestra look on in silent terror as the piano is simply rolled out of the building and through the door to the street. Does it mean the end of

the orchestra? All eyes go to Alma, who is clearly shocked and frightened. After a moment, as though nothing had happened:

ALMA: Let us turn now to . . . to ah—*she leafs through music on podium*—the Beethoven . . .

GISELLE: Madame?—if I could make a suggestion . . .

ALMA: I'm sure this will soon be explained . . .

GISELLE, *desperately:* But why wait till they "explain" it, Madame! I used to play a lot in movie houses . . . on Rue du Four and Boulevard Raspail . . . And I could teach you all kinds of Bal Musette numbers . . . you know, real live stuff that won't bore them. I mean, listen just for a minute!

She plays on her violin—her face perspiring with anxiety—a Bal Musette, lively, dance music. . . .

Enter Frau Lagerführerin Mandel, and Commandant Kramer, with two SS aides.

All but Giselle spring to attention.

TCHAIKOWSKA: Attention!

Giselle looks up from her violin, nearly falls back in a faint at the threatening sight of the big brass, and stands at rigid attention.

MANDEL: At ease. The officers have decided to keep the piano in their club for the use of the members.

KRAMER, *to Alma:* I thought you could manage without it, Madame.

ALMA: Of course, Herr Commandant . . . it was only a little extra sound to fill out, but not imperative at all. We hope the officers will enjoy it.

KRAMER: Which one is Greta, the Dutch girl?

An accordion squeaks . . . it is in Greta's hands.

ALMA: Come!

Greta comes out of the orchestra, accordion in hand. Kramer moves forward, inspecting her fat, square body. She hardly dares glance at him, her eyes lowered.

KRAMER: Open your mouth. *In terror she does so. He peers in at her teeth.* Do you have any disease?

GRETA—*a scared whisper:* No, Herr Commandant.

KRAMER, *to Alma:* Dr. Mengele tells me she's not a very good player.

ALMA: Not very good, no, although not too bad—but she . . . she works quite hard . . .

KRAMER: But you could manage without her.

ALMA, *unwillingly:* Why . . . yes, of course, Herr Commandant.

Cut to Fania, flaring with anger at Alma.

Cut to Kramer, signaling one of the SS aides, who steps forward to Greta, preparing to take her off. Greta stiffens.

KRAMER, *to Greta:* My wife needs someone to look after our little daughters. You look like a nice clean girl.

General relief; Greta is simply rigid. Mandel takes a coat from the second SS aide and hands it to Greta, who quickly and gratefully puts it on. The first aide leads her to exit, and she nearly stumbles in her eagerness to keep up with him, her accordion left behind.

KRAMER, *turning to Alma:* This Sunday you will play in the hospital for the sick and the mental patients. You will have the Beethoven ready.

ALMA: Yes, Herr Commandant. I must ask your . . . toleration, if I may—our cellist has typhus and now without the accordion we may sound a little wanting in the lower . . .

KRAMER: I will send one of the cellists from the men's orchestra—they have several from the Berlin Philharmonic—he can teach one of your violinists by Sunday.

ALMA—*the idea knocks the breath out of her, but . . . :* Why . . . yes, of course, I'm sure we can teach one of our girls by Sunday, yes.

Kramer turns and strolls out.

MANDEL, *as though the orchestra should feel honored:* It will be very interesting, Madame—Dr. Mengele wants to observe the effects of music on the insane.

ALMA: Ah, so!—well, we will do our very best indeed.

Mandel walks over to Fania.

MANDEL, *pleasantly:* And how are you, these days?

FANIA, *swallowing her feelings:* I am quite well . . . of course, we are all very hungry most of the time—that makes it difficult.

MANDEL: I offered to send an extra ration this week before the concert on Sunday, but Madame Alma feels it ought to be earned, as a reward afterwards. You disagree?

Fania glances past Mandel to Alma, who is near enough to have overheard as she turns pages in a score. Alma shoots her a fierce warning glance.

FANIA, *lowering her gaze in defeat:* It's . . . not for me to agree or not . . . with our conductor.

Cut to Alma's room. Alma is pacing up and down, absolutely livid, while Fania stands with lowered gaze—this could be her end.

ALMA: How do you dare make such a comment to her!

FANIA: I don't understand, Madame—I simply told her that we were hungry. . . .

ALMA: When they have managed to play a single piece without mistakes, I will recommend an extra ration—but *I* will decide that, do you understand? *Fania is silent.* There cannot be two leaders. Do you agree or don't you?

FANIA: Why are you doing this?

Alma doesn't understand.

FANIA: We are hungry, Madame! And I saw a chance to tell her! Am I to destroy every last human feeling? She asked and I told her!

ALMA, *a bit cowed, but not quite:* I think we understand each other—that will be all now. *Fania doesn't move.* Yes?—what is it?

FANIA: Nothing. *Makes a move to go.* I am merely trying to decide whether I wish to live.

ALMA: Oh come, Fania—no one dies if they can help it. You must try to be more honest with yourself. Now hurry and finish the Beethoven orchestration—we must give them a superb concert on Sunday.

Alma walks to a table where her scores are, and sits to study them. Fania has been reached, and turns and goes out, a certain inner turmoil showing on her face.

Cut to Etalina, being coached by a young cellist, a thin young man with thick glasses and shaven head. Most of the orchestra is watching them avidly—watching *him*, the women standing around in groups at a respectful distance, the Poles also.

His hands, in close shots, are sensuous and alive and male. The camera bounces such shots off the women's expressions of fascination and desire and deprivation.

Fania tears her gaze from him, and tries to work on her orchestrations—on a table.

Cut to the cellist's hands. He is demonstrating a tremolo. Etalina tries, but she is awkward. He adjusts her arm position.

Cut to Paulette, just entering the dayroom from outside. She is barely strong enough to stand. Michou rushes to her with a cry of joy. Fania sees her, and leaps up to go to her; and Elzvieta also and Etalina.

ETALINA: Paulette! Thank God, I don't have to learn this damned instrument!

Cut to the group helping Paulette to a chair, Paulette is an ascetic-looking, aristocratic young lady.

FANIA: Are you sure you should be out?
ELZVIETA: Was it typhus or what?
ETALINA: She still looks terrible.
FANIA: Sssh! Paulette? What is it?

Paulette is trying to speak but has hardly the strength to. Everyone goes silent, awaiting her words.

PAULETTE: You're to play on Sunday . . .
ETALINA: In the hospital, yes, we know.
FANIA: You don't look to me like you should be walking around, Paulette. . . .

PAULETTE, *stubborn, gallant; she grips Fania's hand to silence her:* They plan . . . to gas . . . all the patients . . . after . . . the concert.

A stunned silence.

FANIA: How do you know this?

PAULETTE: One of the SS women . . . warned me. . . . I knew her once. . . . She used to be . . . one of the . . . chambermaids in our house. So I got out.

Alma enters from her room, sees the gathering, then sees Paulette.

ALMA: Paulette! How wonderful! Are you all better now? We're desperate for you! We're doing the Beethoven Fifth on Sunday!

Paulette gets to her feet, wobbling like a mast being raised.

FANIA: She's had to walk from the hospital, Madame—could she lie down for a bit?

PAULETTE: No! I . . . I can.

She gets to the cello, sits, as though the room is whirling around for her. Etalina rushes and hands her the bow. The orchestra members quickly sit in their places.

ALMA, *at podium:* From the beginning, please.

The Beethoven Fifth begins. Paulette, on the verge of pitching forward, plays the cello. The pall of fear is upon them all now. Fania has resumed her place at the table with her orchestrations. She bends over them, shielding her eyes, a pencil in hand.
    She is moved to glance at the window. There, just outside it, she sees . . .
    Shmuel, at the window. He is pointing at his eyes, which he opens extra wide.

Cut to Fania, startled. Then, lowering her hands from her eyes, forces herself to see, to look—first at Paulette, and the orchestra, and finally at . . .
    Alma, conducting. She is full of joyful tension, pride, wav-

ing her arms, snapping her head in the rhythm and humming the tune loudly, oblivious to everything else.

Cut to Paulette feverishly trying to stay with the music; her desperation—which those around her understand—is the dilemma of rehearsing to play for the doomed.

Cut to Fania, at one end of the dormitory corridor between bunks, wringing out a bra and heavy stockings over a pail. Her expression is tired, deadened; she has been changing, much life is gone from her eyes. Nearby, in dimness, Tchaikowska and another Blockawa are lying in an embrace, kissing; Tchaikowska glances over, and with a sneer . . .

TCHAIKOWSKA: Now you do her laundry? —the contessa?

Fania takes the bra and stockings down the corridor to Paulette's bunk, hangs them to dry there. Paulette is lying awake, but weak.

PAULETTE: Thank you. I'm troubled . . . whether I should have told the other patients—about what's going to happen. What do you think? *Fania shakes her head and shrugs.* Except, what good would it do them to know?
FANIA: I have no answers any more, Paulette.
VOICES: Shut up, will you! Trying to sleep! Sssh!
FANIA: Better go to sleep. . . .

Across the corridor, Charlotte is staring at Michou with something like surprise in her expression, self-wonder. Michou turns her head and sees Charlotte staring at her, and shyly turns away.
    Fania now climbs into her own bunk, lies there open-eyed. Other women are likewise not asleep, but some are.
    Fania lies there in her depression.
    She shuts her eyes against the sounds from outside—the coupling of freight cars, a surge of fierce dogs barking, shouts—her face depleted. Now Charlotte's head appears at the edge of the bunk. Fania turns to her.
    Charlotte timorously asks if she may slide in beside her.

CHARLOTTE: May I?

Fania slides over to make room. Charlotte lies down beside her.

CHARLOTTE, *with a certain urgency:* I just wanted to ask you . . . about Michou.

Now their eyes meet. Fania is surprised, curious.
   Charlotte is innocently fascinated, openly in love but totally unaware of it.

CHARLOTTE: What do you know about her? I see you talking sometimes together.

FANIA: Well . . . she's a militant; sort of engaged to be married; the kind that has everything planned in life. Why?

CHARLOTTE: I don't know! She just seems so different from the others—so full of courage. I love how she always stands up for herself to the SS.

FANIA—*slight pause; she knows now that she is cementing an affair:* That's what she says about you.

CHARLOTTE, *surprised, excited:* She's spoken about me?

FANIA: Quite often. She especially admired your guts. *Slight pause.* And your beauty.

Charlotte looks across the aisle and sees Michou, who is asleep.

Cut to Michou, emphasizing her hungered look in sleep, her smallness and fragility.

Cut to Fania and Charlotte.

CHARLOTTE: She's so beautiful, don't you think? I love her looks.

FANIA: It would be quicker if you told me what you don't like about her.

CHARLOTTE, *shyly laughing:* I don't understand what is happening to me, Fania. Just knowing she's sleeping nearby, that she'll be there tomorrow when I wake—I think of her all day. I could see her face all through my fever . . . I just adore her, Fania.

FANIA: No. You love her, Charlotte.

CHARLOTTE: You mean . . . ?

FANIA: You're seventeen, why not? At seventeen what else is there but love?

CHARLOTTE: But it's impossible.

Fania softly laughs.

CHARLOTTE: Are you laughing at me?

FANIA: After all you've seen and been through here, is that such a disaster?

CHARLOTTE: How stupid I am—I never thought of it as . . .

FANIA: In this place to feel at all may be a blessing.

CHARLOTTE: Do you ever have such . . . feelings?

FANIA, *shaking her head:* I have nothing. Nothing at all any more. Go now, you're still not well, you should sleep.

Charlotte starts to slide out, then turns back and suddenly kisses Fania's hand gratefully.

FANIA—*she smiles, moved:* What a proper young lady you must have been!

Charlotte shyly grins, confessing this, and moves away down the aisle. She pauses as she starts to pass Michou. The latter opens her eyes. Both girls stare in silence at one another— really looking inward, astonished at themselves. Now Michou tenuously reaches out her hand, which Charlotte touches with her own.

Cut to Fania, observing them. A deep, desperate concern for herself is on her face. She closes her eyes and turns over to sleep.

At the distant drone of bombers, Fania slowly opens her eyes. Turns on her back, listening.

Cut to a series of close-ups: Michou, Paulette, Liesle, Etalina, and others; they are opening their eyes, listening, trying to figure out the nationality of the planes.

Now the Polish Blockawas, some in bed with each other, do the same.

Cut to Fania. She has gone to a window and is looking out onto the "street." The sound of the bombers continues.

Cut to the barracks "street," SS guards in uniform carrying rifles—five or six of them converging and looking upward worriedly.

Cut to Fania, turning from the window and momentarily facing the apprehensive, questioning stares of the Blockawas. She starts to pass them; Tchaikowska reaches out and grasps her wrist.

TCHAIKOWSKA, *pointing upward:* American? English? *Fania shrugs, doesn't know. Tchaikowska releases her.* Too late for you anyway.

Fania's face is totally expressionless—yet in this impacted look is torment that another human could do this.

FANIA: Maybe it is too late for the whole human race, Tchaikowska.

She walks past, heading for the dayroom, not her bunk.

Cut to Fania, under a single bulb, alone in the dayroom. She has pencil in hand, orchestrating—but she looks off now, unable to concentrate. Elzvieta appears beside her, sits.

ELZVIETA: So it's going to end after all. *Fania gives her an uncomprehending glance.* Everyone tries to tell you their troubles, don't they.

FANIA: I don't know why, I can't help anyone.

ELZVIETA: You are someone to trust, Fania—maybe it's that you have no ideology, you're satisfied just to be a person.

FANIA: I don't know what I am anymore, Elzvieta. I could drive a nail through my hand, it would hardly matter. I am dying by inches, I know it very well—I've seen too much. *Tiredly wipes her eyes.* Too much and too much and too much . . .

ELZVIETA: I'm one of the most successful actresses in Poland. *Fania looks at her, waiting for the question; Elzvieta, in contrast to Fania, has long hair.* My father was a count; I was brought up in a castle; I have a husband and Marok, my son, who is nine years old. *Slight pause.* I don't know what will happen to us, Fania—you and I, before the end. . . .

FANIA, *with a touch of irony:* Are you saying good-bye to me?

ELZVIETA, *with difficulty:* I only want one Jewish woman to understand. . . . I lie here wondering if it will be worse to survive than not to. For me, I mean. When I first came here I was sure that the Pope, the Christian leaders did not know;

but when they found out they would send planes to bomb out the fires here, the rail tracks that bring them every day. But the trains keep coming and fires continue burning. Do you understand it?

FANIA: Maybe other things are more important to bomb. What are we anyway but a lot of women who can't even menstruate anymore—and some scarecrow men?

ELZVIETA, *suddenly kissing Fania's hand:* Oh, Fania—try to forgive me!

FANIA: You! Why? What did you ever do to me? You were in the Resistance, you tried to fight against this, why should you feel such guilt? It's the other ones who are destroying us—and they only feel innocent! It's all a joke, don't you see? It's all meaningless, and I'm afraid you'll never change that, Elzvieta! *Elzvieta gets up, rejected, full of tears.* I almost pity a person like you more than us. You will survive, and everyone around you will be innocent, from one end of Europe to the other.

Offscreen, we hear the sounds of a train halting, shouts, debarkation noises. Elzvieta turns her eyes toward a window.

Cut to a convoy debarking in the first dawn light. SS and kapos and dogs.

Cut to Elzvieta, riven by the sight now, sinking to her knees at a chair, and crossing herself, praying. Fania studies her for a moment . . . then she goes back to work on her orchestration, forcing herself to refuse this consolation, this false hope and sentiment. She inscribes notes. Something fails in her; she puts down pencil.

FANIA: My memory is falling apart; I'm quite aware of it, a little every day . . . I can't even remember if we got our ration last night . . . did we?

Tchaikowska appears from the dormitory door—she is drinking from a bowl. Now she walks to the exit door of the dayroom, opens it, and throws out the remainder of milk in the bowl, wiping the bowl with a rag.

Elzvieta, still on her knees, watches Tchaikowska returning to the dormitory; she tries to speak calmly. . . .

ELZVIETA: You throw away milk, Tchaikowska?

TCHAIKOWSKA: It was mine.

ELZVIETA: Even so . . .

TCHAIKOWSKA: Our farm is two kilometers from here—they bring it to me, my sisters.

ELZVIETA: But even so . . . to throw it away, when . . .

She breaks off. Tchaikowska looks slightly perplexed.

TCHAIKOWSKA: You saying it's not my milk?

ELZVIETA: Never mind.

TCHAIKOWSKA, *tapping her head:* You read too many books, makes you crazy.

She exits into the dormitory. Elzvieta swallows in her hunger, and, as Fania watches her, she bends her head and more fervently, silently prays.

Cut to the barracks "street," silent and empty for a moment; suddenly the blasts of sirens, whistles, and the howling of pursuit dogs. From all corners SS guards and dog handlers explode onto the street. They are in a chaotic hunt for someone.

Prisoners are being turned out of barracks onto the "street," lined up to be counted, hit, kicked. . . .

Cut to the hunters, crashing into the dayroom with dogs howling. Blockawas are coming out of the dormitory, throwing on clothes. SS women accompany the guards. Alma comes out of her room questioningly.

Cut to the orchestra, fleeing from bunks in the dormitory as hunters rip off blankets, overturn mattresses—screaming in fear of dogs, shouting.

Cut to the players, being driven outside into the "street."

Cut to the "street." Scurrying to form ranks and trying to dress at the same time, the players are calling out their names and coming to attention. Before them stand an SS officer and a dog handler, beside Tchaikowska who is checking names off a roster she holds.

Alma stands at attention before the officer.

TCHAIKOWSKA: All accounted for, Mein Herr.

SS OFFICER, *to Madame Alma:* Do you know Mala?

ALMA: Mala? No, but I have seen her accompanying the Commandant, of course—as an interpreter.

SS OFFICER: She has had no contact at all with your players?

ALMA: No, no, she has never been inside our barracks, Herr Kapitän.

The SS officer now walks off, followed by the handler and dog. Michou is the first to realize.

MICHOU: Mala's escaped! I bet she's gotten out!

The orchestra is electrified. . . .

CHARLOTTE, *to another:* Mala's out!

Blockawas are pushing them back into barracks.

PAULETTE: Fania!—did you hear!

Cut to the "Canada" girls. Deals are going on at their tables, and a girl prisoner comes hurrying up. A quick whisper to one of the dealers.

GIRL: Mala got out . . . and Edek too!

DEALER: With Edek? How!?

GIRL: They got SS uniforms somehow, and took off!

Business stops as three or four dealers cross themselves and bow their heads in prayer.

Cut to Alma, at the podium, going through a score, with Fania alongside her pointing out something on it.

The following lines of dialogue are all in close intimate shots—since they dare not too openly discuss the escape. (All are in their chairs, instruments ready for rehearsal.)

CHARLOTTE: What a romance! Imagine, the two of them together—God!

MICHOU: I saw him once, he's gorgeous—blond, and beautiful teeth. . . .

LIESLE: She's a Belgian, like me. . . .

ESTHER: What Belgian? She's Jewish, like all of us. . . .

LIESLE: Well, I mean . . .

ELZVIETA: Edek is a Pole, though—and they're going to tell the world what's happening here.

ETALINA: Imagine—if they could put a bomb down that chimney!

ELZVIETA: Now the world will know! Let's play for them The Wedding March! . . .

She raises her violin.

CHARLOTTE, *readying her bow on the violin—devoutly:* For Mala and Edek!

MICHOU: Mala and Edek!

Etalina, on time for once, readies her instrument.

Cut to Shmuel, bowing to Alma, his toolbox on his shoulder.

SHMUEL: I'm supposed to diagram the wiring, Madame. I won't disturb you.

Alma nods, lifts her baton, and starts the number.

Shmuel, as the number proceeds, has a piece of paper on which he is tracing the wiring. He follows along one wall to the table in a corner of the room, where Fania is seated with a score she is following, pencil in hand.

Fania senses Shmuel is lingering at a point near her; and as he approaches her, his eyes on the wiring, he exposes the paper in his hand for her to read. She glances at Alma at the end of the room, then leans a little . . .

Cut to the note, reading: ALLIES LANDED IN FRANCE.

Shmuel's hand crumples the paper.

Cut to Shmuel, swallowing the note. Then taking his toolbox and slinging it onto his shoulder, he hurriedly limps away and goes out the exit without turning back.

Fania turns and looks out the window, and sees . . .

The by-now familar arrival of new prisoners as seen from the dayroom window. Shmuel walks out of the shot, his place taken by . . .

Mandel—who is leading Ladislaus, a four-year-old boy, away from his mother, who is at the edge of a crowd of new arrivals, watching, not knowing what to make of it. The mother now calls to him; we can't hear her through the window. Ladislaus is beautiful, and Mandel seems delighted as she gives him a finger to hold on to.

Note: The character of this particular crowd of prisoners is somewhat different—they are Polish peasant families, not Jews. They are innocently "camping" between barracks buildings, far less tensely than the Jews on arrival, and the kids are running about playing, even throwing a ball. Infants are suckling; improvised little cooking fires, etc. . . . So that Ladislaus's mother is only apprehensive as she calls to him, not hysterical at his going off with Mandel.

Cut to the orchestra, continuing to play. Etalina is turning with a look of open fear from the window; she leans to Elzvieta beside her and unable to contain herself, whispers into her ear.

Alma sees this breach of discipline.

ALMA, *furiously:* Etalina!

The music breaks off.

ETALINA, *pointing outside:* Those are Poles, not Jews. . . . They're Aryans, Madame!

MICHOU: Why not? Hitler always said they would kill off the Poles to make room for Germans out there.

ETALINA: But look at them, there must be thousands. . . . They'd never gas that many Aryans! *To Alma:* I think they're going to give them this barracks, Madame!

Mandel and Ladislaus enter.
     Silence. Mandel now picks up Ladislaus to show him off to the orchestra.

MANDEL: Isn't he beautiful?

Only Tchaikowska and the other Blockawas purr and smile. The orchestra sits in silence, not knowing what to make of this or Etalina's theory.

MANDEL, *to Alma:* What's the matter with them?

ALMA: It's nothing, Frau Mandel—there seems to be a rumor that these Aryan Poles will be given our barracks. . . .

MANDEL: Oh, not at all, Madame—in fact, I can tell you that

there will be no further selections from within our camp. Of course we have no room for new arrivals—so for them . . . there will be other arrangements.

Cut to Fania, turning out toward the window; she sees a line of trucks loading the peasants for gassing.

Cut to the child's mother being pushed aboard—but now she is fighting to stay off the truck and looking desperately about for her child.

Cut to Mandel, now fairly surrounded with players who, in their relief, can now express feeling for the beautiful child. Featured here is Marianne, who is chanting a nursery rhyme and tickling his cheek. . . .

MARIANNE: Hoppa, hoppa, Ladislaus
            Softly as a little mouse . . .

Mandel, with an almost girlishly innocent laugh, presses the child's face against her own. Then putting him down, and bending to him, holding his hand.

MANDEL: And now we are going to get you a nice new little suit, and shoes, and a sweet little shirt. *She gives a perfectly happy, proud glance at the orchestra.* Work hard now—we are all expecting an especially fine concert for the hospital on Sunday! *To child:* Come along.

She exits with Ladislaus hanging on to her finger

Cut to the "street," teeming with life a few moments before, now totally cleansed of people. Mandel leads the boy so as to avoid the dying embers of cooking fires, other debris left by the crowd, bundles, cookpots. . . .
    Kapos are policing the area, throwing debris into hand-drawn wagons. A kapo picks up a ball, and as Mandel approaches he bows a little and offers it to her. She accepts it and hands it to Ladislaus and walks on, tenderly holding his hand.

Cut to the players, clustered at the door and windows, watching Mandel going away. They are all confused, yet attracted by this show of humanity.

GISELLE: So she's a human being after all!

ESTHER: She is? Where's the mother?

ETALINA: Still—in a way, Esther . . . I mean at least she adores the child.

ESTHER, *with a wide look of alarm to all:* What's happening here. . . ?

PAULETTE: All she said was that . . .

ESTHER, *shutting her ears with her hands:* One Polack kid she saves and suddenly she's human? What is happening here!

From the podium, Alma calmly, sternly summons them with the tapping of her baton.

ALMA: From the beginning, please! We have a great deal to do before Sunday.

Silently they seat themselves. And Beethoven's Fifth begins.

Cut to the searchlight from a tower, sweeping the street. Sirens sound and the searchlight is extinguished.

Cut to Marianne, singing; she breaks off as the sirens sound. And all lights go out.

As the sirens die out, bombers take over.

The players sit waiting in the dark, eyes turned upward toward the sound. As the sound rises to crescendo, Alma exits into her room; and as she is closing the door she catches Fania's eye. Fania rises, approaches the door.

Cut to Alma's room. Still in darkness, Alma sits. The bombers are fading.

ALMA: I will be leaving you after the Sunday concert, Fania. *Fania is surprised.* They are sending me on a tour to play for the troops. I wanted you to be first to hear the news. *A different camera angle reveals the excitement and pride in her expression.* I am going to be released, Fania! Can you imagine it? I'll play what I like and as I like. They said . . . *Elated now, filling herself:* they said a musician of my caliber ought not be wasted here! . . . What's the matter? I thought you'd be happy for me.

FANIA: Well, I am, of course. But you'll be entertaining men who are fighting to keep us enslaved, won't you.

ALMA: But that is not the point! I . . . *Only an instant's difficulty.* I am German, Fania; I can't help that, and I will play for German soldiers.

FANIA, *changing the hopeless subject:* And what about us? We're going to continue, aren't we?

ALMA: I have suggested you to replace me.

FANIA—*nods, consenting:* Well . . . *A move to leave.* I hope . . . it ends soon for all of us.

She turns to grasp the doorknob.

ALMA: Why are you trying to spoil my happiness?

Fania turns to her, trying to plumb her.

ALMA: I will be playing for honorable men, not these murderers here! Soldiers risk their lives. . . !

FANIA: Why do you need my approval? If it makes you happy then enjoy your happiness.

ALMA: Not all Germans are Nazis, Fania! You are nothing but a racialist if you think so!

FANIA: Alma—you are German, you are free—what more do you want! I agree, it is an extraordinary honor—the only Jew to play a violin for the German Army! My head will explode. . . !

She pulls the door open just as SS Frau Schmidt walks up to it. Shock. Schmidt is the powerhouse who runs the clothing depot and knocked Fania down earlier on for speaking out of line.

ALMA: Why . . . Frau Schmidt . . . come in . . . please!

The lights suddenly go on. All glance up, noting this wordlessly.

SCHMIDT: I wanted to extend my congratulations, Madame Rosé—I have just heard the great news.

ALMA, *ravished:* Oh, thank you, thank you, Frau Schmidt. This is very moving to me, especially coming from you.

SCHMIDT: Yes, but I always express my feelings. I would like you to join me for dinner tonight—a farewell in your honor?

ALMA: I . . . I am overwhelmed, Frau Schmidt. Of course.

SCHMIDT: At eight, then?—in my quarters.

ALMA: Oh, I'll be there. . . . Thank you, thank you.

Schmidt exits. Now, eyes glistening with joy, Alma turns to Fania.

ALMA: Now . . . now you see! That woman, I can tell you, has tried everything to be transferred . . . she is desperate to get out of here, and yet she has the goodness to come and wish me well on my departure.

FANIA, *stunned:* Well I certainly never expected that of her. . . . But who knows what's in the human heart?

ALMA: You judge people, Fania, you are terribly harsh.

Alma is now sprucing herself up for dinner, brushing her skirt, straightening her blouse. . . .

FANIA: And Mandel saved that child. Maybe they figure they're losing the war, so . . .

ALMA, *at the height of her hopes for herself:* Why must everything have a worm in it? Why can't you accept the little hope there is in life?

She is now putting on her coat.

FANIA: I'm all mixed up. Schmidt wanting to get out is really unbelievable, Alma—she's gotten rich running the black market; she's robbed every woman who's landed here . . . every deal in the place has her hand in it. . . .

ALMA, *extending her hand:* I am leaving in the morning, Fania—if we don't see each other . . . Thank you for your help.

FANIA, *taking her hand:* You are totally wrong about practically everything, Alma—but I must say you probably saved us all. And I thank you from my heart.

ALMA: You can thank my refusal to despair, Fania.

FANIA: Yes, I suppose that's true.

Cut to an honor guard, and SS at attention.

The whole orchestra is filing into this room through a doorway. They are in their finest; atmosphere is hushed, eyes widened with curiosity, incredulity at this whole affair.

For at center stands a coffin, flowers on it, the top open. But the orchestra is ranged some yards from it.

When they have all assembled, enter Commandant Kramer, Dr. Mengele, other brass—

And finally Mandel, her finger in the hand of little Ladislaus, who is now dressed in a lovely blue suit, and linen shirt, and tie, and good shined shoes, and holding a teddy bear.

First Kramer, Mengele, Mandel, and the other brass step up and look mournfully into the coffin. Now the orchestra is ordered to pay its respects by a glance from Mandel to Fania.

Cut to Mandel, her eyes filling with tears.

Cut to the orchestra. A feeling of communion; they are starting to weep, without quite knowing why.

Cut to Alma—in the coffin. Fania looks down at Alma dead—she is bewildered, horrified. Then she moves off, her place taken by Paulette, then others. . . . The sound of keening is beginning as they realize it is Alma who has died.

Cut to the black market. Fania is pretending to trade a thick slice of bread for some soap with the chief black marketeer, a brazen girl who is smelling the bread offered.

FANIA: What happened?
BLACK MARKETEER: Schmidt poisoned her at dinner.
FANIA: How do you know!
BLACK MARKETEER: They shot her this morning.
FANIA: Schmidt!?
BLACK MARKETEER—*nods:* Nobody was getting out if she couldn't. 'Specially a Jew.
FANIA: Then she really wanted out!
BLACK MARKETEER: Well, she'd made her pile, why not?

Both their heads suddenly turn to the same direction at a booming sound in the distance.

BLACK MARKETEER, *looking questioningly at Fania:* That thunder or artillery?

They both turn again, listening in the midst of the market.

Cut to Olga, the Ukrainian accordionist, who has apparently inherited the conductorship; she is robot-like in her arm-waving as she leads them in the Fifth Symphony—but it all falls to pieces, and Fania hurries up to the podium.

OLGA, *before Fania can get a word out:* No! I have been appointed and I am going to conduct!

FANIA: Now listen to me!

OLGA: No! I am kapo now and I order you to stop interfering!

FANIA: Olga, dear—you can barely read the notes, you have no idea how to bring in the instruments!

OLGA: Go back to your seat!

FANIA: You'll send us to the gas! Mengele will be there on Sunday—he won't stand for this racket—it's nonsensical! Now let me rehearse, and on Sunday you can stand up in front and wave your arms, but at least we'll be rehearsed!

ETALINA: Hey!—sssh!

All turn to listen . . . once again there is the sound of a distant booming.

ETALINA: God . . . you suppose Mala and Edek found the Russians and are leading them here?

GISELLE: I bet! That was artillery. The Russians are famous for their artillery. . . !

OLGA: All right, listen! *She is desperately trying to fill out an image of authority.* I know a number. It's very famous with us in the Ukraine. We are going to play it. First I.

Olga takes up her accordion and launches into a "Laughing Song," a foot-stomper polka, full of "Ha-ha-ha, hee-hee-hee," etc.

Orchestra looks at her, appalled, some of them starting to giggle.

Blockawas led by Tchaikowska appear and, loving it, begin doing a polka with one another, hands clapping. . . .

There is sharp whistling outside.

Tchaikowska hurries out into the street as players go to the windows. . . .

Cut to a gallows. The hanging of Mala and Edek. They have both been horribly beaten, can barely stand. Mala stumbles to her knees but flings away the hand of the executioner and stands by herself under the noose.

The camera now turns out . . . picking up part of the immense crowd of prisoners forced to watch the executions.

Cut to prisoners, en masse—in fact, the whole camp, tens of thousands, a veritable city of the starved and humiliated, ordered to watch the execution. This is a moment of such immense human import—for one after another, in defiance, they dare to bare their heads before the two doomed lovers and create a sea of shaven heads across a great space, while SS men and kapos club at them to cover themselves.

Cut to the gallows—and the drop. Both Mala and Edek are hanging.

Cut to the sky.

Dissolve from sky to rain.

Cut to the dayroom at night. Rain is falling on the windows. Girls are practicing in a desultory way, breaking off in mid-note to talk quietly together. Fania is at her table; she is playing with a pencil, staring at nothing, her face deeply depressed, deadened.

Now Michou, who is at another window a few yards away, calls in a loud whisper . . .

MICHOU, *pointing outside:* Fania!

Fania looks out the window.

Cut to Marianne, on the "street," just parting from the executioner, a monstrous large man, who grimly pats her ass as she rushes into the barracks.

Cut to Marianne, entering the dayroom from outside, shaking out her coat, and as she passes Michou . . .

MICHOU: With the executioner?

Marianne halts. All around the room the expressions are angrily contemptuous, disgusted.

MICHOU: He killed Mala and Edek, did you know?

MARIANNE: Well, if he didn't, somebody else would've, you can be sure of that.

She starts toward the door to the dormitory, then halts, turns to them all.

MARIANNE: I mean to say, dearies, whose side do you think *you're* on? Because if anybody's not sure you're on the side of the executioners, you ought to go out and ask any prisoner in this camp, and they'll be happy to tell you! *To Michou:* So you can stick your comments you know exactly where, Michou. Any further questions?

She looks about defiantly, smiling, exits into the dormitory, removing her coat.
    The truth of her remarks is in the players' eyes. They avoid one another as the women resume practicing. Esther comes to Fania.

ESTHER: You shouldn't let her get away with that.—I'd answer but nobody listens to what *I* say. . . .

FANIA: But she's right, Esther, what answer is there?

ESTHER: I am *not* on their side—I am only keeping myself for Jerusalem.

FANIA: Good.

ESTHER—*Fania's uninflected, sterilized comment has left her unsatisfied:* What do you mean by that, Fania?

FANIA: That it's good, if you can keep yourself so apart from all this. So clean.

ESTHER, *asking, in a sense:* But we're not responsible for this.

FANIA: Of course not, nothing here is our fault. *Finally agreeing, as it were, to go into it:* All I mean is that we may be innocent, but we have changed. I mean we know a little something about the human race that we didn't know before. And it's not good news.

ESTHER, *anxiously, even angry:* How can you still call them human?

FANIA: Then what are they, Esther?

ESTHER: I don't like the way you . . . you seem to connect such monsters with . . .

Suddenly, Giselle calls out sotto voce—she is sitting with Charlotte.

GISELLE: Mengele!

Dr. Mengele's importance is evident in the way they leap to their feet as he enters. His handsome face is sombre, his uniform dapper under the raincoat which he now opens to take out a baton and Alma's armband, which has some musical insignia on it.

OLGA, *at rigid attention:* Would the Herr Doktor Mengele like to hear some particular music?

Mengele walks past her to the door of Alma's room.

Cut to Mengele, entering Alma's room. He looks about at the empty bed and chair, as though in a sacred place. Then he takes the baton and hangs it up from a nail in the wall above a shelf, and on the shelf he carefully places her armband. Now he steps back and, facing these relics, stands at military attention for a long moment.
   The camera turns past him to discover, through the doorway to the dayroom, Fania looking in, and others jammed in beside her, watching in tense astonishment.

MENGELE: Kapo!
OLGA, *rushing into room:* Herr Doktor Mengele!

She goes to attention.

MENGELE: That is Madame Rosé's baton and armband. They are never to be disturbed. *He faces the relics again.* In Memoriam.

Fania greets this emotional display with incredulity, as do others nearby.
   Now the dread doctor turns and walks into the dayroom, the players quickly and obsequiously making way for him, and standing with attentive respect as he goes by.
   As he passes into the center of the dayroom, his heels clacking on the wooden floor in a slow, pensive measure, the

tension rises—no one is sure why. And he halts instead of leaving them, his back to them. Why has he halted, what is the monster thinking?

Cut to the players. They have risen to a dread tension, their faces rigid.

Cut to Mengele. He turns to them; he has an out-of-this-world look now, an inspired air, as though he had forgotten where he was and only now takes these faces into consciousness. He seems less angry than alarmed, surprised.

Fania, unable to wait for what may come out of him, takes a tenuous step forward and bows a little, propelled by her terror of death, now, at this moment.

FANIA: If the Herr Doktor will permit me—the orchestra is resolved to perform at our absolute best, in memory of our beloved Madame Rosé.

Only now does Mengele turn that gaze on her, as though he heard her from afar. Fania's voice is near trembling.

FANIA: I can assure the Herr Doktor that we are ready to spend every waking moment perfecting our playing. . . . We believe our fallen leader would wish us to continue . . . *Beginning to falter:* to . . . to carry on as she . . . inspired us. . . .

The sound of bombers overhead. Mengele reacts, but in the most outwardly discreet way, with an aborted lift of the head. But the girls understand that he knows the end is near, and this heightens their fear.

He changes under this sound from the sky, and strolls out as though to show unconcern. As soon as he is out of sight several girls break into weeping. Fania feels humiliated, and goes alone to her table. . . .

ETALINA, *weeping:* It's the end! You felt it, didn't you, Fania! He's going to send us to the gas!

PAULETTE, *asking Fania's reaction:* The way he stared at us!

CHARLOTTE: The thing to do is rehearse and rehearse and rehearse! *To Liesle:* To this day you've never gotten the

Beethoven right! Now here, damn you! *She thrusts an accordion at her.* Work on that arpeggio! *She notices Fania looking upward.* What's the matter?

The whole group turns to Fania questioningly—they are scared, panicked. She is listening to the sky.

FANIA: I can't understand why they don't bomb here. They could stop the convoys in one attack on the rails.

ELZVIETA: They're probably afraid they'll hit *us*.

MICHOU: It's political—it always is—but I can't figure out the angles.

ESTHER: They don't want it to seem like it's a war to save the Jews. *They turn to Esther.* They won't risk planes for our sake, and pilots—their people wouldn't like it. *To Fania:* Fania . . . if they do come for us and it's the end . . . I ask you not to do that again and beg for your life. . . .

FANIA, *guiltily:* I was only . . .

ESTHER, *crying out—a kind of love for Fania is in it:* You shouldn't ever beg, Fania!

Cut to Lagerführerin Mandel entering from the rain. She wears a great black cape. She looks ravaged, desolate. She goes to a chair and sits, unhooks her cape. In one hand now is seen . . .

The child's sailor hat. It is held tenderly on her lap.

Cut to Mandel, in a state of near shock; yet an air of self-willed determination too, despite her staring eyes.

Olga, now the kapo, looks to Fania for what to do. Others likewise glance at her. Fania now comes forward and stands before Mandel.

Mandel comes out of her remoteness, looks at Fania.

MANDEL: The duet from *Madame Butterfly*. You and the other one.

Fania turns to the girls—Giselle hurries into the dormitory.

GISELLE, *running off:* Marianne? Come out here . . . !

Mandel now stands and walks to a window looking out at the rain. Meanwhile Charlotte and Etalina have taken up their violins to accompany.

Marianne, half asleep, enters from the dormitory and comes to Fania. And now they wait for Mandel to turn from the window and order them to begin. But she doesn't. So Fania walks across the room to her.

Cut to Fania, arriving beside Mandel, who is staring out at the rain-washed window. Fania's eyes travel down to the hat in the other woman's hand.

FANIA: We are ready to begin, Frau Mandel.

Mandel seems hardly to have heard, keeps on staring. After a moment . . .

FANIA: Is something the matter with the little boy?

Mandel now glances at Fania—there is an air of dissociation coming over the Nazi's face.

MANDEL: It has always been the same—the greatness of a people depends on the sacrifices they are willing to make.

Fania's expression of curiosity collapses—she knows now.

MANDEL: I gave him . . . back.

Now Mandel is straightening with an invoked pride before Fania, stiffening. But she is still struggling with an ancient instinct within her.

MANDEL: Come now, play for me.

She goes to her seat. Fania, nearly insensible, joins Marianne—who greets her with a raised eyebrow to keep their hostility intact. Charlotte's violin starts it off, the duet from Act II.

MARIANNE (*as Suzuki*): *It's daylight! Cio-Cio-San.*
FANIA (*as Butterfly*)—*mimes picking up an infant, cradling it in her arms: He'll come, he'll come, I know he'll come.*
MARIANNE (*as Suzuki*): *I pray you go and rest, for you are weary. And I will call you when he arrives.*
FANIA (*as Butterfly*)—*to her "baby": Sweet thou art sleeping, cradled on my heart . . .*

Cut to Mandel, stunned by the lyric and music; but through her sentimental tears her fanatic stupidity is emerging.

FANIA (*as Butterfly*) (*voice-over*): *Safe in God's keeping, while I must weep apart. Around thy head the moonbeams dart. . . .*

Cut to the group.

FANIA (*as Butterfly*), *rocking the "baby": Sleep my beloved.*
MARIANNE (*as Suzuki*): *Poor Madame Butterfly!*

Cut to Mandel, fighting for control, staring up at Fania. And Fania now takes on a challenging, protesting tone.

FANIA (*as Butterfly*): *Sweet, thou art sleeping, cradled on my heart. Safe in God's keeping, while I must weep apart.*

The sound of bombers . . . coming in fast, tremendous. Sirens.
Mandel comes out of her fog, stands . . . girls are rushing to windows to look up. The lights go out.
The sound of bombers overhead and nearby explosions.
There is screaming; in the darkness, total confusion; but Mandel can be seen rushing out into the night, a determined look on her face.

Cut to the railroad platform. Bombs explode.
Despite everything, deportees are being rushed onto waiting trucks, which roar away.

Cut to a series of close shots: Kramer kicking a deportee. . . . Mandel commanding a woman to board a truck. . . . And Mengele, face streaming, his eyes crazed as he looks skyward; he goes to an SS officer.

MENGELE: Hurry!—faster!

Cut to the warehouse hospital. "The Blue Danube" is in full swing as the shot opens. At one end of the vast shadowy space is the orchestra, "conducted" by Olga.
The few good violinists like Elzvieta and Charlotte saw away as loud as possible.
The Bechstein piano has been brought in and Fania is playing.
The sick, what appear to be hundreds of them, are ranged

in beds; the insane, some of them clinging to walls or to each other like monkeys; about a hundred so-called well prisoners in their uniforms ranged at one end; dozens of SS officers, male and female, in one unified audience sit directly before the players.

Cut to a dancing woman emerging from among the insane; heads turn as she does a long, sweeping waltz by herself; shaven head, cadaverous, a far-out expression.

SS glance at her, amused.

Cut to the prisoners. A humming has started among them to "The Blue Danube."

Cut to Mengele, Kramer, and SS officers. These high brass notice the humming—they take it with uncertainty—is it some kind of demonstration of their humanity?

Cut to the prisoners. They have dared to hum louder—and the fact that it is done in unison and without command or authorization enlivens them more and more.

Cut to Commandant Kramer, starting to get to his feet, when Mengele touches his arm and gestures for him to permit the humming as harmless. Kramer half-willingly concedes, and sits.

Cut to the orchestra. "Blue Danube" ends. With no announcement, in the bleak silence, Olga picks up her accordion. Fania and Paulette immediately come to her and have a quick whispered conversation while trying to appear calm.

FANIA, *sotto voce:* Not the "Laughing Song"!
OLGA: But they want another number!
PAULETTE: But they're all going to the gas, you can't play that!
OLGA: But I don't know any other! What's the difference?

Olga steps from them and begins to play and sing the "Laughing Song," which requires all to join in.

And as it proceeds, some of the insane join in, out of tempo to be sure, and . . .

Kramer is laughing, along with other SS.

Patients in beds are laughing. . . .

Cut to Fania, in her eyes the ultimate agony.

Cut to Mengele, signaling Kramer, who is beside him, and the latter speaks to an aide at his side. The aide gets up and moves out of the shot. . . .

Cut to the orchestra. The "Laughing Song" is continuing.

Cut to a door to the outside, which is opening. Kapos are leading half a dozen patients through it.

Cut to the orchestra. The "Laughing Song" continues; now Paulette sees the kapos leading people out. Her cello slides out of her grasp as she faints. "Laughing Song" is climaxing. Michou is propping up Paulette while attempting to play and laugh.

Cut to the hospital warehouse. Patients, orchestra, and SS are rocking along in the finale, as more patients are being led out through the door.

Cut to the dayroom. Later that night. The players are sitting in darkness while some are at the windows watching a not very distant artillery bombardment—the sky flashes explosions.
    Fania, seated at her table, is staring out the window. She is spiritless now.
    Players' faces, in the flashes of light from outside, are somber, expectant.

Cut to a fire in the dayroom stove, visible through its cracks. Michou is grating a potato into a pan. Charlotte is hungrily looking on. This is very intense business.

Cut to Olga, the new conductor, emerging from Alma's room: She is very officious lately.

OLGA: All right—players? We will begin rehearsal. *Heads turn to her but no one moves.* I order you to rehearse!
ETALINA, *indicating outside:* That's the Russian artillery, Olga.
OLGA: I'm in charge here and I gave no permission to suspend rehearsals!
ETALINA: Stupid, it's all over, don't you understand? The Russians

are out there and we will probably be gassed before they can reach us.

GISELLE: Relax, Olga—we can't rehearse in the dark.

ETALINA: She can—she can't read music anyway.

OLGA—*defeated, she notices Michou:* Where'd you get those potatoes?

MICHOU: I stole them, where else?

OLGA, *pulling her to her feet:* You're coming to Mandel! —I'm reporting you!

From behind her, suddenly, Fania has her by her hair.

FANIA, *quietly:* Stop this, Olga, or we'll stuff a rag in your mouth and strangle you tonight. Let her go.

Olga releases Michou.

CHARLOTTE: She was only making me a pancake, that's all.

FANIA: Sit down, Olga—we may all go tonight.

OLGA: I don't see why.

ETALINA: We've seen it all, dummy, we're the evidence. *Olga unhappily stares out a window.* I feel for her—she finally gets an orchestra to conduct and the war has to end.

Cut to a series of close shots: the players' faces—the exhaustion now, the anxiety, the waiting.

Cut to Etalina, just sitting close to Fania.

ETALINA: I think I saw my mother yesterday. And my two sisters and my father.

FANIA, *coming alert to her from her own preoccupations:* What? Where? What are you talking about?

ETALINA: Yesterday afternoon; that convoy from France; when we were playing outside the freight car; I looked up and . . . I wasn't . . . I wasn't sure, but . . .

Their eyes meet; Fania realizes that she is quite sure, and she reaches around and embraces Etalina, who buries her face in Fania's breast and shakes with weeping.

FANIA: Oh, but what could you have done?

Cut to Lagerführerin Mandel, entering the dayroom. All rise to stand at attention, faces flaring with anxiety. Mandel is

wide-eyed, totally distracted, undone. Etalina is weeping as
she stands at attention.

MANDEL: Has anyone come across that little hat? *Silence. No
one responds. Amazement in faces now.* The little sailor hat. I
seem to have dropped it. No?

Heads shake negatively, rather stunned. Mandel, expressionless, exits.
    The players sit again.
    Etalina has an explosion of weeping.

FANIA, *comforting her:* Sssh . . .

Marianne now comes over to Fania, who is stroking Etalina's
face.

MARIANNE: I just want you to know, Fania, that . . . you
turned your back on me when I needed you, and . . . I
don't want you to think I'm too stupid to know it.

FANIA: What are you talking about? *Marianne bitterly turns
away, as* . . . Are you a little child that I should have locked
in the closet?

Marianne walks away to a window, adamantly bitter.

Cut to Michou, feeding Charlotte pieces of pancake from a
pan, as she would a child.

Cut to Fania, looking with a certain calculation at . . .
    Elzvieta, who blanches and turns from an explosion in the
sky, and crosses herself.
    Fania comes up to her.

FANIA: Elzvieta? *She takes out a small but thick notebook:* I would
like you to keep this. It's my diary—everything is in there
from the first day.

ELZVIETA: No, no. You keep it. You will be all right,
Fania. . . .

FANIA: Take it. Take it, maybe you can publish it in Poland. . . .

ELZVIETA—*starts to take it, then doesn't:* It's impossible, Fania—
I feel like I'm condemning you! You keep it, you will live, I
know you will!

FANIA: I am not sure . . . that I wish to, Elzvieta.

ELZVIETA, *realizing, she looks deeply into Fania's dying eyes:* Oh no . . . no, Fania! No!

She suddenly sweeps Fania into her arms, as . . .
Two troopers enter. These are not SS men; they carry rifles and combat gear.

TROOPER: Jews left! Aryans right! Hurry up!

The players scurry to form up. . . .
Fania and Elzvieta slowly disengage—it's good-bye.

Cut to an open freight car. Dawn is breaking; rain drenches some twenty-five players in this freight car ordinarily used for coal. Fania now is lying on her back with her eyes shut, the players extending their coats to shield her. The train slows.
Nearby two Wehrmacht troopers are huddled over a woodstove; women also cluster around for warmth.
These men are themselves worn out with war, dead-eyed.
Marianne makes her way over to one of the troopers and gives him a flirty look.

MARIANNE: How's it going, soldier?

The trooper's interest is not very great.

MARIANNE: Could a girl ask where you're taking us?

She comes closer—and with mud-streaked face, she smiles.
. . . Now he seems to show some interest in her.

MARIANNE: 'Cause wherever it is, I know how to make a fellow forget his troubles. Where are we heading?

TROOPER, *shrugging:* Who knows? I guess it's to keep you away from the Russians, maybe . . . so you won't be telling them what went on there. Or the Allies either.

MARIANNE: Going to finish us off?

TROOPER: Don't ask me.

The train stops.

Cut to a flat, barren, endless landscape covered with mud.

Cut to an SS officer mounting onto the car; below him on the ground are several other SS plus dogs and handlers.

The officer looks the players over, then points at Marianne. She steps forward. He hands her a club.

SS OFFICER: You are the kapo. Get them out and form up.

Officer hops down and moves off to next car.

Cut to Marianne, who hefts the club in her hand and turns to the players, who all seem to receive the message her spirit emits—they fear her.

MARIANNE: Out, and form up five by five.

She prods Charlotte in the back as she is starting to climb down.

CHARLOTTE: Stop pushing me!

Marianne viciously prods Paulette, who falls to the ground as Michou and Giselle seek to intercede; and Marianne swings and hits Giselle, then goes after Michou, and both escape only by jumping down and falling to their hands and knees. Now Marianne turns to the *pièce de résistance*—
Fania is practically hanging from the supporting hands of Charlotte and Etalina, who are moving her past Marianne.

MARIANNE: She can walk like anybody else.
ETALINA: She's got typhus, Marianne!

She beats their hands away from Fania, who faces her, swaying with a fever. Marianne swings and cracks Fania to the floor of the car.

Cut to a vast barn or warehouse, its floor covered with hundreds of deportees in the final stages of their physical resistance. They are practically on top of one another; and over all a deep, undecipherable groaning of sound, many languages of every European nation.
Now a shaft of daylight flashes across the mass as a door to the outside is opened and through it a straggling column of deportees moves out of this building.
The door closes behind them, followed by . . .

The sound of machine guns.

Cut to the little group of players around Fania, who are wide-eyed, powerless. She is propped up in Paulette's lap now, panting for breath.
Fania opens her eyes . . .

ETALINA, *slapping Fania's hands:* That's better . . . keep your eyes open . . . you've got to live, Fania. . . .

Now Fania, half-unconscious, sees past Etalina . . . to . . .
A woman and man making love against a wall.
A man barely able to crawl, peering into women's faces.

MAN: Rose? Rose Gershowitz?

Cut to a Polish woman, surrounded by the ill and dying, giving birth, with help from another woman.
Machine guns fire in near distance. Along with the baby's first cries.

Cut to Fania, receiving these insanely absurd sounds with a struggle to apprehend. And now she sees . . .
The Polish woman who just gave birth, standing up, swaying a little, wrapping her rags about her as she takes her baby from a woman and holds it naked against herself.

Cut to Fania, ripping the lining out of her coat—which was lying on top of her as a blanket—and gestures for Paulette to hand it on to the Polish woman, which is done. And the baby is wrapped in it.
Light again pours in from the opening door, and another column of deportees is moving to exit and death. And as this column stumbles toward the door, urged on by SS men and kapos . . .
Shmuel appears in the barn door. The light behind him contrasts with the murk within the building, and he seems to blaze in an unearthly luminescence.
He is staring in a sublime silence, as now he lifts his arms in a wordless gesture of deliverance, his eyes filled with miracle, and turning, he starts to gesture behind him. . . .
A British soldier appears beside him and looks into the barn.

Cut to the British soldier. His incredulous, alarmed, half-disgusted, half-furious face fills the screen.

Cut to a panoramic shot: a shouting mass of just-liberated deportees throwing stones. Some of these people are barely able to stand, some fall to their knees and still throw stones at . . .

A truck filled with SS men and women, their arms raised in surrender, trying to dodge the stones. Several trucks are pulling away, filled with SS.

Fania is being half-carried by Michou and Etalina, and others near them.

ETALINA: Please, Fania, you've got to live, you've got to live. . . !

Michou suddenly sees something offscreen, picks up stones and starts throwing. . . .

MICHOU: There she is! Hey rat! Rat!

Paulette and Esther turn to look at . . .

Marianne.

In the midst of the mob, Marianne is being hit by stones thrown by Michou. Other deportees are trying to hold on to Marianne to keep her from escaping. . . .

FANIA'S VOICE: Michou!

Michou turns to . . .

Fania, steadied on her feet by the others, staring at . . . Marianne, frightened, but still full of defiant hatred.

Cut to a British communications soldier, with a radio unit, coming up to Fania.

SOLDIER: Would it be at all possible to say something for the troops?

Fania registers the absurdity of the request.

SOLDIER: It would mean so much, I think . . . unless you feel . . .

She stops him by touching his arm; all her remaining strength is needed as she weakly sings the "Marseillaise."

FANIA:

> *Allons enfants de la Patrie*
> *Le jour de gloire est arrivé*
> *Contre nous de la tyrannie* . . .

Fania's eyes lift to . . .
    The sky. The clouds are in motion.

Cut to a busy, prosperous avenue in Brussels—1978 autos, latest fashions on women, etc. . . .

Cut to a restaurant dining room. The camera discovers Fania at a table, alone. It is a fashionable restaurant, good silver, formal waiters, sophisticated lunch crowd. Fania is smoking, sipping an aperitif, her eye on the entrance door.
    Of course she is now thirty years older, but still vital and attractively done up and dressed. And she sees . . .
    First, Liesle, the miserable mandolin player, who enters and is looking around for her. Fania half-stands, raising her hand. As Liesle starts across the restaurant toward her, Charlotte enters behind her. And she recognizes Liesle.
    Keeping Fania's viewpoint—Charlotte quickly catches up with Liesle, touches her arm; turns, a pause; they shake hands, then Liesle gestures toward Fania's direction and they start off together.

Cut to Liesle and Charlotte arriving at the table; Fania is standing; a pause. It is impossible to speak. Finally, Fania extends both her hands, and the other two grasp them.

FANIA: Liesle! —Charlotte!

They sit, their hands clasped. After a moment . . .

LIESLE: We could hardly believe you were still singing—and here in Brussels!
CHARLOTTE: I'm only here on a visit, imagine? And I saw your interview in the paper!

Words die in them for a moment as they look at one another trying to absorb the fact of their survival, of the absurdity of their lives. Finally . . .

FANIA: What about the others? Did you ever hear anything about Marianne?

LIESLE: Marianne died.

FANIA—*it is still a shock:* Ah!

LIESLE: A few years after the war—I can't recall who told me. She was starting to produce concerts. She had cancer.

CHARLOTTE: I have two children, Fania . . .

FANIA: Charlotte with children! Imagine!

A waiter appears. He knows Fania.

WAITER: Is Madame ready to order or shall we . . . ?

FANIA: In a few minutes, Paul. *With a glance at the other two:* We haven't seen each other in thirty years, so . . . you must ask the chef to give us something extraordinary; something . . . absolutely marvelous!

And she reaches across the table to them and they clasp hands.

Cut to their hands on the white tablecloth, and their numbers tattooed on their wrists.

The camera draws away, and following the waiter as he crosses the restaurant, we resume the normality of life and the irony of it; and now we are outside on the avenue, the bustle of contemporary traffic; and quick close shots of passersby, the life that continues and continues. . . .

FINAL FADE-OUT

I THINK ABOUT YOU
A GREAT DEAL

The Writer enters. Wears shirt and trousers. Carrying a bundle of mail. Sits, goes through letter after letter; of a dozen he removes two of importance, the rest he—after an instant of hesitation— drops into his wastebasket. Instantly, the IMPRISONED ONE *enters, in his forties, wearing rumpled gray clothing. He sits. The* WRITER *does not face him directly.*

WRITER: Yes.

(Slight pause)

Amazing, how often I think of you even though we've barely met. And that was so long ago.

(Reaches into the waste basket, retrieves the letters he dropped in.)

I suppose it happens whenever I get a load of this kind of stuff. Must get fifty pounds of it a month. I'm on the master list, obviously. Look at this. . . . (*Reads off the senders' names.*) "Ban the Bomb," "Planned Parenthood," "Save the Children," "American Indian Fund," "Friends of the Arts," "National Organization for Women," "Fight the Ku Klux Klan," "Amnesty International," "Central Park Conservancy," —whatever that is, "Save the Animals," "Save Africa," "Save the Rain Forests," save, save, save, save. The mind simply cannot take all this seriously. Things just can't be this bad.

(Slight pause)

I must say, though—it does remind me of you. Your situation seems worse than all the others, though . . . I'm not sure why. Maybe it's the immense investment so many of us have made in Socialism. That people who even call themselves Socialist should imprison the imagination. . . . That's really what it is, isn't it—the war on the imagination. And maybe, too, because your prison is probably further West than Vienna. You are almost within range of the sound of our voices. You can almost hear us, I suppose. In effect. Whatever the reason, I really do think about you a great deal.

(Slight pause)

Reminds me of another writer I knew many years ago in New York. Quite talented, we all thought. Poet and playwright. Lot of promise. But he had an active case of claustrophobia. Couldn't bear to enter an elevator. And they had no money so he and his wife lived in this tiny room which drove him crazy—used to walk the streets half the night.—(It was a lot safer to walk the streets at night in those days.) Anyway . . . in desperation he took a job writing advertising copy for . . . I think it was General Motors. Which allowed him to move into a larger apartment, and eased his anxieties. Years passed and I met him again and naturally I was curious about what he was working on. But the poetry had died, the plays too; what he wanted to show me was this thick file of ads he had written. In fact, he was such a favorite, the Company had given him a special office on the ground floor of their skyscraper so he could avoid the elevator. He was middle-aged by this time, and it was quite . . . moving, actually . . . to see how proud he had become of these works in praise of General Motors. In fact, he showed me his different drafts, and pointed out how he had shifted various ideas around until the whole conception was perfected. And I kept watching the look of triumph on his face. And you couldn't help being happy for him—that he had earned so much space around himself. He obviously no longer lived in his old anxiety. Seemed really satisfied with life now, with a solid feeling of accomplishment. His was clearly a successful life . . . that had substituted itself for a poet.

(Slight pause)

I thought about you, then. They have taken away your space, haven't they—because you have refused to write their ads. Amazing how, more than anything, power loves praise. —But there are fifty other conclusions one could draw from this and none of them change anything for you. So I suppose we must raise it all to the moral level.—The moral level is where nothing gets changed. Yet it exists, doesn't it; just as my thinking so often of you exists. In fact, it joins us together, in a way. In some indescribable way we are each other's continuation . . . you in that darkness where they claw and pound at your imagination, and I out here in this space where I think about you . . . a great deal.

(He drops the clump of appeals into the basket.)

There will be another clump tomorrow. And the next day and the next. (*Slight pause*) Imagine . . . if they stopped! Is that possible? Of course not. As long as mornings continue to arrive, the mail will bring these acts of goodness demanding to be done. And they will be done. Somehow. And so we hold your space open for you, dear friend.

The WRITER *goes to his typewriter, and writes. The* IMPRISONED ONE, *after a moment, rises and walks out. The* WRITER *continues to write.*

END

TWO-WAY MIRROR

ELEGY FOR A LADY

CAST

MAN
PROPRIETRESS

*Music: it has a fine, distant fragility, a simple theme, repeated—
like unresolved grief.*

The MAN *appears in a single beam of light, facing the audience.
He is hatless, dressed in a well-fitted overcoat and tweed suit.*

*He stares as though lost in thought, slightly bent forward, perhaps
to concentrate better. He is deep into himself, unaware for the
moment of his surroundings.*

*Light rises behind him, gradually dawning across the stage, re-
veals aspects of what slowly turns out to be a boutique. The shop
consists of its elements without the walls, the fragments seeming to
be suspended in space.*

*A sweater is draped over a bust, a necklace on another bust, a
garter on an upturned plastic thigh, a watch on an upturned
arm, a knitted cap and muffler on a plastic head. Some of these
stand on elements of the countershape, others seem to hang in air.*

As the light rises to normal level the MAN *moves into the boutique.
And now, among the displays a* WOMAN *is discovered standing,
motionless, looking off at an angle in passive thought. She is wearing a white silk blouse and a light beige skirt and high heeled
shoes. The* MAN *moves from object to object and pauses to look into
the display case in the counter where jewellery is kept. As he nears
her, he halts, staring into her profile. Music dies.*

MAN: Can you help me?
PROPRIETRESS (*turns now to look into his eyes*): Yes?
MAN: Do you have anything for a dying woman?
PROPRIETRESS (*startled, she waits a moment for him to continue
and then looks about, trying to imagine*): Well, let me see . . .

677

He waits another instant, then resumes his search, examining a pair of gloves, a blouse.

May I ask you if . . . ?

She breaks off when he does not respond or turn to her. Finally, he does.

MAN: Excuse me?

PROPRIETRESS: I was just wondering if you meant that she was actually . . .

MAN: By the end of the month or so. Apparently.

PROPRIETRESS (*seeking hope*): . . . But it isn't sure.

MAN: I think *she's* sure. But I haven't talked to any doctors or anything like that . . .

PROPRIETRESS: And it's . . . ?

MAN (*cutting in*): So it seems, yes.

PROPRIETRESS (*helpless personal involvement*): Ah.

MAN (*forcing out the words*): . . . I assume you were going to say cancer.

The PROPRIETRESS *nods with a slight inhale of air. Now she glances around at her stock with a new sense of urgency.*

I started to send flowers, but flowers seem so . . . funereal.

PROPRIETRESS: Not necessarily. Some spring flowers?

MAN: What's a spring flower?—daisies?

PROPRIETRESS: Or daffodils. There's a shop two blocks down —Faynton's.

MAN (*considers*): I passed there twice. But I couldn't decide if it should be a bunch of flowers or a plant.

PROPRIETRESS: Well, either would be . . .

MAN: Except that a bunch would fade, wouldn't they?—in a few days?

PROPRIETRESS: But a plant would last. For years, sometimes.

MAN: But there's a suggestion of irony in that. Isn't there?

PROPRIETRESS (*thinks*): Cut flowers, then.

MAN: They don't last at all, though, and she'd have to watch them withering away every morning . . .

PROPRIETRESS: Yes.

Slight pause. He resumes looking at things, handles a bracelet . . . half asking . . .

She is not an older woman.

MAN: She just turned thirty . . . a couple of months ago.

The PROPRIETRESS *inhales sharply.*

I've never really bought her anything. It struck me this afternoon. Nothing important.

PROPRIETRESS (*delicately*): You've known each other very . . .

MAN (*grieving*): That's always hard to remember exactly. I can never figure out whether we met two winters ago or three. (*A little laugh which she joins.*)—She never can either . . . but we've never been able to stay on the subject long enough . . . in fact, on any subject—Except one.

PROPRIETRESS *laughs softly and he joins her for an instant.*

I'm married.

PROPRIETRESS (*nods*): Yes.

MAN: And a lot older, of course.

PROPRIETRESS: Oh, well that's not always a . . . (*She does not finish.*)

MAN: No, but it is in most cases. (*He glances around again.*) I tried to think of a book. But after all the reading I've done nothing occurs to me.

PROPRIETRESS: She is not religious.

MAN: No—Although we never talked about religion. I don't know whether to try to concentrate her mind or distract it. Everything I can think to send her seems ironical; every book seems either too sad or too comical; I can't think of anything that won't increase the pain of it.

PROPRIETRESS: Perhaps you're being too tender. Nothing you could send would be as terrible as what she knows.

He considers this, nods slightly.

People do make a kind of peace with it.

MAN: No; I think in her case the alarm never stops ringing; living is all she ever thought about—She won't answer the phone anymore. She doesn't return my calls for days, a week sometimes. I think, well, maybe she wants me—you know—to disappear, but then she does call back and always makes an excuse for not having called earlier. And she seems so desperate for me to believe her that I forget my resentment and I try to offer to help again and she backs away again . . . and I end up not seeing her for weeks again. (*Slight pause.*) I even wonder sometimes if she's simply trying to tell me there's somebody else. I can't figure out her signal.

PROPRIETRESS: Yes. But then again it might simply be that she . . .

MAN: That's right . . .

PROPRIETRESS: . . . Finds it unbearable to be cheated of someone she loves . . .

MAN: I'm so glad to hear you say that!—it's possible . . . (*With relief, deeper intimacy.*) Sometimes, you know, we're on the phone and suddenly she excuses herself—and there's silence for a whole minute or two. And then she comes back on with a fresh and forward-looking attitude and her voice clear. But a couple of times she's cut out a split second too late, and I hear the rush of sobbing before she can clap her hand to the receiver. And it just burns my mind—and then when she comes back on so optimistically I'm in a terrible conflict; should I insist on talking about the reality, or should I pretend to sort of swim along beside her?

PROPRIETRESS: She's in a hospital.

MAN: Not yet—Although, frankly, I'm not really sure. She's never home anymore. I know that. Unless she's stopped answering her phone altogether.—Even before this happened she would do that; but she's on the phone practically all day in her work so it is understandable. Not that I'm ruling out that she might have been staying elsewhere occasionally.—But of course I've no right to make any demands on her. Or even ask any questions.—What does this sound like to you?

PROPRIETRESS: It sounds like you'd simply like to thank her.

Music resumes behind his speech.

MAN (*with a slight surprise*): Say! That's exactly right, yes! . . . I'd simply like to thank her. I'm so glad it sounds that way.

PROPRIETRESS: Well . . . why not just *do* that?

MAN (*anguished*): But how can I without implying that she's coming to the end . . . ? (*He breaks off.*)

PROPRIETRESS: But she's *said* she's . . . ?

MAN: Not really in so many words; she just . . . as I told you . . . breaks up on the phone or . . .

Music dies away.

PROPRIETRESS (*with anguish now*): Then why are you so sure she's . . . ?

MAN: Because they're evidently operating on her in about ten days. And she won't tell me which hospital.

PROPRIETRESS: . . . When you say evidently . . .

MAN: Well. I know she's had this growth, and there was a pain for awhile—about last summer—but then it passed and she was told it was almost certainly benign. But . . . (*He goes silent; stares at the* PROPRIETRESS.) Amazing.

PROPRIETRESS: Yes?

MAN: I've never mentioned her at all to anyone. And she has never let on about me. I know that . . . and we have close mutual friends who have no idea. And here I walk in and tell you everything, as though . . . (*From an engaging chuckle the breath seems to suddenly go out of him and he sits weakly on a stool, struggling against helplessness.*)

Music resumes.

PROPRIETRESS: Yes?

He makes an attempt to resume looking around the store but it fails.

When you passed here earlier today . . .

MAN (*with great relief*): Yes, that's right, I remember that! You saw me then . . .

PROPRIETRESS: You stared at the window for a very long time.

MAN: I was trying to think of something for her.

Music resumes.

PROPRIETRESS: Yes, I could see you imagining; it moved me deeply—for her sake.

MAN: It's amazing how absolutely nothing is right. I've been all over this part of town. But every single thing makes some kind of statement that is simply . . . not right.

PROPRIETRESS: I'm sure you're going to think of something.

MAN: I hope so!

PROPRIETRESS: Oh I'm sure!

MAN: It's partly, I think, that I don't know what I want to say because I'm not sure what I have a right to say—I mean someone my age ought to be past these feelings.—(*With sudden revulsion.*) I go on as though there's all the time in the world . . . ! (*He stands, quickened, looking at the goods again.*) That kerchief is beautiful.

PROPRIETRESS: It's silk. Paris. (*She unfurls it for him.*)

MAN: Lovely. How would you wear it?

PROPRIETRESS: Any way. Like this . . . (*She drapes it over her shoulders.*)

MAN: Hm.

PROPRIETRESS: Or even as a bandanna. (*She wraps it over her hair.*)

MAN: But she wouldn't do that indoors.

PROPRIETRESS: Well . . . she *could*.

MAN: No. I'm afraid it could taunt her.

PROPRIETRESS (*putting it back on her shoulders*): Well, then—in bed, like this.

MAN (*tempted*): It is the right shade.—You have her colouring, you know;—I can't get over it, walking in off the street like this and blabbing away.

PROPRIETRESS: A thing like that builds up; you never know who you'll suddenly be telling it to.

MAN: Except that you have a look in your eye.

PROPRIETRESS (*smiling*): What kind of look?

MAN (*returns her smile*): You're seeing me. (*Of the scarf, definitely now.*) That isn't right. (*She slips it off. He moves, looking about.*) . . . I think it's also that you're just about her age.

PROPRIETRESS: Why would that matter?

MAN: Someone older usually forgets what thirty was really like.

PROPRIETRESS: But you remember?

MAN: I didn't used to—thirty is far back down the road for me; but when I'm with her it all flows back at the touch of her skin. I feel like a Hindu recalling a former life.

PROPRIETRESS: And what is thirty like?

Music resumes.

MAN: Thirty is an emergency. Thirty is the top of the ridge from where you can see down both sides—the sun and the shadow, your youth and your dying in the same glance. It's the last year to believe that your life can radically change anymore. And now she's caught on that ridge, unable to move.—God . . . (*A surge of anguish.*) . . . how *pleased* with herself she'd gotten lately!—her ambitions and plans really working out . . . (*With a half-proud, half-embarrassed grin.*) although tough too—she can snap your head back with a harsh truth, sometimes. But I don't mind, because all it is is her wide-open desire to live and win. (*He glances around at the objects.*): So it's hard to think of something that won't suggest the end of all that . . . and those eyes closing.

Music dies away.

PROPRIETRESS: I have a kind of warm negligee. That one up there.

MAN (*looks up, studies it for a moment*): But mightn't that look like something after you've had a baby?

PROPRIETRESS: Not necessarily.

MAN: Yes. Like when they stroll around the hospital corridors afterwards. . . . If she's very sick she'd have to be in a hospital gown, wouldn't she?

PROPRIETRESS (*sharply, like a personal rebellion*): But *everybody* doesn't die of it! Not *every* case!

MAN (*explosively*): But she weeps on the phone! I *heard* it!

PROPRIETRESS (*a personal outcry*): Well the thought of disfigurement is terrible, isn't it? (*She turns away, pressing her abdomen. Pause.*) You ought to write, and simply thank her.

MAN (*asking . . .*): But that *has* to sound like a goodbye!

PROPRIETRESS: You sound as though you never had a single intimate talk!

MAN: Oh yes, but not about . . . negative things, somehow.

PROPRIETRESS: You met only for pleasure.

MAN: Yes. But it was also that we both knew there was nowhere it could go. Not at my age. So things tend to float pretty much on the surface . . .

PROPRIETRESS (*smiling*): Still, the point does come . . .

MAN: Surprisingly, yes . . .

PROPRIETRESS: When it begins to be an effort to keep it uncommitted . . .

MAN: Yes, there's a kind of contradiction . . .

PROPRIETRESS:—To care and simultaneously not-care . . .

MAN: You can't find a breakthrough—it's like a fish falling in love with the sun; once he breaks water he can't breathe!— So maybe the whole thing really doesn't amount to anything very much. (*Pause.*)

PROPRIETRESS (*she re-folds a sweater he had opened up*): But you don't always look like this, do you?

MAN: How?

PROPRIETRESS: In pain.

MAN: I guess I'm still unable to understand what she means to me.—I've never felt this way about a death. Even my mother's and father's . . . there has always been some unwelcome, tiny feeling of release; an obligation removed. But in her case, I feel I'm being pulled under myself and suffocated.

The PROPRIETRESS *takes a deeper breath of air and runs a hand down her neck.*

What else do you have that might . . . ? (*He halts as he starts once again to look around at the merchandise.*) . . . Wait! I know—a bed jacket! That's the kind of neutral—healthy people wear them too!

PROPRIETRESS: I haven't any.

MAN: Nothing at all?

PROPRIETRESS: You might try the department stores.

MAN (*greatly relieved*): I will. I think that's what I want. A bed jacket doesn't necessarily *say* anything, you see?

PROPRIETRESS: That's true, there is something non-committal about a bed jacket. Try Saks.

MAN: Yes. Thanks very much.—I never dreamed I'd have such a conversation! (*He starts to button up. With embarrassment . . .*) It really amazes me . . . coming in here like this . . .

PROPRIETRESS: I have an electric kettle if you'd care for a cup of tea.

MAN: . . . Thanks, I wouldn't mind, thanks very much . . . I simply can't get over it, . . . I had no idea all this was in me.

She goes behind the counter, throws a switch; he sits at the counter again.

Are you the owner here? (*He opens his coat again.*)

PROPRIETRESS (*nods, affirmatively, then . . .*): You know, it may be a case of a woman who's simply terrified of an operation, that's all.—I'm that way.

MAN (*thinks, trying to visualise—then . . .*): No, I think it would take a lot more to panic her like this. She's not an hysterical person, except once a month for a few hours, maybe.

PROPRIETRESS: She tends to objectify her situation.

MAN: That's it.

PROPRIETRESS: Sees herself.

MAN: Yes.

PROPRIETRESS: From a distance.

MAN: Yes, she has guts; really cool nerve right up to the moment she flies to pieces.

PROPRIETRESS: She's had to control because she's alone.

MAN: Yes; so something like this must be like opening a shower curtain and a wild animal jumps out.

PROPRIETRESS: She was never married.

MAN: Never. (*He begins to stare off and smile.*)

PROPRIETRESS: Something about her couldn't be.—Unless to you?

MAN (*joyfully*): She has a marvellous, throaty, almost vulgar laugh; it can bend her forward and she even slaps her thigh like a hick comedian . . .

The PROPRIETRESS *begins laughing.*

And gets so helpless she hangs on my arm and nearly pulls me down to the sidewalk.

The PROPRIETRESS *laughs more deeply.*

One time at one of those very tiny café tables we both exploded laughing at the same instant, and our heads shot forward just as the waiter was lowering my omelette between us . . .

She bursts out laughing and slaps her thigh. Music: sharply. He sees this and his smile remains. The tea kettle whistles behind the counter.

PROPRIETRESS: Milk or lemon?

He watches her a moment, smiling.

Lemon?

MAN: Lemon, yes.
(*She goes and pours tea. The* MAN, *with a new anticipatory excitement.*) You're not busy?

Music dies away.

PROPRIETRESS: After Christmas it all dies for a few days. (*She hands him a cup.*)

MAN: It's more like somebody's home in here.

PROPRIETRESS: I try to sell only what I'd conceivably want for myself, yes.

MAN: You're successful.

PROPRIETRESS: In a way. (*Confusing.*) . . . I am, I guess.—Very, in fact.

MAN: But a baby would be better.

PROPRIETRESS (*a flash of resentment, but then truth*): Sometimes. (*She hesitates.*) Often, actually. (*She looks around at the shop.*) It's all simply numbers, figures. Something appalling about business, something totally pointless—like emptying a pail and filling it again every day.—Why?—Do I look unhappy?

MAN: You look like you'd found yourself . . . for the fiftieth time and would love to throw yourself away again.

PROPRIETRESS: You try to avoid hurting people.

MAN: Yes, but it can't be helped sometimes. I've done it.

PROPRIETRESS: No wonder she loves you.

MAN: I'm not so sure. I really don't know anymore.

PROPRIETRESS: Oh, it must be true.

MAN: Why?

PROPRIETRESS: It would be so easy.

MAN: But I'm so old.

PROPRIETRESS: No.

MAN: I'm not sure I want her to. I warned her not to, soon after we started. I said there was no future in it. I said that these things are usually a case of loving yourself and wanting someone else to confirm it, that's all. I said all the blunt and ugly things I could think of.

PROPRIETRESS: And it didn't matter at all. (*Slight pause.*)

MAN: It didn't?

PROPRIETRESS (*with a hard truthfulness*): Of course it mattered—what you said made her stamp on her feelings, and hold part of herself in reserve. It even humiliated her a little.

MAN (*in defence*): But her independence means more to her than any relationship, I think.

PROPRIETRESS: How do you know?—You were the one who ordered her not to love you . . .

MAN: Yes. (*Evading her eyes.*) But there's no tragic error, necessarily—I don't think she wanted to love anyone. In fact, I don't think either of us said or did anything we badly regret—it's Nature that made the mistake; that I should be so much older, and so perfectly healthy and she so young and sick.

PROPRIETRESS (*unnerved, an outburst*): Why do you go on assuming it has to be the end!

He looks at her with surprise.

Thousands of people survive these things. And why couldn't you ask her what exactly it was?

MAN: I couldn't bear to make her say it.

PROPRIETRESS: Then all she's actually said was that an operation . . . ?

MAN: No. Just that the 28th of the month was a big day.

PROPRIETRESS (*almost victoriously*): Well that could mean almost anything.

MAN (*in anguish*): Then why doesn't she let me come and see her!

PROPRIETRESS (*frantically*): Because she doesn't want to load her troubles onto you!

MAN: I've thought of that.

PROPRIETRESS: Of course. It's a matter of pride. Even before this happened, she never encouraged you to just drop in, for instance—did she?

MAN: Oh no. On the contrary.

PROPRIETRESS: Of course not! She wanted her hair to be done and be dressed in something you'd like her in . . .

MAN: Oh, insisted on that, yes.

PROPRIETRESS: Then you can hardly expect her to invite you to see her in hospital! (*Slight pause.*)

MAN: Then it *is* pretty superficial, isn't it?

PROPRIETRESS: Why!—it could be the most important thing in her entire life.

MAN (*pause. Shakes his head*): No. Important—but not the most important. Because neither of us have burned our bridges. As how could we?—If only because of my age?

PROPRIETRESS: Why do you go on about your age? That's only an excuse to escape with.

MAN (*smiles*): But it's the only one I've got, dear.—But whatever age I was, she wouldn't be good to be married to.

PROPRIETRESS (*hurt, almost alarmed*): How can you say that!

MAN: What's wrong in saying it? She's still ambitious for herself, she still needs risks, accomplishments, new expectations; she needs the dangerous mountains not marriage in the valley—marriage would leave her restless, it would never last. (*Pause.*)

PROPRIETRESS (*dryly*): Well, then . . . you were both satisfied . . .

(*As he turns to her, surprised.*) . . . with what you had.

MAN: That's a surprise—I never thought of that. Yes; very nearly. (*He thinks further.*) Almost. Yes. (*Slight pause.*) That's a shock, now.

PROPRIETRESS: To realise that you were almost perfectly happy.

MAN: Almost—You see, there was always—of necessity—something so tentative about it and uncertain, that I never thought of it as perfect, but it was—a perfect chaos. Amazing.

PROPRIETRESS: And your wife?

MAN (*slight pause*): My wife is who I should be married to. We've always helped one another. I'll always be grateful for having her. Especially her kindness.

PROPRIETRESS: She's not ambitious.

MAN: Yes; within bounds. We're partners in a business—advisory service for town planners. She's tremendously competent; I oversee; do less and less, though.

PROPRIETRESS: Why? Isn't it important?

MAN: Certainly is—we've changed whole countrysides for the next hundred years.

PROPRIETRESS: Then why do less and less?

MAN: I won't be here in a hundred years.—That struck me powerfully one morning. (*Pause.*)

PROPRIETRESS: So—all in all—you will survive this.

MAN (*catching the implied rebuke*): That's right. And in a while, whole days will go by when her anguish barely crosses my mind; and then weeks, and then months, I imagine. (*Slight pause.*) And as I say this, I know that at this very moment she may well be keeping herself hidden from me so as not to wound me with her dying.

PROPRIETRESS: Or wound herself.

He looks at her questioningly.

If she doesn't have to look at what she's lost she loses less.—But I don't believe it's as bad as you make it. She's only keeping you away so that you won't see her so frightened of the knife. She has sense.

MAN: But why!—I would try to comfort her!

PROPRIETRESS (*strongly, angrily protesting*): But she doesn't want comfort, she wants her power back! You came to her for happiness, not some torn flesh bleeding on the sheets! She knows how long pity lasts! (*Slight pause.*)

MAN: Then what are you saying?—That there is really no gift I can give her at all?—Is that what you say?

PROPRIETRESS, *silent, lowers her eyes.*

There is really nothing between us, is there—nothing but an . . . uncommitment? (*He grins.*) Maybe that's why it's so hard to think of something to give her . . . She asked me once—as we were getting up at the end of an evening—she said, 'Can you remember all the women you've had?' Because she couldn't remember all the men, she said.

PROPRIETRESS: And did you believe her?

MAN: No. I thought she was merely reassuring me of her indifference—that she'd never become demanding. It chilled me up the spine.

PROPRIETRESS: Really! Why?

MAN: Why say such a thing unless she had a terrific urge to hold onto me?

PROPRIETRESS: But now you've changed your mind . . . *He turns to her surprised.*

MAN: No, I kind of think now she was telling the truth. I think here is some flow of indifference in her, cold and remote, like water flowing in a cave. As there is in me. (*Slight pause.*) I feel you're condemning me now.

PROPRIETRESS: I never condemn anyone; you know that. I can't.

MAN: I know. But still, deep, deep down . . .

PROPRIETRESS: No. I'm helpless not to forgive everything, finally.

MAN: That's your glory, but in some deepest part of you there has to be some touch of contempt . . .

PROPRIETRESS: What are you saying?—You carefully offered only your friendship, didn't you?

MAN: But what more could I offer!

PROPRIETRESS: Then you can't expect what you would have had if you'd committed yourself, can you.

MAN: What I would have had . . . ?

Music resumes.

PROPRIETRESS: Yes!—To be clung to now, to be worn out with weeping, to be staggered with your new loneliness, to be clarified with grief, washed with it, cleansed by a whole sorrow. A lover has to earn that satisfaction. If you couldn't bring yourself to share her life, you can't expect to share her dying. Is that what you'd like?

MAN: I would like to understand what I was to her.

PROPRIETRESS (*protesting*): You were her friend!

MAN (*shakes his head*): There is no such thing. No! No! No! What is a friend who only wants the good news and the bright side? I love her. But I am forbidden to by my commitments, by my age, by my aching joints—great God almighty, I'm sleepy by half-past nine! The whole thing is ludicrous, what could she have seen in me? I can't bear the sight of my face in the mirror—I'm shaving my father every morning!

PROPRIETRESS: Then why not believe her—you were . . . simply one of her friends.

Music dies away.

MAN (*pause*): One of her . . . friends. Yes.—I'll have to try to accept that. (*Slight pause.*) But why doesn't it empty me? Why am I still filled like this? What should I do that I haven't done—or say that I haven't said to make some breakthrough? (*Weeping.*) My God, what am I saying! (*Imploring.*) You know. Tell me!

PROPRIETRESS: Perhaps . . . that it's perfect, just as it is?

He slowly turns from her, absorbing her voice.

That it is all that it could ever have become? (*Pause.*)

MAN: You feel that?—You believe that?

PROPRIETRESS: Yes.

MAN: . . . That we are as close now as we ever can come?

PROPRIETRESS: Yes.—But she believes she's going to make it, she knows she'll live.

MAN: So she's simply . . . momentarily afraid.

PROPRIETRESS: Oh, terribly, yes.

MAN (*with gathering hope*): That's possible; and it's true that she'd never wish to be seen that scared, especially by me. She has contempt for cowardice, she rises to any show of bravery—any! I think you're possibly right; she'll want to see me when she's made it! When she's a winner again!

PROPRIETRESS: I'm sure of it.

MAN: On the other hand . . . (*He breaks off suddenly; as though a hollowness opens beneath him his face goes expressionless.*) . . . it's also possible, isn't it . . . that . . .

PROPRIETRESS (*cutting him off, with dread*): Why go further? You'll know everything soon.

MAN: Not if I can't see her. She won't say the name of the hospital.

PROPRIETRESS (*she touches his hand*): But why go further?

MAN: But if she . . . dies?

PROPRIETRESS: She doesn't expect to.

MAN (*with confidence, an awareness*): Or she does expect to.

And he turns to her; she is filled with love and anguish; he speaks directly to her, gripping her hand in his.

Either way, my being with her now . . . would only deepen it between us when it should not be deepened, because very soon now I will be far too old. If she makes it . . . it would not be good for us—to have shared such agony. It won't cure age, nothing will—*That's* it.

She offers her lips, he kisses her.

It's that she doesn't want it spoiled you see, by deepening.

PROPRIETRESS (*she embraces him, her body pressed to his, an immense longing in it and a sense of a last embrace*): She wants to make it stay exactly as it is . . . forever. (*She presses his face to hers, they kiss.*) How gently! (*He kisses her again. With a near cry of farewell . . .*) Oh how gently! (*He slips from her embrace; a new thought as he looks around the shop. Filled, directed by his grief.*)

MAN: Then what I ought to send her is something she could definitely keep for a long time. (*He is quickened as he looks about, as though he almost knows beforehand what to seek. He moves more quickly from object to object, and at a tray of costume jewellery he halts, draws out a watch on a gold chain.*) Does this work? (*He winds it.*)

PROPRIETRESS: Oh yes, it's exact. It's an antique.

MAN (*puts the watch to his ear, then couches it in his hand, hefts it, then hangs it from the neck of the* PROPRIETRESS *and stands back to look at it on her.*) Yes, it's beautiful.

PROPRIETRESS: I know.

He starts to take out his wallet . . .

Take it.

Music resumes but more rapidly now.

She takes it off her neck and holds it out, hanging it before him; he puts back his wallet. The implication freezes him.

Go ahead—it's just the right thing; it will tell her to be brave each time she looks at it.

He takes the watch and chain and looks at them in his hand.

You never said her name. (*She starts to smile.*)
MAN (*starting to smile*): You never said yours. (*Slight pause.*)
Thank you. Thank you . . . very much.

On each of their faces a grin spreads—of deep familiarity. The light begins to lower; with the smile still on his face he moves away from the setting until he is facing front, staring. The woman and the boutique go dark, vanishing. He strolls away, alone. . . .

Music dies away.

TWO-WAY MIRROR

SOME KIND OF LOVE STORY

CAST

ANGELA
TOM O'TOOLE

The action takes place in ANGELA's bedroom, in an American city. Time: the present.

A bed in a darkened room. A window. The headboard of the bed is white plastic tufting with gold trim, Grand Rapids Baroque. A door upstage to the bathroom. Another at right to the living-room. Skirts, bras, shoes, articles of clothing dropped everywhere. ANGELA *is barely visible sitting up on the bed. The right door opens.*

TOM O'TOOLE *sticks his head in.*

TOM: Are we decent?

ANGELA: Christ's sake, close the door.

TOM: Lemme get in first! (*He shuts the door behind him, pushes back his narrow brimmed hat, unbuttons his raincoat, and is forced to peer through the murky air to see her face.*) Well!—You're sounding nice and spunky, how's it goin' tonight?

ANGELA: Philly out there?

TOM: In the kitchenette, lip-readin' his racin' form.

ANGELA: Say anything to you?

TOM: Nooo. Just laid one of his outraged-husband looks on me again. What do you say I buy you a spaghetti?—Come on.

ANGELA: You can turn on the light. And lock the door, will you?

TOM: What's with the rollers? You going out?

She undoes a roller now that her attention has been drawn to it. He locks the door and switches a lamp on. She is sitting up in bed, permed hair, black slip, pink wrapper. She lights a cigarette.

Jeeze, you really are swollen. You want ice?

ANGELA (*works her jaw, touching it*): It's going down.

TOM (*sitting on a stool beside the bed*): Hope you don't mind, darlin', but a man who takes his fists to his wife ought to be strung up by his testicles one at a time.

ANGELA (*a preoccupied air*): Nobody's perfect. He can't help himself, he's immature.

TOM: Well, maybe I'll understand it sometime—It's amazing, I always leave here with more questions than I came in with.

ANGELA: He's still the father of my daughter. (*She gets off the bed, tidies up the room a bit.*) By the way, she called me from L.A. She's going to apply to the University of California, being she's so fantastic in basketball.

TOM (*dropping into a chair, hat and coat still on*): Well, that'd be nice, wouldn't it? You're lucky to have a kid these days who loves you.

ANGELA: Don't yours?

TOM: Yeah, but they're exceptional. Anyway, I'm unusually love-able. (*He guffaws.*)

ANGELA: What're you laughing at?—It's true. (*Sadly.*) You're probably the most loveable man I've ever met.

TOM (*to get down to business*): You caught me climbin' into bed when you called.

ANGELA: I appreciate you coming, Tom—this had to be my worst day yet. (*She moves to a window to look into the back-yard.*)

TOM: No kiddin'. On the phone you sounded like you seen a ghost.

ANGELA (*a wan smile*): You ever going to love me again?

TOM: Always will, honey—in spirit.

The answer turns her sadder; she restlessly walks in sighing frustration.

I explained it, Ange—

ANGELA: What'd you explain?

TOM: You are part of the case in a certain way; and I can't be concentrating on this case and banging you at the same time. It's all wrong. I'm being as straight as I can with you. —What happened today?

ANGELA: I don't know—it just hit me again like a ton of bricks that Felix is still sitting in that cell.

TOM: That's right; it'll be five years October.

ANGELA: You tend to get used to it after so long but today I simply . . . I couldn't stand it all over again.

TOM: I can't stand it *every* day.

ANGELA (*as though reawakened to his value*): You're a wonderful man, Tom. You're really one of a kind.

TOM: Personally, I wouldn't mind sharin' the distinction, but I don't see too many volunteers on *this* case.

ANGELA (*she looks off, shaking her head with wonder at his character*): Be proud of yourself—I mean with all the great people in this state, the colleges, the churches, the newspapers, and nobody lifts a finger except you . . . I simply can't believe he's still in there!

TOM (*sensing attenuation*): What'd you want to see me about, Ange?

ANGELA (*glances at him, then gets up again, moves*): I'm really teetering. My skin is so tight I could scream.

TOM: What happened today?

ANGELA: God how I love to see you sitting here and the sound of your voice . . . (*At the window.*) . . . Is that drizzle comin' down again?

TOM: But it's kind of warm out; you want to try to walk it off? Come on, I'll take you to the boardwalk, buy you a chowder.

ANGELA (*moves restlessly*): God, how I hate this climate.

TOM: I thought it reminded you of Sweden.

ANGELA: I'm a Finn, not a Swede; I said it was *like* Finland— Not that I was ever *in* Finland.

TOM (*a grin*): So how's my standing tonight?

ANGELA: You're always in my top three; you know that.

TOM (*wryly*): Not always, Ange—last time I was practically wiped off the scoreboard.

ANGELA (*genuinely surprised*): What are you talking about?

TOM: You ordered me never to show my face again, don't you remember?

ANGELA (*vaguely recalling a probability*): Well, you were probably pressuring me, that's all; I will not submit to pressure . . .

TOM: Well, *you* called *me* tonight, kid. So what's it about?

ANGELA: What the hell is this goddam rush, suddenly?

TOM (*laughs*): Rush! You have any idea how long we've been bullshitting around together about this case? It's damn near five years!

ANGELA: And every single thing you know about it came from me and don't you forget it either.

TOM: Well . . . not everything . . .

ANGELA (*a shot of angry indignation*): *Everything!*

TOM (*a sigh*): Well, all right.—But I'm still nowhere.

ANGELA: This is a whole new side of you, isn't it?

TOM (*sensing her fear—gently*): Baby Doll, the last time on Thursday I spent seven-and-one-half hours in this room with you . . .

ANGELA: It was nowhere *near* seven and . . .

TOM (*suppressing explosion*): Until two-thirty a.m. when you give me such a kick in the balls that if it'd landed I'd have gone into orbit. So we can call tonight a strictly professional visit to hear whatever you got to say about the case of Felix Epstein . . . and *nothing else.*—Now what'd you want to tell me?

ANGELA (*dismissing him*): Well, I can't talk to you in a mechanical atmosphere.

TOM (*gets up*): Then goodnight and happy dreams.

ANGELA: What are you doing?

TOM (*a strained laugh*): Gettin' back into my pyjamas!—I have driven here through half an hour of fog and rain!

ANGELA (*open helplessness*): I'm desperate to talk to you! Why don't you give me a chance to open my mouth? (*Turning her back on him, moving . . .*) I mean, shit, if you want a mechanical conversation go see your friendly Ford dealer.

TOM: I'll tell you something, Angela—you're just lucky I'm still in love with you.

ANGELA (*she smiles now, tragically*): You wouldn't be kidding about that if I wasn't a sick woman—I'd have walked you off into the sunset five years ago and don't think I couldn't have done it.

TOM: My wife thinks you could still do it.

ANGELA: Go on, she knows why you see me nowadays.

TOM: Maybe that's why she's talkin' separation.

ANGELA: One of the nicest things about you, Tom, is that you're so obvious when you're full of shit.

TOM: She thinks we're still making it, Angela.

ANGELA (*breaks into a smile, warm and pleasured, gets up and*

comes to him, takes off his hat and kisses the top of his head):
Honestly?

TOM: I mean it. From the way I talk about you she says she can
tell.

ANGELA (*sliding her hand towards his crotch*): Well as long as
she believes it, why don't we again?

TOM (*grasping her wrists*): Y'know . . . I had to give up the
booze twenty years ago, and then the cigarettes because the
doctor told me I have the make-up of an addict. If I went
into you again I'd never come out the rest of my life.

ANGELA (*seizing the respite*): Were you ever really in love,
Tom?

TOM (*hesitates, then nods*): Once.

ANGELA: I don't mean as a kid . . .

TOM: No, I was about twenty-five.

ANGELA: What happened to her?

TOM (*hesitates, then grins in embarrassment*): My mother didn't
approve.

ANGELA: Why not, she wasn't Catholic?

TOM: She was Catholic.

ANGELA (*a wide grin*): A tramp?

TOM: No! But she knew I'd stayed over with her a couple of
times. And we were a strict family, see.

ANGELA: You've still got a lot of priest in you, Tom—I love
that about you.

TOM: You do? I don't. Leaving that woman was the biggest
mistake I ever made. In fact, five or six years later, I was already married but I went back looking for her—I was ready
to leave my wife—But she was gone, nobody knew where.

ANGELA (*romantically*): And you really still think of her?

TOM: More now than ever. In that respect I lived the wrong life.

ANGELA (*she is staring at him, an open expression on her face. On
her knees beside his chair she rests her head on his shoulder*):
Life is so wrong—a man like you ought to be happy all day
and all night long.

ANGELA *sings 'When Irish Eyes Are Smiling'. He corrects a
couple of mistakes.*

TOM (*intimately, breaking into the song*): Tell me the truth,

Angela—are you ever going to unload what you know about the Epstein case?

ANGELA (*slight pause. She is deeply fearful, but taking pleasure, too, in his concern*): I'm so worried about myself, Tom. I think I did some kind of a number today, right in the middle of Crowley Square.

TOM (*grinning*): I know when you're changing the subject, kid.

ANGELA (*angered*): It scared me to death, for Christ's sake!—I'm still shaking!

TOM: What happened?

ANGELA (*a moment to let her indignation sink in*): I'm walking along past the piano store—Ramsey's?

TOM: And?

ANGELA: All I remember next is I'm sitting on the fender of a parked car with a whole crowd of people around me. A couple of young guys were sniggering—like I'd done something indecent or something—they had that look, y'know? (*A deepening of overtly fearful breathing.*) I've really got to get to a doctor, Tom.

TOM: Okay.

ANGELA: I go blotto for longer and longer stretches, I think. Sometimes I get the feeling that I don't know where the hell I been all day, or what I said, or to who I said it.

TOM: You want me to arrange a psychiatrist?

ANGELA: With what, though?

TOM: Maybe I can get one on the tab. You want one?

ANGELA (*a sigh*): I don't know, everyone I ever went to ends up trying to get into my pants. Anyway, I know what they'll tell me—I'm a schizophrenic. So what else is new? Why are you so resentful tonight?

TOM: Honey, it's the same schizophrenia conversation we had fifteen different times, and it's eleven p.m.

ANGELA: What I am trying to tell you is that my heart is hanging by a thread, I haven't got very long. Or is that important?

TOM: Then why don't you tell me what you know before it's too late? The man is still innocent and he's still dying by inches in prison; his wife is a walking wreck, her parents are ready for the morgue, and you have the key to this case,

Angela—I know it as sure as I know my name—and you jerk me around month after month, a crumb here and a crumb there. . . . I'm so exhausted I can't sleep!—And now you take to dragging me out of bed every other night to chat me up? (*She covers her eyes suddenly.*) Maybe it'd be good if you saw Felix again—you haven't been up there in a year, I could drive you . . .

ANGELA (*this touched a nerve*): I don't want to see him.

TOM (*surprised*): You mean *never*?

ANGELA: I've done more for Felix Epstein than you or anybody. I led the fight all by myself, for Christ's sake!

TOM: Honey, I don't know too much about the head, but as one ex-Catholic to another . . .

ANGELA: I'm not 'ex'.

TOM: Well, semi-ex. What's eatin' you alive is not schizophrenia, kid, it's your conscience.

ANGELA (*with shaky sarcasm*): You been talking to your friendly Jewish psychiatrist again, I see.

TOM: He's not my psychiatrist, he's interested in the case.

ANGELA: Well if that's what he thinks I'm up to, you can tell him from me he's full of shit.

TOM: I'll send him an immediate wire. (*He makes to leave.*) I'm really beat . . .

ANGELA (*instantly stopping him*): Wait, I just want you to tell me one thing. Sit down a second. Don't be this way—(*They sit.*) Why are you on this case?

TOM (*shocked—a near screech*): *What*!!

ANGELA (*sharply*): Well, don't be mad, I'm trying to tune myself! They're yelling tonight.

TOM (*quieting*): You're hearing them now? (*She nods. He is awkward making this absurdly obvious explanation.*) Well, the Epsteins hired me to clear Felix, they paid me five thousand dollars.—How do you pop a question like that after all these years?

ANGELA: Simply that if I told you what I know . . . (*A near stutter.*) . . . what, what . . . when would I ever see you again—on television? The great detective who broke the Epstein case . . . ?

TOM: In other words you backed me out of my pyjamas to be the Ladies Home Companion again.

He starts angrily for the door, but she flies to him in what he sees is a genuine terror.

ANGELA: No! Tom, you can't go! Oh, God you can't leave me tonight . . . Tom, Tom, please, you mustn't . . . ! Not tonight! (*She has a grip on him and pulls him back to the chair, forcing him into it.*) . . . you got to stay . . . just a little while . . .

TOM: God Almighty, what has got you so scared?

Trembling, she returns to sit on the bed.

ANGELA: Let's just be peaceful for a while, okay? (*Making conversation.*) What . . . what's it like out?

TOM (*reaching into his side pocket, ignoring her question*): You know what I done?

ANGELA (*grateful for the diversion, smiles, mimicking*): What'd you done?

TOM: Finally bought myself a notebook . . . (*He takes out a black looseleaf notebook.*) This is amazing—you askin' me why I'm in the case—because I sat down after lunch and started making a resume of the case right from day one, and it suddenly jumped off the page at me. (*A grin.*) That I had no explanation why *you* were involved in this case in the first place. At all and whatsoever. That funny?

ANGELA: Why shouldn't I be?

TOM: But why should you be, honey? (*A grinding laugh.*) You never knew Felix before his arrest; *or* the parents. And there you were in the courtroom every single day of the trial, and startin' up a defence committee yet!—I'd just always taken it for granted that you belonged there!

ANGELA: Why not!—I had nothing to do in the daytime and I kept reading about the case in the papers so I came to see.

He glances up at her with a look of open scepticism.

Why don't you come out with it?

She is almost visibly swept by a furiously pleasurable release, a sense of her real self; she stands, throwing out one hip, arms akimbo, mouth distorted into a tough sneer and her voice goes rough as gravel.

What you mean is how does a fuckin' whore come off attending a . . .

TOM: Now wait, I did not call you a . . .

ANGELA: Go on, you're full of shit—you know I've been a hooker!

TOM: I never said . . .

ANGELA: Oh, fuck off, will ya! You've snooped around, say it!—I've hooked the Holiday Inn, Travelodge . . .

TOM: Cut it out, Angela.

ANGELA: . . . Howard Johnson's, Ramada Inn . . . I've spread my ass on every barstool in this misbegotten, reamed-out village . . . why don't you say it?

TOM (*helplessly*): I did not mean that you . . .

ANGELA: Say it!—How does a common slut *presume* . . .

TOM (*erupting*): I did not cast any such aspersion, Angela . . . !

ANGELA (*bending over to shout*): . . . *Presume* to involve herself in high class causes!

TOM (*mystified and alarmed*): What is this?

ANGELA (*she seems actually blind, enraged*): Well, you can get your filthy parish mind off my ass, you Irish mutt!

TOM (*suddenly aware, stepping back from her*): . . . Oh, God, is this a number?

ANGELA (*cupping her breasts to thrust them forward, mimics him*): 'Oh, God!' Grab onto this you jerked-off choir boy . . . come on, get your finger out of your yum-yum and try some of this!

TOM (*holding his head*): Holy God.

ANGELA: Go on, you don't kid me . . . (*Turning and trying to force his hand onto her buttocks.*) Grab hold, you fucking milk-face, you think you're better than anybody else?

TOM: Angela, Jesus . . . !

(*A struggle; he forces her onto the bed. She screams and tries to fight him off, loses her wind, and gasping, as he stands up, watching him . . . pushing his hands off.*)

ANGELA: Well, if you can't get it up get goin'. I've got a line into the street tonight. Tip the hatcheck girl—if you can part with a dollar. And the name is Leontine in case you want to ask for me next time. (*She has gradually lost an inner pressure and seems to fall asleep.* O'TOOLE *goes and bends over her, moved and mystified. He draws a blanket over her. Then he straightens up and peers into the air, goes to the phone and dials.*)

TOM (*sotto voce, with glances toward the bed*): Hello? That you Mrs Levy? Tom O'Toole here. (*Charmingly.*) You sounded like your daughter!—Oh, pretty fair, thanks; the doctor said I could call anytime and I . . .—Oh, thanks very much, I'm really sorry for the hour.—Really!—I never thought you people watched TV! Thanks. (*He waits, glances over to* AN-GELA, *then stares front with a certain eagerness.*) Hey, Josh, how are ya!—(*Nods.*) I'm there now but I might have to hang up, she just blew herself out.—Yeah, just like I described to you. Listen, I just got an idea.—Bad, very bad; really, really off the wall tonight, maybe the worst yet; in fact she just did a new one on me that I never saw before; Leontine, a real house whore. Horrendous vulgarity; you know, right off the knuckles. Listen, I gotta be quick—something just struck me; could a person have delusions, but like inside the delusion is the facts? What I'm trying to say, Josh . . . is that I got a gut feeling tonight that *somebody might really be threatening her life.*—Hell, I don't *know* why, but it's very hard to watch her and believe that she's stoking the whole thing up from inside, you see? I mean if they really want to get rid of her it verifies a lot of what she's been saying, you see?—Right! 'Cause I can't help it, Josh. I still believe that the key to this case is under that pantyhose. (*Listens avidly.*) Oh, she's definitely had Mob connections, that's objective; Johnny Gates kept her something like two years.—Gates? He's the head honcho. Numero Uno. But I checked the apartment house myself and she used to live there, no questions about it.—Listen, I might've given you the wrong idea—everything factual she's told me has stacked up with my own information. (*He laughs.*): No no, I've got great respect for fantasy; look, I was six years on the New York Vice Squad, how fantastic can you get?—Yes, please, go ahead. (*He listens.*) In what sense, my relation? (*Blushingly.*) Well, you must've guessed, didn't you? We rolled around together last spring but I finally decided to go back to the *status quo ante.*—Well, I got some bad feelings; started to wonder if they had her back working for them again.—Ya, basically prostitution. In fact, I think hubby may be the pimp, he's been punching her around again lately and that's typical pimp relationship.—Ya, but I thought she'd gotten out of that a long time ago. Even on the Vice Squad as a young guy I never touched them; I don't even like public swimming pools! (*Sees* ANGELA *moving*.) She's moving around . . .—I read you . . . but see she's got some terrific perceptions, sees right through to your spinal cord . . . she can be terrific company, wonderful sense of humour . . . I mean she's not *always crazy*.—But I think I'm *being* objective; maybe sometimes you've got to go to crazy people for the facts, though . . . maybe facts are what's making them crazy unless I'm bananas too, by this time. (*She is sitting up, looking around*.) Gotta go. (*He hangs up*.) How you doin', dear? (*She turns to him, sharp surprise*.) . . . I been here a few minutes.

ANGELA: How long you been here?

TOM: Few minutes.

ANGELA: Was that Philly knocking?

TOM: I didn't hear any knocking, you must've been dreaming.

ANGELA (*slight pause—she stares at the door*): Would you go and see if they're still out there?

TOM: Who's that, dear?

ANGELA: The cops.

TOM: What cops you mean?

ANGELA: The cruiser. They've been parking a cruiser on the street almost all the time. Didn't you see it when you came?

TOM: . . . Well, no, I didn't notice.

ANGELA: Well, go and take a look out front. Go ahead.

TOM (*suspending disbelief, hoping it is true*.) Okay. (*He unlocks the door, exits, as . . .*)

ANGELA: Look out the bay window—usually towards Rodman Street.

She turns front, fear in her face, an attempt at concentration . . . he re-enters, shuts the door and walks into the room. She rather quickly goes and locks the door, always glancing at him for his report.

TOM: Don't see any cruiser, Angela.

ANGELA: Well, believe me, they're always there.

TOM (*nods . . . only half pretending to disbelieve her*): Cops are leaning on you? (*She barely nods, turns away.*) When did *this* start?

ANGELA: About . . . three, four weeks.

TOM: You mean since I began coming around so much again?

ANGELA: I think so.

TOM: Well, that would be nice, if I'm makin' them nervous. But I have to say it, honey—there's no cruiser down there now.

ANGELA: You're . . . not leaving, are you?

TOM: I'll stay a few minutes, if you want. (*He removes his coat. She goes to the bed and sits. He sits in an armchair.*) Who's Leontine?

ANGELA: Leontine?

TOM: Yeah, you just went into her; she come after me like the wrath of God.

ANGELA: I never heard that name.

TOM: She's quite a broad.

ANGELA: Why—what'd she say?

TOM: Nothin' much. She sounds like a whore in a house. (*This seems to wilt her a little with yet another grief.*) You really don't remember *none* of it?

ANGELA (*pressing her temples apprehensively*): No. But listen . . . there is always a cruiser, Tom. (*He looks at her, silent.*) I'm telling you, they're down there all the time.

TOM (*he takes her hand*): I believe you.

ANGELA (*relief and gratitude on her face*): Even two of them sometimes . . .

TOM: Sit down. (*He puts her in a chair, sits opposite her and claps his hands together to inspire hope.*) I have a feeling tonight is going to break the ice.

ANGELA (*she is glad for their unity, and also digging in against it*): . . . Just let me get my wind a little.

TOM: Good, get your wind. (*Feeling some semblance of control, he spreads out on the chair, chuckles . . .*) I never knew anybody where everytime I see her there's some big surprise —you're a soap opera. I keep waitin' for the next instalment.

ANGELA (*with tragic pride*): Yeah, well—I've had a life, kid.

TOM: Like now with these cruisers you keep seein'—

ANGELA: Not that I 'keep seeing',—they're *there*.

TOM: So what you're telling me is—it's the cops that've got you scared. Right?

She glances at him, loaded with other considerations.

You wouldn't want to give me a definite yes or no on that.

She turns to him, her gaze unreadable.

Okay, then it's yes.

ANGELA: Tom?

TOM: Uh huh?

ANGELA (*another message runs parallel with her words*): You're not realising the problem . . . (*Slight pause.*) I'm talking about *you*.

He was momentarily turned away from her; now he faces her. Slight pause.

TOM: What about me?

ANGELA (*cautiously*): You've got to start being more careful and watch every step you take . . .

TOM (*affects a grin, blushing with anger*): I hope I'm not hearing this right, Angela.

ANGELA (*with apology*): . . . I'm only telling you what I know. You should start being more . . .

TOM (*cutting her off*):—Honey, listen to me. I was a New York cop for twenty-four years; I been threatened by *experts*, so you can imagine that some Mack Sennett Police Department is not my idea of the Holy Terror, y'know? And I wish you would say this in case somebody should happen to ask you . . .

ANGELA (*trying to be testy*): . . . Nobody's asking me anything.

TOM (*seething*): But just in case they did, though—you tell them that I am on the Epstein case to the end of the bitter end . . .

ANGELA: . . . I'm not trying to . . .

TOM: . . . And there is nothing anybody can do about that, Angela—right?

ANGELA: That couldn't be better with me, Tom.

TOM: It wouldn't matter what it was with you, honey, or with anybody else. Get the picture?

ANGELA: You're one of a kind; honestly, Tom, you really stand tall. (*She comes to him, kisses him.*) Take me some place, let me make you happy again. Come on.

TOM (*holding both her hands*): Listen, never be the only one who knows something . . .

ANGELA (*looking contritely at the floor*): I know . . .

TOM: If somebody else knows it too, that's your best protection.

She nods agreement. He mimes playing pool.

The table's all set up, you want to start hittin' a few?

The moment of decision is on her, and she gives him a lost smile and turns away again.

I know you want to, Angie.

ANGELA (*a desperate little laugh*): You know?—Sometimes you talk just like Jimmy Cagney.

TOM (*sighs*): Oh, honey, are we gonna talk about Cagney now?

ANGELA: Well you do, you get that same sweet-and-sour thing. And the same brass balls.

TOM (*flattered despite himself*): Well, let's face it, Cagney was my god. (*Snaps his fingers, still seated he goes into a light little shuffling tap dance with a chuck of his head.*) 'Take me out to the ball game . . .'

ANGELA (*genuinely delighted, relieved*): Hey, wonderful!

TOM: Sure, and Pat O'Brien, Spencer Tracy . . . Christ, all those great Irishmen, tough and honest to a man. The movies in them days was Mick-Heaven. The only crooks were Italians.

ANGELA: You'd been great in a movie.

TOM: What as—the dumbest bookie on the block?

ANGELA: No, something dignified—like the first Irish Pope.

TOM: Jesus, you really like me, don't you.

ANGELA: I adore you, Tom. You've saved my life more than you'll ever know.

She draws him to her on the bed and snuggles onto his lap. He doesn't mind at all, and grins at her.

Do me once more.

TOM: No more, Ange, I'm sorry—it does something to my judgment.

ANGELA: I could make you fly around the room. You're my ideal, Tom.

TOM: Come on, kid.

ANGELA: You know, Father Paulini once said that if I'd known a man like you earlier in my life, I'd have turned out a completely different person. But once my father'd raped me, I always expected a man to go right for my ass.

TOM: Mmmm.

ANGELA (*slaps his cheek lightly*): Can't you get your mind off the case for *one minute* and just talk to me like a person?

TOM: It's after eleven p.m., Ange, I'm tired.

ANGELA: Know what I love? When you talk about being a cop in the old days in New York. Would you?—It soothes me. Talk about the Communion Breakfasts. (*She rests her head on his chest.*) And how important the Church was, right?

TOM (*sighs in boredom—although he likes it, too. He glances down at her, sensing his power . . .*): Oh yeah, the Church was really important in the Department in those days. Like any cop who took money from whores . . . or like dope money . . . the priest lay his head open.

ANGELA: Really? Even dope?

TOM: Sure . . . even the Mafia wouldn't touch dope in those days . . .

ANGELA (*incredulously*): Jesus.

TOM: It was a whole different world. (*Grins.*) Like one time they had me guarding the money in the Yankee Stadium office; great big piles of cash on the table. And I ask one of the officials—bein' that they were getting me for nothin', with the city payin' my salary, and all—if I could maybe get a hot dog sent up. So he says sure, gimme fifty cents, I'll send down. Imagine?—I'm watchin' half a million bucks for them and I couldn't even steal a free dog.

ANGELA: I can just see you there . . . with all that money . . . and nobody even giving you a dog. (*Her fear returns in a sweep and she is suddenly welling up.*) Oh, God, Tom . . .

TOM (*turning her face to him*): What is it, honey . . . come

on, tell me! (*He hesitates before her vulnerability, then suddenly kisses her on the mouth.*)

ANGELA: Come on, Tom—please! Screw me, split me. I'll never
forget that last time. You're a bull. Please! I want you!

*He gets to his feet, disturbed by his unforseen kiss. She is sent
into a real outpouring of sobbing—in mourning, as it were,
for her wasted life which denied her a man like this . . . he
tends to her, smoothing her hair.*

TOM: Listen now—I could arrange protection. I could have
you taken where it's safe. Just tell me what's got you so
scared? (*She reaches for him again . . .*) I'd love to, honey,
but I'm goddamned if I ever change this subject with you
again. It's my professional reputation, my livelihood!

ANGELA (*even here there is a faint air of her improvising*): I'm
going to die.

TOM: I hate hearing you say that.

ANGELA: I can't get air. (*Slight pause.*)

TOM: You been to confession?

ANGELA: Yes. But I . . . (*Breaks off.*)

TOM: You couldn't tell him about this, huh? (*She shakes her
head.*) I wish I was smarter, kid; I wish I could say the right
thing. You don't know how I hate to see you suffering like
this.

ANGELA: You've been wonderful, Tom.

TOM: Why can't you give me a little faith? (*A silent struggle in
her; she touches his face, then turns away.*) Why are these cops
leaning on you, can you just tell me that?

ANGELA (*she is silent for a moment; some resolve seems to harden*):
Tom.

TOM: I'm listening.

ANGELA: I want you to tell me one thing from the heart.—
What's the single main thing you want from this case?

TOM (*uncomprehending*): The single . . . ?

ANGELA: Well is it to get Felix out on the street, or . . . ?

TOM: Well, no, I want the people who put him in there too.

ANGELA: Why? You want revenge or something?

TOM: There's such a thing as the administration of justice,
honey—which in this county, is laying on the floor like a

busted dozen eggs, it is a fucking farce.—But I don't think I understand the question.

ANGELA: . . . Nothing. I was just wondering what you wanted.

TOM: Fair enough,—I'll answer you!—Callaghan's got to be blasted out of the prosecutor's office for falsifying evidence, okay? And Bellanca and his whole crew of detectives for conspiring with him . . . (*Grinning.*) Now tell me why you asked a question like that?

ANGELA: Well, I agree with Bellanca . . .

TOM: Why?—Callaghan's worse; publicly calling me a 'ridiculous pseudo-detective' and trying to lift my license . . . but we're back in this tic-tac-toe again. Are you going to tell me why the cops are so heavy on you, or not? (*She moves as though framing an answer.*) And I beg you on bended knees, don't start wrappin' me in another ball of wool.

ANGELA (*looks down at her hands, almost patently evading*): The thing, y'see, is that I was so humiliated after what my father . . .

TOM (*impatiently*): Darlin', I *know* your father raped you, but . . .

ANGELA: Oh, am I boring you?

TOM: I didn't say you . . .

ANGELA (*fish on the line, she swims away, half sobbing, half furious*): Well, I beg your fucking pardon!

TOM (*furiously*): Angela, I am just about convinced starting this minute that you are full of shit! I don't think you know a goddamned thing about this case and I am going home! Forever!

He picks up his coat; she grabs him.

ANGELA (*in great alarm*): Can't we talk for two minutes without the case . . . ?

TOM: I want an answer to what I asked you—what got you into this in the first place? Where are you comin' from, Angela, what is your connection!

ANGELA (*gripping her head*): I'm going crazy!

TOM: I'm turning into a laughing stock! I walk into the Burrington Court House the other day and I had a hard time not to put a fist through some of the stupid smiles on those cops standing around—they all know I'm still on this case after nearly four years . . .

ANGELA: Well, fuck' em!

TOM (*takes a beat—quietly*): Well, you're really chock full of solutions. I understand a very colourful description of me is goin' around the courthouses—I am the detective who couldn't track a diuretic elephant on a glacier.

ANGELA: A diuretic elephant. . . . ? (*She breaks out laughing.*)

TOM (*grinning*): Gives you a vivid picture, doesn't it?

Their eyes meet and she sees the steel in his eyes and turns away.

All right, baby—take care of yourself. I guess tonight ends it between us, kid. And I may as well tell you straight—I am humiliated. (*He waits for her to start it going again; then . . .*) And I'm sorry for your sake; that you couldn't level with me; cause in my opinion, the reason you're sick is that you lie. (*He starts to leave, he sees her near paralysis of fear.*) It's okay. I've got a whole other way to move ahead. It would've been easier with you but I can make it alone. Take care, kid—I'm out of your life.

He crosses the room to the door, starts getting his arms into his raincoat—stalling, but not too obviously. She watches him in desperation. Her voice trembling, her anxiety pitched high . . .

ANGELA: Can you believe . . . ? (*She breaks off.*)

TOM (*alerted*): Believe what, dear?

ANGELA (*wringing her hands, struggling in fear of going on . . .*): That a man can be a fine and good man and still do something that's . . . just terrible?

TOM (*avid now*): Sure.

ANGELA: I mean a thing . . . that is not really in his nature to do, but that he has to because . . . it's all so . . . (*Almost crying out.*) . . . rotten in this place?

TOM (*more warmly now*): Absolutely. I believe that. If I thought life was straight lines I'd be workin' for the Highway Department. (*Slight pause.*) . . . Like who are you referring to?

She sends him a terrified glance; there is some longing in her look, too. Her breathing now becomes raspy and he helps her to the bed where she sits, gasping and glancing up at him half in terror and half in hope.

I always said you had class, darling, you know why?—'Cause of your conscience; most people would just sign out and butter their own potatoes, but not you. You suffer.

His expectations high, he watches her regain her breathing, but she doesn't venture any further.

Who were you talking about?

She glances at him, but nothing more.

Kid, now listen to me and hold on tight—I am six inches from thinking that *you* were part of the frameup they laid on Felix . . .

ANGELA (*furiously*): How can you be such a stupid son of a bitch!

TOM: . . . And that you're still part of it right now, and trying to keep me from finding out what went down! Which would make you about the lowest cunt since Hitler! (*Pushing up his coat collar.*) Take care of yourself. This time it's for good.

ANGELA (*with breathless veracity, and really trying* not *to break down in weeping*): After five years you don't know the first thing about this case.

TOM (*pause. He turns to her at the door*): . . . Jesus, the way you say that goes right down to my haemorrhoids.

ANGELA: Believe me, darling . . . zee-ro. (*She holds up forefinger and thumb, touching.*)

TOM: You telling me that Felix Epstein is guilty? (*Long pause.*)

ANGELA: Felix is innocent. (*She heaves for breath; a real attack, she lies down.*)

TOM (*goes to her quickly*): What should I do! You want a doctor?

She rises on one arm, gasping.

Tell me what to do!

She rocks back and forth; he bores in filled with aggressive need.

All right, can you confirm one fact—did Callaghan fake the picture that nailed Felix? Or don't you know?

She screams, frightened of him.

—What are you doing? . . . Oh, no, Angela!

She presses her fists against her chest and her elbows against her sides with her shoulders pushed upward as though she were trying to become small, like a young child. He recognises this.

Don't do that—! Please stop that, Angela!

He makes a move toward her.

ANGELA: Don't you touch me! (*She skitters into a corner, blindly staring at him.*)
TOM (*reaching toward her protectively*): Ange . . .

With a frightened scream, she cowers all scrunched up, terror in her face. A sound from her mouth, high and childlike.

Is it 'Emily'?
ANGELA: Don't, please . . . !
TOM: Okay, Emily . . . (*Opening his coat and holding out his palms.*) . . . see? Nothin' on me at all. Okay, darling? Why don't you come out and we get a little ice cream from the corner? Your father's gone, honey—honest, he won't be comin' back tonight.

He takes one step toward her but she reacts in fright so he backs up.

Okay, dear, you stay there and I'll just make a call, Okay? Take your time, have a little nap if you want. (*He goes and sits beside the phone, dials. As he waits, he playfully twiddles his fingers at her.*) Hya, darlin'. (*Into the phone.*) Sorry to bother you again, Mrs Levy . . . thanks a lot. (*To* ANGELA.) How about a chocolate fudge later?—I'm sorry, Josh,—No, no, I hate to bother you so late . . .—Oh, zonked out again, being Emily now, all scrunched up like an eight year old, it's pathetic. Listen, bad news . . . she claims it's the cops leaning on her.—I think it could be, yes. But she's been seeing two police cruisers parked on the block every night . . . but I looked and there's none down there, you see? But why

do I still believe her?—Oh absolutely! I believe her, Josh!—
Except if it was just that I invested so much in her I could
walk away; wasting your time is most of what you do in this
business. (*Listens, a rapt stare now.*) Now *that*'s funny; I was
thinking of Maria all the way down in the car before, like she
was sitting in the seat beside me.—There is a similarity, yes;
the same kind of sexiness, maybe. (*Glances up at* ANGELA. *A
shake of the head, wondrously.*)—So in other words, I've
blown four and a half years . . . on a dream! (*Resistance
hardens his face.*) Except, goddammit, Josh, she was the first
one who told me about Carl Linstrom;—yes, the man who
was seen covered with blood, running away from the Kaplan
house. And now I have four separate witnesses to corrobo-
rate and I can't get the police to make an arrest! You see
what I mean?—She knows too many facts for just a crazy,
fantasising whore . . . ! (ANGELA *sits up, he sees her.*) . . .
We're back on the air, I'll be in touch. (*He hangs up. She
approaches him, staring.*) Well! What do you say, Bubbles—
welcome back! (*She stares at him, puzzled, suspicious. He is
defensive . . .*) I made a little call. (*Her stare is unrelenting.*)
To my friend, the psychiatrist. Sends his regards. (*Her stare
remains.*) I told you—he's my quarterback sometimes. He's
still very interested in the case . . . You know, Felix being
Jewish . . .

ANGELA: Some Jew! He didn't have the balls to join my
committee.

TOM: Well, let's face it kid, neither did anybody else, that was a
one-woman committee. (*He stands.*) Well, take care. I really
got to hit the pike.

ANGELA: Wait, wait . . . we didn't even talk. What've you
been working on lately?

TOM: Oh, nothing great.

ANGELA: Like what?

TOM: Corporation stuff mostly. Big ball bearing company; in
fact—I've got to go out to Phoenix, investigate a guy they're
about to make the vice president.

ANGELA: They still doing that shit?

TOM (*shrugs*): Well, you know—you can't have a homosexual
vice president of a ball bearing company.

ANGELA: But how do you do that?

TOM: Ah, it's boring. I get his old airplane ticket stubs for the past few months; they usually travel on the company account; and see if he's been to some off-the-track town . . . you know, Ashtabula, Ohio; Grim City, Iowa; and I go to the gay bar and show the bartender his picture with a hundred dollar bill clipped to it, and he tells me if he's ever seen him there. I didn't used to mind it, but I don't like it anymore. But . . . (*He shrugs, with a sigh, rubbing two fingers together.*)

ANGELA: And for that he can't be vice president?

TOM: Well, they're scared of blackmail. And you know, he's supposed to be a good example.

ANGELA: To who?

TOM: Who the hell knows anymore? (*At the door.*)

ANGELA (*the same lostness and tension grip her but she no longer pleads for him to stay*): Would you take another look down the street before you go?

TOM: For you, I'll do it. (*He goes, opens the door, exits. She remains absolutely still, facing front. He returns.*) I don't see them.

ANGELA (*awakened*): Heh?

TOM: There's no cruiser down there.

ANGELA: Who?

TOM (*impatiently*): The cruiser! The cops you were so worried about.

ANGELA (*preoccupied*): Oh.

TOM: Oh!—Five minutes ago you were . . . Oh, forget it. I don't see Philly in the living-room. So why don't you try to relax now, Okay?—Maybe I'll see you sometime. (*She is lost in thought. He turns her face to him.*) . . . Ange?

ANGELA: I used to be with Charley.

TOM (*electrified*): . . . Callaghan?

She is silent.

Talking about the prosecutor?

ANGELA (*hard as a nail*): I will deny everything if you ever try to hurt him with it—I'm myself now, Tom, you understand what I'm saying to you? I will never hurt Charley. (*She takes a sudden inhale.*)

TOM (*stunned*): Okay.—Was this like one or two shots or . . . ?

ANGELA: Three, four times a week over two years. We went to Canada and Puerto Rico, couple of times.

TOM: And when did it end? (*Slight pause.*)

ANGELA: He's come back to me.

TOM: You seeing him *now*?

ANGELA (*a sudden expressiveness, closeness*): He's the love of my life, Tom.

TOM: Right.—This is quite a blow to my mind, darlin'. (*Slight pause.*) You mean like . . . you were exercising with him while he was prosecuting Felix?

ANGELA: Yes. (*Slight pause.*)—You don't believe me.

TOM (*slight pause*):—Well . . . it sure ties certain things together. That's the reason you came to the trial every day, is that it?—to buck him up?

ANGELA (*hesitation*): I wasn't there to buck him up. (*Slight pause.*) I was there taking notes—which you saw me do, and which you read.

TOM (*apologetically*): That's right, honey . . .

ANGELA: Some whores can take notes, y'know—I went to Mary Immaculate, which just happens to have the highest academic record in the state. I can also add, subtract and multiply . . .

TOM: Now, don't go off into a . . .

ANGELA (*deeply agitated*): Sometimes I don't understand why the fuck I talk to you at all, O'Toole. I mean, Jesus . . . (*He lets her find her calm as she walks about shaking her head.*) I may come off the street but that don't mean I've still got rocks in my head. I'm going to get out of this situation, you know.

TOM: I hope so, Angela.—Out of what situation?

ANGELA (*retreating*): Never mind. Just don't forget what I said about hurting Charley. I can murder you if you do that.

TOM: How you going to murder me, Ange?

ANGELA: Don't worry, I can do it.

TOM: We're gonna forget you said that, Okay?

ANGELA: I'm not threatening you!

TOM: The second time tonight . . .

ANGELA: I didn't mean that I . . .

TOM: Stop-right-here-Angela! Charley Callaghan has tried to get my Investigator's Licence lifted because I have gotten reversals on two of his biggest cases, just like I am going to do on this one . . .

ANGELA: I did not mean . . . !

TOM: . . . So you can ask me not to hurt Charley but please do not try to scare me with him because that is to laugh! Now what'd you want to say?—I mean I hope you are not conveying some kind of a threat from somebody.

ANGELA: You know?—Sometimes I think you ought to see a psychiatrist.

TOM: Oy gevalt!—Kid, you are going to end me up pluckin' chickens in the funny farm!

ANGELA: But you suspect everything I say! You tell me to trust you, but do you trust me?

TOM: Darlin', look—let's get back to taking those notes during the trial; can I ask what they were for?

ANGELA: 'Cause I knew Felix had nothing to do with Kaplan's murder, and I wanted to prove it.

TOM: I'm still not getting the picture, dear, forgive me. You were in the hammock with Charley at nights and in the days taking notes to *dis*prove his case?

ANGELA: We broke up over the case.

TOM (*impressed*): Oh!

ANGELA: I couldn't stand what it was doing to him. He'd come back from the court and we'd go out to the beach and build a fire and he'd stare into it with tears pouring down his cheeks. Sometimes he would look up into the stars and try to pray. Charley studied for priesthood, you know . . .

TOM: I heard that.

ANGELA: He still does retreats.

TOM: Yeah, well . . . I guess I must've missed his spiritual side.

ANGELA: You have a closed mind: I'm telling you he's a whole other person than you believe.

TOM: Listen, I'm always ready to learn.—What were the tears for though?

ANGELA: . . . We even went to churches in San Juan.

TOM: Together?

ANGELA: Well, we sat in different parts . . .

TOM: In other words, the tears were that he was rigging the Epstein case, or what?

ANGELA *doesn't answer at once.*

Ange? Please.—What were the tears?

ANGELA: It wasn't his fault. The chief of detectives handed him the case, all tied with a ribbon and ready for trial . . .

TOM: Bellanca. (ANGELA *nods.*) So *Bellanca* faked the photograph? (*She nods again.*)

ANGELA: Charley didn't want to touch the case. They made him push it. I know how you hate him, Tom, but you have to believe me . . .

TOM: Tell me something—why did they pick on Felix in the first place? Why him?

ANGELA: Total accident—he just happened to have come to town to visit his uncle, Abe Kaplan; it's exactly like he claimed—he was trying to get Kaplan to take him into the accountancy firm.

TOM: But why did they have to go through that whole charade when they could have just gone out and picked up Linstrom?—They had to know Linstrom was covered with blood that night—they *had* the killer any time they wanted him.

ANGELA (*slight pause*): Because Linstrom was a runner.

TOM: A runner?

ANGELA: For Kaplan. (*Slight pause.*)

TOM: Abe Kaplan was in drugs?

ANGELA: In!—Abe *ran* the drugs in this town.—God, you are stupid. You're pathetic.

TOM (*embarrassed*): I knew Abe was the big loan shark . . .

ANGELA: That was the front.

TOM: . . . So they latched onto Felix . . . tell me again, will ya?

ANGELA (*impatiently*): To make it look like a family argument—the uncle and the nephew . . .

TOM: But Charley's the chief . . . (*She silently assents.*) . . . if he felt so bad about it, why did he have to go ahead and make the case against Felix?

ANGELA *is staring.*

Don't go out on me, will you? (*She stares. He bursts out.*)
This is horrendous.—You cannot go out on me now! Why
couldn't they arrest Linstrom?

ANGELA: Because it could open the whole can of worms.

TOM: What can is that, honey?

ANGELA (*this is deeper than she wanted to go. Barely audible*):
The police connection.

TOM: To the drugs.

ANGELA: That's why they're parking down there.

He gives her an evasive nod.

They are, you know.

*He gives her a deeper nod of assuagement. But his thought has
moved to something else at which he stares now . . .*

They are parking down there, Tom . . . (*She starts angrily
for the door, but he forces her into an embrace.*)

TOM: If I was to ask you, Angela—how do you know Abe Kaplan was in drugs . . . can I ask you that?

ANGELA *doesn't answer at once, moving away from him.*

. . . Because I'm trying to be as objective as I can, you see,
dear? I mean let's face it, Abe was one of the pillars, right?
With the synagogue and the Boys Town and you name it,
and a lot of people are going to find that hard to believe,
you know?

ANGELA (*decides, faces him*): I used to be with Abe.

TOM (*rocked*): . . . No kiddin', *Abe*?

ANGELA: A lot. We went down to Bimini together.

TOM: Bimini.

ANGELA: Twenty, twenty-five times.

TOM: Isn't Bimini one of the . . . ?

ANGELA: I carried for him coming back. I would deliver the
stuff to Bellanca.

A long pause. He moves now, facing front.

That's why I'm so upset with them parking down there, you
see?

TOM (*he sets his jaw*): But they are not parking down there, honey.

ANGELA (*springing up, gripping her head*): They are parking down there!!

He shuts his eyes.

And you . . . you've got to start taking precautions.

TOM: We must be on some kind of wave length together . . . (*He takes a snubnose revolver out of his pocket.*) I never carry this, but I'm leaving the house tonight and, for some reason . . . I stuck it in my pocket before going out the door. (*He puts the gun away.*) Incidentally, if Bellanca's holding any kind of . . . like a drug rap over you, the best thing you could do is level with me, you know; the Feds would protect a witness against drug dealers, they have a witness-protection programme and it's serious . . . You're not going out on me, are you?

ANGELA:—No, I'm here. (*Her voice breaks in the tension and she moves, holding down a sobbing fit.*)

TOM: How long can you go on with this tension? You're going to explode.

She simply shakes her head.

Has anybody said exactly what they want from you?—Is it to get me to stop coming around?—or what?

ANGELA (*staring ahead, almost stupidly*): For me to give him his letters back.

TOM (*this is new . . . he uses a fine degree of charm*): . . . Which letters we talkin' about?

She stares.

Charley wrote you letters?

She turns to him blankly.

About your relationship, or what?

ANGELA: About his struggle.

TOM: Like with his conscience.

She is staring ahead.

—He wrote you a letter about it?

ANGELA (*nodding*): Nine.

TOM: No kiddin'—(*With the faintest tinge of doubt now.*)—nine letters?

ANGELA (*reaches for his hand*): Don't leave me, Tom.

TOM: I'm with you, Ange. And where are they—these letters?

ANGELA: . . . I have them some place.

TOM: Oh.

ANGELA: I always had to have candles for him in the apartment.

TOM: Candles.

ANGELA: It helped him—to look into flames. I was the closest to him, closer than his wife. He couldn't keep it to himself anymore. I begged him. I prayed for him but he had to push the case, or he'd lose everything. I told him, I said, 'You could be anything, you could be President of the United States!—Don't do this to an innocent man, God will take it out of your flesh!'—I thought if he saw me in court taking notes he'd realise that I meant business and I would not let Felix rot in jail . . . and it would make him stop the case. (*She breathes in suddenly, deeply, and the eyes seem to be going blind.*)

TOM: Don't leave me, Angela.

ANGELA (*gripping his hand*): I'm staying. I'm trying . . . Oh, God, Tom, you don't know, you don't know . . .

TOM: Tell me, what, what?

ANGELA: . . . They picked me up off the street today. (*She is in open terror.*)

TOM: Cops?

ANGELA: I lied to you before . . . When I was walking past Ramsey's piano store, they suddenly came up beside me and jammed me into the cruiser, and drove me around, two cops and a detective. Caught my hair in the goddamned door!

TOM: Bastards!—What'd they want?

ANGELA: That if I didn't straighten up I'd be floating in the bay. (*She weeps. He holds her in his arms.*)

TOM (*he turns to the door*): So they're leaning on you for the letters, is that bottom line?

ANGELA *nods.*

Why don't you give them to them?

ANGELA: But I'd never see him again.

TOM: You honest to God see him now?

ANGELA: He comes, once or twice a week. But now it's only to get them back.

TOM: You're not making it with him anymore.

ANGELA: Only once in a while. (*Now she curls up on the bed.*)

TOM: Can I see the letters? (*She doesn't react.*) You want to go somewhere? My valise is in the car. (*She stretches a hand to him, tempted, conflicted.*) Get your coat on, come on, we'll ride somewhere and talk more. (*He holds her hand.*)

ANGELA: I'll die before I hurt him, Tom.

TOM: All right—Suppose you don't show me anything, just read me the relevant parts—you keep them in your hands.— Go on, get them.

She is in a fever of indecision. She gets off the bed, one moment covering her eyes with her hands, the next glancing at him as though trying to judge him. She opens a drawer off the dressing-table; hesitates, then takes out a brush and brushes her hair.

Darlin', listen to me—with that kind of evidence, I can put Felix back on the street by noon tomorrow.

ANGELA (*pressed*): I said I can't hurt Charley!

TOM (*furiously.*): Then why've you told me this?

ANGELA: I can't give you them now.

TOM: When then?

ANGELA: When I can!

He watches her for a long moment.

TOM: Angela—explain to me—why'd you tell me all this?

ANGELA: So you'd help me!

TOM: Help you how?

She looks directly into his eyes in an open appeal.

Are you telling me to drop Felix? You're not telling me that, are you?

She is silent.

Honey—you mean I just drive home now and go to sleep?

She is silent—furiously.

Talk to me.

ANGELA (*scared of him now*): I don't owe Felix Epstein—I fought for him!

TOM: How! You had a cannon and you threw some beanbags! And for five whole years you cold-bloodedly watched me chasing up one dead end after another and never said boo about this?

ANGELA: You never trusted a word I said, did you? Do you trust me even now? You know you don't!

TOM: What other man in your life ever believed in you like I did! How dare you say that to me! I'm damn near a laughing stock for believing in you.—Now give it to me straight— did you call me here tonight to get me to quit this case?

The load on her is crushing . . .

ANGELA: Sssssh!—Don't talk so loud . . .

TOM (*to the door*): Fuck Philly and fuck them!

The violence in the air sends her into quicker movements seeking escape and air . . .

Where are you comin' from, Angela, whose side are you on? What is happening here? (*With a cry in his voice, he grips her.*) Are they running you? Do they make you keep calling me?

ANGELA (*violently breaking from him, shaking a finger at him*): You know . . . you know . . . (*Groping breathlessly, she becomes rigidly straight; a new personality, a terribly austere, dignified lady with upper-class speech.*) . . . it might just be a terribly good idea for you to think a little more highly of me and stop irritating me!

TOM: Who's this now?

ANGELA: You are irritating me!

TOM: I refuse to talk to Renata!

ANGELA: Stop irritating me!

TOM (*even though knowing she is hardly able to hear him—in fact, she is softly hooting to herself as he speaks in order to block off his sounds and mock him*): Irritating *you*! You knew all these years where the bodies were buried and I'm irritating you? You're lucky I quit the booze, your face'd be running down that wall by now! (*Swelling, pulling up his pants.*) The enormity!

ANGELA: Enormity? (*She bursts out laughing rather merrily.*)

TOM: And what if I don't quit? Would that . . . put you in some kind of an emergency?

ANGELA (*as though quite beyond all harm*): Me!

TOM: . . . In other words, sweetie . . . are you trying to tell me that we're not really all that great friends?—Is that it?

ANGELA (*confused, but adopting an indignant stance*): Now you listen . . . !

TOM: You listen to me—this is still the United States of America, you don't have to lay down in front of those punks.

ANGELA: Well, I must say . . . what astounds *me* is how you get to think *you're* such a high grade cultured individual and such a great Catholic . . . !

TOM: All right, Renata, come! I'll find a doctor for you in Boston.

ANGELA: . . . But all you really are is gutteral!

TOM: Will you just blow that out your ass and talk straight?

ANGELA: . . . You can't help it, your whole manner is gutteral because your whole background is gutteral.

TOM: You're not even using the word right.

ANGELA: I mean who do you imagine you fuckin' are—just because you read some magazines without any pictures?

TOM (*eyes rolling upward*): Jesus Christ . . .

ANGELA: *You* have the audacious contempt to call the Lord's name in vain?

TOM (*defeated*): Okay, Renata, let's just forget the whole . . .

ANGELA: *You* can call me Miss Marshall. Stupid bastard.

TOM (*laughs, despite everything*): By this time Miss Renata Marshall ought to know that a respectable lady like her doesn't call people stupid bastards.

ANGELA: Which I would be delighted to do if these stupid bastards had the mental competence to understand any other kind of language, you dumb shit.

TOM: Touché. (*He spreads his arms out.*) Okay, pull out the nails. I want to come down. I'm through, hon . . . for tonight. But I'll be back and we can start *all over again*!

She is surprised, frightened too as the air goes out of her.

(*In a mixture of laughter and fury . . .*)

That's right, Baby. (*Partly toward the door.*) I will never give up until Felix Epstein is walking the street! Plus lover-boy Callaghan gets a long number across the back of his shirt— if, in fact, you ever really laid him at all outside of your mental waterbed!

ANGELA (*exhausted, she starts to droop*): Well, you don't say . . .

TOM: Then where's his letters? Show me one single proof that this is not another one of your spitball delusions?

ANGELA: *My* delusions! *My* delusions! And what about your delusions? All of a sudden *I'm in the United States of America*? (*Tears are pouring into her eyes.*) And *I've* got *delusions*? This town is in the United States? This police force . . . ?

TOM (*his pain surges and he protectively embraces her, chastened*): I gotcha, honey.

ANGELA (*weeping*): Help me—for Christ's sake, Tom!

TOM: Sssh! (*He cuts off her weeping by kissing her mouth and holds her against himself with great force. And turning her face up . . .*) Did you really think you could get me off the case?

ANGELA (*covers her face and sobs in defeat*): My God!
The phone rings: they are both caught off guard. She goes and picks up the phone with high tension, her voice fearful, very faint—clearly, she has some specific caller in mind. Yes? (*Surprised and pleased—charm suddenly warms her voice.*) Oh!— Oh, I'm so sorry, I forgot all about it! (*A near stutter.*) Well . . . well . . . well, yes, sure . . . (*She looks confused at her watch but can't quite focus on it . . . and with a glance at Tom,* sotto voce.) What's the time?

TOM (*sotto voce*): Ten to twelve.

ANGELA (*with a warmly thankful glance at him*): Sure, I can make it, I have have to get dre . . . (*But glancing down at herself, she breaks off.*) . . . in fact, I am dressed already . . . (*Feels her hair, surprised that it is in place.*) . . . in fact, my hair's practically done . . . Ah . . . (*Ineffectually shielding the phone—oddly—with a half-turn away from Tom.*) . . . where is it again? Oh, right! (*Nearly whispering.*) And what's the room? Okay. (*Smiles.*) . . . You too, pussycat! (*She hangs up. She has expanded with a new pleasure-*

shame, an identity that is palpable. She turns to face him.) I had an appointment I forgot all about.

TOM: You did? How come?

ANGELA: I don't know, I just blew it.

TOM: They say that means a person really doesn't want to go.

ANGELA: You got time to drop me?

TOM (*this is more difficult*): . . . Where's that?

ANGELA (*evasively*): Well . . . like the corner of Main and Benson would be okay.

TOM (*an instant—he looks at her almost incredulous, then turns away, and with dry rage, humiliation*): Come on.

ANGELA (*with fresh energy*): Just got to fix my face, be right with you. Put your feet up. (*She turns to go up to the bathroom.*)

TOM (*with an open resentment*): Why don't I drop you right at the hotel instead of on the street—it's only a few more yards? (*She turns back to him, ashamed—as it were—for his sake.*)

ANGELA: . . . The corner would be okay.

He doesn't reply, his head turned angrily away from her, although he is attempting to grin. She breaks the moment, hurries into the bathroom . . . another moment . . . and in a dispirited way he picks up the phone and dials. He waits, greatly tired, an inward look in his deadened face.

TOM: This could be tapped, you want to hang up?—Good, turn it on. You rolling? (*As for a record.*) Abe Kaplan was hit by one of his own crazy runners.—That's correct, he was into drugs, Josh . . . with the detective squad.—Why is it incredible?—Because she was Abe's broad. And Callaghan's too, incidentally. (*He listens.*) Look, talk to you later, I just wanted to tell you this much before I go outside.—No don't worry. I'll be all right—What do you want me to do, call the police?—Well, that's nice of you to offer, but she's only going to twist you around too, isn't she? I mean I've got to stop looking for some red tag that says 'Real' on it; I don't have the education, but I have the feeling and I'm just going to have to follow my nose, wherever it takes me, y'know?— If it's real for me then that's the last question I can ask, right?—Well, I'm not sure yet, but somehow I think I can decide pretty quick now, maybe tonight.—I do, yes . . . I feel kind of relieved now that I've thought of this. And at the same time like in a fog on top of a mountain where the next step is either six inches down or five thousand feet. (*A laugh.*)—It *is* a mystery, but I still have my ignoramus opinion, Josh; I think that somewhere way upstream the corruption is poisoning the water and making us all a little crazy. —Her? No, she's feeling great now! In the toilet getting saddled up for some honcho in the Hilton, and ten minutes ago rasping out her last and final breath! (*He laughs.*)—No, kid, it's not unreal, it's just horrendous!

ANGELA *enters.*

And here she comes now, riding on her elephant, our Lady of the Hilton, looking like seven million bucks!

She laughs delightedly.

You hear her? She's laughing, fulla beans.

ANGELA (*calls into phone*): Hya, Doc!

TOM: Now if only Felix could get the joke—Right, talk to you soon. (*He hangs up.*)

ANGELA: Before we go down—if those cops give me any trouble, we're going to midnight mass at St Jude's, Okay?

He laughs brazenly.

What are you laughing at?

TOM: What cops?

ANGELA (*gesturing toward door*): In the cruiser downstairs.

TOM (*totally loose and lost, he laughs*): What cruiser downstairs?

She looks shaken, distraught.

You stole five years of my life, you goddamn lunatic! I ought to wrap you around a lamp post.

ANGELA (*gathering herself in protest*): But there's always one there!

TOM (*mimicking*): There's always one there! (*Clenching his fists to keep them off her.*) How did you get into my life!!

With a look of apprehensive uncertainty mixed with indigna-

tion, she turns and dashes out the door. He strides about, full of self-hatred.

How did I get into this goddamn dream! My brain died! She murdered my brain . . . !

She enters, rather slowly, glancing at him with a new air of mock indignation. He reads this look, and takes an uncertain few steps toward the door, then halts and turns back to see her looking at herself in her hand mirror with bland assurance. He rushes out the door. She stares front. He re-enters.

ANGELA: Who's crazy now?

TOM: Angela . . . Christ, I'm sorry. Forgive me, will you?

She gives him a peeved look. Approaching her, arms extended . . .

Oh, Darlin' . . . Oh, Ange . . . I can't help it, I love you!

(He starts to embrace her but she frees herself.)

ANGELA: Hey, watch the hair, for Christ sake! I'm serious, you've got to get yourself some help!

TOM (*apologetically*): But, honey, they weren't down there a little while ago . . .

ANGELA: Well, don't cops take leaks?

TOM (*anxious to forestall*): Look . . . what do you say we go and get a ravioli and a nice bottle of wine . . . ?

ANGELA (*imperatively*): I have to go!

TOM (*surprising himself, a cry*): Why! They don't have to run *every thing* in this world! . . . Listen . . . get in my car. Let me take you to Judge McGuire's house—you remember, he and I are close; he'll arrange federal protection; we can bust this case and you can . . . you can start a whole new life, darling. (*She stares into his face.*) And who knows, maybe we could still walk off into that sunset together? (*Taking her hand.*)

ANGELA: I can't.

TOM: Yes you could, if you believed in me.

ANGELA: No, not only you, Tommy,—I think you got me too late; all that went by. Come on, I'm late. (*She takes her coat off a chair, she starts upstage. He rushes to intercept her.*

TOM: Wait! I want to tell you something Dr Levy told me.

ANGELA: Levy! Levy's gutless.

TOM: He said I haven't been in love since I was twenty-five, so you like woke me from the dead, sexually, so . . .

ANGELA: Did he really say that?

TOM: So I handed you almost magical powers, like you could see in the dark through a slab of concrete.

ANGELA: Oh, Tommy . . .

TOM: . . . But I see now that whatever you know you're never going to tell me, because you don't want me off and away. That's it, isn't it—never, never, never.

ANGELA: Listen!—maybe if we could meet for a good long lunch tomorrow . . .

TOM: No more lunches!

ANGELA: Give me one more chance to try to tell you, Tommy; that makes me happier than anything I've ever heard in my life—that I woke you from the dead. How about Pinnochio's, one o'clock?

TOM: No! Come, I'll drop you. I've got a man in jail. I've wasted too much time. (*He gets his coat and hat.*)

ANGELA: So this is it, then?

TOM: This has to be the last long night, yes. But you get evidence, something I can take into court, call me anytime—I just have to get to work, Okay?

ANGELA: Okay. Then I should tell you something to keep in mind. There's a whole side of this case you never even heard of. (*He goes stock still.*) Don't believe it, I don't care—but I have to tell you. You're not just leaving a crazy woman, you're leaving the case. 'Cause I'm the only one alive who knows. There are names that'd knock your head off, all the way to Boston, Washington, Providence and New York. The whole criminal justice system could be picked up by the tail like a dead rat. All you got now is the tip of the tip of the iceberg.—Good Luck. (*She opens the door and glances back.*) You still dropping me or is that out too? (*She sees him wipe a tear from his eye.*) What're you doing? (*She comes to him, incredulously.*) Why are you crying?

TOM (*shrugs, shakes his head*): . . . I guess because I still believe you.

ANGELA (*she draws his face to her and holds him*): I'll be at the corner table at the end of the bar.

TOM: NO!

ANGELA: Please come! (*She lowers her hands.*) Please come! It's all in me, Tom. And you're the only one who can ever get it out. I want to talk . . . quietly and . . . honestly. (*She is staring ahead.*) And then maybe it'll all be there . . . all the rottenness; and then it'll drop away. And then, maybe I could start to change my life. I'm going to expect you. You might just be amazed! (*She goes out. From the next room . . .*) Philly? Where are you? I'll be back in a couple of hours! (*Calling.*) Tom? Are you coming?

TOM (*eyes lifted*): Sorry, Felix . . . but hold on, don't let go, baby!

ANGELA (*from further off, calling*): What are you doing, you're making me late!

TOM (*shutting his eyes*): Dear God . . . make it only one more time!

ANGELA: Tom!

TOM: Yes! Coming, coming, coming . . . (*Hurrying out as the scene quickly blacks out.*)

NOTES AND ESSAYS
ON THE PLAYS

FOREWORD

(*After the Fall*)

THIS play is not "about" something; hopefully, it is something. And primarily it is a way of looking at man and his human nature as the only source of the violence which has come closer and closer to destroying the race. It is a view which does not look toward social or political ideas as the creators of violence, but into the nature of the human being himself. It should be clear now that no people or political system has a monopoly on violence. It is also clear that the one common denominator in all violent acts is the human being.

The first real "story" in the Bible is the murder of Abel. Before this drama there is only a featureless Paradise. But in that Eden there was peace because man had no consciousness of himself nor any knowledge of sex or his separateness from plants or other animals. Presumably we are being told that the human being becomes "himself" in the act of becoming aware of his sinfulness. He "is" what he is ashamed of.

After all, the infraction of Eve is that she opened up the knowledge of good and evil. She presented Adam with a choice. So that where choice begins, Paradise ends. Innocence ends, for what is Paradise but the absence of any need to choose this action? And two alternatives open out of Eden. One is Cain's alternative—or, if you will, Oswald's; to express without limit one's unbridled inner compulsion, in this case to murder, and to plead unawareness as a virtue and a defense. The other course is what roars through the rest of the Bible and all history—the struggle of the human race through the millennia to pacify the destructive impulses of man, to express his wishes for greatness, for wealth, for accomplishment, for love, but without turning law and peace into chaos.

The question which finally comes into the open in this play is, how is that pacification to be attained? Quentin, the central character, arrives on the scene weighed down with a sense of his own pointlessness and the world's. His success as an attorney has crumbled in his hands as he sees only his own egotism in it and no wider goal beyond himself. He has lived through two wrecked marriages. His desperation is too serious, too deadly to permit him to blame others for it. He is desperate for a clear view of his own responsibility for his life, and this because he has recently found a woman he feels he can love, and who loves him; he cannot take another life into his hands hounded as he is by self-doubt. He is faced, in short, with what Eve brought to Adam—the terrifying fact of choice. And to choose, one must know oneself, but no man knows himself who cannot face the murder in him, the sly and everlasting complicity with the forces of destruction. The apple cannot be stuck back on the Tree of Knowledge; once we begin to see, we are doomed and challenged to seek the strength to see more, not less. When Cain was questioned, he stood amazed and asked, "Am I my brother's keeper?" Oswald's first words on being taken were, "I didn't do anything." And what country has ever gone into war proclaiming anything but injured innocence? Murder and violence require Innocence, whether real or cultivated. And through Quentin's agony in this play there runs the everlasting temptation of Innocence, that deep desire to return to when, it seems, he was in fact without blame. To that elusive time, which persists in all our minds, when somehow everything was part of us and we so pleasurably at one with others and everything merely "happened" to us. But the closer he examines those seemingly unified years the clearer it becomes that his Paradise keeps slipping back and back. For there was always his awareness, always the choice, always the conflict between his own needs and desires and the impediments others put in his way. Always, and from the beginning, the panorama of human beings raising up in him and in each other the temptation of the final solution to the problem of being a self at all—the solution of obliterating whatever stands in the way, thus destroying what is loved as well.

This play, then, is a trial; the trial of a man by his own conscience, his own values, his own deeds. The "Listener," who to some will be a psychoanalyst, to others God, is Quentin himself turned at the edge of the abyss to look at his experience, his nature and his time in order to bring to light, to seize and—

innocent no more—to forever guard against his own complicity with Cain, and the world's.

But a work of fiction, like an accident witnessed in the street, inevitably gives rise to many differing accounts. Some will call it a play "about" Puritanism, or "about" incest, or "about" the transformation of guilt into responsibility, or whatever. For me it is as much a fact in itself as a new bridge. And in saying this I only dare to express what so many American writers are trying to bring to pass—the day when our novels, plays, pictures and poems will indeed enter into the business of the day, the mindless flight from our own actual experience, a flight which empties out the soul.

Saturday Evening Post, February 1, 1964

"WITH RESPECT FOR HER AGONY—BUT WITH LOVE"

(*After the Fall*)

I AM not naive enough to have imagined that *After the Fall* would be received as merely another play and evaluated as such, but it is surprising how overwhelmed some otherwise knowledgeable people permit themselves to become by the obvious fact that elements of the author's life are part of the play he writes. The character of Maggie, which in great part seems to underlie the fuss, is not in fact Marilyn Monroe. Maggie is a character in a play about the human animal's unwillingness or inability to discover in himself the seeds of his own destruction. Maggie is in this play because she most perfectly exemplifies the self-destructiveness which finally comes when one views oneself as pure victim. And she most perfectly exemplifies this view because she comes so close to being a pure victim—of parents, of a Puritanical sexual code and of her exploitation as an entertainer.

The character of Maggie is quite obviously treated not only

with respect for her agony but with love. Is it to be imagined that people commit suicide without immense forces of self-destruction let loose in them; that they do it neatly, winsomely, and without the horror which that dreadful act entails?

More immediately to the point, and I dare say this only because I have been charged with cruelty toward the memory of Marilyn Monroe, it is in many cases precisely those who scoffed at her ambitions and in some cases those who were overtly vicious to her both personally and in print who now cry in outrage that Maggie's suffering should be connected with Marilyn's. The hypocrisy which bewildered and finally enraged her in life indeed seems to be following her in death.

Certainly one of the more diverting, if minor, pastimes of literary life is the game of Find the Author: Tolstoy, barely concealed behind Pierre in *War and Peace*; Fitzgerald, behind Dick Diver; Hemingway, behind all his heroes; Goethe, behind Dr. Faustus. Once the author's identity is "discovered" a certain counterfeit of knowingness spreads through the reader's soul, quite as though he had managed to see through an attempt to trick him into believing that the work at hand was art rather than a disguised biography.

It is as though fiction, whether in play or novel form, ought to be derived from the thinnest air or it loses its right to some esthetic category. The fact is that the identification of the artist in his work, while sometimes interesting as gossip, has nothing at all to do with the value of the work—which depends, or ought to, on its general application to other men besides himself. Despite the romantic image of the artist creating strange worlds unrelated to his life, an artwork's human value lies precisely in its unique ability to share experience which otherwise must remain in darkness. Art is witness or it begins the descent to artifice and momentarily fashionable entertainment. This game of identification, in my opinion, is always played by those who will not, or cannot, grapple with the objective meaning of the work at hand. It is a way of reducing a book or play to a species of publicity.

When I speak of art as witness it is simply to give back to art its original function as a vision of life rather than as a spurious comfort. I believe *After the Fall* to be a dramatic statement of a hidden process which underlies the destructiveness hanging over this age. That elements of my life have been publicized to the point where, in some minds, fiction and design seem to have given way to reportage cannot have prevented me from using my own evidence, any more than if my life were unknown. The time may be close or far away, I do not know, but it will come—as it has for certain other of my plays—when the extra-dramatic identification of themes and persons in them will no longer matter.

I would only say now that despite appearances, this play is no more and no less autobiographical than *All My Sons, Death of a Salesman, The Crucible* or *A View from the Bridge*. I have never known, for example, anyone who committed suicide as a result of action by a Congressional committee, but such disasters have been part of my time; and such a suicide is in this play, not because I appeared before an investigation committee but because, in the thematic structure of this play, such a suicide throws light upon the inability of a man to live with the mixture of good and evil in his own nature. Equally, the other characters in *After the Fall* are drawn, not reported; for this theme creates its characters and their fate quite as much as they create the theme.

Finally, what has been called the exculpation of Quentin is not to be found in this work. Indeed, it is one of the play's major points that there is not, and cannot truly be, a divestment of guilt. But there can be—and if life is to be lived, there must be—a recognition of the individual's part in the evil he sees and abhors. To make this point was far more important than even I imagined; instead of taking it to heart, there are those who prefer to turn it on its head and interpret Quentin as somehow seeking to justify himself, when actually he is in search of his responsibility—and discovers it. Evidently this is so unfamiliar an idea to many people that they take the play as an apology. The play is neither an apology nor the arraignment of others; quite simply, overtly and clearly, it is a statement of commitment to one's own actions. Indeed, Quentin's impulse to feel in some concrete way his own authorship of his life and his person extends to his taking on guilt even for what he did *not* do.

The whole business reminds me of the righteous indignation

which greeted Hannah Arendt's controversial book, *Eichmann in Jerusalem*. It seemed to me, reading it, that she was trying to make a spectacularly simple and quite evident point. Namely, that the significant truth about Eichmann was not that he was a monster but that, in order to exercise his monstrousness—to be in a position to murder—he had to have the moral permission of others. In trying to prove her thesis, the author extended that permissiveness even to Jews and to well-meaning Gentiles who, despite all, were less than total in their active opposition to barbarity. But the suggestion that "we" could, in even a remote way, bear responsibility for what "we" abhor was turned upside down by some people so that Miss Arendt was made to seem an apologist for Eichmann.

It is, always and forever, the same struggle: to perceive somehow our own complicity with evil is a horror not to be borne. Much more reassuring to see the world in terms of totally innocent victims and totally evil instigators of the monstrous violence we see all about us. At all costs, never disturb our innocence.

But what is the most innocent place in any country? Is it not the insane asylum? There people drift through life truly innocent, unable to see into themselves at all. The perfection of innocence, indeed, is madness. What Quentin in this play tries desperately to do is to open Maggie's eyes to her own complicity with her destruction; it is an act of love, for it requires that he open himself to his own complicity if his imprecations are to carry any weight; he must, in short, give up his own claim to innocence in order to win her back from self-destruction.

It is, therefore, not that the play is personal which offends some people; it is, in my opinion, that the pain it delivers up is nonliterary; it is too actual; it is not sentimentalized enough. So, all those who in real life laugh at the Maggies of the world, who mock their hopes and take advantage of their ignorance, their vulnerability, their terrible loneliness and need—all those cannot, with a tear or two, "decently" pay their "respects" to the victims of their own hypocrisy. All this the play, thank God, prohibits.

OUR GUILT FOR THE WORLD'S EVIL

(*Incident at Vichy*)

ABOUT ten years ago a European friend of mine told me a story. In 1942, said he, a man he knew was picked up on the street in Vichy, France, during a sudden roundup of Jews, taken to a police station and simply told to wait. Refugees of all sorts had been living in Vichy since the invasion of France because the relatively milder regime of Marshal Pétain had fended off some of the more brutal aspects of German occupation. With false papers, which were not hard to buy, a Jew or a politically suspect person could stay alive in the so-called Unoccupied Zone, which covered the southern half of the country. The racial laws, for one thing, had not been applied by Pétain.

In the police station the arrested man found others waiting to be questioned, and he took his place on line. A door at the front of the line would open, a Vichy policeman would beckon, a suspect would go in. Some soon came out again and walked free into the street. Most did not reappear. The rumor moved down the line that this was a Gestapo operation, and that the circumcised would have to produce immaculate proof of their Gentileness, while the uncircumcised would of course go free.

The friend of my friend was a Jew. As he got closer and closer to the fatal door he became more and more certain that his death was near. Finally, there was only one man between him and that door. Presently, this last man was ordered into the office. Nothing stood between the Jew and a meaningless, abrupt slaughter.

The door opened. The man who had been the last to go in came out. My friend's friend stood paralyzed, waiting for the policeman to appear and beckon him into the office. But instead of walking past him with his pass to freedom, the Gentile who had just come out stopped in front of my friend's friend, thrust his pass into his hand, and whispered for him to go. He went.

He had never before laid eyes on his saviour. He never saw him again.

In the ten years after hearing it, the story kept changing its meaning for me. It never occurred to me that it could be a play until this spring when "Incident at Vichy" suddenly burst open complete in almost all its details. Before that it had been simply a fact, a feature of existence which sometimes brought exhilaration with it, sometimes a vacant wonder, and sometimes even resentment. In any case, I realize that it was a counterpoint to many happenings around me in this past decade.

That faceless, unknown man would pop up in my mind when I read about the people in Queens refusing to call the police while a woman was being stabbed to death on the street outside their windows. He would form himself in the air when I listened to delinquent boys whose many different distortions of character seemed to spring from a common want of human solidarity. Friends troubled by having to do things they disapproved of brought him to mind, people for whom the very concept of choosing their actions was a long forgotten thing. Wherever I felt the seemingly implacable tide of human drift and the withering of will, in myself and in others, this faceless person came to mind. And he appears most clearly and imperatively amid the jumble of emotions surrounding the Negro in this country, and the whole unsettled moral problem of the destruction of the Jews in Europe.

At this point I must say that I think most people seeing this play are quite aware it is not "about Nazism," or a wartime horror tale; they do understand that the underlying issue concerns us now, and that it has to do with our individual relationships with injustice and violence. But since a few critics persist in their inability to differentiate between a play's story and its theme, it is just as well to make those differences plain.

The story as I heard it never presented a "problem"; everyone believes that there are some few heroes among us at all times. In the words of Hermann Broch, "And even if all that is created in this world were to be annihilated, if all its esthetic values were abolished . . . dissolved in skepticism of all law . . . there would yet survive untouched the unity of thought, the ethical postulate." In short, the birth of each man is the rebirth of a claim to justice and requires neither drama nor proof to make it known to us.

What is dark if not unknown is the relationship between those who side with justice and their implication in the evils they oppose. So unknown is it that today in Germany it is still truly incomprehensible to many people how the crude horrors of the Nazi regime could have come to pass, let alone have been tolerated by what had for generations been regarded as one of the genuinely cultured nations of the world. So unknown that here in America where violent crime rises at incredible rates—and, for example, the United Nations has to provide escorts for people leaving the building after dark in the world's greatest city—few people even begin to imagine that they might have some symbolic or even personal connection with this violence.

Without for an instant intending to lift the weight of condemnation Nazism must bear, does its power not become more comprehensible when we see our own helplessness toward the violence in our own streets? How many of us have looked into ourselves for even a grain of its cause? Is it not for us—as it is for the Germans—the others who are doing evil?

The other day on a news broadcast I heard that Edward R. Murrow had been operated on for lung cancer. The fact was hardly announced when the commercial came on—"Kent satisfies best!" We smile, even laugh; we must, lest we scream. And in the laughter, in the smile, we dissolve by that much. Is it possible to say convincingly that this destruction of an ethic also destroys my will to oppose violence in the streets? We do not have many wills, but only one; it cannot be continuously compromised without atrophy setting in altogether.

The first problem is not what to do about it, but to discover our own relationship to evil, its reflection of ourselves. Is it too much to say that those who do not suffer injustice have a vested interest in injustice?

Does any of us know how much of his savings-bank interest is coming from investments in Harlem and Bedford-Stuyvesant real estate, those hovels from which super profits are made by jamming human beings together as no brute animals could be jammed without their dying? Does anyone know how much of his church's income is derived from such sources?

Let the South alone for a moment—who among us has

asked himself how much of his own sense of personal value, how much of his pride in himself is there by virtue of his not being black? And how much of our fear of the Negro comes from the subterranean knowledge that his lowliness has found our consent, and that he is demanding from us what we have taken from him and keep taking from him through our pride?

It was not to set forth a hero, either as a fact of history or as an example for us now, that I wrote this play, but to throw some light on evil. The good and the evil are not compartments but two elements of a transaction. The hero of the play, Prince Von Berg, is mistakenly arrested by a Nazi race "expert." He comes into the detention room with his pride of being on the humane side, the right side, for he has fled his Austria and his rank and privilege rather than be part of a class which oppresses people.

None of the horrors he witnesses are really surprising to him here, nothing is forbidden any more, as he has long known. What he discovers in this place is his own complicity with the force he despises, his own inherited love for a cousin who, in fact, is a Nazi and an oppressor, the material cause, in short, for what before was a general sense of guilt, namely, his own secret joy and relief that, after all, he is not a Jew and will not be destroyed.

Much is made of guilt these days, even some good jokes. Liberalism is seen now as a response to guilt; much of psychiatry has made a business of evaporating guilt; the churches are no longer sure if their age-old insistence on man's guilt is not an unwitting spur to neurosis and even the acting-out of violence; the Roman Catholic Church has only recently decided to lift the Crucifixion guilt from the Jews alone and to spread it evenly over mankind.

I have no "solution" to human guilt in this play, only a kind of remark, no more. I cannot conceive of guilt as having an existence without the existence of injustice. And injustice, like death itself, creates two opposing interests—one more or less profits from it, the other more or less is diminished by it. Those who profit, either psychically or materially, seek to even out the scales by the weight of guilt. A "moral" ounce is taken up to weigh down the otherwise too-light heart which contemplates uneasily its relative freedom from injustice's penalty, the guilt of having been spared.

In my play, the hero is that man whose guilt is no longer general but suddenly a clear transaction—he has been, he sees, not so much an opponent of Nazism but a vessel of guilt for its brutalities. As a man of intense sympathy for others he will survive, but at a price too great for him to pay—the authenticity of his own self-image and his pride. And here I stop; I do not know why any man actually sacrifices himself any more than I know why people commit suicide. The explanation will always be on the other side of the grave, and even that is doubtful.

If they could speak, could the three boys who were murdered in Mississippi really explain why they had to go to the end? More—if each of them could discover for us in his personal history his motives and the last and most obscure corner of his psychology, would we really be any closer to the mystery of why we first require human sacrifices before our guilt can be transformed into responsibility? Is it not an absurdity that the deaths of three young men should make any difference when hundreds have been lynched and beaten to death before them, and tens of thousands humiliated?

The difference, I think, is that these, including Chaney, the young Negro, were not inevitable victims of Mississippi but volunteers. They had transformed guilt into responsibility, and in so doing opened the way to a vision that leaped the pit of remorse and helplessness. And it is no accident that the people of Mississippi at first refused to concede they had been murdered, for they have done everything in their power to deny responsibility for the "character" of the Negro they paternalistically "protect," and here in these three young bodies was the return with interest for their investment in the guilt that does not act.

At the end of "Incident at Vichy," the Prince suddenly hands his pass to a Jew, a psychiatrist, who accepts it in astonishment, in awe and wonder, and walks out to freedom. With that freedom he must accept the guilt of surviving his benefactor. Is he a "good" man for accepting his life this way, or a "bad" one?

That will depend on what he makes of his guilt, of his having survived.

In any case, death, when it takes those we have loved, always hands us a pass. From this transaction with the earth the living take this survivor's reproach; consoling it and at turns denying its existence in us, we constantly regenerate Broch's "unity of thought, the ethical postulate"—the debt, in short, which we owe for living, the debt to the wronged.

It is necessary to say something more about Germany in this context of guilt. I cannot read anyone's mind, let alone a nation's, but one can read the drift of things. About a year ago I wrote some thoughts about the current Frankfurt trials of Nazi war criminals which were published in Germany, among other countries. There was much German mail in response, and a good lot of it furious, in part because I asked the question whether a recrudescence of Nazism was possible again in the future. The significant thing in many letters was a resentment based on the idea that the Nazis and the regime were something apart from the German people. In general, I was giving Germany a "bad name."

Apart from the unintended humor, I think this reaction is to be faced by the world and especially by the Germans. It is, in fact, no good telling people they are guilty. A nation, anymore than an individual, helps nobody by going about beating its chest. I believe, in truth, that blank and emotional charges of a generalized guilt can only help to energize new frustrations in the Germans and send them striving for "dignity" through a new, strident and dangerous nationalism. Again, guilt can become a "morality" in itself if no active path is opened before it, if it is not transformed into responsibility. The fact, unfortunately, is that for too many the destruction of the Jews by Germans has become one of Orwell's non-actions, an event self-propelled and therefore incomprehensible.

But if the darkness that persists over human guilt were to be examined not as an exceptional condition or as illness, but as a concomitant of human nature, perhaps some practical good could come of it instead of endless polemic. If the hostility and aggression which lie hidden in every human being could be accepted as a fact rather than as reprehensible sin, perhaps the race could begin to guard against its ravages, which always take us "unawares," as something from "outside," from the hands of "others."

The reader has probably been nodding in agreement with what I have just said about Germany, but who among us knew enough to be shocked, let alone to protest, at the photographs of the Vietnamese torturing Vietcong prisoners which our press has published? The Vietnamese are wearing United States equipment, are paid by us, and could not torture without us. There is no way around this—the prisoner crying out in agony is *our prisoner.*

It is simply no good saying that the other side probably does the same thing; it is the German's frequent answer when you raise the subject of Nazi atrocities—he begins talking about Mississippi. And more. If he is intelligent he will remind you that the schoolbooks sent to Germany by the United States immediately after the war included the truth about Nazism, but that they were withdrawn soon after when the cold war began, so that a generation has grown up which has been taught nothing about the bloodiest decade in its country's history.

What is the lesson? It is immensely difficult to be human precisely because we cannot detect our own hostility in our own actions. It is tragic, fatal blindness, so old in us, so ingrained, that it underlies the first story in the Bible, the first personage in that Book who can be called human. The Rabbis who collected the Old Testament set Cain at its beginning not out of some interest in criminology but because they understood that the sight of his own crimes is the highest agony a man can know, and the hardest to relate himself to.

"Incident At Vichy" has been called a play whose theme is "Am I my brother's keeper?" Not so. "Am I my own keeper?" is more correct.

Guilt, then, is not a featureless mist but the soul's remorse for its own hostility. We punish ourselves to keep from being punished, and to keep from having to take part in regenerating that "unity of thought, that ethical postulate," which nevertheless is reborn with every child, again and again forever.

New York Times Magazine, January 3, 1965

TO THE ACTORS PERFORMING THIS PLAY: ON STYLE AND POWER

(Incident at Vichy)

THERE is, of course, no substitute for an actor's instincts. If his talents for mimicry and interpretation could flow unobstructed there would be no place for any theoretical discussion of his art. But as every actor knows, he is driven to reach for some objectivity toward himself and his role precisely in order to liberate his subjective grasp of the reality involved. I presume to write about style in particular because the rehearsals of this play so often required the director to speak about style itself, apart from the usual psychological elements of the roles. And in the course of these rehearsals it became clear that style is a mysterious if not a suspect word, and that its implications— sharp, good enunciation, precise gestures, controlled vocal tones, form-imposed rates of speaking speed and so on, connote something close to insincerity and falsehood to many actors.

Playwrights hardly dare to write about acting, chiefly I think, because it is a mystery to them. But in these times it is also because we are surrounded by schools and methods which are nearly secret societies whose arcane signals we cannot interpret. I write not in total ignorance of those signals, but without reference to them; instead, I would reassert what has threatened to become a lost art—the art of interpreting the play rather than the actor's or director's attitude toward it. And I quickly add that I owe great debts to the actors in my plays who have given them life. In fact, I would save the actors from themselves, for I believe that for social and historical reasons outside their control, they have been saddled with distorting ideas about the art which make it harder for them to do their work. I speak of style because it is in the attempt to achieve something more than naturalism in acting that many of these distorting misconceptions seem to come to a head. It is when an actor is called upon to play someone much different from himself that his acting shows, and with it his ideas about himself and the theatre are most nakedly revealed.

For example; in this play American actors were called on to play Europeans. Furthermore, the language of the play is not contemporary American but a created language of a certain formality designed to set the characters apart from Americans and at the same time to permit the expression of their commonness and humanity. Yet, compared with everyday speech, it is a stiffened and avowedly conventionalized—i.e. objectified speech imposed on the play by the nature of the form. In short, from the first moment the audience is asked to accept two seemingly contradictory states; first, they must believe that this is happening *now*, and second, that the play is a creation of the mind rather than a spontaneous event which just happens to be looked-in on by them. Again for reasons of form, we are to be aware that this is being created, but created in order to illuminate a theme. The design of this play is supposed to be seen not concealed.

So that to begin with the usual benchmarks of reality by which the actor can measure his authenticity are changed. His existence as the character cannot be the result of mere verisimilitude, the mimicry of recognizable American types. He must prove his existence not merely by evoking his own personal memories and feelings which the text might suggest, but by depersonalizing those feelings and imagining a new personage to whom they might belong. But even this is only half the problem. For whatever authenticity he may achieve through his evocation of his own relevant feelings and memories, he must subjugate to the rhythmic demands of the text and the imposed physical manner his role requires, a manner which is not American and not native to him.

But it is not merely that he is playing a foreigner, and in several of the roles, foreigners of a class that does not exist in America. It is also that his emotions are called up by his relationship to a theme and a situation rather than to what is more usual in our theatre—his personal life.

In our realistic drama, the symbolic meaning of the play is, so to speak, an after-effect or by-product of the story. The characters themselves only do concrete things and are lost in the swirl of action around them. In fact, any great awareness of what is thematically at stake in the action is a fault in such drama, and this is correct given the nature of that form. Thus the actor is trained to act so as to seem blind to the significance of what he is doing; he is best when he is visceral and without a consciousness of himself. He is observed, rather than the observer. But in this play, given the situation and the nature of the attack upon its mysteries, the actor is called upon to seek to know what his actions and attitudes signify beyond their narrow bounds as acts and thoughts. Because these characters face total destruction everything they do and say becomes objectified to them and must become so for the audience. This open development of the overall meaning decides the idiom in which the play is written, and must rule the way in which it is acted. In short, the nature of style itself becomes of the first importance.

Now with us in America, "style" connotes artifice, a dangerous threat to authenticity, a mannered thing and finally a trick. The word brings with it the sounds of elocution, the danger of posing, and the threat of empty "acting." Above all, it is the opposite of emotion and "truth." It is something one affects rather than something one is. But the fact, I think, is that until style as a concept is understood, the American actor will at best be limited to playing himself, to say nothing of the problem of playing classics or any play of a different culture and a different age.

The trouble, it seems to me, is that style is so largely conceived as an imitation of something while naturalistic action is regarded as the *being* of something. Perhaps the time has come to look into the reality of style, for after all it exists first in society and is only reflected in the theatre. Why, then, should it be so difficult if not impossible to take it to heart as a legitimate human expression?

It seems to me that the nub of the problem is to throw some light on the reality-relationships to style outside the theatre. As an example, consider the beard in America.

A man wearing a beard in this country is expressing a certain attitude toward society. Judges, policemen, executives, admirals, and the power structure as a whole are clean-shaven. The bearded man adopts a convention to protest or separate himself from another convention. The beard in this culture is connected to art, the free spirit, the opponent of Philistinism in all its forms. The function of the beard is to impart to its wearer certain particular values in opposition to power.

Obviously, though, behind the beard many individual differences do exist. One man may grow a beard because his personal deficiencies coincide with his wish to protest—he may have a receding chin or a deformed lip. He may have lost all the hair on his head and wishes to compensate. On the other hand, he may be quite handsome without the beard. In any case, the beard, whatever individual characteristics might lie behind it, nevertheless joins all other beards as a symbol. And it is, beneath every other consideration, a particular attitude toward power. And so it is with style in any of its forms—it is at bottom an expression of the individual's relationship to power.

Thus, when the actor is called upon to play a courtier, a knight, a king, he will exhaust his merely subjective resources before he creates such personages if he approaches them on the purely behavioural, psychological level. He will at best achieve the man *behind* the style, but—to continue the analogy, he will never account for the beard. I believe that so many American attempts to "be" the king or the courtier turn mawkish and unconvincing not only because the American has no experience with these types in his history—although this does contribute to the difficulty of his believing in them. It is equally that he cannot locate the legitimacy of the symbolic function which they carry out in their societies.

But the same problem undoubtedly faced the Elizabethan actor, a plebian, trying to convince his audience that he was indeed a king. If we are to believe Shakespeare, however, the Elizabethan actor must have tended to emphasize the symbolic, heroic side of such figures and lost sight of their individual natures. To these actors, who lived on the fringes of society and to the point where they were finally banned as immoral creatures, it might have been inevitable they should fail to attach common human qualities to royalty, a class they confronted only in power relationships rather than as human equals. Thus the undifferentiated bombast of their acting, and Hamlet's warning plea to check themselves against the models they were to portray.

With us the distortion is opposite. Our actors seek to make

power-figures real by emphasizing their individuality and psychological drives even to the point of trying to speak blank verse in a way that would make it sound like prose—as though there were no style at all, as though the political functions of these characters were non-existent or at best only peripherally involved in their psychology. In fact, the verse form itself can, I think, be shown to be a function of the kind of confrontation classic plays make with power, specifically, the forces controlling the fate of the society, be they mortal or in the hands of the gods.

So it is a fruitless comment to make—that the American is at odds with style because he has had no experience with so to speak stylized figures. There is no reason to think that a Greek actor, as citizen, felt anymore at home with the character of Creon or Oedipus then Laurence Olivier does. Indeed, Olivier might have a relative advantage in that he does not believe in the holiness of Oedipus and can approach the part feeling more equal to it than his ancient predecessors. What he might well suffer from, however, is the absence around him of a society willing and eager to believe in the powerfulness of that fate, that cosmos which the character brings crashing down around his head.

Moreso in America is this true, for here we affect not to notice our obedience, if not our slavery, to differing styles and especially to social power factors which lie behind them. People are immeasurably more aware of the fact that a President plays golf, or owned a haberdashery store, or lifts up dogs by the ears, than that he has the power to kill them. For this is the ultimate reality of power, that it can kill without committing a crime. And once the overlays of custom and sentiment are torn away, this is also the ultimate relevancy of style, namely, its function as weapon and a shield. However secret it may be to us, the greater part of our psychic energy is spent on neutralizing outside forces ranged against us and turning them to our safety. A man's style—his public face, his way of dress and speech and gesture, is his armament against this danger.

The American actor's attitude toward style is an uneasy one not, as is commonly thought, because the society had no feudal history, the absence of which has allegedly deprived him of some race memory of a stratified, class-conscious world. For it is not only the ranks and titles of medieval society that throw him off, it is also Chekhov and Ibsen and Strindberg and, of course, Brecht.

Now it is obvious that actors in any country find it more congenial to play their own countrymen. We know our own in our bones—but even this needs examining; for what our bones know is our society which exists within us as an a priori subjective quantity which does not have to be "understood" any more than the American actor needs to be taught the difference between the way one regards one's doctor and one's pharmacist. In his own society the actor can easily separate the social plumage of one man from that of another, and he does so without thought. But face to face with unfamiliar societies he must approach their reality objectively in the first instance, and with objective reality—as opposed to anything subjective, he distrusts himself.

But this uneasiness is inevitable if one glances at our ordinary attitudes toward class and power. In this country the individual in a position of power moves perilously close to an implicit ludicrousness as he adopts the style of power. Whether mayor or president, in theory he is really no different than his ordinary neighbor. He is hardly more than the deputy of his own office, of which he is only the temporary occupant anyway. Thus it is the office itself which has the grandeur; the individual wielding its powers stands in its shadow and should he take its implications too seriously in terms of a personal style he risks ridicule. And this ridicule is itself an expression of the underlying reality —namely, that in a democracy there is no one who cannot be turned out at a moment's notice. It is this same ridicule which threatens the actor called on to play any aspect of power. The thing is simply lacking in reality; it is not something his deeper emotions can readily absorb.

But the difficulty is only compounded and even confused by seeking to heal it with an almost totally subjective approach such as the present version of "The Method" affords. Quite simply, there is nothing in the subjective life of the actor as a person which can "teach" him to make real what in life is never "real." Even a real king has to learn how to act like one. He must learn how to walk like a king and talk like one, how to eat like one and, of course, history is full of kings who failed their lessons.

And what is obvious in the case of a king is less so in every other rank and kind of man but equally true—we are all taught our styles whether we were raised in a slum or a penthouse. Overtly in the case of the upper middle class which is told in so many words what is permissible and what is not in terms of social and human relationships, and by example in these groups less self-conscious of themselves.

Yet "The Method" turns the actor almost entirely toward his personal psychology for clues to the reality of the part he is to play. And inevitably it has come to the point where every aspect of objectification, be it speech, gesture, or any other means of communication (as opposed to self-identification) is regarded as a kind of encumbrance, at best a necessary evil. It is no accident that so many actors can no longer be heard, and that their voices sound muffled and private and their enunciation impossible to understand. It is not that they cannot speak the language *as persons*, it is that they do not believe in language as a psychological, subjective reality quite as real as anger, pain, anxiety or lust. What at all costs must be truly felt are his own feelings; when they are actual enough to him they will somehow automatically become actual to the audience and to his fellow actors. This is a psychological untruth, however, and a dramatic disaster.

There are, of course, certain feelings which become self-evident as the result of certain actions. A man who stabs someone must be angry; a man who throws his arms around someone must be feeling affection; a man who cannot smile must be sad. But even these actions require further definition, as seemingly definite as they appear. A particular man stabbing someone may not be angry so much as frightened himself; a man throwing his arms around someone may be trying to neutralize the other's animosity and feel nothing like affection at all; a man who cannot smile may feel great joy at the fact that he has finally succeeded in keeping a straight face.

So that the actuality of an emotion, its particularity, and the accuracy with which it is conveyed, depend on far more than the actor generating in himself that emotion *per se*. That process of generation is truly but half the problem of acting. The other half is its communication, which on the stage is done through speech and a modification of gesture which comes from an objectification by the actor, and will not come at all if the actor's attention is solely on what he feels.

In a word, acting has come perilously close to being a species of therapy and has moved too far from art. A too-great absorption in one's own feelings is ordinarily called self-indulgence; and that is what it is on the stage when the crucial step of communication is taken only unwillingly, haltingly, negatively. It needs to be emphasized again that acting is not a private but a social occupation. It is a vulgarization of psychological knowledge to put forward the notion which in effect misled actors have been taught, namely, that to feel a truth is to act it. The insane feel all sorts of truths but it is precisely because those truths have become unrelated to the world outside them, and because they have lost the sheer technique of social communication that they are called insane. An actor moves into the realm of acting and out of the category of non-actors precisely when he communicates and not a moment before, whatever the power of his feelings. The time has arrived when actors can boast of changing a line of Chekhov's because it did not suit the emotion they were feeling at the moment; the time has come when actors declare that the words are merely the vehicles of their emotions and have no life of their own let alone supremacy. It is necessary to say, therefore, that the logical end of such an "art" is the destruction of meaning in the theatre and the raising up of emotion for its own sake. And this can only be the triumph of nihilism in the theatre, the breakdown of any dramatic architecture, the defeat of climax and with it the power of drama to symbolize meaning. To resume the analogy—it is as though a man could truly be born a king without having to learn anything at all beyond feeling like one. It is like being asked to believe that a man in this society grows a beard with no thought whatever of what he looks like to others. It is like being asked to believe in a psychological autonomy, a sealed psychology—which can only exist in the mad.

With the certainty that I am not alone in this, I would like to offer certain examples of rehearsal problems which this false approach engenders, and which have been repeated so often in my experience as to prove their widespread validity.

Rehearsals begin. The actors have little more than an outline of the characters in mind. As they read the script aloud, and later begin to tentatively project bits and pieces of their interpretations of the roles, the director points out contradictions between what they are doing on page 9 and 60, contradictions of attitude which make the character unbelievable or illogical.

Aware that the actor is still not at home with the dynamics of the role, the director projects the final result—either by describing what it must finally seem or by demonstrating through line-readings and action, he places the goal before the actor.

Unseriously now, rather gaily and experimentally, not for a moment intending to adopt as final this particular way of doing the part, the actor shows the director that he can do what is asked. He imitates the result. Quite often—more often than not, in fact, he pulls off an exciting bit of acting. A good step seems to have been taken and he is encouraged to go further in that direction. In short, he has invented something.

Now there sets in the process of making that invention real to himself. Gradually the joy seems to leak out of it, the gaiety evaporates and something like self-consciousness and thought moves in. Finally, the invention which was in itself perhaps near-accurate, and had the appearance of a discovery, is shaved away and shaped to fit the inner sense of truth which the actor is capable of finding within himself. The result, so very often, is that the original image which he succeeded in producing is narrowed to his sense of truth, and it is comparatively meagre as compared with his first attempts. There must be something terribly wrong with a method which so consistently repeats the same kind of self-destruction.

I know full well that at this point I will be reminded—(cursed out is the better phrase)—that this is nothing but a faulty misuse of "The Method." I can only reply that when it reoccurs and reoccurs, and with actors of obvious talent, I am entitled to say that it is not a misuse but an inevitability.

And how could it be otherwise? Look at the contradiction these actors are being asked to overcome. They are being asked to consciously motivate what is essentially an instinctual outburst, an outburst born of their sheer miming ability. What is disgraceful about the ability to project what one does not understand so much as sense and feel? The spurious intellectualization of acting is at the heart of "The Method's" contradiction. The ability to do without knowing why is equal in value to the ability to do after understanding why. I have witnessed one actor after another thinking his part to smithereens. Which is simply to say that his first, tentative attempt was an attempt to communicate. His after-thoughts were in the counter-direction, toward himself.

Thus it was that Harold Clurman, as knowing an adept of "The Method" as any man alive, could rightly answer an actor who asked him "But how can I do this?"—(a sudden emphasis on a word which was required if the next speech was to make any sense)—"Because you have to." The shock if not insult in the actor's face told more about the contemporary misunderstanding than all the words ever written on the subject. It was as though his art were threatened; as though having to subjugate his sense of truth to the text were a violation of his dignity. As though, in short, he were on this stage for some purpose other than the interpretation of his role and this play. And, just to show that he could indeed act so mechanically, so shorn of his inner truth, he "artificially" emphasized the required word—and it was quite wonderful.

Second example. An actor to supposed to play a man on the verge of an outburst of anger. But it is a man with a powerful ability to suppress anger. The problem is show not his suppression alone, or his anger alone, but the process of one in conflict with the other.

The actor appears. He begins to play. One sees a man who is apparently calm. One waits for the anger to appear, for the process of conflict to begin. The actor remains calm, apparently. The scene is over. Nothing has happened.

"You don't seem to be angry," he is told.

"I am furious."

"But we have to see some sign of it."

"It's in everything I've done, in every word."

"It doesn't come out. Maybe you ought to try clenching your hands at some point or even working your jaw."

"What do you want, a tag? I am *being* angry, I don't see why I have to put an arrow on it."

"But right now you are being angry with me and you are certainly showing it."

Hiatus. A sense of insult.

The difference is obvious. Talking angrily with the director and at the same time trying to control his anger, he is being angry *in relation* to someone else, not only himself.

Style, before it can be anything else, is a relation outward. It is indeed a learned behaviour, an objectively learned way of identifying one's social location, and no actor can achieve it until he can see its existence around him in society. The actor for whom any objectification of his inner feelings is somehow a contradiction of feeling, is helpless before the problem of act-ing itself, let alone acting in a style not native to him.

The failure to act in a style is therefore only an amplification into the obvious of his essentially contradictory attitude toward acting itself.

typescript, c. 1964

AUTHOR'S PRODUCTION NOTE

(*The Price*)

A FINE balance of sympathy should be maintained in the play-ing of the roles of Victor and Walter. The actor playing Walter must not regard his attempts to win back Victor's friendship as mere manipulation. From entrance to exit, Walter is attempt-ing to put into action what he has learned about himself, and sympathy will be evoked for him in proportion to the open-ness, the depth of need, the intimations of suffering with which the role is played.

This admonition goes beyond the question of theatrics to the theme of the play. As the world now operates, the qualities of both brothers are necessary to it; surely their respective psychologies and moral values conflict at the heart of the social dilemma. The production must therefore withhold judgment in favor of presenting both men in all their humanity and from their own viewpoints. Actually, each has merely proved to the other what the other has known but dared not face. At the end, demanding of one another what was forfeited to time, each is left touching the structure of his life.

The play can be performed with an intermission, as indicated at the end of Act One, if circumstances require it. But an unbroken performance is preferable.

Collected Plays, vol. 2 (1981)

PREFATORY NOTE

(*The Creation of the World and Other Business*)

SINCE no critic noted what this play was about, a few suggestions are in order. It is in the same line as its predecessors, "After the Fall," "Incident at Vichy," and "The Price," (whose themes also went unremarked,) which from different angles take up the procedure by which humans act out murderous aggression in defense of their innocence.

When this becomes obvious, as when a man runs amok and shoots down strangers or his own family, we concede it exists and put him away if we can catch him. It is called paranoia, a disease, and since it is a disease it naturally does not apply to us but to our neighbors. But even so we usually are deaf to what the paranoic is saying, which is simply that he was innocent but was surrounded by deadly enemies who he had to destroy in order to protect decency, peace, justice, or whatever color of the moral spectrum. These four plays do not, however, attempt a pathology but a viewpoint toward the normal tension by which aggression is kept within bounds.

More accurately, the tension which manages to conceal the fact that aggression exists, and not merely in "society" or "the system" but within us all. But these are not psychological plays. (I have no more interest in psychology in-itself than in bacteriology.) This play in particular deals with man as the creator of institutions, as the projector of gods, the inner engine being his unadmissable fear of himself. That fear springs from the more or less conscious knowledge that he is capable of murdering his own kind, and therefore of being murdered himself. To defend himself he invents ethics, religion, moral standards and the numberless other sublimations which transform aggression into higher and beneficial forms. He is quite rightly proud of his religion, art and ethical arts for their beauty, so much so that he forgets what they succeeded in concealing.

These four plays could not have been conceived, however, if those sublimations worked sufficiently well. They spring, in fact, out of the European holocaust of the Jews, the succession of wars since, the magnifying violence of our peacetime world, our common bewilderment before the unquestionable fact of our rapacity, when every current social system describes its aims as peaceful and democratic.

Quite probably there would have been far less resistance to recognizing the common theme of these plays—I am not speaking of its acceptance—had there been a strong dose of cynicism in them. Had Quentin, in "After the Fall," begun by describing himself as beyond all hope, a thoroughly defeated man, and ended by bravely accepting himself as such, he and the play would have comfortably fallen into a pattern which is called tragic and at least life-like. But he is evidently intolerable because he seeks to find his justification, which of course none of us does, and far from being exemplary is merely excusing himself. Needless to say, no sane author could have imagined this character as an exemplar, given his own admissions, but I did imagine that the spectacle of a man discovering his own murderous impulses—despite his own disgust with them, a particular human procedure might have emerged for the viewer. It did not, excepting for a remarkably few people.

Nor did the announced next-step, the challenge in this procedure make itself felt, anymore than it did in "Incident at Vichy," where it was far more overt, at the very forefront of the play. It was seen as some sort of throw-back to anti-Nazi, World War II melodrama; but the subject of its action is the need a few men feel—and have surely felt, to transcend, to break out of the magnetic pull of self-survival through sacrificing others, rather than passively accepting death. To recognize and accept as real their own aggression and to feel not guilt but responsibility for it *themselves*, however it might have been foisted upon them by a world they never made.

What evolves in "The Price" is the spectre of concealed aggression under a social "inevitability"; the discovery of the man inside the social role through which he sought to survive. Each brother faces the other with his shield of values, his own sublime reasons for acting as he did. The shields disintegrate, the inner surge of each one's survival-thrust is revealed, but the play stops short of levelling a judgement as to which of them is justified, which is the "hero." But, as in "After the Fall" and "Incident at Vichy," it is not to discover an exemplar with whose situation we can find comfortable identification—that cannot be the issue anymore. And this is so because, for one thing, we are not living in monarchies or dictatorships where we have no voice, but in societies where it is no longer possible to draw a line between the depradations of leaders and the population's own drives. What the liberal cannot stomach—and all critics are in this sense liberals, as well as the audiences in theatres, is that our leaders express even us, our own—for example—desires to "pacify" minority races, our own wish to accept the "honor" which is proclaimed exists in the Vietnam peace (aggression). And again, these plays would have been far more easily accepted, in my opinion, had they not persisted in leaving unresolved the question, (which is theatrical and social and ethical), as to who to root for. The point—which is unacceptable—is that to be human is to share in evil; but to engage the future, to act for man, is to keep alive the struggle against one's own patrimony by recognizing it and transforming it into a life-protecting force.

That this theme is not absolutely concealed in my mind is apparent in an occasional letter from strangers, one of which raises the requisite point. A physician in Michigan who saw "Creation" asks, "Why is it that the message of your play, that particular thought about good and evil, about how we are going to handle aggression, about the basic moral question of mankind, cannot be dealt with, cannot be accepted by man in this time? What has occurred to me is that the basic reluctance has to do with a sort of artifice we have created . . . that is, to deny our animal nature. So that the reason God in your play had to deny, had to refuse loving the Devil, was because *man* has to create an ego ideal for himself which is fictitious, but which he needs in order to strive for its attainment. It in interesting that man attempted only to imitate Christ, who turned the aggression against himself, rather than the God who claims to be altogether free of it."

Not I alone but the actors in this play were astonished by the extreme variations in the response of its audiences. One night they sat there as though listening to a foreign language—soundless and inert. The next, the theatre was in an uproar of laughter and at the end people wept. Some nights people walked out angrily muttering while at the same moment others were shouting appreciation. In my experience there has never been such an enigmatic relationship of a play with its audiences. It was not a case of how the story developed—this was the mystery; for some audiences the very first dialogue between God and Adam caused a solemn silence which never relented. For others, it was funny from the first word.

At a minimum, therefore, what we were confronting was some force of conditioning, for the play was played with great consistency every night. It seemed to me that for some people the sight of God coming down from Heaven and speaking with such familiarity, so commonly, and revealing a distinct lack of supernatural foresight; a God experimenting in his creation like an artist; a God surprised by his own inventions—this God was from the first moment either an affront or illegible-as-God. The God in this play, in short, is not sublime enough to suit the religious or superstitious, nor sufficiently outrageous in his mockery of religion to suit the reigning iconoclasm. So he in unrecognizable, he fails to be "God." But this just might have been the point. For this God is possibilities, the infinite choices which life presents and so he cannot be known as a monolithic force is known. He is all forces, including even his most formidable invention, Lucifer. For after all it was out of God that Lucifer came.

Lucifer is God's ultimate irony. Since God insists that basically everything that exists is good, then—says Lucifer—every aspect of every force, every emotion, every idea, is equally good and must be accepted as such by God. But God senses his demise in this attitude, his overthrow. For he can only exist for man if man perceives differences, if some things and some acts have greater value and others have less. Without this discrimination man cannot be but another of the beasts, a failure on God's part to recreate himself in a creature, rather than just another animal.

The power of Lucifer's position is that it does reflect the duality of man, including his perversity. The speciousness in it is its license to destroy. Lucifer not only recognizes aggression but would bless it.

Thus both gods exist as projections of the human's nature, but the leap to a higher consciousness can only be made by recognizing the fact of perversity and then going on to protecting life against its unbridled force.

My own belief is that the failure of the play to evoke a more or less uniform response stems from my faulty assumption that its gods would be recognized as projections of the human tension, as man-created. Those who were able to laugh did so because they saw the irony in the *human* struggle these gods represented, and those who were put-off were either wedded to the idea of man as God's creation, or torn between the two. Which is not to deny a religious element in the play, but it consists not of superstition, but of a belief in the possibility of transcendancy, of awesome mankind straining toward a unified vision of itself.

That unity cannot be attained by denying the existence of the perverse, of aggression, but neither can it be by equating aggression with, for example, love. In a certain sense Lucifer and God in this play are in quotation marks, but in another sense they are all but palpable powers, for the truth is that we do kill in the name of God and sometimes in his name we are magnanimous, and we do give way to perversity or celebrate it in the Devil's name. That a thing is projected does not mean it has no reality, if by reality is meant, power which for all intents and purposes is real. Do we need to prove that for a piece of cloth imprinted with stripes or a star men will commit any atrocity, any act of courage and self-sacrifice? The sublime has

powers indeed, just as a government, conceived and adminis-
tered by men, has powers nevertheless, and they are no less
actual because they are man-made, however sublime they finally appear.

So both gods in this play are sublime and both are necessary,
which is to say, creation and destruction exist irremediably as
human impulses. The Luciferian view is that they cannot be
weighed, that there is no difference between them, since they
both bear the fiat of God's work. God's point, finally, is that
they do indeed exist—a sad necessity, and that man must
choose between them knowing they exist. But why "must"
man choose at all?

In my reading of the Old Testament the first figure with anything to say that reveals a human character, is Cain. Adam and
Eve are reported on, they are briefly noted forces, functions of
God's creation unscarred by characteristics. The image is one
of Eden, and it is Eden because there are no conflicts, and
there are no conflicts because there are no choices. Man, in
short, is not yet man because he lacks differentiation from the
beasts until he strives toward God. God, who is all possibilities,
has left in the Garden the Tree, the possibility of knowing the
difference between good and evil. He forbids man the fruit,
but he is helpless not to leave the tree there. By even passively resisting the eating, Man responds to God's love and
authority, he already *knows*. But before he eats he does not
know remorse, without which the dimensions of choosing are
undefined. Lucifer enters to present the choice as a step toward
Godliness, being-like-God. In a sense he is telling the truth
when he urges man to sin, he is doing God's will, for in choice
is the agony of the God-search. The God in this play is in
conflict, and Lucifer expresses half of it—God's need to en-
hance the consciousness of Man. The imperative, again, is the
process of human evolution, the insatiable need in man to
know. This is the "must," the given.

The Jews who fixed the succession of chapters of the Bible had
first to choose among a mass of material which it is presumed
had no set order. Like several earlier cosmologies it was inevitable that they open their people's spiritual history with an ex-

planation of how the world came to be, the Creation, but why must they have chosen a murder as the first human event in the development of mankind? And not merely a murder but a fratricide?

The socio-historical explanation is that Cain represents a victorious agricultural civilization and Abel the nomadic tribes which were at one time masters of that part of the world and were finally subdued. But even if this is true it does not explain the necessity for setting this conflict at the head of Israel's Holy Book.

It is that without a murder, and the most horrendous kind of murder of a blood brother, God would not be necessary in human affairs but only as a nature God; he would have no moral dimension. By confronting Cain, God becomes more than the Lord of what-is, the Creator, and opens a new dimension of what must-not-be. But if man, who is God-made, is indeed capable of fratricide, on what basis can God believably prohibit him anything his passions lead him to do? Does not this murder prove that Lucifer is right, and man is ungovernable and therefore must logically be accorded every right?

This murder leads all the other stories of the Bible because it raises the questions of whether in the same creature, capable of killing its own kind, is another force powerful enough, reliable enough, to keep it from self-destruction. And of course this force too is God-made. This crisis is the first one and the last, the axis upon which all human relations ultimately turn—whether, in short, what we have come to call morality is more than a social invention and exists on the same primitive level as aggression. For if it is merely a wish born of passive, peace-loving philosophers, the race is finished, or if it exists merely in the mind of a God who hasn't to worry about making a living and succeeding, and fighting for supremacy with other men, it remains a wish laid upon a race which has failed.

The issue is raised in this play not on the level of the moral statutes but in the realm of human behaviour from which those statutes sprang. God, to be sure, has condemned Cain to wander the earth like a vagabond and a fugitive, but he has not killed him. The final decision is up to Adam and Eve, the first human beings to confront a murderer. How will they deal with this son, now that he has killed his brother? God has gone back to heaven, the sun is moving in the sky as unconcerned as ever—how to relate to this fellow?

In short, on what basis do they either condemn him, send him out in the world, or let him live on with them? Eve especially understands, having been second-rate in God's eyes from the beginning, how powerful Cain's resentment was when his offering was scorned and Abel's praised—he did not kill out of sheer perversity, for no reason. She sees that he was victimized, driven beyond his tolerance. Yet she cannot simply take him back as though he had literally no responsibility, as though in some part of him he had not willed his brother's death; and it is simply because her nature, which created Abel as well as Cain, revolts. And this is not a question of laws handed down from above, but of passions welling up from below, the need to recognize the existence of love in herself and to protect its existence rather than to make nothing of it by, in effect, accepting this murder as but another irremediable event. I had supposed that this might point to a biology, so to speak, of morals, an indication that even within the act of giving-birth, of creating a human being, there is evoked a primordial demand for its survival. And that this demand, not the philosophical law-makers' fiats, underlies and forces the elaboration of the protective human codes of civilization. In a word, this play was an attempt to strip away the codes, the civilization, from a family in order to see how and why it would rise from them again, from what passions, from what untutored feelings the law and man's ambiguous relations to God would form out of chaos once more.

typescript, c. 1972

AUTHOR'S NOTE

(*The Poosidin's Resignation*)

The Poosidin fragment was the work only of a couple of late afternoons—playing around in that helpless anger so many of us knew at the time. The principals were so outrageous, it was impossible to feel much more than contempt at their endless lying, self-praise, lugubrious insensitivity to the monstrousness of their deformities. They lodged in my mind, finally, as merely impersonators doing a bloody takeoff on something called greatness. They were fakes, genuine only in their bad acting, so bad as to evoke a certain sympathy for their struggle to seem authentic. They were W. C. Fields playing F. D. Roosevelt in whose shadow they grew up and whose royal self-assurance they felt forced to invoke. I apologize that it isn't better on the page, but I can read it aloud and, in the right mood, can make it sound almost—not quite—as stupefying as the models who inspired it.

Boston University Journal, 1976

CONDITIONS OF FREEDOM: TWO PLAYS OF THE SEVENTIES

(*The Archbishop's Ceiling; The American Clock*)

I

It is pointless any longer to speak of a period as being one of transition—what period isn't?—but the seventies, when both these plays were written, seemed to resist any definition even at the time. *The Archbishop's Ceiling* in some part was a response to this indefinition I sensed around me. Early in the decade the Kent State massacre took place, and while the anti-Vietnam War movement could still mobilize tens of thousands, the freshness had gone out of the wonderful sixties mixture of idealism and bitterness that had sought to project a new unaggressive society based on human connection rather than the values of the market economy. There was a common awareness of exhaustion, to the point where politics and social thought themselves seemed ludicrously out of date and naively ineffectual except as subjects of black comedy. Power everywhere seemed to have transformed itself from a forbidding line of troops into an ectoplasmic lump that simply swallowed up the righteous sword as it struck. Power was also doing its own, often surprising thing.

At least as an atmosphere, there was a not dissimilar disillusion in Eastern Europe and, for different reasons, in France too. As president of International PEN, I had the opportunity to move about in Eastern Europe, as well as in the Soviet Union, and I felt that local differences aside, intellectual life in the whole developed world had been stunned by a common failure to penetrate Power with a more humane and rational point of view. It may have been that the immense sense of relief and the high expectations that rushed in with the defeat of Hitler and Mussolini's fascism had to end in a letdown, but whatever the causes, by the seventies the rational seemed bankrupt as an ultimate sanction, a bar to which to appeal. And with it went a sense of history, even of the evolution of ideas and attitudes.

The ups and downs of disillusionment varied with time and place, however. It was possible to sit with Hungarian writers, for example, while they talked of a new liberalizing trend in their country, at the very moment that in Prague the depths of a merciless repression were being plumbed. There, with the Soviet ousting of Dubček and the crushing of all hope for an egalitarian socialist economy wedded to liberal freedoms of speech and artistic expression, the crash of expectations was especially terrible, for it was in Prague that this novel fusion seemed actually to have begun to function.

The seventies was also the era of the listening device, government's hidden bugs set in place to police the private conversations of its citizens—and not in Soviet areas alone. The White House was bugged, businesses were bugging competitors to defeat their strategies, and Watergate and the publication of the Pentagon Papers (which polls showed a majority of Americans disapproved) demonstrated that the Soviets had little to teach American presidents about domestic espionage. The burgling of psychiatrists' offices to spy out a government official's private life, the widespread bugging by political parties of each other's offices, all testified to the fact that the visible motions of political life were too often merely distractions, while the reality was what was happening in the dark.

Thus, when I found myself in Eastern European living rooms where it was all but absolutely certain that the walls or ceilings were bugged by the regime, it was not, disturbingly enough, an absolutely unfamiliar sensation for me. Of course there were very important differences—basically that an Eastern writer accused of seditious thoughts would have no appeal from his government's decision to hound him into silence, or worse. But the more I reflected on my experiences under bugged ceilings, the more the real issue changed from a purely political one to the question of what effect this surveillance was having on the minds of people who had to live under such ceilings, on whichever side of the Cold War line they happened to be.

Václav Havel, the Czech playwright who was later to serve a long term in prison, one day discovered a bug in his chandelier when house painters lowered it to paint the ceiling; deciding to deliver it to the local police, he said that it was government property that he did not think rightfully belonged to a private person. But the joke was as unappreciated as the eavesdropping itself was undenied. Very recently, in the home of a star Soviet writer, I began to convey the best wishes of a mutual friend, an émigré Russian novelist living in Europe, and the star motioned to me not to continue. Once outside, I asked if he wasn't depressed by having to live in a tapped house. He thought a moment, then shrugged—"I really don't know how I feel. I guess we figure the thing doesn't work!"—and burst out laughing at this jibe at Soviet inefficiency. Was he really all that unaffected by the presence of the unbidden guest? Perhaps so, but even if he had come to accept or at least abide it fatalistically, the bug's presence had changed him nonetheless. In my view it had perhaps dulled some resistance in him to Power's fingers ransacking his pockets every now and then. One learns to *include the bug* in the baggage of one's mind, in the calculus of one's plans and expectations, and this is not without effect.

The occasion, then, of *The Archbishop's Ceiling* is the bug and how people live with it, but the theme is something different. There are a number of adaptations to such a life: one man rails furiously at the ceiling, another questions that a bug is even up there, a third has changes of opinion from day to day; but man is so adaptable—and anyway the bug doesn't seem to be reacting much of the time and may simply be one more nuisance—that resistance to its presence is finally worn down to nothing. And that is when things become interesting, for something like the naked soul begins to loom, some essence in man that is simply unadaptable, ultimate, immutable as the horizon.

What, for instance, becomes of the idea of sincerity, the unmitigated expression of one's feelings and views, when one knows that Power's ear is most probably overhead? Is sincerity shaken by the sheer fact that one has so much as *taken the bug into consideration*? Under such pressure who can resist trying to some degree, however discreet and slight, to characterize himself for the benefit of the ceiling, whether as obedient conformist or even as resistant? And what, in that case, has been done to one's very identity? Does this process not overturn the very notion of an "I" in this kind of world? It would seem that "I" must be singular, not plural, but the art of bureaucracy is to change the "I" of its subjects to "we" at every moment of conscious life. What happens, in short, when people know that they are—at least most probably, if not certainly—at all times talking to Power, whether through a bug or a friend who is really an informer? Is it not something akin to accounting for oneself to a god? After all, most ideas of God see him as omnipresent, invisible, and condign in his judgments; the bug lacks only mercy and love to qualify, it is conscience shorn of moral distinctions.

In this play the most unreconcilable of the writers is clearly the most talented. Sigmund really has no permanent allegiance except to the love of creating art. Sigmund is also the most difficult to get along with, and has perhaps more than his share of cynicism and bitterness, narcissism and contempt for others.

He is also choking with rage and love. In short, he is most alive, something that by itself would fuel his refusal—or constitutional incapacity—to accept the state's arrogant treatment. But with all his vitality, even he in the end must desperately call up a sanction, a sublime force beyond his ego, to sustain him in his opposition to that arrogance; for him it is the sublimity of art, in whose life-giving, creative essence he partakes and shares with other artists whose works he bows to, and in the act transcends the tyranny.

In a sense *Archbishop* begs the question of the existence of the sacred in the political life of man. But it begins to seem now that some kind of charmed circle has to be drawn around each person, across which the state may intrude only at its very real economic and political peril.

Glasnost, which did not exist in the seventies, is to the point here, for it is at bottom a Soviet attempt, born of economic crisis, to break up the perfection of its own social controls in order to open the channels of expression through which the creativity, the initiatives, and the improvisations of individual people may begin to flow and enrich the country. The problem, of course, is how to make this happen in a one-party state that in principle illegalizes opposition. But the wish is as plain as the desperate need of the economy itself, indeed of the regime, for the wisdom of the many and the release of their energies. Finally, the question arises whether, after so many generations of training in submission, the habits of open-minded inquiry and independence can be evoked in a sufficient number of people to make such a policy work.

Late in 1986, when glasnost was a brand-new idea scarcely taken seriously as the main thrust of the new administration, a Russian writer expressing the pre-glasnost view said to me, "What you people in the West don't understand is that we are not a competitive society and we don't wish to be. We want the government to protect us, that is what the government is for. When two Western writers meet, one of them most likely asks the other what he is writing now. Our writers never ask such a question. They are not competing. You have been in our Writers Union and seen those hundreds of writers going in and out, having their lunches, reading newspapers, writing letters, and so on. A big number of those people haven't written anything in years! Some perhaps wrote a few short stories or a novel some years ago—and that was it! They were made members of the Union, got the apartment and the vacation in the south, and it is not so different in any other field. But this is not such a terrible thing to us!"

But, I countered, there were surely some highly talented people who produced a good deal of work.

"Of course! But most are not so talented, so it's just as well they don't write too much anyway. But is it right that they should be thrown out in the streets to starve because they are not talented? We don't think so!"

What he had chosen to omit, of course, was that the mediocrities, of which he was all but admittedly one, usually run things in the Writers Union, something the gifted writers are usually too prickly and independent to be trusted to do. And so the system practically polices itself, stifling creativity and unpalatable truth-telling, and extolling the mediocre. But its main object, to contain any real attempts at change, is effectively secured. The only problem is that unless the system moves faster it may be permanently consigned to an inferior rank among the competing societies.

And so it may well have come to pass that the sanctity of the individual, his right to express his unique sense of reality freely and in public, has become an economic necessity and not alone a political or aesthetic and moral question. If that turns out to be the case, we will have been saved by a kind of economic morality based on necessity, the safest morality of all.

II

The American Clock was begun in the early seventies and did not reach final form until its production at the Mark Taper Forum in Los Angeles in 1984, a version that in turn was movingly and sometimes hilariously interpreted in the Peter Wood production two years later at the British National Theatre. The seemingly endless changes it went through reflected my own search for something like a dramatic resolution to what, after all, was one of the vaster social calamities in history—the Great Depression of the thirties. I have no hesitation in saying that as it now stands, the work is simply as close to such a resolution as I am able to bring it, just as the experience itself remains only partially resolved in the hands of historians. For the humiliating truth about any "period" is its essential chaos, about which any generalization can be no more than just that, a statement to which many exceptions may be taken.

With all its variety, however, there were certain features of the Depression era that set it apart, for they had not existed before in such force and over such a long time. One of the most important of these to me, both as a person living through those years and as a writer contemplating them three decades afterwards, was the introduction into the American psyche of a certain unprecedented *suspense*. Through the twenties the country, for me—and believe I was typical—floated in a reassuring state of nature that merged boundlessly with the sea and the sky; I had never thought of it as even having a system. But the Crash forced us all to enter history willy-nilly, and everyone soon understood that there were other ways of conducting the nation's business—there simply had to be, because the one we had was so persistently not working. It was not only the radicals who were looking at the historical clock and asking how long our system could last, but people of every viewpoint. After all, they were hardly radicals who went to Washington to ask the newly inaugurated President Roosevelt to nationalize the banks, but bankers themselves who had finally confessed their inability to control their own system. The objective situation, in a word, had surfaced; people had taken on a new consciousness that had been rare in more prosperous times, and the alternatives of fascism or socialism were suddenly in the air.

Looking back at it all from the vantage of the early seventies, we seemed to have reinserted the old tabula rasa, the empty slate, into our heads again. Once more we were in a state of nature where no alternatives existed and nothing had grown out of anything else. Conservatism was still damning the liberal New Deal, yearning to dismantle its remaining prestige, but at the same time the Social Security system, unemployment and bank insurance, the regulatory agencies in the stock market— the whole web of rational protections that the nation relied on—were products of the New Deal. We seemed to have lost awareness of community, of what we rightfully owe each other and what we owe ourselves. There seemed a want of any historical sense. America seems constantly in flight to the future; and it is a future made much like the past, a primeval paradise with really no government at all, in which the pioneer heads alone into the unknown forest to carve out his career. The suddenness of the '29 Crash and the chaos that followed offered a pure instance of the impotence of individualist solutions to so vast a crisis. As a society we learned all over again that we are in fact dependent and vulnerable, and that mass social organization does not necessarily weaken moral fiber but may set the stage for great displays of heroism and self-sacrifice and endurance. It may also unleash, as it did in the thirties, a flood of humor and optimism that was far less apparent in seemingly happier years.

When Studs Terkel's *Hard Times* appeared in 1970, the American economy was booming, and it would be another seventeen years before the stock market collapsed to anything like the degree it had in 1929. In any case, in considering his collection of interviews with survivors of the Depression as a partial basis for a play (I would mix my own memories into it as well), I had no prophecy of doom in mind, although in sheer principle it seemed impossible that the market could keep on rising indefinitely. At bottom, quite simply, I wanted to try to show how it was and where we had come from. I wanted to give some sense of life as we lived it when the clock was ticking every day.

The idea was not, strictly speaking, my invention but a common notion of the thirties. And it was a concept that also extended outward to Europe and the Far East; Hitler was clearly preparing to destroy parliamentary governments as soon he organized his armies, just as Franco had destroyed the Spanish Republic, and Japan was manifestly creating a new empire that must one day collide with the interests of Britain and the United States. The clock was ticking everywhere.

Difficulties with the play had to do almost totally with finding a balance between the epic elements and the intimate psychological lives of individuals and families like the Baums. My impulse is usually toward integration of meaning through significant individual action, but the striking new fact of life in the Depression era—unlike the self-sufficient, prosperous seventies—was the swift rise in the common consciousness of the social system. Uncharacteristically, Americans were looking for answers far beyond the bedroom and purely personal relationships, and so the very form of the play should ideally reflect this wider awareness. But how to unify the two elements, objective and subjective, epic and psychological? The sudden and novel impact of the Depression made people in the cities, for example, painfully conscious that thousands of farm families were being forced off their lands in the West by a combination of a collapsed market for farm goods and the unprecedented drought and dust storms. The farmers who remained operating were aware—and openly resentful—that in the cities people could not afford to buy the milk for which they could not get commercially viable prices. The social paradoxes of the collapse were so glaring that it would be false to the era to try to convey its spirit through the life of any one family. Nevertheless the feeling of a unified theatrical event evaded me until the revision for the 1984 Mark Taper production, which I believe came close to striking the balance. But it was in the British National Theatre production two years later that the play's theatrical life was finally achieved. The secret was vaudeville.

Of course the period had much tragedy and was fundamentally a trial and a frustration for those who lived through it, but no time ever created so many comedians and upbeat songs. Jack Benny, Fred Allen, W. C. Fields, Jimmy Durante, Eddie Cantor, Burns and Allen, and Ed Wynn were some of the headliners who came up in that time, and the song lyrics were most often exhilaratingly optimistic: "Love Is Sweeping the Country," "Life Is Just a Bowl of Cherries," "April in Paris," "I'm Getting Sentimental over You," "Who's Afraid of the Big Bad Wolf?" It was, in the pop culture, a romantic time and not at all realistically harsh. The serious writers were putting out books like Nathanael West's *Miss Lonelyhearts*, Erskine Caldwell's *God's Little Acre*, Jack Conroy's *The Disinherited*, André Malraux's *Man's Fate*, Hemingway's *Winner Take Nothing*, and Steinbeck's *In Dubious Battle*, and Edward Hopper was brooding over his stark street scenes, and Reginald Marsh was painting vagrants asleep in the subways, but Broadway had O'Neill's first comedy, *Ah, Wilderness!*, and another comical version of the hard life, *Tobacco Road*, Noel Coward's *Design for Living*, the Gershwins' *Let 'Em Eat Cake*, and some of the best American farces ever written—*Room Service*, *Three Men on a Horse*, and *Brother Rat* among them.

In the Mark Taper production I found myself allowing the material to move through me as it wished—I had dozens of scenes by this time and was shifting them about in search of their hidden emotional as well as ideational linkages. At one point the experience brought to mind a sort of vaudeville where the contiguity of sublime and ridiculous is perfectly acceptable; in vaudeville an imitation of Lincoln doing the Gettysburg Address could easily be followed by Chinese acrobats. So when subsequently Peter Wood asked for my feeling about the style, I could call the play a vaudeville with an assurance born of over a decade of experimentation. He took the hint and ran with it, tossing up the last shreds of a realistic approach, announcing from the opening image that the performance was to be epic and declarative.

Out of darkness, in a brash music hall spotlight, a baseball pitcher appears and tosses a ball from hand to glove as he gets ready on the mound. The other characters saunter on singing snatches of songs of the thirties, and from somewhere in the balcony a man in a boater and striped shirt, bow tie and gartered sleeves—Ted Quinn—whistles "I Found a Million-Dollar Baby in a Five-and-Ten-Cent Store." At one side of the open stage, a five-piece jazz band plays in full view of the audience (impossible in the penurious New York theatre), and the sheer festivity of the occasion is already established.

The most startling, and I think wonderful, invention of all was the treatment of the character of Theodore K. Quinn. This was the actual name of a neighbor of mine, son of a Chicago railroad labor organizer, who had worked himself up from a poor Chicago law student to the vice-presidency of General Electric. The president of GE, Quinn's boss through most of the twenties, was Gerard Swope, a world-famous capitalist and much quoted social thinker, who decided as the thirties dawned that Quinn was to succeed him on his retirement. Quinn, in charge of the consumer products division of the company, had frequently bought up promising smaller manufacturers for Swope, incorporating their plants into the GE giant, but had developed a great fear that this process of cartelization must end in the destruction of democracy itself. Over the years his rationalization had been that he was only taking orders—although in fact it was on his judgment that Swope depended as to which companies to pick up. Then the excuses were threatened by his elevation to the presidency, an office with dictatorial powers at the time. As he would tell me, "Above the president of General Electric stood only God."

The real Ted Quinn had actually been president of GE for a single day, at the end of which he put in his resignation. "I just couldn't stand being the Lord High Executioner himself," he once said to me. He went on to open an advisory service for small businesses and made a good fortune at it. During World War II he was a dollar-a-year head of the Small Business Administration in Washington, seeing to it that the giant concerns did not gobble up all the available steel. Particularly close to his heart was the Amana company, a cooperative.

Quinn also published several books, including *Giant Business, Threat to Democracy* and *Unconscious Public Enemies*, his case against GE-type monopolies. These, along with his antimonopoly testimony before congressional committees, got him obliterated from the roster of former GE executives, and the company actually denied—to journalist Matthew Josephson, who at my behest made an inquiry in 1972—that he had ever so much as worked for GE. However, in the course of time a film director friend of mine who loved to browse in flea markets and old bookstores came on a leather-covered daily diary put out by GE as a gift for its distributors, circa 1930, in which the company directors are listed, and Theodore K. Quinn is right there as vice-president for consumer sales. The fact is that it was he who, among a number of other innovations, conceived of the compact electric refrigerator as a common consumer product, at a time when electric refrigeration was regarded as a purely commercial item, the behemoth used in restaurants, hotels, and the kitchens of wealthy estates.

From the big business viewpoint Quinn's central heresy was that democracy basically depended on a large class of independent entrepreneurs who would keep the market competitive. His fear was that monopoly, which he saw spreading in the American economy despite superficial appearances of competition, would end by crippling the system's former ingenuity and its capacity to produce high-quality goods at reasonable prices. A monopoly has little need to improve its product when it has little need to compete. (First Communist China and then Gorbachev's Russia would be grappling with a very similar dilemma in the years to come.) He loved to reel off a long list of inventions, from the jet engine to the zipper, that were devised by independent inventors rather than corporations and their much advertised laboratories: "The basic things we use and are famous for were conceived in the back of a garage." I knew him in the fifties, when his populist vision was totally out of fashion, and maybe, I feared, an out-of-date relic of a bygone America. But I would hear it again in the seventies and even more loudly in the eighties as a muscle-bound American industrial machine, wallowing for generations in a continental market beyond the reach of foreign competition, was caught flat-footed by German and Japanese competitors. Quinn was a successful businessman interested in money and production, but his vision transcended the market to embrace the nature of the democratic system for which he had a passion, and which he thought doomed if Americans did not understand the real threats to it. He put it starkly once: "It may be all over, I don't know—but I don't want to have to choose between fascism and socialism, because neither one can match a really free, competitive economy and the political liberties it makes possible. If I do have to choose, it'll be socialism, because it harms the people less. But neither one is the way I'd want to go."

Perhaps it was because the style of the National Theatre production was so unashamed in its presentational declarativeness that the Ted Quinn role was given to David Schofield, a tap dancer with a brash Irish mug, for Quinn was forever bragging about—and mocking—his mad love of soft-shoe dancing. And so we had long speeches about the dire consequences of business monopoly delivered by a dancer uncorking a most ebullient soft-shoe all over the stage, supported by some witty jazz played openly before our eyes by a deft band. As Quinn agonizes over whether to accept the presidency of GE, a phone rings at the edge of the stage; plainly, it is as the new president that he must answer it. He taps his way over to it, lifts the receiver, and simply places it gently on the floor and dances joyously away.

It was in the National Theatre that I at last heard the right kind of straightforward epic expressiveness, joyful and celebratory rather than abashed and veiled, as economic and political —which is to say epic—subjects were in the mouths of the characters. In this antic yet thematically precise spirit, accompanied by some forty songs out of the period, the show managed to convey the *seriousness* of the disaster that the Great Depression was, and at the same time its human heart.

There was one more invention that I particularly prized. Alone in her Brooklyn house, Rose Baum sits at the piano, bewildered and discouraged by the endless Depression, and plays some of the popular ballads of the day, breaking off now and then to muse to herself about the neighborhood, the country, her family, her fading hopes. The actress sat at a piano whose keyboard faced the audience, and simply held her hands suspended over the keys while the band pianist a few yards away played the romantic thirties tunes. Gradually a triple reality formed such as I have rarely witnessed in the theatre: first, the objective stage reality of the band pianist playing, but somehow magically directed by Rose's motionless hands over her keyboard; and simultaneously, *the play's memory* of this lost past that we are now discovering again; and finally, the middle-aged actress herself seeming, by virtue of her motionless hands suspended over the keys, to be recalling this moment from her very own life. The style, in short, had fused emotion and conscious awareness, overt intention and subjective feeling—the aim in view from the beginning, more than a decade before.

The Archbishop's Ceiling; The American Clock: Two Plays (1989)

PLAYWRIGHT'S NOTE

(*Elegy for a Lady*)

It never before occurred to me to add a note of explanation to a play in published form. A playwright expects to be misinterpreted to some important degree, but to confront total incomprehension on the part of the critics is a new experience. This is especially strange when among the public there were more than enough people who expressed a perfectly adequate understanding and appreciation of what they had seen. In the hope that the interested audience and readers of this play not be permanently misled I would make certain fundamental observations.

The play is The Man's revery. It is not a dream but the kind of waking projection the mind often ventures into when it is stymied by life. Through this revery he makes it possible to confront if not the dying woman he loves then his fears about the truth of their relationship.

The actor must understand that there are bad implications for his character, and worse yet for hers in this confrontation. The relationship may turn out not to have had any meaning at all, something that would threaten his own reality. But however he may be judged, The Man cannot bear to accept living without the truth whatever it may cost his self-esteem.

The setting should combine a certain super emphasis on dream elements, like the mannikin parts scattered everywhere, and at the same time elements that are real and substantial and logical. Again, this is not a dream; The Man is awake and aware. Actually, he has been searching through stores for something that will signify his inexpressibly contradictory feelings for his beloved. In the end, the "perfection" which The Proprietress discovers is simply the completion, the fullest flowering of their relationship within its given limits, namely, both their natures, his age, the society and the life he has lived. He cannot, in short, have everything and he tastes acceptance of reality, the filling of bounds, a sense of form.

The Proprietress, as he envisions her, is packing up the store's contents from the beginning of the play until the shelves are empty and nothing is left but the bare structure of the set, the occasion of his vision.

The play, being his revery, is basically his viewpoint; thus The Proprietress must be played with the feelings of a woman who loves him but who understands the condition of their relationship. At the same time, however, he is not dreaming and he insists on her having her own autonomy, her determination to deny the imminence of death; he also, in effect, insists on her contradicting him when he knows that she would, in life.

He is in control of this vision but striving to stretch himself to embrace the unpalatable truth and even an ultimate dilemma, if that should turn out to be the case.

Primary to the role of The Man is the impact of his desperation; half-convinced he will never see his lover alive again he is racing time to find out what they meant to each other. It is painful to him that she might die without his having named their relation; he is thirsting for meaning, objectification, he wants to *see*.

Ideally, the part should be played with a doubled vision; he knows that in the literal sense The Proprietress is not his lover; he knows he has created this persona. But at the same time she has the same force for him as his lover. It is simply that within this revery he has the liberty to speak fully, to hurt himself and her, to fill their customarily observed gaps—as he would find it impossible to do in real life—in the hope of achieving a vision of them both in their real connection with one another. Because of her duality in his imagination, being both his lover and an abstract of her, she takes on another dimension of Womankind. But she must not be played "abstractly." She may weep and make her demands even more fully than she might have in life.

It may be asked, why this form, this enigma? The answer is simply that in revery he creates an arena in which to be free to say everything, an area of the imagination where he has the liberty to confront what he suspects she may be feeling in real life. It is also the place—perhaps its primary function for him is this—where he may glimpse the nothingness which is hounding him behind his back, as it were, in the hope of being victorious over it.

Finally, death being so near to both of them they are, needless to say, beyond any sentimentality. This tone may be difficult to grasp, however, in a theatre where all but insouciant irony and romance are feelings outlawed; but the integrative vision, the sense of putting things together, is a powerful feeling which the actor, perhaps unstylishly at present, is entitled to feel.

Elegy for a Lady (1982)

AUTHOR'S NOTE

(*Some Kind of Love Story; Elegy for a Lady*)

The stories and characters of this pair of plays are unrelated to one another but in different ways both works are passionate voyages through the masks of illusion to an ultimate reality. In *Some Kind of Love Story* it is social reality and the corruption of justice which a delusionary woman both conceals and unveils. The search in *Elegy for a Lady* is for the shape and meaning of a sexual relationship that is being brought to a close by a lover's probable death. In both the unreal is an agony to be striven against and, at the same time, accepted as life's condition.

Two-Way Mirror (1984)

AUTHOR'S NOTE

(*Elegy for a Lady*)

It isn't always clear exactly where one stands in psychic space when grief passes up through the body into the mind. To be at once the observer and observed is a split awareness that most people know; but what of the grieved-for stranger, the other who is 'not-me'?—Doesn't it sometimes seem as though he or she is not merely outside oneself but also within and seeing outward through one's own eyes at the same time that he or she is being seen?

There is an anguish, based on desire impossible to realize, that is so unrequited, and therefore so intense, that it tends to fuse all people into one person in a so-to-speak spectral unity, a personification which seems to reflect and clarify these longings and may even reply to them when in the ordinary world of 'I' and 'You' they cannot even be spoken aloud. Nor is this really so strange when one recalls how much of each of us is imagined by the other, how we create one another even as we actually speak and actually touch.

Two-Way Mirror (1984)

CHRONOLOGY

NOTE ON THE TEXTS

NOTES

Chronology

1915   Born Arthur Asher Miller on October 17 in New York City, the second child of Isadore and Augusta ("Gussie") Barnett Miller. (Father emigrated at the age of six from Eastern Europe and joined his parents and six siblings in New York City, where his father Shmuel owned a clothing business on the Lower East Side. As a young man he established his own highly successful business, the Miltex Coat and Suit Company, in Manhattan's garment district. Mother was born in the United States to immigrant parents. Their first child, Kermit, was born three years before Miller.) Family lives in a sixth-floor apartment at 45 West 110th Street, with a view of Central Park.

1916–28 At age six Miller begins attending P.S. 24 on West 111th Street. Sister Joan is born in 1922. Miller celebrates his bar mitzvah in 1928.

1929   Stock market crash devastates family finances and threatens the solvency of Miltex. Family moves to Gravesend in Brooklyn, living in a small house at 1350 Third Street where Miller shares a bedroom with his recently widowed maternal grandfather. Attends James Madison High School on Bedford Avenue.

1930–32 Brother Kermit begins attending New York University in the fall of 1930, while Miller transfers to Abraham Lincoln High School on Ocean Parkway. Works for Miltex in the summer of 1931, carrying samples for salesmen as they make their rounds. In the fall Kermit quits NYU to work full-time for Miltex. Miller makes deliveries for a local bakery before school, then takes new job driving a delivery truck for an auto-supply store.

1933–34 Graduates high school in June 1933. After working at Miltex in the summer, he finds a job paying $15 a week as stock clerk at the Chadick-Delameter auto-parts warehouse at 10th Avenue and West 63rd Street in Manhattan. Reads *Crime and Punishment* during his commute from Brooklyn. Applies unsuccessfully to the University of Michigan twice. Enrolls in classes in history and chemistry at City College of New York's night school but stops

attending after two weeks. Writes to the University of
Michigan and asks that his application be reconsidered
and is accepted on a probationary basis provided he prove
his ability to pay tuition, room, and board. Matriculates at
University of Michigan in Ann Arbor in fall 1934. Rooms
with fellow New Yorker Charles Bleich in a private home.

1935   Works as reporter on school newspaper, *The Michigan
Daily*; does well enough in his courses that the university
rescinds his probationary status and offers him a loan to
help cover expenses. Hitchhikes home for summer break.
In the fall lives in rooming house off-campus. Takes cre-
ative writing course and continues to write for *Michigan
Daily*, covering organizing efforts of the United Auto
Workers and interviewing UAW leader Walter Reuther.

1936   Meets first-year student Mary Grace Slattery and becomes
romantically involved with her. In six days writes his first
play, *No Villain*, which wins $250 Hopwood Award from
the university. Writes "In Memoriam," short story about
a salesman; attempts to adapt it for the stage but aban-
dons the effort. Miltex closes in the summer. Miller revises *No Villain* and submits new version, entitled *They
Too Arise*, to a student playwriting contest sponsored by
the Theatre Guild. Attends performance on Broadway of
Ibsen's *A Doll's House* during his winter break and is
deeply impressed.

1937   Enrolls in playwriting seminar with Professor Kenneth
Rowe. Awarded $1,250 scholarship when *They Too Arise*
wins Theatre Guild competition; the play is staged on
campus and then in Detroit. Miller writes *Honors at
Dawn*, which wins the Hopwood Award. Meets Norman
Rosten, who has come to the university on a Theatre
Guild scholarship to study with Kenneth Rowe. Inter-
views prisoners at nearby Jackson State Penitentiary and
uses the material as the basis of play eventually entitled
The Great Disobedience.

1938   Completes *The Great Disobedience* in March. Graduates
from University of Michigan in June and returns to New
York City, living in the family home in Brooklyn. Writes
new version of *They Too Arise* entitled *The Grass Still
Grows*, which after an enthusiastic response at the literary
agency Leland Hayward and Company is sent to Broadway producers. Miller is hired by the Federal Theatre and
Writers Project and moves into a studio apartment on

East 74th Street in Manhattan, but is then let go when the Project is forced to cut back.

1939   Writes tragedy about the Aztecs' encounter with Cortez called "The Montezuma Play," "The Children of the Sun," and ultimately *The Golden Years*. Collaborates with Norman Rosten on one-act play Listen, *My Children* and *You're Next!*, satire of the House Committee on Un-American Activities, which had investigated the Federal Theatre Project. Radio play *William Ireland's Confession* is performed on CBS on October 19.

1940   Miller marries Mary Slattery in a Catholic ceremony in her hometown in Ohio on August 5. The couple return to New York and move into a Brooklyn Heights apartment. In September, Miller sails alone to South America on a two-week trip to research *The Half-Bridge*, a play set on a merchant ship.

1941   Starts writing novel "The Man Who Had All the Luck" and receives modest advance from Atlantic Monthly Press; when he submits a partial manuscript, it is rejected by the publisher. Travels alone to North Carolina and sketches out ideas and stories for plays; trip is sponsored by Library of Congress to collect dialect speech for the folk division.

1942–43 Begins working the night shift at the Brooklyn Navy Yard. Finishes "The Man Who Had All the Luck" and sends it to Doubleday, Doran, which rejects it. Writes radio plays that are aired on the NBC Dupont Cavalcade of America. Quits job at Brooklyn Navy Yard when he is hired to write *The Story of G.I. Joe*, film adaptation of Ernie Pyle's *Here Is Your War*.

1944   Interviews soldiers at army training camps for *The Story of G.I. Joe* but is fired before script is completed and receives no writing credit on the film; uses material in a book of reportage, *Situation Normal . . .* , published by Harper. Adapts "The Man Who Had All the Luck" into a play and an early version is included in anthology *Cross-Section: A Collection of New American Writing*. Daughter Jane born September 7. *The Man Who Had All the Luck*, directed by Joseph Fields, opens at the Forrest Theatre on November 23 to unfavorable reviews and closes after four performances.

1945   One-act play *That They May Win* is included in anthology *Best One-Act Plays of 1944*. Writes *Focus*, novel about anti-Semitism, which is published by Reynal & Hitchcock and becomes a commercial success.

1946   Completes play *All My Sons*. After Leland Hayward Agency is bought out by MCA, Miller is assigned to Kay Brown, who will represent him for the next four decades. Harold Clurman, formerly of the Group Theatre, reads *All My Sons* and agrees to produce it, with Elia Kazan directing.

1947   After trial runs in New Haven and Boston, *All My Sons* opens on Broadway on January 29 and runs for 328 performances; book version is published by Reynal & Hitchcock. Miller buys house in Roxbury, Connecticut. Works for one week in a Queens factory assembling boxes as "a moral act of solidarity with those who had failed in life." *All My Sons* is named best new play of the 1946–47 season by the New York Drama Critics Circle; Miller and Kazan receive Antoinette Perry ("Tony") Awards for their work on the play. Son Robert is born on May 31. Moves in June to converted stable house at 31 Grace Court in Brooklyn Heights, living in upper floors and renting out two apartments in the building. Publishes essay in *The New York Times* arguing for a subsidized theater that "would lay upon all work and works the standards of art, and not primarily the standards of business men." Declines offer to write the screenplay for Alfred Hitchcock's *Rope*. Works on *Death of a Salesman*. Max Sorensen, leader of the Catholic War Veterans, denounces *All My Sons* as Communist "propaganda," and the War Department prevents it from being staged in the American-occupied Germany. *All My Sons* is performed in the Netherlands and Poland.

1948   Miller travels to Europe for the first time, visiting Italy, Greece, and France. *Focus* is banned by the principal of DeWitt Clinton High School in New York on grounds that it is offensive to Roman Catholics. Film version of *All My Sons*, directed by Irving Reis and starring Edward G. Robinson and Burt Lancaster, is released. *All My Sons* is produced in London and is warmly received, with one critic calling it "the best serious play that America has sent us for some time." Miller completes *Death of a Salesman* and Kazan agrees to direct it. Revises play based on suggestions by Kazan, but does not use revised version after producer Kermit Bloomgarden expresses strong preference for original version.

1949   After successful trial run in Philadelphia, *Death of a Sales-
          man* opens on Broadway on February 10 and runs for 742
          performances. Miller publishes essay "Tragedy and the
          Common Man" in *The New York Times* in February and
          another essay about tragedy and *Death of a Salesman*
          in the *New York Herald-Tribune* the following month.
          Attends Cultural and Scientific Conference for World
          Peace in New York City, a gathering criticized by anti-
          Communist liberals who claim it is too sympathetic to
          Communism, and chairs panel on the arts whose mem-
          bers include Dmitri Shostakovich, Aaron Copland, and
          Clifford Odets. *Death of a Salesman* is named best new
          play of the 1948–49 season by the New York Drama Crit-
          ics Circle and is awarded Pulitzer Prize, Donaldson
          Award, and Antoinette Perry Award; London staging is
          met with an enthusiastic reception. Continues working on
          "The Hook," a screenplay about union corruption on the
          Brooklyn waterfront, and an adaptation of Ibsen's *An
          Enemy of the People*. *Death of a Salesman* is published in
          book form in America and England and becomes first
          play offered as a selection of the Book of the Month
          Club.

1950–51   *Death of a Salesman* tours the U.S. and is staged in Vienna,
          Copenhagen, Düsseldorf, and other European cities.
          Short story "It Takes a Thief," first published in *Collier's*
          three years earlier, is adapted for television and broadcast
          on NBC Cameo Theatre. Adaptation of *An Enemy of the
          People* opens on Broadway on December 28, 1950, and
          runs for 36 performances. Travels with Kazan to Los An-
          geles to seek studio backing for "The Hook." Meets ac-
          tress Marilyn Monroe. Columbia Pictures expresses
          interest in "The Hook," but Miller withdraws screenplay
          after studio executive Harry Cohn asks him to revise
          script along anti-Communist lines. Writes to Monroe, and
          they begin corresponding. Buys house at 155 Willow
          Street in Brooklyn Heights and moves family there. Film
          of *Death of a Salesman*, directed by Laslo Benedek and
          starring Frederic March, is released.

1952   Miller's relations with Kazan deteriorate after Kazan testi-
          fies before the House Committee on Un-American Activi-
          ties on April 10 and names associates he knew to be
          members of the Communist Party. Miller begins re-
          searching and writing play about 17th-century Salem

witch trials and works on it throughout the summer.
Writes several pages of dialogue based on his job at the
auto-parts warehouse that will later be developed into *A
Memory of Two Mondays.*

1953–54   *The Crucible* opens on Broadway on January 22, 1953, to
mixed reviews and runs for 197 performances; it is also
staged in London, and in Paris in Marcel Aymé's French
adaptation, *Les Sorcières de Salem,* starring Yves Montand
and Simone Signoret. When he is invited to Brussels for
the Belgian premiere of the play, Miller's passport application is rejected by the State Department "under regulations denying passports to people believed to be
supporting the Communist movement."

1955   Miller becomes romantically involved with Marilyn Monroe. Writes one-act version of *A View from the Bridge,*
drawing on Brooklyn waterfront research for "The Hook."
Works on screenplay for film about juvenile gangs in
Brooklyn to be made in cooperation with the city government. After a summer tryout on Cape Cod and trial
runs in New Haven and Boston, *A View from the Bridge:
Two One-Act Plays* (*Bridge* and *A Memory of Two Mondays*) opens on Broadway on September 29 and runs for
149 performances. Miller separates from wife in October
and moves into the Chelsea Hotel in Manhattan. City au-
thorities cancel the gang film project after Miller is de-
nounced as "a veteran backer of Communist causes" by
the *New York World-Telegram.*

1956   Settles with wife on terms of divorce in February, and
then spends six weeks near Reno to establish residency for
a Nevada divorce. Works on a two-act version of *A View
from the Bridge* and the introduction to his *Collected
Plays.* Visits Los Angeles to see Monroe, who is filming
Bus Stop. Granted divorce in June. Receives honorary
Doctorate of Humane Letters from the University of
Michigan. Appears before House Committee on Un-
American Activities on June 21 in hearing ostensibly related to his passport application. In his testimony Miller
admits to having attended meetings with Communist
writers in 1947, but he refuses to identify others at these
meetings and denies ever having submitted himself to
"Communist discipline." Marries Marilyn Monroe in civil
ceremony in White Plains, New York, on June 29 and in
a Jewish ceremony in Katonah on July 1. Miller is cited
for contempt by Congress on July 10. Travels to England

with Monroe for honeymoon, where she films *The Prince and the Showgirl* with Laurence Olivier. Returns briefly to New York and writes short story "The Misfits, or Chicken Feed: The Last Frontier of the Quixotic Cowboy." Goes back to London for premiere in October of expanded *A View from the Bridge*, directed by Peter Brook. (Production is staged under the aegis of a private club after the censor refuses to license public performances because of the play's references to homosexuality.)

1957   Miller is convicted of contempt of Congress in federal district court in Washington, D.C., on May 31 after a six-day trial and is sentenced on July 19 to one-month suspended jail term and a $500 fine. Moves with Monroe from 2 Sutton Place to apartment on East 57th Street; also spends time at rented house in Amagansett, Long Island. Monroe has miscarriage in early August. *Arthur Miller's Collected Plays* published. *Les Sorcières de Salem*, film adaptation of *The Crucible* starring Yves Montand and Simone Signoret and with a screenplay by Jean-Paul Sartre, is released in France. *Death of a Salesman* is staged in Moscow. Miller begins adapting "The Misfits" into a screenplay intended as a vehicle for Monroe.

1958   Buys farm in Roxbury. Contacts Frank Lloyd Wright to design new house on the site but declines Wright's proposed plan and instead renovates existing 18th-century farmhouse; buys property adjoining the farm. Completes screenplay of *The Misfits*. Named a member of the National Institute of Arts and Letters. U.S. Court of Appeals for the District of Columbia overturns Miller's conviction for contempt of Congress in August. Miller writes essay "My Wife Marilyn" for *Life* magazine. Monroe suffers another miscarriage.

1959–60   Miller is awarded Gold Medal for Drama from the National Institute of Arts and Letters. Sends completed screenplay of *The Misfits* to John Huston, who agrees to direct the film. Travels with Monroe to Los Angeles, where she is filming *Let's Make Love*. Miller goes to Ireland to work with John Huston on *The Misfits*, but soon returns to California at Monroe's request. Works on rewrites of the *Let's Make Love* script. Monroe has an affair with co-star Yves Montand; Miller returns to Connecticut. They travel to Reno, Nevada, in July 1960 for location shooting for *The Misfits*. Miller meets Ingeborg (Inge) Morath, an Austrian-born photographer sent by the Magnum agency to document the production. In late August, Miller takes Monroe, who is in a fragile mental state and dependent on barbiturates, to Los Angeles to be hospitalized. Returns to New York and moves out of the 57th Street apartment; divorce plans are announced on November 11.

1961   Monroe is granted divorce in Juarez, Mexico, on January 24. Novelization of *The Misfits* by Miller is published shortly before the film is released on February 1. Mother dies on March 6. Miller discovers that *Death of a Salesman* has been filmed in the Soviet Union without his permission. *Uno Sguardo del Ponte*, opera of *A View from the Bridge* by Renzo Rossellini, premieres in Rome and is staged in several European cities; Robert Ward's opera of *The Crucible* is staged in the fall and wins a Pulitzer Prize the following year. Short story "I Don't Need You Anymore" is included in *Prize Stories 1961: The O. Henry Awards*. Filming begins in Brooklyn and Paris for screen version of *A View from the Bridge*, directed by Sidney Lumet with screenplay by Norman Rosten.

1962   One-hour television adaptation of *Focus* is broadcast on NBC. Film of *A View from the Bridge* released in the U.S. in late January. Miller marries Inge Morath in Connecticut on February 17 and the couple depart for honeymoon in Europe. New production of *The Crucible* with essayistic passages read from the stage is presented in Boston. Marilyn Monroe dies from an overdose of barbiturates on August 5. Miller works on *After the Fall*. Daughter Rebecca Augusta born September 15.

1963   As *After the Fall* is planned for production in the inaugural season of the Lincoln Center Repertory Theater, Miller works with director Elia Kazan for the first time since the early 1950s. Writes children's book *Jane's Blanket* for daughter Jane. Joins 47 other playwrights in refusing to allow their plays to be performed in South African theaters enforcing apartheid. *Death of a Salesman* staged as part of the inaugural season of the Guthrie Theater in Minneapolis.

1964   *After the Fall*, starring Jason Robards, premieres on January 23 and runs for 208 performances; among those attending the gala opening are Lady Bird Johnson, Adlai Stevenson, and Ralph Bunche. The play attracts controversy because of its presumed autobiographical elements, particularly concerning Miller's marriage to Monroe. Writes for the *New York Herald-Tribune* about trial in Frankfurt of former SS men who had served at Auschwitz. Returns home and completes draft of play *Incident at Vichy* in three weeks. Film rights for *After the Fall* bought by Carlo Ponti, Ira Steiner, and MGM; Miller works on script but then withdraws from the project because of differences with producers about the screenplay and casting. Makes cuts in *After the Fall* seven months into its run. Directed by Harold Clurman for the Lincoln Center Repertory Company, *Incident at Vichy* premieres on December 3 and runs for 32 performances.

1965   Miller travels to the Soviet Union and Poland. Elected president of PEN International at its annual conference and serves four years in the position. Participates in demonstrations against the Vietnam War and antiwar teach-in at the University of Michigan, and refuses invitation from President Johnson to attend signing of the federal Arts and Humanities Act because "the occasion is so darkened by the Vietnam tragedy that I could not join it with clear conscience" (will maintain his antiwar activism for the duration of the conflict).

1966–67   While in England for production of *Incident at Vichy*, Miller falls ill with hepatitis and is hospitalized. Television version of *Death of a Salesman* is broadcast on CBS on May 8, 1966, with Lee J. Cobb and Mildred Dunnock reprising their roles from the original Broadway production; adaptation of *An Enemy of the People* is broadcast by National Educational Television. Publishes story collection *I Don't Need You Anymore*. A son, Daniel Miller, is born. Miller travels to Abidjan, Ivory Coast, for PEN International conference in July 1967.

1968   *The Price* opens on Broadway on February 7 and runs for 429 performances. Harold Clurman publishes essay "The Merits of Mr. Miller" in *The New York Times* in response to negative assessment of Miller's career by critic Alfred Bermel. Campaigns for Democratic presidential candidate Eugene McCarthy and attends Democratic Party convention in Chicago as delegate from Roxbury. Travels to the Soviet Union and visits Czechoslovakia after Soviet invasion. *The Price* is staged in Tel Aviv.

1969   London production of *The Price* opens in March. Miller refuses to have his work published in Greece as a protest against the Greek military regime. One-act play *The Reason Why* filmed for television at Miller's Roxbury farm. Signs letter condemning the expulsion of Alexander Solzhenitsyn from the Soviet Writers' Union. *In Russia*, the first of several collaborative books with photographer Morath, is published.

1970–71   Miller receives Creative Arts Award from Brandeis University. Russian television production of *The Price* is canceled and Miller's works are banned in the Soviet Union. American television productions of *A Memory of Two Mondays* and *The Price* are broadcast in February 1971.

1972–74   Miller is a delegate to the Democratic National Convention in Miami. After trial run in Washington, *The Creation of the World and Other Business*, comic adaptation of the Book of Genesis, opens in New York on November 30, 1972, and closes after 20 performances. Miller serves as writer-in-residence at University of Michigan. Adapts *The Creation of the World and Other Business* into a musical, *Up from Paradise*, which he directs and plays the onstage role of narrator in a production at the University of Michigan. Writes editorial of support for Soviet physicist Andrei Sakharov's six-day hunger strike in 1974 and criticizes the Nixon administration's silence about Sakharov and other dissidents as a "message . . . that the United States is a moral nullity." Becomes active supporter of Peter Reilly, a teenager from Canaan, Connecticut, who had been convicted of manslaughter in the killing of his mother; believing that Reilly had been coerced into confessing, Miller raises money for Reilly's legal fees and eventually hires a detective to investigate the case. Television version of *After the Fall*, starring Christopher Plummer, is broadcast on NBC on December 10, 1974.

1975–76   *Death of a Salesman*, starring George C. Scott, Teresa Wright, and Harvey Keitel, is revived on Broadway in June 1975 and runs for 71 performances. Persuades *The New York Times* to publish a series of articles about the Peter Reilly case. Appears before Senate subcommittee in November to advocate American pressure on governments that violate human rights and the freedom to publish, emphasizing the situation in Czechoslovakia. Peter Reilly is granted a new trial on March 26, 1976, and the charges against him are dismissed in November (he is fully exonerated in 1977).

1977   *The Archbishop's Ceiling* has world premiere on April 23 at the Kennedy Center in Washington; the play's scheduled New York run is canceled by its producers. *Up from Paradise* is also staged at the Kennedy Center. *In the Country*, a collaboration with Inge Morath, is published.

1978   Miller's version of *An Enemy of the People* is filmed, directed by George Schaefer and starring Steve McQueen, but film never receives wide release. Miller speaks in front of Soviet mission in New York protesting the trials of dissidents Alexander Ginzburg and Anatoli Shcharansky. Visits China with Morath in November. *The Theatre Essays of Arthur Miller* is published. Hour-long comedy *Fame* is broadcast on NBC on November 30.

1979   *Chinese Encounters*, in collaboration with Morath, is published. *The Price* is revived in New York in a successful off-Broadway run, then moves to Broadway; it is also staged at the Spoleto Festival USA in Charleston. Miller accepts offer to write television adaptation of *Playing for Time*, a memoir by Fania Fénelon, who had been forced to play in an orchestra of female prisoners at Auschwitz, and defends controversial casting of Vanessa Redgrave, a supporter of the Palestine Liberation Organization, in the lead role. *Arthur Miller on Home Ground*, documentary by Harry Rasky, is released in November.

1980   Version of *The American Clock* premieres at the Spoleto USA festival. After Miller extensively revises the play, the London production by the National Theatre receives Olivier Award for the season's best new play, but the Broadway production, with his sister Joan playing Rose Baum, closes after 12 performances in November. *Playing for Time* is broadcast on CBS on September 30.

1981   Attends inauguration of French president François Mitterrand. Second volume of *Collected Plays* is published. First New York performance of *Up from Paradise* is staged at the Whitney Museum. Two-act version of *A View from the Bridge* is revived at the Long Wharf Theater in New Haven.

1982   Monologue *I Think About You a Great Deal*, written as a tribute to imprisoned Czech playwright Václav Havel, whom Miller had met in the 1960s, is performed at the International Theatre Festival in Avignon, France. Program of two one-act plays, *Elegy for a Lady* and *Some Kind of Love Story*, runs for six weeks at the Long Wharf.

1983   First Broadway production of the two-act *A View from the Bridge* opens on February 3 and runs for 149 performances. Miller agrees to direct a production of *Death of a Salesman* in Beijing and visits China with Morath from March to May; while they are away, a fire at their Roxbury house destroys many of his papers and possessions.

1984   Receives honorary doctorate from the University of Hartford. Broadway revival of *Death of a Salesman* starring Dustin Hoffman is well received and runs for 185 performances. *Salesman in Beijing*, with photographs by Inge Morath, is published in June. *After the Fall* is revived in New York in October. Miller threatens legal action against avant-garde troupe The Wooster Group for performing a segment of *The Crucible* without permission in their production *L.S.D.*; the troupe closes the play. Receives Kennedy Center Honors for lifetime achievement in the arts.

1985   Under the aegis of PEN, travels with British playwright Harold Pinter to Istanbul for five days in March to conduct inquiries into human-rights abuses and censorship in Turkey. Film of *Death of a Salesman*, starring Dustin Hoffman and directed by Volker Schlöndorff, is screened at the Venice Film Festival in September and is broadcast on CBS; *Private Conversations*, Christian Blackwood's documentary about the making of the film, is shown at the New York Film Festival. *The Archbishop's Ceiling* premieres in England. Miller visits the U.S.S.R. to meet with Soviet writers.

1986   Stage adaptation of *Playing for Time* premieres at theater festival in Edinburgh. Miller travels to the U.S.S.R. in October for a conference in Kyrgyzstan and meets Soviet leader Mikhail Gorbachev at the Kremlin.

1987–88   *All My Sons* is broadcast on the Public Broadcasting System's American Playhouse. *Danger: Memory!*, program of the one-act plays *Clara* and *I Can't Remember Anything*, opens at Lincoln Center in New York. London revival of the two-act *A View from the Bridge* runs for six months. *The Golden Years* is broadcast by the BBC as a radio play. Autobiography *Timebends* is published. *The American Clock* is revived for a run at the Williamstown Theater Festival.

1989   Miller's original screenplay *Everybody Wins* enters production, directed by Karel Reisz and starring Nick Nolte and

Debra Winger. Arthur Miller Centre for American Studies is established at the University of East Anglia, under the directorship of Christopher Bigsby. *The Crucible* is revived at the Long Wharf in New Haven.

1990   *Everybody Wins* is released. Miller travels to Prague for Czech productions of *The Archbishop's Ceiling* and *The Crucible*. *The Archbishop's Ceiling* is performed for the first time in New York. *After the Fall* is revived in London at the Royal National Theatre. Miller travels to South Africa to interview Nelson Mandela for the BBC.

1991   *Clara* is broadcast on the Arts & Entertainment network. *The Ride Down Mt. Morgan* premieres in London in the fall. *The Crucible* is staged in New York as the inaugural offering of the National Actors Theater.

1992   *The Price* is revived on Broadway and runs for 46 performances. One-act version of *The Last Yankee* staged in East Hampton, N.Y. Miller works on "Gellburg," play that will eventually be staged as *Broken Glass*. Directs production of *Death of a Salesman* in Stockholm.

1993   Full-length version of *The Last Yankee* premieres in New York and a production is mounted in London. *The American Clock* is broadcast on the TNT network. Miller receives National Medal of Arts.

1994   *Broken Glass* premieres at the Long Wharf in New Haven in March, starring Ron Silver (soon replaced by David Dukes), Amy Irving, and Ron Rifkin, with Miller revising the play during the production in preparation for its April 24 opening on Broadway; play earns Tony Award nomination for best play, and runs for 73 performances. Miller continues to work on the play for its London staging, and once again wins an Olivier Award for the best new play of the season. With Peter Reilly, becomes involved in the case of Richard Lapointe, a mentally disabled Connecticut man sentenced to life after confessing to the rape and murder of an 88-year-old woman. Oxford University names Miller to a one-year appointment as Professor of Contemporary Theatre.

1995   One-act *The Ryan Interview* is staged in May in New York. Film version of *The Crucible*, with screenplay by Miller, directed by Nicholas Hytner, and starring Daniel Day-Lewis and Winona Ryder, begins shooting; son Robert is one of the producers. PEN American Center organizes tribute to Miller on the occasion of his 80th birthday. *Homely Girl: A Life*, a novella, is published by Viking.

1996   *The Ride Down Mt. Morgan* has its American premiere at the Williamstown Theatre Festival. *Broken Glass* is broadcast on PBS's Masterpiece Theater on October 20, directed by David Thacker; Thacker's revival of *Death of a Salesman* is mounted at the Royal National Theatre. Film version of *The Crucible* is released in November, and Miller's screenplay is published by Penguin.

1997   Screenplay of *The Crucible* receives Academy Award nomination. Roundabout Theater Company revives *All My Sons* in New York, in a production that soon moves to Broadway. Signature Theater Company in New York begins season-long Miller retrospective, staging revivals of *The Last Yankee* and *The American Clock*.

1998   Miller receives Berlin Prize fellowship by the American Academy in Berlin. *Mr. Peters' Connections* premieres as part of the Signature Theater's retrospective. Revised version of *The Ride Down Mt. Morgan*, starring Patrick Stewart, is staged in New York at the Public Theater.

1999   *Death of a Salesman*, starring Brian Dennehy and Elizabeth Franz, is revived on Broadway, runs for 274 performances, and wins four Tony Awards; Miller also receives a lifetime achievement award. William Bolcom's opera of *A View from the Bridge*, with libretto by Miller and Arnold Weinstein, is performed by the Lyric Opera of Chicago in October. *The Price* is revived on Broadway in November and runs for 128 performances.

2000   *The Ride Down Mt. Morgan* is staged on Broadway, with Patrick Stewart reprising his role in the Public Theater production, and runs for 121 performances. In Los Angeles, *The Man Who Had All the Luck* has its first American staging since 1944. *Mr. Peters' Connections* premieres in London, where the National Theatre revives *All My Sons*. *Echoes Down the Corridor: Collected Essays 1944–2001* is published.

2001   Miller's one-act *Untitled* is performed as a prelude to a staging of Havel's *Vanek Plays* in New York. *On Politics and the Art of Acting*, originally a National Endowment for the Humanities lecture, is published. Film adaptation of *Focus*, directed by Neil Slavin and starring William H. Macy and Laura Dern, is released in the fall. At National

Book Awards ceremony in November Miller receives Medal for Distinguished Contribution to American Literature.

2002   Inge Morath dies of lymphoma on January 30. *The Crucible* is revived on Broadway in a production starring Liam Neeson and Laura Linney that runs for 101 performances; *The Man Who Had All the Luck* is also revived on Broadway for 62 performances. Miller meets painter Agnes Barley, who later becomes his companion. *Resurrection Blues* premieres in August at the Guthrie Theater. Bolcom's *A View from the Bridge* is performed at the Metropolitan Opera in New York. Gail Levin's documentary *Making "The Misfits"* is broadcast on PBS in October.

2003   Miller completes *Finishing the Picture*. Brother Kermit dies on October 17.

2004   *After the Fall* is revived on Broadway and runs for 53 performances. *Finishing the Picture* has world premiere at the Goodman Theater in Chicago.

2005   Arthur Miller dies of congestive heart failure in Roxbury on February 10 and is buried in the Roxbury Center Cemetery.

Note on the Texts

This volume contains eleven of Arthur Miller's plays—*After the Fall* (1964), *Incident at Vichy* (1964), *The Price* (1968), *Fame* (1970), *The Reason Why* (1970), *The Creation of the World and Other Business* (1972), *Up from Paradise* (1974), *The American Clock* (1974; revised 1980, 1984), *The Archbishop's Ceiling* (1977; revised 1984), *Elegy for a Lady* (1982), and *Some Kind of Love Story* (1982)—along with a screenplay, *Playing for Time* (1980), and two dramatic sketches, *The Poosidin's Resignation* (1976) and *I Think About You a Great Deal* (1982). These works are presented in the order of their first public performances, the dates of which are noted in parentheses in the preceding list (except for *The Poosidin's Resignation*, which was not performed in public during Miller's lifetime and is included here under 1976, the year in which it was first published). The volume concludes with a selection of Miller's notes and essays on the plays.

In writing his plays, Miller often completed numerous drafts before arriving at a version he considered worthy of the stage. He tended to make further revisions in the course of early readings, rehearsals, and out-of-town previews, and sometimes after opening night. In some cases he made extensive changes after a play's initial performance run was finished (*The American Clock* and *The Archbishop's Ceiling* were both presented in new versions in 1984 after premiering in 1974 and 1977). In other cases he adapted his works, rewriting *After the Fall*, *Fame*, and *The Reason Why* for television, *The Creation of the World and Other Business* as a musical, and the television play *Playing for Time* for the stage.

In the present volume, the texts of Miller's plays have been taken, wherever possible, from editions Miller prepared for readers rather than from working typescripts, acting editions, cast recordings, films, or magazine printings, though in some cases the latter versions may more closely reflect the state of a given play on its opening night. All but three of the plays in the present volume have been taken from such editions. Of those three, two (*Fame* and *The Reason Why*) come from Miller's final typescripts, now among his papers at the Harry Ransom Center, University of Texas at Austin, and one (*Up from Paradise*) from an acting edition (New York: Samuel French, 1984) which contains the only published text. No published version of *The Reason Why* is known, and it is believed to be published in the present volume for the first time. Further information about the composition, performance, and textual history of each play and dramatic sketch is given below, along with a list of the sources from which the pieces gathered in "Notes and Essays on the Plays" have been taken.

After the Fall. Commissioned as the inaugural production of the new Lincoln Center Repertory Company as early as 1960, *After the Fall* opened at the ANTA–Washington Square Theater on January 23, 1964 (directed by Elia Kazan) after a gala preview on January 20 attended by Lady Bird Johnson and other notables. Miller's first play since *A View from the Bridge* (1956), it had taken him at least two years to write, and he drew on unfinished drafts begun even earlier. He read an early version for the cast—titled *After the Fall; or, The Survivor*—on October 24, 1963. The play was first published in the *Saturday Evening Post* on February 1, 1964, and in book form by The Viking Press on February 11; Miller included it without revision in his *Collected Plays*, vol. 2 (New York: The Viking Press, 1981). On Broadway, it ran for 208 performances; toward the end of this run, in mid-August 1964, Miller is reported to have shortened the play by eighteen minutes, but the shorter version remains unpublished. During the summer of 1971, Miller collaborated on a film adaptation, never produced, with Abby Mann. The text of *After the Fall* in the present volume has been taken from Miller's *Collected Plays*, vol. 2.

Incident at Vichy. Miller wrote *Incident at Vichy* "in a couple of months," he told *The New York Times* at the end of June 1964, though he had been "mulling it over for five or six years"; elsewhere he claimed to have finished the play in three weeks. In late August, he read the play to the cast of the Repertory Theater of Lincoln Center, and it opened at the ANTA-Washington Square Theater on December 3, 1964 (directed by Harold Clurman). Miller is not known to have revised the play for subsequent theatrical runs in London and elsewhere, and he was not directly involved in its adaptation for television in 1973. The play was published separately by The Viking Press in 1965 and then included without change in Miller's *Collected Plays*, vol. 2, from which the text in the present volume has been taken.

The Price. After previews in Philadelphia, *The Price* opened on Broadway on February 7, 1968 (directed by Ulu Grosbard), ultimately running for 425 performances. Written mainly in 1967, the play first took shape as part of a script for television, *It Is You, Victor*, begun as early as 1964 and extensively revised in 1966. The television play, about a director rehearsing a group of actors, was never produced. But Miller's collaborator on the project, Ulu Grosbard, was excited by the play described within the play (titled *A Cop and Solomon* in one draft version now at the Ransom Center) and suggested that Miller rewrite it for the stage; it evolved to become *The Price*. A condensed text of *The Price* was published to coincide with the Broadway opening (in the *Saturday Evening Post* on February 10, 1968), and a separate book edition was published by The Viking Press later in the year. The text of *The Price* in the present volume has been taken from the *Collected Plays*, vol. 2, in which Miller included the play in 1981.

Fame and *The Reason Why*. Miller's one-act plays *Fame* and *The Reason Why* premiered off-Broadway, in a production by the New Theater Workshop (directed by Gino Giglio) in November 1970. *Fame* began as a short story, titled "The Recognitions" when it was first published in *Esquire* in July 1966 and "Fame" when Miller included it in his story collection *I Don't Need You Any More* (1967). *The Reason Why* may have been written for a political fundraiser: Miller read a version of it at the "Artists and Writers Scene for Gene," a campaign event for presidential candidate Eugene McCarthy, at the New York nightclub Cheetah on August 14, 1968. Plans for the plays' first performance were announced in early November 1969. They were originally envisioned as part of a triple bill, titled "Behind the Times" after a third play Miller ultimately withheld. (A typescript of *Behind the Times* is now in Miller's papers at the Ransom Center.) Both plays were subsequently filmed for television in separate productions: *The Reason Why* later in November (see Lewis Funke, "Stars Help Arthur Miller Film TV Antiwar Allegory," *The New York Times*, November 17, 1969) and *Fame*, expanded with a new second act, in 1978. (The television version of *Fame* aired as part of NBC's "Hallmark Hall of Fame" on November 30, 1978.) A text of the one-act *Fame* was published in the *Yale Literary Magazine*, a student journal, in March 1971, but Miller is not known to have overseen the details of this publication. No published version of *The Reason Why* is known. In the present volume, the texts of the two plays have been taken from Miller's final typescripts, now at the Harry Ransom Center, The University of Texas at Austin.

The Creation of the World and Other Business. Announcing the completion of his new play *The Creation of the World and Other Business* in September 1971, Miller called it "a catastrophic comedy" and explained that he had begun writing it about a year earlier. It was tentatively scheduled for a Broadway run early in 1972, but the first cast reading did not take place until the end of August. Between this first reading and the play's Broadway opening on November 30, Miller rewrote the play extensively; its first director, Harold Clurman, resigned and was replaced by Gerald Freedman; and it was significantly recast. The play was reportedly "in trouble" from its early stages. (For a more detailed account of its turbulent progress from out-of-town previews to Broadway, see Tom Buckley, "In the Beginning, Miller's 'Creation,'" *The New York Times*, December 5, 1972). The play ran for twenty performances on Broadway and closed on December 16. Miller's final text of the play was published separately in 1973 by both The Viking Press and Dramatists Play Service; it was then collected without major revision in Miller's *Collected Plays*, vol. 2, from which the text in the present volume has been taken.

Up from Paradise: A Musical. Up from Paradise, Miller's musical reworking of the unsuccessful *The Creation of the World and Other Business*, was written in collaboration with composer Stanley Silverman during Miller's tenure as writer-in-residence at the University of Michigan. The show opened at the Power Center for the Performing Arts in Ann Arbor on April 23, 1974, and was later performed at the Kennedy Center's Musical Theatre Lab (1977) in Washington, D.C. and in New York at the Whitney Museum (1981) and the Jewish Repertory Theatre (1983). Plans in 1979 for a Broadway run did not materialize. The text of the musical in the present volume has been taken from the only published version, *Up from Paradise: A Musical* (New York: Samuel French, 1984), which reflects the version of the play performed by the Jewish Repertory Theatre.

The American Clock. By Miller's own account, *The American Clock* went through "seemingly endless changes" before he was satisfied with its "final form": the revised version that premiered at the Mark Taper Forum in Los Angeles in June 1984 (directed by Gordon Davidson) and that opened to considerable acclaim at the British National Theatre in August 1986 (directed by Peter Wood). He had begun writing the play in 1970, soon after the April publication of the book on which it was based, Studs Terkel's *Hard Times: An Oral History of the Great Depression*; an early draft, now at the Ransom Center, is dated July 1970. A reporter visiting Miller a few months after this date found him still at work on the play, "a first draft not quite completed" beside his typewriter (see Joanne Koch, "How Can I Call Him Arthur?," *Chicago Tribune*, January 31, 1971). Miller oversaw a workshop production of the play (then titled *The American Clock: A Mural for Theatre*) while at the University of Michigan; the University Players announced its "world premiere" for their performances on April 24–27, 1974. The play premiered officially on May 24, 1980, at the Spoleto Festival's Dockside Theater in Charleston, South Carolina (directed by Dan Sullivan) after previews at the Harold Clurman Theater in New York beginning on April 29; it also ran at the Mechanic Theater in Baltimore. Revised, it opened on November 20, 1980, at the Biltmore Theater in New York (directed by Vivian Matalon), where it ran for only twelve performances. (The *Times*'s critic Frank Rich, who had admired an earlier version, complained: "Mr. Miller has tinkered with his play to the point of dismantling it.") The first published texts of the play (New York: Dramatists Play Service, 1982; London: Methuen, 1983) predate Miller's final and substantial rewriting of the play after its failure on Broadway. In his memoir *Timebends* (1987), he asserted that his final version restored the play to its "early, uncontaminated" form, "more or less fresh from my desk." The text printed here has been taken from *The Archbishop's Ceiling; The American Clock: Two Plays* (New York: Grove Press, 1989), a readers' edition that Miller prepared after his final revision of *The American Clock* for performance in Los Angeles and London.

The Poosidin's Resignation. The Poosidin's Resignation is not known to have been performed during Miller's lifetime and was probably not intended for performance. The text in the present volume has been taken from the *Boston University Journal* (24.2 [1976]: 5–13), the only published source, where it appeared along with his short story "Ham Sandwich," under the title "Two Short Works."

The Archbishop's Ceiling. Miller began writing *The Archbishop's Ceiling* in December 1975 and finished a version by April 30, 1976, announcing the fact in a theater news column (John Corry, "Broadway") in *The New York Times*: "I'm holding my breath on this one. I'm very pleased with it and now I just want to get it launched." In spite of his early excitement, the play would face setbacks before it was staged: an initial run scheduled for December 1976 at the Long Wharf Theater in New Haven was postponed and then canceled because Miller, the *Times* again reported, was "still working on the final draft of his script." The play ultimately premiered at the Kennedy Center's Eisenhower Theater on April 30, 1977 (directed by Arvin Brown) to unusually negative reviews. Plans for a Broadway run were canceled. Miller rewrote the play extensively after its initial theatrical failure— restoring many elements to their earliest forms and reworking others —and presented it again, at the Cleveland Playhouse in Cleveland, Ohio, on October 12, 1984 (directed by Jonathan Bolt). The revised 1984 text was the basis for a more favorably received British theatrical run, first at the Bristol Old Vic in 1985 (directed by Paul Unwin), and then at The Pit in the Barbican, where it was performed by the Royal Shakespeare Company in 1986 (directed by Nick Hamm). In *Timebends*, Miller blamed his play's early failure on his initial rewriting: "I had hopelessly given way and reshaped a play for what I had come to think of as the Frightened Theatre . . . and was persuaded to personalize what should have been allowed its original epic impulse." The play remained unpublished until 1984, when Methuen in London printed Miller's revised version; an acting edition was published in New York by Dramatists Play Service in 1985. The text of *The Archbishop's Ceiling* in the present volume has been taken from *The Archbishop's Ceiling; The American Clock: Two Plays* (New York: Grove Press, 1989), a readers' edition that incorporates Miller's final revisions of 1984.

Playing for Time. Miller agreed to write the screenplay for the made-for-television movie *Playing for Time* around November 1978. Based on a memoir by Fania Fénelon about her experiences in the Women's Orchestra of Auschwitz (published as *Playing for Time* in the U.S. in 1977 and *Sursis pour l'orchestre* in its original French edition of 1976), the project had been conceived by producer Linda Yellen, who approached Miller through his agent. Initial reports about their project associated it with ABC, but by July 1979, after Vanessa Redgrave agreed to play Fénelon, it had been taken up by CBS. The casting of Redgrave prompted considerable controversy while Miller was writing the screenplay because of Redgrave's support for the Palestine Liberation Organization, but filming began as scheduled in November; *Playing for Time* aired on CBS on September 30, 1980, to a wide audience and critical acclaim. A text of the screenplay was published soon afterward in a mass market paperback (New York: Bantam, 1981), and Miller subsequently included it in his *Collected Plays*, vol. 2 (New York: Viking, 1981). He returned to the screenplay in 1985, adapting it for theatrical performance: a stage version opened at the Studio Theatre in Washington, D.C., on September 22 for a brief run, and a text of this adaptation was published in an acting edition in the same year (Woodstock, IL: Dramatic Publishing Company, 1985). Plans to bring the stage adaptation to Broadway did not materialize. Miller did not claim that the adapted *Playing for Time* was intended as a definitive new form of his original work, displacing the old (unlike his revised versions of *The Archbishop's Ceiling* or *The American Clock*). Instead, the play alters the screenplay quite minimally—with much of the dialogue left unchanged—in order to fit the particular requirements and circumstances of theatrical production. (For further information on Miller's revisions and his handling of his source material, see Christopher Bigsby, *Arthur Miller: A Critical Study* [Cambridge: Cambridge University Press, 2005]). The text of *Playing for Time* in the present volume has been taken from Miller's 1981 *Collected Plays*, vol. 2.

I Think About You a Great Deal. Miller wrote his short monologue *I Think About You a Great Deal* at the request of the Association Internationale de Défense des Artistes, which was organizing "Une nuit pour Václav Havel" in support of the then-imprisoned Czech playwright. The piece was performed on July 21, 1982, at the Festival d'Avignon, an international theatrical festival, along with works by Samuel Beckett, Max Frisch, Eugène Ionesco, Harold Pinter, Tom Stoppard, and others. The text was first published by the Department of Slavic Languages and Literatures at the University of Michigan in *Cross Currents: A Yearbook of Central European Culture* 2 (1983): 23–24, and subsequently collected in *Living in Truth: Twenty-Two*

Essays Published on the Occasion of the Award of the Erasmus Prize to Václav Havel, edited by Jan Vladislav (Amsterdam: Meulenhoff, 1986; London: Faber and Faber, 1987). The text in the present volume has been taken from *Cross Currents*.

Elegy for a Lady and *Some Kind of Love Story*. Miller's one-act plays *Elegy for a Lady* and *Some Kind of Love Story* premiered as a double bill at the Long Wharf Theater in New Haven on October 26, 1982, under the title *Two by A.M.*; Miller himself directed the plays. They were first published in separate acting editions (New York: Dramatists Play Service, 1982, 1983) and then gathered in a readers' edition, with minor revisions, under the title *Two-Way Mirror* (London: Methuen, 1984). The change in the title of the double-bill had been proposed by Christopher Bigsby, who contributed an afterword to the new edition and later claimed Miller's "approval, if some bafflement" at the suggestion (see Bigsby's introduction to the 1995 revised edition of *The Portable Arthur Miller*). The texts printed here are those of the 1984 Methuen *Two-Way Mirror*.

Notes and Essays on the Plays. The list below indicates the sources from which the texts in the section entitled "Notes and Essays on the Plays" have been taken. The pieces have been arranged to follow the order in which the plays were first performed; some were published considerably after the initial performances or are published here for the first time.

Foreword (*After the Fall*): *Saturday Evening Post*, February 1, 1964, p. 32. Printed as a foreword to the first published version of the play; reprinted without change in *The Theater Essays of Arthur Miller*, ed. Robert A. Martin (New York: Viking, 1978), but not published in other editions of the play.

"With Respect for Her Agony—But with Love" (*After the Fall*): *Life*, February 7, 1964, p. 66.

Our Guilt for the World's Evil (*Incident at Vichy*): *New York Times Magazine*, January 3, 1965.

To the Actors Performing This Play: On Style and Power (*Incident at Vichy*): typescript at Ransom Center. No published version is known.

Author's Production Note (*The Price*): *Collected Plays*, vol. 2 (New York: Viking, 1981).

Prefatory Note (*The Creation of the World and Other Business*): typescript, Ransom Center. No published version is known.

Author's Note (*The Poosidin's Resignation*): *Boston University Journal*, vol. 24, no. 2 (1976), pp. 7–13.

Conditions of Freedom: Two Plays of the Seventies (*The Archbishop's*

Ceiling, The American Clock): The Archbishop's Ceiling; The American Clock: Two Plays (New York: Grove Press, 1989).

Author's Note (*Some Kind of Love Story, Elegy for a Lady*): *Some Kind of Love Story* (New York: Dramatists Play Service, 1983).

Playwright's Note (*Elegy for a Lady*): *Elegy for a Lady* (New York: Dramatists Play Service, 1982).

Author's Note (*Elegy for a Lady*): *Two-Way Mirror* (London: Methuen, 1984).

All of the works in the preceding list are published by permission of The Arthur Miller 2004 Literary and Dramatic Trust, with the exception of the "Foreword" to *After the Fall* and the "Author's Production Note" to *The Price*, both published by arrangement with Viking Penguin, a member of Penguin Group (USA), Inc.

This volume presents the texts of the original printings and typescripts chosen for inclusion here, but it does not attempt to reproduce non-textual features of their typographic design. The texts are presented without change, except for the correction of typographical errors. Spelling, punctuation, and capitalization are often expressive features and are not altered, even when inconsistent or irregular. The following is a list of typographical errors corrected, cited by page and line number: 34.29, out the; 46.34, rememer; 93.21, brought; 96.13, MAGGIE: Quentin?; 130.19, them are; 139.32, the the; 206.13, chairs; 224.18, fo this; 230.26, Borsolino; 245.24, ethical!"; 273.7, Ave; 273.39, a way; 275.37, Carribean; 281.22, its; 282.6, Everytime; 307.14, Even; 310.28, then; 334.9, *Sotto.*; 339.33, Caine; 353.35, dumfounded; 364.28, cocyx; 367.12, LINX; 367.34, his; 371.35, thing; 374.3, will if; 374.13, CURIOUSITY; 375.17, arms-length; 382.28, let's; 387.10, your; 387.19, here; 390.15, *opeining*; 390.34, *her*; 392.2, *ENTRACTE*; 393.36, *MUSICIAL*; 396.32, ARCHIPELEGOS; 400.2, ITS; 408.34–35, coming I; 409.6, His; 411.1, whan; 413.3, OF; 419.9, Roses'; 458.12, 16, *"S'Wonderful."*; 462.34, by it's the idea that all of our relationships are basically ruled by money; 492.27–28, *A'Changing."*; 500.27, Gorly, gorly; 537.18, MAYA; 606.10, then; 608.33, fillng; 615.32, somehere; 654.27, greats; 657.32, in; 679.18, Well; 726.6, deadend; 749.14, if; 752.38, is; 754.15, Lawrence; 755.2, medaeval; 755.3, Checkov; 755.13, plummage; 757.22, Checkov's; 758.35, phrase) that; 759.13, alive could; 761.20, amock; 766.16, characterstics.

Notes

In the notes below, the reference numbers denote page and line of this volume (the line count includes chapter headings). No note is made for material included in standard desk-reference works. Quotations from Shakespeare are keyed to *The Riverside Shakespeare*, ed. G. Blakemore Evans (Boston: Houghton Mifflin, 1974). Biblical references are keyed to the King James Version. For further information on Miller's life and works, see Susan C. W. Abbotson, *Critical Companion to Arthur Miller: A Literary Reference to His Life and Work* (New York: Facts On File, 2007); S. K. Bhatia, *Arthur Miller* (London: Heinemann, 1985); Christopher Bigsby, *Arthur Miller, 1915–1962* (Cambridge: Harvard University Press, 2009) and *Arthur Miller, 1962–2005* (London: Weidenfeld and Nicolson, 2011); Christopher Bigsby, ed., *The Cambridge Companion to Arthur Miller* (Cambridge: Cambridge University Press, 1997); Neil Carson, ed., *Arthur Miller: A Collection of Critical Essays* (Englewood, NJ: Prentice Hall, 1969); Mel Gussow, *Conversations with Arthur Miller* (London: Nick Hern Books, 2002); Alice Griffin, *Understanding Arthur Miller* (Columbia, SC: University of South Carolina Press, 1996); Robert A. Martin, *Arthur Miller: New Perspectives* (Englewood, NJ: Prentice Hall, 1982); Arthur Miller, *Timebends: A Life* (New York: Grove, 1987); Benjamin Nelson, *Arthur Miller: Portrait of a Playwright* (New York: McKay, 1970); Matthew C. Roudané, ed., *Conversations with Arthur Miller* (Jackson, MS: University Press of Mississippi, 1987); Dennis Welland, *Miller: The Playwright* (London: Methuen, 1979).

AFTER THE FALL

Original cast:

Quentin	Jason Robards Jr.
Felice	Zohra Lampert
Holga	Salome Jens
Mother	Virginia Kaye
Dan	Michael Strong
Father	Paul Mann
Nurses	Faye Dunaway, Diane Shalet
Doctor	Scott Cunningham
Maggie	Barbara Loden
Elsie	Patricia Roe
Louise	Mariclare Costello
Lou	David J. Stewart

Mickey	Ralph Meeker
Woman with parrot	Crystal Field
Man in the park	Stanley Beck
Carrie	Ruth Attaway
Chairman	David Wayne or Lou Frizzell
Reverend Harley Barnes	Hal Holbrook or Harold Scott
Porter	Jack Waltzer
Secretary	Diane Shalet
Lucas	Harold Scott
Clergyman	James Greene
Others	Stanley Beck, Scott Cunningham, Faye Dunaway, Crystal Field, Lou Frizzell, James Greene, Clint Kimbrough, John Philip Law, Barry Primus, Jim Ray -James, Harold Scott, Diane Shalet, Jack Waltzer

Director: Elia Kazan. Producers: Elia Kazan and Robert L. Whitehead for the Repertory Theater of Lincoln Center. Production design and lighting: Jo Mielziner. Music: David Amram. Costumes: Anna Hill Johnstone. Production state managers: Robert Downing and Frederick DeWilde. Premiered at the ANTA–Washington Square Theater, New York, on January 23, 1964.

21.9   the night of the Dempsey-Tunney fight]   Jack Dempsey (1895–1983) fought Gene Tunney (1897–1978) on September 22, 1927, in a celebrated rematch for the world heavyweight title.

69.20   Idlewild]   Until 1963, the common name for what is now John F. Kennedy International Airport.

77.31   "Little Girl Blue"]   Song with lyrics by Lorenz Hart (1895–1943) and music by Richard Rodgers (1902–1979), from the Broadway musical *Jumbo* (1935).

79.31   El Morocco]   Fashionable New York nightclub, originally a speakeasy, which opened in 1931; its address until 1961 was 154 East 54th Street.

85.28   Gibson Girl]   Ideal type of fashionable feminine beauty of the late 19th and early 20th centuries, derived from the drawings of magazine illustrator Charles Dana Gibson (1867–1944).

INCIDENT AT VICHY

Original cast:

Lebeau	Michael Strong
Bayard	Stanley Beck
Marchand	Paul Mann
Police Guard	C. Thomas Blackwell
Monceau	David J. Stewart
Gypsy	Harold Scott

Waiter	Jack Waltzer
Boy	Ira Lewis
Major	Hal Holbrook
First Detective	Alek Primrose
Old Jew	Will Lee
Second Detective	James Dukas
Leduc	Joseph Wiseman
Police Captain	James Greene
Von Berg	David Wayne
Professor Hoffman	Clinton Kimbrough
Ferrand	Graham Jarvis
Prisoners	Pierre Epstein, Stephen Peters, Tony Lo Bianco, John Vari

Director: Harold Clurman. Producers: Elia Kazan and Robert L. Whitehead. Scenery: Boris Aronson. Lighting: Jean Rosenthal. Costumes: Jane Greenwood. Production stage manager: Frederic DeWilde. Premiered at the ANTA–Washington Square Theatre, New York, on December 3, 1964.

164.26   Cyrano]   Cyrano de Bergerac, protagonist of Edmond Rostand's 1897 play.

181.13   *Hände weg!*]   Hands off!

THE PRICE

Original cast:

Victor Franz	Pat Hingle
Esther Franz	Kate Reid
Gregory Solomon	Harold Gary
Walter Franz	Arthur Kennedy

Director: Ulu Grosbard. Producer: Robert L. Whitehead in association with Robert W. Dowling. Setting and costumes: Boris Aronson. Lighting: Paul Morrison. Production stage manager: Del Hughes. Premiered at the Morosco Theatre, New York, on February 7, 1968.

188.18   Gallagher and Shean]   Edward Gallagher (1873–1929) and Al Shean (1868–1949), a vaudeville and Broadway singing duo popular in the 1910s and 1920s.

202.27   Jimmy Walker's]   James John Walker (1881–1946), New York City mayor from 1926 to 1932.

209.11–12   Jacob . . . the Angel]   See Genesis 32.

FAME

Original cast: Kim Chan, Marilyn Chris, Gene Gross, Rose Roffman, Eli Wallach, Richard Kiley. Director: Gino Giglio. Premiered at New Theater Workshop, New York, in November 1970.

THE REASON WHY

Original cast: See original cast list for *Fame*, above.

284.30–31   dead as Kelcey's ass]   A proverbial phrase.

THE CREATION OF THE WORLD AND OTHER BUSINESS

Original cast:

Adam	Bob Dishy
God	Stephen Elliott
Eve	Zoe Caldwell
Chemuel, the Angel of Mercy	Lou Gilbert
Raphael, an Angel	Dennis Cooley
Azrael, the Angel of Death	Lou Polan
Lucifer	George Grizzard
Cain	Barry Primus
Abel	Mark Lamos

Director: Gerald Freeman. Producer: Robert L. Whitehead. Music: Stanley Silverman. Settings and projections: Boris Aronson. Lighting: Tharon Musser. Costumes: Hal George. Production stage manager: Frederic DeWilde. Opened at the Shubert Theater, New York, on November 30, 1972.

297.22   *unbeschreiblich*]   Indescribable.

299.27   Law of the Conservation of Energy]   Principle of physics, embodied in the First Law of Thermodynamics, stating that energy cannot be created or destroyed, only transformed.

312.4   Adonoi . . . echaud]   From the opening words of the Shema, a Jewish prayer: Adonai is our god, Adonai alone.

UP FROM PARADISE

Original cast (Ann Arbor, MI, 1974):

Narrator	Arthur Miller
God	Bob Bingham
Adam	Allan Nicholls
Eve	Kimberly Farr
Lucifer	Larry Marshall
Cain	Seth Allen
Abel	Dennis Cooley

Director: Arthur Miller. Music: Stanley Silverman. Settings: Alan Billings. Costumes: Zelma Weisfeld. Lighting: R. Craig Wolf. Opened at the Power Center for the Performing Arts, Ann Arbor, Michigan, on April 23, 1974.

Original cast (New York, 1983):

God	Len Cariou
Azrael	Raymond Murcell

Raphael	Avery J. Tracht
Uriel	Richard Frisch
Adam	Austin Pendleton
Eve	Alice Playten
Lucifer	Walter Bobbie
Cain	Paul Ukena Jr.
Abel	Lonny Price

Director: Ran Avni. Sets: Michael C. Smith. Costumes: Marie Anne Chiment. Lighting: Dan Kinsley. Musical Director: Michael Ward. Stage Manager: G. Franklin Heller. Opened at the Jewish Repertory Theatre in New York on October 25, 1983.

391.10   *CAIN . . . new world.*]   A footnote in the 1984 Samuel French edition of the text reads: "He can be played by a grown young man."

THE AMERICAN CLOCK

Original cast (New York, 1980):

Lee Baum	William Atherton
Moe Baum	John Randolph
Clarence, Waiter, Isaac, Jerome, Piano Mover	Donny Burks
Rose Baum	Joan Copeland
Frank, Livermore, Man in Welfare Office, Stanislaus	Ralph Drischell
Grandpa, Kapush	Salem Ludwig
Fanny Margolies, Myrna	Francine Beers
Clayton, Sidney Margolies, Ralph	Robert Harper
Durant, Sheriff, Piano Mover, Toland	Alan North
Tony, Taylor, Dugan	Edward Seamon
Waiter, Bicycle Thief, Rudy, Piano Mover, Ryan	Bill Smitrovich
Joe, Bush	David Chandler
Doris, Isabel, Grace	Marilyn Caskey
Irene	Rosanna Carter
Jeanette Ramsey, Edie, Lucille, Attendant	Susan Sharkey

Director: Vivian Matalon. Scenery: Karl Eigsti. Lighting: Neil Peter Jampolis. Costumes: Robert Wojewodski. Opened at the Biltmore Theatre in New York on November 20, 1980, after performances at the Spoleto Festival's Dockside Theater in Charleston, South Carolina, beginning on May 24, 1980, directed by Dan Sullivan.

Original cast (London, 1986):

Arthur Robinson	Barrie Ingham
Clarence, Isaac	Tommy Eytie

Moe Baum	Michael Bryant
Rose Baum	Sara Kestleman
Lee Baum	Neil Daglish
Grandpa	Peter Gordon
Fanny Margolies, Charleston Dancer	Sally Dexter
Sidney Margolies, Charleston Dancer, Henry Taylor, Ryan	Barry James
Lucille, Diana Morgan, Harriet Taylor	Roz Clifton
Doris Gross, Charley, Edie	Eve Adam
Joey, Broadway Tony, Farmer, Stanislaus	Steven Law
Frank, Servant, Louis Banks, Rudy, Toland	Okon Jones
Dr. Rosman, Grandma Taylor	Edna Dore
Jesse Livermore, Iowa Sheriff, Bush	Alan Haywood
William Durant, Judge Bradley, Dugan	John Normington
Arthur Clayton, Brewster, Mr. Graham, Ralph	Adam Norton
Mrs. Taylor, Miss Fowler, Grace	Judith Coke
Daughters	Annabel Mednick, Valerie Minifie
Servants	Tommy Eytie, Marsha Hunt, Okon Jones, Ellen Thomas, Major Wiley
Frank Howard, Theodore K. Quinn, Mississippi Sheriff, Kapush	David Schofield
Farmer, Chuck	Nicholas Donovan
Bidders	Robert Ralph, Paul Stewart
Marathon Dancers	Roz Clifton, Nicholas Donovan, Annabel Mednick, Adam Norton
Isabel, Irene	Marsha Hunt
Musicians	Robert Lockhart, David Roach, Roy Babbington, Michael Gregory, Peter Pettinger

Director: Peter Wood. Set design: Timothy O'Brien. Costumes: Stephen Lewis. Lighting: Robert Bryan. Musical arrangements: Robert Lockhart. Sound design: Paul Groothuis. Production manager: Michael Cass Jones. Stage manager: Ernest Hall. Opened at the Olivier Theatre of the National Theatre in London on December 18, 1986, after revisions in 1984.

413.3   STUDS TERKEL'S *HARD TIMES*]   Terkel's *Hard Times: An Oral History of the Great Depression* was first published in 1970.

414.12   JESSE LIVERMORE] American stock trader (1877–1940), sometimes called "The Great Bear of Wall Street," known for preserving his wealth by selling short during the crash of 1929.

414.13   WILLIAM DURANT] Automobile magnate (1861–1947), founder of General Motors and Chevrolet. He was bankrupted as a result of the 1929 crash.

417.10   *"Million-Dollar Baby"*] "I Found a Million Dollar Baby (in a Five and Ten Cent Store)," song from the Broadway musical *Billy Rose's Crazy Quilt* (1931), with music by Harry Warren (1893–1981) and lyrics by Mort Dixon (1892–1956) and Billy Rose (1899–1966).

418.24   *"I Can't Give You Anything But Love,"*] Song from the Broadway revue *Blackbirds of 1928* (1928) with music by Jimmy McHugh (1894–1969) and lyrics by Dorothy Fields (1905–1974).

418.28   Charley Paddock] Charlie Paddock (1900–1943), American athlete who broke records in track and field at the 1920 Olympics.

419.16   *"On the Sunny Side of the Street."*] Song from the Broadway musical *The International Revue* (1930) with music by Jimmy McHugh and lyrics by Dorothy Fields.

419.20   Rudy Vallee] Rudy Vallée (1901–1986), singer and actor.

425.22   Jake the Barber] John Factor (1892–1984), Chicago-based racketeer and con man, later a casino operator in Las Vegas.

429.23–24   *" 'Taint Nobody's Bizness"*] Vaudeville blues song (c. 1922) by Porter Grainger (1891–c. 1955) and Everett Robbins (fl. 1920s).

431.16   Germany in 1922] From 1922 to 1923 Germany suffered from hyperinflation, during which, at its height, the price of goods doubled every two days.

435.32–436.2   *the Iowa Hymn . . . His own."*] From the hymn "We Gather Together," originally written in Dutch in 1597 by Adrianus Valerius (c. 1575–1625) and translated by Theodore Baker (1851–1934).

440.11   *"How Long,"*] From the "How Long, How Long Blues" (1928), written by Leroy Carr (1905–1935).

440.30   *"The Joint is Jumpin'"*] 1937 song with music by Fats Waller (1904–1943) and lyrics by Andy Razaf (1895–1973) and J. C. Johnson (1896–1981).

445.30   *"My Baby Just Cares for Me"*] Song from the film *Whoopee!* (1930), with music by Walter Donaldson (1893–1947) and lyrics by Gus Kahn (1886–1941).

451.37   *Coronet* by Manuel Komroff] 1929 popular novel.

452.20   *"Once in a While."*] 1937 song with music by Michael Edwards (1893–1962) and lyrics by Bud Green (1897–1981).

457.3–4   *"In New York City, You Really Got to Know Your Line,"*] From "New York City Blues" (c. 1935), by Huddie Ledbetter (Lead Belly, 1888–1949).

458.3–4   *"He Loves and She Loves,"*] 1927 song with music by George Gershwin (1898–1937) and lyrics by Ira Gershwin (1896–1983).

458.12–13   *Funny Face* . . . *" 'SWonderful."*] The song " 'S Wonderful" appeared in the 1927 musical *Funny Face*, by George and Ira Gershwin.

458.22   *"Do-Do-Do What You Done-Done-Done Before."*] From "Do Do Do," a song in the Broadway musical *Oh, Kay!* (1926), with music by George Gershwin and lyrics by Ira Gershwin.

460.16   *"Love and a Dime"*] Popular song originally written for the 1934 Princeton undergraduate musical *Stags at Bay* by Brooks Bowman (1913–1937).

463.28–29   *"Backbone and Navel Doin' the Belly Rub,"*] Lyric from the traditional American folksong "Things About Coming My Way," adapted in the early 1930s by the Mississippi Sheiks, Tampa Red, and others.

466.35–467.23   ROOSEVELT: Clouds . . . human fortitude.] From Roosevelt's acceptance speech at the Democratic Convention, June 27, 1936.

470.18   WPA] Works Progress Administration, New Deal agency devoted to large-scale public employment, created in April 1935.

471.2   Writers Project] Federal Writers' Project, division of the WPA established in July 1935.

472.8   Felix the Frankfurter] Felix Frankfurter (1882–1965), who served on the U.S. Supreme Court from 1939 to 1962.

473.20–21   Helen Hayes . . . Victoria Regina] Hayes (1900–1993) appeared in Laurence Housman's play on Broadway beginning in 1935.

473.26   Adolphe Menjou] Film actor (1890–1963) famous for his roles in sophisticated comedies.

478.26–27   *Superman* comic strip] Following the debut of Superman in *Action Comics* #1 (June 1938), a syndicated comic strip was launched in January 1939.

479.40–480.2   Hemingway . . . no fucking good."] See chapter twenty-three of Ernest Hemingway's novel *To Have and Have Not* (1937): "a man alone ain't got no bloody fucking chance."

480.16–17   WPA Guide]   One of the principal activities of the Federal
Writers' Project was the preparation of the American Guide Series, a series of
historical and geographical guides to each of the states, published between
1937 and 1941.

492.18   "*We're in the Money.*"]   Song from the film *Gold Diggers of 1933*
(1933), with lyrics by Al Dubin (1891–1945) and music by Harry Warren
(1893–1981).

492.27–28   "*The Times They Are A-Changin'.*"]   Popular song written in
1963 by Bob Dylan (b. 1941).

493.10   "*I Want to Be Happy*"]   Song from the musical *No, No, Nanette*
(1925) with music by Vincent Youmans (1898–1946) and lyrics by Irving Cae-
sar (1895–1996).

493.32   "*Life Is Just a Bowl of Cherries*"]   Popular song (1931) with music
by Ray Henderson (1896–1970) and lyrics by Buddy DeSylva (1895–1950) and
Lew Brown (1893–1958).

THE POOSIDIN'S RESIGNATION

502.17   attack on our Navel off Indochinery]   The U.S. destroyer *Maddox*
was attacked by North Vietnamese torpedo boats in the Gulf of Tonkin on
August 2, 1964, and a second attack on the *Maddox* and another destroyer,
Turner Joy, was reported on August 4, probably as the result of false radar
contacts. President Lyndon Johnson used the attacks to secure congressional
approval of a resolution authorizing "all necessary measures" to "prevent further aggression" in Southeast Asia.

503.11–12   Now let us reason / Together]   Phrase associated with Lyndon
Johnson, from Isaiah 1:18.

503.34   I want that absoloonly clure]   Richard M. Nixon often used variations on the phrase "I want to make one thing perfectly clear."

THE ARCHBISHOP'S CEILING

Original cast (Washington, D.C., 1977):

Adrian	Tony Musante
Sigmund	John Cullum
Maya	Bibi Andersson
Martin	Josef Sommer
Marcus	Douglas Watson
Irina	Bara-Cristen Hansen

Director: Arvin Brown. Producers: Robert L. Whitehead, Roger L. Stevens,
Konrad Matthaei. Scenery: David Jenkins. Costumes: Bill Walker. Lighting:
Ron Wallace. Opened at the Eisenhower Theater, John F. Kennedy Center for
the Performing Arts, Washington, D.C., on April 30, 1977.

Original cast (Cleveland, 1984):

Adrian	Morgan Lund
Maya	Lizbeth MacKay
Marcus	John Buck Jr. ·
Irina	Sharon Bicknell
Sigmund	Thomas S. Oleniacz

Director: Jonathan Bolt. Scenery: Gary C. Eckhart. Costumes: Francis Blau. Lighting: Robert Gould. Opened at the Cleveland Playhouse, Cleveland, Ohio, on October 12, 1984.

529.22   *Grüss Gott*] A colloquial greeting (literally, "God bless you" or "God greet you").

559.16–21   a marvelous line . . . rest."] See the Prologue to Auden's *The Age of Anxiety: A Baroque Eclogue* (1947).

562.4   *Du bist sehr schön*] You are very pretty.

563.9   *"Bei Mir Bist Du Schön,"*] German title of a popular song originally written in Yiddish for the 1932 musical *Men Ken Lebn Nor Men Lost Nisht*, with music by Sholom Secunda (1894–1974) and lyrics by Jacob Jacobs (1890–1977).

573.13–14   in Shakespeare . . . sport."] See *King Lear*, IV.i.36–37.

584.16–19   Malraux . . . Cortázar] André Malraux, French novelist (1901–1976); Gyula Illyés (1902–1983), Hungarian poet and novelist; Heinrich Böll (1917–1985), German novelist; Kōbō Abe (1924–1993), Japanese novelist; Nadine Gordimer (b. 1923), South African novelist; Julio Cortázar (1914–1984), Argentinian novelist and short story writer.

PLAYING FOR TIME

Original cast:

Fania Fénelon	Vanessa Redgrave
Alma Rosé	Jane Alexander
Mala	Maud Adams
Olga	Christine Baranski
Etalina	Robin Bartlett
Elzvieta	Marisa Berenson
Paulette	Verna Bloom
Katrina	Donna Haley
Charlotte	Lenore Harris
Varya	Mady Kaplan
Shmuel	Will Lee
Michou	Anna Levine
Frau Schmidt	Viveca Lindfors
Marianne	Melanie Mayron
Giselle	Marcell Rosenblatt
Dr. Mengele	Max Wright

Frau Lagerführerin Maria Mandel	Shirley Knight
Tchaikowska	Elaine Bromka
Liesle	Faith Catlin
Commandant Kramer	Clarence Felder
Esther	Marta Heflin
Woman on train	Martha Schlamme
SS Officer	Robert Dannon
Chessplayer #2	Thomas Everett
Young Chess Player	Tom Everett
Polish woman	Mary Kay Fager
The Executioner	Huggy-Bear Ferris
German trooper	John Griesemer
Boy Scout	Thomas La Fleur
Ladislaus' mother	Lorraine Lucey
Ladislaus	Robert Lucey
Tattooer	Mary McGonical
Canadian girl	Monica Merriman
Edek	Lee Jay Nelson
British radioman	Peter Phillips
Asthmatic man	Sidney Sandness
Chessplayer #1	Zvee Scooler
German NCO	Dennis Michael Sheppard
Berta	Dorothy Sherwood
British radio operator	Eoin Stewart
Greta	Grace Stover
Blockawa	Phyllis Vanier
SS Sergeant	Spencer Waldron
Prisoner	Rick Washburn

Director: Daniel Mann. Producers: John E. Quill, Linda Yellen. Associate Producer: Louise Ramsay. Music: Brad Fiedel. Cinematography: Arthur J. Ornitz. Film Editing: Jay Freund. Art Direction: Robert Gundlach. Set Decoration: Gary Jones. Costume Design: Ruth Morley. First Assistant Camera: Joseph Di Pasquale. Extras casting: Sylvia Fay. Key Costumer: Eoin Stewart. Title designer: Arnold Skolnick. First aired on the CBS television network on September 30, 1980.

585.3   Fania Fénelon] French pianist and composer (1908–1983), born Fania Goldstein. *Playing for Time* was originally published in France as *Sursis pour l'Orchestre* (*Reprieve for the Orchestra*) in 1976.

592.29   Dr. Mengele] Josef Mengele (1911–1979), SS officer and physician assigned to Auschwitz-Birkenau, 1943–45.

599.34   Alma Rosé] Austrian violinist (1906–1944), niece of Gustav Mahler, daughter of Arnold Rosé who was for fifty years the director of the Vienna Philharmonic. After the German–Austrian Anschluss in 1938 she lived successively in England, the Netherlands, and France, where she was arrested by the Gestapo in 1942. She was deported in 1943 to Auschwitz, where she became leader of the Mädchenorchester von Auschwitz. The cause of her death is disputed.

600.32   "Un bel di"] Soprano aria sung by Cio-Cio San in act 2 of Giacomo Puccini's *Madama Butterfly* (1904).

604.22   von Suppé] Franz von Suppé (1819–1895), Austrian composer of dozens of operettas, some of whose overtures, including those for *Poet and Peasant* (1846) and *Light Cavalry* (1866), became widely popular as concert pieces.

611.15   Drancy] Internment camp on the outskirts of Paris from which 63,000 prisoners were deported to concentration and extermination camps in the period between 1941 and 1944.

612.2   "Stormy Weather"] Song (1933) with music by Harold Arlen (1905–1986) and lyrics by Ted Koehler (1894–1973), first popularized by Ethel Waters.

626.5   Furtwängler] Wilhelm Furtwängler, German conductor (1886–1954).

627.33   "Meditation" from *Thaïs*] Orchestral entr'acte from act 2 of Jules Massenet's 1894 opera.

ELEGY FOR A LADY

Original cast:
Man   Charles Cioffi
Proprietress   Christine Lahti
Director: Arthur Miller. Set: Hugh Landwehr. Music: Stanley Silverman. Costumes: Bill Walker. Lighting: Ronald Wallace. Opened, with *Some Kind of Love Story*, as part of the double bill *2 by A.M.*, at the Long Wharf Theatre, New Haven, Connecticut, October 26, 1982.

SOME KIND OF LOVE STORY

Original cast:
Angela   Christine Lahti
Tom   Charles Cioffi
Director: Arthur Miller. Set: Hugh Landwehr. Music: Stanley Silverman. Costumes: Bill Walker. Lighting: Ronald Wallace. Opened, with *Elegy for a Lady*, as part of the double bill *2 by A.M.*, at the Long Wharf Theatre, New Haven, Connecticut, October 26, 1982.

709.24   Mack Sennett Police Department] Sennett (1880–1960) was the producer, beginning in 1912, of slapstick silent film comedies featuring the Keystone Kops.

720.13   Oy gevalt!]   Yiddish exclamation of exasperation or dismay.

NOTES AND ESSAYS ON THE PLAYS

737.24   Oswald's]   Lee Harvey Oswald (1939–1963), who assassinated President Kennedy on November 22, 1963.

740.15–16   Dick Diver]   Psychiatrist protagonist of F. Scott Fitzgerald's *Tender Is the Night* (1934).

742.1–2   *Eichmann in Jerusalem*]   *Eichmann in Jerusalem: A Report on the Banality of Evil* (1963).

743.1   OUR GUILT . . . EVIL]   Miller's typescript for this article, now at the Harry Ransom Center, University of Texas at Austin, is dated December 17, 1964, and is introduced on a separate page as follows: "The Editor has asked me to set down what I think are some of the contemporary applications of my play, 'Incident at Vichy.' No writer enjoys pointing out the relevancy of his fiction which ought to be clear in the work itself, but in this case, the subject being annihilation and violence, we are all with our faces rubbed into the matter to the point where a wider vision is difficult and ought to be enhanced, if that in fact is possible, by any means at hand. I cannot pretend to have written this play for the fun of it. But first, the background."

744.10–12   the people in Queens . . . windows.]   On March 13, 1964, Kitty Genovese (1935–1964) was stabbed to death near her home in Kew Gardens, Queens; the *New York Times* reported the murder on March 27, 1964, in "Thirty-Eight Who Saw Murder Didn't Call the Police," by Martin Gansberg (1920–1995).

744.33–37   the words of Hermann Broch . . . postulate."]   See *The Sleepwalkers: A Trilogy* (1932) by the Austrian Jewish writer Hermann Broch (1886–1951), as translated from *Die Schlafwandler* (1932) by Willa and Edwin Muir.

746.29–30   Roman Catholic Church . . . from the Jews alone]   See "Nostra Aetate," a document approved by the Second Vatican Council in 1965.

747.13–14   the three boys . . . Mississippi]   Civil rights activists James Chaney, Andrew Goodman, and Michael Schwerner were murdered by Klansmen in Neshoba County, Mississippi, shortly after midnight on June 21, 1964.

748.11–13   I wrote . . . war criminals]   Miller's response to the Frankfurt war crimes trials was first published in "How the Nazi Trials Search the Hearts of All Germans," *New York Herald-Tribune*, March 15, 1964.

753.38–39   Hamlet's warning . . . portray]   See *Hamlet*, III.ii.16–35.

754.26–28   a President plays golf . . . lifts up dogs by the ears]   The references are to Dwight Eisenhower, Harry Truman, and Lyndon Johnson.

759.12–13   Harold Clurman . . . adept of "The Method"]   As a founder (with Lee Strasberg and Cheryl Crawford) of the Group Theatre (1931–41), Clurman (1901–1980) was instrumental in developing an acting style inspired in part by the methods of Konstantin Stanislavski.

770.30   Soviet ousting of Dubček]   Alexander Dubček (1921–1992) became First Secretary of the Czechoslovakia Communist Party in January 1968, and initiated a period of liberalization known as the "Prague Spring" which was ended by the invasion of Warsaw Pact troops in August 1968. He was forced to resign his post in April 1969.

771.4   burgling of psychiatrists' offices]   Following the indictment of Daniel Ellsberg for his role in the publication of the Pentagon Papers in June 1971, the offices of Ellsberg's psychiatrist, Lewis Fielding, were broken into on September 3, 1971, by E. Howard Hunt, G. Gordon Liddy, and others in an attempt to obtain information that could be used to discredit Ellsberg.

776.15   Studs Terkel's *Hard Times*]   See note 413.3.

777.28–31   "Love Is . . . the Big Bad Wolf?"]   "Love Is Sweeping the Country," song by George Gershwin (music) and Ira Gershwin (lyrics) from the musical *Of Thee I Sing* (1931); "Life Is Just a Bowl of Cherries," see note 493.32; "April in Paris," song by Vernon Duke (music) and E. Y. Harburg (lyrics) from the musical *Walk a Little Faster* (1932); "I'm Getting Sentimental over You," song by George Bassman (music) and Ned Washington (lyrics), introduced by the Tommy Dorsey Orchestra in 1932; "Who's Afraid of the Big Bad Wolf," song by Frank Churchill with additional lyrics by Ann Ronell, featured in the Walt Disney cartoon *Three Little Pigs* (1933).

THE LIBRARY OF AMERICA SERIES

The Library of America fosters appreciation and pride in America's literary heritage by publishing, and keeping permanently in print, authoritative editions of America's best and most significant writing. An independent nonprofit organization, it was founded in 1979 with seed funding from the National Endowment for the Humanities and the Ford Foundation.

To subscribe to the series or to order individual copies, please visit www.loa.org or call (800) 964.5778.

*This book is set in 10 point Linotron Galliard,
a face designed for photocomposition by Matthew Carter
and based on the sixteenth-century face Granjon. The paper
is acid-free lightweight opaque and meets the requirements
for permanence of the American National Standards Institute.
The binding material is Brillianta, a woven rayon cloth made
by Van Heek-Scholco Textielfabrieken, Holland. Composition by Dedicated Book Services. Printing by
Malloy Incorporated. Binding by Dekker Book-
binding. Designed by Bruce Campbell.*

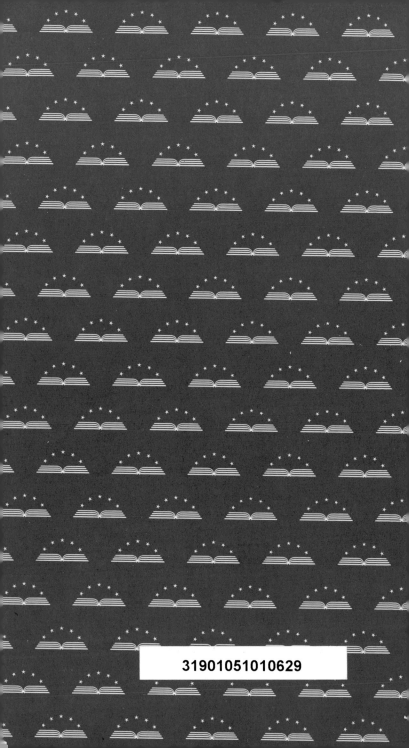